Marketing Management
for Business Students

Contents

The following chapters are from:

Marketing: An Introduction
by Gary Armstrong, Philip Kotler, Michael Harker and
Ross Brennan

A Pearson Custom Publication

Marketing Management for Business Students

A Customised Edition of:

Marketing: An Introduction
by Gary Armstrong, Philip Kotler, Michael Harker
and Ross Brennan

PEARSON
Custom Publishing

Pearson Education Limited
Edinburgh Gate
Harlow
Essex CM20 2JE

And associated companies throughout the world

Visit us on the World Wide Web at:
www.pearsoned.co.uk

First published 2010

This Custom Book Edition © 2010 Published by Pearson Education Limited

Compiled from:

Marketing: An Introduction
by Gary Armstrong, Philip Kotler, Michael Harker and Ross Brennan
ISBN 978 0 273 71395 1
Copyright © Pearson Education Limited 2009

ISBN 978 1 84959 210 9

PART ONE

Defining marketing and the marketing process

CHAPTER 1
Marketing: Managing profitable customer relationships

AFTER STUDYING THIS CHAPTER, YOU SHOULD BE ABLE TO

- define marketing and outline the steps in the marketing process
- explain the importance of understanding customers and the marketplace and identify the five core marketplace concepts
- identify the key elements of a customer-driven marketing strategy and discuss the marketing management orientations that guide marketing strategy
- discuss customer relationship management and identify strategies for creating value *for* customers and capturing value *from* customers in return
- describe the major trends and forces that are changing the marketing landscape in this age of relationships

THE WAY AHEAD Previewing the concepts

We'll start with a simple question: What *is* marketing? Simply put, marketing is managing profitable customer relationships. The aim of marketing is to create value for customers and to capture value in return. Chapter 1 is organised around five steps in the marketing process – from understanding customer needs, to designing customer-driven marketing strategies and programmes, to building customer relationships and capturing value for the firm. Understanding these basic concepts, and forming your own ideas about what they really mean to you, will give you a solid foundation for all that follows.

Our first stop is to look at an organisation that you might not think of as having much need for marketing ideas and concepts – UEFA, the governing body of European football.

Marketing European football

What are the biggest sporting events in the world? Everyone has their own opinion, but if you weigh a number of factors like television audience size, number of countries or teams involved, revenues and expenditure – not to mention the ability to bring much of the world to a halt – then the top five probably include the World Cup, the summer Olympic Games, the European football Championship, the Superbowl and the European Champions League.

Source: Getty Images.

Of these five, two are overseen by UEFA – the Union of European Football Associations.[1] There is a lot at stake here: regional and national pride, global TV audiences in the billions and lots and lots of money. UEFA defines its core purpose as being to promote, protect and develop European football at every level of the game, to promote the principles of unity and solidarity, and to deal with all questions relating to European football.[2] It does this by taking the excitement, the attention and the cash that big tournaments generate and using it to support its other activities.

Because of this, a lot of what UEFA does is marketing-related – whether sponsorship of an event or tournament by a commercial enterprise, a social programme to use the power of sport to alleviate problems like racism, the buying and selling of broadcasting and merchandising rights, public relations and managing relationships with governments, teams and an almost infinite number of journalists – not to mention the fans!

The marketing function of UEFA – people, resources and responsibilities for marketing affairs – is split across four divisions, each with its own focus.[3]

The **Marketing and Media Rights Division** develops marketing and media strategies for all UEFA competitions – the Champions League, the UEFA Cup, the European Football Championships and less prominent competitions like women's football, junior level tournaments and various 'futsal' events (the name is an abbreviation of the Portuguese term **fut**ebol de **sal**ão and the game is an indoor version of the standard sport). It has the responsibility to find the best price for broadcasting rights and agreeing terms and conditions with broadcasting partners and then maintaining relationships with these key partners.

UEFA Marketing and Media Management (UMMM) is the commercial division of UEFA responsible for generating revenue from sponsorship and licensing for competitions, and managing the relationships with all associated commercial partners. In essence, this division sells the rights to be associated with prestigious and exciting international events. It maintains high prices by strictly limiting the number of companies that are given these licences. Euro2008 in Austria and Switzerland had a core sponsorship panel of just ten companies – big global names like Adidas, Coke and Carlsberg. In the 2007–2008 Champions League season, the competition had just five sponsors – Heineken, Mastercard, Vodafone, Ford and Sony. Any number of merchandise items are produced for major tournaments – replica team strips, footballs, and even items for the desk-oriented like mouse mats and coffee mugs.[4]

UEFA Media Technologies SA (UMT) is the service company created by UEFA to support broadcast and sponsorship partners with multimedia content.[5] It links with the TV companies to try to ensure the best possible coverage of games. Untypically, during Euro 2008 the broadcasting of one game – an exciting match between Germany and Turkey – was interrupted by a severe electrical storm which disrupted power supplies. Many national broadcasters and sponsors were very unhappy at the failure of the systems at a critical time.[6] Other than TV, this division is increasingly involved with supporting UEFA's online operations – whether providing and maintaining statistical databases or selling downloadable recordings of games in order to maintain and develop relationships with fans and journalists.

The **Communications and Public Affairs Division** (CPAD) is responsible for public relations activity – such as briefing and supporting the activities of journalists. The division also has the responsibility of managing the work UEFA does with various charity and social groups. For example, CPAD works with the International Red Cross – the 'official charity partner of Euro2008' – among other projects with other organisations that have charitable or social causes to advance through the money and publicity generated by the sport.

That UEFA expends so much effort on marketing activity may surprise you – but think about it – it has brands, it provides services, it has connections and relationships with various publics and it generates significant revenue. One UEFA marketing manager – Philippe Le Floc'h – comments on the Champions League, a competition that alone generated €750m in 2007:

It is the best club competition in the world. It is a competition of champions, the best clubs, and the best players in the world. We have to make sure that whoever comes to the stadium, or watches on television, can fully experience it. We've thought about changing the music, but it is the second most recognised feature after the star ball and we get requests from all over the world for it to be used at weddings.[7]

Is everyone happy at the marketing activities of UEFA? Not quite. Some people aren't convinced that UEFA is sticking to its core mission of supporting football – they worry that it is moving too far towards becoming fully commercialised and that the sport is being used to make some people rich whilst traditional fans are being sidelined.

For Yves Stemmle, Switzerland's opening match against the Czech Republic in the 2008 European soccer championship won't be just about advancing to the next round. It will be about his civil rights.

'They want me to drink only Carlsberg beer and wear things with this,' said Stemmle, 36, pointing to the Euro 2008 logo on his hat as he sat in a Lugano café before a warm-up game with Slovakia. 'They can't tell me what to wear.'

Some fans say UEFA, European soccer's governing body, has put profits ahead of their interests and plans to turn them away from stadiums and 'fan zones' if they wear clothes bearing the logos of companies that aren't tournament sponsors. UEFA estimates the 23-day championship, which begins June 7 in Basel, will generate 2 billion Swiss francs ($1.9 billion) in revenue from media rights, tickets and sponsors. After expenses, it expects to retain 330 million francs to cover administrative costs and fund other tournaments.

A Swiss tabloid, SonntagsBlick, published a caricature showing UEFA President Michel Platini as Moses holding up 11 commandments to heed during the event. The first: Drink only Carlsberg beer. Lamp posts around Zurich are sprouting stickers saying, 'UEFA: We Care About Money,' a play on the group's slogan, 'We Care About Football.'

Organizers of previous events have protected sponsors' rights inside stadiums by refusing entry to groups of fans paid to wear corporate logos. UEFA is

extending its campaign against ambush marketers into fan zones, areas in each of the host cities where supporters gather to watch games on giant TV screens. That has aroused the ire of some fans.

'Fan zones are paid for and run by the city and access is free,' says Patrick Cotting, who lectures on marketing and sponsorships at the University of Lugano and consults for the Euro 2008 organizers in Basel. 'There's no legal precedent that would forbid individuals from entering a public space because they're wearing the wrong T-shirt.'

Copenhagen-based Carlsberg is paying at least 100 million kroner ($21 million) for the sponsorship, its biggest ever, giving it the right to exclusive sales in the eight biggest fan zones in each host city.

'There are plenty of other places in the local cities where fans can drink other beers and we totally respect that,' said Keld Strudahl, head of international marketing for the company.

In Austria, beermaker Ottakringer Brauerei AG is taking advantage of the popular backlash by selling its beer with a red-white-red logo, the colours of Austria's flag, and calling it the 'unofficial fan beer' drunk by 'real fans who want to show their support in whatever way they want'.

'Soccer used to belong to the people,' said Carlo Kuemin, 70, as he huddled under an umbrella in the standing-only curve of Lugano's Cornaredo Stadium during the Switzerland–Slovakia match. 'Not any more. The sponsors

govern the events now. It's all about the money.'

Stemmle, the fan in the café, isn't taking UEFA's actions lying down.

'I have a ticket to the opening match between Switzerland and the Czech Republic,' he said. 'I'm only going to wear things they don't allow.'[8]

UEFA then is an organisation that recognises the need to build and maintain relationships with its stakeholders – including customers. Our example shows, however, that marketing actions can have unintended consequences – care and attention is needed!

Sources: See notes 1–8 at the end of this chapter.

Today's successful organisations have one thing in common: they are strongly customer-focused and heavily committed to marketing. These organisations share a passion for satisfying customer needs in well-defined target markets. They motivate everyone in the organisation to help build lasting customer relationships through superior customer value and satisfaction. As Wal-Mart founder Sam Walton asserted: 'There is only one boss. The customer. And he can fire everybody in the company from the chairman on down, simply by spending his money somewhere else.'

WHAT IS MARKETING?

Marketing, more than any other business function, deals with customers. Although we will soon explore more detailed definitions of marketing, perhaps the simplest definition is this one: marketing is managing profitable customer relationships. The twofold goal of marketing is to attract new customers by promising superior value and to keep and grow current customers by delivering satisfaction.

Tesco states its core purpose as being 'to create value for customers to earn their lifetime loyalty', and that 'no one tries harder for customers'. IKEA's vision is to 'create a better everyday life for the many people'. Dell leads the personal computer industry by consistently making good on its promise to 'be direct'. Dell makes it easy for customers to custom-design their own computers and have them delivered quickly to their home or office. These and other highly successful companies know that if they take care of their customers, market share and profits will follow.

Sound marketing is critical to the success of every organisation. Large for-profit firms such as Procter & Gamble, Toyota and Zara use marketing. But so do not-for-profit organisations such as universities, museums, symphony orchestras and even churches – as seen in Marketing at Work 1.2 (page 27).

You already know a lot about marketing – it's all around you. You see the results of marketing in the abundance of products in your nearby department store. You see marketing in the advertisements on your TV screen, that spice up your magazines, stuff your mailbox or border your Web pages. At home, where you work, and where you study, you see marketing in almost everything you do. Yet, there is much more to marketing than meets the consumer's casual eye. Behind it all is a massive network of people and activities competing for your attention and purchases. Marketing is a set of extremely varied practices, and Europe is a diverse and exciting continent. In this book we will look at Russian beer brands being launched in the UK, French cars being advertised in Germany, Danish foods being sold in Arab supermarkets and European aircraft being sold round the world – and many other examples of marketing in, to and from Europe.

This book will give you a complete and formal introduction to the basic concepts and practices of today's marketing. In this chapter, we begin by defining *marketing* and the marketing process.

Marketing defined

What *is* marketing? Many people think of marketing only as selling and advertising. Even if you have chosen to study marketing deliberately and with forethought, you might think the same. And no wonder – every day we are bombarded with television commercials, direct-mail offers and Internet pop-up ads. However, selling and advertising are only the tip of the marketing iceberg.

Today, marketing must be understood not in the old sense of making a sale – 'telling and selling' – but in the new sense of *satisfying customer needs*. If the marketer does a good job of understanding consumer needs, develops products and services that provide superior customer value, and prices, distributes and promotes them effectively, these products will sell very easily. Thus, selling and advertising are only part of a larger 'marketing mix' – a set of marketing tools that work together to satisfy customer needs and build customer relationships. Marketing is as much attitude as action, as much perspective as planning.

Broadly defined, marketing is a social and managerial process by which individuals and organisations obtain what they need and want through creating and exchanging value with others. In a narrower business context, marketing involves building profitable, value-laden exchange relationships with customers. Hence, we define **marketing** as the process by which companies create value for customers and build strong customer relationships in order to capture value from customers in return.[9]

The marketing process

Figure 1.1 presents a simple five-step model of the marketing process. In the first four steps, companies work to understand consumers, create customer value and build strong customer relationships. In the final step, companies reap the rewards of creating superior customer value. By creating value *for* consumers, they in turn capture value *from* consumers in the form of sales, profits and long-term customer equity.

In this and the next chapter we will examine the steps of this simple model of marketing. In this chapter, we will review each step but focus more on the customer relationship steps – understanding customers, building customer relationships and capturing value from customers. In Chapter 2, we'll look more deeply into the second and third steps – designing marketing strategies and constructing marketing programmes.

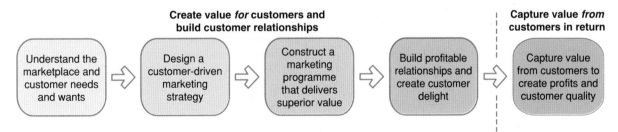

FIGURE 1.1

A simple model of the marketing process

UNDERSTANDING THE MARKETPLACE AND CUSTOMER NEEDS

As a first step, marketers need to understand customer needs and wants and the marketplace within which they operate. We now examine five core customer and marketplace concepts:

1 needs, wants and demands;

2 marketing offers (products, services and experiences);

3 value and satisfaction;

4 exchanges and relationships; and

5 markets.

Customer needs, wants and demands

The most basic concept underlying marketing is that of human needs. Human **needs** are states of felt deprivation. They include basic *physical* needs for food, clothing, warmth and safety; *social* needs for belonging and affection; and *individual* needs for knowledge and self-expression. These needs were not created by marketers; they are a basic part of the human make-up.

Wants are the form human needs take as they are shaped by culture and individual personality. A hungry person *needs* food but *wants* a Big Mac, fries and a soft drink. A person in Mauritius *needs* food but *wants* a mango, rice, lentils and beans. Wants are shaped by one's society and are described in terms of objects that will satisfy needs. When backed by buying power, wants become **demands**. Given their wants and resources, people demand products with benefits that add up to the most value and satisfaction.

Outstanding marketing companies go to great lengths to learn about and understand their customers' needs, wants and demands. They conduct consumer research and analyse mountains of customer data – Tesco collect gigabytes per day through their Clubcards. Marketing people at all levels – including top management – stay close to customers. For example, at Richer Sounds Hi-Fi (**www.richersounds.com**) every after-sales questionnaire filled in and returned by a customer passes across the desk of the founder, Julian Richer, and Harley-Davidson's chairman regularly mounts his Harley and rides with customers to get feedback and ideas.

Market offerings – products, services and experiences

Consumers' needs and wants are fulfilled through a **market offering** – some combination of products, services, information or experiences offered to a market to satisfy a need or want. Market offerings are not limited to physical *products*. They also include *services*, activities or benefits offered for sale that are essentially intangible and do not result in the ownership of anything. Examples include banking, airlines, hotels, accountancy and home repair services. More broadly, market offerings also include other entities, such as *persons*, *places*, *organisations*, *information* and *ideas*. For example, for the International Red Cross, the 'marketing offer' is health education and charitable workplace giving – not to mention efforts in recruiting blood donors.

Many sellers make the mistake of paying more attention to the specific products they offer than to the benefits and experiences produced by these products. These sellers suffer from **marketing myopia**. They are so taken with their products that they focus only on existing wants and lose sight of underlying customer needs.[10] They forget that a product is only a tool to solve a consumer problem. A manufacturer of quarter-inch drill bits may think that the customer needs a drill bit. But what the customer *really* needs is a quarter-inch hole. These sellers will have trouble if a new product comes along that serves the customer's need better or less expensively. The customer will have the same *need* but will *want* the new product.

Smart marketers look beyond the attributes of the products and services they sell. By orchestrating several services and products, they create *brand experiences* for consumers. For example, Europe's biggest theme park is Parque Warner, just outside Madrid. Visiting this is certainly an experience; so is a ride on a Harley-Davidson motorcycle. Your Nikes are more than just shoes: they are an empowering experience that makes you think you can 'just do it'. And you don't just watch AC Milan play: you immerse yourself in the San Siro experience.[11] 'What consumers really want [are offers] that dazzle their senses, touch their hearts, and stimulate their minds', declares one expert. 'They want [offers] that deliver an experience.'[12]

Customer value and satisfaction

Consumers usually face a broad array of products and services that might satisfy a given need. How do they choose among these many market offerings? Customers form expectations about the value and satisfaction that various market offerings will deliver and buy accordingly. Satisfied customers buy again and tell others about their good experiences. Dissatisfied customers often switch to competitors and disparage the product to others.

Marketers must be careful to set the right level of expectations. If they set expectations too low, they may satisfy those who buy but fail to attract enough buyers. If they raise expectations too high, buyers will be disappointed. Customer value and customer satisfaction are key building blocks for developing and managing customer relationships. We will revisit these core concepts later in the chapter.

Exchanges and relationships

Marketing occurs when people decide to satisfy needs and wants through exchange relationships. **Exchange** is the act of obtaining a desired object from someone by offering something in return. In the broadest sense, the marketer tries to bring about a response to some market offering. The response may be more than simply buying or trading products and services. For instance, a political candidate wants votes, a church wants a bigger congregation, an orchestra wants an audience, and a social action group wants to change government policy and public opinion.

Marketing consists of actions taken to build and maintain desirable exchange *relationships* with target audiences involving a product, service, idea or other object. Beyond simply attracting new customers and creating transactions, the goal is to retain customers and grow their business with the company. Marketers want to build strong relationships by consistently delivering superior customer value. We will expand on the important concept of managing customer relationships later in the chapter.

Markets

The concepts of exchange and relationships lead to the concept of a market. A **market** is the set of actual and potential buyers of a product. These buyers share a particular need or want that can be satisfied through exchange relationships.

Marketing means managing markets to bring about profitable customer relationships. However, creating these relationships takes work. Sellers must search for buyers, identify their needs, design good market offerings, set prices for them, promote them, and store and deliver them. Activities such as product development, research, communication, distribution, pricing and service are core marketing activities.

Although we normally think of marketing as being carried on by sellers, buyers also carry on marketing. Consumers do marketing when they search for the goods they need at prices they can afford. Company purchasing agents do marketing when they track down sellers and bargain for good terms.

Figure 1.2 shows the main elements in a modern marketing system. In the usual situation, marketing involves serving a market of final consumers in the face of competitors. The company and their competitors send their respective offers and messages to consumers, either directly or through marketing intermediaries. All the actors in the system are affected by major environmental forces (demographic, economic, physical, technological, political/legal, social/cultural) and we'll discuss these environmental forces in Chapter 3.

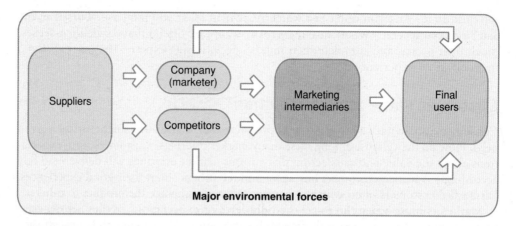

FIGURE 1.2

Elements of a modern marketing system

Each party in the system adds value for the next level. All of the arrows represent relationships that must be developed and managed. Thus, a company's success at building profitable relationships depends not only on its own actions but also on how well the entire system serves the needs of final consumers. Aldi cannot fulfil its promise of low prices unless its suppliers provide merchandise at low costs. And BMW cannot deliver high quality to car buyers unless its dealers provide outstanding sales and service.

DESIGNING A CUSTOMER-DRIVEN MARKETING STRATEGY

Once it fully understands consumers and the marketplace, marketing management can design a customer-driven marketing strategy. We define **marketing management** as the art and science of choosing target markets and building profitable relationships with them. The marketing manager's aim is to find, attract, keep and grow target customers by creating, delivering and communicating superior customer value.

To design a winning marketing strategy, the marketing manager must answer two important questions: What customers will we serve (what's our target market)? and How can we serve these customers best (what's our value proposition)? We will discuss these marketing strategy concepts briefly here, and then look at them in more detail in the next chapter.

Selecting customers to serve

The company must first decide *who* it will serve. It does this by dividing the market into segments of customers (*market segmentation*) and selecting which segments it will go after (*target marketing*). Some people think of marketing management as finding as many customers as possible and increasing demand. But marketing managers know that they cannot serve all customers in every way. By trying to serve all customers, they may not serve any customers well. Instead, the company wants to select only customers that it can serve well and profitably. For example, Marks & Spencer profitably targets the affluent; Lidl profitably targets families with modest means.

Some marketers may even seek *fewer* customers and reduced demand. For example, some public transport systems have trouble meeting demand during peak usage periods. In these and other cases of excess demand, organisations may practice *demarketing* to reduce the number of customers or to shift their demand temporarily or permanently. In order to reduce demand for seats on trains, for example, the London Underground has a price structure to persuade tourists and other leisure travellers to take their trips after the morning rush hour, and many public healthcare organisations across Europe use demarketing to persuade people to use services only when they need them, and not simply when it is convenient.[13]

Thus, marketing managers must decide which customers they want to target, and on the level, timing and nature of their demand. Simply put, marketing management is *customer management* and *demand management*.

Choosing a value proposition

The company must also decide how it will serve targeted customers – how it will *differentiate and position* itself in the marketplace. A company's *value proposition* is the set of benefits or values it promises to deliver to consumers to satisfy their needs. Porsche promises driving performance and excitement: 'What a dog feels like when its leash breaks'. Red Bull energy drink, on the other hand, captures a large part of the energy drink market by promising 'It gives you w-i-i-i-ngs!'

Such value propositions differentiate one brand from another. They answer the customer's question 'Why should I buy your brand rather than a competitor's?' Companies must design strong value propositions that give them the greatest advantage in their target markets.

Marketing management orientations

Marketing management wants to design strategies that will build profitable relationships with target consumers. But what *philosophy* should guide these marketing strategies? What weight should be given to the interests of customers, the organisation and society? Very often, these interests conflict.

There are five alternative concepts under which organisations design and carry out their marketing strategies: the *production, product, selling, marketing* and *societal marketing concepts*.

The production concept

The **production concept** holds that consumers will favour products that are available and highly affordable. Therefore, management should focus on improving production and distribution efficiency. This concept is one of the oldest orientations that guides sellers.

The production concept is still a useful philosophy in some situations. For example, Asian computer maker Legend dominates the highly competitive, price-sensitive Chinese PC market through low labour costs, high production efficiency and mass distribution. However, although useful in some situations, the production concept can lead to marketing myopia. Companies adopting this orientation run a major risk of focusing too narrowly on their own operations and losing sight of the real objective – satisfying customer needs and building customer relationships.

The product concept

The **product concept** holds that consumers will favour products that offer the most in quality, performance and innovative features. Under this concept, marketing strategy focuses on making continuous product improvements.

Product quality and improvement are important parts of most marketing strategies. However, focusing *only* on the company's products can also lead to marketing myopia. For example, some manufacturers believe that if they can 'build a better mousetrap, the world will beat a path to their door'. But they are often rudely shocked. Buyers may well be looking for a better solution to a mouse problem but not necessarily for a better mousetrap. The better solution might be a chemical spray, an exterminating service, or something that works better than a mousetrap. Furthermore, a better mousetrap will not sell unless the manufacturer designs, packages and prices it attractively, places it in convenient distribution channels, brings it to the attention of people who need it, and convinces buyers that it is a better product.

The selling concept

Many companies follow the **selling concept**, which holds that consumers will not buy enough of the firm's products unless it undertakes a large-scale selling and promotion effort. The concept is typically practised with unsought goods – those that buyers do not normally think of buying or contributing to, such as insurance policies or donating blood. These industries must be good at tracking down prospects and selling them on product benefits.

Such aggressive selling, however, carries high risks. It focuses on creating sales transactions rather than on building long-term, profitable customer relationships. The aim often is to sell what the company makes rather than making what the market wants. It assumes that customers who are coaxed into buying the product will like it. Or, if they don't like it, they will possibly forget their disappointment and buy it again later. These are usually poor assumptions.

The marketing concept

The **marketing concept** holds that achieving organisational goals depends on knowing the needs and wants of target markets and delivering the desired satisfactions better than competitors do. Under the marketing concept, customer focus and value are the *paths* to sales and profits. Instead of a product-centered 'make and sell' philosophy, the marketing concept is a customer-centered 'sense and respond' philosophy. It views marketing not as 'hunting' but as 'gardening'. The job is not to find the right customers for your product, but to find the right products for your customers.

Figure 1.3 contrasts the selling concept and the marketing concept. The selling concept takes an *inside-out* perspective. It starts with the factory, focuses on the company's existing products, and calls for heavy selling and promotion to obtain profitable sales. It focuses primarily on customer conquest – getting short-term sales with little concern about who buys or why.

In contrast, the marketing concept takes an *outside-in* perspective. In the words of one Ford executive, 'If we're not customer driven, our cars won't be either'.[14] The marketing concept starts with a well-defined market, focuses on customer needs and integrates all the marketing activities that affect customers. In turn, it leads to profits by creating lasting relationships with the right customers based on customer value and satisfaction.

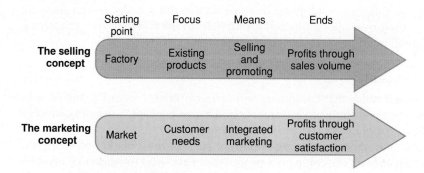

FIGURE 1.3

The selling and marketing concepts contrasted

Implementing the marketing concept often means more than simply responding to customers' stated desires and obvious needs. *Customer-driven* companies research current customers in detail to learn about their desires, gather new product and service ideas and test proposed product improvements. Such customer-driven marketing usually works well when a clear need exists and when customers know what they want.

In many cases, however, customers *don't* know what they want or even what is possible. For example, even 20 years ago, how many consumers would have thought to ask for now commonplace products such as mobile phones, notebook computers, 24-hour online buying and satellite navigation systems in their cars? Such situations call for *customer-driving* marketing – understanding customer needs even better than customers themselves do and creating products and services that meet existing and latent needs, now and in the future. As an executive at 3M puts it: 'Our goal is to lead customers where they want to go before *they* know where they want to go.' In Marketing at Work 1.1 several managers from a variety of firms give their perspectives on what marketing is and how their companies implement it.

MARKETING AT WORK 1.1

Managers on marketing

So how and why do businesses take marketing so seriously? Let's look at the personal perspectives from some current managers working in business today.

Electrolux – the Swedish manufacturer of household appliances – has been in business for nearly a hundred years and currently sells more than 40 million products globally for about €11 billion annually. The corporate motto is '*Thinking of you*' – but is their embracing of the marketing concept more than skin-deep? Richard Sells, the chief innovation officer at Electrolux, gives his take as a designer on the importance of marketing:

I think marketing ultimately is the bringing together of a consumer offer that is relevant and attractive to consumers, so whether you talk about that from the point of view of brand marketing, product marketing, marketing services, the offer in store – ultimately it's about bringing together an offer that is relevant and understanding the

consumer well enough to know that that offer is relevant. Most of the home appliance markets are saturated, and therefore consumers are looking for more sophisticated appliances. They're looking for better designed appliances, things that add some value to their home. They're no longer simply saying, 'OK, I'll have a dishwasher because I've never had one before', and so in that respect it's important that we understand what their needs are. You know, does a product that we are offering give some unique feature. The feeling can be sort of, you know, 'Wow, how did Electrolux know I needed that, because it really does solve my problem.'

Land Rover is a familiar name. For 60 years they have been producing high quality utility vehicles. Colin Green is their director of Global Marketing:

I think marketing at its essence is understanding consumer needs, understanding whether you can satisfy those consumer needs and then presenting

yourself in the marketplace through the principles of the four Ps – Price, Product, Promotion and Place – and getting those activities entirely focused on what the consumer is demanding and how you can meet those needs.

You'd expect a marketing manager to be onside with the idea of the importance of marketing, but what about at the very top level? Philip Popham, the managing director of Land Rover, comments:

For me, marketing is all about positioning your brand and your product correctly. It's about developing and building desirability which really does take away the need for the selling process, it builds desirability of the product so people want it and it builds loyalty. It's about handling the customer in the right way, making him or her proud to be associated with the brand, proud to be associated with the product which he or she has purchased and wanting more of that in the future, that's what good marketing is.

Land Rover and Electrolux are huge companies employing thousands of people and marketing their products globally. What about smaller businesses, is marketing relevant there as well? Acme Whistles has been in business for more than 130 years, with its 100 employees making and selling 6 million whistles per year. Quite simply, they think they make the world's best whistles. Acme products are used by police forces and animal trainers around the globe, by referees in most professional football leagues and in the early 1900s they supplied the whistles for use on the Titanic! Simon Topman, the MD at Acme, explains his take on how marketing is relevant to his business:

Our marketing is undoubtedly affected by the way that we make things. A very good example of that is a tradition that was laid down by Joseph Hudson, our founder, who like any founder of a business was perhaps a little eccentric and a very determined individual. One of the things he used to do was personally blow every whistle before it left the factory. The production now is about 6 million a year so, of course, that isn't possible anymore – but we still do test every single one. Everything that leaves this factory is as we say in our marketing literature: 'Individually tested and guaranteed.' There are rejects, but we find them, not the customers.

Successful marketing for me is linking together all resources of the company with the demand of the customer. So that everybody within this place right down to the cleaners knows what the customer wants and understands that keeping the machinery clean and the floor space around it clean is yet another way of making sure that the plating isn't contaminated, or the solder isn't contaminated, so the whistle looks better and lasts longer. And when you have all that lined up properly, then I think you have a great story to tell, great marketing and a business that's truly tuned in to its customers.

Our ultimate aim is to make sure that that very famous brand name Acme, and our product link with it, is obligatory for the buyers of whistles. That such is the demand by the customer that retailers can't afford to not carry that product. To that extent we educate our entire workforce from the cleaners all the way through to those who are dealing with sales calls on what the customer wants, why the customer wants it, how they want it so that we're filling up that chain all the way from the very bottom right through to the customer. The whole company is focused on that customer – making our product the best they can possibly get, the one they've got to have.

Sources: Corporate websites for Acme Whistles (www.acmewhistles.co.uk), Electrolux (www.electrolux.com/), Land Rover (www.landrover.com/), and interviews with managers conducted by Pearson Education Ltd.

How firms market their products varies from industry to industry, as these images from Electrolux, Acme Whistles and Land Rover show – but there are commonalities as well. *Photos sources*: Electrolux (bottom left); Getty Images/Frank Greenaway (top right); The Advertising Archives (bottom right). All with permission.

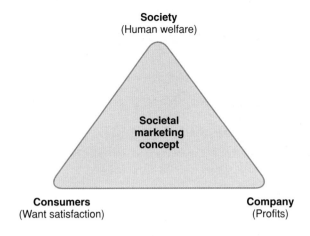

Society
(Human welfare)

**Societal
marketing
concept**

Consumers
(Want satisfaction)

Company
(Profits)

FIGURE 1.4

Three considerations underlying
the societal marketing concept

The societal marketing concept

The **societal marketing concept** questions whether the pure marketing concept over-looks possible conflicts between consumer *short-term wants* and consumer *long-term welfare*. Is a firm that satisfies the immediate needs and wants of target markets always doing what's best for consumers in the long run? The societal marketing concept holds that marketing strategy should deliver value to customers in a way that maintains or improves both the consumer's *and the society's* well-being.

Consider the fast-food industry. You may view today's giant fast-food chains as offering tasty and convenient food at reasonable prices. Yet many consumer nutritionists and environmental groups have voiced concerns. They point to increasing levels of obesity in adults and in children at ever earlier ages – leading to healthy life expectancy figures in cities like Glasgow being the lowest in Europe at about 60 years for a man.[15] What's more, these products are wrapped in convenient packaging, leading to waste and pollution. Thus, in satisfying short-term consumer wants, the highly successful fast-food chains may be harming consumer health and causing environmental problems in the long run.[16]

As Figure 1.4 shows, companies should balance three considerations in setting their marketing strategies: company profits, consumer wants *and* society's interests. Cadbury had a problem in 2007 when warnings for nut-allergy sufferers were missed off the packaging of its Creme Eggs. Despite this happening at Easter, when sales are at their absolute peak, and such allergies affecting only a tiny proportion of the population, Cadbury felt it had no choice but to recall the products.[17]

PREPARING A MARKETING PLAN AND PROGRAMME

The company's marketing strategy outlines which customers the company will serve and how it will create value for these customers. Next, the marketer develops a marketing programme that will actually deliver the intended value to target customers. The marketing programme builds customer relationships by transforming the marketing strategy into action. It consists of the firm's *marketing mix*, the set of marketing tools the firm uses to implement its marketing strategy.

The major marketing mix tools are classified into four broad groups, called the *four Ps* of marketing: product, price, place and promotion. To deliver on its value proposition, the firm must first create a need-satisfying market offering (product). It must decide how much it will charge for the offer (price) and how it will make the offer available to target consumers (place). Finally, it must communicate with target customers about the offer and persuade them of its merits (promotion). We will explore marketing programmes and the marketing mix in much more detail in later chapters.

MAKING CONNECTIONS Linking the concepts

What have you learned so far about marketing? For the moment, set aside the more formal definitions we've examined and try to develop your own understanding of marketing.

■ In *your own words*, what *is* marketing? Write down *your* definition. Does your definition include such key concepts as customer value and relationships?

■ What does marketing *mean* to you? How does it affect your life on a daily basis?

■ What brand of trainers did you purchase last? Describe your relationship with Nike, New Balance, Reebok, Adidas, or whichever company made the shoes you purchased.

BUILDING CUSTOMER RELATIONSHIPS

The first three steps in the marketing process – understanding the marketplace and customer needs, designing a customer-driven marketing strategy and constructing marketing programmes – all lead up to the fourth and most important step: building profitable customer relationships.

Managing marketing relationships

The necessity of managing the organisation's relationships, sometimes called *relationship marketing* or, popularly, *customer relationship management (CRM)*, is perhaps the most important new idea in modern marketing. Until recently, CRM has been defined narrowly as a customer data management activity. By this definition, it involves managing detailed information about individual customers and carefully managing customer 'touch points' in order to maximise customer loyalty – that is, the company uses its data about past transactions and interactions as a corporate memory, to help it more effectively engage with its customers in the present. We will discuss this narrower CRM activity in Chapter 4, which deals with managing marketing information.

More recently, however, customer relationship management has taken on a broader meaning. In this broader sense, **customer relationship management** is the overall process of building and maintaining profitable customer relationships by delivering superior customer value and satisfaction. It deals with all aspects of acquiring, keeping and growing customers – the opening case of UEFA showed how complex this can be.

Relationship building blocks: customer value and satisfaction

The key to building lasting customer relationships is to create superior customer value and satisfaction. Satisfied customers are more likely to be loyal customers and to give the company a larger share of their business for longer.

Customer value Attracting and retaining customers can be a difficult task. Customers often face a bewildering array of products and services from which to choose. A customer buys from the firm that offers the highest **customer perceived value** – the customer's evaluation of the difference between all the benefits and all the costs of a market offering relative to those of competing offers.

For example, Toyota Prius hybrid car owners gain a number of benefits. The most obvious benefit is fuel efficiency and hence reduced running costs. However, by purchasing a Prius the owners may also receive some status and image values. Driving a Prius makes owners feel and appear more environmentally responsible. When deciding whether to purchase a Prius, customers will weigh these and other perceived values of owning the car against the money, effort and psychic costs of acquiring it. Moreover, they will compare the value of owning a Prius against that of owning another hybrid or non-hybrid car. They will select the brand that gives them the greatest perceived value. Other drivers may prioritise other factors rather than efficiency and environmental impact – such as performance and social status reinforcement. These people would be more likely to buy a Ferrari or a Mercedes.

Customers often do not judge product values and costs accurately or objectively. They act on *perceived* value. For example, is the Prius really the most economical choice? Running costs may be significantly cheaper, but an alternative like a Skoda might be much cheaper to buy. In reality, it might take years to save enough in reduced fuel costs to offset the car's higher price. However, Prius buyers perceive that they are getting real value. A recent survey of the ownership experiences of 69,000 new car buyers showed that Prius owners *perceived* more overall value for their money than buyers of any other new car.[18] How many of them are likely to have considered it objectively – even to the extent of some calculations on the back of an envelope?

Customer satisfaction Customer satisfaction depends on the product's perceived performance relative to a buyer's expectations. If the product's performance falls short of expectations, the customer is dissatisfied. If performance matches expectations, the customer is satisfied. If performance exceeds expectations, the customer is highly satisfied or delighted.

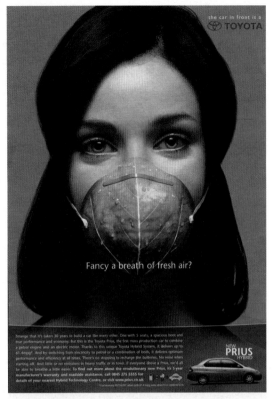

Perceived customer value: when deciding to purchase a Prius, customers will weigh its benefits against the benefits of owning another hybrid or non-hybrid brand.

Outstanding marketing companies go out of their way to keep important customers satisfied. Highly satisfied customers make repeat purchases and tell others about their good experiences with the product. Most studies show that higher levels of customer satisfaction lead to greater customer loyalty, which in turn results in better company performance.[19] The key is to match customer expectations with company performance. Smart companies aim to *delight* customers by promising only what they can deliver, then delivering *more* than they promise.

However, although the customer-centred firm seeks to deliver high customer satisfaction relative to competitors, it does not attempt to *maximise* customer satisfaction. A company can always increase customer satisfaction by lowering its price or increasing its services. But this may result in lower profits. Thus, the purpose of marketing is to generate customer value profitably. This requires a very delicate balance: The marketer must continue to generate more customer value and satisfaction but not 'give away the house'.

Customer relationship levels and tools

Companies can build customer relationships at many levels, depending on the nature of the target market. At one extreme, a company with many low-margin customers may seek to develop *basic relationships* with them. For example, Tesco has handed out millions of Clubcard loyalty cards which it uses to collect and analyse data on the shopping habits of a good proportion of the UK population. At the other extreme, in markets with few customers and high margins, sellers want to create *full partnerships* with key customers. This is often the case where one business is selling to another – P&G customer teams work closely with Sainsbury's, Asda, Carrefour and other major supermarkets – but also where the product is customised or tailored to the specific needs of a specific customer – such as a bespoke suit. In between these two extreme situations, other levels of customer relationships are appropriate.

Beyond offering consistently high value and satisfaction, marketers can use specific marketing tools to develop stronger bonds with consumers. For example, many companies now offer *frequency marketing programmes* that reward customers who buy frequently or in large amounts. Airlines offer frequent-flyer programmes and hotels give room upgrades to their frequent guests.

Building customer relationships. Porsche helps to maintain the community spirit of Porsche owners by sponsoring and endorsing owners' clubs across Europe.

Source: http://www.porscheclubgb.com/. With permission: Porsche.

Other companies sponsor *club marketing programmes* that offer members special discounts and create member communities. For example, Porsche, the German sports car manufacturer, sponsors owners' clubs in many countries around the world. As well as organising purely social events like dinners, track days and charity fund-raising events, the clubs also run trips to the Porsche manufacturing and development centres in Stuttgart, Leipzig and Weissach. Porsche as a commercial enterprise has a brand and human presence at all of these events and makes sure that the relationships with current owners are maintained and developed over time.[20]

To build customer relationships, companies can add structural ties as well as financial and social benefits. A business marketer might supply customers with special equipment or online linkages that help them manage their orders, payroll or inventory. As we'll discuss in detail in Chapter 11, Smiths – an offshoot of the well-known high street newsagent WHSmith – uses web-based software with its thousands of customers to manage the inventory and logistical difficulties in distributing millions of newspapers and magazines daily.

The changing nature of customer relationships

Dramatic changes are occurring in the ways in which companies are relating to their customers. Yesterday's companies focused on mass marketing to all customers at arm's length. Today's companies are building more direct and lasting relationships with more carefully selected customers. Here are some important trends in the way companies are relating to their customers.

Relating with more carefully selected customers

Few firms today still practise true mass marketing – selling in a standardised way to any customer who comes along. Today, most marketers realise that they don't want relationships with every customer. Instead, companies now are targeting fewer, more profitable customers. Called *selective relationship management*, many companies now use customer profitability analysis to weed out customers that cost them money and to target ones that are profitable for pampering. Once they identify profitable customers, firms can create attractive offers and special handling to capture these customers and earn their loyalty.

But what should the company do with unprofitable customers? If it can't turn them into profitable ones, it may even want to 'fire' customers that are too unreasonable or that cost more to serve than they are worth. For example, banks now routinely assess customer profitability based on such factors as an account's average balances, account activity, services usage, branch visits and other variables. For most banks, profitable customers with large balances are pampered with premium services, whereas unprofitable, low-balance ones get the cold shoulder. The Dutch bank ING Direct selects accounts differently. It seeks relationships with customers who don't need or want expensive pampering while firing those who do.

ING Direct is the fast-food chain of financial services. With a handful of offerings including savings accounts, mortgages and CDs and home equity loans, the bank is about as no-frills as it gets. Yet its profits are downright gaudy. ING Direct's secret? Selective relationship management. The bank lures low-maintenance customers with high interest rates. Then, to offset that generosity, the bank does 91 per cent of its transactions online and offers bare-bones service. In fact, ING Direct USA routinely 'fires' overly demanding customers. By ditching clients who need the direction, hand-holding and personalised service of a branch bank, the company has driven its cost per account to a third of the industry average.

ING Direct USA CEO Arkadi Kuhlmann explains: 'We need to keep expenses down, which doesn't work when customers want a lot of [hand-holding]. If the average customer phone call costs us $5.25 and the average account revenue is $12 per month, all it takes is 100,000 misbehaving customers for costs to go through the roof. So when a customer calls too many times or wants too many exceptions to the rule, our sales associate can basically say: Look, this doesn't fit you. You need to go back to your community bank and get the kind of contact you're comfortable with . . . It's all about finding customers who are comfortable with a self-serve business; we try to get you in and out fast . . . Even though our touch is light and short, it's all about how you feel in the end. The smile at a take-out window can be just as satisfying as good service at a sit-down restaurant. While this makes for some unhappy customers, [those are the] ones you want out the door anyway.'[21]

Selective relationship management: ING Direct seeks relationships with customers who don't need or want expensive pampering, routinely 'firing' overly demanding customers. The bank lures low-maintenance customers with high interest rates and no fees or minimums. 'No bull!'

Source: ING Direct. With permission.

Of course, marketing strategies and tactics like this can cause significant issues for society as a whole – as we saw with the dissatisfied football fans in the UEFA case – and we'll discuss these in Chapter 16.

Relating for the long term

Just as companies are being more selective about which customers they choose to serve, they are serving chosen customers in a deeper, more lasting way. Today's companies are going beyond designing strategies to *attract* new customers and create *transactions* with them. They are using customer relationship management to *retain* current customers and build profitable, long-term *relationships* with them. The new view is that marketing is the science and art of creating, developing and sustaining interactive relationships with profitable customers.[22]

Why the new emphasis on retaining and developing/growing customers? In the past, growing markets and an upbeat economy meant a plentiful supply of new customers. However, companies today face some new marketing realities. Changing demographics, more sophisticated competitors, and overcapacity in many industries mean that there are fewer customers to go around. Many companies are now fighting for shares of flat or fading markets.

As a result, the costs of attracting new consumers are rising. In fact, on average, it can cost a lot more to attract a new customer than it does to keep a current customer satisfied – meaning that some investment in keeping current customers can save a lot further down the line.

Relating directly

Beyond connecting more deeply with their customers, many companies are also connecting more *directly*. In fact, direct marketing is booming. Consumers can now buy virtually any product without going to a shop – by telephone, mail-order catalogues, kiosks and online. Businesses routinely shop on the Web for items ranging from standard office supplies to high-priced, high-tech computer equipment.

Some companies sell *only* via direct channels – firms such as Dell, Expedia and Amazon.com, to name only a few. Other companies use direct connections to supplement their other communications and distribution channels. For example, XBox 360 consoles and games are available from many high-street retailers, but once set up and connected to the Web customers can buy new games, add-ons for games they already own, music and films through the online marketplace – as well as being able to purchase trailers and demos of new games.

Some marketers have hailed direct marketing as the 'marketing model of the next century'. They envision a day when all buying and selling will involve direct connections between companies and their customers. Others, although agreeing that direct marketing will play a growing and important role, see it as just one more way to approach the marketplace. We will take a closer look at the world of direct marketing in Chapters 13 and 14.

Partner relationship management

When it comes to creating customer value and building strong customer relationships, today's marketers know that they can't go it alone. They must work closely with a variety of marketing partners. In addition to being good at *customer relationship management*, marketers must also be good at **partner relationship management**. Major changes are occurring in how marketers partner with others inside and outside the company jointly to bring more value to customers.

Partners inside the company

Traditionally, marketers have been charged with understanding customers and representing customer needs to different company departments. The old thinking was that marketing is done only by marketing, sales, and customer support people. However, in today's more connected world, marketing no longer has sole ownership of customer interactions. Every functional area can interact with customers, especially electronically. The new thinking is that every employee must be customer-focused. David Packard, late co-founder of Hewlett-Packard, wisely said, 'Marketing is far too important to be left only to the marketing department'.[23] This has led to the idea of 'the part-time marketer' – someone who works for the organisation but not in the marketing department who has, nevertheless, the opportunity to impact positively or negatively upon how customers think about the firm. Technicians can make a good or bad impression, as can shop-floor staff and anyone who answers the phone when a customer calls.[24]

Today, rather than letting each department go its own way, firms are linking all departments in the cause of creating customer value. Rather than assigning only sales and marketing people to customers, they are forming cross-functional customer teams. Marketing at Work 1.1 gave the perspectives of those not employed as marketers but who nevertheless understood the importance of marketing in their roles as senior managers or product designers. As an example of this culture, P&G assigns 'customer development teams' to each of its major retailer accounts. These teams – consisting of sales and marketing people, operations specialists, market and financial analysts and others – coordinate the efforts of many P&G departments towards helping the retailer be more successful.

Marketing partners outside the firm

Changes are also occurring in how marketers connect with their suppliers, channel partners and even competitors. Most companies today are networked companies, relying heavily on partnerships with other firms.

Marketing channels consist of distributors, retailers and others who connect the company to its buyers. The *supply chain* describes a longer channel, stretching from raw materials to components to final products that are carried to final buyers. For example, the supply chain for personal computers consists of suppliers of computer chips and other components, the computer manufacturer, and the distributors, retailers and others who sell the computers.

Through *supply chain management*, many companies today are strengthening their connections with partners all along the supply chain. They know that their fortunes rest not just on how well they perform. Success at building customer relationships also rests on how well their entire supply chain performs against competitors' supply chains. These companies don't just treat suppliers as vendors and distributors as customers. They treat both as partners in delivering customer value. On the one hand, for example, Mercedes works closely with carefully selected suppliers to improve quality and operations efficiency. On the other hand, it works with its franchise dealers to provide top-grade sales and service support that will bring customers in the door and keep them coming back.

Beyond managing the supply chain, today's companies are also discovering that they need *strategic* partners if they hope to be effective. In the new, more competitive global environment, going it alone is going out of style. *Strategic alliances* are booming across almost all industries and services. For example, Dell joins forces with software creators such as Oracle and Microsoft to help boost business sales of its servers and their software. And Volkswagen is working jointly with agricultural processing firm Archer Daniels Midland further to develop and utilise biodiesel fuel.

Sometimes even competitors work together for mutual benefit. For example oral-care competitors Procter & Gamble and Philips joined forces to create the innovative IntelliClean system, a combination power toothbrush and toothpaste dispensing system. And Sony has partnered with Ericsson to produce mobile phone handsets – the Japanese electronics giant brings decades of experience in manufacturing high quality handheld gadgets and the Swedish telecoms giant brings detailed knowledge of mobile phones in respect of design and use by customers.[25]

CAPTURING VALUE FROM CUSTOMERS

The first four steps in the marketing process involve building customer relationships by creating and delivering superior customer value. The final step involves capturing value in return, in the form of current and future sales,

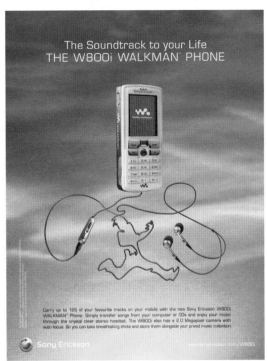

The Soundtrack to your Life
THE W800i WALKMAN PHONE

Carry up to 195 of your favourite tracks on your mobile with the new Sony Ericsson W800i WALKMAN Phone. Simply transfer songs from your computer or CDs and enjoy your music through the crystal clear stereo headset. The W800i also has a 2.0 Megapixel camera with auto focus. So you can take breathtaking shots and store them alongside your prized music collection.

Sony Ericsson

Partnership relationship management: both Sony and Ericsson benefit from working together. Sony brings manufacturing excellence and Ericsson understands the markets and customers.

market share and profits. By creating superior customer value, the firm creates highly satisfied customers who stay loyal and buy more. This, in turn, means greater long-run returns for the firm. Here, we discuss the outcomes of creating customer value: customer loyalty and retention, share of market and share of customer, and customer equity.

Creating customer loyalty and retention

Good customer relationship management creates customer delight. In turn, delighted customers remain loyal and talk favourably to others about the company and its products. Studies show big differences in the loyalty of customers who are less satisfied, somewhat satisfied and completely satisfied. Even a slight drop from complete satisfaction can create an enormous drop in loyalty. Thus, the aim of customer relationship management is to create not just customer satisfaction, but customer delight.[26]

Companies are realising that losing a customer means losing more than a single sale. It means losing the entire stream of purchases that the customer would make over a lifetime of patronage. For example, Porsche believe that someone who buys a new Porsche will typically replace it with a new car after seven years. Five years after purchase, the company starts to target these owners with letters and other communications to make sure their next car is a Porsche as well – if this works, that is another £70,000 in revenue. Indeed, Lexus estimates that a single satisfied and loyal customer is worth $600,000 in lifetime sales. You almost certainly visit a supermarket once a week or more – you may not spend much per visit, but consider how this sum adds up over a year or two. Thus, working to retain and grow customers makes good economic sense. In fact, a company can lose money on a specific transaction but still benefit greatly from a long-term relationship. Banks recognise this when putting together account packages for students. While at university, it is likely they will cost rather than make their bank money – because of reduced rate loans and overdrafts, low-level balances and often free gifts for account opening. When the student becomes a full-time worker four or five years later that is the point at which that customer will begin to become profitable – statistics tell us that you are more likely to get divorced than change your bank.[27]

This means that companies must aim high in building customer relationships. Customer delight creates an emotional relationship with a product or service, not just a rational preference.

Growing share of customer

Beyond simply retaining good customers to capture customer lifetime value, good customer relationship management can help marketers to increase their **share of customer** – the share they get of the customer's purchasing in their product categories. Thus, banks want to increase 'share of wallet'. Supermarkets and restaurants want to get more 'share of stomach'. Car companies want to increase 'share of garage' and airlines want greater 'share of travel'.

To increase share of customer, firms can offer greater variety to current customers. Or they can train employees to cross-sell and up-sell in order to market more products and services to existing customers. For example, Amazon is highly skilled at managing and developing relationships with its customers to increase its share of each customer's purchases. Originally an online bookseller, Amazon now offers customers music, DVDs, gifts, toys, consumer electronics, office products and home improvement items. In addition, based on each customer's purchase history, the company recommends related products that might be of interest – and the more you buy the better they become at predicting what else will interest you. In this way, Amazon captures a greater share of each customer's spending budget.

Building customer equity

We can now see the importance of not just acquiring customers, but of keeping and growing them as well. Customer relationship management takes a long-term view. Companies want not only to create profitable customers, but to 'own' them for life, capture their **customer lifetime value**, and earn a greater share of their purchases.

What is customer equity?

The ultimate aim of customer relationship management is to produce high *customer equity*.[28] **Customer equity** is the combined discounted customer lifetime values of all of the company's current and potential customers. Clearly, the more loyal the firm's profitable customers, the higher the firm's customer equity. Customer equity may be a better measure of a firm's performance than current sales or market share. Whereas sales and market share reflect the past, customer equity suggests the future. Consider the US car manufacturer Cadillac:

> In the 1970s and 1980s Cadillac had some of the most loyal customers in the industry. To an entire generation of car buyers, the name 'Cadillac' defined American luxury. Cadillac's share of the luxury car market reached a whopping 51 per cent in 1976. Based on market share and sales, the brand's future looked rosy. However, measures of customer equity would have painted a bleaker picture. Cadillac customers were getting older (average age 60) and average customer lifetime value was falling. Many Cadillac buyers were on their last car. Thus, although Cadillac's market share was good, its customer equity was not. Compare this with BMW. Its more youthful and vigorous image didn't win BMW the early market share war. However, it did win BMW younger customers with higher customer lifetime values. The result? In the years that followed, BMW's market share and profits soared while Cadillac's fortunes eroded badly. Thus, market share is not the answer. We should care not just about current sales but also about future sales. Customer lifetime value and customer equity are the name of the game. Recognising this, Cadillac is now making the Caddy cool again by targeting a younger generation of consumers with new high-performance models and its highly successful Break Through advertising campaign.[29]

Building the right relationships with the right customers

Companies should manage customer equity carefully. They should view customers as assets that need to be managed and maximised. But not all customers, not even all loyal customers, are good investments. Surprisingly, some loyal customers can be unprofitable, and some disloyal customers can be profitable. Which customers should the company acquire and retain? 'Up to a point, the choice is obvious: Keep the consistent big spenders and lose the erratic small spenders,' says one expert. 'But what about the erratic big spenders and the consistent small spenders? It's often unclear whether they should be acquired or retained, and at what cost.'[30]

The company can classify customers according to their potential profitability and manage its relationships with them accordingly. Figure 1.5 classifies customers into one of four relationship groups, according to their profitability and projected loyalty.[31] Each group requires a different relationship management strategy. 'Strangers' show low profitability and little projected loyalty. There is little fit between the company's offerings and their needs. The relationship management strategy for these customers is simple: don't invest anything in them.

'Butterflies' are profitable but not loyal. There is a good fit between the company's offerings and their needs. However, as with real butterflies, we can enjoy them for only a short while and then they're gone. Efforts to convert butterflies into loyal customers are rarely successful. Instead, the company should enjoy the butterflies for the moment.

	Butterflies	True Friends
High profitability	Good fit between company's offerings and customer's needs; high profit potential	Good fit between company's offerings and customer's needs; highest profit potential
Low profitability	**Strangers** Little fit between company's offerings and customer's needs; lowest profit potential	**Barnacles** Limited fit between company's offerings and customer's needs; low profit potential

Potential profitability (vertical axis)

Short-term customers | Long-term customers

Projected loyalty

FIGURE 1.5

Customer relationship groups

Source: Reprinted by permission of *Harvard Business Review*. Exhibit adapted from 'The Mismanagement of Customer Loyalty', by Werner Reinartz and V. Kumar, July 2002, p. 93. Copyright © 2002 by the Harvard Business School Publishing Corporation; all rights reserved.

It should use promotional blitzes to attract them, create satisfying and profitable transactions with them, and then cease investing in them until the next time around.

'True friends' are both profitable and loyal. There is a strong fit between their needs and the company's offerings. The firm wants to make continuous relationship investments to delight these customers and nurture, retain and grow them. It wants to turn true friends into 'true believers', who come back regularly and tell others about their good experiences with the company.

'Barnacles' are highly loyal but not very profitable. There is a limited fit between their needs and the company's offerings. An example is smaller bank customers who bank regularly but do not generate enough returns to cover the costs of maintaining their accounts. Like barnacles on the hull of a ship, they create drag. Barnacles are perhaps the most problematic customers. The company might be able to improve their profitability by selling them more, raising their fees, or reducing service to them. However, if they cannot be made profitable, they should be 'fired'.

The point here is an important one: different types of customer require different relationship management strategies. The goal is to build the *right relationships* with the *right customers*.

MAKING CONNECTIONS Linking the concepts

We've covered a lot of territory. Again, slow down for a moment and develop *your own* thoughts about marketing.

■ In *your own words*, what *is* marketing and what does it seek to accomplish?

■ How well does Renault manage its relationships with customers? What customer relationship management strategy does it use? Compare the relationship management strategies of Tesco and Asda.

■ Think of a company for which you are a 'true friend'. What strategy does this company use to manage its relationship with you?

THE NEW MARKETING LANDSCAPE

As the world spins on, dramatic changes are occurring in the marketplace. Richard Love of Hewlett-Packard observes, 'The pace of change is so rapid that the ability to change has now become a competitive advantage.' As the marketplace changes, so must those who serve it.

In this section, we examine the major trends and forces that are changing the marketing landscape and challenging marketing strategy. We look at four major developments: the new digital age, rapid globalisation, the call for more ethics and social responsibility, and the growth in not-for-profit marketing.

The new digital age

The Internet has and is continuing to revolutionise how companies create value for customers and build and maintain customer relationships. The digital age has fundamentally changed customers' notions of convenience, speed, price, product information and service. Thus, today's marketing requires new thinking and action. Companies need to retain most of the skills and practices that have worked in the past. But they will also need to add major new competencies and practices if they hope to grow and prosper in the changing digital environment. Now, more than ever before, we are all connected to each other and to things near and far in the world around us. Where it once took weeks or months to travel across Europe, we can now travel around the globe in only hours or days. Where it once took days or weeks to receive news about important world events, we now see them as they are occurring through live satellite broadcasts. Where it once took weeks to correspond with others in distant places, they are now only moments away by phone or email.

The technology boom has created exciting new ways to learn about and track customers, and to create products and services tailored to individual customer needs. Technology is also helping companies to distribute products more efficiently and effectively. And it's helping them to communicate with customers in large groups or one-to-one.

Through video conferencing, marketing researchers at a company's headquarters in Paris can look in on focus groups in Prague without ever stepping onto a plane. With only a few clicks of a mouse button, a direct marketer can tap into online data services to learn anything from what car you drive to what you read to what flavour of ice cream you prefer. Or, using today's powerful computers, marketers can create their own detailed customer databases and use them to target individual customers with offers designed to meet their specific needs.

Technology has also brought a new wave of communication and advertising tools – on mobile phones, podcasts, and even in virtual online worlds like Second Life. Marketers can use these tools to zero in on selected customers with carefully targeted messages. Through e-commerce, customers can learn about, design, order and pay for products and services, without ever leaving home. Then, through the marvels of express delivery, they can receive their purchases in less than 24 hours. From virtual reality displays that test new products to online virtual stores that sell them, the technology boom is affecting every aspect of marketing.

The Internet

Today, the **Internet** links individuals and businesses of all types to each other and to information all around the world. It allows anytime, anywhere connections to information, entertainment and communication. Companies are using the Internet to build closer relationships with customers and marketing partners. Beyond competing in traditional market*places*, they now have access to exciting new market*spaces*.

These days, it's hard to find a company that doesn't use the Web in a significant way – or one that doesn't have new opportunities and challenges for marketers. We will explore the impact of the new digital age in more detail in Chapter 14.

Rapid globalisation

As they are redefining their relationships with customers and partners, marketers are also taking a fresh look at the ways in which they connect with the broader world around them. In a rapidly shrinking world, many marketers are now connected *globally* with their customers and marketing partners.

Today, almost every company, large or small, is touched in some way by global competition. Your local florist might buy its flowers from the Netherlands, while BMW and Mercedes compete in their home market of Germany with giant Japanese rivals like Toyota and Nissan. A fledgling Internet retailer finds itself receiving orders from all over the world at the same time as an Italian consumer goods producer introduces new products into emerging markets abroad.

Coca-Cola offers a mind-boggling 400 different brands in more than 200 countries. MTV has joined the elite of global brands, delivering localised versions of its music channels in 30 languages to 161 countries.[32]

Today, companies are not only trying to sell more of their locally produced goods in international markets, they also are buying more supplies and components abroad. For example, Isaac Mizrahi, one of America's top fashion designers, may choose cloth woven from Australian wool with designs printed in Italy. He will design a dress and email the drawing to a Hong Kong agent, who will place the order with a Chinese factory. Finished dresses will be flown to New York, where they will be redistributed to department and speciality stores around the country.

Thus, managers in countries around the world are increasingly taking a global, not just local, view of the company's industry, competitors and opportunities. They are asking: What is global marketing? How does it differ from domestic marketing? How do global competitors and forces affect our business? To what extent should we 'go global'? We will discuss the global marketplace in more detail in Chapter 15.

The call for more ethics and social responsibility

Marketers are re-examining their relationships with social values and responsibilities and with the very Earth that sustains us. As the worldwide consumerism and environmentalism movements mature, today's marketers are being called on to take greater responsibility for the social and environmental impact of their actions – whether it be the place of manufacture, the packaging surrounding the product or how far the finished item travels before being sold. Corporate ethics and social responsibility have become hot topics for almost every business and few companies can ignore the renewed and very demanding environmental movement.

The social responsibility and environmental movements will place even stricter demands on companies in the future. Some companies resist these movements, budging only when forced by legislation or organised consumer outcries. More forward-looking companies, however, readily accept their responsibilities to the world around them. They view socially responsible actions as an opportunity to do well by doing good. They seek ways to profit by serving the best long-term interests of their customers and communities.

Some companies – such as Ben & Jerry's, Bodyshop, the Co-op and others – are practising 'caring capitalism', setting themselves apart by being civic-minded and responsible. They are building social responsibility and action into their company value and mission statements. For example, the financial services division of the Co-op – the Co-operative Bank – is a leader in respect of investing the money of its clients. Armaments manufacturers, industries which pollute heavily and companies that provide poor conditions for their staff are all on the Co-op's investment blacklist. In turn, the supermarket portion of the business has been a pioneer on many consumer rights issues – genetically modified foods, sourcing from sustainable resources and clear labelling on all foods. We will revisit the relationship between marketing and social responsibility in greater detail in Chapter 16.

The growth of not-for-profit sector marketing

In the past, marketing has been most widely applied in the for-profit business sector. In recent years, however, marketing also has become a major part of the strategies of many not-for-profit organisations, such as universities, hospitals, museums, orchestras and even churches. Many performing arts groups – even Russia's famous Mariinsky company, which usually performs opera and ballet to packed houses – face huge operating deficits that they must cover by more aggressive donor marketing from businesses like Gazprom, BP and Total, for example.[33] Finally, many long-standing not-for-profit organisations – the YMCA, the Salvation Army, the Scouts and, of course, the organisations we see in Marketing at Work 1.2 – are now modernising their missions and 'products' to attract more members, visitors or donors.[34]

The Mariinsky theatre in St Petersburg, Russia, uses marketing to raise money from sponsors.

Source: Photo by Maria Smirnova.

MARKETING AT WORK 1.2

The marketing domain

That commercial organisations use marketing techniques and ideas to support branded manufactured goods like motorcycles, cars or electronic items is probably something you expected. That being said, do marketing ideas have validity and value in other contexts? Neil Rami, managing director of Marketing Birmingham is someone who thinks they do:

I think like any city we're in a global competitive environment and because of the size and the scale of this city we do operate globally. You know, we have the largest event and conference sector per head of population in Western Europe, that means that we're competing for business

Cities, charities and cathedrals can put marketing concepts and ideas to good use as profit-making enterprises.
Source: Photos from Corbis/Peter Adams (left); Getty Images (right).

not only with Paris, Detroit, Barcelona – the conventional conference centres – but also

with Johannesburg, Dubai and increasingly China and the Asian subcontinent.

Ultimately for me marketing is about informing people's views, it's about increasing their propensity to buy, and it's about doing that in a profitable way. That's no different when it comes to the marketing of cities, whether you're in Liverpool, Newcastle, London or Birmingham, we're all in the same business. My job is to increase people's propensity to visit Birmingham and to do it cost-effectively. We're not a profit-making business but we very much require resources, both financial and human capital to promote the city and marketing effectively is a requirement.

Taking it further, do the benefits of being marketing-oriented apply to organisations that have priorities other than the bottom line? Lucy Caldicott, head of fundraising at VSO, thinks that they do:

Fund-raising is what in a corporate environment you'd call sales and its exactly the same in that it's about generating revenue for your organisation. In my past I've worked for American Express in direct marketing so I came from a very strong brand organisation with quite a history of using sophisticated direct marketing techniques and that is exactly the sort of way a lot of charities raise money. The skills that you develop in a marketing function in a company are completely transferable to charity work. For example, the [VSO] communications team is responsible for the brand and what the brand means and how we live the brand and the kind of words we use to describe ourselves. Also, fund-raising is a

hugely competitive environment so there are hundreds and hundreds of charities competing for funds.

Vicky Starnes, head of marketing at VSO, adds:

Here at VSO we're marketing the opportunity for people to make a difference first hand, and also to have the experience of a lifetime. We're looking for professionals to volunteer overseas, for anything up to two years, working with a partner organisation in a developing country. And together with the local community they're working to change people's lives and really tackle poverty in the country where they're working. I think marketing for volunteer recruitment is quite a special kind of marketing. Really what we're asking people to do is give up up to two years' worth of their lives, and commit that to us at VSO, and the communities that they're trying to help. We need to be very targeted in reaching the right kind of professionals, because if we don't have the right kind of opportunities for somebody to actually do their work and make a difference with it, there's no point us sending them out there. I think in a more conventional charitable organisation people would be really looking to attract funds from the general public, they'll be calling on emotive motivations and topics, and trying to show people how their money could be used and why they should be giving money. The marketing we're doing here at VSO to recruit volunteers is totally different from that, because we're appealing to people for their professional skills.

Commercial enterprises like Electrolux and Land Rover obviously have a need for marketing, and we've just seen how charities and cities can benefit as well. How about a cathedral – surely they don't need to know anything about marketing? Mark McVey, head of marketing and PR for St Paul's Cathedral in London, disagrees:

Previously I've worked at Hampton Court and the Tower of London and the basic product we have is very similar in terms of we are trying to attract the same audience, the same market. Tourists are typically coming to London for short breaks. They might set aside one day to do attractions and they'll most probably want to have two or three visits within that day. And we need to make sure that we are actually within their radar to be able to ensure that they come to us on that particular day. One of our greatest competitors is our exterior image, and we need to ensure that they know about what there is to do and see inside. My role as marketing manager is to try to ensure that we get as many people inside the building as possible. It's clearly important for income generation because we need to be able to have enough money to keep this great building going – and we only do that by getting them inside. We don't have a huge marketing budget and therefore we need to be rather clever with the resources we've got. We don't advertise in the conventional sense – we're adopting a much more subtle approach in talking to the tour operators, people that are putting on educational visits, so that we can then influence them, tell them of the benefits of St Paul's, how we can work with them and how we can enhance the packages that they're putting together.

We've developed our website, and that is now becoming an effective marketing tool. We have our marketing leaflets that we produce in the sort of hundreds of thousands that are distributed round all of the tourist information centres and hotels. We attend a number of trade fairs to get our message out to the wider market.

I think marketing has become more relevant since London became a much more competitive place. Up until seven or eight years ago we could just open our doors, and people would flock in, even though we were charging.

Now that we've got the free museums, it's become a much more crowded marketplace and therefore we have got to make sure that we hold on to our market share.

Canon Lucy Wingate – who holds a more traditional position at St Paul's – also recognises the importance of marketing:

We're such an iconic building, we've got a relationship with people all over the world. We're one of the 'Top 20 most recognised buildings' in the world along with the White House and the Taj Mahal, so we've got those kinds of constituencies to think about when we're thinking about how the building relates to other people. We can't pick one group, and just target that market if I can use that kind of

language, we can't just say 'We're going to describe ourselves or even sell ourselves to one particular type of person'. It just doesn't work like that. We're very conscious of our history, and I suppose what we would say is that we're part of the cultural memory of the UK, and of Christianity in particular. Our core activity is the services that we hold and providing what we might call 'sacred space' within a 24/7 modern city like London. All of our visitors who come and pay, and all of our marketing, will be to support that core business.

Sources: Organisational websites for VSO (www.vso.org.uk), Marketing Birmingham (www.marketingbirmingham.com) and St Paul's Cathedral (www.stpauls.co.uk), and interviews with representatives by Pearson Education Ltd.

Government agencies have also shown an increased interest in marketing. For example, the national defence forces of most European countries – who rely on volunteers rather than conscripts – have a marketing plan to attract recruits, and various government agencies across the Continent are now designing *social marketing campaigns* to encourage energy conservation and concern for the environment or to discourage smoking, excessive drinking and drug use.

SO, WHAT IS MARKETING? PULLING IT ALL TOGETHER

At the start of this chapter, Figure 1.1 presented a simple model of the marketing process. Now that we've discussed all of the steps in the process, Figure 1.6 presents an expanded model that will help you pull it all together. What is marketing? Simply put, marketing is the process of building profitable customer relationships by creating value for customers and capturing value in return.

The first four steps of the marketing process focus on creating value for customers. The company first gains a full understanding of the marketplace by researching customer needs and managing marketing information. It then designs a customer-driven marketing strategy based on the answers to two simple questions. The first question is: What consumers will we serve? (market segmentation and targeting). Good marketing companies know that they cannot serve all customers in every way. Instead, they need to focus their resources on the customers they can serve best and most profitably. The second marketing strategy question is: How can we best serve targeted customers?

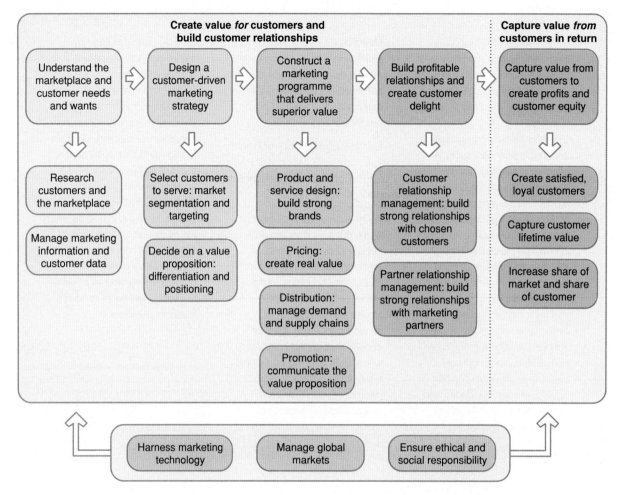

FIGURE 1.6

An expanded model of the marketing process

(differentiation and positioning). Here, the marketer outlines a value proposition that spells out what values the company will deliver in order to win target customers.

With its marketing strategy decided, the company now constructs a marketing programme – consisting of the four marketing mix elements, or the four Ps – that transforms the marketing strategy into real value for customers. The company develops product offers and creates strong brand identities for them. It prices these offers to create real customer value and distributes the offers to make them available to target customers. Finally, the company designs promotional programmes that communicate the value proposition to target customers and persuade them to act on the market offering.

Perhaps the most important step in the marketing process involves building value-laden, profitable relationships with target customers. Throughout the process, marketers practise customer relationship management to create customer satisfaction and delight. In creating customer value and relationships, however, the company cannot go it alone. It must work closely with marketing partners both inside the company and throughout the marketing system. Thus, beyond practising good customer relationship management, firms must also practise good partner relationship management.

The first four steps in the marketing process create value *for* customers. In the final step, the company reaps the rewards of its strong customer relationships by capturing value *from* customers. Delivering superior customer value creates highly satisfied customers who will buy more and will buy again. This helps the company to capture customer lifetime value and greater share of customer. The result is increased long-term customer equity for the firm.

Finally, in the face of today's changing marketing landscape, companies must take into account three additional factors. In building customer and partner relationships, they must harness marketing technology, take advantage of global opportunities, and ensure that they act in an ethical and socially responsible way.

Figure 1.6 provides a good road map to future chapters of the text. Chapters 1 and 2 introduce the marketing process, with a focus on building customer relationships and capturing value from customers. Chapters 3, 4, and 5 address the first step of the marketing process – understanding the marketing environment, managing marketing information, and understanding consumer behaviour. In Chapter 6, we look more deeply into the two major marketing strategy decisions: selecting which customers to serve (segmentation and targeting) and deciding on a value proposition (differentiation and positioning). Chapters 7 to 13 discuss the marketing mix variables, one by one. Then, the final three chapters examine the special marketing factors: marketing technology in the digital age, global marketing, and marketing ethics and social responsibility.

So, here we go, down the road to learning marketing. We hope you'll enjoy the journey!

THE JOURNEY YOU'VE TAKEN Reviewing the concepts

Today's successful companies – whether large or small, for-profit or not-for-profit, domestic or global – share a strong customer focus and a heavy commitment to marketing. The goal of marketing is to build and manage profitable customer relationships. Marketing seeks to attract new customers by promising superior value and to keep and grow current customers by delivering satisfaction. Marketing operates within a dynamic global environment, which can quickly make yesterday's winning strategies obsolete. To be successful, companies will have to be strongly market-focused.

1 Define marketing and outline the steps in the marketing process.

Marketing is the process by which companies create value for customers and build strong customer relationships in order to capture value from customers in return.

The marketing process involves five steps. The first four steps create value for customers. First, marketers need to understand the marketplace and customer needs and wants. Next, marketers design a customer-driven marketing strategy with the goal of getting, keeping and growing target customers. In the third step, marketers construct a marketing programme that actually delivers superior value. All of these steps form the basis for the fourth step, building profitable customer relationships and creating customer delight. In the final step, the company reaps the rewards of strong customer relationships by capturing value from customers.

2 Explain the importance of understanding customers and the marketplace, and identify the five core marketplace concepts.

Outstanding marketing companies go to great lengths to learn about and understand their customers' needs, wants and demands. This understanding helps them to design want-satisfying market offerings and build value-laden customer relationships by which they can capture customer lifetime value and greater share of customer. The result is increased long-term customer equity for the firm.

The core marketplace concepts are needs, wants and demands; market offerings (products, services and experiences); value and satisfaction; exchange and relationships; and markets. Wants are the form taken by human needs when shaped by culture and individual personality. When backed by buying power, wants become demands. Companies address needs by putting forth a value proposition, a set of benefits that they promise to consumers to satisfy their needs. The value proposition is fulfilled through a market offering, which delivers customer value and satisfaction, resulting in long-term exchange relationships with customers.

3 Identify the key elements of a customer-driven marketing strategy and discuss marketing management orientations that guide marketing strategy.

To design a winning marketing strategy, the company must first decide *whom* it will serve. It does this by dividing the market into segments of customers (*market segmentation*) and selecting which segments it will cultivate (*target marketing*). Next, the company must decide *how* it will serve targeted customers (how it will *differentiate and position* itself in the marketplace).

Marketing management can adopt one of five competing market orientations. The *production concept* holds that management's task is to improve production efficiency and bring down prices. The *product concept* holds that consumers favour products that offer the most in quality, performance and innovative features; thus, little promotional effort is required. The *selling concept* holds that consumers will not buy enough of the organisation's products unless it undertakes a large-scale selling and promotion effort. The *marketing concept* holds that achieving organisational goals depends on determining the needs and wants of target markets and delivering the desired satisfactions more effectively and efficiently than competitors do. The *societal marketing concept* holds that generating customer satisfaction *and* long-term societal well-being are the keys to both achieving the company's goals and fulfilling its responsibilities.

4 Discuss customer relationship management, and identify strategies for creating value *for* customers and capturing value *from* customers in return.

Broadly defined, *customer relationship management* is the process of building and maintaining profitable customer relationships by delivering superior customer value and satisfaction. The aim of customer relationship management is to produce high *customer equity*, the total combined customer lifetime values of all of the company's customers. The key to building lasting relationships is the creation of superior *customer value* and *satisfaction*.

Companies want not only to acquire profitable customers, but to build relationships that will keep them and grow 'share of customer'. Different types of customer require different customer relationship management strategies. The marketer's aim is to build the *right relationships* with the *right customers*. In return for creating value *for* targeted customers, the company captures value *from* customers in the form of profits and customer equity.

In building customer relationships, good marketers realise that they cannot go it alone. They must work closely with marketing partners inside and outside the company. In addition to being good at customer relationship management, they must also be good at *partner relationship management*.

5 Describe the major trends and forces that are changing the marketing landscape in this new age of relationships.

As the world spins on, dramatic changes are occurring in the marketing arena. The boom in computer, telecommunications, information, transportation and other technologies has created exciting new ways to learn about and track customers, and to create products and services tailored to individual customer needs.

In a rapidly shrinking world, many marketers are now connected *globally* with their customers and marketing partners. Today, almost every company, large or small, is touched in some way by global competition. Today's marketers are also re-examining their ethical and societal responsibilities. Marketers are being called upon to take greater responsibility for the social and environmental impact of their actions. In the past, marketing has been most widely applied in the for-profit business sector. In recent years, however, marketing has also become a major part of the strategies of many not-for-profit organisations, such as colleges, hospitals, museums, symphony orchestras and even churches.

Pulling it all together, as discussed throughout the chapter the major new developments in marketing can be summed up in a single word: *relationships*. Today, marketers of all kinds are taking advantage of new opportunities for building relationships with their customers, their marketing partners, and the world around them.

NAVIGATING THE KEY TERMS

NOTES AND REFERENCES

1 http://www.uefa.com/.

2 http://www.uefa.com/uefa/aboutuefa/index.html.

3 http://www.uefa.com/uefa/keytopics/kind=131072/index.html.

4 http://www.euro2008.uefa.com/countries/cities/city=1191/news/
newsid=726502.html#euro+merchandise+proving.

5 http://www.sportandtechnology.com/features/0532.html.

6 http://www.sportbusiness.com/news/167372/storms-knock-out-euro-2008-global-television-feed.

7 http://www.guardian.co.uk/football/2007/feb/15/newsstory.sport.

8 http://www.bloomberg.com/apps/news?pid=20670001&refer=europe&sid=aAgM1tkB5W.
© 2008 Bloomberg L.P. All rights reserved. Used with permission.

9 The American Marketing Association offers this definition: 'Marketing is an organizational
function and a set of processes for creating, communicating, and delivering value to
customers and for managing customer relationships in ways that benefit the organization
and its stakeholders.' Accessed at http://www.marketingpower.com/mg-dictionary-
view1862.php?, September 2005. See also Lisa M. Keefe, 'What Is the Meaning of
"Marketing"', *Marketing News*, 15 September 2004, pp. 17–18; and Chekitan S. Dev and
Don E. Schultz, 'A Customer-Focused Approach Can Bring the Current Marketing Mix
into the 21st Century', *Marketing Management*, January–February 2005, pp. 18–24.

10 See Theodore Levitt's classic article, 'Marketing Myopia', *Harvard Business Review*,
July–August 1960, pp. 45–56. For more recent discussions, see James R. Stock, 'Marketing
Myopia Revisited: Lessons for Logistics', *International Journal of Physical Distribution &
Logistics Management*, **2**(1/2), 2002, pp. 12–21; and Yves Doz, Jose Santos and Peter J.
Williamson, 'Marketing Myopia Re-Visited: Why Every Company Needs to Learn from
the World', *Ivey Business Journal*, January–February 2004, p. 1.

11 http://www.parquewarner.com/; http://www.acmilan.com/InfoPage.aspx?id=42776.

12 See Erika Rasmusson, 'Marketing More than a Product', *Sales & Marketing Management*,
February 2000, p. 99; and Lawrence A. Crosby and Sheree L. Johnson, 'Managing
Experiences', *Marketing Management*, January–February 2005, pp. 12–14.

13 See F. Lega, 'Developing a marketing function in public healthcare systems: A framework
for action', *Health Policy*, October 2006, **78**(2/3), pp. 340–52.

14 See David Lewis, 'Southwest Staff Go Nuts (for Customers!)', Sales & Marketing Institute,
accessed at www.salesmarketing.org.nz/article623.html, May 2005. For more on market
orientation and firm performance, see Ahmet H. Kirca, Satish Jayachandran and William O.
Bearden, 'Marketing Orientation: A Meta-Analytic Review and Assessment of Its
Antecedents and Impact on Performance', *Journal of Marketing*, April 2005, pp. 24–41.

15 See 'Healthy Life Expectancy in Scotland', available from http://www.scotland.gov.uk/
Topics/Statistics/Browse/Health/TrendLifeExpectancy/LinkLifeExpectancySummary.

16 See 'Deep Fried Mars Mar Myth is Dispelled', BBC: http://news.bbc.co.uk/1/hi/scotland/
4103415.stm or 'America's Most Fattening Burger', *Time*, 3 January 2005, p. 186; and
'For the Health-Unconscious, Era of Mammoth Burger Is Here', *Wall Street Journal*,
27 January 2005, p. B.1.

17 'How Effective are Product Recalls?', BBC:
http://news.bbc.co.uk/1/hi/magazine/6379389.stm.

18 'The 2004 Total Value Awards: Incentives Don't Correlate to Value Says Strategic Vision',
Strategic Vision, 4 October 2004, accessed at www.strategicvision.com, February 2005;
Chad Lawhorn, 'Gas Costs Steer Study into Hybrids', *Knight Ridder Tribune Business News*,
29 April 2005, p. 1; and Ronald D. White, 'Car Buyers Think Hard and Long Distance
about Mileage', *Los Angeles Times*, 30 April 2005, p. C.1.

19 Catherine Arnold, 'Satisfaction's the Name of the Game', *Marketing News*, 15 October
2004, pp. 39, 45; Eugene W. Anderson, Claes Fornell and Sanal K. Mazvancheryl,
'Customer Satisfaction and Shareholder Value', *Journal of Marketing*, October 2004,
pp. 172–85; and Christian Homburg, Nicole Koschate and Wayne D. Hoyer, 'Do Satisfied
Customers Really Pay More? A Study Between Customer Satisfaction and Willingness to
Pay', *Journal of Marketing*, April 2005, pp. 84–96.

20 See for example http://www.porscheclubgb.com/Default.aspx.

21 ING Web page at: www.ingdirect.co.uk, accessed Augst 2008. Other information
adapted from Elizabeth Esfahani, 'How to Get Tough with Bad Customers', *Business 2.0*,
October 2004, p. 52. See also Amey Stone, 'Bare Bones, Plump Profits', *BusinessWeek*,
14 March, 2005, p. 88.

22 See E. Gummesson, *Total Relationship Marketing* (Oxford: Butterworth-Heinemann, 1999);
C. Grönroos, *Service Management and Marketing: Customer Management in Service
Competition* (London: Wiley, 1990); and M.J. Harker, 'Relationship Marketing Defined',
Marketing Intelligence and Planning, 17(1), 1999, pp. 13–21.

23 Philip Kotler and Kevin Lane Keller, *Marketing Management*, 12th edn (Upper Saddle River,
NJ: Prentice Hall, 2006), p. 27.

24 See E. Gummesson, 'Marketing Orientation Revisited: The Crucial Role of the Part-Time
Marketer', *European Journal of Marketing*, 25(2), 1991, pp. 60–75.

25 http://www.sonyericsson.com/cws/corporate/company/aboutus/profile.

26 For more discussion of customer loyalty, see Fred Reichheld and Christine Detrick,
'Loyalty: A Prescription for Cutting Costs', *Marketing Management*, September–October
2003, pp. 24–5; Jacquelyn S. Thomas, Robert C. Blattberg and Edward J. Fox,
'Recapturing Lost Customers', *Journal of Marketing Research*, February 2004,
pp. 31–45, and Clara Agustin and Jagdip Singh, 'Curvilinear Effects of Consumer
Loyalty Determinants in Relational Exchanges', *Journal of Marketing Research*,
February 2005, pp. 96–108.

27 http://business.timesonline.co.uk/tol/business/money/savings/article1302837.ece;
http://www.guardian.co.uk/money/2008/jun/14/banks.currentaccounts.

28 See Roland T. Rust, Valerie A. Zeithaml and Katherine A. Lemon, *Driving Customer Equity*
(New York Free Press 2000); Robert C. Blattberg, Gary Getz and Jacquelyn S. Thomas,
Customer Equity (Boston, MA: Harvard business School Press, 2001); Rust, Lemon and
Zeithaml, 'Return on Marketing: Using Customer Equity to Focus Marketing Strategy',
Journal of Marketing, January 2004, pp. 109–27; James D. Lenskold, 'Customer-Centered
Marketing ROI', *Marketing Management*, January/February 2004, pp. 26–32; and Rust,
Zeithaml and Lemon, 'Customer-Centered Brand Management', *Harvard Business Review*,
September 2004, p. 110.

29 This example is adapted from information in Rust, Lemon and Zeithaml, 'Where Should the Next Marketing Dollar Go?', *Marketing Management*, September–October 2001, pp. 24–8. Also see David Welch and David Kiley, 'Can Caddy's Driver Make GM Cool?', *BusinessWeek*, 20 September 2004, pp. 105–6; John K. Teahen Jr, 'Cadillac Kid: "Gotta Compete" ', *Knight Ridder Tribune Business News*, 7 May 2005, p. 1.

30 Ravi Dhar and Rashi Glazer, 'Hedging Customers', *Harvard Business Review*, May 2003, pp. 86–92.

31 Werner Reinartz and V. Kumar, 'The Mismanagement of Customer Loyalty', *Harvard Business Review*, July 2002, pp. 86–94. For more on customer equity management, see Sunil Gupta, Donald R. Lehman and Jennifer Ames Stuart, 'Valuing Customers', *Journal of Marketing Research*, February 2004, pp. 7–18; Michael D. Johnson and Fred Selnes, 'Customer Portfolio Management: Toward a Dynamic Theory of Exchange Relationships', *Journal of Marketing*, April 2004, pp. 1–17; Sunil Gupta and Donald R. Lehman, *Managing Customers as Investments* (Philadelphia: Wharton School Publishing, 2005); and Roland T. Rust, Katherine N. Lemon and Das Narayandas, *Customer Equity Management* (Upper Saddle River, NJ: Prentice Hall, 2005).

32 'MTV's Search for Global Harmony', *Financial Times*: http://www.ft.com/cms/s/0/f52e958c-3631-11dd-8bb8-0000779fd2ac.html.

33 http://www.mariinsky.ru/en/about/sponsors/.

34 For other examples, and for a good review of non-profit marketing, see Philip Kotler and Alan R. Andreasen, *Strategic Marketing for Nonprofit Organizations*, 6th edn (Upper Saddle River, NJ: Prentice Hall, 2003); Philip Kotler and Karen Fox, *Strategic Marketing for Educational Institutions* (Upper Saddle River, NJ: Prentice Hall, 1995); Norman Shawchuck, Philip Kotler, Bruce Wren and Gustave Rath, *Marketing for Congregations: Choosing to Serve People More Effectively* (Nashville, TN: Abingdon Press, 1993); Philip Kotler, John Bowen and James Makens, *Marketing for Hospitality and Tourism*, 3rd edn (Upper Saddle River, NJ: Prentice Hall, 2003); and 'The Nonprofit Marketing Landscape', special section, *Journal of Business Research*, June 2005, pp. 797–862.

CHAPTER 2

Company and marketing strategy: Partnering to build customer relationships

AFTER STUDYING THIS CHAPTER, YOU SHOULD BE ABLE TO

- explain company-wide strategic planning and its four steps
- discuss how to design business portfolios and develop growth strategies
- explain marketing's role in strategic planning and how marketing works with its partners to create and deliver customer value
- describe the elements of a customer-driven marketing strategy and mix, and the forces that influence it
- list the marketing management functions, including the elements of a marketing plan, and discuss the importance of measuring and managing return on marketing

THE WAY AHEAD Previewing the concepts

Ready to travel on? In the first chapter, we explored the marketing process by which companies create value for consumers in order to capture value in return. On this leg of our journey, we dig deeper into steps two and three of the marketing process – designing customer-driven marketing strategies and constructing marketing programmes. To begin, we look at the organisation's overall strategic planning. Next, we discuss how marketers, guided by the strategic plan, work closely with others inside and outside the firm to serve customers. We then examine marketing strategy and planning – how marketers choose target markets, position their market offerings, develop a marketing mix and manage their marketing programmes. Finally, we look at the important step of measuring and managing return on marketing investment.

First stop: Nike. During the past several decades, Nike has forever changed the rules of sports marketing strategy. In the process, it has built the Nike swoosh into one of the world's best-known brand symbols. But the Nike we know today is far, far different from the brash young start-up company of 40 years ago. As Nike has grown and matured – moving from maverick to mainstream – its marketing strategy has matured as well. To stay on top in the intensely competitive sports apparel business, Nike will have to keep finding fresh ways to bring value to its customers.

Nike

The Nike 'swoosh' – it's everywhere! Just for fun, try counting the swooshes whenever you pick up the sports pages or watch a pickup basketball game or tune into a televised golf match. Through innovative marketing, Nike has built the ever-present swoosh into one of the best-known brand symbols on the planet. But 40-some years ago, when young CPA Phil Knight and college track coach Bill Bowerman co-founded the company, Nike was just a brash, young upstart in the athletic footwear industry.

In those early days, Knight and Bowerman ran Nike without formal planning. In 1964, the pair chipped in $500 apiece to start Blue Ribbon Sports. In 1970, Bowerman dreamed up a new sneaker tread by stuffing a piece of rubber into his wife's waffle iron. The Waffle Trainer quickly became the nation's best-selling training shoe. In 1972, the company became Nike, named after the Greek goddess of victory. The swoosh was designed by a graduate student for a fee of $35. By 1979, Nike owned 50 per cent of the US running shoe market. It all seemed easy then. Running was in, sneakers were hot, and Nike had the right stuff.

During the 1980s, under Phil Knight's leadership, Nike revolutionised sports marketing. To build its brand image and market share, Nike spent lavishly on big-name endorsements, splashy promotional events, and in-your-face 'Just Do It' ads. At Nike, however, good marketing meant more than just promotional hype and promises – it meant consistently building strong relationships with customers based on real value. Nike's initial success resulted from the technical superiority of its running and basketball shoes. To this day, Nike leads the

Source: PA Photos/Luis M. Alvarez/AP.

industry in research-and-development spending.

But Nike gave customers much more than good athletic gear. Customers didn't just wear their Nikes, they *experienced* them. As the company stated on its Web page (**www.nike.com**), 'Nike has always known the truth – it's not so much the shoes but where they take you.' Beyond shoes, apparel and equipment, Nike marketed a way of life, a sports culture, a just-do-it attitude. As Phil Knight said at the time: 'Basically, our culture and our style is to be a rebel.' The company was built on a genuine passion for sports, a maverick disregard for convention, and a belief in hard work and serious sports performance.

Throughout 1980s and 1990s, still playing the role of the upstart underdog, Nike sprinted ahead of its competition. Between 1988 and 1997, Nike's revenues grew at an annual rate of 21 per cent; annual return to

investors averaged a staggering 47 per cent. Nike leveraged its brand strength, moving aggressively into new product categories, sports and regions of the world. The company slapped its familiar swoosh logo on everything from sunglasses and soccer balls to batting gloves and hockey sticks. Nike invaded a dozen new sports, including baseball, golf, ice and street hockey, skateboarding, wall climbing and hiking. It seemed that things couldn't be going any better.

In the late 1990s, however, Nike stumbled and its sales slipped. The whole industry suffered a setback, as a 'brown shoe' craze for hiking and outdoor shoe styles ate into the athletic sneaker business. Moreover, Nike's creative juices seemed to run dry. Unexciting new sneaker designs collected dust on retailer shelves as buyers wanting a new look switched to competing brands. To make matters worse, Nike was fighting off allegations that it was over-commercialising sports and exploiting child labour in Asian sweatshops.

But Nike's biggest obstacle may have been its own incredible success. The brand appeared to suffer from big-brand backlash, and the swoosh may have become too common to be cool. As sales moved past the $10 billion mark, Nike moved from maverick to mainstream. Rooting for Nike was like rooting for Microsoft. Instead of anti-establishment, Nike *was* the establishment. Once the brat of sports marketing, Nike now had to grow up and act its age.

And grow up it has. In recent years, Nike's marketing strategy has matured. The company still spends hundreds of millions of dollars each year on very creative advertising, innovative brand-building promotions, and big-name endorsers. For example, Nike signed basketball phenomenon LeBron James to a $90 million endorsement contract a few years back, and in the Athens Olympics, Nike athletes brought home 50 gold medals plus dozens more silver and bronze. But Nike has toned down its anti-establishment attitude – its marketing is a bit less edgy. And the company is now devoting much more attention to mundane marketing details. 'Gone are the days when Nike execs, working on little more than hunches, would do just about anything and spend just about any amount in the quest for publicity and market share,' says one Nike observer. 'More and more, Nike is searching for the right balance between its creative and its business sides, relying on a newfound financial and managerial discipline to drive growth.'

The new Nike has returned to the basics – focusing on innovation,

methodically assessing new market opportunities, developing new product lines, and reworking its information and distribution systems. According to the industry observer:

In the old days, Nike operated pretty much on [marketing] instinct. It took a guess as to how many pairs of shoes to churn out and hoped it could cram them all onto retailers' shelves. Not anymore. Nike has overhauled its computer systems to get the right number of sneakers to more places in the world more quickly. [It] also overhauled its supply-chain system, which often left retailers either desperately awaiting delivery of hot shoes or struggling to get rid of the duds. The old jerry-built compilation strung together 27 different computer systems worldwide, most of which couldn't talk with the others . . . Nike has spent $500 million to build a new system. [Now, according to Nike,] the percentage of shoes it makes without a firm order from a retailer has fallen from 30 per cent to 3 per cent, while the lead time for getting new sneaker styles to market has been cut to six months from nine.

The old seat-of-the-pants Nike had difficulty going global; at the new Nike, more than 50 per cent of sales now come from international markets, and these markets are growing rapidly. The old Nike also stumbled with its acquisitions, trying to force its own super-heated marketing culture onto them. The new Nike has learned to give its acquired brands some independence. As a result, acquisitions such as Cole Haan dress shoes, Converse retro-

style sneakers, Hurley International skateboard gear, Bauer in-line and hockey skates, and Starter Official affordable sneakers now account for more than 10 per cent of Nike's revenues and a quarter of its sales growth.

The new, more-mature Nike is once again achieving stunning results. In the past four years, Nike's sales have grown 50 per cent to more than $14 billion. The company captures a 40 per cent share of the US branded athletic footwear market; the next-biggest competitor is Reebok at 13 per cent. A relative newcomer to soccer, Nike recently became the top football boot marketer in Europe, with a 35 per cent market share, edging out long-time leader Adidas, at 31 per cent. Nike's evolving marketing prowess over the years has also been good for investors. An investment of $1,000 in Nike in 1980 would be worth more than $64,000 today. And founder Phil Knight's 27 per cent stake in Nike is worth $6.2 billion, making him one of the world's richest people.

To stay on top, however, Nike will have to keep its marketing strategy fresh, finding new ways to deliver the kind of innovation and value that built the brand so powerfully in the past. No longer the rebellious, anti-establishment upstart, Nike must continually reassess and rekindle its meaning to customers. Says Knight, 'Now that we've [grown so large], there's a fine line between being a rebel and being a bully. [To our customers,] we have to be beautiful as well as big.'[1]

Sources: See note 1 at the end of this chapter.

Marketing strategies and programmes are guided by broader, companywide strategic plans. So, to understand the role of marketing, we must first understand the organisation's overall strategic planning process. Like Nike, all companies must look ahead and develop long-term strategies to meet the changing conditions in their industries and ensure long-term survival.

COMPANY-WIDE STRATEGIC PLANNING: DEFINING MARKETING'S ROLE

Each company must find the overall plan for long-term survival and growth that makes the most sense given its specific situation, opportunities, objectives and resources. This is the focus of **strategic planning** – the process of developing and maintaining a strategic fit between the organisation's goals and capabilities and its changing marketing opportunities.

Strategic planning sets the stage for the rest of the planning in the firm. Companies usually prepare annual plans long-range plans and strategic plans. The annual and long-range plans deal with the company's current businesses and how to keep them going. In contrast, the strategic plan involves adapting the firm to take advantage of opportunities in its constantly changing environment.

At the corporate level, the company starts the strategic planning process by defining its overall purpose and mission (see Figure 2.1). This mission is then turned into detailed supporting objectives that guide the whole company. Next, headquarters decides what portfolio of businesses and products is best for the company and how much support to give each one. In turn, each business and product develops detailed marketing and other departmental plans that support the company-wide plan. Thus, marketing planning occurs at the business unit, product and market levels. It supports company strategic planning with more detailed plans for specific marketing opportunities.[2]

Defining a market-oriented mission

An organisation exists to accomplish something. At first, it has a clear purpose or mission, but over time its mission may become unclear as the organisation grows, adds new products and markets, or faces new conditions in the environment. When management senses that the organisation is drifting, it must renew its search for purpose. It is time to ask: What is our business? Who is the customer? What do consumers value? What *should* our business be? These simple-sounding questions are among the most difficult the company will ever have to answer. Successful companies continuously raise these questions and answer them carefully and completely.

Many organisations develop formal mission statements that answer these questions. A **mission statement** is a statement of the organisation's purpose – what it wants to

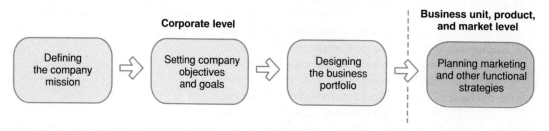

FIGURE 2.1

Steps in strategic planning

accomplish in the larger environment. Studies have shown that firms with well-crafted mission statements have better organisational and financial performance.[3]

Some companies define their missions only in product or technology terms ('We make and sell furniture' or 'We are a chemical-processing firm'). But mission statements should be *market-oriented* and defined in terms of customer needs. Products and technologies eventually become outdated, but basic market needs may last forever.

A market-oriented mission statement defines the business in terms of satisfying basic customer needs. For example, the Blackwell Publishing mission is not just to publish books, but 'to provide an expert publishing service to other experts – authors, editors, librarians, researchers, teachers and their students, societies and professionals – enabling them to do their jobs better'. Likewise, eBay's mission isn't simply to hold online auctions and trading. Instead, it connects individual buyers and sellers in 'the world's online marketplace'. Its mission is to be a unique Web community in which people can shop around, have fun and get to know each other, for example by chatting at the eBay Café. Table 2.1 provides several other examples of product-oriented versus market-oriented business definitions.

Management should avoid making its mission too narrow or too broad. A pencil manufacturer that says it is in the communication equipment business is stating its mission too broadly. Missions should be *realistic*. Singapore Airlines would be deluding itself if it adopted the mission to become the world's largest airline. Missions should also be *specific*. Many mission statements are written for public relations purposes and lack specific, workable guidelines. Such generic statements sound good but provide little real

TABLE 2.1 Market-oriented business definitions

Company	Product-oriented definition	Market-oriented definition
Allied Irish Bank	We run banks	We offer a distinctive value proposition to our customers by providing them with a distinctive combination of best products, best service, best relationships and best delivery
Amazon.com	We sell books, videos, CDs, toys, consumer electronics, hardware, housewares and other products	We make the Internet buying experience fast, easy and enjoyable – we're the place where you can find and discover anything you want to buy online
Asda	We run discount stores	We deliver low prices every day and give ordinary people the chance to buy the same things as rich people
Disney	We run theme parks	We create fantasies – a place where America still works the way it's supposed to
B&Q	We sell tools and home repair and improvement items	We enable consumers to achieve the homes of their dreams
eBay	We hold online auctions	We connect individual buyers and sellers in the world's online marketplace, a unique Web community in which they can shop around, have fun and get to know each other
Nike	We sell shoes	We help people experience the emotion of competition, winning and crushing competitors
Revlon	We make cosmetics	We sell lifestyle and self-expression; success and status; memories, hopes and dreams
Ritz-Carlton Hotels	We rent rooms	We create the Ritz-Carlton experience – one that enlivens the senses, instils well-being, and fulfils even the unexpressed wishes and needs of our guests

The mission of the World Association of Girl Guides is 'to enable girls and young women to develop their fullest potential as responsible citizens of the world'.

guidance or inspiration. Missions should fit the *market environment*. For example, the World Association of Girl Guides and Girl Scouts no longer concentrates on preparing girls to fulfil traditional female roles in society, but has as its mission 'to enable girls and young women to develop their fullest potential as responsible citizens of the world', and 'aims to engage and empower young women, so that they can make a difference in their communities'.[4]

The organisation should also base its mission on its *distinctive competencies*. Finally, mission statements should be *motivating*. A company's mission should not be stated as making more sales or profits – profits are only a reward for undertaking a useful activity. A company's employees need to feel that their work is significant and that it contributes to people's lives. For example, Microsoft's aim is to help people to 'realize their potential' – 'your potential, our passion' says the company. Google's mission is to 'organise the world's information and make it universally accessible and useful'.

Setting company objectives and goals

The company needs to turn its mission into detailed supporting objectives for each level of management. Each manager should have objectives and be responsible for reaching them. For example, Monsanto operates globally in the agricultural biotechnology business. It defines its mission as 'improving the future of farming . . . improving the future of food . . . abundantly and safely'. It seeks to help feed the world's rapidly growing population while at the same time sustaining the environment. Monsanto ads ask us to 'Imagine innovative agriculture that creates incredible things today'.

This mission leads to a hierarchy of objectives, including business objectives and marketing objectives. Monsanto's overall objective is to build profitable customer relationships by developing better agricultural products and getting them to market faster at lower costs. It does this by researching products that safely help crops produce more nutrition and higher yields without chemical spraying. But research is expensive and requires improved profits to plough back into research programmes. So improving profits becomes another major Monsanto objective. Profits can be improved by increasing sales or reducing costs. Sales can be increased by improving the company's share of existing markets, by entering new markets, or both. These goals then become the company's current marketing objectives.[5]

Marketing strategies and programmes must be developed to support these marketing objectives. To increase its European market share, Monsanto might increase its products' availability and promotion. To enter new markets, the company may cut prices and target large farms in several different countries. These are its broad marketing strategies. Each broad marketing strategy must then be defined in greater detail. For example, increasing the product's promotion may require more salespeople and more advertising; if so, both requirements will have to be spelled out. In this way, the firm's mission is translated into a set of objectives for the current period.

Marketing at Work 2.1 provides an insight into the strategic dilemmas that can face a growing company as it considers what the implications of growing beyond its domestic market are for its mission, overall goals and marketing programmes. The top management team at a Taiwanese company contemplates the strategic issues raised by possible entry into the European market.

Monsanto defines its mission as 'improving the future of farming . . . improving the future of food . . . abundantly and safely'.

Designing the business portfolio

Guided by the company's mission statement and objectives, management now must plan its **business portfolio** – the collection of businesses and products that make up the company. The best business portfolio is the one that best fits the company's strengths and weaknesses to opportunities in the environment. Business portfolio planning involves two steps. First, the company must analyse its *current* business portfolio and decide which businesses should receive more, less, or no investment. Second, it must shape the *future* portfolio by developing strategies for growth and downsizing.

Analysing the current business portfolio

The major activity in strategic planning is business **portfolio analysis,** whereby management evaluates the products and businesses making up the company. The company will want to put strong resources into its more profitable businesses and phase down or drop its weaker ones.

Management's first step is to identify the key businesses making up the company. These can be called the strategic business units. A *strategic business unit* (SBU) is a unit of the company that has a separate mission and objectives and that can be planned independently from other company businesses. An SBU can be a company division, a product line within a division, or sometimes a single product or brand.

The next step in business portfolio analysis calls for management to assess the attractiveness of its various SBUs and decide how much support each deserves. Most companies are well advised to 'stick to their knitting' when designing their business portfolios. It's usually a good idea to focus on adding products and businesses that fit closely with the firm's core philosophy and competencies.

Branding in international markets: Martas Precision Slides

Dr Paurav Shukla (Senior Lecturer), Dr Steve Hogan (Principal Lecturer) and Ina Chang (Researcher), *Brighton Business School, University of Brighton, UK*

It was a mid-summer morning in Taipei, and Gary Chen was standing in the boardroom, thinking wistfully of his days as a management student when the kind of decision he was now facing as CEO and President had been discussed dispassionately in a study group preparing for class. As Gary knew only too well from his prior experience, real-world decisions were never as clear-cut as they had seemed in business classes. This morning he was gathering his entire executive team to discuss the company's strategy for future growth. The team had shown great understanding and commitment since the company's foundation in 1997 but the decision now facing them was likely to be the most critically important yet. Two clear strategic options appeared open for the future and it was unlikely that they could pursue both. After many hours of pre-meeting discussion, Gary knew that most of the experienced team members were leaning in one direction while his intuition as well as that of some of the younger team members was pointing in the other. A final decision had to be hammered out today, and hopefully agreed unanimously, to avoid creating any serious rift within the management team.

As he watched the team filing into the room, Gary reflected that they were actually fortunate to have the two options. The alternatives had emerged from a process of experimentation and discovery during a time of immense uncertainty about how the company could meet its ambition of becoming a global leader in the furniture fitting market. The senior members expected the original business proposition of producing generic products for a range of domestic and international customers to remain in place, given the past phenomenal growth of the company and the dynamic markets it was serving. Some of the newer, internationally educated team members, however, were pointing towards a change of strategy and advocating the creation of a strong global Martas brand. Gary closed the door and started the meeting: 'This is your company. What kind of company do you want it to be? I see two clear options with no middle path. Let's discuss the future.'

Company background

The Chen family entered the furniture fitting and hardware sector in the 1990s with the establishment of Martas Precision Slides Limited, a company with a strong focus on customer orientation, innovation and quality. The company was an offshoot of the Chien-Tai Hardware Company which had had a successful track record in the furniture industry for more than two decades.

Martas was started with an initial capital investment of 90 million Taiwanese dollars (US$ 2.75 million) at a time when Taiwan was being heralded as the 'Furniture Kingdom of the East'. The furniture fitting and hardware sector covers a wide range of products but Martas founders identified the drawer slides market as having the highest growth prospects both nationally and internationally. At that time there were only five drawer slide manufacturers in Taiwan with products that met the required international standards. Although Martas was perceived as a newcomer to the Taiwanese furniture fitting industry, the company's senior management team had many decades of relevant experience gained in South-East Asia. In early 2000, the team realised that the company was ready for market expansion and started looking at opportunities to enter European markets. New staff were employed in senior positions to lead the company into this new phase of development and growth.

The major product produced by Martas is a precision ball-bearing slide with assorted designs and functions for application in a range of furniture fitting situations including household appliances (cabinets and wardrobes) and office equipment (drawers, keyboard sliders). The company has a collective management decision-making culture which successfully fosters innovation and discussion across all levels. A hierarchy of management exists but employees at all levels are encouraged to put forward their ideas for improving products and processes. In order to hold on to talented people with a common goal, Martas aims to establish a comfortable working environment in which continuous learning and development can flourish.

By the end of 2001, Martas had become involved as original equipment manufacturer (OEM) by manufacturing a set of ball-bearing slide products for international companies. The slides had to pass through many rigorous quality tests imposed by European industrial customers. Within three years, Martas was already recognised as a well-known generic product manufacturer in the international furniture fitting market which was reflected in its turnover of more than US$ 6.1 million. The strategic focus on customer orientation, product innovation and quality par excellence developed by the initial senior management team had paid off. However, although the company already had a presence in a number of developed markets in Europe and North America through generic product sales, the major part of its business was coming from just one single market – mainland China – which was a concern should political or economic problems occur in that market.

The target was to achieve turnover of US$ 20 million within the coming decade but it was becoming clear that the company might have to review its strategic focus and look beyond the Chinese market to achieve this target. Europe was perceived to be a lucrative potential market by the management but the company had only made generic industrial sales to customers who then sold on the slides under their own brand names. It was becoming apparent that selling branded product offered image advantages, better customer loyalty and higher returns in comparison to generic sales. Martas's problem was that their own brand would need to be built from scratch and they had limited experience of how this should be done and what the implications for the business might be.

The European furniture market

The furniture market growth on both the office and household fronts had a direct impact on the Martas products. The overall global furniture market was worth around £130 billion in 2003. China Council for the Promotion of International Trade (CCPIT) reported that Europe was the largest furniture market in the world with a 45 per cent share of the global furniture market, ahead of both North America (19 per cent) and Asia-Pacific (25 per cent). According to the UK Foreign and Commonwealth Office (FCO), European countries also dominate the imported furniture market. Italy, Germany, France, Spain and Finland were identified as the largest importers with the Italians, in particular, playing a leading role.

European consumers were characterised as 'quality of life' pursuers and it was observed that they paid more attention to the perceived value of products rather than to price considerations. European furniture taste was described as 'good looking and practical' and at the same time 'full of traditional impression with artistic perception'. Cultural differences between EU Member States were, however, evident and therefore a company had to adapt its strategic thinking to match these. For example, Italians were highly interested in a link with Renaissance design in their furniture while English traditional style furniture was attractive to other nationalities. There was a good amount of export-import business between European countries themselves. For example, the Danish furniture industry exported over 80 per cent of its furniture production to other EU members and in particular to Germany, Sweden and the UK. After some initial analysis, the younger team members at Martas were proposing to target first the German and the British markets with the new brand on the basis of market size, import potential and openness to international brands.

Germany remained one of the largest furniture markets in Europe with its domestic production accounting for 30 per cent of total European furniture output. Most German manufacturers focused on their domestic market, with external trade being mainly conducted within the EU. Nearly 87 per cent of all imported furniture into Germany arrived from EU sources in 2003, although imports from Eastern Europe and Asia were increasing rapidly.

The British furniture market was segmented into office furniture, upholstered furniture, kitchen furniture, and furniture parts. Demand for household furniture market in the UK was expected to rise by 3–4 per cent every five years. In relation to the consumer market, one study indicated that almost 50 per cent of UK consumers seemed dissatisfied with their existing furniture and were looking for an alternative. This meant that the demand was set to increase in future within the marketplace.

It was also felt that the cultural characteristics of those two countries would assist foreign companies like Martas to adapt to the different business working practices. The young executives had prepared a comparative index on social characteristics and the environmental policies of both countries. Both countries were concerned about environmental issues, so that decisions on product design, manufacturing, materials used and packaging were considered very important. Even if the product was to be targeted towards the business market, Martas executives were aware that demand was ultimately based upon consumer trends. This derived demand was therefore seen as an important feature in marketing Martas branded products in Europe. The consumer behaviour and market segmentation of the UK and German markets seemed to be fairly similar and so the Martas team considered that they would be able use similar segmentation and targeting strategies in both markets. However, the product was likely to need some modification to reflect different consumer furniture preferences. The team was confident that Martas products could meet the high European standards expected and believed that they had now enough experience of dealing with European firms through their generic products for the company to launch its own brand offering. The future of the company for them was clear. Branding would bring further focus, clear and consistent product and presence, increased awareness and loyalty, through which they would be able to enjoy higher turnover and profit and meet their targeted growth objectives.

The final decision

Although the idea of branding Martas products and its advantages was strongly supported by the younger executives, unsurprisingly there was some resistance to the idea. Those opposed argued on the basis of the company's experience, reputation, expertise and success in selling generic product. 'Why do we need to change so radically, particularly with our limited European experience?' was a typical question raised.

Gary, trying to remain neutral and at the same time allowing everyone's views to be heard, emphasised that it was not a good idea for the team to delay the decision on this issue. A decision one way or the other needed to be made for the company to allocate resources and plan

accordingly for the future. But which direction should they go? It was a dilemma.

Sources: We would like to thank Gary Chen, Managing Director of Martas Precision Slides for his support in the development of this case study. Additional sources: J. Donovan, 2004, *Market Report – Household Furniture*, KeyNote; China Council for the Promotion of International Trade, http://app.ccpit.org/; Foreign Commonwealth Office, http://www.fco.gov.uk; World Furniture Online, 2005, *Exhibitions in the Wood, Furniture and Furnishings Sector*, available from: http://www.worldfurnitureonline.com/dbsys/services/fairs.html, accessed: 24 September 2005; ICEX, 2004, *Spain: The Furniture Sector. Consumer Goods Division*, Spanish Institute for Foreign Trade, available from: http://www.icex.es, accessed: 15 July 2005; X.H. Chen, 2005, *International Economic and Trade Information: Denmark Furniture Market Overview*, Bejing WTO Affairs Information Network, SMEs Trade Promotion Net, available from: http://www.bjwto.org/tp/Article_Show.asp?ArticleID=2406, accessed: 16 July 2005.

The purpose of strategic planning is to find ways in which the company can best use its strengths to take advantage of attractive opportunities in the environment. So most standard portfolio analysis methods evaluate SBUs on two important dimensions – the attractiveness of the SBU's market or industry and the strength of the SBU's position in that market or industry. The best-known portfolio planning method was developed by the Boston Consulting Group, a leading management consulting firm.[6]

The Boston Consulting Group approach Using the Boston Consulting Group (BCG) approach, a company classifies all its SBUs according to the **growth–share matrix** shown in Figure 2.2. On the vertical axis, *market growth rate* provides a measure of market

FIGURE 2.2

The BCG Growth–Share Matrix

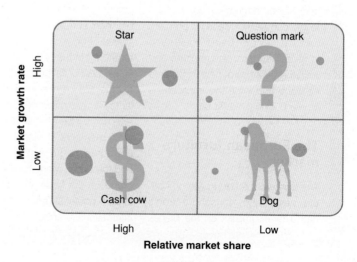

attractiveness. On the horizontal axis, *relative market share* serves as a measure of company strength in the market. The growth–share matrix defines four types of SBUs:

- *Stars*. Stars are high-growth, high-share businesses or products. They often need heavy investment to finance their rapid growth. Eventually their growth will slow down, and they will turn into cash cows.

- *Cash cows*. Cash cows are low-growth, high-share businesses or products. These established and successful SBUs need less investment to hold their market share. Thus, they produce a lot of cash that the company uses to pay its bills and to support other SBUs that need investment.

- *Question marks*. Question marks are low-share business units in high-growth markets. They require a lot of cash to hold their share, let alone increase it. Management has to think hard about which question marks it should try to build into stars and which should be phased out.

- *Dogs*. Dogs are low-growth, low-share businesses and products. They may generate enough cash to maintain themselves but do not promise to be large sources of cash.

The ten circles in the growth–share matrix represent a company's ten current SBUs. The company has two stars, two cash cows, three question marks and three dogs. The areas of the circles are proportional to each SBU's sales value. This company is in fair shape, although not in good shape. It wants to invest in the more promising question marks to make them stars and to maintain the stars so that they will become cash cows as their markets mature. Fortunately, it has two good-sized cash cows. The income from these cash cows will help finance the company's question marks, stars and dogs. The company should take some decisive action concerning its dogs and its question marks. The picture would be worse if the company had no stars, if it had too many dogs, or if it had only one weak cash cow.

Once it has classified its SBUs, the company must determine what role each will play in the future. One of four strategies can be pursued for each SBU. The company can invest more in the business unit in order to *build* its share. Or it can invest just enough to *hold* the SBU's share at the current level. It can *harvest* the SBU, milking its short-term cash flow regardless of the long-term effect. Finally, the company can *divest* the SBU by selling it or phasing it out and using the resources elsewhere.

As time passes, SBUs change their positions in the growth–share matrix. Each SBU has a life cycle. Many SBUs start out as question marks and move into the star category if they succeed. They later become cash cows as market growth falls, then finally die off or turn into dogs toward the end of their life cycle. The company needs to add new products and units continuously so that some of them will become stars and, eventually, cash cows that will help finance other SBUs.

Problems with matrix approaches The BCG and other formal methods revolutionised strategic planning. However, such centralised approaches have limitations. They can be difficult, time-consuming and costly to implement. Management may find it difficult to define SBUs and measure market share and growth. In addition, these approaches focus on classifying *current* businesses but provide little advice for *future* planning.

Formal planning approaches can also place too much emphasis on market-share growth or growth through entry into attractive new markets. Using these approaches, many companies plunged into unrelated and new high-growth businesses that they did not know how to manage – with very bad results. At the same time, these companies were often too quick to abandon, sell, or milk to death their healthy mature businesses. As a result, many companies that diversified too broadly in the past now are narrowing their focus and getting back to the basics of serving one or a few industries that they know best.

Because of such problems, many companies have dropped formal matrix methods in favour of more customised approaches that are better suited to their specific situations. Moreover, unlike former strategic planning efforts, which rested mostly in the hands of senior managers at company headquarters, today's strategic planning has been decentralised. Increasingly, companies are placing responsibility for strategic planning in the hands of cross-functional teams of divisional managers who are close to their markets.

Developing strategies for growth and downsizing

Beyond evaluating current businesses, designing the business portfolio involves finding businesses and products the company should consider in the future. Companies need growth if they are to compete more effectively, satisfy their stakeholders and attract top talent. 'Growth is pure oxygen,' states one executive. 'It creates a vital, enthusiastic corporation where people see genuine opportunity.' At the same time, a firm must be careful not to make growth itself an objective. The company's objective must be 'profitable growth'.

Marketing has the main responsibility for achieving profitable growth for the company. Marketing must identify, evaluate and select market opportunities, and lay down strategies for capturing them. One useful device for identifying growth opportunities is the **product–market expansion grid**, shown in Figure 2.3.[7] We apply it here to Starbucks:

More than 20 years ago, Howard Schultz hit on the idea of bringing a European-style coffee house to America. People needed to slow down, he believed – to 'smell the coffee' and enjoy life a little more. The result was Starbucks. This coffee house doesn't sell just coffee, it sells *The Starbucks Experience*. 'There's the Starbucks ambience', notes an analyst, 'The music. The comfy velvety chairs. The smells. The hissing steam.' Says Starbucks Chairman Schultz, 'We aren't in the coffee business, serving people. We are in the people business, serving coffee.' People around the globe now flock to Starbucks, making it a powerhouse premium brand. Some 30 million customers now visit the company's more than 9,200 stores worldwide each week.

Growth is the engine that keeps Starbucks perking – the company targets (and regularly achieves) substantial revenue growth exceeding 20 per cent each year. Starbucks's success, however, has drawn a full litter of copycats, ranging from direct competitors such as Caribou Coffee to fast-food merchants (such as McDonald's McCafé) and even discounters (Wal-Mart's Kicks Coffee). To maintain its phenomenal growth in an increasingly overcaffeinated marketplace, Starbucks must brew up an ambitious, multipronged growth strategy.[8]

First, Starbucks's management might consider whether the company can achieve deeper **market penetration** – making more sales to current customers without changing its products. It might add new stores in current market areas to make it easier for more customers to visit. In fact, Starbucks is adding an average of 28 stores a week, 52 weeks a year – its ultimate goal is 30,000 stores worldwide. Improvements in advertising, prices, service, menu selection, or store design might encourage customers to stop by more often, stay longer, or to buy more during each visit. For example, Starbucks has

FIGURE 2.3

The product–market expansion grid

	Existing products	New products
Existing markets	Market penetration	Product development
New markets	Market development	Diversification

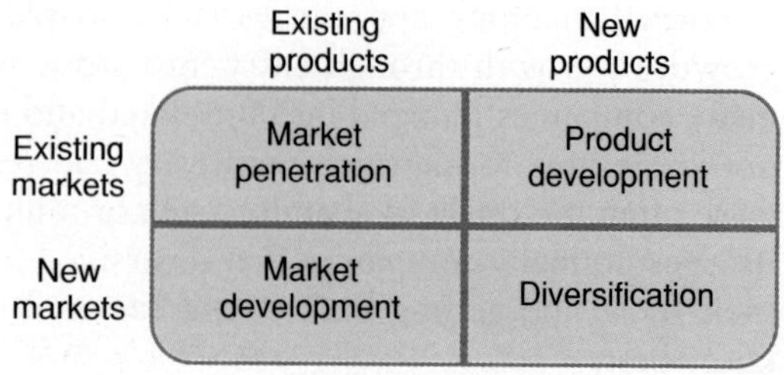

added drive-through windows to many of its stores. A company debit card lets customers prepay for coffee and snacks or give the gift of Starbucks to family and friends. And to get customers to hang around longer, Starbucks now offers T-Mobile Hot-Spot wireless Internet access in many of its stores.

Second, its management might consider possibilities for **market development** – identifying and developing new markets for its current products. For instance, managers could review new *demographic markets*. Perhaps new groups – such as older people or different ethnic groups – could be encouraged to visit Starbucks coffee shops for the first time or to buy more from them. Managers also could review new *geographical markets*. Starbucks is expanding rapidly in new global markets. In 1996, Starbucks had only 11 coffee houses outside North America. It now has more than 2,650, with plenty of room to grow. 'We're just scratching the surface in China,' says Starbucks's CEO. 'We have 150 stores and the potential for more than 2,000 there.'

Strategies for growth: to maintain its phenomenal growth in an increasingly over-caffeinated marketplace, Starbucks has brewed up an ambitious, multipronged growth strategy.

Source: Corbis/Marc Asnin.

Third, management could consider **product development** – offering modified or new products to current markets. For example, Starbucks has introduced new reduced-calorie options, such as Frappuccino Light Blended Beverages. It recently added Chantico, an indulgent, chocolate beverage to its menu to draw in more non-coffee drinkers.

Fourth, Starbucks might consider **diversification** – starting up or buying businesses outside its current products and markets. For example, in 1999 Starbucks purchased Hear Music, which was so successful that it spurred the creation of the new Starbucks entertainment division. It is also installing kiosks (called Media Bars) in select Starbucks stores that let customers download music and burn their own CDs while sipping their lattes.

In a more extreme diversification, Starbucks might consider leveraging its strong brand name by making and marketing a line of branded casual clothing consistent with the 'Starbucks Experience'. However, this would probably be unwise. Companies that diversify too broadly into unfamiliar products or industries can lose their market focus, something that some critics are already concerned about with Starbucks.

Companies must not only develop strategies for *growing* their business portfolios but also strategies for **downsizing** them. There are many reasons why a firm might want to abandon products or markets. The market environment might change, making some of the company's products or markets less profitable. The firm may have grown too fast or entered areas where it lacks experience. This can occur when a firm enters too many foreign markets without the proper research or when a company introduces new products that do not offer superior customer value. Finally, some products or business units simply age and die. One marketing expert summarises the problem this way:

Companies spend vast amounts of money and time launching new brands, leveraging existing ones, and acquiring rivals. They create line extensions and brand extensions, not to mention channel extensions and sub-brands, to cater to the growing number of niche segments in every market . . . Surprisingly, most businesses do not examine their brand portfolios from time to time to check if they might be selling too many brands, identify weak ones, and kill unprofitable ones. They tend to ignore loss-making brands rather than merge them with healthy brands, sell them off, or drop them. Consequently, most portfolios have become [jammed] with loss-making and marginally profitable brands. Moreover, the surprising truth is that most brands don't make money for companies. Many corporations generate fewer than 80 to 90 per cent of their profits from fewer than 20 per cent of the brands they sell, while they lose money or barely break even on many of the other brands in their portfolios.[9]

When a firm finds brands or businesses that are unprofitable or that no longer fit its overall strategy, it must carefully prune, harvest or divest them. Weak businesses usually require a disproportionate amount of management attention. Managers should focus on promising growth opportunities, not fritter away energy trying to salvage fading ones.

PLANNING MARKETING: PARTNERING TO BUILD CUSTOMER RELATIONSHIPS

The company's strategic plan establishes what kinds of businesses the company will operate in and its objectives for each. Then, within each business unit, more detailed planning takes place. The major functional departments in each unit – marketing, finance, accounting, purchasing, operations, information systems, human resources and others – must work together to accomplish strategic objectives.

Marketing plays a key role in the company's strategic planning in several ways. First, marketing provides a guiding *philosophy* – the marketing concept – that suggests that company strategy should revolve around building profitable relationships with important consumer groups. Second, marketing provides *inputs* to strategic planners by helping to identify attractive market opportunities and by assessing the firm's potential to take advantage of them. Finally, within individual business units, marketing designs *strategies* for reaching the unit's objectives. Once the unit's objectives are set, marketing's task is to help carry them out profitably.

Customer value and satisfaction are important ingredients in the marketer's formula for success. However, as we noted in Chapter 1, marketers alone cannot produce superior value for customers. Although it plays a leading role, marketing can be only a partner in attracting keeping and growing customers. In addition to *customer relationship management*, marketers must also practise *partner relationship management*. They must work closely with partners in other company departments to form an effective *value chain* that serves the customer. Moreover, they must partner effectively with other companies in the marketing system to form a competitively superior *value-delivery network*. We now take a closer look at the concepts of a company value chain and value-delivery network.

Partnering with other company departments

Each company department can be thought of as a link in the company's **value chain**.[10] That is, each department carries out value-creating activities to design, produce, market, deliver and support the firm's products. The firm's success depends not only on how well each department performs its work but also on how well the activities of various departments are coordinated.

For example, the French group Carrefour is the second largest retailer in the world and the largest retailer in Europe. Carrefour's goal is to create customer value and satisfaction by providing shoppers with the products they want at the lowest possible prices. Marketers at Carrefour play an important role. They learn what customers need and stock the stores' shelves with the desired products at unbeatable low prices. They prepare advertising and merchandising programmes and assist shoppers with customer service. Through these and other activities, Carrefour's marketers help deliver value to customers.

However, the marketing department needs help from the company's other departments. Carrefour's ability to offer the right products at low prices depends on the purchasing department's skill in developing the needed suppliers and buying from them at low cost. Carrefour's information technology department must provide fast and accurate information about which products are selling in each store. And its operations people must provide effective, low-cost merchandise handling.

The value chain: Carrefour's ability to offer the right products at low prices depends on the contributions of people from all departments: marketing, purchasing, information systems and operations.

Source: Corbis/Ellipsa.

A company's value chain is only as strong as its weakest link. Success depends on how well each department performs its work of adding customer value and on how well the activities of various departments are coordinated. At Carrefour, if purchasing can't wring the lowest prices from suppliers, or if operations can't distribute merchandise at the lowest costs, then marketing can't deliver on its promise of lowest prices.

Ideally, then, a company's different functions should work in harmony to produce value for consumers. But, in practice, departmental relations are full of conflicts and misunderstandings. The marketing department takes the consumer's point of view. But when marketing tries to develop customer satisfaction, it can cause other departments to do a poorer job *in their terms*. Marketing department actions can increase purchasing costs, disrupt production schedules, increase inventories and create budget headaches. Thus, the other departments may resist the marketing department's efforts.

Yet marketers must find ways to get all departments to 'think consumer' and to develop a smoothly functioning value chain. Marketing management can best gain support for its goal of customer satisfaction by working to understand the company's other departments. Marketing managers need to work closely with managers of other functions to develop a system of functional plans under which the different departments can work together to accomplish the company's overall strategic objectives.

Jack Welch, General Electric's highly regarded former CEO, told his employees: 'Companies can't give job security. Only customers can!' He emphasised that all General Electric people, regardless of their department, have an impact on customer satisfaction and retention. His message: 'If you are not thinking customer, you are not thinking.'[11]

Partnering with others in the marketing system

In its quest to create customer value, the firm needs to look beyond its own value chain and into the value chains of its suppliers, distributors and, ultimately, customers. Consider McDonald's. McDonald's 31,500 restaurants worldwide serve more than 50 million customers daily, capturing a more than a 40 per cent share of the burger market.[12] People do not swarm to McDonald's only because they love the chain's hamburgers. In fact, consumers typically rank McDonald's behind major competitors in taste. Consumers flock to the McDonald's *system*, not just to its food products. Throughout the world, McDonald's finely-tuned system delivers a high standard of what the company calls QSCV – quality, service, cleanliness and value. McDonald's is effective only to the extent that it successfully partners with its franchisees, suppliers and others jointly to deliver exceptionally high customer value.

More companies today are partnering with the other members of the supply chain to improve the performance of the customer **value-delivery network**. For example, Toyota knows the importance of building close relationships with its suppliers. In fact, it even includes the phrase 'achieve supplier satisfaction' in its mission statement.

Achieving satisfying supplier relationships has been a cornerstone of Toyota's stunning success. Competitors often alienate their suppliers through self-serving, heavy-handed dealings. Some competitors 'set annual cost-reduction targets [for the parts they buy],' says one supplier. 'To realize those targets, they'll do anything. [They've unleashed] a reign of terror, and it gets worse every year.' Says another, '[Ford] seems to send its people to "hate school" so that they learn how to hate suppliers.' By contrast, in survey after survey, car industry suppliers rate Toyota as their most preferred customer. Rather than bullying suppliers, Toyota partners with them and helps them to meet its very high expectations. It learns about their businesses, conducts joint improvement activities, helps train their employees, gives daily performance feedback, and actively seeks out supplier concerns. Says one delighted Toyota supplier, 'Toyota helped us dramatically improve our production system. We started by making one component, and as we improved, [Toyota] rewarded us with orders for more components. Toyota is our best customer.'

Such high supplier satisfaction means that Toyota can rely on suppliers to help it improve its own quality, reduce costs and develop new products quickly. For example, when Toyota recently launched a programme to reduce prices by 30 per cent on 170 parts that it would buy for its next generation of cars, suppliers didn't complain. Instead, they pitched in, trusting that Toyota would help them achieve the targeted reductions, in turn making them more competitive and profitable in the future. In all, creating satisfied suppliers helps Toyota to produce lower-cost, higher-quality cars, which in turn results in more satisfied customers.[13]

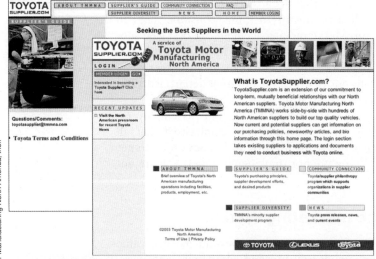

Source: Toyota Motor Manufacturing North America, Inc..

Increasingly in today's marketplace, competition no longer takes place between individual competitors. Rather, it takes place between the entire value-delivery networks created by these competitors. Thus, Toyota's performance against Ford depends on the quality of Toyota's overall value-delivery network versus Ford's. Even if Toyota makes the best cars, it might lose in the marketplace if Ford's dealer network provides more customer-satisfying sales and service.

Toyota partners with its suppliers and helps them meet its very high expectations. Creating satisfied suppliers helps Toyota produce lower-cost, higher-quality cars, which in turn results in more satisfied customers.

MAKING CONNECTIONS Linking the concepts

Here's a good place to pause for a moment to think about and apply what you've read in the first part of this chapter.

■ Why are we talking about companywide strategic planning in a marketing text? What *does* strategic planning have to do with marketing?

■ What are Starbucks's mission and strategy? What role does marketing play in helping Starbucks to accomplish its mission and strategy?

■ What roles do other Starbucks departments play, and how can Starbucks's marketers partner with these departments to maximise overall customer value?

MARKETING STRATEGY AND THE MARKETING MIX

The strategic plan defines the company's overall mission and objectives. Marketing's role and activities are shown in Figure 2.4, which summarises the major activities involved in managing marketing strategy and the marketing mix.

Consumers stand in the centre. The goal is to build strong and profitable customer relationships. Next comes **marketing strategy** – the marketing logic by which the company hopes to achieve these profitable relationships. Through market segmentation, targeting and positioning, the company decides which customers it will serve and how. It identifies the total market, then divides it into smaller segments, selects the most promising segments, and focuses on serving and satisfying customers in these segments.

Guided by marketing strategy, the company designs a *marketing mix* made up of factors under its control. To find the best marketing strategy and mix, the company engages in marketing analysis, planning, implementation and control. Through these activities, the company watches and adapts to the actors and forces in the marketing environment. We will now look briefly at each activity. Then, in later chapters, we will discuss each one in more depth.

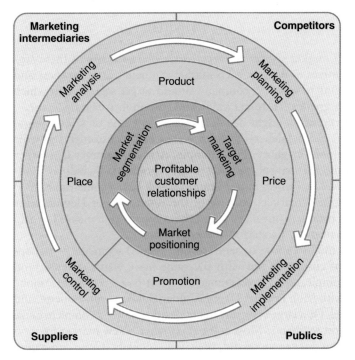

FIGURE 2.4

Managing marketing strategy and the marketing mix

Customer-centred marketing strategy

As we emphasised throughout Chapter 1, to succeed in today's competitive marketplace, companies need to be customer-centred. They must win customers from competitors, then keep and grow them by delivering greater value. But before it can satisfy customers, a company must first understand their needs and wants. Thus, sound marketing requires a careful customer analysis.

Companies know that they cannot profitably serve all consumers in a given market – at least not all consumers in the same way. There are too many different kinds of consumers with too many different kinds of needs. And most companies are in a position to serve some segments better than others. Thus, each company must divide up the total market, choose the best segments, and design strategies for profitably serving chosen segments. This process involves three steps: *market segmentation*, *target marketing* and *market positioning*.

Market segmentation

The market consists of many types of customers, products and needs. The marketer has to determine which segments offer the best opportunities. Consumers can be grouped and served in various ways based on geographic, demographic, psychographic and behavioural factors. The process of dividing a market into distinct groups of buyers who have different needs, characteristics or behaviour and who might require separate products or marketing programmes is called **market segmentation**.

Every market has segments, but not all ways of segmenting a market are equally useful. For example, Nurofen (a leading painkiller provided by Reckitt Benckiser plc) would gain little by distinguishing between low-income and high-income painkiller users if both respond in the same way to marketing efforts. A **market segment** consists of consumers who respond in a similar way to a given set of marketing efforts. In the car market, for example, consumers who want the biggest, most comfortable car regardless of price make up one market segment. Customers who care mainly about price and running costs make up another segment. It would be difficult to make one car model that was the first choice of consumers in both segments. Companies are wise to focus their efforts on meeting the distinct needs of individual market segments.

Target marketing

After a company has defined market segments, it can enter one or many of these segments. **Target marketing** involves evaluating each market segment's attractiveness and selecting one or more segments to enter. A company should target segments in which it can profitably generate the greatest customer value and sustain it over time.

A company with limited resources might decide to serve only one or a few special segments or 'market niches'. Such 'nichers' specialise in serving customer segments that major competitors overlook or ignore. For example, Arm & Hammer is a leader in providing consumer goods that use baking soda as an ingredient, including toothpaste, deodorants and others. The Danish butter brand Lurpak has become established as a leader in many international markets because of the reputation of Denmark for producing high quality dairy products (for more about the company that makes Lurpak, Arla Foods, you'll have to wait until the start of the next chapter).

Alternatively, a company might choose to serve several related segments – perhaps those with different kinds of customers but with the same basic wants. French food manufacturer Danone, for example, offers a wide range of yogurt-based products. Danone targets very young children with Mon Premier Danone, older children with Danette, and adults with Activia and Actimel. Or a large company might decide to offer a complete range of products to serve all market segments. Most companies enter a new market by serving a single segment, and if this proves successful, they add segments. Large companies eventually seek full market coverage. They want to be the General Motors of their industry.

GM says that it makes a car for every 'person, purse, and personality'. The leading company normally has different products designed to meet the special needs of each segment.

Market positioning

After a company has decided which market segments to enter, it must decide what positions it wants to occupy in those segments. A product's *position* is the place the product occupies relative to competitors in consumers' minds. Marketers want to develop unique market positions for their products. If a product is perceived to be exactly like others on the market, consumers would have no reason to buy it.

Market positioning is arranging for a product to occupy a clear, distinctive and desirable place relative to competing products in the minds of target consumers. As one positioning expert puts it, positioning is 'how you differentiate your product or company in the mind of your prospect. It's why a shopper will pay a little more for your brand. The trick is to figure out how to express the difference.'[14] Thus, marketers plan positions that distinguish their products from competing brands and give them the greatest advantage in their target markets.

BMW makes 'the ultimate driving machine', Sainsbury's is 'where good food costs less', and Kenco claim to be 'the real coffee experts'. MasterCard tell us that 'There are some things money can't buy. For everything else there's MasterCard.' Visa is 'everywhere you want to be'. Tesco says 'every little helps'. Such deceptively simple statements form the backbone of a product's marketing strategy.

In positioning its product, the company first identifies possible competitive advantages upon which to build the position. The company can offer greater customer value either by charging lower prices than competitors do or by offering more benefits to justify higher prices. But if the company *promises* greater value, it must then *deliver* that greater value. Thus, effective positioning begins with actually *differentiating* the company's market offering so that it gives consumers more value. Once the company has chosen a desired position, it must take strong steps to deliver and communicate that position to target consumers. The company's entire marketing programme should support the chosen positioning strategy.

Developing the marketing mix

After deciding on its overall marketing strategy, the company is ready to begin planning the details of the marketing mix, one of the major concepts in modern marketing. The **marketing mix** is the set of controllable, tactical marketing tools that the firm blends to produce the response it wants in the target market. The marketing mix consists of everything the firm can do to influence the demand for its product. The many possibilities can be collected into four groups of variables known as the 'four Ps': *product*, *price*, *place* and *promotion*. In service markets the 'four Ps' are often extended to 'seven Ps' by the addition of *people*, *process* and *physical* evidence. But for the moment we will concentrate on product, price, place and promotion. Figure 2.5 shows the marketing tools under each P.

Product means the goods and services combination the company offers to the target market. Thus, a Peugeot 207 product (produced by PSA Peugeot Citroën) consists of nuts and bolts, spark plugs, pistons, headlights and thousands of other parts. Peugeot offers several 207 models and dozens of optional features. The car comes fully serviced and with a comprehensive warranty that is as much a part of the product as the steering wheel.

Price is the amount of money customers have to pay to obtain the product. PSA Peugeot Citroën calculates suggested retail prices that its dealers might charge for each 207. But Peugeot dealers rarely charge the full list price. Instead, they negotiate the price with each customer, offering discounts, trade-in allowances and credit terms. These actions adjust prices for the current competitive situation and bring them into line with the buyer's perception of the car's value.

FIGURE 2.5

The four Ps of the marketing mix

Place includes company activities that make the product available to target consumers. Peugeot partners with a large body of independently owned dealerships that sell the company's many different models. Peugeot selects its dealers carefully and supports them strongly. The dealers keep an inventory of Peugeot cars, demonstrate them to potential buyers, negotiate prices, close sales and service the cars after the sale.

Promotion means activities that communicate the merits of the product and persuade target customers to buy it. Peugeot spends more than €1.0 billion each year on advertising, about €300 per vehicle, to tell consumers about the company and its many products. Dealership salespeople assist potential buyers and persuade them that Peugeot is the best car for them. Peugeot and its dealers offer special promotions – sales, cash rebates, low financing rates – as added purchase incentives.

An effective marketing programme blends all of the marketing mix elements into a coordinated programme designed to achieve the company's marketing objectives by delivering value to consumers. The marketing mix constitutes the company's tactical tool kit for establishing strong positioning in target markets.

Some critics think that the four Ps may omit or underemphasise certain important activities. For example, they ask, 'Where are services?' Just because they don't start with a *P* doesn't justify omitting them. The answer is that services, such as banking, airline and retailing services, are products too. We might call them *service products*. 'Where is packaging?' the critics might ask. Marketers would answer that they include packaging as just one of many product decisions. All said, as Figure 2.5 suggests, many marketing activities that might appear to be left out of the marketing mix are subsumed under one of the four Ps. The issue is not whether there should be four, six or ten Ps so much as what framework is most helpful in designing marketing programmes.

There is another concern, however, that is valid. It holds that the four Ps concept takes the seller's view of the market, not the buyer's view. From the buyer's viewpoint, in this age of customer relationships, the four Ps might be better described as the four Cs:[15]

4Ps	4Cs
Product	Customer solution
Price	Customer cost
Place	Convenience
Promotion	Communication

Thus, while marketers see themselves as selling products, customers see themselves as buying value or solutions to their problems. And customers are interested in more than just the price; they are interested in the total costs of obtaining, using and disposing of a product. Customers want the product and service to be as conveniently available as possible. Finally, they want two-way communication. Marketers would do well to think through the four Cs first and then build the four Ps on that platform.

MANAGING THE MARKETING EFFORT

In addition to being good at the *marketing* in marketing management, companies also need to pay attention to the *management*. Managing the marketing process requires the four marketing management functions shown in Figure 2.6 – *analysis*, *planning*, *implementation* and *control*. The company first develops company-wide strategic plans, and then translates them into marketing and other plans for each division, product and brand. Through implementation, the company turns the plans into actions. Control consists of measuring and evaluating the results of marketing activities and taking corrective action where needed. Finally, marketing analysis provides information and evaluations needed for all of the other marketing activities.

Marketing analysis

Managing the marketing function begins with a complete analysis of the company's situation. The marketer should conduct a **SWOT analysis**, by which it evaluates the company's overall strengths (S), weaknesses (W), opportunities (O) and threats (T) (see Figure 2.7). Strengths include internal capabilities, resources, and positive situational factors that may help the company to serve its customers and achieve its objectives. Weaknesses include internal limitations and negative situational factors that may interfere with the company's performance. Opportunities are favourable factors or trends in the external environment that the company may be able to exploit to its advantage. And threats are unfavourable external factors or trends that may present challenges to performance.

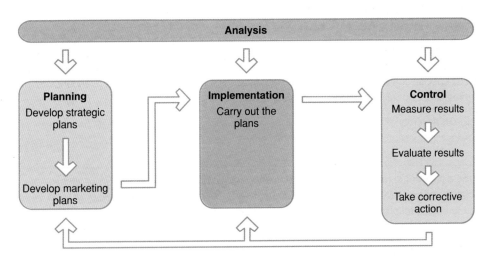

FIGURE 2.6

Marketing analysis, planning, implementation and control

FIGURE 2.7

SWOT analysis

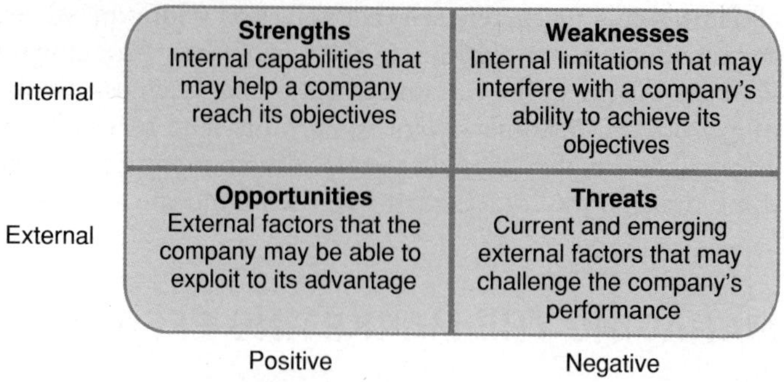

TABLE 2.2 Contents of a marketing plan

Section	Purpose
Executive summary	Presents a brief summary of the main goals and recommendations of the plan for management review, helping top management to find the plan's major points quickly. A table of contents should follow the executive summary.
Current marketing situation	Describes the target market and company's position in it, including information about the market, product performance, competition and distribution. This section includes: ■ A *market description* that defines the market and major segments, then reviews customer needs and factors in the marketing environment that may affect customer purchasing. ■ A *product review* that shows sales, prices and gross margins of the major products in the product line. ■ A review of *competition*, which identifies major competitors and assesses their market positions and strategies for product quality, pricing, distribution and promotion. ■ A review of *distribution*, which evaluates recent sales trends and other developments in major distribution channels.
Threats and opportunities analysis	Assesses major threats and opportunities that the product might face, helping management to anticipate important positive or negative developments that might have an impact on the firm and its strategies.
Objectives and issues	States the marketing objectives that the company would like to attain during the plan's term and discusses key issues that will affect their attainment. For example, if the goal is to achieve a 15 per cent market share, this section looks at how this goal might be achieved.
Marketing strategy	Outlines the broad marketing logic by which the business unit hopes to achieve its marketing objectives and the specifics of target markets, positioning and marketing expenditure levels. It outlines specific strategies for each marketing mix element and explains how each responds to the threats, opportunities and critical issues spelled out earlier in the plan.
Action programmes	Spells out how marketing strategies will be turned into specific action programmes that answer the following questions: *What* will be done? *When* will it be done? *Who* is responsible for doing it? *How* much will it cost?
Budgets	Details a supporting marketing budget that is essentially a projected profit-and-loss statement. It shows expected revenues (forecasted number of units sold and the average net price) and expected costs (of production, distribution and marketing). The difference is the projected profit. Once approved by higher management, the budget becomes the basis for materials buying, production scheduling, personnel planning and marketing operations.
Controls	Outlines the control that will be used to monitor progress and allow higher management to review implementation results and spot products that are not meeting their goals.

The company must analyse its markets and marketing environment to find attractive opportunities and identify environmental threats. It must analyse company strengths and weaknesses as well as current and possible marketing actions to determine which opportunities it can best pursue. The goal is to match the company's strengths to attractive opportunities in the environment, while eliminating or overcoming the weaknesses and minimising the threats. Marketing analysis provides inputs to each of the other marketing management functions. We discuss marketing analysis more fully in Chapter 3.

Marketing planning

Through strategic planning, the company decides what it wants to do with each business unit. Marketing planning involves deciding on marketing strategies that will help the company attain its overall strategic objectives. A detailed marketing plan is needed for each business, product or brand. What does a marketing plan look like? Our discussion focuses on product or brand marketing plans.

Table 2.2 outlines the major sections of a typical product or brand marketing plan. (See Appendix 1 for a sample marketing plan.) The plan begins with an executive summary, which quickly overviews major assessments, goals and recommendations. The main section of the plan presents a detailed analysis of the current marketing situation as well as potential threats and opportunities. It next states major objectives for the brand and outlines the specifics of a marketing strategy for achieving them.

A marketing strategy consists of specific strategies for target markets, positioning, the marketing mix and marketing expenditure levels. In this section, the planner explains how each strategy responds to the threats, opportunities and critical issues spelled out earlier in the plan. Additional sections of the marketing plan lay out an action programme for implementing the marketing strategy along with the details of a supporting marketing budget. The last section outlines the controls that will be used to monitor progress and take corrective action.

Marketing implementation

Planning good strategies is only a start towards successful marketing. A brilliant marketing strategy counts for little if the company fails to implement it properly. **Marketing implementation** is the process that turns marketing *plans* into marketing *actions* in order to accomplish strategic marketing objectives. Whereas marketing planning addresses the *what* and *why* of marketing activities, implementation addresses the *who*, *where*, *when* and *how*.

Many managers think that 'doing things right' (implementation) is as important as, or even more important than, 'doing the right things' (strategy). The fact is that both are critical to success, and companies can gain competitive advantages through effective implementation. One firm can have essentially the same strategy as another, yet win in the marketplace through faster or better execution. Still, implementation is difficult – it is often easier to think up good marketing strategies than it is to carry them out. For example, the Danish industrial air-conditioning company Danfoss had a clear strategic vision to be a global leader in its core business, and a clear strategy to implement this by developing close relationships with its customers using a relationship marketing approach. The vision and the strategy were only the start, and had to be implemented through a detailed and lengthy process of gathering and analysing customer service information in order to understand and deliver what customers really wanted (see Marketing at Work 2.2).

MARKETING AT WORK 2.2

Implementing customer relationship strategy at Danfoss

Professor Adam Lindgreen,
Department of Marketing and
Business Strategy, Hull University
Business School, UK, **Dr Martin**
Hingley, *Harper Adams University*
College, UK, **Professor Michael**
Beverland, *RMIT University,*
Melbourne, Australia, **Jesper**
Krogh Jørgensen, *Stig*
Jørgensen & Partners, Denmark
and **John D. Nicholson,**
Department of Marketing and
Business Strategy, Hull University
Business School, UK

A lot of business-to-business companies talk about the need to develop closer relationships with their customers. In many cases this remains an unfulfilled wish, because they fail to invest in the basic tools to understand exactly what their customers want and exactly how their customers feel about what they are getting. Danish company Danfoss invested some serious time and money so that the desire of the management to get closer to their customers was matched by the information and the systems to enable them to really make it happen.

With 22,600 employees and net sales of DKK 22.2 billion in 2007, Danfoss ranks among the largest industrial companies in Denmark. The company's broad vision reflects its desire to become a global leader within its core businesses, as well as a highly respected company that improves quality of life through advanced customer application technologies that also create value for stakeholders. The company consists of 110 sales subsidiaries across the world, classified into 13 business units within three divisions: refrigeration and air conditioning, heating, and motion controls. The global group produces products in 70 factories spread across 25 different countries and leads several industries in terms of research and development, production, and the sales and service of mechanical and electronic components.

Danfoss has for many years measured its customers' satisfaction using customer perception studies. At the beginning of 2003, however, the executive board of the Heating Division initiated a process with the goal of improving and coordinating its local customer surveys. In 2005, some of the elements from the solution developed by the Heating Division were absorbed, adopted and further developed to prepare for a company-wide and global roll out. The following sections describe this two-step process.

The first step: The process within the Heating Division

In 2003, the Danfoss Heating Division initiated a project to improve its customer surveys. The management team had a very clear idea of what they wanted to achieve: the objective was to develop a unified approach for the entire division to improve its ability to benchmark results, make the survey results more operational, and thereby improve their relevance and value for the frontline staff.

In this process, the Heating Division of Danfoss turned to Stig Jørgensen & Partners, a management consulting company that has specialised in the field of developing and implementing global solutions for measuring and managing customer loyalty. Together with the team at Danfoss, Stig Jørgensen & Partners developed and implemented a new solution that meets the requirements of the divisional management.

Danfoss is a Danish company with global reach, which has recently implemented a comprehensive new strategy to gather better customer information and develop improved customer relationships.
Source: http://www.danfoss.com/NewsAndEvents/PressCenter/PhotoGallery/PhotoGallery.htm.

In short, the solution would create a knowledge base that could summarise the drivers of customer loyalty, the overall loyalty toward Danfoss Heating, and the division's 'share of wallet' among its existing customers. With such knowledge, Danfoss Heating could involve all its sales managers and employees in improving its customer relationships. Furthermore, the project aimed eventually to improve sales and marketing activities by measuring their effects on customer loyalty, and increase sales growth through greater share of customers' spending. Finally, Stig Jørgensen & Partners hoped to help Danfoss identify, select and implement some cost-effective loyalty and sales growth improvement projects and provide customers with more relevant services, more effective customer-facing processes and better customer experiences.

From May 2003 to the end of 2005, the '4C programme' was created: Customer loyalty, Competence development, Cultural change and Customer relationship management. This program was designed to increase the effectiveness of the sales, service, and marketing processes within the Heating Division by analysing, developing and capitalising on customer loyalty. As a 'health check' for the division, the project attempted to help the company prioritise and improve its relationships with various direct and indirect customers so as to ensure future profitable growth.

The second step: The process within the Danfoss Sales Programme (DSP)

In 2005, Danfoss established the global, group-wide DSP that forms part of the Danfoss Business System (DBS). This was a change initiative designed to achieve global operational excellence throughout the group's value chain.

One of the working principles of DSP is to use the division's best existing methods and tools within the fields of sales and marketing. At the end of 2005, it was decided that DSP should use the customer loyalty measurement concept developed by the Heating Division. Because DSP already had the necessary support processes and tools in place, it only needed to integrate and further develop the core measurement methods and tools used by the Heating Division.

One of the key elements is the Customer Insight tool, with which Danfoss can follow developments in its market and obtain an objective evaluation of how well it is doing. The overview analysis from the Customer Insight tool includes details not only of the marketplace but also of customer satisfaction, customer loyalty, average share of wallet per customer, and loyalty drivers for each specific customer segment, which then can be combined with existing internal data about customers and their purchase patterns.

A key building block of the Customer Insight tool is the use of structured customer surveys (with telephone-based and online data captures); a unique Loyalty Simulator® analysis tool uses customer feedback to identify the key drivers of customer loyalty among existing customers. Danfoss can upload the data and receive an automatic report in return. These easily understood summary reports go to frontline staff and form the basis of the information that sales managers and sales engineers use when they communicate with customers. With more customer information than ever before, including individual customer reports, Danfoss's sales engineers are in a far better position to understand what makes customers tick, and have a strong, objective basis for effective cross-selling (that is, selling additional products and services to existing customers).

It also has become possible to give existing target customers better information about new products and services based on their specific business needs and their perceptions of Danfoss's performance and ability to fulfil those needs. Last but not least, the customer surveys function as a fact-based 'voice of customer' that the different sales companies can use as input for selecting and utilising the various other sales and marketing improvement modules provided by DSP.

Results

In general terms the new system enables Danfoss to understand the specific needs of individual business customers, and to conduct market segment analysis using concrete, customer-based information. More specifically, the Customer Insight tool helps to increase sales to individual customers, makes it clearer which are the most important customers, reduces the risk of customers defecting to competitors, and increases the efficiency of the sales engineers. Certainly, the pioneers of the system, the Heating Division, have seen excellent financial performance recently. In Sweden, the Heating Division doubled its sales growth. It was estimated that the investment in the new customer survey system was repaid within seven months. The management team were very happy with the return on this investment. Danfoss has gained market share as a result of improved customer insight. If nothing else, it

▶

has more detailed information about its customers, including their preferred product ranges and sales, service, and marketing activities. Sales engineers can now approach customers armed with much more information, and offer new business opportunities. Danfoss uses the information generated through the project as the basis of its marketing activities; it considers the project an ongoing process. Its marketing strategy is now based on concrete customer information combined with excellent analytical tools. The key question for Danfoss now? How can it be made even better!

In an increasingly connected world, people at all levels of the marketing system must work together to implement marketing strategies and plans. At Bosch, for example, marketing implementation for the company's power tools, outdoor equipment and other products requires day-to-day decisions and actions by thousands of people both inside and outside the organisation. Marketing managers make decisions about target segments, branding, packaging, pricing, promotion and distribution. They talk with engineering about product design, with manufacturing about production and inventory levels, and with finance about funding and cash flows. They also connect with outside people, such as advertising agencies to plan ad campaigns and the news media to obtain publicity support. The sales force urges Homebase, Argos, B&Q and other retailers to advertise Bosch products, provide ample shelf space and use company displays.

Successful marketing implementation depends on how well the company blends its people, organisational structure, decision and reward systems, and company culture into a cohesive action programme that supports its strategies. At all levels, the company must be staffed by people who have the needed skills, motivation and personal characteristics. The company's formal organisation structure plays an important role in implementing marketing strategy; so do its decision and reward systems. For example, if a company's compensation system rewards managers for short-term profit results, they will have little incentive to work toward long-term market-building objectives.

Finally, to be successfully implemented, the firm's marketing strategies must fit with its company culture, the system of values and beliefs shared by people in the organisation. The most successful companies have almost cult-like cultures built around strong, market-oriented missions. At companies such as Ryanair, Innocent and BMW employees share such a powerful vision that they have a very strong sense of what's right for their company.

Marketing department organisation

The company must design a marketing organisation that can carry out marketing strategies and plans. If the company is very small, one person might do all of the research, selling, advertising, customer service and other marketing work. As the company expands, a marketing department emerges to plan and carry out marketing activities. In large companies, this department contains many specialists. Thus, PSA Peugeot Citroën and Nestlé have product and market managers, sales managers and salespeople, market researchers, advertising experts, and many other specialists. To head up such large marketing organisations, many companies have now created a *chief marketing officer* (or CMO) position.

Modern marketing departments can be arranged in several ways. The most common form of marketing organisation is the *functional organisation*. Under this organisation, different marketing activities are headed by a functional specialist – a sales manager, advertising manager, marketing research manager, customer service manager, or new-product manager. A company that sells across the country or internationally often uses a *geographic organisation*. Its sales and marketing people are assigned to specific countries, regions and districts. Geographic organisation allows salespeople to settle into a territory, get to know their customers, and work with a minimum of travel time and cost.

Companies with many very different products or brands often create a *product management organisation*. Using this approach, a product manager develops and implements a complete strategy and marketing programme for a specific product or brand. Product management first appeared at Procter & Gamble in 1929. A new company soap, Camay, was not doing well, and a young P&G executive was assigned to give his exclusive attention to developing and promoting this product. He was successful, and the company soon added other product managers.[16] Since then, many firms, especially consumer products companies, have set up product management organisations.

For companies that sell one product line to many different types of markets and customers that have different needs and preferences, a *market* or *customer management organisation* might be best. A market management organisation is similar to the product management organisation. Market managers are responsible for developing marketing strategies and plans for their specific markets or customers. This system's main advantage is that the company is organised around the needs of specific customer segments.

Large companies that produce many different products flowing into many different geographic and customer markets usually employ some *combination* of the functional, geographic, product and market organisation forms. This ensures that each function, product and market receives its share of management attention. However, it can also add costly layers of management and reduce organisational flexibility. Still, the benefits of organisational specialisation usually outweigh the drawbacks.

Marketing organisation has become an increasingly important issue in recent years. As we discussed in Chapter 1, many companies are finding that today's marketing environment calls for less focus on products, brands and territories and more focus on customers and customer relationships. More and more companies are shifting their brand management focus towards *customer management* – moving away from managing just product or brand profitability and towards managing customer profitability and customer equity. And many companies now organise their marketing operations around major customers. For example, companies such as Nestlé and Bosch have large teams, or even whole divisions, set up to serve large customers like Asda, Homebase or Carrefour.

Marketing control

Because many surprises occur during the implementation of marketing plans, the marketing department must practise constant marketing control. **Marketing control** involves evaluating the results of marketing strategies and plans and taking corrective action to ensure that objectives are attained. Marketing control involves four steps. Management first sets specific marketing goals. It then measures its performance in the marketplace and evaluates the causes of any differences between expected and actual performance. Finally, management takes corrective action to close the gaps between its goals and its performance. This may require changing the action programmes or even changing the goals.

Operating control involves checking ongoing performance against the annual plan and taking corrective action when necessary. Its purpose is to ensure that the company achieves the sales, profits and other goals set out in its annual plan. It also involves determining the profitability of different products, territories, markets and channels.

Strategic control involves looking at whether the company's basic strategies are well matched to its opportunities. Marketing strategies and programmes can quickly become outdated, and each company should periodically reassess its overall approach to the marketplace. A major tool for such strategic control is a **marketing audit**. The marketing audit is a comprehensive, systematic, independent and periodic examination of a company's environment, objectives, strategies and activities to determine problem areas and opportunities. The audit provides good input for a plan of action to improve the company's marketing performance.[17]

The marketing audit covers *all* major marketing areas of a business, not just a few trouble spots. It assesses the marketing environment, marketing strategy, marketing organisation, marketing systems, marketing mix, and marketing productivity and profitability. The audit is normally conducted by an objective and experienced outside party. The findings may come as a surprise – and sometimes as a shock – to management. Management then decides which actions make sense and how and when to implement them.

MEASURING AND MANAGING RETURN ON MARKETING

Marketing managers must ensure that their marketing expenditure is being wisely invested. In the past, many marketers spent freely on big, expensive marketing programmes, often without thinking carefully about the financial returns on their spending. They believed that marketing produces intangible outcomes, which do not lend themselves readily to measures of productivity or return. But all that is changing:

> For years, corporate marketers have walked into budget meetings like neighborhood junkies. They couldn't always justify how well they spent past handouts or what difference it all made. They just wanted more money – for flashy TV ads, for big-ticket events, for, you know, getting out the message and building up the brand. But those heady days of blind budget increases are fast being replaced with a new mantra: measurement and accountability. Armed with reams of data, increasingly sophisticated tools, and growing evidence that the old tricks simply don't work, there's hardly a marketing executive today who isn't demanding a more scientific approach to help defend marketing strategies in front of the chief financial officer. Marketers want to know the actual return on investment (ROI) of each dollar. They want to know it often, not just annually . . . Companies in every segment of business have become obsessed with honing the science of measuring marketing performance. 'Marketers have been pretty unaccountable for many years,' notes one expert. 'Now they are under big pressure to estimate their impact.'[18]

In response, marketers are developing better measures of *return on marketing*. **Return on marketing** (or *marketing ROI*) is the net return from a marketing investment divided by the costs of the marketing investment. It measures the profits generated by investments in marketing activities.

It's true that marketing returns can be difficult to measure. In measuring financial ROI, both the *R* and the *I* are uniformly measured in money terms. But there is as yet no consistent definition of marketing ROI. 'It's tough to measure, more so than for other business expenses,' says one analyst. 'You can imagine buying a piece of equipment . . . and then measuring the productivity gains that result from the purchase,' he says. 'But in marketing, benefits like advertising impact aren't easily put into dollar returns. It takes a leap of faith to come up with a number.'[19]

A company can assess return on marketing in terms of standard marketing performance measures, such as brand awareness, sales or market share. Increasingly, however, marketers are using customer-centred measures of marketing impact, such as customer acquisition, customer retention and customer lifetime value. Figure 2.8 views marketing expenditures as investments that produce returns in the form of more profitable customer relationships.[20] Marketing investments result in improved customer value and satisfaction, which in turn increases customer attraction and retention. This increases individual customer lifetime values and the firm's overall customer equity. Increased customer equity, in relation to the cost of the marketing investments, determines return on marketing.

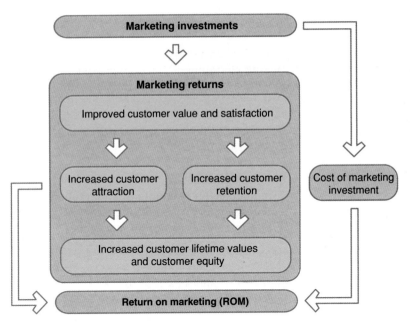

FIGURE 2.8

Return on marketing

Source: Reprinted with permission from *Journal of Marketing*, published by the American Marketing Association, Roland T. Rust, Katherine N. Lemon and Valerie A. Zeithamal, January 2004, p. 112.

Regardless of how it's defined or measured, the return on marketing concept is here to stay. 'All good marketers live and die by measurements of their results,' states the marketing productivity consultant. 'Projections are made, marketing is delivered, results are measured, and the knowledge is applied to guide future marketing . . . The return on marketing investments is integral to strategic decisions at [all levels] of the business.'[21]

THE JOURNEY YOU'VE TAKEN Reviewing the concepts

In Chapter 1, we defined *marketing* and outlined the steps in the marketing process. In this chapter, we examined company-wide strategic planning and marketing's role in the organisation. Then, we looked more deeply into marketing strategy and the marketing mix, and reviewed the major marketing management functions. So you've now had a pretty good overview of the fundamentals of modern marketing. In future chapters, we'll expand on these fundamentals.

1 Explain company-wide strategic planning and its four steps.

Strategic planning sets the stage for the rest of the company's planning. Marketing contributes to strategic planning, and the overall plan defines marketing's role in the company. Although formal planning offers a variety of benefits to companies, not all companies use it or use it well.

Strategic planning involves developing a strategy for long-term survival and growth. It consists of four steps: defining the company's mission, setting goals and objectives, designing a business portfolio, and developing functional plans. *Defining a clear company mission* begins with drafting a formal mission statement, which should be market-oriented, realistic, specific, motivating and consistent with the market environment. The mission is then transformed into detailed *supporting goals and objectives* to guide the entire company. Based on those goals and objectives, headquarters designs a *business portfolio*, deciding which businesses and products should receive more or fewer resources. In turn, each business and product unit must develop *detailed marketing plans* in line with the company-wide plan.

2 Discuss how to design business portfolios and develop strategies for growth and downsizing.

Guided by the company's mission statement and objectives, management plans its *business portfolio*, or the collection of businesses and products that make up the company. The firm wants to produce a business portfolio that best fits its strengths and weaknesses to opportunities in the environment. To do this, it must analyse and adjust its *current* business portfolio and develop growth and downsizing strategies for adjusting the *future* portfolio. The company might use a formal portfolio-planning method. But many companies are now designing more customised portfolio-planning approaches that better suit their unique situations. The *product/market expansion grid* suggests four possible growth paths: market penetration, market development, product development and diversification.

3 Assess marketing's role in strategic planning and explain how marketers partner with others inside and outside the firm to build profitable customer relationships.

Under the strategic plan, the major functional departments – marketing, finance, accounting, purchasing, operations, information systems, human resources, and others – must work together to accomplish strategic objectives. Marketing plays a key role in the company's strategic planning by providing a *marketing-concept philosophy* and *inputs* regarding attractive market opportunities. Within individual business units, marketing designs *strategies* for reaching the unit's objectives and helps to carry them out profitably.

Marketers alone cannot produce superior value for customers. A company's success depends on how well each department performs its customer value-adding activities and how well the departments work together to serve the customer. Thus, marketers must practise *partner relationship management*. They must work closely with partners in other company departments to form an effective *value chain* that serves the customer. And they must partner effectively with other companies in the marketing system to form a competitively superior *value-delivery network*.

4 Describe the elements of a customer-driven marketing strategy and mix, and the forces that influence it.

Consumer relationships are at the centre of marketing strategy and programmes. Through market segmentation, target marketing and market positioning, the company divides the total market into smaller segments, selects segments it can best serve, and decides how it wants to bring value to target consumers. It then designs a *marketing mix* to produce the response it wants in the target market. The marketing mix consists of product, price, place and promotion decisions.

5 List the marketing management functions, including the elements of a marketing plan, and discuss the importance of measuring and managing return on marketing.

To find the best strategy and mix and to put them into action, the company engages in marketing analysis, planning, implementation and control. The main components of a *marketing plan* are the executive summary, current marketing situation, threats and opportunities, objectives and issues, marketing strategies, action programmes, budgets and controls. To plan good strategies is often easier than to carry them out. To be successful, companies must also be effective at *implementation* – turning marketing strategies into marketing actions.

Much of the responsibility for implementation goes to the company's marketing department. Marketing departments can be organised in one or a combination of ways: *functional marketing organisation*, *geographic organisation, product management organisation*, or *market management organisation*. In this age of customer relationships, more and more companies are now changing their organisational focus from product or territory management to customer relationship management. Marketing organisations carry out *marketing control*, both operating control and strategic control. They use *marketing audits* to determine marketing opportunities and problems and to recommend short-term and long-term actions to improve overall marketing performance.

Marketing managers must ensure that their marketing budget is being well spent. Today's marketers face growing pressures to show that they are adding value in line with their costs. In response, marketers are developing better measures of *return on marketing*. Increasingly, they are using customer-centred measures of marketing impact as a key input into their strategic decision-making.

NAVIGATING THE KEY TERMS

NOTES AND REFERENCES

1 Quotes and other information from Stanley Holmes, 'The New Nike', *BusinessWeek*, 20 September 2004, pp. 78–86; 'Nike, Inc.', *Hoover's Company Records*, 15 May 2005, p. 14254; Daniel Roth, 'Can Nike Still Do It Without Phil Knight?' *Fortune*, 4 April 2005, pp. 59–68; and www.nikebiz.com, May 2005.

2 For a more detailed discussion of corporate- and business-level strategic planning as they apply to marketing, see Philip Kotler and Kevin Lane Keller, *Marketing Management*, 12th edn (Upper Saddle River, NJ: Prentice Hall, 2006), Chapter 2.

3 See Forest David and Fred David, 'It's Time to Redraft Your Mission Statement', *The Journal of Business Strategy*, January/February 2003, pp. 11–15; 'Crafting Mission Statements', *Association Management*, January 2004, p. 23; and Charles N. Toftoy and Joydeep Chartterjee, 'Mission Statements and the Small Business', *Business Strategy Review*, Autumn 2004, pp. 41–4.

4 http://www.wagggsworld.org/en/about/scouting.

5 Monsanto Company Pledge Report, accessed at http://monsanto.com/monsanto/layout/our_pledge/default.asp, July 2005.

6 The following discussion is based in part on information found at www.bcg.com/this_is_bcg/mission/growth_share_matrix.jsp, December 2005. For more on strategic planning, see Dennis Rheault, 'Freshening Up Strategic Planning: More than Fill-in-the-Blanks', *The Journal of Business Strategy*, 24(6), 2004, pp. 33–7; Anthony Lavia, 'Strategic Planning in Times of Turmoil', *Business Communications Review*, March 2004, pp. 56–60; Rita Gunther McGrath and Ian C. MacMillan. 'Market Busting', *Harvard Business Review*, March 2005, pp. 80–9.

7 H. Igor Ansoff, 'Strategies for Diversification', *Harvard Business Review*, September–October 1957, pp. 113–24. Also see Kevin Lane Keller, *Strategic Brand Management*, 2nd edn (Upper Saddle River, NJ: Prentice Hall, 2003), pp. 576–8; and Kotler and Keller, *Marketing Management*, pp. 47–8.

8 Quotes and information in the Starbucks examples and in the growth discussion that follows are from Monica Soto Ouchi, 'Starbucks Ratchets Up Growth Forecast', *Knight Ridder Tribune News*, 15 October 2004, p. 1; Stanley Holmes, 'First the Music, Then the Coffee', *BusinessWeek*, 22 November 2004, p. 66; Barbara Clements, *Knight Ridder Tribune News*, 28 April 2005, p. 1; and Patricia Sellers, 'Starbucks: The Next Generation', *Fortune*, 4 April 2005, p. 30.

9 Nirmalya Kumar, 'Kill a Brand, Keep a Customer', *Harvard Business Review*, December 2003, pp. 87–95.

10 Michael E. Porter, *Competitive Advantage: Creating and Sustaining Superior Performance* (New York: Free Press, 1985); and Michel E. Porter, 'What Is Strategy?' *Harvard Business Review*, November–December 1996, pp. 61–78. See also Kim B. Clark, et al., *Harvard Business School on Managing the Value Chain* (Boston: Harvard Business School Press, 2000); 'Buyer Value and the Value Chain', *Business Owner*, September–October 2003, p. 1; and 'The Value Chain,' accessed at www.quickmba.com/strategy/value-chain/, July 2005.

11 Philip Kotler, *Kotler on Marketing* (New York: The Free Press, 1999), pp. 20–2. See also Philip Kotler, *Marketing Insights from A to Z* (Hoboken, NJ: Wiley, 2003), pp. 102–7.

12 McDonald's Corporation Investor Fact Sheet January 2004, accessed at www.mcdonalds.com/corp/invest/pub/2004_fact_sheet.html; 'McDonald's Corporation,' *Hoover's Company Records*, 1 May 2005, p. 135045; and 'McDonald's Fetes 50th Birthday, Opens Anniversary Restaurant', *Knight Ridder Tribune Business News*, 15 April 2005, p. 1.

13 Quotes and other information from Jeffery K. Liker and Thomas Y. Choi, 'Building Deep Supplier Relationships', *Harvard Business Review*, December 2004, pp. 104–13; and Lindsey Chappell, 'Toyota Aims to Satisfy Its Suppliers', *Automotive News*, 21 February 2005, p. 10.

14 Jack Trout, 'Branding Can't Exist without Positioning', *Advertising Age*, 14 March 2005, p. 28.

15 The four Ps classification was first suggested by E. Jerome McCarthy, *Basic Marketing: A Managerial Approach* (Homewood, IL: Irwin, 1960). For the 4Cs, other proposed classifications, and more discussion, see Robert Lauterborn, 'New Marketing Litany: 4P's Passé; C-Words Take Over', *Advertising Age*, 1 October 1990, p. 26; Elliott Ettenberg, 'Goodbye 4Ps, Hello 4Rs', *Marketing Magazine*, 14 April 2003, p. 8; Michael R. Hyman, 'Revising the Structural Framework for Marketing Management', *Journal of Business Research*, September 2004, p. 923; and Don E. Schultz, 'New Definition of Marketing Reinforces Idea of Integration', *Marketing News*, 15 January 2005, p. 8.

16 For more on brand and product management, see Keller, *Strategic Brand Management*, 2nd edn.

17 For details, see Kotler and Keller, *Marketing Management*, 12th edn, pp. 719–25. Also see Neil A. Morgan, Bruce H. Clark and Rich Gooner, 'Marketing Productivity, Marketing Audits, and Systems for Marketing Performance Assessment: Integrating Multiple Perspectives', *Journal of Marketing*, May 2002, pp. 363–75.

18 Diane Brady, 'Making Marketing Measure Up', *Business Week*, 13 December 2004, pp. 112–13; and 'Kotler Readies World for One-on-One', *Point*, June 2005, p. 3.

19 Mark McMaster, 'ROI: More Vital than Ever', *Sales & Marketing Management*, January 2002, pp. 51–2. Also see Paul Hyde, Ed Landry and Andrew Tipping, 'Are CMOs Irrelevant?' Association of National Advertisers/Booz, Allen, Hamilton white paper, p. 4, accessed at www.ana.net/mrc/ANABoozwhitepaper, June 2005.

20 For a full discussion of this model and details on customer-centred measures of return on marketing, see Roland T. Rust, Katherine N. Lemon and Valerie A. Zeithaml, 'Return on Marketing: Using Customer Equity to Focus Marketing Strategy', *Journal of Marketing*, January 2004, pp. 109–27; and Roland T. Rust, Katherine N. Lemon and Das Narayandas, *Customer Equity Management* (Upper Saddle River, NJ: Prentice Hall, 2005).

21 James D. Lenskold, 'Marketing ROI: Playing to Win', *Marketing Management*, May–June 2002, pp. 30–6. Also see Lenskold, *Marketing ROI: The Path to Campaign, Customer, and Corporate Profitability* (New York: McGraw-Hill, 2003); and Rishad Tobaccowala, 'The High Cost of Arrogance and the Need to Focus on Outputs', *Point*, May 2005, p. 6.

PART TWO VIDEO CASE:
Making an effort to understand your customers

Now that you should have some idea about the basic concepts and objectives of marketing you should have realised that understanding both the context of the organisation you work for and the patterns in the behaviour of your customers are issues that must be confronted if the firm is to succeed. In this section of the book we will consider these problems – how companies understand their customers and how they acknowledge forces and trends within their environments. This video case has marketers from half a dozen companies talking about how they view these problems and try to mitigate or solve them. Amongst the interviewees are representatives from Ikea who discuss problems arising from operating in many different countries and cultures simultaneously, managers from a family company that sells eggs to health and safety conscious consumers and executives from HSBC who discuss how they came to understand a new market.

Go to **www.pearsoned.co.uk/armstrong** to watch this video case, and then consider the following questions:

1. Do any of these marketers reveal insights into environmental pressures or aspects of consumer behaviour that surprise you?

2. Can you think of effective solutions to any of the issues discussed? Do you agree with the plans currently in place?

PART TWO

Understanding the marketplace and consumers

CHAPTER 3
The marketing environment

AFTER STUDYING THIS CHAPTER, YOU SHOULD BE ABLE TO

- describe the environmental forces that affect the company's ability to serve its customers
- explain how changes in the demographic and economic environments affect marketing decisions
- identify the major trends in the firm's natural and technological environments
- explain the key changes in the political and cultural environments
- discuss how companies can react to the marketing environment

THE WAY AHEAD Previewing the concepts

In Part One (Chapters 1 and 2), you learned about the basic concepts of marketing and the steps in the marketing process for building profitable relationships with targeted consumers. In Part Two, as you continue your journey towards learning about marketing, we'll look deeper into the first step of the marketing process – understanding the marketplace and customer needs and wants. In this chapter, you'll discover that marketing does not operate in a vacuum but rather in a complex and changing environment. Other *actors* in this environment – suppliers, intermediaries, customers, competitors, publics and others – may work with or against the company. Major environmental *forces* – demographic, economic, natural, technological, political and cultural – shape marketing opportunities, pose threats, and affect the company's ability to serve customers and develop lasting relationships with them. To understand marketing, and to develop effective marketing strategies, you must first understand the context in which marketing operates.

To illustrate just how swiftly and how unexpectedly serious damage can be inflicted on a company by something entirely outside its control, we start off by looking at the Danish company Arla Foods, and the damage that it suffered in Middle Eastern markets after a Danish newspaper published cartoons that many people of the Islamic faith found offensive. Through no fault of its own, Arla found its brand reputation damaged, its relationships with customers and retailers undermined, and its sales slashed. Read on to see how they set out to put this right.

The boycott of Arla Foods in the Middle East

Dr Ibrahim Abosag, *Lecturer in Marketing, Manchester Business School, University of Manchester, UK*

The Danish company Arla Foods is a global dairy group with production facilities in 11 countries and sales offices in 24 countries, which sells its products in over 100 countries. Arla started its operation in the Middle East some 40 years ago. Soon after its entry into the Middle East market it became the market leader, mainly because of the absence of any credible local competitors. Over the years, Arla has maintained its position as market leader in the Middle East in cheese, butter and cream production. In the mid-1980s, Arla started to operate the Danya Foods dairy in Saudi Arabia's capital, Riyadh. The production facilities in Riyadh are seen to enhance and strengthen its position as market leader in the region. It employs more than 1,200 people across the Middle East, mostly in Saudi Arabia. From its early days in the Middle East until the end of 2005, Arla enjoyed excellent brand recognition, and according to the executive director of the Overseas Division, Finn Hansen (2005), 'consumer awareness of our brands is on a par with, say, Coca-Cola'.

However, in early 2006 Arla lost its market lead because of a boycott of Danish products in many parts of the Middle East. The publication in 2005 by a Danish tabloid newspaper of a series of cartoon caricatures of the Prophet Muhammad sparked uproar across the Middle East. Consumers started to boycott Danish products and a trade boycott followed shortly after; major local retailers such as Al-Othaim Holding and Azizia Panda announced the withdrawal of all Danish products from their shelves. Arla Foods' brands such as Lurpak butter, Puck cream cheese, Three Cows white cheese and Dano powdered milk, felt the double impact of both the consumer and the trade boycott. The most intense boycotting campaigns were carried out in Saudi Arabia, the biggest market in the Middle East. Arla Foods' products were withdrawn from more than 50,000 stores across the region in less than five days, losing over 60 per cent of its market. The main Saudi competitor Almarai took advantage of the cartoon crisis and took the lead in the market. In 2008, Almarai was still the market leader.

The campaigners were successful in posting the images of Danish brands on the internet calling upon consumers to boycott these brands. Also, mobile phone messages carrying boycott lists of Danish products were widely circulated. Similarly, a number of retail stores put all Danish brands, including Arlas's, in a special section on one side of the store accompanied by a large notice calling on consumers not to buy. At the same time, Western stores doing business in the region tried to limit the damage to their own reputations. For example, the French-owned supermarket chain Carrefour stopped selling Danish goods, while several firms, including the Swiss food multinational Nestlé, placed advertisements in Saudi newspapers to counter rumours that their products were made in Denmark.

Product boycotts are not new, but this one was organised, widespread and quite devastating in its impact. Demonstrations were organised and in some countries they reached riot level. Two drivers of Arla official cars and distribution lorries were attacked. The headquarters premises were stoned and threats were issued by demonstrators. The impact was such that Arla was forced to close its plant in Riyadh, lay off employees in Denmark for ten weeks and postpone its plan to double sales in the region by 2010.

Over 40 years of marketing investment and brand building had been undermined in a blink of an eye. With a large-scale boycott happening and no previous experience of anything like this, the whole situation was new to the senior managers of Arla Foods. There were no tried and tested damage limitation

Arla Foods owns leading dairy brands in the Middle East.
Photo source: Arla Foods. With permission.

strategies because the campaign was unprecedented. Faced with an unenviable task, the general manager Erik Folden and the marketing manager Torben Terp Hansen in Arla Foods' headquarters in Saudi Arabia considered ways of restoring faith in Arla Foods' brands. They realised that successful boycotts can have a short-term impact on sales and a long-term impact on a company's most precious asset, its reputation. The main intention was to protect the brand by distancing Arla Foods' brands from the trigger of the boycott.

The initial reaction from Arla was to keep silent. 'Consumer sentiments were high and we knew it was not the right time yet to address our society. "Silence is golden" and we kept it for almost 45 days' (Torben Terp Hansen). During this period, Arla Foods' executives worked on developing 'a comeback strategy' involving seven steps. The first step was to distance themselves from the cartoons, a message that was communicated by Arla managers widely through newspapers and TV stations. The second step revolved around the International Support of the Prophet Conference on 23 March 2006 in Bahrain. The conference discussed Arla Foods' statement and issued a religious recommendation to exempt the company from any boycott. The Bahrain statement cleared Arla of any responsibility and emphasised that Arla should not be punished for the action of others.

In the third step, the company made the Bahrain statement public. To serve this purpose, a statement was published in all newspapers and TV channels thanking the conference for removing Arla Foods from the boycott list. The Bahrain statement was attached alongside the company's statement. A printed version of the statement was placed on the doors of outlets. Soon after, Arla Foods organised a Press and Trade Conference in Riyadh, which was attended by the major retailers and spearheaded by Al-Othaim Holding. The aim was to persuade the retailers to make a collective decision to accept Arla Foods back onto their shelves. Although Arla Foods was successful in restarting its relationships with some of the retailers, it failed to secure the support from the big retailer Azizia Panda who continued to boycott Arla products. Nonetheless, Arla published another 'thank you statement' through the media for those retailers who accepted Arla Foods back. The statement contained the logos of the retailers who agreed to sell Arla Foods brands.

The fourth step was getting back to the stores. Now the retailers were safe in taking back Arla products because Arla had distanced itself from the cartoons. Reuters television covered the return of Arla Foods' brands to stores across the region. Despite all of the statements and coverage, some customers maintained their boycott. This meant that step five had to focus on promotion. Given the huge product stock returns from markets since the boycott started, and because customers are price sensitive, heavy consumer and trade offers were made to entice retailers and consumers to break their boycott.

In step six Arla concentrated on corporate and brand communication. Two main messages were at the heart of its communication. Firstly, it informed the public about its position on the cartoons. Secondly, it reminded consumers about the long heritage Arla Foods had in the region. The communication platform for all brands was aligned with the corporate one and phrases such as '40 years with you' and 'together for generations' were used. Brand communication was designed to show understanding of the region's values, culture and sentiments. However, this communication strategy was essentially a short-term measure. Two months later, the strategy was replaced in step seven by the long-term brand communication. This was seen as an important step to regain the hearts and minds of consumers. To achieve this, heavy investments were made into charities, social activities and social responsibility campaigns: product donations, ties with official governmental bodies, children's cancer activities, and donations of ambulances to Saudi Red Crescent. These activities, which endured for some considerable time, were designed to improve the perception of Arla Foods across the Middle East, and specifically in Saudi Arabia.

A year after the boycott started, at the end of 2006, Arla Foods had recovered most of its market share in most Middle Eastern countries with the exception of Saudi Arabia where it had only recovered 50 per cent. By early 2008 Arla Foods had managed to recover 70 per cent of its market in Saudi Arabia.

The boycott against Arla lasted a lot longer than many others. A similar boycott of American products faded quite quickly, in only a few weeks. The intensity and the scale of the boycott against the American products did not force American companies to react in the way Arla Foods had to. Even in 2008, Arla still had more work to do to repair all of the damage inflicted by the boycott.

Source: With thanks to Torben Terp Hansen, General Manager of Arla Foods, Lebanon.

Marketers need to be good at building relationships with customers, others in the company and external partners. To do this effectively, they must understand the major environmental forces that surround all of these relationships. A company's **marketing environment** consists of the actors and forces outside marketing that affect marketing management's ability to build and maintain successful relationships with target customers. Successful companies know the vital importance of constantly watching and adapting to the changing environment.

The environment continues to change rapidly, and both consumers and marketers wonder what the future will bring. More than any other group in the company, marketers must be the trend trackers and opportunity seekers. Although every manager in an organisation needs to observe the outside environment, marketers have two special aptitudes. They have disciplined methods – marketing research and marketing intelligence – for collecting information about the marketing environment. They also spend more time in the customer and competitor environments. By carefully studying the environment, marketers can adapt their strategies to meet new marketplace challenges and opportunities.

The marketing environment is made up of a *microenvironment* and a *macroenvironment*. The **microenvironment** consists of the actors close to the company that affect its ability to serve its customers – the company, suppliers, marketing intermediaries, customer markets, competitors and publics. The **macroenvironment** consists of the larger societal forces that affect the microenvironment – demographic, economic, natural, technological, political and cultural forces. We look first at the company's microenvironment.

THE COMPANY'S MICROENVIRONMENT

Marketing management's job is to build relationships with customers by creating customer value and satisfaction. However, marketing managers cannot do this alone. Figure 3.1 shows the major actors in the marketer's microenvironment. Marketing success will require building relationships with other company departments, suppliers, marketing intermediaries, customers, competitors and various publics, which combine to make up the company's value delivery network.

The company

In designing marketing plans, marketing management takes other company groups into account – groups such as top management, finance, research and development (R&D), purchasing, operations and accounting. All these interrelated groups form the internal environment. Top management sets the company's mission, objectives, broad strategies and policies. Marketing managers make decisions within the strategies and plans made by top management.

FIGURE 3.1

Actors in the microenvironment

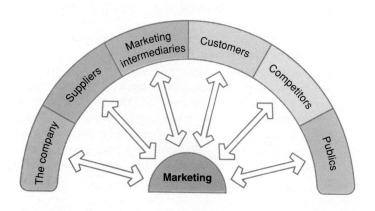

Marketing managers must also work closely with other company departments. Finance is concerned with finding and using funds to carry out the marketing plan. The R&D department focuses on designing safe and attractive products. Purchasing worries about getting supplies and materials, whereas operations is responsible for producing and distributing the desired quality and quantity of products. Accounting has to measure revenues and costs to help marketing know how well it is achieving its objectives. Together, all of these departments have an impact on the marketing department's plans and actions. Under the marketing concept, all of these functions must 'think consumer'. They should work in harmony to provide superior customer value and satisfaction.

Suppliers

Suppliers form an important link in the company's overall customer value delivery system. They provide the resources needed by the company to produce its goods and services. Supplier problems can seriously affect marketing. Marketing managers must watch supply availability – supply shortages or delays, labour strikes and other events can cost sales in the short term and damage customer satisfaction in the long term. Marketing managers also monitor the price trends of their key inputs. Rising supply costs may force price increases that can harm the company's sales volume.

Most marketers today treat their suppliers as partners in creating and delivering customer value. Tesco goes to great lengths to work with its suppliers. For example, it helps them to test new products in its stores. Tesco has signed up to the Office of Fair Trading supermarket Code of Practice on the treatment of suppliers, which means that it undertakes to treat suppliers fairly at all times and to avoid such practices as delaying payments to suppliers or insisting that suppliers contribute financially to supermarket promotional activities. In the most recent audit by the Office of Fair Trading Tesco was found to be implementing this Code effectively.

Marketing intermediaries

Marketing intermediaries help the company to promote, sell and distribute its goods to final buyers. They include resellers, physical distribution firms, marketing services agencies and financial intermediaries. *Resellers* are distribution channel firms that help the company find customers or make sales to them. These include wholesalers and retailers, who buy and resell merchandise. Selecting and partnering with resellers is not easy. No longer do manufacturers have many small, independent resellers from which to choose. They now face large and growing reseller organisations such as Tesco, Carrefour, Aldi and Fnac. These organisations frequently have enough power to dictate terms or even shut the manufacturer out of large markets.

Physical distribution firms help the company to stock and move goods from their points of origin to their destinations. Working with warehouse and transportation firms, a company must determine the best ways to store and ship goods, balancing factors such as cost, delivery, speed and safety. *Marketing services agencies* are the marketing research firms, advertising agencies, media firms and marketing consulting firms that help the company target and promote its products to the right markets. *Financial intermediaries* include banks, credit companies, insurance companies and other businesses that help finance transactions or insure against the risks associated with the buying and selling of goods.

Like suppliers, marketing intermediaries form an important component of the company's overall value delivery system. In its quest to create satisfying customer relationships, the company must do more than just optimise its own performance. It must partner effectively with marketing intermediaries to optimise the performance of the entire system.

Thus, today's marketers recognise the importance of working with their intermediaries as partners rather than simply as channels through which they sell their products. For example, when Coca-Cola signs on as the exclusive drinks provider for a fast-food chain, such as McDonald's or Subway, it provides much more than just soft drinks. It also pledges powerful marketing support.

Coke assigns cross-functional teams dedicated to understanding the finer points of each retail partner's business. It conducts a staggering amount of research on beverage consumers and shares these insights with its partners. It analyses the demographics of geographical areas and helps partners to determine which Coke brands are preferred in their areas. Coca-Cola has even studied the design of drive-through menu boards to better understand which layouts, fonts, letter sizes, colours and visuals induce consumers to order more food and drink.[1]

Customers

The company needs to study five types of customer markets closely. *Consumer markets* consist of individuals and households that buy goods and services for personal consumption. *Business markets* buy goods and services for further processing or for use in their production process, whereas *reseller markets* buy goods and services to resell at a profit. *Government markets* are made up of government agencies that buy goods and services to produce public services or transfer the goods and services to others who need them. Finally, *international markets* consist of these buyers in other countries, including consumers, producers, resellers and governments. Each market type has special characteristics that call for careful study by the seller.

Competitors

The marketing concept states that to be successful a company must provide greater customer value and satisfaction than its competitors do. Thus, marketers must do more than simply adapt to the needs of target consumers. They also must gain strategic advantage by positioning their offerings strongly against competitors' offerings in the minds of consumers.

No single competitive marketing strategy is best for all companies. Each firm should consider its own size and industry position compared to those of its competitors. Large firms with dominant positions in an industry can use certain strategies that smaller firms cannot afford. But being large is not enough. There are winning strategies for large firms, but there are also losing ones. And small firms can develop strategies that give them better rates of return than large firms enjoy.

Publics

The company's marketing environment also includes various publics. A **public** is any group that has an actual or potential interest in or impact on an organisation's ability to achieve its objectives. We can identify seven types of publics.

- *Financial publics* influence the company's ability to obtain funds. Banks, investment houses and shareholders are the major financial publics.
- *Media publics* carry news, features and editorial opinion. They include newspapers, magazines, websites, and radio and television stations.
- *Government publics*. Management must take government developments into account. Marketers must often consult the company's lawyers on issues of product safety, truth in advertising, and other matters.

- *Citizen-action publics*. A company's marketing decisions may be questioned by consumer organisations, environmental groups, minority groups and others. Its public relations department can help it stay in touch with consumer and citizen groups.

- *Local publics* include neighbourhood residents and community organisations. Large companies usually appoint a community relations officer to deal with the community, attend meetings, answer questions and contribute to worthwhile causes.

- *General public*. A company needs to be concerned about the general public's attitude toward its products and activities. The public's image of the company affects its buying.

- *Internal publics* include workers, managers, volunteers and the board of directors. Large companies use newsletters and other means to inform and motivate their internal publics. When employees feel good about their company, this positive attitude spills over to external publics.

A company can prepare marketing plans for these major publics as well as for its customer markets. Suppose the company wants a specific response from a particular public, such as goodwill, favourable word of mouth, or donations of time or money. The company would have to design an offer to this public that is attractive enough to produce the desired response.

THE COMPANY'S MACROENVIRONMENT

The company and all of the other actors operate in a larger macroenvironment of forces that shape opportunities and pose threats to the company. Figure 3.2 shows the six major forces in the company's macroenvironment. In the remaining sections of this chapter, we examine these forces and show how they affect marketing plans.

Demographic environment

Demography is the study of human populations in terms of size, density, location, age, gender, race, occupation and other statistics. The demographic environment is of major interest to marketers because it involves people, and people make up markets. The world population is growing at an explosive rate. It now totals more than 6.6 billion and will exceed 8.1 billion by the year 2030.[2] The world's large and highly diverse population poses both opportunities and challenges.

Changes in the world demographic environment have major implications for business. For example, consider China. More than a quarter of a century ago, to curb its rapidly growing population, the Chinese government passed regulations limiting families to one child each. As a result, Chinese children – known as 'little emperors and empresses' – are being showered with attention and luxuries under what's known as the 'six-pocket

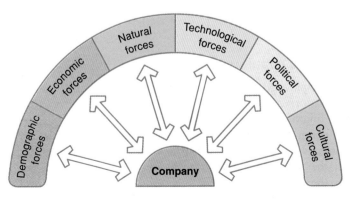

FIGURE 3.2

Major forces
in the company's
macroenvironment

syndrome'. As many as six adults – two parents and four doting grandparents – may be indulging the whims of each 'only child'. Parents in the average Beijing household now spend about 40 per cent of their income on their cherished only child. Among other things, this trend has created huge market opportunities for children's educational products.

In China's increasingly competitive society, parents these days are desperate to give Junior an early edge. That's creating opportunities for companies peddling educational offerings aimed at kids. Disney, for example, is moving full speed into educational products. Magic English, a €225 Disney package that includes workbooks, flash cards, and 26 videodisks, has been phenomenally successful. Disney has also launched interactive educational CD-ROMs featuring the likes of Winnie the Pooh and *101 Dalmations'* Cruella DeVille. Disney isn't alone in catering to the lucrative Chinese coddled-kiddies market. For example, Time Warner is testing the waters in Shanghai with an interactive language course called English Time. The 200-lesson, 40-CD set takes as long as four years for a child to complete. Time Warner is expecting strong sales, despite the €3,300 price tag.[3]

Source: Mark Leong/Redux/eyevine.

Demographics and business: Chinese regulations limiting families to one child have resulted in what is known as the 'six-pocket syndrome'. Chinese children are being showered with attention and luxuries, creating opportunities for marketers.

Interestingly, the one-child policy is creating another major Chinese demographic development – a rapidly ageing population. In what some deem a potential 'demographic earthquake', by 2004 58 per cent of the Chinese population was aged over 40. And because of the one-child policy, close to 75 per cent of all Chinese households will be childless, either because they chose to have no children or because their only child has left the nest. The result is an ageing society that will need to be more self-reliant, which in turn will cause a large growth in service markets such as education for older people, leisure clubs and nursing homes.[4]

Thus, marketers keep close track of demographic trends and developments in their markets, both at home and abroad. They track changing age and family structures, geographic population shifts, educational characteristics and population diversity. Here, we discuss the most important demographic trends in Europe.

Changing age structure of the population

The population of the 27 Member States of the EU stood at more than 493 million in 2007.[5] It is very difficult to forecast the EU population because of the very large inward and outward flows of migrants, and because the population of the EU depends on when, and whether, new countries such as Turkey are allowed to join. Net inward migration to the EU is expected to be the biggest factor leading to population growth, since the natural growth of the population (where births exceed deaths) is expected to decline as families across the EU choose to have fewer children. Birth rates in the richest countries of the EU, such as the UK, France and Italy, are already well below the 'replacement level' (where births and deaths are just in balance). The single most important demographic trend in the EU is the changing age structure of the population. Internationally, in Europe, North America and several other parts of the world (such as Australia and New Zealand) there are three generational groups that are considered particularly important by marketers – the baby boomers, Generation X and Generation Y.

The baby boomers This is the generation born between 1946 and 1964, a period when birth rates in countries affected by the Second World War rose sharply (hence the 'baby boom'). Since then, the **baby boomers** have become one of the most powerful forces shaping the marketing environment. The baby boomers have now grown to maturity, many of them are property owners, and they account for around a quarter of the population.

Marketers have typically paid the most attention to the smaller upper crust of the boomer generation – the more educated, mobile and wealthy segments. These segments have gone by many names. In the 1980s, they were called 'yuppies' (young urban professionals), and 'DINKs' (dual-income, no-kids couples). In the 1990s, yuppies and DINKs gave way to a new breed, with names such as 'DEWKs' (dual-earners with kids) and 'MOBYs' (mother older, baby younger). Now, to the chagrin of many in this generation, they are acquiring such titles as 'WOOFs' (well-off older folks) or even 'GRUMPIES' (just what the name suggests).

As a group, the baby boomers are the most affluent Europeans. However, although the more affluent boomers have grabbed most of the headlines, baby boomers cut across all walks of life, creating a diverse set of target segments for businesses. There are wealthy boomers but also boomers with more modest means.

The youngest boomers are now in their early forties; the oldest are entering their sixties. Thus, the boomers have evolved from the 'youthquake generation' to the 'backache generation'. The maturing boomers are rethinking the purpose and value of their work, responsibilities and relationships. They are approaching life with a new stability and reasonableness in the way they live, think, eat and spend. As they reach their peak earning and spending years, the boomers constitute a lucrative market for new housing and home remodelling, financial services, travel and entertainment, eating out, health and fitness products, and high-priced cars and other luxuries.

It would be a mistake to think of the boomers as ageing, staid retirees. In fact, the boomers are spending large amounts each year on *anti*-ageing products and services. And unlike previous generations, boomers are likely to postpone retirement. Many boomers are rediscovering the excitement of life and have the money to enjoy themselves.

Generation X The baby boom was followed by a 'birth dearth', creating another generation of people born between 1965 and 1976. The term '**Generation X**' was made famous in the book of that name by Douglas Coupland, published in 1991, although the term had been in use for several years before Coupland wrote his book.[6] They are named 'Generation X' because they lie in the shadow of the boomers and lack obvious distinguishing characteristics. Others call them the 'baby busters,' the 'yiffies' (young, individualistic, freedom-minded few), or the 'generation caught in the middle' (between the larger baby boomers and later Generation Ys).

The Generation Xers are defined as much by their shared experiences as by their age. Increasing divorce rates and higher employment for their mothers made them the first generation of latchkey kids (left to look after themselves after school). They grew up during the 1970s and 1980s, which were particularly troubled times in the world economy, with rampant inflation and high unemployment. Having grown up in times of recession when companies ceased to offer 'lifetime employment' and started to reduce their workforces ('downsizing'), they developed a more cautious economic outlook. They care about the environment and respond favourably to socially responsible companies. Although they seek success, they are less materialistic; they prize experience, not acquisition. They are cautious romantics who want a better quality of life and are more interested in job satisfaction than in sacrificing personal happiness and growth for promotion. Often, family comes first, career second.

As a result, the Gen Xers are a more sceptical bunch. 'Marketing to Gen Xers is difficult,' says one marketer, 'and it's all about word of mouth. You can't tell them you're good, and they have zero interest in a slick brochure that says so. You have to rely on somebody they know and trust to give you instant credibility. They have a lot of "filters" in place.'[7]

Once labelled as 'the MTV generation' and viewed as body-piercing slackers who whined about 'McJobs', the GenXers have now grown up and are beginning to take over. The GenXers are displacing the lifestyles, culture and materialistic values of the baby boomers. Very soon they will overtake the baby boomers as a primary market for almost every product category.[8] With so much potential, many companies are focusing on Gen Xers as an important target segment.

Generation Y Both the baby boomers and Gen Xers will one day be passing the reins to **Generation Y** (also called echo boomers). This is the generation born between 1977 and 1994, when the number of births increased as the baby boomers entered their child-bearing years. The echo boom has created a large teen and young adult market.

Older members of Generation Y have now graduated from university and are moving up in their careers. Like the trailing edge of the Generation Xers ahead of them, one distinguishing characteristic of Generation Y is their utter fluency and comfort with computer, digital and Internet technology. In the richer countries of the EU nine out of ten teens have a home computer, 73 per cent of teens surf the Internet every day, and over 80 per cent of 15–19-year-olds own a mobile phone. In all, they are an impatient, now-oriented bunch. 'Blame it on the relentless and dizzying pace of the Internet, 24-hour cable news cycles, cell phones, and TiVo for creating the on-demand, gotta-get-it-now universe in which we live,' says one observer. 'Perhaps nowhere is the trend more pronounced than among the Gen Y set.'[9]

Generation Y represents an attractive target for marketers. However, reaching this message-saturated segment effectively requires creative marketing approaches. For example, the popularity of action sports with Gen Yers has provided creative marketing opportunities for products ranging from clothes to video games, films and even beverages. Red Bull's edgy and irreverent positioning makes it a natural for the action-sport crowd. Red Bull has become a true action-sports supporter. It sponsors the Red Bull Air Race World Series and the Red Bull X-Alps adventure racing event, is endorsed by athletes from a wide range of sports including cricket, football and athletics, and sponsors top adventure sports stars such as the amazing Austrian base jumping star Felix Baumgartner (if you were unaware of Felix's exploits, you should really check them out at **www.felixbaumgartner.com**).

The motor industry is aggressively targeting this future generation of car buyers. For example, BMW offers a motor sports training programme for young drivers, some of whom are too young to have a licence. As a part of its 'Ultimate Driving Experience' tour, BMW offers go-kart drivers between the ages of 15 and 23 an array of scholarships, training and race experience to help develop their racing careers. 'We are courting teenagers,' says a BMW marketing executive. 'BMW is the premier brand for youth, so we have a reason to work harder with the next generation.'[10]

New brands and new services have emerged to deliver what the Generation Y market wants, while simultaneously providing marketers with a more effective means to communicate with them. Setanta, a provider of premium TV sports channels, is an excellent example (see Marketing at Work 3.1).

MARKETING AT WORK 3.1

Setanta: Pub channel to global sports broadcaster

Sean Ennis, *Department of Marketing, University of Strathclyde, Scotland*

Setanta Television has undergone a major transformation since its inception in 1990. Two Irishmen, living in London at the time, were very frustrated when they could not access a World Cup football game involving their home country against Holland. Given the large Irish diaspora based in London, they approached FIFA and persuaded them to sell them the rights to a feed of the game. They hired out their local pub and charged people £5 to watch it.

Over the next couple of years they expanded this initiative and acquired the rights from the Gaelic Athletic Association (GAA) to transmit broadcasts of the Irish championship games to the Irish diaspora in the United Kingdom, North America and Australia.

Fast forward to the present decade and Setanta entered into a deal with the Scottish Premier League to show a number of games. In early 2007, they had over 250,000 customers.

Perhaps of more significance was the appointment in April 2007, of a UK director of brand marketing to develop further business and take Setanta from its overdependence on the Irish diaspora and move it to a position where it could be recognised as a major holder of global sports TV rights in the UK. In the preceding months, prior to the appointment of the UK director, Setanta acquired the rights to broadcast rugby (Magners League), golf (American PGA tournaments) and various European football games from various leagues.

Perhaps its most significant move was successfully to launch a bid, in partnership with ITV, for TV rights to show the England football team's home fixtures and some FA Cup games. Setanta now reaches into over 100 million homes worldwide and operates more sports channels than any other independent broadcaster in Ireland and the UK.

The European Union, worried by the increasing dominance of Sky television, allowed a number of competitors such as Virgin Media, BT and Freeview, as well as Setanta, to bid for various packages from the English Premier League. In this case, Setanta bid £392 million for 46 live matches.

The UK director of brand marketing, Timothy Ryan, set a target of 1 million subscribers by the end of 2007, growing to 1.9 million by year end 2009. The major marketing initiative was to offer a subscription to its package of nine digital channels (including RacingUK) for £10 per month. They backed this campaign by allocating a budget of £5 million and employing the services of Desmond Lynam (a well-known TV personality) and a host of present and former sportspeople to encourage people to take out a subscription.

One of its key selling points is that it is 'platform neutral'. Although the costs to the viewer can vary, depending on which platform, it is available on Sky, Freeview, Virgin Media and BT Vision.

Sky remains the dominant platform for broadcasting sport by a very large measure. Currently over 6 million of its 8 million subscribers take out the sports package.

In summary, while Sky continues to dominate the sports broadcasting rights, Setanta has made inroads into the market. In part, this has been driven by the legislative environment, where the EU has demanded that one group should not hold exclusive rights to football in England.

The changing face of UK football

The biggest winner arising from the emergence of pay-per-view, dedicated sports channels is the Premier League in England: a body that represents the 20 clubs in arguably the richest football league in the world. In fact, the actions of the EU, ostensibly to create competition, have only succeeded in driving up the value of the broadcasting rights to very high levels. This allows clubs to pay very high – some would say too high – wages to footballers. It can be argued that this provides a very entertaining league where fans are exposed to the best players in the world on a regular basis. Many clubs, such as Arsenal, Manchester United and Manchester City, on the back of the inflow of revenue, have built new stadia or significantly improved existing ones. All-seater stadia are now the order of the day.

In tandem with these developments, most clubs have invested significantly in broadening the fan base and increasing commercial opportunities through branding, merchandising and international expansion (through developing linkages with clubs in key markets such as China and Japan). This has led to more revenue streams flowing into the clubs. By building the brand value, clubs are also able to attract more lucrative sponsorship deals across a number of different platforms: for example, shirt advertising, perimeter advertising, naming rights for stadia, stands and so on.

On the face of it, everything points to a very positive situation in English football. However, so far we have ignored one key interest group in our discussions: the fan.

Fans, by contrast, have had to face up to inexorable price increases in season tickets and admission to individual matches. Few clubs in the Premier League have ever seen fit to reduce their prices, apart from a couple of struggling clubs who perennially finish in the middle of the table. The arrival of very successful businesspeople to the domain of club ownership, has meant that, increasingly, hard-nosed business principles are employed to judge the effectiveness and efficiency of the clubs. While success is measured by the number of trophies won, it is also judged by the level of profitability and return on investment that accrues at the end of the financial year. While the attitude of Roman Abramovich, a Russian industrialist who owns Chelsea, may be viewed as fairly philanthropic, the American businessmen who own Manchester United seek a serious return on their investment and are unlikely to be swayed by misty-eyed sentimentality.

It is no longer possible to watch premier football on 'free-to-air' television due to the increasing dominance of BSkyB and more recently, Setanta. Despite the arguments about creating a more competitive market, the actions of the EU have meant that the individual viewer now has to take out an extra subscription to gain access to the televised games.

As well as having to pay to watch football on the television, fans are also facing increasing costs in terms of food and beverage at games.

While football games traditionally took place on Saturday afternoons at 3 pm, increasingly games are played on Sunday morning, Friday and Monday evenings and at other potentially inconvenient times for the fans. The sight of bleary-eyed supporters making their way from the north-east of England to London for a 12.30 kick-off has become a regular occurrence. As the TV companies are effectively bankrolling the industry, it can be argued that they are entitled to fix the schedules in order to maximise their audiences.

Since the inception of the Premier League in 1992, attendances have risen, challenging the fears of the football administrators who felt that blanket coverage of live football would only encourage spectators to stay at home or go to the pub to watch the games. But in the last couple of years, attendances at some of the struggling Premier League clubs have shown signs of decline. Some fans and football journalists have expressed the view that the product has become predictable and 'tired'. Despite these worrying observations, revenues continue to increase and the likes of Setanta seek to spread their involvement in this league.

The future?

Over the next five years or so, it is anticipated that football fans will make increasing use of mobile technology to access games, watch clips of goal action and make greater use of PCs to view games. The powerful clubs in the UK and Europe are also looking with increasingly envious eyes at the potential revenue that can be generated from running their own subscription-based TV channel. It does not take a genius to work out the potential revenue that could be generated for Manchester United from running such a service across the globe, targeting growth markets such as China, the Gulf region and North America. If 250,000 people worldwide were prepared to pay the equivalent of £10 to view an individual league game or pay £250 for a TV season ticket to view all games in the regular season, it suddenly becomes a significant source of revenue.

In a further attempt to capitalise on the global interest in the Premier League, football administrators recently put forward a proposal to have each of the member clubs play one regular league game in a foreign city. While this initiative received a lot of negative comments from UEFA and other European football clubs, it has not entirely disappeared off the radar. Indeed it is likely that it will emerge again over the next couple of years, albeit in a reduced format.

In summary, football in the UK has never been as strong financially as it is today. Money appears to flow into the coffers of the premier clubs, sparking off a virtuous (or vicious) circle of escalating salaries for players. The concept of the fan is also changing. The traditional fan who attends each game and buys a season ticket is joined by virtual fans from all over the world who watch the game in downtown Hong Kong, access the game via their laptop through a pirate TV channel or get the highlights of the game sent to their mobile phone. The product is showing signs of tiredness and may possibly need rejuvenation, either in the format of the league or the introduction of clubs such as Celtic and Rangers from the neighbouring Scottish league. This is possibly a longer-term prospect. The concept of a more structured European league also continues to fester in the background.

There is no doubt that the emergence of BSkyB in the 1990s and the subsequent evolution of Setanta, has had a profound impact on the structure, shape and direction of the football industry in the United Kingdom. It remains to be seen what direction this sector will take in the next decade.

Sources: 'Analysis: Setanta puts itself on the satellite map', *Marketing Week*, 30 November 2006, p. 14; Jeremy Lee, 'Setanta pushes into Sky territory', *Marketing Week*, 11 April 2007, p. 19; Raymond Snoddy, 'Fans are losers in Premiership TV fight', *Marketing*, 10 May 2006, p. 18; 'Sports Broadcasting – SETANTA: Football pitch hots up', *Marketing Week*, 2 August 2007, p. 22.

Generational marketing Do marketers have to create separate products and marketing programmes for each generation? Some experts warn that marketers have to be careful about turning off one generation each time they craft a product or message that appeals effectively to another. Others caution that each generation spans decades of time and many socio-economic levels. For example, marketers often split the baby boomers into three smaller groups – leading boomers, core boomers and trailing boomers – each with its own beliefs and behaviours. Similarly, they split Generation Y into Gen Y adults and Gen Y teens. Thus, marketers need to form more precise age-specific segments within each group. More importantly, defining people by their birth date may be less effective than segmenting them by their lifestyle or life stage.

The changing family

The 'traditional household' consists of a husband, wife and children (and sometimes grandparents). But this stereotypical notion of a household is becoming less and less representative of the way modern society really is.

In Europe today, married couples with children now make up only about 34 per cent of households, and this percentage is falling. The average size of a household is about 2.5 people, but this varies considerably across Europe, standing, for example, at 3.1 in Ireland and 2.2 in Germany. More people are divorcing or separating, choosing not to marry, marrying later, or marrying without intending to have children. Marketers must increasingly consider the special needs of non-traditional households, because they are now growing more rapidly than traditional households. Each group has distinctive needs and buying habits. The type of household that is forecast to grow fastest across Europe for the next two decades is the single-person household. This trend will be seen all across Europe, but the proportion of people living in single-person households now and in the future varies considerably from nation to nation. For example, the proportion of the population living in single-person households in the Mediterranean countries and in Ireland is typically around 5–10 per cent, while in northern European countries like Denmark, Sweden, Finland and Germany it is typically 15–20 per cent.[11]

Women are making up an increasing proportion of the working population. In 2006 in the EU 72 per cent of men aged 15–64 were in paid employment, compared to 57 per cent of women of the same age group. Again, this figure varies considerably across Europe: for example, 73 per cent of women in Denmark were in paid employment, and only 46 per cent of women in Italy.[12] The significant number of women in the workforce has spawned the child day-care business and increased consumption of career-oriented women's clothing, financial services, and convenience foods and services.

Geographic shifts in population

This is a period of great migratory movements between and within countries. Net migration is the difference between immigration (the number of people entering a country) and emigration (the number of people leaving). In recent years the number of immigrants from the rest of the world into Europe has considerably exceeded the number of emigrants; it is estimated that net inward migration into the EU was between 1.5 million and 2 million people each year from 2002 to 2005. Within the EU countries there has been a net migration of people westwards; that is to say that Western European countries, particularly the United Kingdom and Germany, have seen large inflows of population from countries in Eastern Europe. Such population shifts interest marketers because people in different geographical regions buy differently. Tobacco consumption provides a good way of understanding this; in Finland 23 per cent of adults smoke (27 per cent of men, 20 per cent of women), in France, 27 per cent of adults smoke (33 per cent of men, 21 per cent of women), in Denmark 30 per cent of adults smoke (32 per cent of men, 29 per cent of women), while in Hungary 42 per cent of adults smoke (53 per cent of men, 30 per cent of women).[13] As workers from Eastern European countries such as

Hungary move west to find jobs, marketers have to ask themselves whether their consumption behaviour will resemble more the country where they were born, or the country where they choose to work.

The shift in where people live has also caused a shift in where they work. For example, the migration toward metropolitan and suburban areas has resulted in a rapid increase in the number of people who 'telecommute' – work at home or in a remote office and conduct their business by phone, fax, modem, or the Internet. This trend, in turn, has created a booming SOHO (small office/home office) market.

A better-educated, more white-collar, more professional population

The European population is becoming better educated, and European workers are increasingly employed in professional or 'white collar' (managerial or equivalent) jobs. This generalisation is valid more or less everywhere across the Continent. For example, in Spain the proportion of people achieving a tertiary educational qualification (that is, a qualification beyond secondary school level) increased from 37 per cent in 1991 to 67 per cent in 2006, and in Ukraine that proportion increased from 47 per cent to 73 per cent. The number of students enrolled in tertiary education in the EU has increased steadily over the last decade and is expected to continue to grow; for example, the growth in the number of students in tertiary education between 1994 and 2004 was 25 per cent in Spain, 35 per cent in the United Kingdom, 59 per cent in Ireland and 83 per cent in Sweden. Governments across Europe recognise that economic success is increasingly dependent on having a well-educated population, and are investing in education. Typically, public spending on education in European countries runs at about 5 per cent of gross domestic product (GDP, a measure of the total national income).[14] The rising number of educated people will increase the demand for good quality products, books, magazines, travel, personal computers and Internet services. Over the next decade job growth is likely to be strongest for professional workers and weakest for jobs in manufacturing.

Increasing diversity

Countries vary in their ethnic and racial make-up. For example, in Japan almost everyone is Japanese. The situation is very different in the United Kingdom, with people from virtually all nations. Roughly 20 per cent of the births in the UK are to mothers born outside the country. Taking England alone, in 2005 it was estimated that 84.7 per cent of the population was White British, and another 4.4 per cent was White but not British (including Irish people and immigrants from Eastern Europe). The largest ethnic minority group in England was Asian (very largely of Indian, Pakistani or Bangladeshi origin), who made up 5.3 per cent of the population, followed by the Black population at 2.7 per cent (fairly equally divided between people of African and of Caribbean origin).[15] Focusing in even more tightly on London alone, it is estimated that a third of Londoners were born outside the UK, but Londoners born outside the UK made up a higher proportion, around 38 per cent, of London's labour force; they are more likely to be parents than Londoners born in the UK.

Marketers in the public and private sectors often have to factor in the ethnic composition of their markets when devising marketing strategies. Lloyds TSB bank has launched an Islamic bank account (which conforms to Islamic, Shariah law) aimed at a predominantly Asian target market that practises Islam. The Mayor of London's office makes publicity and information material available in Arabic, Bengali, Chinese, Greek, Gujurati, Hindi, Punjabi, Turkish, Urdu and Vietnamese as well as English. In a multiracial city, like London, opportunities for marketers to turn a profit by serving the specific needs of particular ethnic groups abound – just ask **www.afrotherapy.com** of London (suppliers of hair care and beauty products for those with black skin), **www.ranifashions.com** of Luton near London (suppliers of traditional Indian clothing) or the food store Polish Specialities of Hammersmith in west London.

Diversity goes beyond ethnic heritage. For example, many major companies have recently begun explicitly to target gay and lesbian consumers. Evidence from countries in which a gay lifestyle is widely accepted, such as the UK, the USA and Germany, suggests that gay men and lesbians represent a tremendous marketing opportunity – being, on average, better educated, more likely to be in a professional job, and better paid. In addition, gay men and lesbians tend to be early adopters of trends that eventually are adopted by the mainstream. For example, according to one expert, 'in the weeks following an episode of the Bravo hit show *Queer Eye for the Straight Guy* – in which five gay men, known as the Fab 5,

Multicultural marketing: an increasing number of businesses in Europe target the large, and often affluent, ethnic minority markets.

Source: http://www.ranifashions.com/

make over a low-maintenance straight man – many businesses whose products are featured have seen a significant sales boost'. Lucky Brand jeans saw a 17 per cent sales jump for the two months following a mention on *Queer Eye*.[16]

Companies in several industries are now waking up to the needs and potential of the gay and lesbian segment. For example, Gay.com, a website that attracts more than 2 million unique visitors each month from more than 100 countries, has also attracted a diverse set of well-known advertisers, such as American Express, Halo pet care products, Delta Airlines and a number of different holiday destinations. In fact, holiday companies and holiday destinations have recently demonstrated a particularly strong interest in the large amounts of money that are being spent in what is called the 'gay tourism' or 'pink tourism' market.[17] A wide range of cities around the world are vying to attract gay and lesbian tourists. Many of them provide detailed information through their websites, and other media, to prospective gay and lesbian tourists. For example, the city of Manchester in northern England claims that: 'Manchester's gay scene is famously one of Britain's friendliest, busiest and most welcoming. There's a huge range of stylish bars and clubs in the Gay Village and while here you'll find shopping heaven, an arts scene to match anywhere in Europe, and more trendy restaurants than you can shake a credit card at.'[18] The city of Melbourne, Australia says: 'Life's a party, or at least it should be, and Melbourne's gay and lesbian community certainly know how to enjoy it',[19] and gay and lesbian tourists eager to visit Germany can find out everything they need to know at the 'Gayfriendly Germany' section of the official German tourism website.[20]

MAKING CONNECTIONS Linking the concepts

Pull over here for a moment and think about how deeply these demographic factors affect all of us and, as a result, marketers' strategies.

- Apply these demographic developments to your own life. Think of some specific examples of how the changing demographic factors affect you and your buying behaviour.
- Identify a specific company that has done a good job of reacting to the shifting demographic environment – generational segments (baby boomers, Generation X or Generation Y), the changing family and increased diversity. Compare this company to one that's done a poor job.

Economic environment

Markets require buying power as well as people. The **economic environment** consists of factors that affect consumer purchasing power and spending patterns. Nations vary greatly in their levels and distribution of income. Some countries have *subsistence economies* – they consume most of their own agricultural and industrial output. These countries offer few market opportunities. At the other extreme are *industrial economies*, which constitute rich markets for many different kinds of goods. Marketers must pay close attention to major trends and consumer spending patterns both across and within their world markets. The following are some of the major economic trends in Europe.

Changes in income

The general trend in incomes throughout the EU over the last two decades has been upwards. This can be seen in the first four columns of Table 3.1, which show GDP per capita (a measure of how much income per head is created in the economy), for five selected EU Member States, together with an EU average. The five nations shown in Table 3.1 have been chosen to show the range of income per head to be found across the EU; Germany and the United Kingdom represent the richest group of nations, Spain represents the 'middle income' group of nations, and Lithuania and Poland represent the poorer nations of the EU, with income per head at about 50 per cent of the EU average. However, a closer inspection will show that the growth rate of income per head has been far higher in the poorer nations than in the richer nations, indicating a narrowing of the income gap between Europe's richest countries and its poorest countries. During the period from 1996 to 2005, when average EU GDP per capita rose by 43.5 per cent, GDP per capita in Lithuania rose by 114 per cent. When looking at figures like these it is important to remember that the largest economies in the EU are far larger than the smaller economies. Germany alone represents over a fifth of EU GDP, and the four largest economies combined – Germany, the UK, France and Italy – represent two-thirds of EU GDP. At the other end of the scale, there are ten EU member countries that each represent less than 1 per cent of total EU GDP – the Czech Republic, Cyprus, Latvia, Lithuania, Luxembourg, Hungary, Malta, Slovenia and Slovakia.

The growth of consumer spending in the EU was adversely affected in 2008–2009 by the so-called credit crunch. Although this problem largely originated in the USA, where banks had lent large sums of money to people who, it turned out, did not have

TABLE 3.1 Key economic indicators for the EU and five individual EU Member States

	1996	2005	Percentage of EU average 2005	2006		1996	2001	2006
	GDP per capita (in euros)			Inequality of income distribution (income quintile share ratio)	Percentage of consumer spending on food and non-alcoholic beverages			
EU	16,300	23,400	100	4.8	EU	14.3	13.1	12.7
Germany	19,200	25,700	109.8	4.1	Germany	12.1	11.6	11.0
United Kingdom	17,800	27,300	116.8	5.4	United Kingdom	11.2	9.6	9.1
Spain	14,200	23,100	98.7	5.3	Spain	16.9	14.5	13.8
Lithuania	5,700	12,200	52.1	6.3	Lithuania	38.8	29.2	25.8
Poland	6,900	11,700	49.9	5.6	Poland	26.4	22.9	20.9

the means to repay it, it was also felt throughout the EU, particularly in countries such as the UK where consumers had borrowed heavily to buy houses, cars and durable consumer goods. As a consequence the supply of funds banks had to lend to consumers diminished sharply, and a lot of consumers found themselves worse off when their short-term discounted mortgage deals came to an end and they had to refinance at a higher interest rate. These financially squeezed consumers have adjusted to their changing financial situations and are spending more carefully. *Value marketing* has become the watchword for many marketers. Rather than offering high quality at a high price, or lesser quality at very low prices, marketers are looking for ways to offer today's more financially cautious buyers greater value – just the right combination of product quality and good service at a fair price.

Marketers should pay attention to *income distribution* as well as average income. Income distribution in Europe is very skewed. At the top are *upper-class* consumers, whose spending patterns are not affected by current economic events and who are a major market for luxury goods. There is a comfortable *middle class* that is fairly careful about its spending but can still afford the good life some of the time. The *working class* must stick close to the basics of food, clothing and shelter and must try hard to save. Finally, the *underclass* (persons on welfare and many pensioners) must count their pennies when making even the most basic purchases.

While the first four columns of Table 3.1 demonstrate the inequality of incomes between European nations, the fifth column shows the 'inequality of income distribution' within selected countries. We already know that, on average, income per head in Lithuania is about a half of income per head in Germany; now we can see that the income distribution *within* Lithuania is much more unequal than the income distribution within Germany. People in the top fifth of income earners in Lithuania earn on average 6.3 times as much as those in the bottom fifth, while in Germany the ratio is only 4.1. This distribution of income creates a tiered market. Many companies – such as Rolex and Dior – aggressively target the affluent. Others – such as Aldi and Lidl – target those with more modest means. Still other companies tailor their marketing offers across a range of markets, from the affluent to the less affluent.

Changing consumer spending patterns

Table 3.1 also shows the proportion of total expenditures made by European households on food and non-alcoholic beverages – essential purchases that no one can do without. This shows that consumers at different income levels have different spending patterns. Some of these differences were noted over a century ago by Ernst Engel, who studied how people shifted their spending as their income rose. He found that as family income rises, the percentage spent on food declines, the percentage spent on housing remains about constant (except for such utilities as gas, electricity and public services, which decrease), and both the percentage spent on most other categories and that devoted to savings increase. **Engel's laws** generally have been supported by later studies. The information in the final columns of Table 3.1 shows that the proportion of European consumer expenditure going on essentials has declined as average incomes across Europe have risen; it also shows that the proportion of income spent on essentials is much higher in the poorer countries of Europe than in richer countries such as the UK and Germany. However, since incomes are rising fast in poorer countries, such as Lithuania and Poland, the proportion of income spent on essentials is declining much faster here than elsewhere in Europe.

Changes in major economic variables such as income, cost of living, interest rates, and savings and borrowing patterns have a large impact on the marketplace. Companies watch these variables by using economic forecasting. Businesses do not have to be wiped out by an economic downturn or caught short in a boom. With adequate warning, they can take advantage of changes in the economic environment.

Natural environment

The **natural environment** involves the natural resources that are needed as inputs by marketers or that are affected by marketing activities. Environmental concerns have grown steadily during the past three decades. In many cities around the world, air and water pollution have reached dangerous levels. World concern continues to mount about the possibilities of global warming, and many environmentalists fear that soon we will be buried in our own rubbish.

Marketers should be aware of several trends in the natural environment. The first involves growing *shortages of raw materials*. Once upon a time air and water may have seemed to be infinite resources, but few people believe this today. Air pollution chokes many of the world's large cities, and water shortages are already a big problem in some parts of the world. Renewable resources, such as forests and food, also have to be used wisely. Non-renewable resources, such as oil, coal and various minerals, are likely to become more difficult to find and increasingly expensive. Firms making products that require these scarce resources face large cost increases, even if the materials do remain available.

A second environmental trend is *increased pollution*. Industry will almost always damage the quality of the natural environment. Consider the disposal of chemical and nuclear wastes, the dangerous mercury levels in the oceans, the quantity of chemical pollutants in the soil and food supply, and the littering of the environment with non-biodegradable bottles, plastics and other packaging materials.

A third trend is *increased government intervention* in natural resource management. The governments of different countries vary in their concern and efforts to promote a clean environment. Some, like the German government, vigorously pursue environmental quality. Others, especially many poorer nations, do little about pollution, largely because they lack the needed funds or political will. Even the richer nations lack the vast funds and political accord needed to mount a worldwide environmental effort. The general hope is that companies around the world will accept more social responsibility, and that less expensive devices can be found to control and reduce pollution.

Concern for the natural environment has spawned the so-called green movement. Today, enlightened companies go beyond what government regulations dictate. They are developing *environmentally sustainable* strategies and practices in an effort to create a world economy that the planet can support indefinitely. They are responding to consumer demands with products that do less damage to the environment. For example, the Volkswagen 'Blue Motion' range of cars delivers far better fuel economy and causes less damage to the environment for each kilometre travelled than previous generations of vehicles. We will return to the theme of sustainability in Chapter 16.

Other companies are developing recyclable or biodegradable packaging, recycled materials and components, better pollution controls, and more energy-efficient operations. Public transport operator Stagecoach has announced plans to run the first carbon-neutral bus network in the UK, by offsetting the emissions from its fleet of buses with a huge tree-planting scheme. McDonald's has a long-standing rainforest policy and a commitment to purchasing recycled products and to energy-efficient restaurant construction techniques. Panasonic Europe is investing in technology to reduce the environmental impact of its factories, by using filtration systems for

Source: Volkswagon Group.

Responding to consumer demands for more environmentally responsible products, Volkswagen has created the Blue Motion range of cars.

waste water that go far beyond regulatory requirements, by exercising strict control over exhaust emissions, and by keeping energy consumption to a minimum.

These companies are looking to do more than just good deeds. More and more, companies are recognising the link between a healthy ecology and a healthy economy. They are learning that environmentally responsible actions can also be good business (see Marketing at Work 3.2).[21]

Technological environment

The **technological environment** is perhaps the most dramatic force now shaping our destiny. Technology has released such wonders as antibiotics, organ transplants, mobile phones, laptop computers and the Internet. It also has released such horrors as nuclear missiles, chemical weapons and assault rifles. It has created such mixed blessings as the car, television and credit cards.

Our attitude toward technology depends on whether we are more impressed with its wonders or its blunders. For example, what would you think about having a tiny little transmitter implanted in all of the products you buy that would allow tracking products from their point of production through use and disposal? On the one hand, it would provide many advantages to both buyers and sellers. On the other hand, it could be a bit scary. Either way, it's already happening:

> Envision a world in which every product contains a tiny transmitter, loaded with information. As you stroll through the supermarket aisles, shelf sensors detect your selections and beam ads to your shopping cart screen, offering special deals on related products. As your cart fills, scanners detect that you might be buying for a dinner party; the screen suggests a wine to go with the meal you've planned. When you leave the store, exit scanners total up your purchases and automatically charge them to your credit card. At home, readers track what goes into and out of your pantry, updating your shopping list when stocks run low. For Sunday dinner, you pop a Butterball turkey into your 'smart oven', which follows instructions from an embedded chip and cooks the bird to perfection.
>
> Seem far-fetched? Not really. In fact, it might soon become a reality, thanks to tiny radio-frequency identification (RFID) transmitters – or 'smart chips' – that can be embedded in the products you buy. Beyond benefits to consumers, the RFID chips also give producers and retailers an amazing new way to track their products electronically – anywhere in the world, any time, automatically – from factories, to warehouses, to retail shelves, to recycling centres.[22]

The technological environment changes rapidly. Think of all of today's common products that were not available 100 years ago, or even 30 years ago. Anyone who died 150 years ago did not know about cars, planes, radios or the electric light. Someone who died only 80 years ago did not know about television, aerosol cans, automatic dishwashers, air conditioners, antibiotics or computers. Anyone who died during the Second World War did not know about photocopying, synthetic detergents, tape recorders, birth control pills or communications satellites. Even people who died as recently as the 1960s did not know about personal computers, mobile phones, DVD players or the Internet.

New technologies create new markets and opportunities. However, every new technology replaces an older technology. Transistors damaged the vacuum tube (valve) industry, photocopying damaged the carbon-paper business, the car damaged the railway business, CDs damaged the record industry, and in turn music and video downloads are damaging the CD and DVD businesses. When old industries fought or ignored new technologies, their businesses declined. Thus, marketers should watch the technological environment closely. Companies that do not keep up will soon find their products outdated. And they will miss new product and market opportunities.

Gibson: Making money *and* leaving the world a better place

If a tree falls in the rainforest and no one is there to trumpet its eco-friendliness, does it still make a sound? It might – if that wood is destined for an electric guitar. Gibson Guitar, the iconic guitar maker, has worked since the late 1980s to make its wood supply environmentally sustainable. Gibson's electric-guitar division recently switched to 100 per cent fair-trade-certified wood. Other Gibson divisions, including Baldwin Piano, plan to follow suit.

Yet unlike Starbucks, The Body Shop, and other businesses that eagerly brandish their green deeds, Gibson CEO Henry Juszkiewicz doesn't much care to flaunt his environmental credentials (the guy drives a Hummer, after all). What matters to him is ensuring that Gibson has enough exotic wood, mostly mahogany, to keep making guitars for generations.

'We're mercenaries. We're a company. We're for-profit,' Juszkiewicz says in his Nashville office, packed with so many music-industry mementos it looks like his own private Hard Rock Café. 'I'm not a conservationist.' High-end guitar enthusiasts, after all, demand that their instruments be made of exotic woods. But prices for exotics can swing wildly, governed by an unsteady supply and the threat that some species may be placed on an extinction watch list.

Juszkiewicz wanted to eliminate the guesswork by building a network of growers rather than relying on brokers scouring world markets for the best prices. He approached the Rainforest Alliance, a non-profit conservation group, to discuss buying wood from Mexican suppliers certified as sustainable. (Such growers are graded against environmental, labour, and community standards – and for responsible harvesting.)

But that hardly made a dent in Gibson's sourcing problems. So the company hired away two Rainforest Alliance employees to source wood in Costa Rica and Brazil. 'Within the first year of hiring these guys, they were able to develop significant sources,' Juszkiewicz says. 'We went from less than 1 per cent usage of certified product to something like 80 per cent.' Since then, Gibson has forged a direct relationship with growers in Guatemala. That provides both stability of supply and quality, since Gibson is able to instruct farmers on its exacting specifications.

Initially, Juszkiewicz says, Gibson paid a premium for purchasing wood this way. Now buying direct creates modest savings – and the relationships help curb traditional slash-and-burn harvesting, which threatens supplies of precious woods. 'In the short run, a slight price increase won't necessarily hurt them because a guitar is a higher-value product,' says an industry expert. 'In the long run, it helps ensure that they can tap this supply not just in 5 years but in 50 years.'

Tensie Whelan, executive director of the Rainforest Alliance, says she's seeing a critical mass of CEOs discovering that environmentally friendly practices can be good business. But she still teases Juszkiewicz, one of the first: 'He'll say he's a businessman, that he's just out to make money. But believe me, he's passionate about wanting to leave the world a better place.'

Source: Adapted from Ryan Underwood, 'In Tune with the Environment', *Fast Company*, December 19, 2007.

Gibson Guitar works to make its exotic hardwood supply environmentally sustainable. The company has learned that environmentally friendly practices can also be good business. *Photo sources*: © PNC/zefa/Corbis (background); Gibson Les Paul image © Gibson Guitar Corp. Used with express written permission of Gibson Guitar Corp.

One of the keys to developing and exploiting new technologies is spending on research and development (R&D). Total EU R&D spending reached an estimated €210 billion in 2006, just over 1.8 per cent of GDP – the EU target is to raise R&D spending to 3 per cent of GDP by 2010. The EU countries with the highest R&D intensity are Sweden (3.82 per cent of GDP) and Finland (3.45 per cent of GDP), while those countries from Eastern Europe that have joined the EU more recently tend to have lower R&D intensity – 0.48 per cent of GDP in Bulgaria, 0.49 per cent in Slovakia. Scientists today are researching a wide range of promising new products and services, ranging from practical solar energy, electric cars and cancer cures to voice-controlled computers and genetically engineered food crops.

Technological environment: technology is perhaps the most dramatic force shaping the marketing environment. Here, a herder makes a call on his mobile phone.

Source: Getty Images/Joseph Van Os.

Today's research is carried out usually by research teams rather than by lone inventors such as Louis Pasteur, George Stephenson or Karl Benz. Many companies are adding marketing people to R&D teams to try to obtain a stronger marketing orientation. Scientists also speculate on fantasy products, such as flying cars, three-dimensional televisions and space colonies. The challenge in each case is not only technical but also commercial – to make *practical, affordable* versions of these products.

As products and technology become more complex, the public needs to know that these are safe. Thus, government agencies investigate and ban potentially unsafe products. In the European Union, the European Food Safety Authority (EFSA) works with the European Commission, the European Parliament and the authorities in individual countries to assess and eliminate food safety risks. The European Commissioner for Consumer Affairs is in charge of promoting consumer interests, health and safety throughout the EU. This involves working with national consumer protection organisations and recommending regulations to protect consumer interests. Such regulations can result in much higher research costs and in longer times between new-product ideas and their introduction. Marketers should be aware of these regulations when applying new technologies and developing new products.

Political environment

Marketing decisions are strongly affected by developments in the political environment. The **political environment** consists of laws, government agencies and pressure groups that influence or limit various organisations and individuals in a given society.

The European Union

How the European Union was created By 2007 the European Union had expanded to include 27 countries with a combined population of 493 million people. The largest member states in terms of population are Germany (82.4 million), France (62.9 million), the United Kingdom (60.4 million), Italy (58.8 million), Spain (43.8 million) and Poland (38.2 million). Altogether, the EU represents the third largest population block in the world after China and India. If the three countries under consideration as candidates for EU membership – Croatia, the Former Yugoslav Republic of Macedonia, and Turkey – were to join, then the combined population would be close to 600 million. How did such a large and economically powerful international union come about?

The origins of the European Union can be traced back at least as far as the 1950s. Initially there were six members of the European Coal and Steel Community (ECSC), which was established by Belgium, France, Germany, Italy, Luxembourg and the Netherlands in 1952. Politically, the principal motivation behind greater European cooperation could be found in the aftermath of the Second World War (1939–45), during which the major countries of Europe fought each other to a standstill and largely destroyed Europe's industrial capacity. In particular, the cooperation between those great European powers, and rivals, France and Germany was symbolic of the desire to avoid further major conflicts. (Remember that, at the time, this was 'West Germany', since Germany had been partitioned into East, the German Democratic Republic, and West, the Federal Republic of Germany, after the War. German reunification was not to occur until 1990.)

The most prominent forerunner of the European Union was the European Economic Community (EEC), established by the six members of the ECSC in 1957 by the Treaty of Rome. During the next 30 years the EEC expanded periodically; Denmark, Ireland and the UK joined in 1973, Greece in 1981, Spain and Portugal in 1986. Then, in 1987, the Single European Act was passed which was designed to make real progress towards the goal of having a 'single European market'. By the beginning of 1993 the economic reforms to implement the Single European Act had been completed, establishing the free movement of goods, services, people and money within the EEC. In principle, nationals of the EEC states could work wherever they wished within the Community, and businesses could buy and sell as easily across national borders within the EEC as they could within their own countries. Around the same time, in 1992, the Treaty of Maastricht was signed, which was to lead to the creation of the single European currency (the euro) and to closer cooperation between member states on foreign and domestic policy. It was with the Maastricht Treaty that the name 'European Economic Community' was dropped in favour of the new term 'European Union' (EU).

Further major expansion of the European Union followed, with three new member states joining in 1995, ten in 2004 and a further two joining in 2007 to make up 27 in all. Here are all 27, with the year in which they joined the EU, or its predecessors (the ECSC or the EEC):

1952: Belgium, France, Germany, Italy, Luxembourg, the Netherlands

1973: Denmark, Ireland, the United Kingdom

1981: Greece

1986: Spain, Portugal

1995: Austria, Finland, Sweden

2004: Czech Republic, Estonia, Latvia, Lithuania, Hungary, Poland, Slovenia, Slovakia, Cyprus, Malta

2007: Bulgaria, Romania

The objectives of the EU Initially, the main driving force behind European cooperation was the desire to avoid further major conflicts between the member states, and to promote peace more widely within Europe. However, the two principal factors promoting closer European cooperation for the last three or four decades have been politics and economics. Politically, there have always been some within Europe who wish to promote the concept of a 'United States of Europe', that is, ever-closer political union leading eventually to the creation of a European superstate. Economically, the main argument for closer European cooperation is that, through the creation of a huge single market for goods, services, labour and capital in Europe, all of the member states will reap substantial economic benefits. For example, by eliminating the barriers to the free movement of labour, skilled workers can travel across Europe to wherever they are most needed, and employers in search of skilled labour need not restrict themselves to the local economy but can search among all of the member states. Both the political and economic goals of the EU are reflected in the formal objectives, to be found in the key treaties that are the foundation of the Union.

The following are the formal, stated objectives of the EU:

> To promote economic progress and social progress and a high level of employment and to achieve balanced and sustainable development, in particular through the creation of an area without internal frontiers, through the strengthening of economic and social cohesion and through the establishment of economic and monetary union, ultimately including a single currency . . .
>
> To assert its identity on the international scene, in particular through the implementation of a common foreign and security policy including the progressive framing of a common defence policy, which might lead to a common defence . . .
>
> To strengthen the protection of the rights and interests of the nationals of Member States through the introduction of a citizenship of the Union,
>
> To maintain and develop the Union as an area of freedom, security and justice, in which the free movement of persons is assured in conjunction with appropriate measures with respect to external border controls, asylum, immigration and the prevention and combating of crime,
>
> To maintain in full the *acquis communautaire* and build on it with a view to considering to what extent the policies and forms of cooperation introduced by this Treaty may need to be revised with the aim of ensuring the effectiveness of the mechanisms and the institutions of the Community.[23]

The *acquis communautaire* refers to the accumulated body of European laws developed by the EU so far; this covers a wide range of subjects, including the free movement of people, goods, services and money within the EU, laws on free competition, intellectual property, public procurement and many other topics.

Legislation regulating business

Even the most liberal advocates of free-market economies agree that the system works best with at least some regulation. Well-conceived regulation can encourage competition and ensure fair markets for goods and services. Thus, governments develop *public policy* to guide commerce – sets of laws and regulations that limit business for the good of society as a whole. Almost every marketing activity is subject to a wide range of laws and regulations.

Increasing legislation Legislation affecting business around the world has increased steadily over the years. Europe has many laws covering issues such as competition, fair trade practices, environmental protection, product safety, truth in advertising, consumer privacy, packaging and labelling, pricing and other important areas. The European Commission has been active in establishing a new framework of laws covering competitive behaviour, product standards, product liability, and commercial transactions for the nations of the European Union.

Of course, marketers must become familiar with the relevant legislation in whichever markets they operate around the world. For example, Norway bans several forms of sales promotion – trading stamps, contests, premiums – as being inappropriate or unfair ways of promoting products. Thailand requires food processors selling national brands to market low price brands also, so that low-income consumers can find economy brands on the shelves. In India, food companies must obtain special approval to launch brands that duplicate those already existing on the market, such as additional cola drinks or new brands of rice.

Understanding the public policy implications of a particular marketing activity is not a simple matter. For example, in Europe, there are laws created at the EU and at the national levels, and these regulations often overlap – one of the goals of the EU is progressively to harmonise national laws so that the same legal system applies throughout the Union, but it will be quite a while before that goal is achieved. For example, food products sold in Athens are governed both by relevant EU and Greek national laws. Moreover, regulations are constantly changing – what was allowed last year may now be prohibited, and what was prohibited may now be allowed. Marketers must work hard to keep up with changes in regulations and their interpretations.

Business legislation has been enacted for a number of reasons. The first is to *protect companies* from each other. Although business executives may praise competition, they sometimes try to neutralise it when it threatens them. So laws are passed to define and prevent unfair competition. In Europe, such laws are enforced by the Directorate General for Competition and by national competition authorities such as the Office of Fair Trading in the UK, the Competition Authority in Ireland, the Konkurrensverket in Sweden, and the Conseil de la Concurrence in France.

The second purpose of government regulation is to *protect consumers* from unfair business practices. Some firms, if left alone, would make shoddy products, tell lies in their advertising, and deceive consumers through their packaging and pricing. Unfair business practices have been defined and sanctions are enforced by various agencies.

The third purpose of government regulation is to *protect the interests of society* against unrestrained business behaviour. Profitable business activity does not always create a better quality of life. Regulation arises to ensure that firms take responsibility for the social costs of their production or products.

Changing government agency enforcement International marketers will encounter dozens, or even hundreds, of agencies set up to enforce trade policies and regulations. We have mentioned several of those that will be found in Europe in the preceding paragraphs, while in the USA, for example, businesses have to consider the Federal Trade Commission, the Food and Drug Administration and the Federal Communications Commission, among others. Because such government agencies have some discretion in enforcing the laws, they can have a major impact on a company's marketing performance. Few of these agencies employ marketing professionals, however, so that it can be difficult to get them to understand the impact that their actions can have on company marketing strategies.

New laws and their enforcement will continue to increase. Business executives must watch these developments when planning their products and marketing programmes. Marketers need to know about the major laws protecting competition, consumers and society. They need to understand these laws at the local, state, national and international levels.

Increased emphasis on ethics and socially responsible actions

Written regulations cannot possibly cover all potential marketing abuses, and existing laws are often difficult to enforce. However, beyond written laws and regulations, business is also governed by social codes and rules of professional ethics.

Socially responsible behaviour Enlightened companies encourage their managers to look beyond what the regulatory system allows and simply 'do the right thing'. These socially responsible firms actively seek out ways to protect the long-term interests of their consumers and the environment.

The recent rash of business scandals and increased concerns about the environment have created fresh interest in the issues of ethics and social responsibility. Almost every aspect of marketing involves such issues. Unfortunately, because these issues usually involve conflicting interests, well-meaning people can honestly disagree about the right course of action in a given situation. Thus, many industrial and professional trade associations have suggested codes of ethics. And more companies are now developing policies, guidelines and other responses to complex social responsibility issues.

The boom in e-commerce and Internet marketing has created a new set of social and ethical issues. Online privacy issues are the primary concern. For example, website visitors often provide extensive personal information that might leave them open to abuse by unscrupulous marketers. Moreover, both Intel and Microsoft have been accused of covert, high-tech computer chip and software invasions of customers' personal computers to obtain information for marketing purposes. Most companies are now careful to disclose fully their Internet privacy policies.[24]

Throughout the text, we present examples that summarise the main public policy and social responsibility issues surrounding major marketing decisions. These exhibits discuss the legal issues that marketers should understand and the common ethical and societal concerns that marketers face. In Chapter 16 we discuss a broad range of societal marketing issues in greater depth.

Cause-related marketing To exercise their social responsibility and build more positive images, many companies are now linking themselves to worthwhile causes. These days, every product seems to be tied to some cause. Buy women's underwear or swimwear from a Debenhams store and support breast cancer research. Shop at Tesco and collect free vouchers that your local school can use to buy computer equipment. Purchase Habitat Coffee and help Habitat for Humanity build a house for a needy family. Pay for these purchases with the right credit or debit card and you can support a local cultural arts group or help fight heart disease.

Cause-related marketing has become a primary form of corporate giving. It lets companies 'do well by doing good' by linking purchases of the company's products or services with fund-raising for worthwhile causes or charitable organisations. Companies now sponsor dozens of cause-related marketing campaigns each year. Many are backed by large budgets and a full complement of marketing activities. Consider this example:

> In May 2004, Nike began selling simple yellow synthetic silicon rubber bracelets – stamped with the phrase 'Live Strong' – at Niketown outlets around the country. The price was $1, and proceeds were given to the Lance Armstrong Foundation, the non-profit charitable organisation associated with the champion cyclist, who is also a Nike athlete and famous cancer survivor. 'Live Strong' is the foundation's motto; yellow echoes the colour of the lead rider's jersey in the Tour de France. Nike paid for the entire first run of five million bracelets, meaning that 100 per cent of the proceeds, plus another $1 million Nike threw in, went straight to the foundation.
>
> Sales really took off when the Tour de France got under way that summer. Armstrong wore the wristband and so did his whole team. As the tour wore on, competitors and even officials started wearing them. As Armstrong cruised to his record-setting sixth consecutive Tour de France victory, celebrities started wearing them, and suddenly the bracelets were everywhere – a charitable must-have. In less than a year, the foundation had sold more than 40 million 'Live Strong' bracelets for $1 each. On one day alone, the Foundation sold an amazing 900,000 bracelets when Armstrong appeared on 'The Oprah Winfrey Show' and Winfrey challenged her viewers to break the previous single-day record of 382,000.[25]

Cause-related marketing has stirred some controversy. Critics worry that cause-related marketing is more a strategy for selling than a strategy for giving – that 'cause-related' marketing is really 'cause-exploitative' marketing. Thus, companies using cause-related marketing might find themselves walking a fine line between increased sales and an improved image, and facing charges of exploitation.

However, if handled well, cause-related marketing can greatly benefit both the company and the cause. The company gains an effective marketing tool while building a more positive public image. The charitable organisation or cause gains greater visibility and important new sources of funding.

Cultural environment

The **cultural environment** is made up of institutions and other forces that affect a society's basic values, perceptions, preferences and behaviours. People grow up in a particular society that shapes their basic beliefs and values. They absorb a worldview that defines their relationships with others. The following cultural characteristics can affect marketing decision-making.

Persistence of cultural values

People in a given society hold many beliefs and values. Their core beliefs and values have a high degree of persistence. For example, most Europeans believe in working, getting married, giving to charity and being honest. These beliefs shape more specific attitudes and behaviours found in everyday life. *Core* beliefs and values are passed on from parents to children and are reinforced by schools, churches, business and government.

Secondary beliefs and values are more open to change. Believing in marriage is a core belief; believing that people should get married early in life is a secondary belief. Marketers have some chance of changing secondary values but little chance of changing core values. For example, family-planning marketers could argue more effectively that people should get married later than that they should not get married at all.

Shifts in secondary cultural values

Although core values are fairly persistent, cultural swings do take place. Consider the impact of popular music groups, film stars and other celebrities on young people's hairstyling and clothing norms. Marketers want to predict cultural shifts in order to spot new opportunities or threats. Several firms offer 'futures' forecasts in this connection, such as the Yankelovich Monitor, Market Facts' BrainWaves Group, and the Trends Research Institute.

The Yankelovich Monitor has tracked consumer value trends for years. At the dawn of the twenty-first century, it looked back to capture lessons from the past decade that might offer insight into the 2000s.[26] Yankelovich maintains that the 'decade drivers' for the 2000s will primarily come from the baby boomers and Generation X. The baby boomers will be driven by four factors: 'adventure' (fuelled by a sense of youthfulness), 'smarts' (fuelled by a sense of empowerment and willingness to accept change), 'intergenerational support' (caring for younger and older, often in non-traditional arrangements), and 'retreading' (embracing early retirement with second career or phase of their work life). Generation X will be driven by three factors: 'redefining the good life' (being highly motivated to improve their economic well-being and remain in control), 'new rituals' (returning to traditional values but with a tolerant mindset and active lifestyle), and 'cutting and pasting' (balancing work, play, sleep, family and other aspects of their lives).

The major cultural values of a society are expressed in people's views of themselves and others, as well as in their views of organisations, society, nature and the universe.

People's views of themselves People vary in their emphasis on serving themselves versus serving others. Some people seek personal pleasure, wanting fun, change and escape. Others seek self-realisation through religion, recreation, or the avid pursuit of careers or other life goals. People use products, brands and services as a means of self-expression, and they buy products and services that match their views of themselves.

Yankelovich Monitor recently discovered a conflicted consumer segment whose purchases are motivated by self-views of both duty and fun:

> Yankelovich's Monitor has identified a paradoxical consumer segment motivated equally by duty and fun. Comprising more than one-third of the population, these folks want to have their cake and rely on it, too. 'Duty and Fun' consumers agree that 'duty should always come before pleasure' *and* say that they 'try to have as much fun as they can now and let the future take care of itself'. Their split personalities indicate an internal struggle that affects everyday life and buying. To reach these conflicted consumers, marketers must give them something that makes them smile at the register, while offering sound payment options, guarantees, testimonials, and other forms of assurance. For example, PetSmart permits shoppers to bring their pets shopping, allowing duty and fun to happily coexist. And with its hybrid Prius, Toyota merges a respected company brand (duty) and leading-edge technology (fun), turning what could have been a fuddy-duddy failure into a ride for those sold on dutiful fun.[27]

People's views of others Recently, observers have noted a shift from a 'me society' to a 'we society' in which more people want to be with and serve others.

> After years of serious 'nesting' – staying close to the security and creature comforts of home and hearth – people are now venturing out of their homes to hang out in the real world. The nesting instinct has gone in and out of fashion before. When the first big wave hit in the early '80s, trend watchers coined the term 'cocooning' to describe the surge of boomers buying their first homes and filling them up with oversize furniture and fancy gadgets. The dot-com boom set off another round, partly fuelled by cool home gizmos like plasma TVs and PlayStations. Though many expected 9/11 to send people even deeper into nesting mode, sociologists say it actually got people out looking for companionship. After being hunkered down through terror alerts and the war in Iraq, many people were naturally itching to get out. Marketers are beginning to address the shift.[28]

More and more, people want to get out of the house and be with others. This trend suggests a greater demand for 'social support' products and services that improve direct communication between people, such as health clubs and family vacations.

People's views of organisations People vary in their attitudes toward corporations, government agencies, trade unions, universities and other organisations. By and large, people are willing to work for major organisations and expect them, in turn, to carry out society's work.

The late 1980s saw a sharp decrease in confidence in and loyalty towards business and political organisations and institutions. In the workplace, there has been an overall decline in organisational loyalty. During the 1990s, waves of company downsizings bred cynicism and distrust. And in this decade, corporate scandals at Enron, WorldCom, Tyco International and other large companies have resulted in a further loss of confidence in big business. Many people today see work not as a source of satisfaction but as a required chore to earn money to enjoy their non-work hours. This trend suggests that organisations need to find new ways to win consumer and employee confidence.

People's views of society People vary in their attitudes toward their society; conservatives defend the status quo, liberals want to change it, malcontents want to leave it. People's orientation to their society influences their consumption patterns and attitudes toward the marketplace.

People's views of nature People vary in their attitudes toward the natural world. Some feel ruled by it, others feel in harmony with it, and still others seek to master it. A long-term trend has been people's growing mastery over nature through technology and the belief that nature is bountiful. More recently, however, people have recognised that nature is finite and fragile, that it can be destroyed or spoiled by human activities.

This renewed love of things natural has created a sizeable 'lifestyles of health and sustainability' (LOHAS) market: consumers who seek out everything from natural, organic and nutritional products to fuel-efficient cars and alternative medicine. Business has responded by offering more products and services catering to such interests. The global market for organic food and drink was estimated to be worth around €25 billion in 2006; Europe is the largest organic food market in the world, followed by North America in second place. Within Europe Germany is the largest overall organic consumer followed by the UK, but although Germans and the British are avid consumers of organic produce, the share of the food market taken by organic products is highest in Switzerland and Austria, at 6 per cent of the market, compared with 3 per cent in Germany and 1.6 per cent in the UK. Many European companies have emerged to exploit this large and growing market opportunity – for example, Biopark Markt GmbH in Germany (organic meat suppliers), St Merryn Meat Ltd in the UK (a slaughterhouse that supplies organic meat to supermarkets), and Bodin et Fils SA in France (the largest European supplier of organic poultry).

People's views of the universe Finally, people vary in their beliefs about the origin of the universe and their place in it. It is very difficult to make generalisations about the religious faith of Europeans. Many European countries, such as France, Italy and Ireland, are predominantly Christian, while others, like Albania, are predominantly Muslim. The largest candidate for membership of the EU, Turkey, is overwhelmingly a Muslim country. However, the extent of religious observance and the significance of religion in people's lives varies considerably across the Continent. Church attendance is much higher in Ireland than elsewhere in Europe, for example. The great majority of Irish people say that they attend a formal religious ceremony regularly, but only a minority of people in the UK says the same thing. In many parts of Europe there is evidence that attendance at religious ceremonies is declining. Nevertheless, religion itself, and cultural practices associated with religion, remain important factors influencing the behaviour of European consumers. For example, there is a tradition in the Roman Catholic Church of not eating meat on Fridays, but eating fish is deemed to be perfectly acceptable. Even though the religious basis for this tradition is not at all clear, the cultural tradition lives on and the Irish Sea Fisheries Board reports that 30 per cent of the wet fish sold in Ireland is sold on a Friday.[29]

MAKING CONNECTIONS Linking the concepts

Slow down and take a break. You've now read about a large number of environmental forces. How are all of these environments *linked* with each other? With company marketing strategy?

■ How are major demographic forces linked with economic changes? With major cultural trends? How are the natural and technological environments linked? Think of an example of a company that has recognised one of these links and turned it into a marketing opportunity.

■ Is the marketing environment uncontrollable – something that the company can only prepare for and react to? Or can companies be proactive in changing environmental factors? Think of a good example that makes your point, then read on.

RESPONDING TO THE MARKETING ENVIRONMENT

Someone once observed, 'There are three kinds of companies: those who make things happen, those who watch things happen, and those who wonder what's happened.'[30] Many companies view the marketing environment as an uncontrollable element to which they must react and adapt. They passively accept the marketing environment and do not try to change it. They analyse the environmental forces and design strategies that will help the company avoid the threats and take advantage of the opportunities the environment provides.

Other companies take a *proactive* stance toward the marketing environment. Rather than simply watching and reacting, these firms take aggressive actions to affect the publics and forces in their marketing environment. Such companies hire lobbyists – people whose profession is to persuade politicians of a point of view – to influence legislation affecting their industries and stage media events to gain favourable press coverage. They run advertorials (advertisements expressing editorial points of view) to shape public opinion. They pursue legal actions and make complaints to regulators to keep competitors in line, and they form contractual agreements to control their distribution channels better.

Often, companies can find positive ways to overcome seemingly uncontrollable environmental constraints. For example:

> Cathay Pacific Airlines . . . determined that many travellers were avoiding Hong Kong because of lengthy delays at immigration. Rather than assuming that this was a problem they could not solve, Cathay's senior staff asked the Hong Kong government how to avoid these immigration delays. After lengthy discussions, the airline agreed to make an annual grant-in-aid to the government to hire more immigration inspectors – but these reinforcements would service primarily the Cathay Pacific gates. The reduced waiting period increased customer value and thus strengthened [Cathay's competitive advantage].[31]

Marketing management cannot always control environmental forces. In many cases, it must settle for simply watching and reacting to the environment. For example, a company would have little success trying to influence geographic population shifts, the economic environment, or major cultural values. But whenever possible, smart marketing managers will take a *proactive* rather than *reactive* approach to the marketing environment.

THE JOURNEY YOU'VE TAKEN Reviewing the concepts

In this chapter and the next two chapters, you'll examine the environments of marketing and how companies analyse these environments to understand the marketplace and consumers better. Companies must constantly watch and manage the *marketing environment* in order to seek opportunities and ward off threats. The marketing environment comprises all the actors and forces influencing the company's ability to transact business effectively with its target market.

1 **Describe the environmental forces that affect the company's ability to serve its customers.**

The company's *microenvironment* consists of other actors close to the company that combine to form the company's value delivery network or that affect its ability to serve its customers. It includes the company's *internal environment* – its several departments and management levels – as it influences marketing decision-making. *Marketing-channel firms* – suppliers and marketing intermediaries, including resellers, physical distribution firms, marketing services agencies and financial intermediaries – cooperate to create customer value. Five types of customer *markets* include consumer, business, reseller, government and international markets. *Competitors* vie with the company in an effort to serve customers better. Finally, various *publics* have an actual or potential interest in or impact on the company's ability to meet its objectives.

The *macroenvironment* consists of larger societal forces that affect the entire microenvironment. The six forces making up the company's macro-environment include demographic, economic, natural, technological, political and cultural. These forces shape opportunities and pose threats to the company.

2 Explain how changes in the demographic and economic environments affect marketing decisions.

Demography is the study of the characteristics of human populations. Today's *demographic environment* shows a changing age structure, shifting family profiles, geographic population shifts, a better-educated and more white-collar population, and increasing diversity. The *economic environment* consists of factors that affect buying power and patterns. The economic environment is characterised by more consumer concern for value and shifting consumer spending patterns. Today's squeezed consumers are seeking greater value – just the right combination of good quality and service at a fair price. The distribution of income also is shifting. The rich have grown richer, the middle class has shrunk, and the poor have remained poor, leading to a two-tiered market. Many companies now tailor their marketing offers to two different markets – the affluent and the less affluent.

3 Identify the major trends in the firm's natural and technological environments.

The *natural environment* shows three major trends: shortages of certain raw materials, higher pollu-

tion levels, and more government intervention in natural resource management. Environmental concerns create marketing opportunities for alert companies. The marketer should watch for four major trends in the *technological environment*: the rapid pace of technological change, high R&D budgets, the concentration by companies on minor product improvements, and increased government regulation. Companies that fail to keep up with technological change will miss out on new product and marketing opportunities.

4 Explain the key changes in the political and cultural environments.

The *political environment* consists of laws, agencies and groups that influence or limit marketing actions. The political environment has undergone three changes that affect marketing worldwide: increasing legislation regulating business, strong government agency enforcement, and greater emphasis on ethics and socially responsible actions. The *cultural environment* is made up of institutions and forces that affect a society's values, perceptions, preferences and behaviours. The environment shows long-term trends toward a 'we society,' a lessening trust of institutions, greater appreciation for nature, and the search for more meaningful and enduring values.

5 Discuss how companies can react to the marketing environment.

Companies can passively accept the marketing environment as an uncontrollable element to which they must adapt, avoiding threats and taking advantage of opportunities as they arise. Or they can take a *proactive* stance, working to change the environment rather than simply reacting to it. Whenever possible, companies should try to be proactive rather than reactive.

NAVIGATING THE KEY TERMS

NOTES AND REFERENCES

1 See Sarah Lorge, 'The Coke Advantage', *Sales & Marketing Management*, December 1998, p. 17; and Chad Terhune 'Coke Wins a 10-Year Contract From Subway, Ousting PepsiCo', *Wall Street Journal*, 28 November 2003, p. B.3.

2 World POPClock, US Census Bureau, accessed online at www.census.gov, July 2005. This website provides continuously updated projections of the US and world populations.

3 Adapted from Frederik Balfour, 'Educating the "Little Emperors": There's a Big Market for Products That Help China's Coddled Kids Get Ahead', *Business Week*, 10 November 2003, p. 22. See also Clay Chandler, 'Little Emperors', *Fortune*, 4 October 2004, pp. 138–50.

4 See 'China's Golden Oldies', *The Economist*, 26 February 2005, p. 74.

5 http://epp.eurostat.ec.europa.eu, accessed 16 May 2008.

6 Anushka Asthana and Vanessa Thorpe, 'Whatever happened to the original Generation X?', *The Observer*, 23 January 2005, available from http://www.guardian.co.uk/uk/2005/jan/23/britishidentity.anushkaasthana.

7 'Mixed Success: One Who Targeted Gen X and Succeeded – Sort Of', *Journal of Financial Planning*, February 2004, p. 15. Also see Neil Leslie, 'Farther Along on the X Axis', *American Demographics*, May 2004, pp. 21–4.

8 See 'Overlooked and Under X-Plointed', *American Demographics*, May 2004, p. 48; and Howard Schneider, 'Grunge Marketing', *Mortgage Banking*, November 2004, p. 106.

9 Tobi Elkin, 'Gen Y Quizzed about On-Demand', *Advertising Age*, 14 February 2003, p. 37. See also Rebecca Gardyn, 'Born to Be Wired', *American Demographics*, April 2003, pp. 14–15; Noah Rubin Brier, 'Coming of Age', *American Demographics*, November 2004, pp. 16–20; and Michael A. Belch, Kathleen A. Krentler and Laura A. Willis-Flurry, 'Teen Internet Mavens: Influence in Family Decision Making', *Journal of Business Research*, May 2005, pp. 569–75.

10 See 'Automakers Mix It up to Chase Young Buyers', *Automotive News*, 26 April 2004, p. 28B; and 'Elusive Gen Y Demand Edgier Marketing', *Automotive News*, 25 April 2005, p. 28B.

11 'Trends in Households in the European Union: 1995–2025', Eurostat, 2003, available at http://epp.eurostat.ec.europa.eu/cache/ity_offpub/ks-nk-03-024/en/ks-nk-03-024-en.pdf.

12 'The Life of Women and Men in Europe: A Statistical Portrait', Eurostat, 2008, available at http://epp.eurostat.ec.europa.eu/cache/ity_offpub/ks-80-07-135/en/ks-80-07-135-en.pdf.

13 World Health Organisation information obtained from http://www.who.int/tobacco/global_data/country_profiles/euro/en/, accessed 17 May 2008.

14 Information obtained from UNESCO, accessed at http://stats.uis.unesco.org, 18 May 2008.

15 'Social Trends 38: 2008 edition', 2008, Office for National Statistics, available at http://www.statistics.gov.uk/socialtrends38/.

16 Ellen Florian, 'Queer Eye Makes Over the Economy', *Fortune*, 9 February 2004, p. 38. See also Gillian K. Oakenfull and Timothy B. Greenlee, 'Queer Eye for a Gay Guy: Using Market-Specific Symbols in Advertising to Attract Gay Consumers Without Alienating the Mainstream', *Psychology and Marketing*, May 2005, pp. 421ff.

17 Howard L. Hughes, 'Pink Tourism: Holidays of Gay Men and Lesbians', 2006, CABI Publishing.

18 Information accessed at http://www.visitmanchester.com, May 2008.

19 Information accessed at http://www.visitvictoria.com, May 2008.

20 Information accessed at http://www.germany-tourism.co.uk/EGB/attractions_events/gaygermany.htm, May 2008.

21 Information from 'Pollution Prevention Pays', accessed at http://solutions.3m.com/wps/ portal/_l/en_US/_s.155/113842/_s.155/115848, June 2005; and 'Sustainability Key to UPS's Environmental Initiatives', accessed at www.pressroom.ups.com/mediakits/factsheet/0,2305,1140,00.html, June 2005.

22 Ann Bednarz, 'IBM Has Some Tall RFID Plans', *Network World*, 2 May 2005, pp. 17–18; Jack Neff, 'P&G Products to Wear Wire', *Advertising Age*, 15 December 2004, pp. 1, 32; Tom Van Riper, 'Retailers Eye RFID Technology to Make Shopping Easier', *Knight Ridder Tribune Business News*, 23 May 2005, p. 1; and information accessed online at www.autoidlabs.org, August 2005.

23 'Consolidated Versions of the Treaty on European Union and of the Treaty Establishing the European Community', *Official Journal of the European Communities*, 2002.

24 For more on online privacy, see Eric Goldman, 'The Internet Privacy Fallacy', *Computer and Internet Lawyer*, January 2003, p. 20; 'The Spies in Your Computer', *New York Times*, 18 February 2004, p. A18; Amir M. Hormozi, 'Cookies and Privacy', *Information Systems Security*, January/February 2005, pp. 51–60; and Alan R. Peslak, 'Internet Privacy Policies: A Review and Survey of the Fortune 50', *Information Resources Management Journal*, January–March 2005, pp. 29ff.

25 Adapted from Rob Walker, 'Yellow Fever', *New York Times Magazine*, 29 August 2004, p. 23; with information from Zan Dubin Scott, 'Style & Culture; On Wrist Watch; Ribbons, Make Way for Rubber', *Los Angeles Times*, 20 March 2005, p. E.25.

26 For more on Yankelovich Monitor, see /www.yankelovich.com/y-monitor.asp.

27 Adapted from Becky Ebenkamp, 'Fun/Duty Now, for the Future', *Brandweek*, 5 January 2004, p. 16.

28 Portions of this example are adapted from information in Eileen Daspin, 'The End of Nesting', *Wall Street Journal*, 16 May 2003, p. W1. Also see 'The Cocoon Cracks Open', *Brandweek*, 28 April 2003, pp. 32–6; and Dan Lippe, 'Gimme Shelter', *Advertising Age*, special report, 5 April 2004, pp. S1–S8.

29 Information accessed at http://www.independent.ie/national-news, June 2008.

30 See Philip Kotler, *Kotler on Marketing* (New York: Free Press, 1999), p. 3; and Kotler, *Marketing Insights from A to Z* (Hoboken, NJ: John Wiley & Sons, 2003), pp. 23–4.

31 Howard E. Butz Jr and Leonard D. Goodstein, 'Measuring Customer Value: Gaining the Strategic Advantage', *Organisational Dynamics*, Winter 1996, pp. 66–7.

CHAPTER 5
Consumer and business buyer behaviour

AFTER STUDYING THIS CHAPTER, YOU SHOULD BE ABLE TO

- understand the consumer market and the major factors that influence consumer buyer behaviour
- identify and discuss the stages in the buyer decision process
- describe the adoption and diffusion process for new products
- define the business market and identify the major factors that influence business buyer behaviour
- list and define the steps in the business buying decision process

THE WAY AHEAD Previewing the concepts

In the previous chapter, you studied how marketers obtain, analyse and use information to understand the marketplace and to assess marketing programmes. In this chapter, you'll continue your marketing journey with a closer look at the most important element of the marketplace – customers. The aim of marketing is to affect how customers think about and behave towards the organisation and its marketing offers. To affect the *whats, whens* and *hows* of buying behaviour marketers must first understand the *whys*. We look first at *final consumer* buying influences and processes and then at the buying behaviour of *business customers*. You'll see that understanding buying behaviour is an essential but very difficult task.

Our first point of interest: the huge Airbus A380, a new aircraft that is designed to carry a lot of passengers, or a lot of freight, over vast distances. There's little doubt that the A380 is a brilliant conception, delivering not just massive carrying capacity and state-of-the-art technology, but also environmental benefits such as increased fuel efficiency and lower noise. But what is going to make or break the commercial success of this plane are the buying decisions made by airline executives; those buying decisions, in turn, are driven by the buying decisions of their customers. Let's take a look at what lies behind all of those important decisions.

Airbus A380

George S. Low, *Associate Professor of Marketing, M.J. Neeley School of Business, Texas Christian University, USA*

Marketing strategy situation

Airbus is one of the leading aircraft manufacturers in the global aircraft industry. Their newest addition to their aircraft product line is the A380, an extremely large, two-floor plane that can be used as either a passenger or freight plane. Development of this project began in late 2000, with production beginning in early 2002. It was expected that the A380 would be ready for delivery by 2007; however, starting in 2005 delays began to occur because of manufacturing problems. Three delays occurred, and the delivery date was pushed back to 2010. These production delays have resulted in an expected $6 billion loss in earnings along with a struggle to keep customers onboard; FedEx has already pulled out of a deal for ten A380s and bought Boeing's 777 instead. Airbus's top salesman, John Leahy, has responded to these delays by re-negotiating contracts and attempting to keep customers from bailing out like FedEx did. His strategy is to persuade customers to take discounts on future orders as opposed to the cash compensation they were originally expecting. Airbus knew there was risk involved when they came up with the plans for the A380, but they were not prepared for the delays, the loss in earnings, or the strain on the company's reputation.

Company background

Airbus is a sub-company of the European Aeronautic Defence & Space Co., EADS. EADS decided to

Source: Alamy Images/Antony Nettle.

invest in an organisation that could rival America's aerospace giants, such as Boeing, and so created Airbus – the European equivalent. Airbus is based in France, but has offices throughout Europe and the United States, and deals with most of its costs in euros and sterling. The main mission of Airbus is to 'meet the needs of airlines and operators by producing the most modern and comprehensive aircraft family on the market, complemented by the highest standard of product support'. They remain environmentally conscious and continue to work towards building quieter and more fuel-efficient aircraft. The company has a good reputation in the minds of the public but also has the reputation of being very politically-oriented. Airbus is sometimes thought of as succeeding thanks to public subsidies, but not being a very robust commercial operation.

The global aviation industry is extremely cut-throat so introducing any new product is risky, but there is a constant attempt to develop newer planes with better technology. At the same time, both passenger and freight air traffic are expected to grow over the next ten years. The hope is that the A380, because of

its very large capacity, will enable a growth in air journeys by both people and freight while restricting growth in the total number of flights. However, there is, of course, risk involved in the launching of the Airbus A380, since it is just as likely that no change in the industry will occur and the 'A380 is a very large aircraft for a very small market'.

Customers

The main customers that Airbus is focused on are the major airlines, paying passengers and freight customers. The large planes are able to provide something for everyone since they can carry more cargo, but are also state of the art when it comes to luxury and style for high paying travellers. Some of the companies that have already ordered A380s are FedEx, UPS, Emirates, Thai Airways and Singapore Airlines. Singapore Airlines is first in line for deliveries of the plane, while FedEx was angered by the delays and pulled out of the deal.

There's a close relationship between the decisions made by operators of passenger airlines about which planes to buy, and the decisions made by the airline operators' customers about which airline they will fly with. A lot of people are involved in making the decision about which planes an airline should buy. It is a long-term decision that will affect the future of the company. Airline engineers analyse the aircraft from a number of angles: operating efficiency, safety, maintenance costs, and so on. Airline accountants focus on the lifetime costs associated with owning and operating the aircraft. The purchase price of an aircraft, despite being a very large sum of money, is only one part of the total costs involved in owning and operating an aircraft. Airline marketers are interested in how their customers will respond to the new aircraft. This, of course, involves understanding their own customers' behaviour, with a key focus on the different market segments that they serve. Passengers in first class pay top prices and expect the very best in terms of comfort and service. Business class passengers want somewhere they can get on with their work and maybe sleep in reasonable comfort to get ready for an important meeting. The rest of the passengers (that's most of us who ever fly) would like a pleasant journey, but mainly they just want to arrive safely, on time, and with their luggage intact. Before making the decision about which type of aircraft to buy, the airline operator analyses the extent to which each competing product can deliver the features and benefits that it wants to provide to its customers. Of course, different airlines themselves have different priorities: some are luxury airlines offering the best of everything, while others are budget airlines that aim to get you to your destination safely and on time but with a minimum of additional services. Consequently, different airlines, wishing to offer their customers different types of experience, will have different buying criteria when considering which aircraft to buy.

As well as passenger airlines, Airbus wants to sell the A380 to freight operators, like UPS and FedEx. These operators don't have to worry about the needs of passengers, but that doesn't make them any less demanding. The aircraft is one of the primary tools that these companies use to deliver on their promises to their customers. They sell their services to both businesses and to consumers. Although you might only want to send a package across the Atlantic once a year (to your brother in the USA every Christmas), there are plenty of business customers that are sending lots of packages across the ocean every day. So the freight operators have to deliver a reliable, secure, high-speed service to both business customers and private consumers, and they know that the right choice of aircraft is vital if they are going to make this happen.

The A380

Airbus chose a double-deck configuration because the structure required is significantly lighter than a single deck with twin tails. The design of the A380 was meant to be able to use existing airport infrastructure with minor modifications to the airports, and direct operating costs per seat 15–20 per cent less than those for the 747–400. The plane also has more floor space and more seating than the previous largest aircraft. The main cabin is about 20 inches wider than the Boeing 747's, and has economy passengers seated ten across, while the upper-deck economy class has eight seats across. Airbus wants to provide customers with wider seats and aisles for greater comfort. The name 380 was chosen because the 8 represents the cross-section of the twin decks. The wings are also quite long, almost

20 per cent longer than the 747's; even so, they are flexible and able to bend almost 4 metres during take-off and landing.

The innovative technology can be seen first by the pilots in the cockpit. The electronics include an environmental surveillance system which integrates weather radar, traffic alert and collision avoidance and a ground-proximity warning system. This allows pilots to see easily what type of weather they are flying into as well as what the weather will be in the next couple of hours. The technology also allows pilots to locate other planes easily and avoid any potential accidents, making the plane safer for both customers and cargo. The ground-proximity system provides another safety feature as it makes landing easier for the pilots. Additionally, the A380 uses new technology in an attempt to have a larger range, lower fuel burn and emissions, and less noise. Airbus says it is more fuel-efficient than a car – and it averages about 90.6 mpg per passenger.

Another luxury from the A380 is the low noise. The four huge Rolls-Royce engines emit little more than a low hum, even during take-off when engine noise is usually most noticeable. Landing is also quiet, the landing gear can barely be heard as it descends. It is easy to talk to passengers across the aisle and in adjoining rows without raising your voice. This provides the customers with a pleasant voyage as there is no annoying engine noise and conversation is not disrupted by turbulence or loud landings and take-offs. Sounds like a great product! But whether or not it succeeds depends on a whole range of buying decisions. Will airline operators believe that the A380 is the best plane to buy to serve their customers? Will freight operators be persuaded that it is the best product to meet the demands of their business and private customers? And, perhaps most important, will air passengers decide that they want to fly with operators who use the A380, because it makes their journeys that little bit more pleasant?

Sources: Doris Burke, 'Anatomy of an A380', *Fortune Magazine*, 5 March 2007, **155**(4), pp. 101–8; Nelson D. Schwartz, 'Big Plane, Big Problems', *Fortune Magazine*, 5 March 2007, **155**(4), pp. 95–8; Airbus Corporation Web-

site, http://www.airbus.com/en/corporate/ethics/mission_values/; 'Airbus' New Flight Plan', *The Wall Street Journal*, 9 March 2007; Rod Stone, 'Airbus Parent EADS Appoints Rudiger Grube as Co-Chairman', *The Wall Street Journal*, 5 April 2007; Andrew Lee, 'The A380 is a Gamble Worth Taking', *The Engineer*, 10 February 2005; 'Airbus A380 Completes Test flight', *BBC News*, 27 April 2005; Robert Wall, 'Schedule UPSet', *Aviation Week & Space Technology*, 5 March 2007, **166**(10); 'The Airbus 380', Airliners.net, 9 April 2007, http://www.airliners.net/info/stats.main?id=29; Noelle Knox, 'A380 Makes Massive Debut', *USA Today*, 19 January 2005;

'Airbus A380: A Whale of a Plane!', *BBC News*, 10 May 2005; Carol Matlock, 'Aloft on Airbus' Giant New A380', *BusinessWeek Online*, 8 February 2007; Greg Lindsay, 'Airbust? A380 Hits Marketing Turbulence', *Advertising Age*, 2 April 2007, **78**(14); Marc Graser, 'The Nonproduct Placement that Boosts Airbus', *Advertising Age*, 9 May 2005; Barbara Peterson, 'Airbus A380: Taking the Largest Passenger Jet for a Test Drive', *Popular Mechanics*, 22 March 2007, http://www.popularmechanics.com/bolgs/science_news/4213543.html.

The Airbus A380 example shows that many different factors affect business and consumer buying behaviour. Buying behaviour is never simple, yet understanding it is the essential task of marketing management. First we explore the dynamics of the consumer market and consumer buyer behaviour. We then examine business markets and the business buying process.

CONSUMER MARKETS AND CONSUMER BUYER BEHAVIOUR

Consumer buyer behaviour refers to the buying behaviour of final consumers – individuals and households who buy goods and services for personal consumption. All of these final consumers combine to make up the **consumer market**. The European Union consumer market consists of more than 490 million people who consume many trillions of euros' worth of goods and services each year, making it one of the most attractive consumer markets in the world. The world consumer market consists of more than 6.4 *billion* people.[1]

Consumers around the world vary tremendously in age, income, education level and tastes. They also buy an incredible variety of goods and services. The ways in which these diverse consumers connect with each other and with other elements of the world around them influence their choices among various products, services and companies. Here we examine the fascinating array of factors that affect consumer behaviour.

Model of consumer behaviour

Consumers make many buying decisions every day. Most large companies research consumer buying decisions in great detail to answer questions about what consumers buy, where they buy, how and how much they buy, when they buy, and why they buy. Marketers can study actual consumer purchases to find out what they buy, where and how much. But learning about the *whys* of consumer buying behaviour is not so easy – the answers are often locked deep within the consumer's head.

Penetrating the dark recesses of the consumer's mind is no easy task. Often, consumers themselves don't know exactly what influences their purchases. 'Ninety-five per cent of the thought, emotion, and learning [that drive our purchases] occur in the unconscious mind – that is, without our awareness,' notes one consumer behaviour expert.[2]

The central question for marketers is: how do consumers respond to various marketing efforts the company might use? The starting point is the stimulus-response model

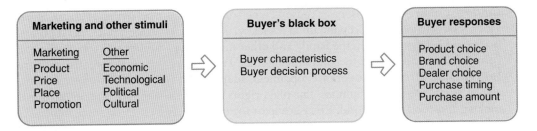

FIGURE 5.1

Model of buyer behaviour

of buyer behaviour shown in Figure 5.1. This figure shows that marketing and other stimuli enter the consumer's 'black box' and produce certain responses. Marketers must figure out what is in the buyer's black box.

At the most basic level marketing stimuli consist of the 'marketing mix': product, price, place and promotion for goods, with the addition of people, physical evidence and process for service products. Other stimuli include major forces and events in the buyer's environment: economic, technological, political and cultural. All these inputs enter the buyer's mind where they are turned into a set of observable buyer responses: product choice, brand choice, dealer choice, purchase timing and purchase amount.

The marketer wants to understand how the stimuli are changed into responses inside the consumer's mind. There are two components: first, the buyer's characteristics influence how he or she perceives and reacts to the stimuli; second, the buyer's decision process itself affects the buyer's behaviour. We look first at buyer characteristics as they affect buying behaviour and then discuss the buyer decision process.

Characteristics affecting consumer behaviour

Consumer purchases are influenced strongly by cultural, social, personal and psychological characteristics, as shown in Figure 5.2. For the most part, marketers cannot control such factors, but they must take them into account.

Cultural Factors

Cultural factors exert a broad and deep influence on consumer behaviour. The marketer needs to understand the role played by the buyer's *culture*, *subculture* and *social class*.

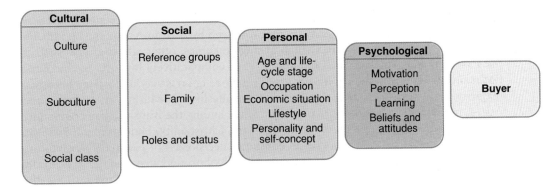

FIGURE 5.2

Factors influencing consumer behaviour

Culture   **Culture** is the most basic cause of a person's wants and behaviour. Human behaviour is largely learned. Growing up in a society, a child learns basic values, perceptions, wants and behaviours from the family and other important institutions. For example, the former Prime Minister of the United Kingdom, Tony Blair, identified a number of core British values: creativity, tolerance, openness, adaptability, work and self-improvement, strong communities and families, fair play, rights and responsibilities, and an outward-looking approach to the world. Every group or society has a culture, and cultural influences on buying behaviour may vary greatly from country to country. Failure to adjust to these differences can result in ineffective marketing or embarrassing mistakes.

Marketers are always trying to spot *cultural shifts* in order to discover new products that might be wanted. For example, the cultural shift toward greater concern about health and fitness has created a huge industry for health and fitness services, exercise equipment and clothing, more-natural foods, and a variety of diets. The shift toward informality has resulted in more demand for casual clothing and simpler home furnishings.

Subculture   Each culture contains smaller **subcultures**, or groups of people with shared value systems based on common life experiences and situations. Subcultures include nationalities, religions, racial groups and geographic regions. Many subcultures make up important market segments, and marketers often design products and marketing programmes tailored to their needs. Ethnic minorities are an example of subculture groups. It is estimated that there are 5.5 million ethnic minority consumers in Britain, and the value of the ethnic minority market as a whole is estimated to be £12 billion a year.[3] Britain has seen several waves of immigration during the last 60 years, including migrants from the Republic of Ireland, the Caribbean, the Indian subcontinent, Africa, Cyprus and Hong Kong. A new wave of immigration from Eastern Europe recently followed the expansion of the European Union in 2004 and 2005. Several ethnic minority groups tend to have more children than the white indigenous population, making them an important target market for baby products companies and for any company that is targeting younger consumers. The ethnic minority market in Britain has a younger age structure than the indigenous population. In the late 1990s only 31 per cent of white British people were aged under 24, compared with 48 per cent of the ethnic minority population.

In geographical terms, ethnic minority groups in Britain are heavily concentrated in the major cities of England, and nearly half live in Greater London. The high geographical concentration makes it easier to devise targeted marketing strategies for ethnic minority groups. However, while there are specialist ethnic minority media (such as radio stations, television stations and newspapers) in Britain, they are nowhere near as well developed as in the United States of America.

The consumer buying behaviour of ethnic minority groups in Britain is influenced by many factors, among which income levels, religion and family structure can be considered particularly important. The British Chinese community has the highest average income level among ethnic minority groups, followed by African-Asians and by Indians. While these groups have relatively high average incomes, other ethnic groups such as the Pakistani and Bangladeshi communities have comparatively low average incomes. For many members of ethnic minority groups their religion is very important. The great majority of British Pakistanis and British Bangladeshis are Muslim, most white and Afro-Caribbean British people are Christian, while among the British Indian community several religions are represented, including Islam, Christianity, Hinduism and Sikhism. Religion can play an important role in consumer decisions. For example, Muslims are forbidden to eat certain foods or to consume alcohol, and may require specifically designed financial services products that do not involve the payment of interest. Finally, family structures vary considerably between ethnic groups. Since they have more children, ethnic minority groups tend to have larger families than the indigenous white community. Additionally, among some Asian subcultures the traditional extended family, where multiple generations live together under the same roof, still exists, although this structure seems to be in decline among British Asians.

Having identified a gap in the market for financial services aimed at the large Muslim minority in Britain, Lloyds TSB launched a range of Shariah (Islamic law) approved financial services, including an Islamic current account and a Shariah-approved home finance service. Muslims signing up to any of these products could rest assured that their money would always be handled in accordance with Shariah. The money that account holders placed with the bank would not be used for any interest-based business activities. In order to reassure Muslim customers of the integrity of the service, Lloyds TSB recruited a committee of religious and legal advisers of the Islamic faith.

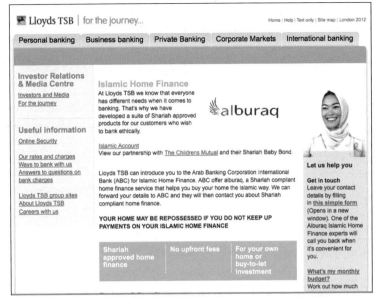

Lloyds TSB is offering services designed to meet the specific needs of people of the Islamic faith.

The worldwide population of people aged over 60 is growing faster than any other age group, and is expected to double from today's 605 million to around 1.2 billion by 2025. Although other countries are also ageing, European countries are ageing faster than those of any other continent. By 2050 it is estimated that 35 per cent of Europe's population will be aged over 60. In the longer term the ageing population represents a considerable public policy challenge, since there will be fewer workers and more retired people. Major efforts by both governments and private firms are going into the promotion of pension plans to persuade younger people that they need to start saving early for retirement. For the moment, however, mature consumers are better off financially than are younger consumer groups. Because mature consumers have more time and money, they are an ideal market for exotic travel, restaurants, high-tech home entertainment products, leisure goods and services, designer furniture and fashions, financial services and health care services.[4]

Their desire to look as young as they feel also makes more mature consumers good candidates for cosmetics and personal care products, health foods, fitness products and other items that combat the effects of ageing. The best strategy is to appeal to their active, multidimensional lives. For example, Kellogg's aired a TV spot for All-Bran cereal in which individuals ranging in age from 53 to 81 are featured playing ice hockey, water skiing, running hurdles, and playing baseball, all to the tune of 'Wild Thing'. A Pepsi ad features a young man in the middle of a mosh pit at a rock concert who turns around to see his father rocking out nearby. And an Aetna commercial portrays someone who, after retiring from a career as a lawyer, fulfils a lifelong dream of becoming an archeologist.[5]

Social class   Almost every society has some form of social class structure. **Social classes** are society's relatively permanent and ordered divisions whose members share similar values, interests and behaviours. Social scientists have identified the ten European social classes shown in Table 5.1.

Social class is not determined by a single factor, such as income, but is measured as a combination of occupation, income, education, wealth and other variables. In some social systems, members of different classes are reared for certain roles and cannot

TABLE 5.1 The European socio-economic classification

ESeC class		Common term	Employment regulation
1	Large employers, higher grade professional, administrative and managerial occupations	Higher salariat	Service relationship
2	Lower grade professional, administrative and managerial occupations and higher grade technician and supervisory occupations	Lower salariat	Service relationship (modified)
3	Intermediate occupations	Higher grade white collar workers	Mixed
4	Small employer and self-employed occupations (exc. agriculture etc.)	Petit bourgeoisie or independents	–
5	Self-employed occupations (agriculture etc.)	Petit bourgeoisie or independents	–
6	Lower supervisory and lower technician occupations	Higher grade blue collar workers	Mixed
7	Lower services, sales and clerical occupations	Lower grade white collar workers	Labour contract (modified)
8	Lower technical occupations	Skilled workers	Labour contract (modified)
9	Routine occupations	Semi- and non-skilled workers	Labour contract
10	Never worked and long-term unemployed	Unemployed	–

Source: http://www.iser.essex.ac.uk/research/esec/user-guide/the-european-socio-economic-classification.

change their social positions. In Europe, however, the lines between social classes are not fixed and rigid; people can move to a higher social class or drop into a lower one. Marketers are interested in social class because people within a given social class tend to exhibit similar buying behaviour. Social classes show distinct product and brand preferences in areas such as clothing, home furnishings, leisure activity and cars.

Social factors

A consumer's behaviour is also influenced by social factors, such as the consumer's *small groups*, *family*, and *social roles* and *status*.

Groups A person's behaviour is influenced by many small **groups**. Groups that have a direct influence and to which a person belongs are called membership groups. In contrast, reference groups serve as direct (face-to-face) or indirect points of comparison or reference in forming a person's attitudes or behaviour. People are often influenced by reference groups to which they do not belong. For example, an aspirational group is one to which the individual wishes to belong, as when a young boy hopes someday to emulate Thierry Henry and play soccer for France and for great club sides like Arsenal and Barcelona.

Marketers try to identify the reference groups of their target markets. Reference groups expose a person to new behaviours and lifestyles, influence the person's attitudes and self-concept, and create pressures to conform that may affect the person's product and brand choices. The importance of group influence varies across products and brands. It tends to be strongest when the product is visible to others whom the buyer respects.

Manufacturers of products and brands subjected to strong group influence must figure out how to reach **opinion leaders** – people within a reference group who, because of special skills, knowledge, personality, or other characteristics, exert influence on others. Some experts call this 10 per cent of Europeans *the influentials* or *leading adopters*. These consumers 'drive trends, influence mass opinion and, most importantly, sell a great many products,' says one expert. They often use their big circle of acquaintances to 'spread their knowledge on what's good and what's bad'.[6]

Many marketers try to identify opinion leaders for their products and direct marketing efforts toward them. They use *buzz marketing* by enlisting or even creating opinion leaders to spread the word about their brands.

Sneeze, a London marketing agency, uses *buzz marketing* to create successful word-of-mouth campaigns for its clients.

Two or three years ago, a Premiership football club (I'm not allowed to tell you which one) was trying to sign up fans to its text bulletin service. For 25p a message (working out at around £100 a year), fans would get a text whenever something interesting happened at the club – team selections, injury updates, half-time scores, that sort of thing.

Despite promoting the service in club literature, on its website, and with armies of attractive girls handing out leaflets on match days, the club could not get the rate of new subscriptions to rise above a disappointing 20 a week. So it hired a small marketing agency called Sneeze.

'We got a group of 14 or 16 actors, who were all football fans, but pretended to be fans [of the unnamed club],' explains Graham Goodkind, Sneeze's founder and chairman. 'And they went round bars and clubs around the ground, in groups of two, saying that one of their mates had been sacked from work because he kept on getting these text messages and talking to everyone about it, and his boss had had enough and given him the boot. So they were going round with this petition trying to get his job back – kind of a vaguely plausible story.

'And then the actors would pull out of their pocket some crumpled-up leaflet, which was for the text subscription service. They'd have a mobile phone in their pocket, and they'd show them how it worked. "What's the harm in that?" they'd say. And they could have these conversations with lots of people – that was the beauty of it. Two people could spend maybe 20 minutes or half an hour in each pub, working the whole pub. We did it at two home games and reckon we got about 4,000 people on the petition in total.'

The petition went in the bin, of course, but subscriptions to the club's texting service soared. 'The week after we had done the activity it went up to 120 sign-ups,' says Goodkind, who is also boss of the Frank PR agency. 'Then you saw that after that it was 125, and the next week was 75, and the next week was 60. That was the talkability, because obviously if you get that service you tell your mates about it. We saw a massive effectiveness.'[7]

Family Family members can strongly influence buyer behaviour. The family is the most important consumer buying organisation in society, and it has been researched extensively. Marketers are interested in the roles and influence of the husband, wife and children on the purchase of different products and services.

Husband–wife involvement varies widely by product category and by stage in the buying process. Buying roles change with evolving consumer lifestyles. For example, in many countries, the wife has traditionally been the main purchasing agent for the family in the areas of food, household products and clothing. But with a growing proportion of women holding jobs outside the home and the willingness of husbands to do more of the family's purchasing, all this is changing. The traditional division of labour between men and women in the family, with men earning the money and women running the home, is already a distant memory in many European countries and is breaking down elsewhere. The traditional buying roles of men and women are also breaking down.[8]

Such changes suggest that marketers in industries that have sold their products only to men or only to women are now courting the opposite sex. For example, consider Barbara K Enterprises:

It's no surprise that many women feel awkward using home-repair tools designed for men. Enter Barbara Kavovit, CEO of Barbara K Enterprises. A self-made woman, Barbara entered the home improvement business by starting her own construction company, passing out fliers and going door-to-door in Westchester County, New York. Seven years later, she created a lifestyle brand that offers innovative, women-friendly home repair and improvement products. On a mission to 'inspire women to become more self-reliant and confident in their own abilities', and to help them overcome the fear factor of do-it-yourself home repair, Barbara K has developed a strong market niche. More than 70 per cent of female home owners do minor home repairs themselves, and 37 per cent say they would rather work on a home improvement project than cook or shop. For these women, Barbara K Enterprises has created a line of high-quality tools and accessories, from hammers and cordless drills to putty knives and pliers. The tools are shaped for smaller hands, have spring-assisted grips, are guaranteed for life, and come in stylish blue and black designs – not pink! Last year, the company sold more than $5 million worth of tools and tool kits emblazoned with the Barbara K name, at stores such as Target, Ace Hardware, and Bed Bath & Beyond.[9]

Children may also have a strong influence on family buying decisions. For example, children as young as age 6 may influence the family car purchase decision. Recognising this fact, Vauxhall launched a new kid-focused ad campaign for its Zafira and Meriva models. Whereas most other multi-purpose vehicle (MPV) ads have focused on selling

Source: Vauxhall General Motors.

features that are important to adults, like carrying home large purchases from the DIY store, Vauxhall used George, Harry and Amir, three young boys, as the stars of their TV campaign. The light-hearted campaign portrayed the boys as the mature, thoughtful members of the family and their parents as argumentative and disorganised. Supported by newspaper advertising that drove home the features and benefits of the products, the TV campaign concentrated on getting the message across to kids, and their parents, that this car was designed with them in mind.

Vauxhall got the message across to kids that the Zafira and the Meriva were designed with them in mind.

Roles and status A person belongs to many groups – family, clubs, organisations. The person's position in each group can be defined in terms of both role and status. A role consists of the activities people are expected to perform according to the persons around them. Each role carries a status reflecting the general esteem given to it by society.

People usually choose products appropriate to their roles and status. Consider the various roles a working mother plays. In her company, she plays the role of a brand manager; in her family, she plays the role of wife and mother; at her favourite sporting events, she plays the role of avid fan. As a brand manager, she will buy the kind of clothing that reflects her role and status in her company.

Personal factors

A buyer's decisions are also influenced by personal characteristics such as the buyer's *age and life-cycle stage*, *occupation*, *economic situation*, *lifestyle* and *personality and self-concept*.

Age and life-cycle stage People change the goods and services they buy over their lifetimes. Tastes in food, clothes, furniture and recreation are often age-related. Buying is also shaped by the stage of the family life cycle – the stages through which families might pass as they mature over time. Marketers often define their target markets in terms of life-cycle stage and develop appropriate products and marketing plans for each stage.

Traditional family life-cycle stages include young singles and married couples with children. Today, however, marketers are increasingly catering to a growing number of alternative, non-traditional stages such as unmarried couples, singles marrying later in life, childless couples, same-sex couples, single parents, extended parents (those with young adult children returning home), and others.

Sony recently overhauled its marketing approach in order to target products and services to consumers based on their life stages. It created a new unit called the Consumer Segment Marketing Division, which has identified seven life-stage segments. They include, among others, Gen Y (under 25), Young Professionals/DINKs (double income no kids, 25 to 34), Families (35 to 54), and Zoomers (55 and over). A recent Sony ad aimed at Zoomers, people who have just retired or are close to doing so, shows a man living his dream by going into outer space. The ad deals not just with going into retirement, but with the psychological life-stage changes that go with it. 'The goal is to get closer to consumers,' says a Sony segment marketing executive.[10]

Occupation A person's occupation affects the goods and services bought. Blue-collar workers tend to buy more rugged work clothes, whereas executives buy more business suits. Marketers try to identify the occupational groups that have an above-average interest in their products and services. A company can even specialise in making products needed by a given occupational group. For example, Goliath Footwear from West Yorkshire in the UK specialises in rugged, durable, no-nonsense safety boots – including the Furnace Masters, a line of safety boots designed for people working with molten metals, which are heat resistant up to 300 degrees centigrade, and feature quick-release fasteners so that they can be removed speedily in the event of a molten metal splash.

Economic situation A person's economic situation will affect product choice. Marketers of income-sensitive goods watch trends in personal income, savings and interest rates. If economic indicators point to a recession, marketers can take steps to redesign, reposition and reprice their products closely. Some marketers target consumers who have lots of money and resources, charging prices to match. For example, Rolex positions it luxury watches as 'a tribute to elegance, an object of passion, a symbol for all time'. Other marketers target consumers with more modest means. Timex makes more affordable watches that are renowned for their reliability and durability, epitomised by the famous Timex Ironman Triathlon model, designed to withstand the toughest sporting conditions.

Lifestyle People coming from the same subculture, social class and occupation may have quite different lifestyles. **Lifestyle** is a person's pattern of living as expressed in his or her psychographics. It involves measuring consumers' major AIO dimensions – activities (work, hobbies, shopping, sports, social events), interests (food, fashion, family, recreation) and opinions (about themselves, social issues, business, products). Lifestyle captures something more than the person's social class or personality. It profiles a person's whole pattern of acting and interacting in the world.

Several research firms have developed lifestyle classifications. The most widely used is SRI Consulting's *Values and Lifestyles (VALS)* typology. VALS classifies people according to how they spend their time and money. It divides consumers into eight groups based on two major dimensions: primary motivation and resources. *Primary motivations* include ideals, achievement and self-expression. According to SRI Consulting, consumers who are primarily motivated by ideals are guided by knowledge and principles. Consumers who are primarily motivated by *achievement* look for products and services that demonstrate success to their peers. Consumers who are primarily motivated by *self-expression* desire social or physical activity, variety and risk.

Consumers within each orientation are further classified into those with *high resources* and those with *low resources*, depending on whether they have high or low levels of income, education, health, self-confidence, energy and other factors. Consumers with either very high or very low levels of resources are classified without regard to their primary motivations (Innovators, Survivors). Innovators are people with so many resources that they exhibit all three primary motivations in varying degrees. In contrast, Survivors are people with so few resources that they do not show a strong primary motivation. They must focus on meeting needs rather than fulfilling desires.

One study identified five key food-related lifestyle segments in Croatia as follows:

■ The *relaxed* segment, representing 13 per cent of the population. They have no clear buying motives and the quality of food is not particularly important to them; they are influenced by friends and by the mass media. Buying and preparing food is not a major concern of this segment.

■ The *traditionalist* segment accounts for 27 per cent of the population. Cooking and eating food are considered to be important social events for this segment, and members of the family like to help out at meal times. They enjoy shopping for food and like to experiment with new recipes.

■ The *modern* segment, representing 32 per cent of the population. The members of this segment do not like to spend too much time on buying, preparing and cooking food; they make detailed shopping lists and plan their food shopping trips carefully. Their main motivation is to reduce the amount of time they spend on buying and cooking food.

■ The *concerned* segment makes up only around 11 per cent of the population. They are particularly interested in the safety and nutritional value of the food that they buy, and are convinced of the advantages of organic food. This segment tends to be relatively old and with above average incomes. Members of this segment pay a lot of attention to the information on food product labels.

■ The *hedonist* segment, representing 17 per cent of the population. This segment tends to comprise older consumers with lower than average education and income. Their main motivation is to enjoy the food that they eat. Women who belong to this segment spend a lot of time shopping for food and take pride in their cooking abilities.[11]

Lifestyle segmentation can also be used to understand how consumers use the Internet, computers and other technology. Forrester developed its 'Technographics' scheme, which segments consumers according to motivation, desire and ability to invest in technology. The framework splits people into ten categories, including:

■ *Fast Forwards*: the biggest spenders on computer technology. Fast Forwards are career-focused, time-strapped, driven, and top users of technology.

■ *New Age Nurturers*: also big spenders. However, they are focused on technology for home uses, such as family education and entertainment.

■ *Mouse Potatoes*: consumers who are dedicated to interactive entertainment and willing to spend for the latest in 'technotainment'.

■ *Techno-Strivers*: consumers who are up-and-coming believers in technology for career advancement.

■ *Traditionalists*: small-town folks, suspicious of technology beyond the basics.[12]

Delta Airlines used Technographics to target online ticket sales better. It created marketing campaigns for time-strapped Fast Forwards and New Age Nurturers, and eliminated Technology Pessimists (those sceptical of technology) from its list of targets. When used carefully, the lifestyle concept can help marketers understand changing consumer values and how they affect buying behaviour.

Personality and self-concept Each person's distinct personality influences his or her buying behaviour. **Personality** refers to the unique psychological characteristics that lead to relatively consistent and lasting responses to one's own environment. Personality is usually described in terms of traits such as self-confidence, dominance, sociability, autonomy, defensiveness, adaptability and aggressiveness. Personality can be useful in analysing consumer behaviour for certain product or brand choices. For example, coffee marketers have discovered that heavy coffee drinkers tend to be high on sociability. Thus, to attract customers, Starbucks and other coffeehouses create environments in which people can relax and socialise over a cup of steaming coffee.

The idea is that brands also have personalities, and that consumers are likely to choose brands with personalities that match their own. A *brand personality* is the specific mix of human traits that may be attributed to a particular brand. One researcher identified five brand personality traits:

1 Sincerity (down-to-earth, honest, wholesome and cheerful)

2 Excitement (daring, spirited, imaginative and up to date)

3 Competence (reliable, intelligent and successful)

4 Sophistication (upper class and charming)

5 Ruggedness (outdoorsy and tough)[13]

The researcher found that a number of well-known brands tended to be strongly associated with one particular trait: Levi's with 'ruggedness', MTV with 'excitement', CNN with 'competence', and Campbell's with 'sincerity'. Hence, these brands will attract people who are high on the same personality traits.

Many marketers use a concept related to personality – a person's *self-concept* (also called *self-image*). The basic self-concept premiss is that people's possessions contribute to and reflect their identities; that is, 'we are what we have'. Thus, in order to understand consumer behaviour, the marketer must first understand the relationship between consumer self-concept and possessions.

Brand personality: well-known brands tend to be strongly associated with one or more traits. Red Bull is associated with extreme 'excitement'.

Source: Alamy Images/Tony Lockhart.

Psychological factors

A person's buying choices are further influenced by four major psychological factors: *motivation*, *perception*, *learning* and *beliefs and attitudes*.

Motivation A person has many needs at any given time. Some are biological, arising from states of tension such as hunger, thirst or discomfort. Others are psychological, arising from the need for recognition, esteem or belonging. A need becomes a motive when it is aroused to a sufficient level of intensity. A **motive (or drive)** is a need that is sufficiently pressing to direct the person to seek satisfaction. Psychologists have developed theories of human motivation. Two of the most popular – the theories of Sigmund Freud and Abraham Maslow – have quite different meanings for consumer analysis and marketing.

Sigmund Freud assumed that people are largely unconscious about the real psychological forces shaping their behaviour. He saw the person as growing up and repressing many urges. These urges are never eliminated or under perfect control; they emerge in dreams, in slips of the tongue, in neurotic and obsessive behaviour, or ultimately in psychoses.

Freud's theory suggests that a person's buying decisions are affected by subconscious motives that even the buyer may not fully understand. Thus, an ageing baby boomer who buys a sporty BMW 330Ci convertible might explain that he simply likes the feel of the wind in his thinning hair. At a deeper level, he may be trying to impress others with his success. At a still deeper level, he may be buying the car to feel young and independent again.

The term *motivation research* refers to qualitative research designed to probe consumers' hidden, subconscious motivations. Consumers often don't know or can't describe just why they act as they do. Thus, motivation researchers use a variety of probing techniques to uncover underlying emotions and attitudes toward brands and buying situations. These sometimes bizarre techniques range from sentence completion, word association, and inkblot or cartoon interpretation tests, to having consumers form daydreams and fantasies about brands or buying situations. One writer offers the following tongue-in-cheek summary of a motivation research session:

> Good morning, ladies and gentlemen. We've called you here today for a little consumer research. Now, lie down on the couch, toss your inhibitions out the window, and let's try a little free association. First, think about brands as if they were your *friends*. Imagine you could talk to your TV dinner. What would he say? And what would you say to him? . . . Now, think of your shampoo as an animal. Go on, don't be shy. Would it be a panda or a lion? A snake or a wooly worm? For our final exercise, let's all sit up and pull out our magic markers. Draw a picture of a typical cake-mix user. Would she wear an apron or a negligee? A business suit or a can-can dress?[14]

Such projective techniques seem pretty strange, and some marketers dismiss such motivation research as mumbo-jumbo. But many marketers routinely use such touchy-feely approaches to dig deeply into consumer psyches and develop better marketing strategies.

Many companies employ teams of psychologists, anthropologists, and other social scientists to carry out motivation research. One ad agency routinely conducts one-to-one, therapy-like interviews to delve into the inner workings of consumers. Another company asks consumers to describe their favourite brands as animals or cars (say, Volkswagens versus Peugeots) in order to assess the prestige associated with various brands. Still others rely on hypnosis, dream therapy, or soft lights and mood music to plumb the murky depths of consumer psyches.

Abraham Maslow sought to explain why people are driven by particular needs at particular times. Why does one person spend much time and energy on personal safety and another on gaining the esteem of others? Maslow's answer is that human needs are arranged in a hierarchy, as shown in Figure 5.3, from the most pressing at the bottom to the least pressing at the top.[15] They include *physiological* needs, *safety* needs, *social* needs, *esteem* needs and *self-actualisation* needs.

A person tries to satisfy the most important need first. When that need is satisfied, it will stop being a motivator and the person will then try to satisfy the next most important need. For example, starving people (physiological need) will not take an interest in the latest happenings in the art world (self-actualisation needs), nor in how they are seen or esteemed by others (social or esteem needs), nor even in whether they are breathing clean air (safety needs). But as each important need is satisfied, the next most important need will come into play.

Perception A motivated person is ready to act. How the person acts is influenced by his or her own perception of the situation. All of us learn by the flow of information through our five senses: sight, hearing, smell, touch and taste. However, each of us receives, organises and interprets this sensory information in an individual way. **Perception** is the process by which people select, organise and interpret information to form a meaningful picture of the world.

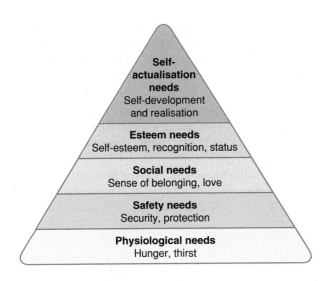

FIGURE 5.3

Maslow's hierarchy of needs

Source: Adapted from A.H. Maslow (1970) *Motivation and Personality*, 2nd edn.

People can form different perceptions of the same stimulus because of three perceptual processes: selective attention, selective distortion and selective retention. People are exposed to a great many stimuli every day. For example, one analyst estimates that people are exposed to about 5,000 ads every day.[16] It is impossible for a person to pay attention to all these stimuli. *Selective attention* – the tendency for people to screen out most of the information to which they are exposed – means that marketers have to work especially hard to attract the consumer's attention.

Even noticed stimuli do not always come across in the intended way. Each person fits incoming information into an existing mindset. *Selective distortion* describes the tendency of people to interpret information in a way that will support what they already believe. For example, if you distrust a company, you might perceive even honest ads from the company as questionable. Selective distortion means that marketers must try to understand the mindsets of consumers and how these will affect interpretations of advertising and sales information.

People will also forget much of what they learn. They tend to retain information that supports their attitudes and beliefs. Because of *selective retention*, consumers are likely to remember good points made about a brand they favour and to forget good points made about competing brands. Because of selective exposure, distortion and retention, marketers have to work hard to get their messages through. This fact explains why marketers use so much drama and repetition in sending messages to their market.

Interestingly, although most marketers worry about whether their offers will be perceived at all, some consumers worry that they will be affected by marketing messages without even knowing it – through *subliminal advertising*. In 1957, a researcher announced that he had flashed the phrases 'Eat popcorn' and 'Drink Coca-Cola' on a screen in a New Jersey movie theatre every five seconds for 1/300th of a second. He reported that although viewers did not consciously recognise these messages, they absorbed them subconsciously and bought 58 per cent more popcorn and 18 per cent more Coke. Suddenly advertisers and consumer-protection groups became intensely interested in subliminal perception. Although the researcher later admitted to making up the data, the issue has not died. Some consumers still fear that they are being manipulated by subliminal messages.

Numerous studies by psychologists and consumer researchers have found no link between subliminal messages and consumer behaviour. It appears that subliminal advertising simply doesn't have the power attributed to it by its critics. Most advertisers scoff at the notion of an industry conspiracy to manipulate consumers through 'invisible' messages. Says one industry insider: '[Some consumers believe we are] wizards who can manipulate them at will. Ha! Snort! Oh my sides! As we know, just between us, most of [us] have difficulty getting a 2 per cent increase in sales with the help of $50 million in media and extremely liminal images of sex, money, power, and other [motivators] of human emotion. The very idea of [us] as puppeteers, cruelly pulling the strings of consumer marionettes, is almost too much to bear.'[17]

Learning When people act, they learn. **Learning** describes changes in an individual's behaviour arising from experience. Learning theorists say that most human behaviour is learned. Learning occurs through the interplay of drives, stimuli, cues, responses and reinforcement.

A *drive* is a strong internal stimulus that calls for action. A drive becomes a motive when it is directed toward a particular *stimulus object*. For example, a person's drive for self-actualisation might motivate him or her to look into buying a digital camera. The consumer's response to the idea of buying a camera is conditioned by the surrounding cues. *Cues* are minor stimuli that determine when, where and how the person responds. For example, the person might spot several camera brands in a shop window, hear of a special sale price, or discuss cameras with a friend. These are all cues that might influence a consumer's *response* to his or her interest in buying the product.

Suppose the consumer buys a Pentax digital camera. If the experience is rewarding, the consumer will probably use the camera more and more, and his or her response will be *reinforced*. Then, the next time the consumer shops for a camera, or for binoculars or some similar product, the probability is greater that he or she will buy a Pentax product. The practical significance of learning theory for marketers is that they can build up demand for a product by associating it with strong drives, using motivating cues, and providing positive reinforcement.

Beliefs and attitudes Through doing and learning, people acquire beliefs and attitudes. These, in turn, influence their buying behaviour. A *belief* is a descriptive thought that a person has about something. Beliefs may be based on real knowledge, opinion or faith, and may or may not carry an emotional charge. Marketers are interested in the beliefs that people formulate about specific products and services, because these beliefs make up product and brand images that affect buying behaviour. If some of the beliefs are wrong and prevent purchase, the marketer will want to launch a campaign to correct them.

People have attitudes regarding religion, politics, clothes, music, food, and almost everything else. *Attitude* describes a person's relatively consistent evaluations, feelings and tendencies toward an object or idea. Attitudes put people into a frame of mind of liking or disliking things, of moving towards or away from them. Our digital camera buyer may hold attitudes such as 'Buy the best', 'The Japanese make the best electronics products in the world', and 'Creativity and self-expression are among the most important things in life'. If so, the Pentax camera would fit well into the consumer's existing attitudes.

Attitudes are difficult to change. A person's attitudes fit into a pattern, and to change one attitude may require difficult adjustments in many others. Thus, a company should usually try to fit its products into existing attitudes rather than attempt to change attitudes. Of course, there are exceptions in which the cost of trying to change attitudes may pay off handsomely. The traditional and dull Scottish breakfast of porridge oats has recently received a substantial boost from changes in lifestyles, greater awareness of healthy eating, and some clever marketing:

Oats have traditionally never enjoyed the sexiest image. But today even the most stylish and faddish foodie will happily admit to starting the day with a bowl of porridge.

Wheat free, low on the Glycaemic Index – which means they are slow energy releasing – and low in calories and fat, oats tick all the boxes as a nutritious and versatile food du jour.

Unlike a slice of white bread or a sugary bowl of cereal for example, the complex carbs in oats help balance blood sugar levels and leave you feeling full up for longer – an excellent way to refuel and curb hunger pangs.

Rich in fibre and protein, their nutritional benefits are also a huge plus. Studies have shown that oats can lower cholesterol, reduce high blood pressure and even improve libido. If further evidence was needed of their super-food status, Britain's longest-living man, David Henderson from Montrose, survived to the ripe old age of 109 and put his long life and good health down to his daily bowl of porridge.

In an age when we are more aware than ever that we are what we eat, it was not long before the rather plain little oat underwent a glamorous makeover. Witness the Scott's Porage Oats advert featuring a young lady ogling up a ruggedly handsome porridge-eating Scotsman's kilt. Soon after this, oatcakes appeared in deliberately more modern flavours – Nairns brought out cracked black pepper oatcakes, closely followed by stem ginger, mixed berry and fruit and spice varieties. Word spread of their appeal as a versatile, healthy snack and before long, oats were flying off shelves in all their forms. Sainsbury's reported a 60 per cent increase in oat sales in the last six months, and according to reports by market researchers TNS last year, oats are now Britain's second favourite breakfast cereal, with the oat industry bringing in £79 million per year.

Scots have long appreciated the benefits of oats. Native to Eurasia, they are the seeds of cereals belonging to the Avena genus and have been grown in Scotland for centuries. They have a lower summer heat requirement and greater tolerance of rain than cereals such as wheat, rye or barley, so are well suited to the Scottish climate. Our forefathers mixed them with a little fat to create oatcakes, one of the first convenience foods, a handy-sized and portable alternative to bread, but with the huge advantage that once baked they kept for long periods.

Scottish chieftains carried around small sacks of oatmeal when travelling by horseback and baked oatcakes on the back of their iron shields for sustenance. Today a pack of emergency oatcakes in the pocket does the same job for the you-are-what-you-eat generation, proving that a good thing will stand the test of time.[18]

We can now appreciate the many forces acting on consumer behaviour. The consumer's choice results from the complex interplay of cultural, social, personal and psychological factors.

The buyer decision process

Now that we have looked at the influences that affect buyers, we are ready to look at how consumers make buying decisions. Figure 5.4 shows that the buyer decision process consists of five stages: *need recognition, information search, evaluation of alternatives, purchase decision* and *post-purchase behaviour*. Clearly, the buying process starts long before the actual purchase and continues long after. Marketers need to focus on the entire buying process rather than on just the purchase decision.[19]

The figure suggests that consumers pass through all five stages with every purchase. But in more routine purchases, consumers often skip or reverse some of these stages. A woman buying her regular brand of toothpaste would recognise the need and go right to the purchase decision, skipping information search and evaluation. However, we use the model in Figure 5.4 because it shows all the considerations that arise when a consumer faces a new and complex purchase situation.

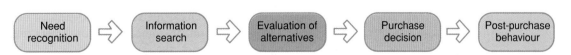

FIGURE 5.4

Buyer decision process

Need recognition

The buying process starts with *need recognition*: the buyer recognises a problem or need. The need can be triggered by *internal stimuli* when one of the person's normal needs – hunger, thirst, sex – rises to a level high enough to become a drive. A need can also be triggered by *external stimuli*. For example, an advertisement or a discussion with a friend might get you thinking about buying a new car. At this stage, the marketer should research consumers to find out what kinds of needs or problems arise, what brought them about, and how they led the consumer to this particular product.

Information search

An interested consumer may or may not search for more information. If the consumer's drive is strong and a satisfying product is near at hand, the consumer is likely to buy it then. If not, the consumer may store the need in memory or undertake an *information search* related to the need. For example, once you've decided you need a new mobile phone, you will probably pay more attention to phone advertisements, phones owned by friends and conversations about phones. Or you may actively look for reading material, email friends and gather information in other ways. The amount of searching you do will depend on the strength of your drive, the amount of information you start with, the ease of obtaining more information, the value you place on additional information and the satisfaction you get from searching.

Consumers can obtain information from any of several sources. These include *personal sources* (family, friends, neighbours, acquaintances), *commercial sources* (advertising, salespeople, 'websites' dealers, packaging, displays), *public sources* (mass media, consumer-rating organisations, Internet searches) and *experiential sources* (handling, examining, using the product). The relative influence of these information sources varies with the product and the buyer. Generally, the consumer receives the most information about a product from commercial sources – those controlled by the marketer. The most effective sources, however, tend to be personal. Commercial sources normally *inform* the buyer, but personal sources *legitimise* or *evaluate* products for the buyer. As one marketer states, 'It's rare that an advertising campaign can be as effective as a neighbor leaning over the fence and saying, "This is a wonderful product".'[20]

As more information is obtained, the consumer's awareness and knowledge of the available brands and features increases. In your phone information search, you may learn about the several brands available. This might help you to drop certain brands from consideration. A company must design its marketing mix to make prospects aware of and knowledgeable about its brand. It should carefully identify consumers' sources of information and the importance of each source.

Evaluation of alternatives

We have seen how the consumer uses information to arrive at a set of final brand choices. How does the consumer choose among the alternative brands? The marketer needs to know about *alternative evaluation*: that is, how the consumer processes information to arrive at brand choices. Unfortunately, consumers do not use a simple and single evaluation process in all buying situations. Instead, several evaluation processes are at work.

The consumer arrives at attitudes toward different brands through some evaluation procedure. How consumers go about evaluating purchase alternatives depends on the individual consumer and the specific buying situation. In some cases, consumers use careful calculations and logical thinking. At other times, the same consumers do little or no evaluating; instead they buy on impulse and rely on intuition. Sometimes consumers make buying decisions on their own; sometimes they turn to friends, consumer guides, or salespeople for buying advice.

Suppose you've narrowed your phone choices to three brands. And suppose that you are primarily interested in four attributes – style, features, guarantee and price. By this time, you've probably formed beliefs about how each brand rates on each attribute. Clearly, if one phone rated best on all the attributes, we could predict that you would choose it. However, the brands will no doubt vary in appeal. You might base your buying decision on only one attribute, and your choice would be easy to predict. If you wanted style above everything else, you would buy the phone that you think has the best styling. But most buyers consider several attributes, each with different importance. If we knew the importance that you assigned to each of the four attributes, we could predict your phone choice more reliably.

Marketers should study buyers to find out how they actually evaluate brand alternatives. If they know what evaluative processes go on, marketers can take steps to influence the buyer's decision.

Purchase decision

In the evaluation stage, the consumer ranks brands and forms purchase intentions. Generally, the consumer's *purchase decision* will be to buy the most preferred brand, but two factors can come between the purchase *intention* and the purchase *decision*. The first factor is the *attitudes of others*. If someone important to you thinks that you should buy the latest phone, then the chances of your buying an older model are reduced.

The second factor is *unexpected situational factors*. The consumer may form a purchase intention based on factors such as expected income, expected price and expected product benefits. However, unexpected events may change the purchase intention. For example, the economy might take a turn for the worse, a close competitor might drop its price, or a friend might report being disappointed in your preferred phone. Thus, preferences and even purchase intentions do not always result in actual purchase choice.

Post-purchase behaviour

The marketer's job does not end when the product is bought. After purchasing the product, the consumer will be satisfied or dissatisfied and will engage in *post-purchase behaviour* of interest to the marketer. What determines whether the buyer is satisfied or dissatisfied with a purchase? The answer lies in the relationship between the *consumer's expectations* and the product's *perceived performance*. If the product falls short of expectations, the consumer is disappointed; if it meets expectations, the consumer is satisfied; if it exceeds expectations, the consumer is delighted.

The larger the gap between expectations and performance, the greater the consumer's dissatisfaction. This suggests that sellers should promise only what their brands can deliver so that buyers are satisfied. Some sellers might even understate product performance levels to boost later consumer satisfaction. For example, Boeing's salespeople tend to be conservative when they estimate the potential benefits of their aircraft. They almost always underestimate fuel efficiency – they promise a 5 per cent savings that turns out to be 8 per cent. Customers are delighted with better than expected performance; they buy again and tell other potential customers that Boeing lives up to its promises.

Almost all major purchases result in **cognitive dissonance**, or discomfort caused by post-purchase conflict. After the purchase, consumers are satisfied with the benefits of the chosen brand and are glad to avoid the drawbacks of the brands not bought. However, every purchase involves compromise. Consumers feel uneasy about acquiring the drawbacks of the chosen brand and about losing the benefits of the brands not purchased. Thus, consumers feel at least some post-purchase dissonance for every purchase.[21]

Why is it so important to satisfy the customer? Customer satisfaction is a key to building profitable relationships with consumers – to keeping and growing consumers and reaping their customer lifetime value. Satisfied customers buy a product again, talk favourably to others about the product, pay less attention to competing brands and advertising, and buy other products from the company. Many marketers go beyond merely *meeting* the expectations of customers – they aim to *delight* the customer. Marketing at Work 5.1 illustrates the buying decision process for both consumer and business buyers of ceramic tiles, and the market research process that one company went through to try to work out how to delight its customers.

MARKETING AT WORK 5.1

The Tile Warehouse: Getting customer-focused

Caroline Tynan, *Professor of Marketing, and* **Sally McKechnie**, *Associate Professor in Marketing, Nottingham University Business School, UK*

The Tile Warehouse is a small family business based in the East Midlands of England, which sells a broad range of ceramic and natural stone floor and wall coverings and ancillary products/services to retail and commercial customers in this region. It was founded in 1980 by John and Marie Lockwood as The Tile Studio, a high street tile boutique, offering a selection of high quality ceramic tiles for the discerning retail customer. At the time the market for ceramic tiles was still in the early stages of growth and UK customer preferences were relatively underdeveloped compared to those in mainland Europe. Nevertheless company sales (by value and volume) were disappointing over the initial years of trading. Demand for ceramic floor and wall coverings was stronger in the commercial sector than the retail sector. Since most of the commercial tiling specialists were based in the South East of England, John and Marie recognised an

opportunity to reinvent and rebrand the business by establishing it as a northern front runner in selling tiles and tile-related products on a wholesale basis. So in 1985, once they had found a suitable out-of-town warehouse site, they closed down the high street boutique and began serving tradesmen (tilers and decorators), professionals (architects and interior designers) as well as retail customers, under the new trading name of The Tile Warehouse.

Clearly John and Marie had made the right move because over the next ten years the business enjoyed growing turnover and healthy profits. However, their good fortune changed in the mid-1990s as competition in the region increased significantly. This period had witnessed not only the rapid growth of DIY multiples in the UK (such as Texas Homecare, Homebase, Do It All and Great Mills) offering building materials and decorative products for homes and gardens to meet a rising level of consumer demand for home improvement products, but also consolidation as multiples repositioned themselves towards particular product groups. Many general DIY multiples offered ceramic tiles as part of their product mix because of the growth opportunity, and consequently the 'DIY sheds' entered the low priced end of the ceramic tiles marketplace. At

the same time specialist wholesalers (that is, category killers such as Topps Tiles) also moved in and began driving prices down even further. Inevitably The Tile Warehouse found itself struggling to compete as an independent specialist against the unprecedentedly low prices offered by the competition.

For the company this was a real blow. John had spent his working life 'in the business of selling tiles' and had always taken a pride in the in-depth specialist product knowledge and expertise of the company's long-serving staff. In the late 1990s the industry was becoming more cut-throat and customer needs were changing. John knew that the future survival of the company could not be taken for granted; they would now have to try to differentiate themselves from the encroaching competition and protect their margins by focusing on selling tiles in the middle to high price range instead. Over the next couple of years the company put the sales staff through various sales and customer service training courses. An immediate result was winning a national award for 'Excellence in Independent Retail' in 2003. Unfortunately this investment in training did not yield the increase in sales they had hoped for. In mid 2004 John and Marie called a family conference with their son Joe, who had carved a successful marketing career in the European film industry over the past ten years, and invited him to take his place in the family business. Joe had already been toying with the idea of taking a career break and agreed to join the business for a two-year period with the remit of bringing in his marketing expertise to develop and implement a marketing strategy for The Tile Warehouse.

When he arrived in 2005 the company had just won the national award for independent retail excellence for the second time. However, Joe knew that this was not the time for the company to become complacent. His first major task was to establish how best to differentiate The Tile Warehouse from Topps Tiles at the low-price end of the market, and from the DIY multiples in the low- to medium-price category. Furthermore, as the company sold ceramic tiles to both the retail and commercial sectors, he knew from experience that it was important to examine information on market trends and buying behaviour.

Clearly a major issue would be to obtain up-to-date and relevant information which he could then best use to differentiate and deliver The Tile Warehouse's offering for both types of customers. Joe's first step was to check with John what market information was available on file. Unlike in his previous workplace where this information was to hand and regularly updated, Joe was dismayed to find that apart from a collection of trade directories and publications from the tiling trade association, trade press clippings and regular internal sales analysis reports, much of the sales and marketing information was in John's head!

Joe proceeded to hire two marketing assistants, Gavin and Lucy, who had just graduated with business degrees from local universities. Gavin was asked to analyse the marketing environment using information gathered from secondary sources, and Lucy was hired to assist Joe with the website design and implementation of direct marketing campaigns. While marketing information was

being gathered and an electronic presence planned, Joe focused on developing a new complementary brand dedicated to serving the specific needs of all professional technical specifiers of ceramic tiles in the commercial sector (such as architects, designers and building consultants) based in the region. Recognising that commercial contracts are normally procured directly from tile manufacturers, John had for some time spotted an opening for the company to build profitable relationships with specifiers of small- to medium-sized contracts. With his parents' approval, Joe launched Prospec UK.

The Tile Warehouse brand continued to appeal to consumers and business buyers. Essentially, when it comes to interior design decisions, consumers have to decide whether to choose, purchase and fit tiles themselves or to use the services of a professional interior designer or a design specialist at a kitchen or bathroom centre. Hence the overlap in the area of interior design services in Figure 5.5.

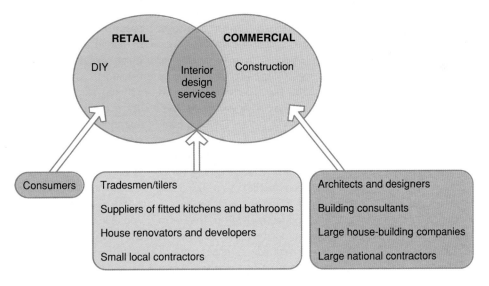

FIGURE 5.5

Ceramic tile market by market sector and customer type

Source: Internal company report.

Gavin's analysis of market trends data from industry reports and internal documents revealed that the UK ceramic tiles market was growing at an average of between 5 and 6 per cent pa and was expected to continue at this rate within the foreseeable future. While the markets for DIY and interior design services were highly fragmented, UK consumer tastes in interior design were becoming more cosmopolitan and influenced by a rise in home improvement-related television programming. As far as the tiling industry was concerned, it was important to recognise that consumer preferences for wall and floor coverings would be affected by changing fashions and an increased interest in DIY projects, making prospects good in the retail sector. Although dominated by multiples, there was still room for the independents. By comparison, in the commercial sector forecasts were somewhat mixed with growth in private and public sector building projects expected to rise, particularly in light of recent central and local government initiatives, but the area of private house-building becoming less buoyant.

Joe still needed to understand more about the buying behaviour for ceramic tiles. Apart from being able to identify the types of consumer households they ought to be targeting for advertising and direct marketing campaigns (mainly wealthy and affluent households in urban and suburban areas), he now had two brands to manage, and a wide variety of business buyers to serve on a limited budget and with a very small team. He commissioned a local market research agency to run some focus groups and in-depth interviews with a sample of consumers, trade/small commercial customers and large commercial customers to examine their perceptions of the company, explore their buying behaviour for ceramic tile-related products and services, and identify how they would prefer the company to communicate with them.

A summary of the main findings of the qualitative study with regard to buying behaviour are provided in Table 5.2.

Overall, the research revealed that purchasing decisions are made individually or jointly for consumer and trade buyers, and jointly for large business buyers. In the examples of joint decision-making described, a number of individuals were identified as participants in the buying decision-making process. Although the composition is not fixed, Joe realised that the company needed to be monitoring more closely who exactly is involved in existing and potential purchases and the roles that participants play in the buying decision.

Normally consumers shopped in couples for tiles and made several trips to outlets before making any purchase. A combination of a low level of product involvement, a high level of perceived risk and disappointment at the lack of interior design advice and expertise amongst showroom staff resulted in advice being sought from a number of sources. Many had never bought ceramic tiles before and wanted to see modern showroom displays. Some wanted to be offered a complete tiling solution that included professional installation of tiles (a 'supply and fit' service). For trade/small commercial buyers buying tiles tended to be a straight rebuy or a modified rebuy situation. They were mainly concerned about the provision of technical advice, price, convenience (location and opening hours) and stock availability. Showroom displays were also important as they helped to visualise what their customers are looking for. Finally, each of the three buying situations applied to the large commercial buyers, many of which attached great importance to compliance with technical standards and the company's green credentials with respect to product sourcing. Technical advice and product range mattered as well.

The Tile Warehouse in its early stages had no formal marketing information system or marketing specialist expertise. Its clear market position, supported by selling and limited advertising and public relations activities, had been sufficient to make the company very successful. However, once customer expectations and the nature of competition began to change in an increasingly tough marketplace, the company had to become more customer-focused if it was going to be able successfully to differentiate itself in both market sectors from its cost-focused competitors.

When trying to introduce a marketing orientation into the company Joe was hampered by the constraints common in small firms such as the limited availability of money, time and marketing awareness. This was made more difficult by having to straddle two sectors, which exhibited different buying behaviours and buying situations, with the same staff and within a single outlet. While acknowledging that getting the family business customer-focused was much harder than expected, without being able to understand the impact of retail and commercial developments on the business, especially buying behaviour for ceramic tiles, Joe would not have been able to make progress in successfully repositioning the company. Without being able to establish the similarities and differences in the buying behaviour of consumer and business buyers of ceramic tiles, the marketing team

TABLE 5.2 Buying behaviour for ceramic tiles by customer type

Customer type	Consumer	Trade/small commercial	Large commercial
Decision-making	Individual Joint	Individual (solo operator) Joint (specialist contractors)	n/a Joint
Buying situation	New buy Modified rebuy	Straight rebuy Modified rebuy New buy	Straight rebuy Modified rebuy New buy
Buying centre members (examples given)	Spouse/partner Friends and family members Interior designer Tradesperson/tiler	Tradesperson/tiler Consumer or builder/contractor Supplier of fitted kitchens/bathrooms Interior designer	Architect/designer Purchasing manager Contract manager Builder/contractor Secretary
Choice criteria	Customer service Interior design advice and expertise Fresh and modern showroom displays Specialist product knowledge Product quality Provision of 'supply and fit' service Provision of samples	Price Location Customer service Technical advice Stock availability Product range Product quality Opening hours Fresh and modern showroom displays Provision of 'supply and fit' service Provision of samples	Product quality – conformity to international technical standards and ethical/greener product sourcing Customer service Technical advice Product range Online catalogue Provision of samples Delivery time

Source: Internal company report.

would not have been able to identify common factors in buying behaviour. As a result, while continuing to deliver excellent customer service, they have built efficiencies in developing different service elements and marketing communications for consumer and business offers, generated new sales leads and improved their approach to customer account management.

Sources: This case study has been produced as part of a Knowledge Transfer Partnership between the Tile Warehouse and Nottingham University Business School. The authors wish to thank Joe Lockwood and Gavin Llewellyn for their assistance with the preparation of the case study and Andrew Darwent for his valuable advice throughout the project partnership. Additional sources: Key Note Report (2005) *The Construction Industry*; Key Note (2006) *DIY and Home Improvements Industry*; Key Note (2006) *Ceramic Tiles and Wallcoverings*; Mintel (2006) *Carpets and Other Floorcoverings – UK*; Internal company documents; company websites: www.thetilewarehouse.com, www.propsectiles.com; The Tile Association website: www.tiles.org.uk.

A dissatisfied consumer responds differently. Bad word-of-mouth often travels farther and faster than good word of mouth. It can quickly damage consumer attitudes about a company and its products. But companies cannot simply rely on dissatisfied customers to volunteer their complaints when they are dissatisfied. Most unhappy customers never tell the company about their problem. Therefore, a company should measure customer satisfaction regularly. It should set up systems that *encourage* customers to complain. In this way, the company can learn how well it is doing and how it can improve.

But what should companies do about dissatisfied customers? At a minimum, most companies offer free telephone numbers and websites to handle complaints and enquiries.

For example, floorcare products company Vax offers extensive consumer advice to Australian consumers at **www.vax.com.au** and to British consumers at **www.vax.co.uk** but is also very conscious that consumers may have individual problems that need the assistance of a customer care adviser:

> At Vax we are dedicated to ensuring that you are happy with your floorcare appliance. Should you be unhappy for any reason, our dedicated helpline can help you. All our advisers are fully trained and will be able to help you solve any problems, quickly and easily. (**www.vax.co.uk/support/careline.php**)

Consumers in the UK can telephone the Vax Careline on 0870 606 1248, while Australian consumers have their own Vaxcare telephone number, 1300 364 040.

By studying the overall buyer decision, marketers may be able to find ways to help consumers move through it. For example, if consumers are not buying a new product because they do not perceive a need for it, marketing might launch advertising messages that trigger the need and show how the product solves consumers' problems. If consumers know about the product but are not buying because they hold unfavourable attitudes toward it, the marketer must find ways either to change the product or change consumer perceptions.

The buyer decision process for new products

We have looked at the stages buyers go through in trying to satisfy a need. Buyers may pass quickly or slowly through these stages, and some of the stages may even be reversed. Much depends on the nature of the buyer, the product and the buying situation.

We now look at how buyers approach the purchase of new products. A **new product** is a good, service or idea that is perceived by some potential customers as new. It may have been around for a while, but our interest is in how consumers learn about products for the first time and make decisions on whether to adopt them. We define the **adoption process** as 'the mental process through which an individual passes from first learning about an innovation to final adoption', and *adoption* as the decision by an individual to become a regular user of the product.[22]

Stages in the adoption process

Consumers go through five stages in the process of adopting a new product:

- *Awareness:* The consumer becomes aware of the new product, but lacks information about it.
- *Interest:* The consumer seeks information about the new product.
- *Evaluation:* The consumer considers whether trying the new product makes sense.
- *Trial:* The consumer tries the new product on a small scale to improve his or her estimate of its value.
- *Adoption:* The consumer decides to make full and regular use of the new product.

This model suggests that the new product marketer should think about how to help consumers move through these stages. A manufacturer of high-definition televisions (HDTVs) may discover that many consumers in the interest stage do not move to the trial stage because of uncertainty and the large investment. If these same consumers were willing to use HDTVs on a trial basis for a small fee, the manufacturer could consider offering a trial-use plan with an option to buy.

Individual differences in innovativeness

People differ greatly in their readiness to try new products. In each product area, there are 'consumption pioneers' and early adopters. Other individuals adopt new products

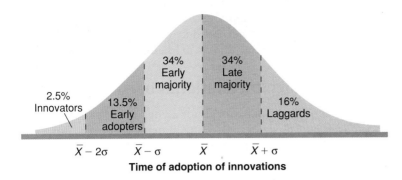

FIGURE 5.6

Adopter categorisation on the basis of relative time of adoption of innovations

Source: Reprinted with the permission of The Free Press, a Division of Simon & Schuster, Inc., from *Diffusion of Innovations*, 5th edn, by Everett M. Rogers. Copyright © 1995, 2003 by Everett M. Rogers. Copyright © 1962, 1971, 1983 by The Free Press. All rights reserved.

much later. People can be classified into the adopter categories shown in Figure 5.6. After a slow start, an increasing number of people adopt the new product. The number of adopters reaches a peak and then drops off as fewer non-adopters remain. Innovators are defined as the first 2.5 per cent of the buyers to adopt a new idea (those beyond two standard deviations from mean adoption time); the early adopters are the next 13.5 per cent (between one and two standard deviations); and so on.

The five adopter groups have differing values. *Innovators* are adventurous – they try new ideas at some risk. *Early adopters* are guided by respect – they are opinion leaders in their communities and adopt new ideas early but carefully. The *early majority* are deliberate – although they are rarely leaders, they adopt new ideas before the average person. The *late majority* are sceptical – they adopt an innovation only after a majority of people have tried it. Finally, *laggards* are tradition bound – they are suspicious of changes and adopt the innovation only when it has become something of a tradition itself.

This adopter classification suggests that an innovating firm should research the characteristics of innovators and early adopters and should direct marketing efforts toward them. In general, innovators tend to be relatively younger, better educated, and higher in income than later adopters and non-adopters. They are more receptive to unfamiliar things, rely more on their own values and judgement, and are more willing to take risks. They are less brand loyal and more likely to take advantage of special promotions such as discounts, coupons and samples.

Influence of product characteristics on rate of adoption

The characteristics of the new product affect its rate of adoption. Some products catch on almost overnight (iPod), whereas others take a long time to gain acceptance (HDTV). Five characteristics are especially important in influencing an innovation's rate of adoption. For example, consider the characteristics of HDTV in relation to the rate of adoption:

- *Relative advantage*: the degree to which the innovation appears superior to existing products. The greater the perceived relative advantage of using HDTV – say, in picture quality and ease of viewing – the sooner HDTVs will be adopted.

- *Compatibility*: the degree to which the innovation fits the values and experiences of potential consumers. HDTV, for example, is highly compatible with the lifestyles found in upper middle-class homes. However, it is not very compatible with the programming and broadcasting systems currently available to consumers.

- *Complexity*: the degree to which the innovation is difficult to understand or use. HDTVs are not very complex and, therefore, once more programming is available and prices come down, will take less time to penetrate European homes than more complex innovations.

- *Divisibility*: the degree to which the innovation may be tried on a limited basis. HDTVs are still very expensive. To the extent that people can lease them with an option to buy, their rate of adoption will increase.

- *Communicability*: the degree to which the results of using the innovation can be observed or described to others. Because HDTV lends itself to demonstration and description, its use will spread faster among consumers.

Other characteristics influence the rate of adoption, such as initial and ongoing costs, risk and uncertainty, and social approval. The new product marketer has to research all these factors when developing the new product and its marketing programme.

Consumer behaviour across international borders

Understanding consumer behaviour is difficult enough for companies marketing within the borders of a single country. For companies operating in many countries, however, understanding and serving the needs of consumers can be daunting. Although consumers in different countries may have some things in common, their values, attitudes and behaviours often vary greatly. International marketers must understand such differences and adjust their products and marketing programmes accordingly.

Sometimes the differences are obvious. For example, in the United Kingdom, where most people eat cereal regularly for breakfast, Kellogg's focuses its marketing on persuading consumers to select a Kellogg's brand rather than a competitor's brand. In France, however, where most people prefer croissants and coffee or no breakfast at all, Kellogg's advertising simply attempts to convince people that they should eat cereal for breakfast. Its packaging includes step-by-step instructions on how to prepare cereal. In India, where many consumers eat heavy, fried breakfasts and many consumers skip the meal altogether, Kellogg's advertising attempts to convince buyers to switch to a lighter, more nutritious breakfast diet.

Often, differences across international markets are more subtle. They may result from physical differences in consumers and their environments. For example, Remington makes smaller electric shavers to fit the smaller hands of Japanese consumers. Other differences result from varying customs. In Japan, for example, where humility and deference are considered great virtues, pushy, hard-hitting sales approaches are considered offensive. Failing to understand such differences in customs and behaviours from one country to another can spell disaster for a marketer's international products and programmes.

Marketers must decide on the degree to which they will adapt their products and marketing programmes to meet the unique cultures and needs of consumers in various markets. On the one hand, they want to standardise their offerings in order to simplify operations and take advantage of cost economies. On the other hand, adapting marketing efforts within each country results in products and programmes that better satisfy the needs of local consumers. The question of whether to adapt or standardise the marketing mix across international markets has created a lively debate in recent years.

MAKING CONNECTIONS Linking the concepts

Here's a good place to take some time out and apply the concepts you've examined in the first part of this chapter.

■ Think about a specific major purchase you've made recently. What buying process did you follow? What major factors influenced your decision?

■ Pick a company that we've discussed in a previous chapter – Setanta, Arla, Boots or another. How does the company you chose use its understanding of customers and their buying behaviour to build better customer relationships?

■ Think about a company like Intel, which sells its products to computer makers and other businesses rather than to final consumers. How would Intel's marketing to business customers differ from Starbucks's marketing to final consumers? The second part of the chapter deals with this issue.

BUSINESS MARKETS AND BUSINESS BUYER BEHAVIOUR

In one way or another, most large companies sell to other organisations. Companies such as Boeing, IBM, Caterpillar, Corus and countless other firms sell *most* of their products to other businesses. Even large consumer products companies, which make products used by final consumers, must first sell their products to other businesses. For example, Procter & Gamble makes many familiar consumer brands – personal care products like Dove, Lux, Sunsilk and Signal, home care products such as Cif, Comfort, Domestos and Surf, food products like Bertolli, Knorr, Slim-Fast and Hellman's, and others. But to sell these products to consumers, Procter & Gamble must first sell them to the wholesalers and retailers that serve the consumer market.

Business buyer behaviour refers to the buying behaviour of the organisations that buy goods and services for use in the production of other products and services that are sold, rented, or supplied to others. It also includes the behaviour of retailing and wholesaling firms that acquire goods to resell or rent them to others at a profit. In the *business buying process*, business buyers determine which products and services their organisations need to purchase, and then find, evaluate and choose among alternative suppliers and brands. *Business-to-business (B-to-B) marketers* must do their best to understand business markets and business buyer behaviour.

Business markets

The business market is *huge*. In fact, business markets involve far more money and goods than do consumer markets. For example, think about the large number of business transactions involved in the production and sale of a single set of Pirelli tyres. Various suppliers sell Pirelli the rubber, steel, equipment and other goods that it needs to produce the tyres. Pirelli then sells the finished tyres to retailers, who in turn sell them to consumers. Thus, many sets of *business* purchases were made for only one set of *consumer* purchases. In addition, Pirelli sells tyres as original equipment to manufacturers who install them on new vehicles, and as replacement tyres to companies that maintain their own fleets of company cars, trucks, buses or other vehicles.

Characteristics of business markets

In some ways, business markets are similar to consumer markets. Both involve people who assume buying roles and make purchase decisions to satisfy needs. However, business markets differ in many ways from consumer markets. The main differences are in *market structure and demand*, the *nature of the buying unit*, and the *types of decisions and the decision process* involved.

Market structure and demand

The business marketer normally deals with *far fewer but far larger buyers* than the consumer marketer does. Even in large business markets, a few buyers often account for most of the purchasing. For example, when Pirelli sells replacement tyres to final consumers, its potential market includes the owners of the millions of cars currently in use in the European Union and around the world. But Pirelli's fate in the business market depends on getting orders from one of only a handful of large car makers. Similarly, Black & Decker sells its power tools and outdoor equipment to tens of millions of consumers worldwide. However, it must sell these products through DIY retail outlets – such as B&Q and Homebase in the UK and Ireland, Brico in Italy, and Bauhaus in Germany – which provide its key routes to the market.

Business markets are also *more geographically concentrated*. Further, business demand is **derived demand** – it derives ultimately from the demand for consumer goods. Hewlett-Packard and Dell buy Intel microprocessor chips because consumers buy personal computers. If consumer demand for PCs drops, so will the demand for computer chips.

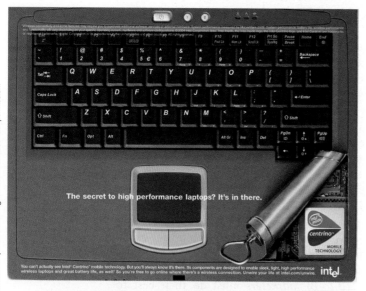

Derived demand: Intel's long-running 'Intel Inside' advertising campaign boosts demand for Intel chips and for the computers containing them.

Therefore, B-to-B marketers sometimes promote their products directly to final consumers to increase business demand. For example, Intel's long-running 'Intel Inside' advertising campaign sells personal computers to buyers on the virtues of Intel microprocessors. The increased demand for Intel chips boosts demand for the PCs containing them, and both Intel and its business partners win.

Similarly, W.L. Gore promotes Gore-Tex® directly to final consumers as a key branded ingredient in waterproof and breathable outdoor clothing – from mountaineering or sailing jackets through to winter ice-climbing boots. You see Gore-Tex® hangtags on clothing lines such as Scarpa mountaineering boots, Henri-Lloyd sailing foul-weather gear, and The North Face walking and mountaineering jackets. By making Gore-Tex® familiar and attractive to final buyers, W.L. Gore also makes the products containing it more attractive.

Nature of the buying unit

Compared with consumer purchases, a business purchase usually involves *more decision participants* and a *more professional purchasing effort*. Often, business buying is done by trained purchasing agents who spend their working lives learning how to buy better. The more complex the purchase, the more likely it is that several people will participate in the decision-making process. Buying committees made up of technical experts and top management are common in the buying of major goods.

Beyond this, many companies are now upgrading their purchasing functions to 'supply management' or 'supplier development' functions. B-to-B marketers now face a new breed of higher-level, better-trained supply managers. These supply managers sometimes seem to know more about the supplier company than it knows about itself. Therefore, business marketers must have well-trained marketers and salespeople to deal with these well-trained buyers.

Types of decisions and the decision process

Business buyers usually face *more complex* buying decisions than do consumer buyers. Purchases often involve large sums of money, complex technical and economic considerations, and interactions among many people at many levels of the buyer's organisation. Because the purchases are more complex, business buyers may take longer to make their decisions. The business buying process also tends to be *more formalised* than the consumer buying process. Large business purchases usually call for detailed product specifications, written purchase orders, careful supplier searches and formal approval.

Finally, in the business buying process, buyer and seller are often much *more dependent* on each other. Consumer marketers are often at a distance from their customers. In contrast, B-to-B marketers may roll up their sleeves and work closely with their customers during all stages of the buying process – from helping customers define problems, to finding solutions, to supporting after-sale operation. They often customise their offerings to individual customer needs.

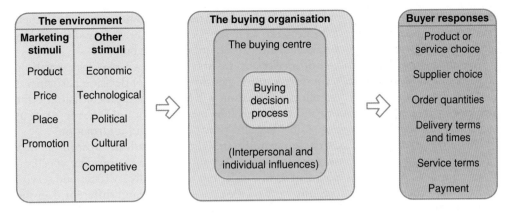

FIGURE 5.7

A model of business buyer behaviour

Business buyer behaviour

At the most basic level, marketers want to know how business buyers will respond to various marketing stimuli. Figure 5.7 shows a model of business buyer behaviour. In this model, marketing and other stimuli affect the buying organisation and produce certain buyer responses. As with consumer buying, the marketing stimuli for business buying consist of the Four Ps: product, price, place and promotion (plus people, physical evidence and service delivery process for service products). Other stimuli include major forces in the environment: economic, technological, political, cultural and competitive. These stimuli enter the organisation and are turned into buyer responses: product or service choice; supplier choice; order quantities; and delivery, service and payment terms. In order to design good marketing mix strategies, the marketer must understand what happens within the organisation to turn stimuli into purchase responses.

Within the organisation, buying activity consists of two major parts: the buying centre, made up of all the people involved in the buying decision, and the buying-decision process. The model shows that the buying centre and the buying decision process are influenced by internal organisational, interpersonal and individual factors as well as by external environmental factors.

The model in Figure 5.7 suggests four questions about business buyer behaviour. What buying decisions do business buyers make? Who participates in the buying process? What are the major influences on buyers? How do business buyers make their buying decisions?

Major types of buying situations

There are three major types of buying situations.[23] At one extreme is the *straight rebuy*, which is a fairly routine decision. At the other extreme is the *new task*, which may call for thorough research. In the middle is the *modified rebuy*, which requires some research.

In a **straight rebuy**, the buyer reorders something without any modifications. It is usually handled on a routine basis by the purchasing department. Based on past buying satisfaction, the buyer simply chooses from the various suppliers on its list. 'In' suppliers try to maintain product and service quality. They often propose automatic reordering systems so that the purchasing agent will save reordering time. 'Out' suppliers try to offer something new or exploit dissatisfaction so that the buyer will consider them.

In a **modified rebuy**, the buyer wants to modify product specifications, prices, terms or suppliers. The modified rebuy usually involves more decision participants than does the straight rebuy. The in suppliers may become nervous and feel pressured to put their best foot forward to protect an account. Out suppliers may see the modified rebuy situation as an opportunity to make a better offer and gain new business.

A company buying a product or service for the first time faces a **new task** situation. In such cases, the greater the cost or risk, the larger the number of decision participants and the greater their efforts to collect information will be. The new task situation is the marketer's greatest opportunity and challenge. The marketer not only tries to reach as many key buying influences as possible but also provides help and information.

The buyer makes the fewest decisions in the straight rebuy and the most in the new task decision. In the new task situation, the buyer must decide on product specifications, suppliers, price limits, payment terms, order quantities, delivery times and service terms. The order of these decisions varies with each situation, and different decision participants influence each choice.

Many business buyers prefer to buy a packaged solution to a problem from a single seller. Instead of buying and putting all the components together, the buyer may ask sellers to supply the components *and* assemble the package or system. The sale often goes to the firm that provides the most complete system meeting the customer's needs. Thus, **systems selling** is often a key business marketing strategy for winning and holding accounts. For example, Veolia Environnement provides a complete solution for its customers' industrial waste problems:

> Veolia Environnement is a 25 billion euro turnover company that few consumers will ever have heard of. Yet it operates all round the world, generating 48 per cent of its revenue from France, 33 per cent from elsewhere in Europe, 10 per cent from the Americas, and 9 per cent from the rest of the world. Veolia Environnement has subsidiaries in 27 European countries, from France and Portugal in the west to Russia in the east. Industrial waste management is one of Veolia's key business areas. The company can simply arrange to collect and dispose of waste products on behalf of manufacturing, commercial and public sector organisations, but promotes its 'integrated solutions and total waste management' to businesses that want their waste systems professionally managed from start to finish. For example, Veolia offers a complete range of integrated industrial site waste management services, including high pressure water jetting, tank and vessel cleaning, emergency response, chemical cleaning, on-site processing, chemical decontamination and land decontamination. Many municipal authorities across Europe also use Veolia's integrated waste management solutions to deliver their statutory obligation to provide waste and recycling services to local communities.[24]

Participants in the business buying process

Who does the buying of the trillions of euros' worth of goods and services needed by business organisations? The decision-making unit of a buying organisation is called its **buying centre**: all the individuals and units that participate in the business decision-making process. The buying centre includes all members of the organisation who play a role in the purchase decision process. This group includes the actual users of the product or service, those who make the buying decision, those who influence the buying decision, those who do the actual buying, and those who control buying information.

The buying centre is not a fixed and formally identified unit within the buying organisation. It is a set of buying roles assumed by different people for different purchases. Within the organisation, the size and make-up of the buying centre will vary for different products and for different buying situations. For some routine purchases, one person – say a buyer – may assume all the buying centre roles and serve as the only person involved in the buying decision. For more complex purchases, the buying centre may include 20 or 30 people from different levels and departments in the organisation.

The buying centre concept presents a major marketing challenge. The business marketer must learn who participates in the decision, each participant's relative influence, and what evaluation criteria each decision participant uses. For example, the Malaysian company San Miguel Woven Products sells disposable surgical gowns to hospitals. It identifies the hospital personnel involved in this buying decision as the purchasing manager, the operating room administrator and the surgeons. Each participant plays a different role. The purchasing manager analyses whether the hospital should buy disposable gowns or reusable gowns. If analysis favours disposable gowns, then the operating room administrator compares competing products and prices and makes a choice. This administrator considers the gown's absorbency, antiseptic quality, design and cost, and normally buys the brand that meets requirements at the lowest cost. Finally, surgeons affect the decision later by reporting their satisfaction or dissatisfaction with the brand.

The buying centre usually includes some obvious participants who are involved formally in the buying decision. For example, the decision to buy a corporate jet will probably involve the company's CEO, chief pilot, a purchasing agent, some legal staff, a member of top management and others formally charged with the buying decision. It may also involve less obvious, informal participants, some of whom may actually make or strongly affect the buying decision. Sometimes, even the people in the buying centre are not aware of all the buying participants. For example, the decision about which corporate jet to buy may actually be made by a corporate board member who has an interest in flying and who knows a lot about aircraft. This board member may work behind the scenes to sway the decision. Many business buying decisions result from the complex interactions of ever-changing buying centre participants.

Major influences on business buyers

Business buyers are subject to many influences when they make their buying decisions. Some marketers assume that the major influences are economic. They think buyers will favour the supplier who offers the lowest price or the best product or the most service. They concentrate on offering strong economic benefits to buyers. However, business buyers respond to both economic and personal factors. Far from being cold, calculating and impersonal, business buyers are human and social as well. They react to both reason and emotion.

Today, most business-to-business marketers recognise that emotion plays an important role in business buying decisions. For example, you might expect that an advertisement promoting large trucks to corporate fleet buyers would stress objective technical, performance and economic factors. However, a recent ad for Volvo heavy-duty trucks shows two drivers arm-wrestling and claims, 'It solves all your fleet problems. Except who gets to drive.' It turns out that, in the face of an industry-wide driver shortage, the type of truck a fleet provides can help it to attract qualified drivers. The Volvo ad stresses the raw beauty of the truck and its comfort and roominess, features that make it more appealing to drivers. The ad concludes that Volvo trucks are 'built to make fleets more profitable and drivers a lot more possessive'.

Figure 5.8 lists various groups of influences on business buyers – environmental, organisational, interpersonal and individual. *Environmental factors* play a major role. For example, buyer behaviour can be heavily influenced by factors in the current and expected economic environment, such as the level of primary demand, the economic outlook and the cost of money. Another environmental factor is shortages in key materials. Many companies now are more willing to buy and hold larger inventories of scarce materials to ensure adequate supply. Business buyers are also affected by technological, political and competitive developments in the environment. Finally, culture and customs can strongly influence business buyer reactions to the marketer's behaviour and strategies, especially in the international marketing environment (see Marketing at Work 5.2).

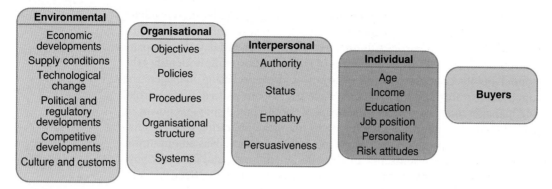

FIGURE 5.8

Major influences on business buyer behaviour

International marketing manners: When in Rome, do as the Romans do

Picture this: The imaginary American firm Consolidated Amalgamation, Inc. thinks it's time that the rest of the world enjoyed the same fine products it has offered American consumers for two generations. It dispatches Vice President Harry E. Slicksmile to Europe, Africa and Asia to explore the territory. Mr Slicksmile stops first in London, where he makes short work of some bankers – he rings them up on the phone. He handles Parisians with similar ease. After securing a table at La Tour d'Argent, he greets his luncheon guest, the director of an industrial engineering firm, with the words, 'Just call me Harry, Jacques'.

In Germany, Mr Slicksmile is a powerhouse. Whisking through a lavish, state-of-the-art marketing presentation, complete with flip charts and audiovisuals, he shows 'em that this all-American boy *knows* how to make a buck. Heading on to Milan, Harry strikes up a conversation with the Japanese businessman

sitting next to him on the plane. He flips his card onto the guy's tray and, when the two say goodbye, shakes hands warmly and clasps the man's right arm. Later, for his appointment with the owner of an Italian packaging design firm, our hero wears his comfy corduroy sports coat, khaki trousers, and favourite casual shoes. Everybody knows Italians are zany and laid back.

Mr Slicksmile next swings through Saudi Arabia, where he coolly presents a potential client with a multimillion-dollar proposal in a classy pigskin binder. His final stop is Beijing, China, where he talks business over lunch with a group of Chinese executives. After completing the meal, he drops his chopsticks into his bowl of rice and presents each guest with an elegant Tiffany clock as a reminder of his visit.

A great tour, sure to generate a pile of orders, right? Wrong. Six months later, Consolidated Amalgamation has nothing to show for the trip but a stack of bills. Abroad, they weren't wild about Harry.

This hypothetical case has been exaggerated for emphasis. Americans are seldom such dolts. But experts say success in international

business has a lot to do with knowing the territory and its people.

Poor Harry tried all right, but in all the wrong ways. The British do not, as a rule, make deals over the phone as much as Americans do. It's not so much a 'cultural' difference as a difference in approach. A proper Frenchman neither likes instant familiarity – questions about family, church, or alma mater – nor refers to strangers by their first names. 'That poor fellow, Jacques, probably wouldn't show anything, but he'd recoil. He'd *not* be pleased,' explains an expert on French business practices. 'It's considered poor taste,' he continues. 'Even after months of business dealings, I'd wait for him or her to make the invitation [to use first names] . . . You are always right, in Europe, to say "Mister".'

Harry's flashy presentation would likely have been a flop with the Germans, who dislike overstatement and showiness. According to one German expert, however, German businessmen have become accustomed to dealing with Americans. Although differences in body language and customs remain, the past 20 years have softened them. 'I hugged an American woman at a business meeting last night,' he said. 'That would be normal in France, but [older] Germans still have difficulty [with the custom].' He says that calling secretaries by their first names would still be considered rude: 'They have a right to be called by the surname. You'd certainly ask – and get – permission first.' In Germany, people address each other formally and correctly – someone with two doctorates (which is fairly common) must be referred to as 'Herr Doktor Doktor'.

When Harry Slicksmile grabbed his new Japanese acquaintance by the arm, the executive probably considered him disrespectful and presumptuous. Japan, like many Asian countries, is a 'no-contact culture' in which even shaking hands is a strange experience. Harry made matters worse by tossing his business card. Japanese people revere the business card as an extension of self and as an indicator of rank. They do not *hand* it to people, they *present* it – with both hands. In addition, the Japanese are sticklers about rank. Unlike Americans, they don't heap praise on subordinates in a room; they will praise only the highest-ranking official present.

Hapless Harry also goofed when he assumed that Italians are like Hollywood's stereotypes of them. The flair for design and style that has characterised Italian culture for

centuries is embodied in the businesspeople of Milan and Rome. They dress beautifully and admire flair, but they dislike garishness or impropriety in others' attire.

To the Saudi Arabians, the pigskin binder would have been considered vile. An American salesman who really did present such a binder was unceremoniously tossed out and his company was blacklisted from working with Saudi businesses. In China, Harry casually dropping his chopsticks could have been misinterpreted as an act of aggression. Stabbing chopsticks into a bowl of rice and leaving them signifies death to the Chinese. The clocks Harry offered as gifts might have confirmed such dark intentions. To 'give a clock' in Chinese sounds the same as 'seeing someone off to his end'.

Thus, to compete successfully in global markets, or even to deal effectively with international firms in their home markets, companies must help their managers to understand the needs, customs and cultures of international business buyers. 'When doing business in a foreign country and a foreign culture – particularly a non-Western culture – assume nothing,' advises an international business specialist. 'Take nothing for granted. Turn every stone. Ask every question. Dig into every detail. Because cultures really

Companies must help their managers understand international customers and customs. For example, Japanese people revere the business card as an extension of self; they do not hand it out but present it.
Source: BLOOMimage/Getty Images.

are different, and those differences can have a major impact.' So the old advice is still good advice: when in Rome, do as the Romans do.

Sources: Portions adapted from Susan Harte, 'When in Rome, You Should Learn to Do What the Romans Do', *The Atlanta Journal-Constitution*, 22 January 1990, pp. D1, D6. Additional examples can be found in David A. Ricks, *Blunders in International Business Around the World* (Malden, MA: Blackwell Publishing, 2000); Terri Morrison, Wayne A. Conway and Joseph J. Douress, *Dun & Bradstreet's Guide to Doing Business* (Upper Saddle River, NJ: Prentice Hall, 2000); James K. Sebenius, 'The Hidden Challenge of Cross-Border Negotiatons', *Harvard Business Review*, March 2002, pp. 76–85; Ross Thompson, 'Lost in Translation', *Medical Marketing and Media*, March 2005, p. 82; and information accessed at www. executiveplanet.com, December 2005.

Business buyer behaviour is also influenced strongly by *organisational factors*. Each buying organisation has its own objectives, policies, procedures, structure and systems, and the business marketer must understand these factors well. Questions such as these arise: How many people are involved in the buying decision? Who are they? What are their evaluative criteria? What are the company's policies and limits on its buyers?

The buying centre usually includes many participants who influence each other, so *interpersonal factors* also influence the business buying process. However, it is often difficult to assess such interpersonal factors and group dynamics. Buying centre participants do not wear tags that label them as 'key decision maker' or 'not influential'. Nor do buying centre participants with the highest rank always have the most influence. Participants may influence the buying decision because they control rewards and punishments, are well liked, have special expertise, or have a special relationship with other important participants. Interpersonal factors are often very subtle. Whenever possible, business marketers must try to understand these factors and design strategies that take them into account.

Finally, business buyers are influenced by *individual factors*. Each participant in the business buying decision process brings in personal motives, perceptions and preferences. These individual factors are affected by personal characteristics such as age, income, education, professional identification, personality and attitudes toward risk. Also, buyers have different buying styles. Some may be technical types who make in-depth analyses of competitive proposals before choosing a supplier. Other buyers may be intuitive negotiators who are adept at pitting the sellers against one another for the best deal.

The business buying process

Figure 5.9 lists the eight stages of the business buying process.[25] Buyers who face a new task buying situation usually go through all stages of the buying process. Buyers making modified or straight rebuys may skip some of the stages. We will examine these steps for the typical new task buying situation.

Problem recognition The buying process begins when someone in the company recognises a problem or need that can be met by acquiring a specific product or service. *Problem recognition* can result from internal or external stimuli. Internally, the company may decide to launch a new product that requires new production equipment and materials. Or a machine may break down and need new parts. Perhaps a purchasing manager is unhappy with a current supplier's product quality, service or prices. Externally, the buyer may get some new ideas at a trade show, see an ad, or receive a call from a salesperson who offers a better product or a lower price. In fact, in their advertising, business marketers often alert customers to potential problems and then show how their products provide solutions.

General need description Having recognised a need, the buyer next prepares a general *need description* that describes the characteristics and quantity of the needed item. For standard items, this process presents few problems. For complex items, however, the buyer may have to work with others – engineers, users, consultants – to define the item. The team may want to rank the importance of reliability, durability, price and other attributes desired in the item. In this phase, the alert business marketer can help the buyers define their needs and provide information about the value of different product characteristics.

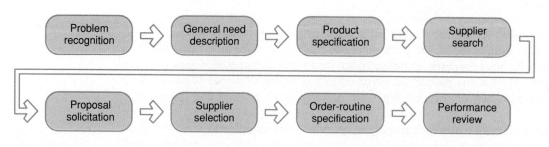

FIGURE 5.9

Stages of the business buying process

Product specification The buying organisation next develops the item's technical product specifications, often with the help of a value analysis engineering team. **Value analysis** is an approach to cost reduction in which components are studied carefully to determine if they can be redesigned, standardised, or made by less costly methods of production. The team decides on the best product characteristics and specifies them accordingly. Sellers, too, can use value analysis as a tool to help secure a new account. By showing buyers a better way to make an object, outside sellers can turn straight rebuy situations into new task situations that give them a chance to obtain new business.

Supplier search The buyer now conducts a *supplier search* to find the best vendors. The buyer can compile a small list of qualified suppliers by reviewing trade directories, doing a computer search, or phoning other companies for recommendations. Today, more and more companies are turning to the Internet to find suppliers. For marketers, this has levelled the playing field – the Internet gives smaller suppliers many of the same advantages as larger competitors.

The newer the buying task, and the more complex and costly the item, the greater the amount of time the buyer will spend searching for suppliers. The supplier's task is to get listed in major directories and build a good reputation in the marketplace. Salespeople should watch for companies in the process of searching for suppliers and make certain that their firm is considered.

Proposal solicitation In the *proposal solicitation* stage of the business buying process, the buyer invites qualified suppliers to submit proposals. In response, some suppliers will send only a catalogue or a salesperson. However, when the item is complex or expensive, the buyer will usually require detailed written proposals or formal presentations from each potential supplier.

Business marketers must be skilled in researching, writing and presenting proposals in response to buyer proposal solicitations. Proposals should be marketing documents, not just technical documents. Presentations should inspire confidence and should make the marketer's company stand out from the competition.

Supplier selection The members of the buying centre now review the proposals and select a supplier or suppliers. During *supplier selection*, the buying centre often will draw up a list of the desired supplier attributes and their relative importance. In one survey, purchasing executives listed the following attributes as most important in influencing the relationship between supplier and customer: quality products and services, on-time delivery, ethical corporate behaviour, honest communication and competitive prices. Other important factors include repair and servicing capabilities, technical aid and advice, geographic location, performance history and reputation. The members of the buying centre will rate suppliers against these attributes and identify the best suppliers.

Buyers may attempt to negotiate with preferred suppliers for better prices and terms before making the final selections. In the end, they may select a single supplier or a few suppliers. Many buyers prefer multiple sources of supplies to avoid being totally dependent on one supplier and to allow comparisons of prices and performance of several suppliers over time. Today's supplier development managers want to develop a full network of supplier partners that can help the company bring more value to its customers.

Order-routine specification The buyer now prepares an *order-routine specification*. It includes the final order with the chosen supplier or suppliers and lists items such as technical specifications, quantity needed, expected time of delivery, return policies and warranties. In the case of maintenance, repair and operating items, buyers may use blanket contracts rather than periodic purchase orders. A blanket contract creates a long-term relationship in which the supplier promises to resupply the buyer as needed at agreed prices for a set time period.

Many large buyers now practice *vendor-managed inventory*, in which they turn over ordering and inventory responsibilities to their suppliers. Under such systems, buyers share sales and inventory information directly with key suppliers. The suppliers then monitor inventories and replenish stock automatically as needed.

Performance review In this stage, the buyer reviews supplier performance. The buyer may contact users and ask them to rate their satisfaction. The *performance review* may lead the buyer to continue, modify or drop the arrangement. The seller's job is to monitor the same factors used by the buyer to make sure that the seller is giving the expected satisfaction.

The eight-stage buying process model provides a simple view of business buying as it might occur in a new task buying situation. The actual process is usually much more complex. In the modified rebuy or straight rebuy situation, some of these stages would be compressed or bypassed. Each organisation buys in its own way, and each buying situation has unique requirements.

Different buying centre participants may be involved at different stages of the process. Although certain buying process steps usually do occur, buyers do not always follow them in the same order, and they may add other steps. Often, buyers will repeat certain stages of the process. Finally, a customer relationship might involve many different types of purchases ongoing at a given time, all in different stages of the buying process. The seller must manage the total customer relationship, not just individual purchases.

E-procurement: buying electronically and on the Internet

During the past few years, advances in information technology have changed the face of the business-to-business marketing process. Electronic and online purchasing, often called *e-procurement*, has grown rapidly.

Companies can do e-procurement in any of several ways. They can set up their own *company buying sites*. For example, General Electric operates a company trading site on which it posts its buying needs and invites bids, negotiates terms and places orders. Or the company can create extranet links with key suppliers. For instance, they can create direct procurement accounts with suppliers like Dell or Staples through which company buyers can purchase equipment, materials, and supplies.

B-to-B marketers can help customers who wish to purchase online by creating well designed, easy-to-use websites. For example, *BtoB* magazine regularly rates Hewlett-Packard's B-to-B website among very best.

> The HP site consists of some 1,900 site areas and 2.5 million pages. It integrates an enormous amount of product and company information, putting it within only a few mouse clicks of customers' computers. IT buying-decision makers can enter the site, click directly into their customer segment – large enterprise business; small or medium business; or government, health, or educational institution – and quickly find product overviews, detailed technical information, and purchasing solutions. The site lets customers create customized catalogs for frequently purchased products, set up automatic approval routing for orders, and conduct end-to-end transaction processing. To build deeper, more personalized online relationships with customers, HP.com features flash demos that show how to use the site, e-newsletters, live chats with sales reps, online classes, and real-time customer support. The site has really paid off. Roughly 55 per cent of the company's total sales now come from the website.[26]

E-procurement gives buyers access to new suppliers, lowers purchasing costs, and hastens order processing and delivery. In turn, business marketers can connect with customers online to share marketing information, sell products and services, provide customer support services and maintain ongoing customer relationships.

So far, most of the products bought online are MRO materials – maintenance, repair and operations. For instance, the London Borough of Barnet purchases everything from chickens to lightbulbs over the Internet. National Semiconductor has automated almost all of the company's 3,500 monthly requisitions to buy materials ranging from the sterile booties worn in its fabrication plants to state-of-the-art software. General Electric, one of the world's biggest purchasers, plans to be buying *all* of its general operating and industrial supplies online within the next few years.

The actual amount of money spent on these types of MRO materials pales in comparison with the amount spent for items such as aircraft parts, computer systems and steel tubing. Yet, MRO materials make up 80 per cent of all business orders and the transaction costs for order processing are high. Thus, companies have much to gain by streamlining the MRO buying process on the Web.

Business-to-business e-procurement yields many benefits. First, it shaves transaction costs and results in more efficient purchasing for both buyers and suppliers. A Web-powered purchasing program eliminates the paperwork associated with traditional requisition and ordering procedures. One recent study found that e-procurement cuts down requisition-to-order costs by an average of 58 per cent.[27]

E-procurement reduces the time between order and delivery. Time savings are particularly dramatic for companies with many overseas suppliers. Adaptec, a leading supplier of computer storage, used an extranet to tie all of its Taiwanese chip suppliers together in a kind of virtual family. Now messages from Adaptec flow in seconds from its headquarters to its Asian partners, and Adaptec has reduced the time between the order and delivery of its chips from as long as 16 weeks to just 55 days – the same turnaround time for companies that build their own chips.

Finally, beyond the cost and time savings, e-procurement frees purchasing people to focus on more strategic issues. For many purchasing professionals, going online means reducing drudgery and paperwork, and spending more time managing inventory and working creatively with suppliers. 'That is the key,' says the H-P executive. 'You can now focus people on value-added activities. Procurement professionals can now find different sources and work with suppliers to reduce costs and to develop new products.'[28]

The rapidly expanding use of e-purchasing, however, also presents some problems. For example, at the same time as the Web makes it possible for suppliers and customers to share business data and even collaborate on product design, it can also erode decades-old customer–supplier relationships. Many firms are using the Web to search for better suppliers.

E-purchasing can also create potential security disasters. Although email and home banking transactions can be protected through basic encryption, the secure environment that businesses need to carry out confidential interactions is often still lacking. Companies are spending millions for research on defensive strategies to keep hackers at bay. Cisco Systems, for example, specifies the types of routers, firewalls and security procedures that its partners must use to safeguard extranet connections. In fact, the company goes even further – it sends its own security engineers to examine a partner's defences and holds the partner liable for any security breach that originates from its computer.

THE JOURNEY YOU'VE TAKEN Reviewing the concepts

This chapter is the last of three chapters that address understanding the marketplace and consumers. Here, we've looked closely at consumers and their buying behaviour. The European Union consumer market consists of around 500 million people who consume many trillions of euros' worth of goods and services each year. The business market involves far more euros and items than the consumer market. Final consumers and business buyers vary greatly in their characteristics and circumstances. Understanding *consumer* and *business buyer behaviour* is one of the biggest challenges marketers face.

1 Describe the consumer market and the major factors that influence consumer buyer behaviour.

The *consumer market* consists of all the individuals and households who buy or acquire goods and services for personal consumption. A simple stimulus-response model of consumer behaviour suggests that marketing stimuli and other major forces enter the consumer's 'black box'. This black box has two parts: buyer characteristics and the buyer's decision process. Once in the black box, the inputs result in observable buyer responses, such as product choice, brand choice, dealer choice, purchase timing and purchase amount.

Consumer buyer behaviour is influenced by four key sets of buyer characteristics: cultural, social, personal and psychological. Understanding these factors can help marketers to identify interested buyers and to shape products and appeals to serve consumer needs better. *Culture* is the most basic determinant of a person's wants and behaviour. People in different cultural, subcultural and social class groups have different product and brand preferences. *Social factors* – such as small group and family influences – strongly affect product and brand choices, as do *personal characteristics*, such as age, life-cycle stage, occupation, economic circumstances, lifestyle and personality. Finally, consumer buying behaviour is influenced by four major sets of *psychological factors* – motivation, perception, learning, and beliefs and attitudes. Each of these factors provides a different perspective for understanding the workings of the buyer's black box.

2 Identify and discuss the stages in the buyer decision process.

When making a purchase, the buyer goes through a decision process consisting of need recognition, information search, evaluation of alternatives, purchase decision and post-purchase behaviour. During *need recognition*, the consumer recognises a problem or need that could be satisfied by a product or service. Once the need is recognised, the consumer moves into the *information search* stage. With information in hand, the consumer proceeds to *alternative evaluation* and assesses brands in the choice set. From there, the consumer makes a *purchase decision* and actually buys the product. In the final stage of the buyer decision process, *post-purchase behaviour*, the consumer takes action based on satisfaction or dissatisfaction. The marketer's job is to understand the buyer's behaviour at each stage and the influences that are operating.

3 Describe the adoption and diffusion process for new products.

The product *adoption process* comprises five stages: awareness, interest, evaluation, trial and adoption. New product marketers must think about how to help consumers move through these stages. With regard to the *diffusion process* for new products, consumers respond at different rates, depending on consumer and product characteristics. Consumers may be innovators, early adopters, early majority, late majority or laggards. Each group may require different marketing approaches. Marketers often try to bring their new products to the attention of potential early adopters, especially those who are opinion leaders.

4 Define the business market and identify the major factors that influence business buyer behaviour.

The *business market* comprises all organisations that buy goods and services for use in the production of other products and services or for the purpose of reselling or renting them to others at a profit. As compared to consumer markets, business markets usually have fewer, larger buyers who are more geographically concentrated. Business demand is derived demand, and the business buying decision usually involves more, and more professional, buyers.

Business buyers make decisions that vary with the three types of *buying situations*: straight rebuys, modified rebuys and new tasks. The decision-making unit of a buying organisation – the *buying centre* – can consist of many different persons playing many different roles. The business marketer needs to know the following: Who are the major buying centre participants? In what decisions do they exercise influence and to what degree? What evaluation criteria does each decision participant use? The business marketer also needs to understand the major environmental, organisational, interpersonal and individual influences on the buying process.

5   **List and define the steps in the business buying decision process.**

The *business buying decision process* itself can be quite involved, with eight basic stages: problem recognition, general need description, product specification, supplier search, proposal solicitation, supplier selection, order-routine specification and performance review. Buyers who face a new task buying situation usually go through all stages of the buying process. Buyers making modified or straight rebuys may skip some of the stages. Companies must manage the overall customer relationship, which often includes many different buying decisions in various stages of the buying decision process.

Recent advances in information technology have given birth to 'e-purchasing', by which business buyers are purchasing all kinds of products and services electronically, either through electronic data interchange links (EDI) or on the Internet. Such cyberbuying gives buyers access to new suppliers, lowers purchasing costs, and hastens order processing and delivery. However, it can also erode customer–supplier relationships and create potential security problems. Still, business marketers are increasingly connecting with customers online to share marketing information, sell products and services provide customer support services and maintain ongoing customer relationships.

NAVIGATING THE KEY TERMS

Adoption process 168
Business buyer behaviour 171
Buying centre 174
Cognitive dissonance 163
Consumer buyer behaviour 148
Consumer market 148
Culture 150
Derived demand 171

Groups 152
Learning 160
Lifestyle 155
Modified rebuy 173
Motive (or drive) 157
New product 168
New task 174
Opinion leaders 152

Perception 158
Personality 156
Social classes 151
Straight rebuy 173
Subculture 150
Systems selling 174
Value analysis 179

NOTES AND REFERENCES

1   World POPClock, US Census Bureau, www.census.gov, July 2005. This website provides continuously updated projections of the US and world populations.

2   Brad Weiners, 'Getting Inside – Way Inside – Your Customer's Head', *Business 2.0*, April 2003, pp. 54–5.

3   Dawn Burton, 'Incorporating ethnicity into marketing intelligence and planning', *Marketing Intelligence and Planning*, **20**(7), 2002, pp. 442–51. Ahmad Jamal, 'Marketing in a multicultural world: The interplay of marketing, ethnicity and consumption', *European Journal of Marketing*, **37**(11/12), 2003, pp. 1599–620.

4 See Peter Francese, 'Older and Wealthier', *American Demographics*, November 2002, pp. 40–1; Alison Stein Wellner, 'The Next 25 Years', *American Demographics*, April 2003, pp. 24–7; and information accessed at www.census.gov, April 2005.

5 See D. Allen Kerr, 'Where There's Gray, There's Green', *Marketing News*, 25 May 1998, p. 2; Laura Petrecca, 'Savvy, Aging Boomers Buy into Pharma Mantra', *Advertising Age*, 8 July 2002, pp. S8–S9; Peter Francese, 'Consumers Today', *American Demographics*, April 2003, pp. 28–9; and Robin Goldwyn Blumenthal, 'Gray Is Good', *Barron's*, 22 March 2004, p. 37.

6 See Edward Keller and Jonathan Berry, *The Influentials* (New York, NY: The Free Press, 2003); John Battelle, 'The Net of Influence', *Business 2.0*, March 2004, p. 70; Alicia Clegg, 'Following the Leaders', *Marketing Week*, 30 September 2004, pp. 47–9; Ronald E. Goldsmith, 'The Influentials', *Journal of Product & Brand Management*, 2005, pp. 371–2; and Matthew Creamer, 'Study: Go Traditional to Influence Influencers', *Advertising Age*, 7 March 2005, p. 8.

7 L. Benedictus, 'Psst! Have you heard?' *The Guardian*, 30 January 2007. Copyright Guardian News and Media Ltd 2007.

8 See Sharon Goldman Edry, 'No Longer Just Fun and Games', *American Demographics*, May 2001, pp. 36–8; Hillary Chura, 'Marketing Messages for Women Fall Short', *Advertising Age*, 23 September 2002, pp. 4, 14–15; and Pallavi Gogoi, 'I Am Woman, Hear Me Shop', *BusinessWeek Online*, 14 February 2005, accessed at www.bwonline.com.

9 See Johneen Manning, 'Female Em-POWER-Ing Tools, Handywomen Rejoice!', GFKA.com, November 2003; Allen P. Roberts Jr, 'Barbara K: How I Did It. With Great Power Tools Comes Great Responsibility', *Inc.*, May 2005, pp. 112–14; and information accessed at www.barbarak.com, July 2005.

10 Tobi Elkin, 'Sony Marketing Aims at Lifestyle Segments', *Advertising Age*, 18 March 2002, pp. 3, 72; and Kenneth Hein, 'When Is Enough Enough?', *Brandweek*, 2 December 2002, pp. 26–8.

11 T. Kesic and S. Piri-Rajh, 'Market segmentation on the basis of food-related lifestyles of Croatian Families', *British Food Journal*, 105(3), 2003, pp. 162–74.

12 Information accessed at www.forrester.com/Data/ConsumerTechno, July 2005; and Colin Chung, 'Quantitative Research Approach to Understanding How Consumers Adopt Technology-Related Products and Services', accessed at www.onetooneinteractive.com/advisor_chung.html, July 2005.

13 Jennifer Aaker, 'Dimensions of Measuring Brand Personality', *Journal of Marketing Research*, August 1997, pp. 347–56. See also Aaker, 'The Malleable Self: The Role of Self Expression in Persuasion', *Journal of Marketing Research*, May 1999, pp. 45–57; and Audrey Azoulay and Jean-Noel Kapferer, 'Do Brand Personality Scales Really Measure Brand Personality?', *Journal of Brand Management*, November 2003, p. 143.

14 Annetta Miller and Dody Tsiantar, 'Psyching Out Consumers', *Newsweek*, 27 February 1989, pp. 46–7. See also Alison Stein Wellner, 'Research on a Shoestring,' *American Demographics*, April 2001, pp. 38–9; and Leon G. Schiffman and Leslie L. Kanuk, *Consumer Behaviour*, 8th edn (Upper Saddle River, NJ: Prentice Hall, 2004), chapter 4.

15 See Abraham H. Maslow, 'A Theory of Human Motivation', *Psychological Review*, 50 (1943), pp. 370–96. See also Maslow, *Motivation and Personality*, 3rd edn (New York: HarperCollins Publishers, 1987); and Barbara Marx Hubbard, 'Seeking Our Future Potentials', *The Futurist*, May 1998, pp. 29–32.

16 Charles Pappas, 'Ad Nauseam', *Advertising Age*, 10 July 2000, pp. 16–18.

17 Bob Garfield, ' "Subliminal" Seduction and Other Urban Myths', *Advertising Age*, 18 September 2000, pp. 4, 105. See also 'We Have Ways of Making You Think', *Marketing Week*, 25 September 2003, p. 14; and Si Cantwell, 'Common Sense; Scrutiny Helps Catch Catchy Ads', *Wilmington Star-News*, 1 April 2004, p. 1B.

18 C. Sawers, 'Porridge is the new fast food', *The Scotsman*, 17 August 2005.

19 For a deeper discussion of the buyer decision process, see Philip Kotler and Kevin Lane Keller, *Marketing Management*, 12th edn (Upper Saddle River, NJ: Prentice Hall, 2006), pp. 191–203.

20 Duglas Pruden and Terry G. Vavra, 'Controlling the Grapevine', *Marketing Management*, July–August 2004, pp. 25–30.

21 See Leon Festinger, *A Theory of Cognitive Dissonance* (Stanford, CA: Stanford University Press, 1957); Schiffman and Kanuk, *Consumer Behaviour*, pp. 219–20; Patti Williams and Jennifer L. Aaker, 'Can Mixed Emotions Peacefully Coexist?', March 2002, pp. 636–49; Adam Ferrier, 'Young Are Not Marketing Savvy; They're Suckers', *B&T Weekly*, 22 October 2004, p. 13; and 'Cognitive Dissonance and the Stability of Service Quality Perceptions', *The Journal of Services Marketing*, 2004, pp. 433ff.

22 The following discussion draws from the work of Everett M. Rogers. See his *Diffusion of Innovations*, 5th edn (New York: Free Press, 2003). See also Eric Waarts, Yvonne M. van Everdingen and Jos van Hillegersberg, 'The Dynamics of Factors Affecting the Adoption of Innovations', *The Journal of Product Innovation Management*, November 2002, pp. 412–23; Chaun-Fong Shih and Alladi Venkatesh, 'Beyond Adoption: Development and Application of a Use-Diffusion Model', *Journal of Marketing*, January 2004, pp. 59–72; and Richard R. Nelson, Alexander Peterhansl and Bhaven Sampat, 'Why and How Innovations Get Adopted: A Tale of Four Models', *Industrial and Corporate Change*, October 2004, pp. 679–99.

23 Patrick J. Robinson, Charles W. Faris and Yoram Wind, *Industrial Buying Behaviour and Creative Marketing* (Boston: Allyn & Bacon, 1967). See also James C. Anderson and James A. Narus, *Business Market Management*, 2nd edn (Upper Saddle River, NJ: Prentice Hall, 2004), ch. 3.

24 Based on information from www.veoliaenvironnement.com.

25 Robinson, Faris and Wind, *Industrial Buying Behaviour*, p. 14.

26 Kate Maddox, '#1 Hewlett-Packard Co.: www.hp.com', *BtoB*, 11 August 2003, p. 1; and 'Great Web Sites: www.hp.com', *BtoB Online*, 13 September 2004, accessed at www.btobonline.com/article.cms?articleId=21878.

27 Demir Barlas, 'E-Procurement: Steady Value', *Line56.com*, 4 January 2005, accessed at www.line56.com.

28 Michael A. Verespej, 'E-Procurement Explosion', *Industry Week*, March 2002, pp. 25–8.

PART THREE VIDEO CASE:
Putting marketing into action

Now that we've fully explored the context in which marketing is 'done' we move on to consider the details, decisions and the processes of putting together a comprehensive marketing strategy. In this video case, we hear from marketers working in three very different companies in three very different sectors of the economy. Hiscox, a provider of specialist insurance policies, Royal Enfield, manufacturers of motorcycles and Inamo – a restaurant in London. As you watch them discuss their strategic and tactical decision making, consider the commonality between the problems they face in respect of understanding their customers, communicating and developing profitable relationships with them and producing goods and services that these customers will be keen on.

Go to **www.pearsoned.co.uk/armstrong** to watch this video case, and then consider the following questions:

1. Do all three firms have a good understanding of the wants and needs of their customers?

2. Do Hiscox and Royal Enfield face a more complex set of problems than Inamo? If so, why do you think this is?

3. In terms of putting together their bundle of products and services they offer to consumers, is there any commonality between these three different companies?

PART THREE

Designing a customer-driven marketing strategy and marketing mix

CHAPTER 6

Segmentation, targeting and positioning: Building the right relationships with the right customers

AFTER STUDYING THIS CHAPTER, YOU SHOULD BE ABLE TO

- define the three steps of target marketing: market segmentation, target marketing and market positioning
- list and discuss the major bases for segmenting consumer and business markets
- explain how companies identify attractive market segments and choose a target marketing strategy
- discuss how companies position their products for maximum competitive advantage in the marketplace

THE WAY AHEAD Previewing the concepts

So far, you've learned what marketing is and also about the importance of understanding consumers and the marketplace environment. With that as background, you're now ready to delve deeper into marketing strategy and tactics. This chapter looks further into key marketing strategy decisions – how to divide up markets into meaningful customer groups (market segmentation), choose which customer groups to serve (target marketing), and create market offerings that best serve targeted customers (positioning). Then, the chapters that follow explore the tactical marketing tools – the Four Ps – by which marketers bring these strategies to life.

As an opening example of segmentation, targeting and position at work, let's look first at Baltika, Russia's biggest brewer. The Baltika story provides a great example of how smart marketers use segmentation, targeting and positioning to succeed.

Baltika: Segmenting the beer market in Russia and the West

Maria Smirnova, *Graduate School of Management, St Petersburg State University, Russia*

Source: Getty Images.

Ever heard of Baltika? If not, chances are you will become familiar with it shortly. Baltika is Russia's leading beer brand – to many Russians, Baltika *is* beer.

Baltika is considered by many to be the first true domestic Russian beer 'brand'. Before it, old Soviet products were state-produced. Baltika Brewery was in fact originally opened as a state-owned and managed company before becoming a joint-stock company in the economic reforms of the 1990s. It is now one of the world's biggest beer producers and Russia's largest FMCG company, running ten breweries and directly employing 12,500 people in the production of more than 540 million hectolitres per year. Baltika owns more than 1,500 rail wagons to aid distribution – the second biggest fleet after the Russian state railway.

From the very beginning, Baltika beer was conceived as a beer of the very highest European quality that would be brewed according to classical techniques. In order to achieve this, management invested in the reconstruction and development of the enterprise – bringing in advanced equipment and technologies to allow the production of the highest quality beers. The success of this programme has made Baltika the leader in the Russian beer market – a position that the company has held since 1996. This is no mean feat – contrary to western perceptions, Russia is not the easiest country in which to market alcoholic drinks, particularly beer. Certainly, the country and its people have a reputation for

enjoying drinking but tough regulation and ingrained cultural preferences for other types of drink in an increasingly competitive market mean that success has never been assured. Furthermore, unlike many other world beer markets, the Russian market is very fragmented and the shares of the main players are not big. Baltika is the one exception; the company is twice as big as its nearest competitor.

As a brand, Baltika brand is consistently rated amongst Russia's top three when evaluated on criteria of market position, stability and capacity for overcoming geographic borders and cultural barriers. Baltika today is Europe's first beer brand in terms of volume.

The right beer for the right drinker

Baltika has a portfolio of sub-brands, the most popular of which are the number '3' and '7' beers (see Table 6.1). The numbering system is unique to Baltika and Russia – marketing was not a concept widely understood in Soviet Russia so rather than emotive or intriguing names, numbers were used instead. Over time, there has been no reason

to change as everyone in Russia knows and understands the system. Baltika believes that the means to continued success lies in supplying 'the right beer to the right people' – that is, in segmenting the market and supplying each segment with an appropriate product. The company recognises that it is still in a developing market. Consumer brand loyalty is quite low and regional pride is high, so Baltika uses its network of breweries across Russia to provide consumers with 'local' products. Having this portfolio means that customers can still experiment and switch but stay with Baltika.

This is a very simple approach, but Baltika also uses more sophisticated marketing techniques to take the whole Russian market and break it down into segments. To do this they use a three-dimensional matrix model of the market created after extensive and continuing market research, with dimensions labelled 'price', 'need states' and 'occasions'. In this matrix, segments are given descriptive names like 'safe and smart' which represents conservative drinkers who prefer innovations and changes to their drinks to be minor, 'health and well-being' which contains the drinkers who are most

TABLE 6.1 Baltika brands

Brand name	Launched	Characteristics
Baltika No. 0	2001	Non-alcoholic
Baltika No. 1	1992	Light
Baltika No. 2 Pale	2004	Light and fresh
Baltika No. 3 Classic	1992	Golden and smooth
Baltika No. 4 Original	1992	Dark and bitter
Baltika No. 5 Gold	2002	Premium beer
Baltika No. 6 Porter	1995	Porter-type beer
Baltika No. 7 Export	1994	Premium export beer
Baltika No. 8 Wheat	2001	Fruity wheat beer
Baltika No. 9 Extra	1998	Strong and pale
Baltika Cooler	2006	Refreshing

concerned about the impact of beer on their health and waistline – Baltika introduced Russia's first non-alcoholic beer just for this segment, calling it Baltika No. 0. A third example of a segment is the 'sophisticates', who will pay a high price for a premium and exotic product. Baltika caters to this group using its licensed production of Kronenbourg 1664 – a brand perceived as being complex and foreign.

Baltika markets its products to each segment by varying the way in which it uses pricing, packaging and promotional tools like advertising. For example, for the more price and value conscious drinkers, Baltika introduced 1 litre cans to be sold through supermarkets. For socialisers at bars who are paying more, the same beer is put into glass bottles with a distinctive shape.

Using its modelling, Baltika has noticed that some segments are growing more rapidly than others, and is hoping to track this evolving market environment by updating its portfolio through innovation and licensing – as they did with Baltika No. 0. As average income levels rise, drinkers are trading up from value brands (a segment in decline) to mid-price products in greater numbers, and the new brand – Baltika Cooler – has a 60 per cent share of this segment filled with young urbanites.

As the company grows, it is looking more and more to expand into international markets. Baltika recognises wisely that just because it has put a lot of effort into segmenting the Russian beer market does not mean that foreign markets can be broken up in the same way. The company believes that the strategic positioning of beer in international markets is essentially based around two main price segments – premium and mainstream, and that Baltika brands can best be positioned in Western markets as a premium/speciality beer. Close to home, in the CIS nations, which tend to be geographical neighbours of Russia, Baltika has fallen naturally into a premium position attractive to young, professional adults with good incomes who are attracted to a non-Western brand.

In the USA the leading brand Baltika exports is No. 9 (a strong beer that symbolises self-confidence), and the brand is promoted through sponsorship of sports events – especially ice hockey with its Eastern European following. The favourite alcoholic beverage for Russian Americans is beer. Of imported beers, their first preference is now Baltika.

This targeting of the Russian immigrant community in foreign markets is not limited to the USA. Baltika's president, Anton Artemiev, said recently 'The UK is a country very much inhabited by Russian speakers – in London alone there are 300,000 Russian-speaking people, a lot of high-society people who spend a week in Moscow and a week in London, going back and forth.'

Catering successfully to these ethnic/cultural segments has given Baltika a foothold in Western countries – but can Baltika take the next step and move into the rest of the market, and what about countries in which there is no substantial ethnic Russian population? Further segmentation work will be required.

Sources: Institutional Investor Rating of Annual Russian Business Leader Studies, available from: http://www.beer-union.com/search.php?search=Baltika; Baltika press releases, available from: http://eng.baltika.ru/; stories from: www.beer-union.com; *Business Week Russia*, 'The Best Russian Brands', http://www.ourfishbowl.com; *Baltika driving Russian premium beer growth*, from: http://cee-foodindustry.com/; *Stepping Out – A story about Russian companies promoting their brands abroad*, by Dmitri Frol, available from: http://www.ethnicusa.com; *Alcohol Preferences of Russian Americans*, Global Advertising Strategies, Market Data, Research Products, 13 March 2006; *'Baltika' Named Russia's Best Exporter*, from: www.fis.ru, 21 June 2007; interviews with Marcho Kuyumdzhiev, Vice President for Marketing at Baltika Breweries, and Anna Balakina, Marketing Manager, International Marketing Group.

FIGURE 6.1

Steps in market segmentation, targeting and positioning

Companies today recognise that they cannot appeal to all buyers in the marketplace, or at least not to all buyers in the same way. Buyers are too numerous, too widely scattered, and too varied in their needs and buying practices. Moreover, the companies themselves vary widely in their abilities to serve different segments of the market. Instead, a company must identify the parts of the market that it can serve best and most profitably. It needs to design strategies to build the *right* relationships with the *right* customers.

Thus, most companies are being choosier about the customers with whom they wish to build relationships. Most have moved away from mass marketing and toward *market segmentation and targeting* – identifying market segments, selecting one or more of them, and developing products and marketing programmes tailored to each. Instead of scattering their marketing efforts (the 'shotgun' approach), firms are focusing on the buyers who have greater interest in the values they create best (the 'rifle' approach).

Figure 6.1 shows the three major steps in target marketing. The first is **market segmentation** – dividing a market into smaller groups of buyers with distinct needs, characteristics or behaviours who might require separate products or marketing mixes. The company identifies different ways to segment the market and develops profiles of the resulting market segments. The second step is **target marketing** – evaluating each market segment's attractiveness and selecting one or more of the market segments to enter. The third step is **market positioning** – setting the competitive positioning for the product and creating a detailed marketing mix. We discuss each of these steps in turn.

MARKET SEGMENTATION

Markets consist of buyers, and buyers differ in one or more ways. They may differ in their wants, how they intend to use the product, resources, locations, buying attitudes and buying practices. Through market segmentation, companies divide large, heterogeneous markets into smaller segments that can be reached more efficiently and effectively with products and services that match their unique needs. In this section, we discuss four important segmentation topics: segmenting consumer markets, segmenting business markets, segmenting international markets and requirements for effective segmentation.

Segmenting consumer markets

There is no single way to segment a market. A marketer has to try different segmentation variables, alone and in combination, to find the best way to view the market structure. Table 6.2 outlines the major variables that might be used in segmenting consumer markets. Here we look at the major *geographic, demographic, psychographic* and *behavioural* variables.

TABLE 6.2 Major segmentation variables for consumer markets

Geographic

World region or country	Europe (Western, Southern, Northern, Eastern), North America, Africa, Asia-Pacific, UK, Belgium, Kenya, Japan
Country region	French regions – Alsace, Limousin, Picardie; English counties – Yorkshire, Essex, Cornwall; Italian provinces – Campania, Lazio, Tuscany
Town/city size	Under 5,000; 5–20,000; 20–50,000; 50–100,000; 100–250,000; 250–500,000; 500–1,000,000; 1–4,000,000; over 4 million
Population density	Urban, suburban, rural
Climate	Mediterranean, arctic, temperate, tropical

Demographic

Age	Under 6, 6–11, 12–19, 20–34, 35–49, 50–64, 65+
Gender	Male, female
Family size	1–2, 3–4, 5+
Life-cycle stage	Young, single; young married, no children; young, married with children; older, married with children; older, married, no children under 18; older, single; other
Income	Under €10,000; €10–20,000; €20–30,000; €30–50,000; €50–100,000; €100,000 and over
Occupation	Professional and technical; managers, officials and proprietors; clerical; sales; craftspeople; supervisors; operatives; farmers; retired; students; unemployed; homemakers
Education	Elementary or less; secondary; college; graduate; postgraduate
Religious beliefs	Buddhist, Christian, Muslim, Hindu, Jew, agnostic, atheist
Ethnicity	English, Irish, Scots, Welsh, in the UK; Catalan, Castilian, Anadalusians in Spain; Flemings and Walloons in Belgium
Generation	Baby Boomer, Generation X, Generation Y
Nationality	British, French, Spanish, Russian

Psychographic

Social class	Lower lowers, upper lowers, working class, middle class, upper middles, lower uppers, upper uppers
Lifestyle	Achievers, strivers, survivors
Personality	Compulsive, gregarious, authoritarian, ambitious

Behavioural

Occasions	Regular, special, one-off
Benefits	Quality, service, economy, convenience, speed
User status	Non-user, ex-user, potential user, first-time user, regular user
User rates	Light user, medium user, heavy user
Loyalty status	None, medium, strong, absolute
Readiness stage	Unaware, aware, informed, interested, desirous, intending to buy
Attitude towards product	Enthusiastic, positive, indifferent, negative, hostile

Geographic segmentation

Geographic segmentation is about dividing the market into different geographical sectors. These sectors might be continents, nations, regions, cities, or even a single street. A company may decide to operate in one or a few of these geographical areas – or to operate in all areas but pay attention to geographical differences in needs and wants – as Baltika does when using local breweries to brew local beers.[1]

Many companies today are localising their products, advertising, promotion and sales efforts to fit the needs of individual regions, cities and even neighbourhoods. For example, Asda has supermarkets across the UK. The mix of products in the shop is influenced by the characteristics of the local area. Wealth levels, ethnic diversity, local industries and delicacies with a traditional geographic home will all have an impact on what is available and these products will often be sourced from the local area.

Asda stores in Scotland will stock a wider range of haggis, Lincolnshire stores have a wider variety of sausages and local favourites like 'chine' – a shoulder cut of pork, partly boned, filled with parsley, sold cooked and eaten cold. The rise in the number of people living in the UK of Polish origin is reflected by the addition of Polish foods and drinks to the shelves – brands like Zywiec beer and Pamapol ready meals. In time, some of these products will cross into the mainstream – the 1990s saw naan breads move from being a niche category product to the mass market.

If you think of the family board game Monopoly, you probably think of the London version. This was an adaptation of the original 1930s US version which had streets and landmarks from Atlantic City in New Jersey. The London version was marketed across the British Commonwealth set of nations – but there now exists a great variety of different sets. The German 'standard' version is based on Berlin, the French on Paris, the Norwegian on Oslo and the Austrian combines places from eight different cities across the country. The version for Swansea in Wales is printed in English and Welsh, and Belgian boards have French and Flemish text. Other than these national versions, many local cities across Europe have their own version – Rotterdam in the Netherlands, Milan in Italy and Barcelona and Seville in Spain. Cities are able to lobby the producer – Parker Brothers – to produce a version of their own city.

Other companies are seeking to cultivate as-yet untapped geographic territory. For example, many multiple retailers in Germany have begun implementing plans for expansion into Eastern Europe, and Russian companies are hoping to exploit opportunities after consolidating their position in domestic markets – Baltica is not an exception in this regard.

In contrast, other retailers are developing new store concepts that will give them access to higher-density urban areas. For example, IKEA is introducing stores in the centre of cities.[2] It is placing these stores in high-density markets, such as London and Amsterdam, where full-size stores are impractical. Similarly, Tesco has a large number of small 'cornerstore'-sized supermarkets called Tesco Express, locating them in central locations near concentrations of office workers and transportation hubs like stations, and it is no coincidence that Aldi often has supermarkets near concentrations of students.

Demographic segmentation

Demographic segmentation divides the market into groups based on variables such as age, gender, family size, family life cycle, income, occupation, education, religion, race, generation and nationality. Demographic factors are the most popular bases for segmenting customer groups. One reason is that consumer needs, wants and usage rates often vary closely in line with demographic variables. Another is that demographic variables are easier to measure than most other types of variables. Even when market segments are first defined using other bases, such as benefits sought or behaviour, their demographic characteristics must be known in order to assess the size of the target market and to reach it efficiently.

Age and life-cycle stage Consumer needs and wants change with age. Some companies use **age and life-cycle segmentation**, offering different products or using different marketing approaches for different age and life-cycle groups. For example, Gap has branched out to target people at different ages and life stages. In addition to its standard line of clothing, the retailer now offers babyGap, GapKids, GapBody and GapMaternity.

Marketers must be careful to guard against stereotypes when using age and life-cycle segmentation, especially in this era of social change. For example, although some 70-year-olds require wheelchairs, others play tennis. Similarly, whereas some 40-year-old couples are sending their children off to university, others are just beginning new families. Thus, age is often a poor predictor of a person's life cycle, health, work or family status, needs and buying power. Companies marketing to mature consumers usually employ positive images and appeals. For example, ads for Dove 'Pro-Age' – designed to improve the elasticity and appearance of the 'maturing skin' of women over 50 – feature attractive older women and uplifting messages.[3]

Gender **Gender segmentation** has long been used in clothing, cosmetics, toiletries and magazines. For example, Berghaus, manufacturers of gear for outdoor activities, has sought advice from female climbers and hikers at the design stage for the last 20 years. European car manufacturers like Renault, Seat and Fiat are producing cars with stylings, accessories and features specifically to appeal to women. Bramdean Asset Management now has a specific division – called Bramdiva – specialising in managing the wealth of women.[4]

Nike has recently stepped up its efforts to capture the women's sports clothing market. It wasn't until 2000 that Nike made women's shoes using moulds made from women's feet, rather than simply using a small man's foot mould. Since then, however, Nike has changed its approach to women. It has overhauled its women's apparel line – called Nikewomen – to create better fitting, more colourful, more fashionable workout clothes for women. Its revamped nikewomen.com website now features the apparel, along with workout trend highlights. And Nike is opening Nikewomen stores in several major cities.[5]

Age and life-cycle segmentation: Dove recognises that middle-aged consumers use cosmetics for different purposes compared with the young.

Source: The Advertising Archives.

Income **Income segmentation** has long been used by the marketers of products and services such as cars, boats, clothing, cosmetics, financial services and travel. Many companies target affluent consumers with luxury goods and convenience services. Stores such as Harrods in London or Quartier 206 in Berlin pitch everything from expensive jewellery and fine fashions to glazed Australian apricots priced at £20 a pound.[6] Credit-card companies offer elite credit cards dripping with perks for those who spend thousands a month, rather than thousands a year.

To cater to its very best customers, Harrods has created its 'Harrods Rewards' programme. Every pound spent means one point credited to your account. Collect 500 points and you receive a gift voucher for £5 – but spend more and that's when the real benefits start. Make it to level 'Green' by spending between £500 and £5,000 in a year and you'll be entitled to free delivery, complimentary tea and coffee in the lounges and access to special in-store events such as couture fashion shows. Spending £5–10,000 takes you to 'Gold' level, meaning that alterations to clothes bought at Harrods are done without additional payment. Beyond 'Gold' there is 'Black', requiring an annual spend of more than £10,000. Achieving this brings you the services of a team of personal shoppers who will give you their full attention – as you recline comfortably in an armchair drinking camomile tea they will bring products to you. Harrods isn't the only company to recognise the potential of perks for cardholders – American Express have a card just for their very, very best customers (see Marketing at Work 6.1).

However, not all companies that use income segmentation target the affluent. For example, many retailers – such as Aldi and Lidl – successfully target low- and middle-income groups. More than half the sales in such stores come from shoppers with family incomes under £15,000. When Aldi scouts out locations for new stores, they look for lower middle-class districts where people wear less expensive shoes and drive old cars.

Coddling the well-heeled

Some companies go to extremes to pamper big spenders. From department stores like Harrods, to car makers like Mercedes and BMW, to hotel chains like Ritz-Carlton and Four Seasons, such companies give their well-heeled customers exactly what they need – and even more.

For example, concierge services are no longer the sole province of five-star hotels and fancy credit cards. They are starting to show up at airlines, retailers, and even electronic-goods makers. Sony Electronics, for instance, offers a service for its wealthiest customers, called Cierge, that provides a free personal shopper and early access to new gadgets, as well as 'white-glove' help with the installation.

Targeting affluent consumers: Visa's Signature card is targeted at the 'new affluent'. It offers no pre-set spending limit, 24-hour concierge services and loads of 'upgrades, perks and discounts . . . It's not just everywhere you want to be, it's everything you ever wanted.'
Source: Thunderbird image used with permission of Ford Motor Company. Visa USA advert used with permission of Visa USA © 2004 Visa USA, Inc.

(Translation: They will send someone over to set up the new gear.)

And then there's British Airways' 'At Your Service' programme – available to a hand-picked few of the airline's gold-level elite customers. There's almost nothing that the service won't do for members – tracking down hard-to-get Wimbledon tickets, for example, or running errands around town, sitting in a member's home to wait for a delivery, or even planning your wedding, right down to the cake.

But when it comes to stalking the well-to-do, perhaps nowhere is the competition greater than in the credit-card industry. To rise above the credit-card clutter and to attract high-end card holders, the major credit-card companies have created a new top tier of super-premium cards – Visa's Infinite card (Signature in the USA), MasterCard's World card, American Express's super-elite Centurion card. Affluent customers are extremely profitable. While premium cards represent only 1.5 per cent of the consumer credit cards issued by Visa, MasterCard and American Express, they account for 20 per cent of the spending. And well-to-do cardholders tend to default a lot less, too.

The World MasterCard programme targets what it calls the 'mass affluent' and reaches 15 million wealthy households. Visa's Infinite card zeroes in on 'new affluent' households, those with incomes exceeding £70,000. Its 7 million cardholders account for 3 per cent of Visa's consumer credit cards but 18 per cent of Visa sales. Both cards feature a pack of special privileges. For its Infinite card, Visa advertises, 'It's not just everywhere you want to be, it's everything you ever wanted.' In addition to the basics, such as no

pre-set spending limit and 24-hour concierge services, Visa promises 'upgrades, perks, and discounts' at major airlines, restaurants and hotels, and special treatment at partners like the Ritz-Carlton and watchmaker Audemars Piguet.

But when it comes to premium cards, the American Express Centurion card is the 'elite of the elite' for luxury card carriers. This mysterious, much-coveted black credit card is issued by invitation only, to customers who *spend* more than £80,000 a year on other AmEx cards and meet other not-so-clear requirements. Then, the select few who do receive the card pay a £1,200 annual fee just for the privilege of carrying it.

But the Centurion card comes dripping with perks and prestige. The elusive plastic, with its elegant matte finish, is coveted by big spenders. 'A black card is plastic bling-bling,' says an industry observer, 'a way for celebrities, athletes, and major business people to express their status.'

A real T-shirt-and-jeans kind of guy, Peter H. Shankman certainly doesn't look like a high roller, but American Express knows better. After he was snubbed by salesmen at a Giorgio Armani boutique on Fifth Avenue in New York recently, the 31-year-old publicist saw 'an unbelievable attitude reversal' at the cash register when he whipped out his black AmEx Centurion Card. In June, a RadioShack cashier refused the card, thinking it was a fake. '"Trust me," I said, "run the card",' recalls the chief executive of Geek Factory, a public-relations and marketing firm. 'I could buy a Learjet with this thing.'

An exaggeration, perhaps. But AmEx's little black card is decidedly the 'It' card for big spenders. Some would-be customers go to absurd lengths to get what they see as a must-have status symbol. Hopefuls have written poems to plead their cases. Others say they'll pay the fee but swear not to use the card – they want it just for show. 'Every week I get phone calls or letters, often from prominent people, asking me for the card,' says AmEx's head of consumer cards, Alfred F. Kelly Jr. Who, he won't say. In fact, AmEx deliberately builds an air of mystery around the sleek card, keeping hush-hush such details as the number of cards in circulation. Analysts say AmEx earns back many times what it spends on perks for black-card customers in both marketing buzz and fees.

Basic services on the Centurion card include a personal travel counsellor and concierge, available 24/7. Beyond that, almost anything

goes. Feel like shopping at Bergdorf Goodman or Saks Fifth Avenue at midnight? No problem. Travelling abroad in first class? Take a pal – the extra ticket is free. The royal treatment often requires elaborate planning. One AmEx concierge arranged a bachelor party for 25, which involved a four-day trip that included 11 penthouse suites, travel by private jet, and a meet-and-greet with an owner of the Sacramento Kings basketball team. The tab was more than $300,000.

How did Shankman earn his card? All the travel and entertainment charges he racks up hosting his clients prompted AmEx to send it to him. It arrived in December, along with a 43-page manual. Recently, Shankman sought reservations for Spice Market, an often-overbooked restaurant in Manhattan, to impress a friend. He called his concierge. 'Half an hour later it was done,' says Shankman. Membership does have its privileges.

So, how many people actually have a Centurion card? 'About the same number of people who can afford a Mercedes Maybach,' says Desiree Fish, a spokeswoman for American Express, referring to a luxury car that can list for more than £150,000. The best guess is that only about 5,000 people worldwide have a Centurion card in their back pocket.

Sources: American Express example adapted from Mara Der Hovanesian, 'This Black Card Gives You Carte Blanche', *BusinessWeek*, 9 August 2004, p. 54. Quotes and other information from David Carr, 'No Name, but Plenty of Bling-Bling for Show', *New York Times*, 13 September 2004, p. C11; Eleena de Lisser, 'How to Get an Airline to Wait for Your Plumber – In Battle for Biggest Spenders, British Airways, Sony Roll Out Hotel-Style 'Concierge' Service', *Wall Street Journal*, 2 July 2002, p. D1; James Tenser, 'Cards Play Their Luxury Hand Right', *Advertising Age*, 13 September 2004, pp. S13–S14; Eric Dash, 'New Spots for the Credit Card Companies Show Fierce Competition for the High-End Consumer', *New York Times*, 11 May 2005, p. C8; and www.visa.com and www.mastercard.com, August 2007.

Psychographic segmentation

Psychographic segmentation divides buyers into different groups based on social class, lifestyle or personality characteristics. People in the same demographic group can have very different psychographic make-ups.

In Chapter 5 we discussed how the products people buy reflect their *lifestyles*. As a result, marketers often segment their markets by consumer lifestyles. Saga, who started by creating holiday packages for the over 50s, have expanded into a range of financial services for the elderly, and have found it necessary to offer a range of products that take account of the widely differing lifestyles – in regard to activity, desire to travel and plans for the future. Old people are not all the same, are planning to enjoy their retirement in different ways, and they certainly aren't all planning on leaving their money to their children! Vegetarians, people with hobbies and dedicated supporters of a football team are examples of how lifestyle choices can impact on consumption decisions.[7]

Marketers have also used *personality* variables to segment markets. For example, marketing for Honda motor scooters *appears* to target young men about town. But it is *actually* aimed at a much broader personality group. One old ad, for example, showed a delighted child bouncing up and down on his bed while the announcer says, 'You've been trying to get there all your life.' The ad reminded viewers of the euphoric feelings they got when they broke away from authority and did things their parents told them not to do. Thus, Honda is appealing to the rebellious, independent child in all of us. In fact, 22 per cent of scooter riders are retired. 'The older buyers are buying them for kicks,' says one elderly customer. 'They never had the opportunity to do this as kids.'[8]

Behavioural segmentation

Behavioural segmentation divides buyers into groups based on their knowledge, attitudes, uses, or responses to a product. Many marketers believe that behaviour variables are the best starting point for building market segments.

Occasions Buyers can be grouped according to occasions when they get the idea to buy, actually make their purchase, or use the purchased item. **Occasion segmentation** can help firms build up product usage. For example, eggs are most often consumed at breakfast. But the wonderfully named British Egg Information Service – an industry body – promotes the use of eggs in other meals, providing recipes and other resources in a bid to increase egg consumption.[9]

Some special days such as Mother's Day and Father's Day, were originally promoted partly to increase the sale of chocolates, flowers, and especially cards – earning them the nickname of 'Hallmark Holidays'. Many marketers prepare special offers and ads for special days in the calendar. Cadbury begins heavy promotion of its Creme Eggs in the run-up to Easter – after Easter, these campaigns come to an almost immediate halt. Some companies focus on specific, important events in people's lives. Anichini in Florence provides hand-made clothes for Christenings – important events in a traditionally Catholic country. Confetti provides a wide range of items for weddings – invitations, cake decorations and of course 174 different types of confetti![10]

Kodak, Konica, Fuji and other camera makers use occasion segmentation in designing and marketing their single-use cameras. By mixing lenses, film speeds and accessories, they have developed special disposable cameras for about any picture-taking occasion, from underwater photography to taking baby pictures. The Kodak Water and Sport single-use camera is water resistant to a depth of 50 feet and features a shock-proof frame, a sunscreen and scratch resistant lens, and 800 speed film. 'It survives where your regular camera won't!' claims Kodak.[11]

Benefits sought A powerful form of segmentation is to group buyers according to the different *benefits* that they seek from the product. **Benefit segmentation** requires finding the major benefits people look for in the product class, the kinds of people who look for each benefit, and the major brands that deliver each benefit. For instance, our chapter-opening example pointed out that Baltika has identified many different segments of beer-drinkers. Proctor & Gamble have a range of detergents matched to segments. Each segment seeks a unique combination of benefits, from cleaning and bleaching to economy, fabric softening, fresh smell, strength or mildness, and lots of suds or only a few.

Champion athletic wear segments its markets according to benefits that different consumers seek from their active wear. For example, 'Fit and Polish' consumers seek a balance between function and style – they exercise for results but want to look good doing it. 'Serious Sports Competitors' exercise heavily and live in and love their active wear – they seek performance and function. By contrast, 'Value-Seeking Mums' have low sports interest and low active wear involvement – they buy for the family and seek durability and value. Thus, each segment seeks a different mix of benefits. Champion must target the benefit segment or segments that it can serve best and most profitably using appeals that match each segment's benefit preferences.

User status Markets can be segmented into non-users, ex-users, potential users, first-time users and regular users of a product. For example, blood banks cannot rely only on regular donors. They must also recruit new first-time donors and remind ex-donors

– each will require different marketing appeals. Included in the potential user group are consumers facing life-stage changes – such as newly-weds and new parents – who can be turned into heavy users. For example, P&G acquires the names of parents-to-be and showers them with product samples and ads for its Pampers and other baby products in order to capture a share of their future purchases. It invites them to join MyPampers.com, giving them access to expert parenting advice, an email newspaper, and coupons and special offers.

Usage rate Markets can also be segmented into light, medium and heavy product users. Heavy users are often a small percentage of the market but account for a high proportion of total consumption. For example, in the fast-food industry, heavy users make up only 20 per cent of patrons but eat up about 60 per cent of all the food served. A single heavy user, typically a single male in his 20s or 30s who doesn't know how to cook, might spend as much as £20 in a day at fast-food restaurants and visit them more than 20 times a month. Despite claims by some consumers that the fast-food chains are damaging their health, these heavy users are extremely loyal. 'They insist they don't need saving,' says one analyst, 'protesting that they are far from the clueless fatties anti-fast-food activists make them out to be.' Even the heaviest users 'would have to be stupid not to know that you can't eat only burgers and fries and not exercise,' he says.[12]

Interestingly, although fast-food companies such as Burger King, McDonald's and KFC depend a lot on heavy users and do all they can to keep them satisfied with every visit, these companies often target light users with their ads and promotions. The heavy users will visit the restaurants regardless. The company's marketing budget is instead focused on trying to convince light users that they want a burger in the first place.

Loyalty status A market can also be segmented by consumer loyalty. Consumers can be loyal to brands (Berghaus), stores (John Lewis), and companies (Volvo). Buyers can be divided into groups according to their degree of loyalty. Some consumers are completely loyal – they buy one brand all the time. For example, Apple has a small but almost cult-like following of loyal users:

It's the 'Cult of the Mac', and it's populated by 'macolytes'. Urbandictionary.com defines a *macolyte* as 'One who is fanatically devoted to Apple products, especially the Macintosh computer. Also know as a Mac Zealot.' (Sample usage: 'He's a macolyte; don't even "think" of mentioning Microsoft within earshot.') How about Anna Zisa, a graphic designer from Milan who doesn't really like tattoos but stenciled an Apple tat on her behind. 'It just felt like the most me thing to have,' says Zisa. 'I like computers. The apple looks good and sexy. All the comments I have heard have been positive, even from Linux and Windows users.' And then there's Taylor Barcroft, who has spent the last 11 years travelling the country in an RV on a mission to be the Mac cult's ultimate 'multimedia historical videographer'. He goes to every Macworld Expo, huge trade shows centered on the Mac, as well as all kinds of other tech shows – and videotapes anything and everything Apple. He's accumulated more than 3,000 hours of footage. And he's never been paid a dime to do any of this, living off an inheritance. Barcroft owns 17 Macs. Such fanatically loyal users helped keep Apple afloat during the lean years, and they are now at the forefront of Apple's burgeoning iPod-iTunes empire.[13]

Others consumers are somewhat loyal – they are loyal to two or three brands of a given product or favour one brand while sometimes buying others. Still other buyers show no loyalty to any brand. They either want something different each time they buy or they buy whatever's on sale.

A company can learn a lot by analysing loyalty patterns in its market. It should start by studying its own loyal customers. For example, by studying 'macolytes', Apple can better pinpoint its target market and develop marketing appeals. By studying its less loyal buyers, the company can detect which brands are most competitive with its own. By looking at customers who are shifting away from its brand, the company can learn about its marketing weaknesses.

Using multiple segmentation bases

Marketers rarely limit their segmentation analysis to only one or a few variables. Rather, they are increasingly using multiple segmentation bases in an effort to identify smaller, better-defined target groups – as Baltika did with its modelling. Thus, a bank may not only identify a group of wealthy retired adults but also, within that group, distinguish several segments based on their current income, assets, savings and risk preferences, housing and lifestyles.

One good example of multivariable segmentation is 'geodemographic' segmentation. Several business information services – such as Claritas, Experian, Acxiom and MapInfo – have arisen to help marketing planners link census and transaction data with consumer lifestyle patterns the better to segment their markets down to postcodes, streets, and even households. One of the leading lifestyle segmentation systems is Experian's Mosaic consumer classification system. The Mosaic system classifies every UK household based on a host of demographic factors – such as age, educational level, income, occupation, family composition, ethnicity and housing – and behavioural and life-style factors – such as purchases, free-time activities and media preferences. Mosaic Global extends this across 380 million households in 26 countries. Utilising Mosaic, marketers can use where you live to paint a surprisingly precise picture of who you are and what you might buy.

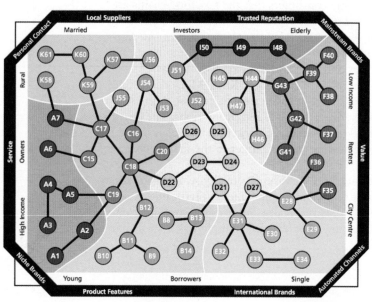

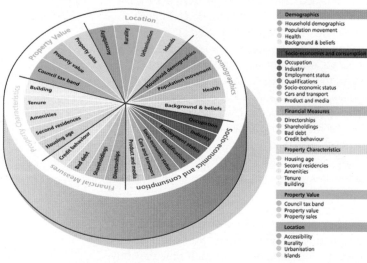

One of the leading lifestyle segmentation systems is Experian's Mosaic consumer classification.

Mosaic classifies UK households into 61 unique lifestyle types aggregated into 11 lifestyle groups.[14] Mosaic segments carry such exotic names as 'High-Technologists', 'Coronation Street' and 'New Urban Colonists'. 'Those image-triggered nicknames save a lot of time and technical research jargon explaining what you mean,' says one marketer. 'It's the names that bring the clusters to life,' says another.[15]

Regardless of what you call the categories, such systems can help marketers to segment people and locations into marketable groups of like-minded consumers. Each segment exhibits unique characteristics

Group	Group Description	% Households	Type	Type Description	% Households
A	Symbols of Success	9.62	A01	Global Connections	0.72
			A02	Cultural Leadership	0.92
			A03	Corporate Chieftains	1.12
			A04	Golden Empty Nesters	1.33
			A05	Provincial Privilege	1.66
			A06	High Technologists	1.82
			A07	Semi-Rural Seclusion	2.04
B	Happy Families	10.76	B08	Just Moving In	0.91
			B09	Fledgling Nurseries	1.18
			B10	Upscale New Owners	1.35
			B11	Families Making Good	2.32
			B12	Middle Rung Families	2.86
			B13	Burdened Optimists	1.96
			B14	In Military Quarters	0.17
C	Suburban Comfort	15.10	C15	Close to Retirement	2.81
			C16	Conservative Values	2.84
			C17	Small Time Business	2.93
			C18	Sprawling Subtopia	3.08
			C19	Original Suburbs	2.41
			C20	Asian Enterprise	1.02
D	Ties of Community	16.04	D21	Respectable Rows	2.65
			D22	Affluent Blue Collar	3.12
			D23	Industrial Grit	3.82
			D24	Coronation Street	2.81
			D25	Town Centre Refuge	1.13
			D26	South Asian Industry	0.88
			D27	Settled Minorities	1.62
E	Urban Intelligence	7.19	E28	Counter Cultural Mix	1.36
			E29	City Adventurers	1.27
			E30	New Urban Colonists	1.36
			E31	Caring Professionals	1.08
			E32	Dinky Developments	1.10
			E33	Town Gown Transition	0.76
			E34	University Challenge	0.26

→

Group	Group Description	% Households	Type	Type Description	% Households
F	Welfare Borderline	6.43	F35	Bedsit Beneficiaries	0.71
			F36	Metro Multiculture	1.67
			F37	Upper Floor Families	1.72
			F38	Tower Block Living	0.49
			F39	Dignified Dependency	1.34
			F40	Sharing a Staircase	0.50
G	Municipal Dependency	6.71	G41	Families on Benefits	1.21
			G42	Low Horizons	2.64
			G43	Ex-industrial Legacy	2.86
H	Blue Collar Enterprise	11.01	H44	Rustbelt Resilience	3.00
			H45	Older Right to Buy	2.67
			H46	White Van Culture	3.17
			H47	New Town Materialism	2.17
I	Twilight Subsistence	3.88	I48	Old People in Flats	0.83
			I49	Low Income Elderly	1.63
			I50	Cared for Pensioners	1.43
J	Grey Perspectives	7.88	J51	Sepia Memories	0.75
			J52	Childfree Serenity	1.34
			J53	High Spending Elders	1.53
			J54	Bungalow Retirement	1.26
			J55	Small Town Seniors	2.71
			J56	Tourist Attendants	0.30
K	Rural Isolation	5.39	K57	Summer Playgrounds	0.29
			K58	Greenbelt Guardians	1.74
			K59	Parochial Villagers	1.64
			K60	Pastoral Symphony	1.31
			K61	Upland Hill Farmers	0.41

and buying behaviour. For example, 'Corporate Chieftains' are well set in their careers, live in a large house in an economically advantaged part of the country. They prize discretion and understatement and look for these in the luxury brands they consume. The 'Child-free Serene' are often retired but independent. They are likely to have sold the family home for another property on the coast or abroad in sunnier climes. They support traditional activities and brands, and respond best to advertising in which the product benefits are clearly stated. When shopping, they appreciate items with a strong regional, heritage or craft-based proposition.

Such segmentation provides a powerful tool for marketers of all kinds. For example, the Bonati Institute, an advanced arthroscopic spinal surgery facility, used Prizm, a US equivalent of Mosaic, to help target prospective clients. The Institute wanted to know what its potential clients were like, where they lived and how to reach them. Claritas began by sorting 5,000 previous Bonati Institute patients into Prizm segments and ranking the segments according to their demographic, lifestyle and media behaviours. It found that the best target groups were middle-income consumers who were not aware of their orthopaedic-related choices. Armed with this information, the Institute devised a precisely targeted direct mail campaign to inform the best potential clients about a seminar series on spinal surgery technology. The results were immediate: seminar attendance increased 20 per cent, producing a substantial increase in scheduled surgeries.[16]

Segmenting business markets

Consumer and business marketers use many of the same variables to segment their markets. Business buyers can be segmented geographically, demographically (industry, company size), or by benefits sought, user status, usage rate and loyalty status. Yet, business marketers also use some additional variables, such as customer *operating characteristics*, *purchasing approaches*, *situational factors* and *personal characteristics*. By going after segments instead of the whole market, companies can deliver just the right value proposition to each segment served and capture more value in return.

Almost every company serves at least some business markets. For example, you probably know American Express as a company that offers personal credit cards to consumers. But American Express also targets businesses in three other segments – merchants, corporations and small businesses. It has developed distinct marketing programmes for each segment. In the merchants segment, American Express focuses on convincing new merchants to accept the card and on managing relationships with those that already do. For larger corporate customers, the company offers a corporate card programme, which includes extensive employee expenses and travel management services. It also offers this segment a wide range of asset management, retirement planning and financial education services. Finally, for small business customers, American Express has created the OPEN: Small Business Network, 'the one place that's all about small business'. Small business cardholders can access the network for everything from account and expense management software to expert small-business management advice and connecting with other small business owners to share ideas and get recommendations.[17]

Many companies set up separate systems for dealing with larger or multiple-location customers. For example, Steelcase, a major producer of office furniture, first segments customers into ten industries, including banking, insurance and electronics. Next, company salespeople work with independent Steelcase dealers to handle smaller, local or regional Steelcase customers in each segment. But many national, multiple-location customers, such as Exxon/Mobile or IBM, have special needs that may reach beyond the scope of individual dealers. So Steelcase uses national account managers to help its dealer networks handle its national accounts – we'll talk about this practice more in Chapter 13.

Within a given target industry and customer size, the company can segment by purchase approaches and criteria. As in consumer segmentation, many marketers believe that *buying behaviour* and *benefits* provide the best basis for segmenting business markets.[18]

Segmenting international markets

Few companies have either the resources or the will to operate in all, or even most, of the countries that dot the globe. Although some large companies, such as Coca-Cola or Sony, sell products in more than 200 countries, most international firms focus on a smaller set. Operating in many countries presents new challenges. Different countries, even those that are close together, can vary greatly in their economic, cultural and political make-up. Thus, just as they do within their domestic markets, international firms need to group their world markets into segments with distinct buying needs and behaviours.

Companies can segment international markets using one or a combination of several variables. They can segment by *geographic location*, grouping countries by regions such as Western Europe, the Pacific Rim, the Middle East, or Africa. Geographic segmentation assumes that nations close to one another will have many common traits and behaviours. Although this is often the case, there are many exceptions. For example, although Austria and Germany have much in common, both differ culturally and economically from the neighbouring Czech Republic. Even within a region, consumers can differ widely. For example, some marketers lump all Central and South American countries together. However, the Dominican Republic is no more like Brazil than Italy is like Sweden. Many Central and South Americans don't even speak Spanish, including 140 million Portuguese-speaking Brazilians and the millions in other countries who speak a variety of Indian dialects.

World markets can also be segmented on the basis of *economic factors*. For example, countries might be grouped by population income levels or by their overall level of economic development. A company's economic structure shapes its population's product and service needs and, therefore, the marketing opportunities it offers. Countries can be segmented by *political and legal factors* such as the type and stability of government, receptivity to foreign firms, monetary regulations and the amount of bureaucracy. Such factors can play a crucial role in a company's choice of which countries to enter and how. *Cultural factors* can also be used, grouping markets according to common languages, religions, values and attitudes, customs and behavioural patterns.

Segmenting international markets based on geographic, economic, political, cultural and other factors assumes that segments should consist of clusters of countries. However, many companies use a different approach called **intermarket segmentation**. They form segments of consumers who have similar needs and buying behaviour even though they are located in different countries. For example, Mercedes-Benz targets the world's well-to-do, regardless of their country.

MTV targets the world's teenagers. The world's 1.2 billion teens have a lot in common: they study, shop and sleep. They are exposed to many of the same major issues: love, crime, homelessness, ecology and working parents. In many ways, they have more in common with each other than with their parents. 'Last year I was in seventeen different countries,' says one expert, 'and it's pretty difficult to find anything that is different, other than language, among a teenager in Japan, a teenager in the UK, and a teenager in China.' MTV bridges the gap between cultures, appealing to what teens around the world have in common. Sony, Reebok, Nike and many other firms also actively target global teens. For example, Sprite's 'Image is nothing – obey your thirst' theme appeals to teens the world over.[19]

Requirements for effective segmentation

Clearly, there are many ways to segment a market, but not all segmentations are effective. For example, buyers of table salt could be divided into blonde and brunette customers. But hair colour obviously does not affect the purchase of salt. Furthermore, if all salt buyers bought the same amount of salt each month, believed that all salt is the same, and wanted to pay the same price, the company would not benefit from segmenting this market.

To be useful, market segments must be:

■ *Measurable*: The size, purchasing power, and profiles of the segments can be measured. Certain segmentation variables are difficult to measure. For example, there are 8 million left-handed people in the UK[20] – almost equalling the combined populations of Norway and Ireland. Yet few products are targeted toward this left-handed segment. The major problem may be that the segment is hard to identify and measure. There are no data on the demographics of lefties, and national government census agencies do not keep track of left-handedness. Private data companies keep reams of statistics on other demographic segments but not on handedness.

■ *Accessible*: The market segments can be effectively reached and served. Suppose a fragrance company finds that heavy users of its brand are single men and women who stay out late and socialise a lot. Unless this group lives or shops at certain places and is exposed to certain media, its members will be difficult to reach.

■ *Substantial*: The market segments are large or profitable enough to serve. A segment should be the largest possible homogenous group worth pursuing with a tailored marketing programme. It would not pay, for example, for a car manufacturer to develop cars especially for people whose height is greater than seven feet.

■ *Differentiable*: The segments are conceptually distinguishable and respond differently to different marketing mix elements and programmes. If married and unmarried women respond similarly to a sale on perfume, they do not constitute separate segments.

■ *Actionable*: Effective programmes can be designed for attracting and serving the segments. For example, although one small airline identified seven market segments, its staff was too small to develop separate marketing programmes for each segment.

MAKING CONNECTIONS Linking the concepts

Slow down a bit and smell the roses. How do the companies you do business with employ the segmentation concepts you're reading about here?

■ Can you identify specific companies, other than the examples already discussed, that practise the different types of segmentation just discussed?

■ Using the segmentation bases you've just read about, segment the UK footwear market. Describe each of the major segments and sub-segments. Keep these segments in mind as you read the next section on target market.

TARGET MARKETING

Market segmentation reveals the firm's market segment opportunities. The firm now has to evaluate the various segments and decide how many and which segments it can serve best. We now look at how companies evaluate and select target segments.

Evaluating market segments

In evaluating different market segments, a firm must look at three factors: segment size and growth, segment structural attractiveness, and company objectives and resources. The company must first collect and analyse data on current segment sales, growth rates and expected profitability for various segments. It will be interested in segments that have the right size and growth characteristics. But 'right size and growth' is a relative matter. The largest, fastest-growing segments are not always the most attractive ones for every company. Smaller companies may lack the skills and resources needed to serve the larger segments. Or they may find these segments too competitive. Such companies may target segments that are smaller and less attractive in an absolute sense, but that are potentially more profitable for them.

The company also needs to examine major structural factors that affect long-term segment attractiveness.[21] For example, a segment is less attractive if it already contains many strong and aggressive *competitors*. The existence of many actual or potential *substitute products* may limit prices and the profits that can be earned in a segment. The relative *power of buyers* also affects segment attractiveness. Buyers with strong bargaining power relative to sellers will try to force prices down, demand more services, and set competitors against one another – all at the expense of seller profitability. Finally, a segment may be less attractive if it contains *powerful suppliers* who can control prices or reduce the quality or quantity of ordered goods and services.

Even if a segment has the right size and growth and is structurally attractive, the company must consider its own objectives and resources. Some attractive segments can be dismissed quickly because they do not mesh with the company's long-term objectives. Or the company may lack the skills and resources needed to succeed in an attractive segment. The company should enter only segments in which it can offer superior value and gain advantages over competitors.

Selecting target market segments

After evaluating different segments, the company must now decide which and how many segments it will target. A **target market** consists of a set of buyers who share common needs or characteristics that the company decides to serve.

Because buyers have unique needs and wants, a seller could potentially view each buyer as a separate target market. Ideally, then, a seller might design a separate marketing programme for each buyer. However, although some companies do attempt to serve buyers individually, most face larger numbers of smaller buyers and do not find individual targeting worthwhile. Instead, they look for broader segments of buyers. More generally, target marketing can be carried out at several different levels. Figure 6.2 shows that companies can target very broadly (undifferentiated marketing), very narrowly (micromarketing), or somewhere in between (differentiated or concentrated marketing).

Undifferentiated marketing

Using an **undifferentiated marketing** (or **mass marketing**) strategy, a firm might decide to ignore market segment differences and target the whole market with one offer. This mass-marketing strategy focuses on what is *common* in the needs of consumers rather than on what is *different*. The company designs a product and a marketing programme that will appeal to the largest number of buyers.

As noted earlier in the chapter, most modern marketers have strong doubts about this strategy. Difficulties arise in developing a product or brand that will satisfy all consumers. Moreover, mass marketers often have trouble competing with more focused firms that do a better job of satisfying the needs of specific segments and niches.

Differentiated marketing

Using a **differentiated marketing** (or **segmented marketing**) strategy, a firm decides to target several market segments and designs separate offers for each. General Motors tries to produce a car for every 'purse, purpose, and personality'. Gap Inc. has created three different retail store formats – Gap, Banana Republic and Old Navy – to serve the varied needs of different fashion segments. And Estée Lauder offers hundreds of different products aimed at carefully defined segments:

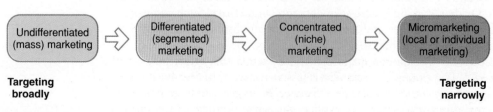

Targeting broadly · **Targeting narrowly**

FIGURE 6.2

Target marketing strategies

 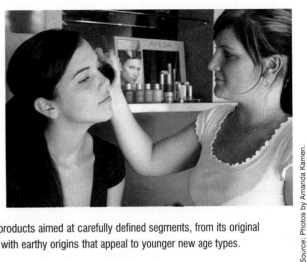

Differentiated marketing: Estée Lauder offers hundreds of different products aimed at carefully defined segments, from its original Estée Lauder brand appealing to age 50+ baby boomers to Aveda, with earthy origins that appeal to younger new age types.

Source: Photos by Amanda Kamen.

Estée Lauder is an expert in creating differentiated brands that serve the tastes of different market segments. Five of the top-ten best-selling prestige perfumes in the United States belong to Estée Lauder. So do eight of the top-ten prestige make-up brands. There's the original Estée Lauder brand, with its gold and blue packaging, which appeals to older, 50+ baby boomers. Then there's Clinique, the company's most popular brand, perfect for the middle-aged mom with no time to waste and for younger women attracted to its classic free gift offers. For young, fashion-forward consumers, there's M.A.C., which provides make-up for clients like Girls' Aloud and Dita von Teese. For the young and trendy, there's the Stila line, containing lots of shimmer and uniquely packaged in clever containers. And, for the New Age type, there's upscale Aveda, with its salon, make-up and lifestyle products, based on the art and science of earthy origins and pure flower and plant essences, celebrating the connection between Mother Nature and human nature.[22]

By offering product and marketing variations to segments, companies hope for higher sales and a stronger position within each market segment. Developing a stronger position within several segments creates more total sales than undifferentiated marketing across all segments. Estée Lauder's combined brands give it a much greater market share than any single brand could. The Estée Lauder and Clinique brands alone reap a combined 40 per cent share of the prestige cosmetics market.

But differentiated marketing also increases the costs of doing business. A firm usually finds it more expensive to develop and produce, say, 10 units of 10 different products than 100 units of one product. Developing separate marketing plans for the separate segments requires extra marketing research, forecasting, sales analysis, promotion planning and channel management. As well as this, trying to reach different market segments with different advertising increases promotion costs. Thus, the company must weigh increased sales against increased costs when deciding on a differentiated marketing strategy.

Concentrated marketing

A third market coverage strategy, **concentrated marketing** (or **niche marketing**), is especially appealing when company resources are limited. Instead of going after a small share of a large market, the firm goes after a large share of one or a few smaller segments or niches. For example, Oshkosh Truck is the world's largest producer of airport rescue trucks and front-loading concrete mixers. Tetra sells 80 per cent of the world's tropical fish food, and Steiner Optical captures 80 per cent of the world's military binoculars market.

Through concentrated marketing, the firm achieves a strong market position because of its greater knowledge of consumer needs in the niches it serves and the special reputation it acquires. It can market more *effectively* by fine-tuning its products, prices and programmes to the needs of carefully defined segments. It can also market more *efficiently*, targeting its products or services, channels and communications programmes only towards consumers that it can serve best and most profitably.

Whereas segments are fairly large and normally attract several competitors, niches are smaller and may attract only one or a few competitors. Niching offers smaller companies an opportunity to compete by focusing their limited resources on serving niches that may be unimportant to or overlooked by larger competitors. Consider Apple Computer. Although it once enjoyed a better than 13 per cent market share, Apple is now a market nicher, capturing less than 4 per cent of the world computer market. Rather than competing head-on with other PC makers as they slash prices and focus on volume, Apple invests in research and development, making it the industry trendsetter. For example, when the company introduced iTunes, it captured more than 70 per cent of the music download market. Such innovation has created a loyal base of consumers who are willing to pay more for Apple's cutting-edge products.

Many companies start as nichers to get a foothold against larger, more resourceful competitors, then grow into broader competitors. For example, Ryanair began by providing a cheaper, no-frills service between southern Ireland and London using just one plane – it is now a serious player in world aviation. In contrast, as markets change, some mega-marketers develop niche markets to create sales growth. For example, in recent years, Pepsi has introduced several niche products, such as Sierra Mist, Pepsi Edge, Mountain Dew Code Red, and Mountain Dew LiveWire. Initially, these brands combined accounted for barely 5 per cent of Pepsi's overall soft-drink sales. However, Sierra Mist has now blossomed into Pepsi's fastest-growing beverage brand, and Code Red and LiveWire have revitalised the Mountain Dew brand. Says Pepsi-Cola North America's chief marketing officer, 'The era of the mass brand has been over for a long time.'[23]

Today, the low cost of setting up shop on the Internet makes it even more profitable to serve seemingly minuscule niches. Small businesses, in particular, are realising riches from serving small niches on the Web. Here is a 'Webpreneur' who achieved astonishing results:

> Sixty-two-year-old British artist Jacquie Lawson taught herself to use a computer only a few years ago. In 2004, her online business had sales of $1.7 million. What does she sell? Online cards. Lawson occupies a coveted niche in the electronic world: a profitable, subscription-based website (**www.jacquielawson.com**) where she sells her highly stylized e-cards without a bit of advertising. While the giants offer hundreds of e-cards for every occasion, Lawson offers only about 50 in total, the majority of which she intricately designed herself. Revenue comes solely from 300,000 members – 81 per cent from the United States – who pay $8 a year. Lawson's success with a business model that has stumped many media giants speaks to both the Internet's egalitarian nature and her own stubborn belief that doing it her way is the right way. With a renewal rate of 70 per cent and more new members subscribing every day, sales will reach an estimated $5 million next year.[24]

Concentrated marketing can be highly profitable. At the same time, it involves higher-than-normal risks. Companies that rely on one or a few segments for all of their business will suffer greatly if the segment turns sour. Or larger competitors may decide to enter the same segment with greater resources. For these reasons, many companies prefer to diversify in several market segments.

Micromarketing

Differentiated and concentrated marketers tailor their offers and marketing programmes to meet the needs of various market segments and niches. At the same time, however, they do not customise their offers to each individual customer. **Micromarketing** is the practice of tailoring products and marketing programmes to suit the tastes of specific individuals and locations. Rather than seeing a customer in every individual, micro-marketers see the individual in every customer. Micromarketing includes *local marketing* and *individual marketing*.

Local marketing **Local marketing** involves tailoring brands and promotions to the needs and wants of local customer groups – cities, neighbourhoods, and even specific stores. Citibank provides different mixes of banking services in each of its branches, depending on neighbourhood demographics. Kraft helps supermarket chains iden-tify the specific cheese assortments and shelf positioning that will optimise cheese sales in low-income, middle-income and high-income stores and in different ethnic communities.

Local marketing has some drawbacks. It can drive up manufacturing and marketing costs by reducing economies of scale. It can also create logistics problems as companies try to meet the varied requirements of different regional and local markets. Further, a brand's overall image might be diluted if the product and message vary too much in different localities.

Still, as companies face increasingly fragmented markets, and as new supporting technologies develop, the advantages of local marketing often outweigh the drawbacks. Local marketing helps a company to market more effectively in the face of pronounced regional and local differences in demographics and lifestyles. It also meets the needs of the company's first-line customers – retailers – who prefer more fine-tuned product assortments for their neighbourhoods.

Individual marketing In the extreme, micromarketing becomes **individual marketing** – tailoring products and marketing programmes to the needs and preferences of indi-vidual customers. Individual marketing has also been labelled *one-to-one marketing*, *mass customisation* and *markets-of-one marketing*. We'll discuss this issue in depth in Chapter 13 in the section on Direct Marketing but here is an outline.

The widespread use of mass marketing has obscured the fact that for centuries con-sumers were served as individuals: the tailor custom-made the suit, the cobbler designed shoes for the individual, the cabinetmaker made furniture to order. Today, however, new technologies are permitting many companies to return to customised marketing. More powerful computers, detailed databases, robotic produc-tion and flexible manufacturing, and interactive communication media such as email and the Internet – all have combined to foster 'mass customisa-tion'. *Mass customisation* is the process through which firms interact one-to-one with masses of customers to design products and services tailor-made to individual needs.[25]

Dell creates custom-configured computers and Ford lets buyers 'build a vehicle' from a palette of options. Ice hockey stick maker Branches Hockey lets customers choose from more than two-dozen options – including stick length, blade patterns and blade curve – and turns out a customised stick in

Individual marketing: the UK's Driver and Vehicle Licensing Authority (DVLA) recognises that some people will pay for personalised number plates for their cars.

Source: http://www.dvla-som-co.uk/home/. Crown Copyright.

five days. Visitors to Nike's NikeID website can personalise their trainers by choosing from hundreds of colours and putting an embroidered word or phrase on the tongue. Even government agencies get in on the act. Visit the UK's vehicle licensing agency, DVLA, and you can choose your next licence plate letter/number combination.

Companies selling all kinds of products – from computers, foods, clothing and golf clubs to fire engines – are customising their offerings to the needs of individual buyers. 'Morelli's Gelato' in the Harrods Food Hall will produce a little tub of ice cream made up to your personal recipe in just twenty-four hours. They have been requested to produce ice creams for weddings – champagne and strawberry; flavours for the experimentally inclined – parmesan and pear; even the downright weird – fancy a tub of mushroom sorbet? Someone did, and Morelli's had it ready the next day.

Consumer goods marketers aren't the only ones going one-to-one. Business-to-business marketers are also finding new ways to customise their offerings. For example, John Deere manufactures seeding equipment that can be configured in more than 2 million versions to individual customer specifications. The seeders are produced one at a time, in any sequence, on a single production line.

Mass customisation provides a way to stand out against competitors. Consider Oshkosh Truck:

Oshkosh Truck specialises in making heavy-duty fire, airport-rescue, cement, garbage, snow-removal, ambulance and military vehicles. According to one account, 'Whether you need to plough your way through sand or snow, Oshkosh has your vehicle, by gosh.' Oshkosh has grown rapidly and profitably over the past decade. What's its secret? Mass customisation – the ability to personalise its products and services to the needs of individual customers. For example, when firefighters order a truck from Oshkosh, it's an event. They travel to the plant to watch the vehicle, which may cost as much as $800,000, take shape. The firefighters can choose from 19,000 options. A stripped-down fire truck costs $130,000, but 75 per cent of Oshkosh's customers order lots of extras, like hideaway stairs, ladders, special doors, compartments and firefighting foam systems for those difficult-to-extinguish fires. Some bring along paint chips so they can customise the colour of their fleet. Others are content just to admire the vehicles, down to the water tanks and hideaway ladders. 'Some chiefs even bring their wives; we encourage it,' says the president of Pierce Manufacturing, Oshkosh's firefighting unit. 'Buying a fire truck is a very personal thing.' Indeed, Pierce customers are in town so often that the Holiday Inn renamed its lounge the Hook and Ladder. Through such customisation and personalisation, Oshkosh has gained a big edge over its languishing larger rivals.[26]

Unlike mass production, which eliminates the need for human interaction, one-to-one has made relationships with customers more important than ever. Just as mass production was the marketing principle of the last century, mass customisation is becoming a marketing principle for the twenty-first century. The world appears to be coming full circle – from the good old days when customers were treated as individuals, to mass marketing when nobody knew your name, and back again.

The move towards individual marketing mirrors the trend in consumer *self-marketing*. Increasingly, individual customers are taking more responsibility for determining which products and brands to buy. Consider two business buyers with two different purchasing styles. The first sees several salespeople, each trying to persuade him to buy his or her product. The second sees no salespeople but rather logs on to the Internet. She searches for information on available products; interacts electronically with various suppliers, users and product analysts; and then makes up her own mind about the best offer. The second purchasing agent has taken more responsibility for the buying process, and the marketer has had less influence over her buying decision.

As the trend towards more interactive dialogue and less advertising monologue continues, self-marketing will grow in importance. As more buyers look up consumer reports, join Internet product discussion forums, and place orders via phone or online, marketers will have to influence the buying process in new ways. They will need to involve customers more in all phases of the product development and buying processes, increasing opportunities for buyers to practice self-marketing.

Choosing a target marketing strategy

Companies need to consider many factors when choosing a target marketing strategy. Which strategy is best depends on *company resources*. When the firm's resources are limited, concentrated marketing makes the most sense. The best strategy also depends on the degree of *product variability*. Undifferentiated marketing is more suited for uniform products such as grapefruit or steel. Products that can vary in design, such as cameras and cars, are more suited to differentiation or concentration. The *product's life-cycle stage* also must be considered. When a firm introduces a new product, it may be practical to launch only one version, and undifferentiated marketing or concentrated marketing may make the most sense. In the mature stage of the product life cycle, however, differentiated marketing begins to make more sense.

Another factor is *market variability*. If most buyers have the same tastes, buy the same amounts, and react in the same way to marketing efforts, undifferentiated marketing is appropriate. Finally, *competitors' marketing strategies* are important. When competitors use differentiated or concentrated marketing, undifferentiated marketing can be suicidal. Conversely, when competitors use undifferentiated marketing, a firm can gain an advantage by using differentiated or concentrated marketing.

Socially responsible target marketing

Smart targeting helps companies to be more efficient and effective by focusing on the segments that they can satisfy best and most profitably. Targeting also benefits consumers – companies reach specific groups of consumers with offers carefully tailored to satisfy their needs. However, target marketing sometimes generates controversy and concern. The biggest issues usually involve the targeting of vulnerable or disadvantaged consumers with controversial or potentially harmful products.

For example, over the years, the breakfast cereal industry has been heavily criticised for its marketing efforts directed toward children. Critics worry that high-powered advertising appeals presented through the mouths of lovable animated characters will overwhelm children's defences. The marketers of toys and other children's products have been similarly battered, often with good justification.

Other problems arise when the marketing of adult products spills over into the kid segment – intentionally or unintentionally. For example, governments and citizen action groups have accused breweries of targeting under-age drinkers with 'alcopop' type drinks. Some critics have even called for a complete ban on advertising to children in the UK, and in several European countries like Sweden severe restrictions are already in place.[27] To encourage responsible advertising, the Children's Advertising Review Unit, the US advertising industry's self-regulatory agency, has published extensive children's advertising guidelines that recognise the special needs of child audiences.

Cigarette, beer and fast-food marketers have also generated much controversy in recent years by their attempts to target vulnerable groups. For example, McDonald's and other chains have drawn criticism for pitching their high-fat, salt-laden fare to low-income people. Similarly, R.J. Reynolds took heavy flak in the early 1990s when it announced plans to market Uptown, a menthol cigarette targeted toward low-income blacks in US cities. It quickly dropped the brand in the face of a loud public outcry and heavy pressure from black leaders.

The meteoric growth of the Internet and other carefully targeted direct media has raised fresh concerns about potential targeting abuses. The Internet allows increasing refinement of audiences and, in turn, more precise targeting. This might help makers of questionable products or deceptive advertisers to victimise more readily the most vulnerable audiences. Unscrupulous marketers can now send tailor-made deceptive messages directly to the computers of millions of unsuspecting consumers.

Not all attempts to target children, minorities or other special segments draw such criticism. In fact, most provide benefits to targeted consumers. For example, Colgate makes a large selection of toothbrushes and toothpaste flavours and packages for children – from Colgate Barbie, Blues Clues, and SpongeBob SquarePants Sparkling Bubble Fruit toothpastes to Colgate Lego Bionicle and Bratz character toothbrushes.

Thus, in target marketing, the issue is not really *who* is targeted but rather *how* and for *what*. Controversies arise when marketers attempt to profit at the expense of targeted segments – when they unfairly target vulnerable segments or target them with questionable products or tactics. Socially responsible marketing calls for segmentation and targeting that serve not just the interests of the company but also the interests of those targeted.

MAKING CONNECTIONS Linking the concepts

Time to coast for a bit and take stock.

■ At the last Making Connections, you segmented the UK footwear market. Refer to Figure 6.2 and select two companies that serve this market. Describe their segmentation and targeting strategies. Can you come up with one that targets many different segments versus another that focuses on only one or a few segments?

■ How does each company you chose differentiate its market offering and image? Has each done a good job of establishing this differentiation in the minds of targeted consumers? The final section in this chapter deals with such positioning issues.

POSITIONING FOR COMPETITIVE ADVANTAGE

Beyond deciding which segments of the market it will target, the company must decide what positions it wants to occupy in those segments. A **product's position** is the way the product is *defined by consumers* on important attributes – the place the product occupies in consumers' minds relative to competing products. 'Products are created in the factory, but brands are created in the mind,' says one positioning expert.[28]

In the car market, the Vauxhall (Opel) Astra and Ford Focus are positioned on economy, Mercedes and BMW on luxury, and Porsche and Ferrari on performance. Volvo positions powerfully on safety. And Toyota positions its fuel-efficient, hybrid Prius as a high-tech solution to the energy shortage. 'How far will you go to save the planet?', it asks.

Consumers are overloaded with information about products and services. They cannot re-evaluate products every time they make a buying decision. To simplify the buying process, consumers organise products, services and companies into categories and 'position' them in their minds. A product's position is the complex set of perceptions, impressions and feelings that consumers have for the product compared with competing products.

Consumers position products with or without the help of marketers. But marketers do not want to leave their products' positions to chance. They must *plan* positions that will give their products the greatest advantage in selected target markets, and they must design marketing mixes to create these planned positions.

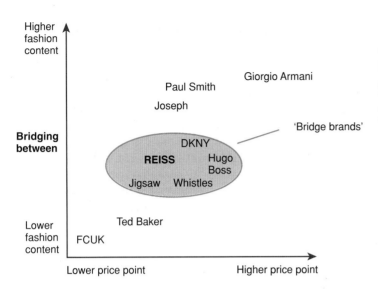

FIGURE 6.3

A positioning map based on consumer perceptions

Source: From L. Quinn, T. Hines and D. Bennison (2007) 'Making sense of market segmentation: A fashion retailing case', *European Journal of Marketing*, **41**(5/6). © Emerald Group Publishing Limited, all rights reserved.

Positioning maps

In planning their positioning strategies, marketers often prepare *perceptual positioning maps*, which show consumer perceptions of their brands versus competing products on important buying dimensions. Figure 6.3 shows a positioning map based on consumer perceptions of fashion retailers in the UK produced on behalf of Reiss.[29] In this example, the retailers are mapped on the basis of consumer perception of their prices and the level of 'fashion content', criteria that the researchers found to explain the situation best. Remember – these have not been objectively measured, it is all about consumer perception. From this map, Reiss can see that it is perceived as being relatively low-priced and at about the midpoint with respect to fashion content. The map also shows which are its closest competitors – that is, the other fashion retailers that customers think of as being similar to Reiss. Management at Reiss must consider the implications of this map for their positioning strategy – is this where they want the firm to be? If not, where is their preferred location, and what actions must be taken to manoeuvre the company there?

Choosing a positioning strategy

Some firms find it easy to choose their positioning strategy. For example, a firm well known for quality in certain segments will go for this position in a new segment if there are enough buyers seeking quality. But in many cases, two or more firms will go after the same position. Then, each will have to find other ways to set itself apart. Each firm must differentiate its offer by building a unique bundle of benefits that appeals to a substantial group within the segment.

The positioning task consists of three steps: identifying a set of possible competitive advantages upon which to build a position, choosing the right competitive advantages and selecting an overall positioning strategy. The company must then effectively communicate and deliver the chosen position to the market.

Identifying possible competitive advantages

To build profitable relationships with target customers, marketers must understand customer needs better than competitors do and deliver more value. To the extent that a company can position itself as providing superior value, it gains **competitive advantage**. But solid positions cannot be built on empty promises. If a company positions its product as *offering* the best quality and service, it must then *deliver* the promised quality and service. Thus, positioning begins with actually *differentiating* the company's market offering so that it will give consumers superior value.

To find points of differentiation, marketers must think through the customer's entire experience with the company's product or service. An alert company can find ways to differentiate itself at every customer contact point. In what specific ways can a company differentiate itself or its market offer? It can differentiate along the lines of *product, services, channels, people* or *image*.

Product differentiation takes place along a continuum. At one extreme we find physical products that allow little variation: chicken, steel, aspirin. Yet even here some meaningful differentiation is possible. For example, many European farmers are successfully charging a premium price after adopting – or implying the adoption – of 'organic' production methods. At the other extreme are products that can be highly differentiated, such as cars, clothing and furniture. Such products can be differentiated on features, performance, or style and design. Thus, Volvo provides new and better safety features; Whirlpool designs its dishwasher to run more quietly; Bose positions its speakers on their striking design and sound characteristics. Similarly, companies can differentiate their products on such attributes as consistency, durability, reliability or repairability.

Beyond differentiating its physical product, a firm can also differentiate the services that accompany the product. Some companies gain *services differentiation* through speedy, convenient or careful delivery. For example, Ocado delivers groceries to your home, like many other companies, but Ocado will do so in a one-hour window of your choice and has an easy to use website. Installation service can also differentiate one company from another, as can repair services. Many a car buyer will gladly pay a little more and travel a little further to buy a car from a dealer that provides top-notch repair services.

Some companies gain service differentiation by providing customer training service or consulting services – data, information systems, and advising services that buyers need.

Firms that practise *channel differentiation* gain competitive advantage through the way they design their channel's coverage, expertise and performance. **Amazon.com**, Dell, and Avon set themselves apart with their high-quality direct channels. Caterpillar's success in the construction equipment industry is based on superior channels. Its dealers worldwide are renowned for their first-rate service.

Companies can gain a strong competitive advantage through *people differentiation* – hiring and training better people than their competitors do. Disney people are known to be friendly and upbeat. Singapore Airlines enjoys an excellent reputation, largely because of the grace of its flight attendants. People differentiation requires that a company selects its customer-contact people carefully and trains them well. For example, Disney trains its theme park people thoroughly to ensure that they are competent, courteous and friendly – from the hotel check-in agents, to the monorail drivers, to the ride attendants, to the people who sweep Main Street USA. Each employee is carefully trained to understand customers and to 'make people happy'.

Even when competing offers look the same, buyers may perceive a difference based on company or brand *image differentiation*. A company or brand image should convey the product's distinctive benefits and positioning. Developing a strong and distinctive image calls for creativity and hard work. A company cannot develop an image in the public's mind overnight using only a few advertisements. If Radisson means quality, this image must be supported by everything the company says and does in or around its hotels.

Symbols – such as the McDonald's golden arches, the Nike swoosh, or Google's colourful logo – can provide strong company or brand recognition and image differentiation. The company might build a brand around a famous person, as Nike did in the 1980s with its Air Jordan basketball shoes and does with Tiger Woods golfing products now. Some companies even become associated with colours, such as Sainsbury's (orange), IBM (blue) or UPS (brown). The chosen symbols, characters and other image elements must be communicated through advertising that conveys the company's or brand's personality.

Choosing the right competitive advantages

Suppose a company is fortunate enough to discover several potential competitive advantages. It must now choose the ones on which it will build its positioning strategy. It must decide *how many* differences to promote and *which ones*.

How many differences to promote? Many marketers think that companies should aggressively promote only one benefit to the target market. Ad man Rosser Reeves, for example, said a company should develop a *unique selling proposition* (USP) for each brand and stick to it. Each brand should pick an attribute and tout itself as 'number one' on that attribute. Buyers tend to remember number one better, especially in an over-communicated society. Thus, Crest toothpaste consistently promotes its anti-cavity protection and Asda promotes low prices.

Other marketers think that companies should position themselves on more than one differentiator. This may be necessary if two or more firms are claiming to be best on the same attribute. Today, in a time when the mass market is fragmenting into many small segments, companies are trying to broaden their positioning strategies to appeal to more segments. For example, Lush produces cosmetics and toiletries that are not only hand-made, but also from ingredients that have not been tested on animals, appealing to those who want either or both ethics and luxury in their toiletries. However, as companies increase the number of claims for their brands, they risk disbelief and a loss of clear positioning.

Which differences to promote? Not all brand differences are meaningful or worthwhile; not every difference makes a good differentiator. Each difference has the potential to create company costs as well as customer benefits. A difference is worth establishing to the extent that it satisfies the following criteria:

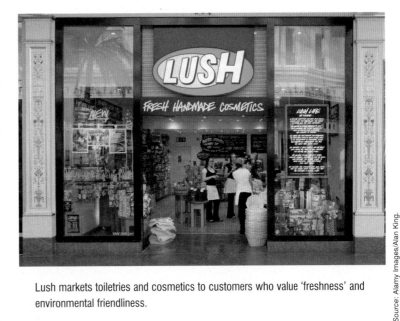

Lush markets toiletries and cosmetics to customers who value 'freshness' and environmental friendliness.

Source: Alamy Images/Alan King.

- ■ *Important*: The difference delivers a highly valued benefit to target buyers.

- ■ *Distinctive*: Competitors do not offer the difference, or the company can offer it in a more distinctive way.

- ■ *Superior*: The difference is superior to other ways that customers might obtain the same benefit.

- ■ *Communicable*: The difference is communicable and visible to buyers.

- ■ *Pre-emptive*: Competitors cannot easily copy the difference.

- ■ *Affordable*: Buyers can afford to pay for the difference.

- ■ *Profitable*: The company can introduce the difference profitably.

Many companies have introduced differentiations that failed one or more of these tests. When the Westin Stamford Hotel in Singapore advertised that it was the world's tallest hotel, it was a distinction that was not important to most tourists – in fact, it turned many off. Polaroid's Polarvision, which produced instantly developed home movies, sank without trace too. Although Polarvision was distinctive and even pre-emptive, it was inferior to another way of capturing motion, namely, camcorders. Thus, choosing competitive advantages upon which to position a product or service can be difficult, yet such choices may be crucial to success.

Selecting an overall positioning strategy

The full positioning of a brand is called the brand's **value proposition** – the full mix of benefits upon which the brand is positioned. It is the answer to the customer's question 'Why should I buy your brand?' Volvo's value proposition hinges on safety but also includes reliability, roominess and styling, all for a price that is higher than average but seems fair for this mix of benefits.

Figure 6.4 shows possible value propositions upon which a company might position its products. In the figure, the five green cells represent winning value propositions – positioning that gives the company competitive advantage. The red cells, however, represent losing value propositions. The centre yellow cell represents at best a marginal proposition. In the following sections, we discuss the five winning value propositions upon which companies can position their products: more for more, more for the same, the same for less, less for much less and more for less.

More for more 'More-for-more' positioning involves providing the most upscale product or service and charging a higher price to cover the higher costs. Radisson Hotels, Mont Blanc writing instruments, BMW cars – each claims superior quality, craftsmanship, durability, performance or style and charges a price to match. Not only is the market offering high in quality, it also gives prestige to the buyer. It symbolises status and a loftier lifestyle. Often, the price difference exceeds the actual increment in quality.

Sellers offering 'only the best' can be found in every product and service category, from hotels, restaurants, food and fashion to cars and household appliances. Consumers are sometimes surprised, even delighted, when a new competitor enters a category with an unusually high-priced brand. Starbucks coffee entered as a very expensive brand in a largely commodity category. Dyson came in as a premium vacuum cleaner with a price to match, touting 'No clogged bags, no clogged filters, and no loss of suction means only one thing. It's a Dyson.'

In general, companies should be on the lookout for opportunities to introduce a 'more-for-more' brand in any underdeveloped product or service category. Yet 'more-for-more' brands can be vulnerable. They often invite imitators who claim the same quality but at a lower price. Luxury goods that sell well during good times may be at risk during economic downturns when buyers become more cautious in their spending.

FIGURE 6.4

Possible value propositions

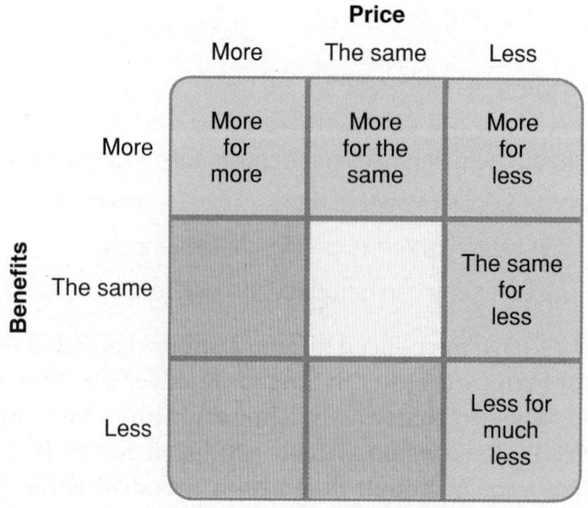

More for the same Companies can attack a competitor's more-for-more positioning by introducing a brand offering comparable quality but at a lower price. For example, Toyota introduced its Lexus line with a 'more-for-the-same' value proposition versus Mercedes and BMW. Its headline read: 'Perhaps the first time in history that trading a £40,000 car for a £20,000 car could be considered trading up.' It communicated the high quality of its new Lexus through rave reviews in car magazines and through a widely distributed videotape showing side-by-side comparisons of Lexus and Mercedes cars. It published surveys showing that Lexus dealers were providing customers with better sales and service experiences than were Mercedes dealerships. Many Mercedes owners switched to Lexus, and the Lexus repurchase rate has been 60 per cent, twice the industry average.

The same for less Offering 'the same for less' can be a powerful value proposition – everyone likes a good deal. For example, Dell offers equivalent quality computers at a lower 'price for performance'. Discount stores such as Wal-Mart and 'category killers' such as Toys 'R' Us and Tesco use this positioning. They don't claim to offer different or better products. Instead, they offer many of the same brands as department stores and speciality stores but at deep discounts based on superior purchasing power and lower-cost operations. Other companies develop imitative but lower-priced brands in an effort to lure customers away from the market leader. For example, AMD makes less expensive versions of Intel's market-leading microprocessor chips.

Less for much less A market almost always exists for products that offer less and therefore cost less. Few people need, want or can afford 'the very best' in everything they buy. In many cases, consumers will gladly settle for less than optimal performance or give up some of the bells and whistles in exchange for a lower price. For example, many travellers seeking accommodation prefer not to pay for what they consider unnecessary extras, such as a pool, attached restaurant, or mints on the pillow. Hotel chains such as Travelodge suspend some of these amenities and charge less accordingly.

'Less-for–much-less' positioning involves meeting consumers' lower performance or quality requirements at a much lower price. Retailers like Colruyt in Belgium, Dia-Mart in France and Lidl and Aldi across Europe (but originally from Germany) are examples of this type of positioning. Ryanair also practices less-for-much-less positioning. It charges incredibly low prices by not serving food, not assigning seats, and not using travel agents (see Marketing at Work 6.2).

More for less Of course, the winning value proposition would be to offer 'more for less'. Many companies claim to do this. And, in the short run, some companies can actually achieve such lofty positions. For example, when it first opened for business in the USA, Home Depot had arguably the best product selection, the best service, *and* the lowest prices compared to local hardware stores and other home improvement chains.

Yet in the long run, companies will find it very difficult to sustain such best-of-both positioning. Offering more usually costs more, making it difficult to deliver on the 'for-less' promise. Companies that try to deliver both may lose out to more focused competitors. For example, facing determined competition from Asda, Sainsbury's must now decide whether it wants to compete primarily on superior service or on lower prices.

All said, each brand must adopt a positioning strategy designed to serve the needs and wants of its target markets. 'More for more' will draw one target market, 'less for much less' will draw another, and so on. Thus, in any market, there is usually room for many different companies, each successfully occupying different positions.

The important thing is that each company must develop its own winning positioning strategy, one that makes it special to its target consumers. Offering only 'the same for the same' provides no competitive advantage, leaving the firm in the middle of the pack.

MARKETING AT WORK 6.2

Ryanair's value proposition: Less for much less

All businesses start small, even airlines. Ryanair was founded in 1985, flying its single small plane between Waterford in Ireland and London. It is now one of Europe's biggest carriers in terms of passengers per year – having experienced rapid growth since 2000, as shown in the chart below – and became the first airline anywhere in the world to fly 4 million passengers internationally in a single month.[30]

Up until 1992, Ryanair had no clear positioning strategy, and did well to break even. Then came the appointment of a dynamic and focused new Chief Executive – Michael O'Leary. Given the task of turning round the organisation, O'Leary examined the business model of Southwest Airlines in the USA – the original low-cost carrier – and considered how that model could be imported into the newly deregulated EU airlines sector.[31] In essence, Ryanair adopted a positioning strategy of 'less for much less' – to provide basic air travel with no frills or thrills at prices a fraction of those of its competitors.

In order to offer low prices on airfares while still making a profit, Ryanair is required to keep a very close eye on its costs – all organisations need to keep an eye on costs, but a fundamental requirement of Ryanair's positioning as a low-price carrier is a fixation with cost reduction and efficiency improvements. Indeed, Ryanair management has a reputation for being able to spot innovative new ways to save money.

How does Ryanair reduce costs? In a word, ruthlessly. Every aspect of the operation is continually under review to establish where costs can be trimmed – or passed on to others – and efficiency improved. In the words of Michael Cawley, Chief Operating Officer:

Can we do what we are doing at a reduced cost? Can we achieve what we want to achieve a different way? How can we hand on those cost savings to the customer? You cannot exist by just reducing prices. You can only exist profitably by reducing costs by at least as much.[32]

Ryanair only uses one type of aeroplane, often purchased second-hand – Boeing 737-800s. This simplifies maintenance and repair which in turn requires fewer support staff to manage and maintain the fleet. It also means that pilots only need to be qualified to fly the one plane, reducing retraining costs and giving both economies of scale and weight when negotiating with Boeing for spares or updates. The planes themselves are not equipped with the sophisticated passenger entertainment systems found on carriers like BA or Virgin – saving money on purchase and upkeep. In flight, passengers are not provided with complimentary meals, and must pay extra for any snacks or drinks they require – as well as an extra source of revenue on top of ticket price, Ryanair doesn't require a complex logistical system to support catering. Ryanair is experimenting with new technology that will allow the safe use of mobile phones in-flight, but only because they will receive a revenue stream in the form of a proportion of the 'roaming fees' from the mobile phone service networks. Speaking of mobile phones, Ryanair made the news when it required staff to cease recharging their personal mobiles at work to save the company money.[33]

Required by law to provide onboard safety information for passengers, Ryanair has chosen not to provide the usual plastic coated sheets to be found next to the sick-bags on most planes but rather has them mounted on the back of the seat in front, meaning there are no stolen or damaged ones to be replaced. This parsimoniousness is continued

Ryanair offers a classic 'less for much less' proposition – the drive to cut costs is apparent across all of the firm's activities.
Source: http://www.ryanair.com/site/EN/.

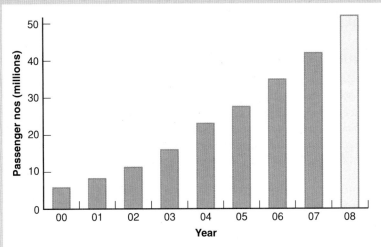

FIGURE 6.5

Ryanair passenger numbers, 2000–2007

Source: http://www.ryanair.com.

in the rest of the interior fixtures and fittings – the seats don't recline, there are no detachable headrests and the windows have no blinds! Seats are upholstered in leather – not for luxury but for reasons of longevity and ease of maintenance.

In choosing its routes, Ryanair avoids 'brand-name' airports like Heathrow, Charles De Gaulle and Schiphol as an explicit part of its strategy, preferring to use less well known regional hubs nearby, for example London Stansted, Paris-Beauvais and Eindhoven.[34] In doing so, Ryanair believes it improves turnaround time, isn't required to pay premium fees for services and facilities like baggage-handling and refuelling, but the additional costs to passengers of significant transit distances at either end of the journey is often a sore point between Ryanair, customer groups and regulatory bodies.[35] Ryanair even grounds part of its fleet over the winter months when demand for flights is lower, a decision unique amongst airlines.[36]

The streamlining of ground operations, a one-model fleet and the use of regional airports have led to remarkable efficiency gains with respect to competitors. In 2003, Ryanair employed fewer than 2,000 staff to fly 24 million passengers. In the same year, Lufthansa required 39,000 employees to fly 37 million.[37] This is a per-employee productivity ratio of more than 12 to 1.

The deviation from standard industry practice continues in areas of the business not directly connected with flying. Faced with a £3 million quotation for producing the first website for the firm, Ryanair instead turned to students at a local university, bargaining them down to less than £15,000.[38] Ryanair produces all its own advertisements in-house, rather than paying an external agency. This has sometimes led to confrontations with bodies such as the Advertising Standards Authority in the UK and its equivalents in other European countries like Belgium and Norway over the use of unpleasant, deceptive or inaccurate language in its communications.

Some 96 per cent of all tickets are sold via Ryanair.com, removing booking agency fees and most of the transaction costs. Some costs, such as fees payable to Visa or MasterCard for processing, are passed on to the passenger at the point of booking (£4 in 2007). Passengers also pay an additional fee for each item of luggage they wish to place in the hold.[39] At check-in, passengers are not assigned a specific seat.

Such ruthlessness does not always win friends or make good headlines.

In recent times, Ryanair lost a case against a disabled passenger who acted to reclaim a fee imposed for the use of a wheelchair in the airports at either end of his journey. Ryanair's position that they were merely passing on the cost imposed on them by the airport operator failed to impress the County Court.[40] Indeed, while most passengers are satisfied, or at least feel they get what they pay for, an outcome of the strategy is that Ryanair has developed a poor reputation for customer service.[41] Several websites exist to report and collate stories about poor customer service from Ryanair.[42]

So what is the future for Ryanair? The company faces significant challenges in respect of legislation, taxation and concerns about the environmental impact of the aviation industry,[43] with Ryanair already fighting to have the sector less heavily regulated at the state and supra-state level within Europe, with specific targets of protectionism, state subsidy of national carriers and monopolies on airport management services.[44] Regardless, the obsession with cost control will stay, and the positioning of the business will remain '*less for much less*'.

Sources: See notes 30–44 at the end of this chapter.

Companies offering one of the three losing value propositions – 'the same for more', 'less for more', and 'less for the same' – will inevitably fail. Customers soon realise that they've been underserved, tell others and abandon the brand.

Developing a positioning statement

Company and brand positioning should be summed up in a **positioning statement**. The statement should follow the form: *To (target segment and need) our (brand) is (concept) that (point-of-difference)*.[45] For example: *'To busy, mobile professionals who need always to be in the loop, BlackBerry is a wireless connectivity solution that allows you to stay connected to data, people and resources while on the go, easily and reliably – more so than competing technologies.'* Sometimes a positioning statement is more detailed:

> To young, active soft-drink consumers who have little time for sleep, Red Bull is the soft drink that gives you more energy than any other brand because it has the highest level of caffeine. With Red Bull, you can stay alert and keep going even when you haven't been able to get a good night's sleep.

Note that the positioning first states the product's membership in a category (Red Bull is a soft drink, first marketed in Austria but based on a traditional Thai drink[46]) and then shows its point of difference from other members of the category (has more caffeine and distinctive ingredients like taurine). Placing a brand in a specific category suggests similarities that it might share with other products in the category. But the case for the brand's superiority is made on its points of difference.

Sometimes marketers put a brand in a surprisingly different category before indicating the points of difference. DiGiorno's is a frozen pizza whose crust rises when the pizza is heated. But instead of putting it in the frozen pizza category, the marketers positioned it in the delivered pizza category. Their ad shows party guests asking which pizza delivery service the host used. But, says the host, 'It's not delivery, its DiGiorno!' This helped highlight DiGiorno's fresh quality and superior taste over the normal frozen pizza.

Communicating and delivering the chosen position

Once it has chosen a position, the company must take strong steps to deliver and communicate the desired position to target consumers. All the company's marketing mix efforts must support the positioning strategy.

Positioning the company calls for concrete action, not just talk. If the company decides to build a position on better quality and service, it must first *deliver* that position. Designing the marketing mix – product, price, place and promotion – involves working out the tactical details of the positioning strategy. Thus, a firm that seizes on a more-for-more position knows that it must produce high-quality products, charge a high price, distribute through high-quality dealers and advertise in high-quality media. It must hire and train more service people, find retailers who have a good reputation for service, and develop sales and advertising messages that broadcast its superior service. This is the only way to build a consistent and believable more-for-more position.

Companies often find it easier to come up with a good positioning strategy than to implement it. Establishing a position or changing one usually takes a long time. In contrast, positions that have taken years to build can quickly be lost. Once a company has built the desired position, it must take care to maintain the position through consistent performance and communication. It must closely monitor and adapt the position over time to match changes in consumer needs and competitors' strategies. However, the company should avoid abrupt changes that might confuse consumers. Instead, a product's position should evolve gradually as it adapts to the ever-changing marketing environment.

THE JOURNEY YOU'VE TAKEN Reviewing the concepts

It's time to stop and stretch your legs. In this chapter, you've learned about the major elements of marketing strategy: segmentation, targeting and positioning. Marketers know that they cannot appeal to all buyers in their markets, or at least not to all buyers in the same way. Buyers are too numerous, too widely scattered, and too varied in their needs and buying practices. Therefore, most companies today practice target marketing – identifying market segments, selecting one or more of them, and developing products and marketing mixes tailored to each.

1 **Define the three steps of target marketing: market segmentation, target marketing and market positioning.**

Market segmentation is the act of dividing a market into distinct groups of buyers with different needs, characteristics or behaviours who might require separate products or marketing mixes. Once the groups have been identified, target marketing evaluates each market segment's attractiveness and selects one or more segments to serve. Target marketing involves designing strategies to build the right relationships with the right customers. Market positioning consists of deciding how best to serve target customers – setting the competitive positioning for the product and creating a detailed marketing plan.

2 **List and discuss the major bases for segmenting consumer and business markets.**

There is no single way to segment a market. Therefore, the marketer tries different variables to see which give the best segmentation opportunities. For consumer marketing, the major segmentation variables are geographic, demographic, psychographic and behavioural. In geographic segmentation, the market is divided into different geographical units such as nations, regions, states, counties, cities or neighbourhoods. In demographic segmentation, the market is divided into groups based on demographic variables, including age, gender, family size, family life cycle, income, occupation, education, religion, race, generation and nationality. In psychographic segmentation, the market is divided into different groups based on social class, lifestyle or personality characteristics.

In behavioural segmentation, the market is divided into groups based on consumers' knowledge, attitudes, uses or responses to a product.

Business marketers use many of the same variables to segment their markets. But business markets can also be segmented by business consumer demographics (industry, company size), operating characteristics, purchasing approaches, situational factors and personal characteristics. The effectiveness of segmentation analysis depends on finding segments that are measurable, accessible, substantial, differentiable and actionable.

3 **Explain how companies identify attractive market segments and choose a target marketing strategy.**

To target the best market segments, the company first evaluates each segment's size and growth characteristics, structural attractiveness, and compatibility with company objectives and resources. It then chooses one of four target marketing strategies – ranging from very broad to very narrow targeting. The seller can ignore segment differences and target broadly using undifferentiated (or mass) marketing. This involves mass producing, mass distributing and mass promoting the same product in about the same way to all consumers. Or the seller can adopt differentiated marketing – developing different market offers for several segments. Concentrated marketing (or niche marketing) involves focusing on only one or a few market segments. Finally, micromarketing is the practice of tailoring products and marketing programmes to suit the tastes of specific individuals and locations. Micromarketing includes local marketing and individual marketing. Which targeting strategy is best depends on company resources, product variability, product life-cycle stage, market variability and competitive marketing strategies.

4 **Discuss how companies position their products for maximum competitive advantage in the marketplace.**

Once a company has decided which segments to enter, it must decide on its market positioning strategy – on which positions to occupy in its chosen segments. The positioning task consists of three steps: identifying a set of possible competitive advantages upon which to build a position, choosing the right competitive advantages and selecting an overall positioning strategy. The brand's full positioning is called its *value proposition* – the full mix of benefits upon which the brand is positioned. In general, companies can choose from one of five winning value propositions upon which to position their products: more for more, more for the same, the same for less, less for much less or more for less. Company and brand positioning are summarised in positioning statements that state the target segment and need, positioning concept and specific points of difference. The company must then effectively communicate and deliver the chosen position to the market.

NAVIGATING THE KEY TERMS

Age and life-cycle segmentation 194
Behavioural segmentation 198
Benefit segmentation 198
Competitive advantage 213
Concentrated (or niche)
   marketing 207
Demographic segmentation 194
Differentiated (or segmented)
   marketing 206

Gender segmentation 195
Geographic segmentation 193
Income segmentation 195
Individual marketing 209
Intermarket segmentation 204
Local marketing 209
Market positioning 192
Market segmentation 192
Micromarketing 209

Occasion segmentation 198
Positioning statement 220
Product position 212
Psychographic segmentation 197
Target market 206
Target marketing 192
Undifferentiated (or mass) marketing 206
Value proposition 216

NOTES AND REFERENCES

1 See S. Paliwoda and S. Marinova, 'The marketing challenges within the enlarged Single European Market', *European Journal of Marketing*, **41**(3/4), 2007, pp. 233–44.

2 http://news.bbc.co.uk/1/hi/england/coventry_warwickshire/4649843.stm.

3 http://www.doveproage.com/.

4 http://www.bramdean.com/wealth_management/bramdiva; http://search.ft.com/ftArticle?queryText=Bramdiva&y=5&aje=true&x=16&id=051119000459.

5 See Fara Warner, 'Nike Changes Strategy on Women's Apparel', *New York Times*, 16 May 2005, accessed at www.nytimes.com.

6 http://www.harrods.com/Cultures/en-GB/Home/homepageindex.htm; http://www.quartier206.com/.

7 See for examples: J. Ansell, T. Harrison and T. Archibald, 'Identifying cross-selling opportunities, using lifestyle segmentation and survival analysis', *Marketing Intelligence & Planning*, **25**(4), 2007, pp. 394–410 or S. Richbell and V. Kite, 'Night shoppers in the "open 24 hours" supermarket: a profile', *International Journal of Retail & Distribution Management*, **35**(1), 2007, pp. 54–68

8 See Maureen Wallenfang, 'Appleton, Wis.-Area Dealers See Increase in Moped Sales', *Knight Ridder Tribune Business News*, 15 August 2004, p. 1; and Honda's website at www.powersports.honda.com/scooters/ (July 2005).

9 http://www.britegg.co.uk/.

10 http://www.confetti.co.uk/category/view/7695.do.

11 Information from www.kodak.com, July 2005.

12 See Jennifer Ordonez, 'Fast-Food Lovers, Unite!', *Newsweek*, 24 May 2004, p. 56.

13 See Alan T. Sarasevic, 'Author plumbs bottomless depth of Mac worship', *San Francisco Chronicle*, 12 December 2004, available at http://www.sfgate.com/cgi-bin/article.cgi?file= /chronicle/archive/2004/12/12/BUG7BA9Q791.DTL&type=business.

14 http://www.business-strategies.co.uk/upload/downloads/mosaic%20uk%20brochure.pdf.

15 John Fetto, 'American Neighborhoods' First Page', *American Demographics*, July–August 2003, p. 34.

16 Example from http://www.clusterbigip1.claritas.com/claritas/Default.jsp?main=2, accessed April 2005.

17 Information from http://home.americanexpress.com/home/mt_personal.shtml, accessed August 2007.

18 For more on segmenting business markets, see Turan Senguder, 'An Evaluation of Consumer and Business Segmentation Approaches', *Journal of the Academy of Business*, March 2003, pp. 618–24; and James C. Anderson and James A. Narus, *Business Market Management*, 2nd edn (Upper Saddle River, NJ: Prentice Hall, 2004), pp. 45–52.

19 See Arundhati Parmar, 'Global Youth United', *Marketing News*, 28 October 2002, pp. 1, 49; 'Teen Spirit', *Global Cosmetic Industry*, March 2004, p. 23; Johnnie L. Roberts, 'World Tour', *Newsweek*, 6 June 2005, pp. 34–6; and the MTV Worldwide website, www.mtv.com/mtvinternational.

20 http://news.bbc.co.uk/1/hi/magazine/6943871.stm.

21 See Michael Porter, *Competitive Advantage* (New York: Free Press, 1985), pp. 4–8, 234–6. For more recent discussions, see Stanley Slater and Eric Olson, 'A Fresh Look at Industry and Market Analysis', *Business Horizons*, January–February 2002, p. 15–22; Kenneth Sawka and Bill Fiora, 'The Four Analytical Techniques Every Analyst Must Know: 2. Porter's Five Forces Analysis', *Competitive Intelligence Magazine*, May–June 2003, p. 57; and Philip Kotler and Kevin Lane Keller, *Marketing Management*, 12th edn (Upper Saddle River, NJ: Prentice Hall, 2006), pp. 342–3.

22 Nina Munk, 'Why Women Find Lauder Mesmerizing', *Fortune*, 25 May 1998, pp. 97–106; Christine Bittar, 'New Faces, Same Name', *Brandweek*, 11 March 2002, pp. 28–34; Robin Givhan, 'Estee Lauder, Sending a Message in a Bottle', *The Washington Post*, 26 April 2004, p. C.01; and information accessed at www.elcompanies.com, www.stila.com, and www.macmakeup.com, July 2005.

23 See Gerry Khermouch, 'Call it the Pepsi Blue Generation', *BusinessWeek*, 3 February 2003, p. 96; Kathleen Sampey, 'Sweet on Sierra Mist', *Adweek*, 2 February 2004, p. 20; and Nat Ives, 'Mountain Dew Double-Dose for Times Square Passers-By', *New York Times*, 8 April 2004, p. C9.

24 Gwendolyn Bounds, 'How an Artist Fell Into a Profitable Online Card Business', *Wall Street Journal*, 21 December 2004, p. B1.

25 For a good discussion of mass customisation and relationship building, see Don Peppers and Martha Rogers, *Managing Customers Relationships: A Strategic Framework* (Hoboken, NJ: John Wiley & Sons, 2004), ch. 10.

26 Adapted from information found in Mark Tatge, 'Red Bodies, Black Ink', *Forbes*, 18 September 2000, p. 114; 'Oshkosh Truck Corporation', *Hoover's Company Profiles*, 1 June 2005, p. 14345; and information accessed at www.oshkoshtruckcorporation.com, August 2005.

27 http://www.sweden.gov.se/sb/d/3011/a/19038; http://europa.eu/scadplus/leg/en/lvb/l24030a.htm.

28 Jack Trout, 'Branding Can't Exist without Positioning', *Advertising Age*, 14 March 2005, p. 28.

29 http://www.reiss.co.uk/; positioning map reproduced from L. Quinn, T. Hines and D. Bennison, 'Making sense of market segmentation: a fashion retailing case', *European Journal of Marketing*, **41**(5/6), 2007, pp. 439–65.

30 http://www.ryanair.com/site/EN/about.php?page=About&pos=HEAD.

31 R. Lachenauer et al. (2006) *Hardball Strategies*, 2nd edn, Harvard Business Review: http://harvardbusinessonline.hbsp.harvard.edu/b02/en/common/item_detail.jhtml?referral= 1933&id=1050&profileId=258013138&_DARGS=/b02/en/includes/product_upsell_ display_center.jhtml_A&_DAV=.

32 http://www.ericsson.com/telecomreport/article.asp?aid=10&tid=85&ma=1&msa=3.

33 http://news.scotsman.com/uk.cfm?id=433412005.

34 http://www.ryanair.com/site/about/invest/docs/Strategy.pdf.

35 http://news.bbc.co.uk/1/hi/business/6957882.stm.

36 http://www.ft.com/cms/s/3afe4938-3f41-11dc-b034-0000779fd2ac,Authorised= false.html?_i_location=http%3A%2F%2Fwww.ft.com%2Fcms%2Fs%2F3afe4938- 3f41-11dc-b034-0000779fd2ac.html&_i_referer=.

37 A. Ruddock, 'Keeping up with O'Leary', *Management Today*, September 2003, pp. 48.

38 http://books.guardian.co.uk/reviews/biography/0,,2146959,00.html.

39 http://money.guardian.co.uk/consumernews/story/0,,2152518,00.html.

40 http://news.bbc.co.uk/1/hi/england/essex/3994913.stm.

41 http://www.rte.ie/business/2006/1026/ryanair.html.

42 http://www.ryanaircampaign.org/; http://www.guardian.co.uk/consumer/story/0,,1812983,00.html.

43 http://www.direct.gov.uk/en/Nl1/Newsroom/DG_10020511.

44 http://search.ft.com/ftArticle?queryText=ryanair&aje=true&id=070710004899; http://www.ft.com/cms/s/7d295dc2-45e3-11dc-b359-0000779fd2ac.html; http://business.guardian.co.uk/story/0,,2145673,00.html.

45 See Bobby J. Calder and Steven J. Reagan, 'Brand Design', in Dawn Iacobucci, ed., *Kellogg on Marketing* (New York: John Wiley & Sons, 2001), p. 61.

46 http://www.redbull.com/images/historysection/pdf/1/Red_Bulls_Good_Buzz.pdf.

CHAPTER 7

Product, services and branding strategy

AFTER STUDYING THIS CHAPTER, YOU SHOULD BE ABLE TO

- define *product* and the major classifications of products and services
- describe the decisions companies make regarding their individual products and services, product lines and product mixes
- discuss branding strategy – the decisions companies make in building and managing their brands
- identify the four characteristics that affect the marketing of a service and the additional marketing considerations that services require
- discuss two additional product issues: socially responsible product decisions and international product and services marketing

THE WAY AHEAD Previewing the concepts

Now that you've had a good look at marketing strategy, we'll take a deeper look at the marketing mix – the tactical tools that marketers use to implement their strategies. In this and the next chapter we'll study how companies develop and manage products and brands. Then, in the chapters that follow, we'll look at pricing, distribution and marketing communication tools. The product is usually the first and most basic marketing consideration. We'll start with a seemingly simple question: what *is* a product? As it turns out, however, the answer is not so simple.

First stop on this leg of the journey: a supremely elegant English brand that has become known around the world as a statement of sophistication, taste and quality – Dunhill. What is the magic ingredient that makes a brand invented for pioneering, and usually very eccentric, English motoring gentlemen in the nineteenth century relevant to well-off consumers of good taste around the world today? How is it that a brand that was invented to sell motoring accessories in England nearly 120 years ago can be used to sell gorgeous pens, fragrances and chess sets today?

Alfred Dunhill Ltd: Reconciling tradition and innovation in product and brand management

Dr Kim Lehman and Dr John Byrom, *School of Management, University of Tasmania, Australia*

Alfred Dunhill would probably not be surprised if he were to walk into a twenty-first century Dunhill store. Certainly he might if he were to visit a store in Shanghai, Dubai, Hong Kong or New Delhi, since he would only know the original retail outlet in St James's, London – which remains the spiritual home of Alfred Dunhill Ltd – and the New York and Paris stores. While he might be surprised by the global reach of the brand, he would still see some of his famous motoring accessories dotted about. But he would surely recognise that aura of discreet, but nonetheless luxurious, style and the continuation of his own fascination with innovative high quality products. Still, Dunhill has come a long way since Alfred took over his father's saddlery business in 1893. Though it is now owned by Swiss-based luxury goods conglomerate Compagnie Financière Richemont SA, it ranks as one of the most well-known British brands in the world. It is still seen as one of those masculine, but gentlemanly, brands that hark back to times gone by.

What would no doubt please Alfred Dunhill, and remind him of his own day, is the way Dunhill still specialises in the market it helped to create all those years ago, supplying luxury gentlemen's accessories, designed in the English style. When Dunhill's tagline was 'Everything for the car but the motor', the firm aimed to provide the still embryonic motoring market with all the extras drivers might need, since cars were little more than a chassis and an engine at the time. Alfred coined the term 'Motorites' to describe the range of products he invented to sell in his elegant shop in central London. That market, though, was made up largely of wealthy, eccentric men prepared to brave technology most people thought would not last very long. Nowadays there may well not be enough gentleman adventurers to form a viable market segment for any firm, but an astute firm will retain the 'spirit' of the past, repackage it for the modern consumer, and carefully manage their products and brand to suit.

Keeping the traditions of the brand alive needs to be a priority for firms, like Dunhill, that seek to incorporate their history into their marketing communications. This is no different from a firm that, for example, is known for its value for money. Such a firm would incorporate into its branding communications clues to the consumer as to where its products sit in relation to others – their position in other words – then use branding to build an image upon which the consumer can draw when it comes time to purchase.

Branding, then, encompasses the associations that come to mind when consumers think about a brand, as well as all instances of contact that customers may have with a brand. For Dunhill, their retail stores and licensed outlets must reinforce the brand. Linked to this is how Dunhill uses brand identity, which involves those facets of the brand that represent the brand visually and verbally – logos, taglines, colours and so on. These facets are constructions of the firm concerned. Dunhill crafts a brand identity to support its position as a retailer of superior, luxury goods for men, continually and consistently communicating the message of tradition and heritage through their advertising. The firm understands that simply claiming a tradition since 1893 is not sufficient to impress today's highly informed consumers. It must be demonstrated in a tangible way.

A significant part of the Dunhill brand is its reputation for innovation and invention. This is true even in relation to their retail outlets. The current London store has a fitting room with a unique lighting system that can reproduce the natural lighting of any city in the world at any time of the day. A gentleman, no matter where they may be from, can assess his suit in just the right lighting! Clearly, Dunhill has never only just been about the 'gentlemanly' product range, it was also about that quirky, eccentric side to the English identity. One example oft-told is Alfred Dunhill's invention of 'Bobby-finders', a combined binocular/goggle that

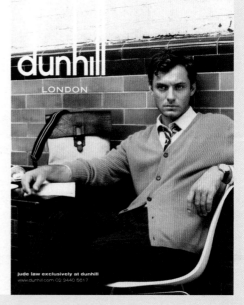

claimed to be useful in detecting police hiding by the roadside, waiting to catch unsuspecting motorists who might be speeding. Stemming from a speeding ticket handed out to Alfred, the 'Bobby-finder' is one slightly eccentric example. There are, though, numerous, more mainstream instances of product innovation. The 'Unique' petrol cigarette lighter became almost a cult item in the 1920s, as did the 'Aquarium' table lighter of the 1940s.

Today, on a more commercial level, the firm exploits this tradition of innovation by drawing on the products of the past. Dunhill maintains an archive of products that feels like a first-class museum, which is used as a source of inspiration for their designers. Items in the archive have provided the inspiration for new products that can be as innovative today as those in the archive were in years gone by. The archive plays a core role in the business. It serves as a reminder of the brand's history, of the variety and quality of products over the years, and is a source of inspiration to energise the creative team to continue that tradition. In a manner of speaking, Dunhill view their archive as an embodiment of the DNA of the brand. There is, then, a storehouse of corporate memory that competing firms can only dream of.

The products that come from this reference to the past are not just reproductions of previous items. The archive 'informs' the design, it does not control it. There is little value in designing, manufacturing and retailing a product that does not communicate with the current market. One example of how this works for Dunhill is their 'Sidecar' collection, launched in 2004. This collection, which included a range of writing instruments and leather goods, was inspired by the motorcycle sidecars produced by Dunhill in their early

years – part of the firm's 'Motorites for Motorcyclists' that first appeared in a 1905 product catalogue. One product in the Sidecar collection particularly illustrates the Dunhill philosophy. A limited edition fountain pen, the Sidecar Limousette, was included, with only 1893 produced, to celebrate the year in which Alfred Dunhill took over the business. These subtleties are part of the English style that is carefully cultivated by Dunhill.

It is this very 'Englishness' that is perhaps at the heart of the brand's appeal in the global marketplace. Dunhill have now successfully packaged their brand for a number of international markets. Alfred Dunhill opened his first New York store in 1921 and the Paris store in 1924. The latter, in Rue de la Paix, has become something of a landmark in the French capital, much as the St James's store has in London. In the 1920s to be able to state 'London, Paris, New York' on your marque was symbolic of an internationally successful brand. It wasn't until 1966 that Dunhill ventured to Asia, opening a store in Hong Kong in that year. Now Dunhill is represented throughout the Far East, the Indian subcontinent and the Middle East. These 'out-posts' of the Dunhill brand, the wholly-owned stores in particular, all communicate the same message as the original three stores – style, restrained luxury and quality gentlemen's accoutrements. Indeed, items from the Dunhill archive collection sometimes travel throughout the firm's global network, tangibly to reinforce the brand's heritage. It would not be unusual to see a collection of 1930s Dunhill Art Deco silver and lacquer cigarette lighters and timepieces on display in the Tokyo store, for example. Both the London and Paris store have continual exhibition displays from the Dunhill archive, including many

items from the very early motoring days. Visitors are literally immersed in the Dunhill brand!

For Dunhill, then, there are two things that are fundamental to their appeal to sophisticated, wealthy customers. The first is authenticity: of the brand and of the products. That authenticity is underpinned by the history and traditions of the firm. A customer might say: 'I go to Dunhill because I know Dunhill has been around for a hundred years, and it stands for something.' Buying into that tradition, that heritage – very important in the Asian market – is an important facet of the Dunhill brand that needs to be carefully managed. However, the brand image can only survive so long as the products are perceived as stylish, well designed and beautifully made, and deliver on the brand promise. Of course, the product must also make the buyer feel good about themselves, and make other people feel impressed; perhaps make the buyer feel 20 years younger, or make them look taller and a lot more sexy! Remember, luxury products are about much more than their physical attributes. They are also about feeling good.

The second fundamental aspect of the Dunhill brand is its relevance to the current market and its consumer. So, while there is no doubt that authenticity and heritage are very important, the product line has to be in tune with the spirit of the times. If it's not, it will fail – consumers are not going to buy simply because of the heritage of the brand. In other words, a heritage brand, if it's not counterbalanced by good quality products with a contemporary feel, can actually become a millstone, because the image of the brand will be diluted, relegating it to being thought of as simply old-fashioned.

The challenge for brands like Dunhill, that rely on their heritage as part of their branding, is to reconcile that with the constant need to remain relevant to the modern consumer. Global retailing, where the same stores appear in every major city, means that consumers throughout the world can now choose from a myriad of luxury brands, many with similar brand promises. In some ways Dunhill has a distinct advantage. It has always had a reputation for producing quirky, innovative, but above all, high-quality men's accessories. It can take risks with its products, and revisit classic ideas and designs. But it would be an unwise strategy to lose sight of those facets of the brand that made it famous. Perhaps the trick might be to remain true to Alfred Dunhill's original vision. He aimed to fill his store with products customers could not find anywhere else. People would visit London, come to Dunhill, and expect to find something new, different and exciting. That is a product and branding strategy still valid in today's world – and one which still works for Dunhill.

Clearly, there is a lot more to the products Dunhill sells than simply a nice pen or a bottle of perfume – Dunhill sells something far more complex than just consumer commodities. This chapter begins with a deceptively simple question: what is a product? After answering this question, we look at ways to classify products in consumer and business markets. Then we discuss the important decisions that marketers make regarding individual products, product lines and product mixes. Next, we look into the critically important issue of how marketers build and manage brands. Finally, we examine the characteristics and marketing requirements of a special form of product – services.

WHAT IS A PRODUCT?

We define a **product** as anything that can be offered to a market for attention, acquisition, use or consumption that might satisfy a want or need. Products include more than just tangible goods. Broadly defined, products include physical objects, services, events, persons, places, organisations, ideas or mixes of these entities. Throughout this text, we use the term *product* broadly to include any or all of these entities. Thus, an Apple iPod, a Toyota Avensis and a Nokia mobile phone are products. But so are a skiing holiday, HSBC banking services and advice from your family doctor.

Because of their importance in the world economy, we give special attention to services. **Services** are a form of product that consists of activities, benefits or satisfactions offered for sale that are essentially intangible and do not result in the ownership of anything. Examples are banking, hotel, airline, retail, accounting and home-repair services. We will look at services more closely later in this chapter.

Products, services and experiences

Product is a key element in the overall *market offering*. Marketing-mix planning begins with formulating an offering that brings value to target customers. This offering becomes the basis upon which the company builds profitable relationships with customers.

A company's market offering often includes both tangible goods and services. Each component can be a minor or a major part of the total offer. At one extreme, the offer may consist of a *pure tangible good*, such as soap, toothpaste or salt – no services accompany the product. At the other extreme are *pure services*, for which the offer consists primarily of a service. Examples include having your teeth checked by a dentist or financial services. Between these two extremes, however, many goods-and-services combinations are possible.

Because of a proliferation of products and competitors, many companies are moving to a new level in creating value for their customers. To differentiate their offers, beyond simply making products and delivering services, they are creating and managing customer *experiences* with their products or company.

Experiences have always been important in the entertainment industry – Disney has long manufactured memories through its movies and theme parks. Today, however, all kinds of firms are recasting their traditional goods and services to create experiences. For example, Ireland's top visitor attraction is the Guinness Storehouse in Dublin. Hundreds of thousands of people visit every year to enjoy the complete Guinness *experience*. This is a great deal more than simply enjoying a drink of Ireland's world famous beer:

Traditionally the unique attraction of Ireland as a tourist destination has been the level and depth of contact tourists have with Irish people. This is especially the case with tourists who wish to connect with their Irish heritage and who consider Ireland to be a second home. As an internationally recognised and acclaimed visitor experience the Guinness Storehouse has consistently been the top visitor attraction in Ireland since it opened its doors in late 2000. Diageo, which Guinness is part of, have successfully leveraged the association of Ireland as a destination and the rich history attached to the Guinness brand into a viable and leading focal point for tourists when they visit Ireland.[1]

The Guinness Brewery Storehouse, Dublin, Ireland.

Source: Alamy Images/AR Photo.

Companies that market experiences realise that customers are really buying much more than just products and services. They are buying what those offers will *do* for them.

Levels of product and services

Product planners need to think about products and services on three levels (see Figure 7.1). Each level adds more customer value. The most basic level is the ***core benefit***, which addresses the question, ***what is the buyer really buying?*** When designing products, marketers must first define the core, problem-solving benefits or services that consumers seek. A woman buying lipstick buys more than lip colour. Charles Revson of Revlon saw this early: 'In the factory, we make cosmetics; in the store, we sell hope.' And young parents buying a Sony Cyber-shot are buying more than a digital camera. They are buying a convenient, high-quality way to capture important moments and memories.

At the second level, product planners must turn the core benefit into an ***actual product***. They need to develop product and service features, design, a quality level, a brand name and packaging. For example, the Sony digital camera is an actual product. Its name, parts, styling, features, packaging and other attributes have all been combined carefully to deliver the core benefit of capturing memories.

Finally, product planners must build an ***augmented product*** around the core benefit and actual product by offering additional consumer services and benefits. Sony must offer more than just a digital camera. It must provide consumers with a complete solution to their picture-taking problems. Thus, when consumers buy a Sony digital camera, Sony and

FIGURE 7.1

Three levels of product

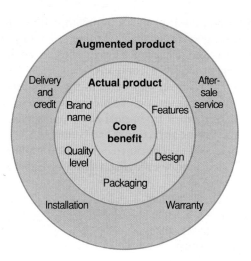

its dealers might also give buyers a warranty on parts and workmanship, instructions on how to use the camera, quick repair services when needed, and a free telephone number to call if they have problems or questions.

Consumers see products as complex bundles of benefits that satisfy their needs. When developing products, marketers must first identify the *core* consumer needs the product will satisfy. They must then design the *actual* product and find ways to *augment* it in order to create the bundle of benefits that will provide the most satisfying customer experience.

Product and service classifications

Products and services fall into two broad classes based on the types of consumers that use them – *consumer products* and *industrial products*. Broadly defined, products also include other marketable entities such as experiences, organisations, persons, places and ideas.

Consumer products

Consumer products are products and services bought by final consumers for personal consumption. Marketers usually classify these products and services further based on how consumers go about buying them. Consumer products include *convenience products*, *shopping products*, *speciality products* and *unsought products*. These products differ in the ways consumers buy them and therefore in how they are marketed (see Table 7.1).

Convenience products are consumer products and services that the customer usually buys frequently, immediately and with a minimum of comparison and buying effort. Examples include soap, chocolate, newspapers and fast food. Convenience products are usually inexpensive, and marketers place them in many locations to make them readily available when customers need them.

Shopping products are less frequently purchased consumer products and services that customers compare carefully on suitability, quality, price and style. When buying shopping products and services, consumers spend a lot of time and effort gathering information and making comparisons. Examples include furniture, clothing, used cars, major appliances, and hotel and airline services. Shopping products marketers usually distribute their products through fewer outlets but provide deeper sales support to help customers in their comparison efforts.

Speciality products are consumer products and services with unique characteristics or brand identification for which a significant group of buyers is willing to make a

TABLE 7.1 Marketing considerations for consumer products

Marketing considerations	Type of consumer Product			
	Convenience	Shopping	Speciality	Unsought
Customer buying behaviour	Frequent purchase, little planning, little comparison or shopping effort, low customer involvement	Less frequent purchase, much planing and shopping effort, comparison of brands on price, quality, style	Strong brand preference and loyalty, special purchase effort, little comparison of brands, low price sensitivity	Little product awareness, knowledge (or, if aware, little or even negative interest)
Price	Low price	High price	Higher price	Varies
Distribution	Widespread distribution, convenient locations	Selective distribution in fewer outlets	Exclusive distribution in only one or a few outlets per market area	Varies
Promotion	Mass promotion by the producer	Advertising and personal selling by both producer and resellers	More carefully targeted promotion by both producer and resellers	Aggressive advertising and personal selling by producer and resellers
Examples	Toothpaste, magazines, laundry detergent	Major appliances, televisions, furniture, clothing	Luxury goods, such as Rolex watches or fine crystal	Life insurance, Red Cross blood donations

special purchase effort. Examples include specific brands and types of cars, high-priced photographic equipment, designer clothes, and the services of medical or legal specialists. A Porsche sports car, for example, is a speciality product because buyers are usually willing to travel great distances to buy one. Buyers normally do not compare speciality products. They invest only the time needed to reach dealers carrying the wanted products.

Unsought products are consumer products that the consumer either does not know about or knows about but does not normally think of buying. Most major new innovations are unsought until the consumer becomes aware of them through advertising. Classic examples of known but unsought products and services are life insurance, pre-planned funeral services and personal pensions. By their very nature, unsought products require a lot of advertising, personal selling and other marketing efforts.

Industrial products

Industrial products are those purchased for further processing or for use in conducting a business. Thus, the distinction between a consumer product and an industrial product is based on the *purpose* for which the product is bought. If a consumer buys a lawnmower for use around home, the lawnmower is a consumer product. If the same consumer buys the same lawnmower for use in a landscaping business, the lawnmower is an industrial product.

The three groups of industrial products and services include materials and parts, capital items, and supplies and services. *Materials and parts* include raw materials and manufactured materials and parts. Raw materials consist of farm products (wheat, cotton, livestock, fruits, vegetables) and natural products (fish, wood, crude oil, iron ore). Manufactured materials and parts consist of component materials (iron, yarn, cement, wires) and component parts (small motors, tyres, castings). Most manufactured materials and parts are sold directly to industrial users. Price and service are the major marketing factors; branding and advertising tend to be less important.

Capital items are industrial products that aid in the buyer's production or operations, including installations and accessory equipment. Installations consist of major purchases such as buildings (factories, offices) and fixed equipment (generators, drill presses, large computer systems). Accessory equipment includes portable factory equipment and tools (hand tools, fork-lift trucks) and office equipment (computers, fax machines, desks). They have a shorter life than installations and simply aid in the production process.

The final group of business products is *supplies and services*. Supplies include operating supplies (lubricants, coal, paper, pencils) and repair and maintenance items (paint, nails, brooms). Supplies are the convenience products of the industrial field because they are usually purchased with a minimum of effort or comparison. Business services include maintenance and repair services (window cleaning, computer repair) and business advisory services (legal, management consulting, advertising). Such services are usually supplied under contract.

Organisations, persons, places and ideas

In addition to tangible products and services, in recent years marketers have broadened the concept of a product to include other market offerings – organisations, persons, places and ideas.

Organisations often carry out activities to 'sell' the organisation itself. *Organisation marketing* consists of activities undertaken to create, maintain or change the attitudes and behaviour of target consumers towards an organisation. Both profit and not-for-profit organisations practise organisation marketing. Business firms sponsor public relations or corporate advertising campaigns to polish their images. *Corporate image advertising* is a major tool companies use to market themselves to various publics. For example, Dutch bank ABN AMRO ads say 'While some are focused on us, we are focused on you', and the French oil company Total tells us that 'our energy is your energy'. Similarly, not-for-profit organisations, such as churches, universities, charities, museums and performing arts groups, market their organisations in order to raise funds and attract members or patrons.

People can also be thought of as products. *Person marketing* consists of activities undertaken to create, maintain or change attitudes or behaviour towards particular people. People ranging from presidents, entertainers and sports figures to professionals such as doctors, lawyers and architects use person marketing to build their reputations and increase business. Businesses, charities, sports teams and other organisations also use person marketing. Creating or associating with well-known personalities often helps these organisations achieve their goals better. That's why more than a dozen different companies – including Nike, Apple, Tag Heuer, Buick, American Express, Wheaties and Accenture – combine to pay more than $70 million a year to link themselves with golf superstar Tiger Woods.[2]

The skilful use of person marketing can turn a person's name into a powerhouse brand. You can buy a wide range of clothing marketed under the Björn Borg brand name, a vast array of golfing gear endorsed by Ryder Cup golf star Sergio Garcia, and you can make yourself

People can develop strong personal brands. Sir Alan Sugar has established a personal brand because of his business, charity and media work.

smell nice with a Roger Federer cologne set. And businessman Alan Sugar has not only established the brand name of his business – Amstrad – but also has now become a well-known personal brand as a result of his many appearances on television, notably in *The Apprentice* where his legendary business acumen attracts millions of dedicated viewers. Like a number of successful businesspeople, Sir Alan uses his strong personal brand to support philanthropic work, for example through the Alan Sugar Foundation.

Place marketing involves activities undertaken to create, maintain or change attitudes or behaviour towards particular places. Cities, states, regions, and even entire nations compete to attract tourists, new residents, conventions, and company offices and factories. Stratford-upon-Avon in England promotes itself as the birthplace of Shakespeare, Dublin – 'the fair city' – advertises itself as a cultural capital with a youthful population where everyone will have fun, while Durban, South Africa, calls itself 'the playground of the Zulu kingdom', promoting both its African heritage and its beautiful coastline. The Iceland Tourist Board invites visitors to Iceland by advertising that it has 'Discoveries the Entire Year'. Icelandair, the only airline that serves the island, partners with the tourist board to sell world travellers on the wonders of Iceland – everything from geothermal spas and glacier tours to midnight golf and clubbing.[3]

Ideas can also be marketed. In one sense, all marketing is the marketing of an idea, whether it is the general idea of brushing your teeth or the specific idea that Arm & Hammer Enamel Care toothpaste will help to protect the enamel on your teeth. Here, however, we narrow our focus to the marketing of *social ideas*. This area has been called **social marketing**, defined by the Social Marketing Institute as the use of commercial marketing concepts and tools in programmes designed to influence individuals' behaviour to improve their well-being and that of society.[4]

Social marketing programmes include public health campaigns to reduce smoking, alcoholism, drug abuse and overeating. Other social marketing efforts include environmental campaigns to promote wilderness protection, clean air and conservation. Still others address issues such as family planning, human rights and racial equality. The European Commission has recently developed a pan-European multimedia advertising campaign to try to convince Europeans to stop smoking, or never to start smoking in the first place – take a look at the start of Chapter 16 if you would like to know more about this now.

But social marketing involves much more than just advertising – the Social Marketing Institute (SMI) encourages the use of a broad range of marketing tools. 'Social marketing goes well beyond the promotional '*P*' of the marketing mix to include every other element to achieve its social change objectives,' says the SMI's executive director.[5]

PRODUCT AND SERVICE DECISIONS

Marketers make product and service decisions at three levels: individual product decisions, product line decisions and product mix decisions. We discuss each in turn.

Individual product and service decisions

Figure 7.2 shows the important decisions in the development and marketing of individual products and services. We will focus on decisions about *product attributes*, *branding*, *packaging*, *labelling* and *product support services*.

Product and service attributes

Developing a product or service involves defining the benefits that it will offer. These benefits are communicated and delivered by product attributes such as *quality*, *features*, and *style and design*.

FIGURE 7.2

Individual product decisions

Product quality Product quality is one of the marketer's major positioning tools. Quality has a direct impact on product or service performance; thus, it is closely linked to customer value and satisfaction. In the narrowest sense, quality can be defined as 'freedom from defects'. But most customer-centred companies go beyond this narrow definition. Instead, they define quality in terms of creating customer value and satisfaction. For example, Siemens defines quality this way: 'Quality is when our customers come back and our products don't.'[6] We emphasised above that a product may be either a tangible good or an intangible service, and in a service business quality has been defined as 'the extent to which the service delivered meets the customer's expectations'.[7]

Total quality management (TQM) is an approach in which all the company's people are involved in constantly improving the quality of products, services and business processes. Companies large and small have credited TQM with greatly improving their market shares and profits. Over the years, however, many companies have encountered problems in implementing TQM. Some companies viewed TQM as a magic cure-all and created token total quality programmes that applied quality principles only superficially. Still others became obsessed with narrowly defined TQM principles and lost sight of broader concerns for customer value and satisfaction. As a result, many such programmes failed, causing a backlash against TQM.

When applied in the context of creating customer satisfaction, however, *total quality* principles remain a requirement for success. Although many firms don't use the TQM label any more, for most top companies customer-driven quality has become a way of doing business. Today, companies are taking a 'return on quality' approach, viewing quality as an investment and holding quality efforts accountable for bottom-line results.[8]

Product quality has two dimensions – level and consistency. In developing a product, the marketer must first choose a *quality level* that will support the product's positioning. Here, product quality means *performance quality* – the ability of a product to perform its functions. For example, a BMW provides higher performance quality than a Fiat: it is better engineered and lasts longer. Companies rarely try to offer the highest possible performance quality level – few customers want or can afford the high levels of quality offered in products such as a Rolls-Royce car, a €1,000 Louis Vuitton handbag or a Rolex watch. Instead, companies choose a quality level that matches target market needs and the quality levels of competing products.

Beyond quality level, high quality can mean high levels of consistency. Here, product quality means *conformance quality* – freedom from defects and *consistency* in delivering a targeted level of performance. All companies should strive for high levels of conformance quality. In this sense, a Ford can have just as much quality as a Rolls-Royce. Although a Ford doesn't have all the same features as a Rolls-Royce, it can as consistently deliver the quality that customers pay for and expect.

Many companies today have turned customer-driven quality into a potent strategic weapon. They have created customer satisfaction and value by consistently and profitably meeting customers' needs and preferences for quality.

Product features A product can be offered with varying features. A stripped-down model, one without any extras, is the starting point. The company can create higher-level models by adding more features. Features are a competitive tool for differentiating the company's product from competitors' products. Being the first producer to introduce a needed and valued new feature is one of the most effective ways to compete.

How can a company identify new features and decide which ones to add to its product? The company should periodically survey buyers who have used the product and ask these questions: How do you like the product? Which specific features of the product do you like most? Which features could we add to improve the product? The answers provide the company with a rich list of feature ideas. The company can then assess each feature's *value* to customers versus its *cost* to the company. Features that customers value little in relation to costs should be dropped; those that customers value highly in relation to costs should be added.

Product style and design Another way to add customer value is through distinctive *product style and design*. Design is a larger concept than style. *Style* simply describes the appearance of a product. Styles can be eye-catching or yawn-producing. A sensational style may grab attention and produce pleasing aesthetics, but it does not necessarily make the product *perform* better. Unlike style, *design* is more than skin deep – it goes to the very heart of a product. Good design contributes to a product's usefulness as well as to its looks.

Good design begins with a deep understanding of customer needs. More than simply creating product or service attributes, it involves shaping the customer's product-use experience. Consider the design process behind Invotek's Strawboard.

Invotek Solutions began life as Poole Partitionings in 1973, a specialist manufacturer of simple aluminium frames.

Like most companies in the partitioning business, Invotek's traditional material of choice has always been plasterboard. It's cheap, fireproof and relatively soundproof.

But there's a problem. Not only is the material not biodegradable, but gypsum-based products such as plasterboard can also be hazardous if combined with other unstable products in landfill. New regulations tackling this issue led Invotek to seek a better, more sustainable alternative.

For Simon Coleman, Commercial Director at Invotek, the change in regulations represented more of an opportunity than a threat to his business: 'It gave us the chance to explore a potentially radical solution,' he explains. 'We could have chosen a mainstream alternative, such as chipboard, ply or MDF, but since they all have environmentally unsound production processes, we didn't feel we'd be making a significant impact to our own environmental footprint.'

Instead, after some intensive desk research, Coleman came across the possibility of using a by-product of wheat straw.

Coleman approached Compak UK, an agrifibre engineering business which manufactures solid compressed sheets from straw waste. The two companies began collaborating on the development of an entirely new partitioning solution.

Invotek's five-strong team of designers was central to the development of the new solution, from the production process and manufacturing specifications to the appearance of the finished product. As with any groundbreaking innovation, there were a number of challenges to be overcome, but nothing the team couldn't handle. 'Over the years we have developed a culture of innovation and design,' says Coleman. 'It means we can respond better to customers' needs, and we are agile enough to adapt our solutions and solve any problems as they arise.'

The resulting product – Strawboard – is biodegradable, easily recycled, produced from a sustainable source, structurally sound, easy to fit and secure, resistant to fire and high impacts and performs well in acoustic testing.

'It wasn't enough just to be environmentally friendly, Strawboard has to perform both practically and financially,' says Coleman. 'We have to be able to demonstrate to environmentally considerate architects and interior designers that Strawboard not only complies with long-term waste acceptance criteria, but provides a very adaptable alternative for plaster surfaces and partitioning.'

The first project using the new material went ahead in July 2006 with the refurbishment of school classrooms at Winton Primary School in Bournemouth. Shortly after, Invotek was short-listed for Most Innovative Product at the 100% Detail/RIBA Journal Innovations Awards.

Since then, it's not just the company name that has changed. Constant design innovation, driven by customer demand, new materials and cutting-edge techniques, has transformed the business. Invotek now boasts an extensive product range, employs 40 people and turned over an impressive £5.5 million in 2004.

Simon Coleman says the company has experienced a 'natural evolution' from its engineering roots and has become an increasingly design-led business. 'The only way to gain competitive advantage in this sector is to offer something unique,' he says. 'And to do that you have to design something.'

Design is central to Invotek's product development, and it's the customers and users who drive the innovation process. 'We listen to what customers say and value their input,' says Coleman. 'In a competitive industry like partitioning you have to be one step ahead.' Listening to the feedback of its customer base – largely architects and designers – Invotek is able to anticipate new trends and capitalise on opportunities. 'Customers are our eyes and ears,' says Coleman. 'They drive our appetite for design and innovation. If enough people are asking for a particular type of product or service then we try to find out how we can give it to them.'

As a result, Invotek has continued to refine its product range. Even though the original Invotek 75 range, developed in 1975, still accounts for approximately 50 per cent of total sales, the past 30 years have seen the range expanded to include a number of other products including glass partitions and movable wall systems. 'Flexibility is an important factor for our customers and we have sought to respond to their needs by adapting what we do best,' says Coleman.

And the Strawboard launch was similarly a response to customer demand for a sustainable alternative to plasterboard. 'It's not just the regulators that are driving the need for more sustainable solutions; our customers want them too,' Coleman explains. 'Our first project with Strawboard was in a school, and it was important for them to be able to source building materials manufactured with the environment in mind.'

He, and the rest of the company, are determined to keep innovating. 'Innovative products such as Strawboard are the result of our continual investment in design, research and development,' says Coleman, 'and those disciplines have been the cornerstones of our consistent growth over the years. We expect our return on investment for the Strawboard product to reach £1 million by the end of 2007.'[9]

Invotek developed Stawboard as a cost-effective, biodegradable, environmentally-friendly new product for use in their partitioning products.

Thus, product designers should think less about product attributes and technical specifications and more about how customers will use and benefit from the product.

Branding

Perhaps the most distinctive skill of professional marketers is their ability to build and manage brands. A **brand** is a name, term, sign, symbol or design, or a combination of these, that identifies the maker or seller of a product or service. Consumers view a brand as an important part of a product, and branding can add value to a product. For example, most consumers would perceive a bottle of Chanel perfume as a high-quality, expensive product. But the same perfume in an unmarked bottle would probably be viewed as lower in quality, even if the fragrance was identical.

Branding has become so strong that today hardly anything goes unbranded. Salt is packaged in branded containers, common screws and staples are packaged with a distributor's label, and car parts – spark plugs, tyres, filters – bear brand names that differ from those of the car makers.

Branding helps buyers in many ways. Brand names help consumers identify products that might benefit them. Brands also say something about product quality and consistency – buyers who always buy the same brand know that they will get the same features, benefits and quality each time they buy. Branding also gives the seller several advantages. The brand name becomes the basis on which a whole story can be built about a product's special qualities. The seller's brand name and trademark provide legal protection for unique product features that otherwise might be copied by competitors. And branding helps the seller to segment markets. For example, Nestlé can offer Cheerios, Shredded Wheat, Shreddies, Fitnesse and many other cereal brands, not just one general product for all consumers.

Building and managing brands is perhaps the marketer's most important task. We will discuss branding strategy in more detail later in the chapter.

Packaging

Packaging involves designing and producing the container or wrapper for a product. The package includes a product's primary container (the tube holding Colgate Total toothpaste). It may also include a secondary package that is thrown away when the product is about to be used (the cardboard box containing the tube of Colgate). Finally, it can include a shipping package necessary to store, identify and ship the product (a corrugated box carrying six dozen tubes of Colgate). Labelling, printed information appearing on or with the package, is also part of packaging.

Traditionally, the primary function of the package was to contain and protect the product. In recent times, however, numerous factors have made packaging an important marketing tool. Increased competition and clutter on retail store shelves means that packages must now perform many sales tasks – from attracting attention, to describing the product, to making the sale.

Companies are realising the power of good packaging to create instant consumer recognition of the company or brand. For example, in an average supermarket, which stocks 15,000 to 17,000 items, the typical shopper passes by some 300 items per minute, and more than 60 per cent of all purchases are made on impulse. In this highly competitive environment, the package may be the seller's last chance to influence buyers. 'Not long ago, the package was merely the product's receptacle, and the brand message was elsewhere – usually on TV,' says a packaging expert. But changes in the marketplace environment are now 'making the package itself an increasingly important selling medium'.[10]

Innovative packaging can give a company an advantage over competitors. Sometimes even seemingly small packaging improvements can make a big difference. For example, paint company Dutch Boy (despite the name it's an American brand) came up with a long overdue innovation – paint in plastic Twist and Pour containers with twist-off caps and pour spouts. More than 50 per cent of Dutch Boy's customers are now buying the plastic containers, and new stores, like Wal-Mart and Sears, are carrying it. It recently followed up with another innovation – the Ready to Roll paint container with a built-in roller tray. The container is easy to open and close, easier to transport, and neater and easier to use than previous alternatives.

In contrast, poorly designed packages can cause headaches for consumers and lost sales for the company. In recent years, product safety has also become a major packaging concern. We have all learned to deal with hard-to-open 'childproof' packaging. And after the rash of product tampering scares during the 1980s, most drug producers and food makers now put their products in tamper-resistant packages. In making packaging decisions, the company must also heed growing environmental concerns. Fortunately, many companies have gone 'green' by reducing their packaging and using environmentally responsible packaging materials.

Labelling

Labels may range from simple tags attached to products to complex graphics that are part of the package. They perform several functions. At the very least, the label *identifies* the product or brand, such as the name Outspan stamped on oranges. The label might also *describe* several things about the product – who made it, where it was made, when it was made, its contents, how it is to be used and how to use it safely. Finally, the label might help to *promote* the product and support its positioning.

For example, in the never-ending search for ways to stand out, the clothing industry seems to be rediscovering the promotional value of the product label.

> Some clothing labels send strong messages. A 'booklet tag' hanging from a workout garment might reinforce the brand's positioning, describing in detail how the garment is used by certain high-profile athletes or what types of special materials are used in its construction. Other brasher statements include pocket flashers and 'lenticular tags', which generate 3-D or animation effects. At the other extreme, tagless heat-transfer labels are replacing sewn-in woven labels, promising ultimate comfort. Even low-key labels are using more brilliant colours or elaborate graphics, beautifying the product and reinforcing the brand message. Rich treatments on labels add pizzazz to luxury items; futuristic tags support emerging technical, man-made fabrications; tags adorned with playful characters evoke a sense of fun for kids' garments. 'The product label is a key cog in branding strategy,' says a labelling expert. 'The look, feel, or even smell of the label – if done creatively – can complement a brand.'[11]

Along with the positives, labelling also raises concerns. There has been a long history of legal concerns about packaging and labels. Labels can mislead customers, fail to describe important ingredients, or fail to include needed safety warnings. As a result, several European laws regulate labelling, while individual countries have their own laws which often supplement EU legislation. Agreed EU-wide controls on food labelling were introduced with Directive 79/112 in 1979. Additional controls have been added and amendments introduced to produce a complex array of labelling requirements. In 2000, the original 1979 Directive and its amendments were consolidated into a single new Directive – 2000/13/EC.

Directive 2000/13/EC is concerned with the labelling of foodstuffs to be delivered to the final consumer, and those to be delivered to catering outlets such as restaurants and canteens. The basic principle is that the labelling must not mislead the purchaser about the product, for example with respect to the characteristics, quantity, properties or origins of the foodstuff. Article 3 of the Directive specifies a range of information that must be provided on all foodstuffs, including a list of ingredients, the shelf life (or for highly perishable products a 'use by' date), details of origin, the name and address of the manufacturer, and any special storage conditions or conditions of use.

Product support services

Customer service is another element of product strategy. A company's offer usually includes some support services, which can be a minor or a major part of the total offering. Later in the chapter we will discuss services as products in themselves. Here, we discuss services that augment actual products.

The first step is to survey customers periodically to assess the value of current services and to obtain ideas for new ones. For example, the Disability and Carers Service of the UK government's Department for Work and Pensions conducts regular customer service surveys. The 2006/2007 customer service survey found that 86 per cent of customers were satisfied with the service overall, and that more than half (56 per cent) were very satisfied. By using the data from the survey the Disability and Carers Service was able to identify aspects of customer service that customers think are important, but with which they are currently relatively less satisfied, so that improvements could be made. For example, customers wanted the forms that they have to fill in to be easier to complete, and the questions that they are asked easier to understand. As a result of acting on this kind of information, the Disability and Carers Service is achieving rising levels of customer satisfaction and declining numbers of complaints.[12]

Many companies are now using a sophisticated mix of phone, e-mail, fax, Internet and interactive voice and data technologies to provide support services that were not possible before. Consider the following example:

> Some online merchants are watching where you surf, then opening a chat window on your screen to ask – just as they would in the store – if you have questions about the goods they see you eyeing. For example, at the Scion website, clicking on the Scion Chat button puts you in real-time touch with someone who can answer your questions or help you to design your personalised Scion. Last year, Hewlett-Packard began sending pop-up chat boxes to visitors who were shopping on HP.com's pages for digital photography products. If a shopper loiters a few minutes over some gear, up pops a photo of an attractive woman with the words, 'Hello, need information? An HP live chat representative is standing by to assist you.' Click on 'Go' and type a question, and a live sales agent responds immediately.[13]

Product line decisions

Beyond decisions about individual products and services, product strategy also calls for building a product line. A **product line** is a group of products that are closely related because they function in a similar manner, are sold to the same customer groups, are marketed through the same types of outlets, or fall within given price ranges. For example, Nike produces several lines of athletic shoes and clothing, Nokia produces several lines of telecommunications products, and HSBC produces several lines of financial services.

The major product line decision involves *product line length* – the number of items in the product line. The line is too short if the manager can increase profits by adding items; the line is too long if the manager can increase profits by dropping items. The company should manage its product lines carefully. Product lines tend to lengthen over time, and most companies eventually need to prune unnecessary or unprofitable items from their lines to increase overall profitability. Managers need to conduct a periodic *product-line analysis* to assess each product item's sales and profits and to understand how each item contributes to the line's performance.

Product line length is influenced by company objectives and resources. For example, one objective might be to allow for upselling. Thus BMW wants to move customers up from its 1-series and 3-series models to 5- and 7-series models. Another objective might be to allow cross-selling: Hewlett-Packard sells printers as well as cartridges. Still another objective might be to protect against economic swings: Arcadia Group runs several different chains of clothing stores catering for different target markets and different income categories to try to reduce the impact of economic fluctuations (these include Burton, Dorothy Perkins, Miss Selfridge, Evans and Top Shop).

A company can lengthen its product line in two ways: by *line stretching* or by *line filling*. **Product line stretching** occurs when a company lengthens its product line beyond its current range. The company can stretch its line downwards, upwards, or both ways.

Companies located at the upper end of the market can stretch their lines *downwards*. A company may stretch downwards to plug a market hole that otherwise would attract a new competitor or to respond to a competitor's attack on the upper end. Or it may add low-end products because it finds faster growth taking place in the low-end segments. DaimlerChrysler stretched its Mercedes line downwards for all these reasons. Facing a slow-growth luxury car market and attacks by Japanese car makers on its high-end positioning, it successfully introduced its Mercedes C-Class cars. These models sell in the €30,000 range without harming the firm's ability to sell other Mercedes at much higher prices.

Companies at the lower end of a market can stretch their product lines *upwards*. Sometimes, companies stretch upwards in order to add prestige to their current products. Or they may be attracted by a faster growth rate or higher margins at the higher end. For example, each of the leading Japanese car companies introduced an upmarket automobile: Toyota launched Lexus, Nissan launched Infinity and Honda launched Acura. They used entirely new names rather than their own names.

Companies in the middle range of the market may decide to stretch their lines in *both directions*. Marriott did this with its hotel product line. Along with regular Marriott hotels, it has added new branded hotel lines to serve both the upper and lower ends of the market. Renaissance aims to attract and please top executives; Marriott, upper and middle managers; Courtyard, salespeople and other 'road warriors'; and Fairfield Inn, vacationers and business travellers on a tight travel budget. ExecuStay by Marriott provides temporary housing for those relocating or away on long-term assignments of 30 days or longer. Marriott's Residence Inn provides a relaxed, residential atmosphere – a home away from home for people who travel for a living. Marriott TownePlace Suites provide a comfortable atmosphere at a moderate price for extended-stay travellers. And Marriott SpringHill Suites have 25 per cent more space than an average hotel room – offering a separate living and work space for business travellers.[14] The major risk with this strategy is that some travellers will trade down after finding that the lower-price hotels in the Marriott chain give them pretty much everything they want. However, Marriott would rather capture its customers who move downwards than lose them to competitors.

An alternative to product line stretching is *product line filling* – adding more items within the present range of the line. There are several reasons for product line filling: reaching for extra profits, satisfying dealers, using excess capacity, being the leading full-line company and plugging holes to keep out competitors. Sony filled its Walkman line by adding solar-powered and waterproof Walkmans, and ultralight models for exercisers in a variety of formats. However, line filling is overdone if it results in cannibalisation and customer confusion. The company should ensure that new items are noticeably different from existing ones.

Product mix decisions

An organisation with several product lines has a product mix. A **product mix** (or **product portfolio**) consists of all the product lines and items that a particular seller offers for sale. Avon's product mix consists of five major product lines: beauty products, wellness products, jewellery and accessories, gifts, and 'inspirational' products (inspiring gifts, books, music and home accents). Each product line consists of several sublines. For example, the beauty line breaks down into make-up, skin care, bath and beauty, fragrance, salon and spa, and outdoor protection products. Each line and subline has many individual items. Altogether, Avon's product mix includes 1,300 items. In contrast, 3M markets more than 60,000 products, a typical hypermarket stocks 100,000 to 120,000 items, and General Electric manufactures as many as 250,000 items.

A company's product mix has four important dimensions: width, length, depth and consistency. Product mix *width* refers to the number of different product lines the company carries. For example, Colgate markets a fairly wide product mix, consisting of dozens of brands that you can 'trust to care for yourself, your home, and the ones you love'. This product mix is organised into five major product lines: oral care, personal care, household care, fabric care and pet nutrition.

Product mix *length* and *depth* refer to the total number of items the company carries within its product lines (length) and the number of items carried within a specific line (depth). Consider two major consumer products companies, Unilever and Colgate. Unilever typically carries many brands within each line. For example, its personal-care line includes Lifebuoy, Lux, Pond's, Sunsilk and Dove (product line length). The Dove brand alone is used on soaps, body washes, shampoos, conditioners and deodorants (product line depth). To illustrate product line *depth* further consider Colgate's line of toothpastes, which come in 11 varieties, ranging from Colgate Total, Colgate Tartar Control, Colgate 2in1 and Colgate Cavity Protection to Colgate Sensitive, Colgate Fresh Confidence, Colgate Max Fresh, Colgate Simply White, Colgate Sparkling White, Colgate Kids Toothpastes and Colgate Baking Soda & Peroxide. Then, each variety comes in its own special forms and formulations. For example, you can buy Colgate Total in regular, mint fresh stripe, whitening paste and gel, advanced fresh gel or 2in1 liquid gel versions.[15]

Finally, the *consistency* of the product mix refers to how closely related the various product lines are in end use, production requirements, distribution channels, or in some other way. Colgate's product lines are consistent in so far as they are consumer products that go through the same distribution channels. The lines are less consistent in so far as they perform different functions for buyers.

These product mix dimensions provide the methods of defining the company's product strategy. The company can increase its business in four ways. It can add new product lines, widening its product mix. In this way, its new lines build on the company's reputation in its other lines. The company can lengthen its existing product lines to become a more full-line company. Or it can add more versions of each product and thus deepen its product mix. Finally, the company can pursue more product line consistency – or less – depending on whether it wants to have a strong reputation in a single field or in several fields.

BRANDING STRATEGY: BUILDING STRONG BRANDS

Some analysts see brands as *the* major enduring asset of a company, outlasting the company's specific products and facilities. John Stewart, co-founder of Quaker Oats, once said, 'If this business were split up, I would give you the land and bricks and mortar, and I would keep the brands and trademarks, and I would fare better than you.' A former CEO of McDonald's agrees: 'If every asset we own, every building, and every piece of equipment were destroyed in a terrible natural disaster, we would be able to borrow all the money to replace it very quickly because of the value of our brand . . . The brand is more valuable than the totality of all these assets.'[16]

Thus, brands are powerful assets that must be carefully developed and managed. In this section, we examine the key strategies for building and managing brands.

Brand equity

Brands are more than just names and symbols. Brands represent consumers' perceptions and feelings about a product and its performance – everything that the product or service *means* to consumers. In the final analysis, brands exist in the minds of consumers.

The real value of a strong brand is its power to capture consumer preference and loyalty. Brands vary in the amount of power and value they have in the marketplace. Some brands, such as Coca-Cola, Mercedes, Nike, Disney and others, become larger-than-life icons that maintain their power in the market for years, even generations. These brands win in the marketplace not simply because they deliver unique benefits or reliable service. Rather, they succeed because they forge deep connections with customers.

A powerful brand has high *brand equity*. **Brand equity** is the positive differential effect that knowing the brand name has on customer response to the product or service. One measure of a brand's equity is the extent to which customers are willing to pay more for the brand. One study found that 72 per cent of customers would pay a 20 per cent premium for their brand of choice relative to the closest competing brand; 40 per cent said they would pay a 50 per cent premium.[17] Heinz lovers are willing to pay a 100 per cent premium. Loyal Coke drinkers will pay a 50 per cent premium and Volvo users a 40 per cent premium.

A brand with strong brand equity is a very valuable asset. *Brand valuation* is the process of estimating the total financial value of a brand. Consulting firm Interbrand specialises in this work. According to Interbrand the world's most valuable brands in 2007 were Coca-Cola (estimated value $65 billion), Microsoft ($59 billion) and IBM ($57 billion). The most valuable European brand in 2007 was Nokia, fifth in the global list at an estimated $34 billion, and the second most valuable was Mercedes-Benz, at $24 billion.[18] (See also Table 15.2 for 2008 rankings, page 526.)

High brand equity provides a company with many competitive advantages. A powerful brand enjoys a high level of consumer brand awareness and loyalty. Because consumers expect stores to carry the brand, the company has more leverage in bargaining with resellers. Because the brand name carries high credibility, the company can more easily launch line and brand extensions, as when Coca-Cola used its well-known brand to introduce Diet Coke and Vanilla Coke, and when Unilever extended the Dove brand to include shampoos and conditioners. A powerful brand offers the company some defence against fierce price competition.

Above all, a powerful brand forms the basis for building strong and profitable customer relationships. Therefore, the fundamental asset underlying brand equity is *customer equity* – the value of the customer relationships that the brand creates. A powerful brand is important, but what it really represents is a profitable set of loyal customers. The proper focus of marketing is building customer equity, with brand management serving as a major marketing tool.[19]

Building strong brands

Branding poses challenging decisions to the marketer. Figure 7.3 shows that the major brand strategy decisions involve brand positioning, brand name selection, brand sponsorship and brand development.

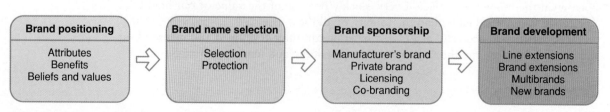

FIGURE 7.3

Major brand strategy decisions

Brand positioning

Marketers need to position their brands clearly in target customers' minds. They can position brands at any of three levels.[20] At the lowest level, they can position the brand on *product attributes*. Thus, marketers of Aquafresh toothpaste can talk about the product's innovative ingredients and good taste. However, attributes are the least desirable level for brand positioning. Competitors can easily copy attributes. More important, customers are not interested in attributes as such; they are interested in what the attributes will do for them.

A brand can be better positioned by associating its name with a desirable *benefit*. Thus, Aquafresh marketers can go beyond the brand's ingredients and talk about the resulting decay prevention or teeth whitening benefits. Some successful brands positioned on benefits are Volvo (safety), Duracell (extended use), The North Face (adventure), FedEx (guaranteed on-time delivery), Nike (performance) and Lexus (quality).

The strongest brands go beyond attribute or benefit positioning. They are positioned on strong *beliefs and values*. These brands deliver emotional benefits. Thus, Aquafresh's marketers can talk not just about ingredients and decay-prevention benefits, but about how these give customers 'a whole new experience of clean'.[21] Successful brands engage customers on a deep, emotional level. Brands such as Starbucks, Vans Skate Shoes and Nokia rely less on a product's tangible attributes and more on creating surprise, passion and excitement surrounding a brand.

When positioning a brand, the marketer should establish a mission for the brand and a vision of what the brand must be and do. A brand is the company's promise to deliver a specific set of features, benefits, services and experiences consistently to the buyers. The brand promise must be simple and honest. The Travel Inn hotel chain, for example, offers clean rooms, low prices and good service but does not promise expensive furniture or large bathrooms. In contrast, Ritz-Carlton offers luxurious rooms and a truly memorable experience but does not promise low prices.

Brand name selection

A good name can add greatly to a product's success. However, finding the best brand name is a difficult task. It begins with a careful review of the product and its benefits, the target market and proposed marketing strategies. After that, naming a brand becomes part science, part art and a measure of instinct (see Marketing at Work 7.1).

Desirable qualities for a brand name include the following:

1 It should suggest something about the product's benefits and qualities. Examples: Aquafresh (toothpaste), Jungle Formula (insect repellent), Mr Sheen (furniture polish).

2 It should be easy to pronounce, recognise and remember. Short names help. Examples: Daz, Dove, Cif. But longer ones are sometimes effective. Examples: 'Vanish Carpet Powershot' carpet cleaner, 'I Can't Believe It's Not Butter' margarine.

3 The brand name should be distinctive. Examples: Lexus, Kodak, Oracle.

4 It should be extendable: Amazon.com began as an online bookseller but chose a name that would allow expansion into other categories.

5 The name should translate easily into foreign languages. Before spending $100 million to change its name to Exxon, Standard Oil of New Jersey tested several names in 54 languages in more than 150 foreign markets. It found that the name Enco referred to a stalled engine when pronounced in Japanese.

6 It should be capable of registration and legal protection. A brand name cannot be registered if it infringes on existing brand names.

Once chosen, the brand name must be protected. Many firms try to build a brand name that will eventually become identified with the product category. Brand names

MARKETING AT WORK 7.1

Naming brands: Just how much does a name matter?

As the year 2009 dawned, British consumers, now spending rather more time than usual in front of their television sets as a result of the harsh economic climate, found one of their favourite insurance companies – Norwich Union – persuading them that in the future it should be called 'Aviva', and that this was a really good idea. It is reasonable to suppose that rather a lot of those consumers were a bit confused by the whole idea. After all, Norwich Union had great brand recognition in the UK, and the name is derived from the name of a town in eastern England (Norwich) where the company was founded in 1797; not a particularly famous town outside the UK, but a well-loved town by the British, famous for a football team of modest success (known as 'the Canaries' because they play in yellow kit – their fans are known as the 'Yellow Army'), and close to some family-friendly holiday resorts on the North Sea coast. So, Norwich, a well-liked town, and Norwich Union, a well-known name.

Why, then, 'Aviva'? The name has no literal meaning in English, although it does raise associations with French (à vivre) and Spanish (viva) expressions with which many English people are familiar, and which have generally 'lively' meanings. The Aviva company was formed in 2002 by a merger between Norwich Union and CGU plc, with the aim of creating an insurance company to compete on the global stage. CGU plc itself had a 'modern' sounding name; names formed solely of letters became something of a fashion in the 1990s (for example, British Telecommunications became simply

BT). CGU was formed in 1998 when insurance companies Commercial Union and General Accident merged. In May 2002, this company merged with Norwich Union to form CGNU, and then in April 2002 the shareholders approved the change of name to Aviva. So, by the time that Aviva was trying to persuade British consumers to drop 'Norwich Union' and to think 'Aviva' as the top-of-mind brand name, Aviva had been the legal company name for nearly seven years.

The strategic reasoning behind the name change was explained at the Aviva website:

> *'As a global company, we need a name and a brand that will be recognised anywhere. The name Aviva brings together more than 40 different trading names around the world. It's perfect for us because it's short, memorable and feels positive and lively.'*

Of course, another key advantage of 'Aviva' over 'Norwich Union' is that it takes a lot less effort to type! If you take a quick look at the standard English-language computer keyboard you will see that the least accomplished keyboard user can probably manage a-v-i-v-a without too much difficulty (you might also reflect that a-v-a-v-a would have been even easier). Why is this important? Well, the truth is that more and more consumer insurance services, like car insurance, travel insurance and home insurance, are being sold direct over the Internet. So a name that is easy to remember, easy to type, and easy to spell is a definite advantage. In fact, 'Norwich' is a particular problem even for people born and brought up in England because of that silent 'w' in the middle; it is an easily misspelt word. Online marketing of insurance is a cut-throat business. If the consumer doesn't get the desired website first time around, then it is very easy to opt for another provider, particularly if the name is simpler to type.

Naming brands: there's some science to it, and some basic rules to be heeded, but there's also a big dose of art and more than a little instinct.
Source: John Kuczala.

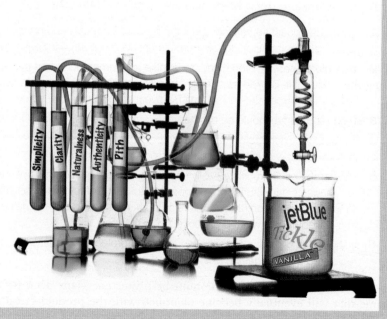

By the way, there really is an insurance company – one of Aviva's rivals – called 'AXA', and its website is 'axa.com'. This company was created in 1982 by the amalgamation of a French and a Canadian insurance company; the name AXA was adopted in 1985 long before anyone had the slightest idea that it would be so convenient for the Internet age. For people using an English language 'QWERTY' keyboard it is difficult to think of a simpler name to type.

Now, there are probably quite a few sceptics out there who think that names cannot matter all that much. Surely, you might argue, it is a question of how good a service the company is selling, what kind of price it offers, and the perceived value delivered to the customer that make the difference, not the name. There is nothing wrong with that argument. However, there are a lot of companies out there offering excellent products and services at highly competitive prices that deliver high levels of customer value. A supposedly 'little thing' like the name just might make enough difference

to matter. In their best-selling book *Freakonomics*, Steven Levitt and Stephen Dubner presented some fascinating, perhaps disturbing, information about the link between an individual person's name and their life-chances. Extensive evidence from the USA in the 1990s shows big differences between the better-off and the poorer members of society in terms of the names given to children. The chances are very strong that Alexandra and her brother Benjamin come from a well-off, highly educated white family, while Cody and his sister Amber come from a badly-off, poorly educated white family. This does *not* mean that the choice of a child's name directly affects their life-chances. However, it clearly *does* mean that people's names carry a lot of extra information over and above simply how to address them. In simple terms, names *matter*. The same goes for companies and brands.

In recent years the trend in marketing and business has been away from the rather meaningless names that were preferred in the 1990s, and

towards names that have some intrinsic significance. Management consultant 'Accenture' and the business-to-business online service provider 'Covisint' represented the previous wave of names; they both sound interesting, but appear to mean nothing in particular. Such names probably work best when there are few of them, so that the curiosity of the name intrigues the customer. On the other hand names like 'Subway' and 'Blockbuster' carry real meaning for the customer (a 'sub' is short for 'submarine', which bears a passing resemblance to the kind of bread they sell in Subway fast-food franchises; a 'blockbuster' is a must-see movie). Of course, 'Aviva' with which we started this case study, is not a particularly meaningful name. Which makes it all the more intriguing to see whether the new name will succeed with customers.

Sources: www.aviva.com; www.open2.net/management_organisation/online_branding.html; www.axa.com; Steven D. Levitt and Stephen J. Dubner, *Freakonomics: A Rogue Economist Explores the Hidden Side of Everything*, London: Penguin Books, 2006.

such as Kleenex, Levi's, Sellotape, Elastoplast and Formica have succeeded in this way. However, their very success may threaten the company's rights to the name. Many originally protected brand names – such as cellophane, aspirin, nylon, kerosene, linoleum, yo-yo, trampoline, escalator, thermos and shredded wheat – are now generic names that any seller can use. To protect their brands, marketers present them carefully using the word 'brand' and the registered trademark symbol, as in 'Elastoplast®'.

Brand sponsorship

A manufacturer has four sponsorship options. The product may be launched as a *manufacturer's brand* (or national brand), as when Kellogg's and IBM sell their output under their own manufacturer's brand names. Or the manufacturer may sell to resellers who give it a *private brand* (also called a *store brand* or *distributor brand*). Although most manufacturers create their own brand names, others market *licensed brands*. Finally, two companies can join forces and *co-brand* a product.

Manufacturers' brands versus private brands Manufacturers' brands have long dominated the retail scene. In recent times, however, an increasing number of retailers and wholesalers have created their own **private brands** (or **store brands**). And in many industries, these private brands are giving manufacturers' brands a real run for their money:

It seems that almost every retailer now carries its own store brands. In the UK Tesco offers several different options across its own 'Tesco' range of brands. You can have the standard Tesco brand (for example, Tesco Daily Care freshmint toothpaste), the low-priced 'value' brand (for example, Tesco Value Kitchen Towel), or the premium 'finest' brand (for example, Tesco Finest Aftersun Lotion). The Spar chain of supermarkets, which you can find in virtually every European country, stocks a wide variety of Spar branded products in many different product categories: 'Each of the SPAR brand goods has been developed and benchmarked against our competitors to ensure that we're offering the best possible product for the price, and of course, the kind of quality you expect. SPAR Brand gives you an outstanding alternative to the major brands that will help you save money.'[22]

Source: Alamy Images/Photomax.

An increasing number of retailers, like Spar, have created their own store brands.

In the so-called *battle of the brands* between manufacturers' and private brands, retailers have many advantages. They control what products they stock, where they go on the shelf, what prices they charge and which ones they will feature in local circulars. Most retailers also charge manufacturers *slotting fees* – payments from the manufacturers before the retailers will accept new products and find 'slots' for them on their shelves.

Private brands can be hard to establish and costly to stock and promote. However, they also yield higher profit margins for the reseller. And they give resellers exclusive products that cannot be bought from competitors, resulting in greater store traffic and loyalty. Retailers price their store brands lower than comparable manufacturers' brands, thereby appealing to budget-conscious shoppers, especially in difficult economic times. And most shoppers believe that store brands are often made by one of the larger manufacturers anyway.

To fend off private brands, leading brand marketers will have to invest in R&D to bring out new brands, new features and continuous quality improvements. They must design strong advertising programmes to maintain high awareness and preference. They must find ways to 'partner' with major distributors in a search for distribution economies and improved joint performance.

Licensing Most manufacturers take years and spend millions to create their own brand names. However, some companies license names or symbols previously created by other manufacturers, names of well-known celebrities, or characters from popular films and books. For a fee, any of these can provide an instant and proven brand name.

Clothing and accessories sellers pay large royalties to adorn their products – from blouses to ties, and linens to luggage – with the names or initials of well-known fashion innovators such as Calvin Klein, Tommy Hilfiger, Gucci or Armani. Sellers of children's products attach an almost endless list of character names to clothing, toys, school supplies, linens, dolls, lunch boxes, cereals and other items. Licensed character names range from classics such as Sesame Street, Disney, Peanuts, Winnie the Pooh, the Muppets, and Scooby Doo characters to the more recent Ice Age, Surf's Up, Star Wars and Harry Potter characters.

The fastest-growing licensing category is corporate brand licensing, as more and more for-profit and not-for-profit organisations are licensing their names to generate additional revenues and brand recognition. Coca-Cola, for example, has some 320 licensees in 57 countries producing more than 10,000 products, ranging from baby clothes and boxer shorts to earrings, a Coca-Cola Barbie doll, and even a fishing lure shaped like a tiny coke can. Each year, licensees sell more than €1 billion worth of licensed Coca-Cola products.[23]

Co-branding Although companies have been **co-branding** products for many years, there has been a recent resurgence in co-branded products. Co-branding occurs when two established brand names of different companies are used on the same product, and has been defined as 'pairing two or more branded products (constituent brands) to form a separate and unique product (composite brand)'.[24] For example, car maker Ford and fashion brand Eddie Bauer co-branded a sport utility vehicle – the Ford Explorer, Eddie Bauer edition. According to Swedish expert Henrik Uggla: 'Corporate brands can exploit pre-established benefits and credibility by licensing ingredient brands . . . Gore-Tex collaborates with strong corporate brands such as Ecco and BOSS, it has stronger purchase intent scores in the apparel category than corporate brands such as Nike, Levi's and Ecco . . . The Adidas corporate [*sic*] have reinforced its brand values and reached new target groups through corporate co-branding with the New Zealand Rugby Union and the All Blacks.'[25] In most co-branding situations, one company licenses another company's well-known brand to use in combination with its own.[26]

Co-branding offers many advantages. Because each brand dominates in a different category, the combined brands create broader consumer appeal and greater brand equity. Co-branding also allows a company to expand its existing brand into a category it might otherwise have difficulty entering alone.

Co-branding also has limitations. Such relationships usually involve complex legal contracts and licences. Co-branding partners must carefully coordinate their advertising, sales promotion and other marketing efforts. Finally, when co-branding, each partner must trust that the other will take good care of its brand.

Brand development

A company has four choices when it comes to developing brands (see Figure 7.4). It can introduce *line extensions* (existing brand names extended to new forms, sizes and flavours of an existing product category), *brand extensions* (existing brand names extended to new product categories), *multibrands* (new brand names introduced in the same product category), or *new brands* (new brand names in new product categories).

Line extensions Line extensions occur when a company introduces additional items in a given product category under the same brand name, such as new flavours, forms, colours, ingredients or package sizes. Thus, Nestlé introduced several line extensions to its Ski yoghurt range, including new yogurt flavours, Ski Up & Go yogurt with cereal and fruit, Ski Smooth (with no fruit pieces) and Ski Fat Free. The vast majority of all new-product activity consists of line extensions.

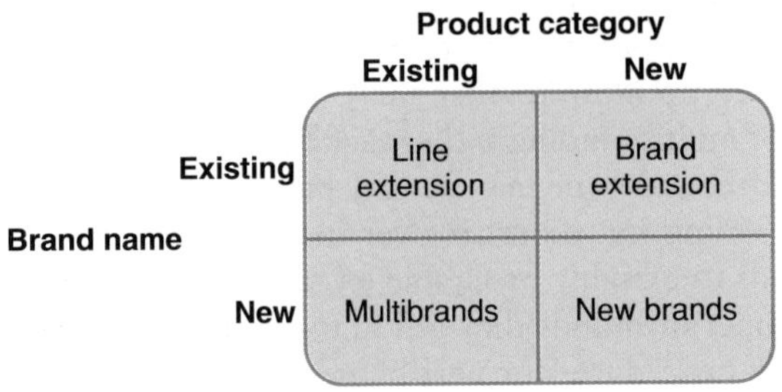

Brand name	Product category	
	Existing	New
Existing	Line extension	Brand extension
New	Multibrands	New brands

FIGURE 7.4

Brand development strategies

A company might introduce line extensions as a low-cost, low-risk way to introduce new products. Or it might want to meet consumer desires for variety, to use excess capacity, or simply to command more shelf space from resellers. However, line extensions involve some risks. An overextended brand name might lose its specific meaning, or heavily extended brands can cause consumer confusion or frustration.

Want a Coke? Not so easy. Pick from more than 16 varieties. In zero-calorie versions alone, Coke comes in three subbrands – Diet Coke, Diet Coke with Splenda, and Coca-Cola Zero. Throw in the flavoured and free versions – Diet Vanilla Coke, Diet Cherry Coke, Diet Coke with Lemon, Diet Coke with Lime, and Caffeine-Free Diet Coke – and you reach a dizzying eight diets from Coke. And that doesn't count 'mid-calorie' Coca-Cola C2. Each subbrand has its own hype – Diet Coke lets you 'live your life', while Coke Zero gives you 'real Coca-Cola taste and zero calories'. And Coca-Cola C2 has '$1/2$ the carbs, $1/2$ the calories, all the great taste'. But it's unlikely that many consumers fully appreciate the differences. Instead, the glut of extensions will likely cause what one expert calls 'profusion confusion'. Laments one cola consumer, 'How many versions of Diet Coke do they need?'[27]

Another risk is that sales of an extension may come at the expense of other items in the line. A line extension works best when it takes sales away from competing brands, not when it 'cannibalises' the company's other items.

Brand extensions A **brand extension** involves the use of a successful brand name to launch new or modified products in a new category. For example, Kimberly-Clark extended its market-leading Huggies brand from disposable nappies to a full line of toiletries for tots, from shampoos, lotions, and nappy-rash ointments to baby wash, disposable washcloths and disposable changing pads. Victorinox extended its venerable Swiss Army brand from multi-tool knives to products ranging from cutlery and ball point pens to watches, luggage and apparel.

Brand extensions: Victorinox, originally known for 'Swiss Army' pocket knives, now offers a range of high quality consumer products.

A brand extension gives a new product instant recognition and faster acceptance. It also saves the high advertising costs usually required to build a new brand name. At the same time, a brand extension strategy involves some risk. While Richard Branson's business empire Virgin has succeeded with ventures ranging from the original record stores (a business sold to Zavvi Entertainment Group in 2007) to railway travel and an airline, it has also failed with several attempted brand extensions, into vodka, clothing and cosmetics, for example.[28] The extension may confuse the image of the main brand. And if a brand extension fails, it may harm consumer attitudes toward the other products carrying the same brand name. Further, a brand name may not be appropriate to a particular new product, even if it is well made and satisfying – would you consider buying Texaco milk or HSBC sausages? Companies that are tempted to transfer a brand name must research how well the brand's associations fit the new product.[29]

Multibrands Companies often introduce additional brands in the same category. Thus, Procter & Gamble markets many different brands in each of its product categories. *Multibranding* offers a way to establish different features and appeal to different buying motives. It also allows a company to lock up more reseller shelf space.

A major drawback of multibranding is that each brand might obtain only a small market share, and none may be very profitable. The company may end up spreading its resources over many brands instead of building a few brands to a highly profitable level. These companies should reduce the number of brands they sell in a given category and set up tighter screening procedures for new brands.

New brands A company might believe that the power of its existing brand name is waning and a new brand name is needed. Or a company may create a new brand name when it enters a new product category for which none of the company's current brand names is appropriate. For example, UK airline British Midland created the 'bmi baby' brand to compete in the budget air travel sector. Japan's Matsushita uses separate names for its different families of consumer electronics products: Panasonic, Technics, National and Quasar.

As with multibranding, offering too many new brands can result in a company spreading its resources too thin. And in some industries, such as consumer packaged goods, consumers and retailers have become concerned that there are already too many brands, with too few differences between them. Thus, Procter & Gamble, Nestlé and other large consumer-product marketers are now pursuing *megabrand* strategies – weeding out weaker brands and focusing their marketing budgets only on brands that can achieve the number-one or number-two market share positions in their categories.

Managing brands

Companies must manage their brands carefully. First, the brand's positioning must be continuously communicated to consumers. Major brand marketers often spend huge amounts on advertising to create brand awareness and to build preference and loyalty. For example, McDonald's spends more than $317 million a year to promote its brand.[30]

Such advertising campaigns can help to create name recognition, brand knowledge, and maybe even some brand preference. However, the fact is that brands are not maintained by advertising but by the *brand experience*. Today, customers come to know a brand through a wide range of contacts and touch points. These include advertising, but also personal experience with the brand, word-of-mouth, personal interactions with company people, company Web pages and many other contacts. The company must put as much care into managing these touch points as it does into producing its ads. 'A brand is a living entity,' says former Disney chief executive Michael Eisner, 'and it is enriched or undermined cumulatively over time, the product of a thousand small gestures.'[31]

The brand's positioning will not take hold fully unless everyone in the company lives the brand. Therefore the company needs to train its people to be customer-centred. Even better, the company should carry on internal brand building to help employees to understand and be enthusiastic about the brand promise. Many companies go even further by training and encouraging their distributors and dealers to serve their customers well. But it is important to remember that brands and branding are key issues for small businesses, not just for multinational organisations with large product portfolios. Small companies need to develop and nurture their brand and its position in the market just as carefully as the well-known international consumer products companies. In Marketing at Work 7.2 we can see how a small Irish company, Cloon Keen, worked very hard to establish its brand at a premium position in the market for scented candles.

All of this suggests that managing a company's brand assets can no longer be left only to brand managers. Brand managers do not have enough power or scope to do all the things necessary to build and enhance their brands. Moreover, brand managers often pursue short-term results, whereas managing brands as assets calls for longer-term strategy. Thus, some companies are now setting up brand asset management teams to manage their major brands. Canada Dry and Colgate-Palmolive have appointed **brand-equity managers** to maintain and protect their brands' images, associations and quality, and to prevent short-term actions by overeager brand managers from hurting the brand.

MARKETING AT WORK 7.2

Cloon Keen Atelier: Developing a premium brand

Ann M. Torres, *Marketing Department, Cairns Graduate School of Business and Economics, National University of Ireland*

Margaret Mangan, co-founder of Cloon Keen Atelier, always had a passion for scent; she believes scent forms the heart of her products. Cloon Keen develops high-quality products where fragrance, design and functionality are blended carefully to create a mood of authenticity and pleasure. The challenge for Cloon Keen, a small operator, is to pursue a strategy that reinforces its chosen market position as it develops new products and markets.

In June 2002, Margaret Mangan and Julian Checkley established Cloon Keen Candles in Galway, Ireland, and began making their hand-poured candles. In the early days of their start-up, Margaret spent a number of weeks travelling around Ireland to find shops that are a good fit for Cloon Keen candles, primarily high-end gift and craft shops as well as upmarket home interior and furniture shops with a modern flair. Margaret's sales drive was successful, as she secured orders from over 60 retailers across the country. To their credit, Cloon Keen has retained about 90 per cent of their original retailers. Despite their achievement with retailers, the firm is shifting its focus towards developing its own retail initiatives, which are ultimately more profitable.

In August 2005, Cloon Keen Atelier opened their retail premises in the heart of Galway city. In designing the shop interior, they took particular care to develop an atmosphere that

reflected the brand. The shop has a warm, modern look that is clean and uncluttered, but not quite minimalist. An opening in Ceardlann Spiddal Craft Village in July 2006 was an opportunity for Cloon Keen to open another retail outlet in Spiddal, Co. Galway. Conveniently located 15 km from Galway city, Ceardlann is also a scenic tourist destination, where visitors can see Cloon Keen's master chandlers pour candles, and can then purchase the finished product from the adjoining shop. Although the studio shop reflects aspects found in the Kirwan's Lane venue, the Ceardlann retail venue was tailored to showcase the craft studio and its environs. The effect is sufficiently similar to recognise Cloon Keen's *look*, but suitably different to intrigue customers with variety.

How do you create a premium, branded candle product? Cloon Keen employs the expertise of three perfumers to create fragrances exclusively for their range of 35 scented candles; they never use generic scents. The quality of fragrance is especially important. Cloon Keen uses authentic aromas, which do not smell harsh, bitter or 'chemical'. Superior quality wax and cotton wicks are used to ensure optimum absorption and diffusion of fragrance. The craft for producing premium candles requires a highly scientific approach. For example, each scent requires a different wick to ensure the candle burns effectively; spicy scents require a thicker cotton wick than sweet scents. Additionally, softer wax is more effective in scented candles, as harder wax disperses fragrance poorly. Cloon Keen assembles 300 to 400 units per week, which increases to 1,500 to 2,000 units per week during the busiest period between September and December.

The next product venture is a line of Cloon Keen branded soaps, creams and lotions in two scents: Lavender and Linden Blossom. The prototypes were in development during 2006 and 2007, and were going into production in spring 2008. Other products (such as shower gel, body scrub, bath oil, shampoo and hair conditioner) will be added as a natural progression to their line. In time, the plan is to create a signature perfume to serve as the brand's hallmark.

Price is a key issue in positioning the products in the premium sector of the market. Cloon Keen produces two lines of premium-scented candles. The gourmet collection, priced at €13.95 per unit, is packaged in tins and is a playful, funky product. It comes in scents such as Basil and Lime Pesto, Crazy as Coconut, Just Baked Apple Pie, Fresh Linen, and Swedish Sauna. Irish consumers generally prefer the softer floral scents in the gourmet range, such as Wild Irish Lavender and Galway Honeysuckle; these floral scents are among Cloon Keen's best sellers. The spa collection of luxury candles, priced at €14.95 per unit, came into production in 2005. This line offers more sophisticated, subtle scents such as Exotic Woods and Fig Tree; its sumptuous packaging reflects its more sensuous, indulgent qualities.

Cloon Keen's pricing strategy reflects its positioning as a quality producer. Margaret and Julian follow a policy of offering exceptionally high quality for the price they charge and regularly monitor rivals' price levels to ensure their products remain competitive. Cloon Keen's average sales per square foot is €430 and compares favourably with established competitors in the home interiors market. With the launch of its personal care products, Cloon Keen expects average sales per square foot to increase to €650.

Cloon Keen actively manage their brand. Margaret and Julian believe that Cloon Keen's brand values have greatly facilitated in generating word-of-mouth to build a loyal customer base. Cloon Keen's brand is based on offering accessible pricing for superior products, and a unique store experience through its upscale store design, attentive customer service and product presentation. Cloon Keen strives for authenticity in its branding approach. The combination of smell, touch and sight in Cloon Keen's retail ambiance is meant to inspire and heighten the customer's experience. As a speciality retailer, Cloon Keen is being positioned as a worthy alternative to the high-priced designer brands offered in department stores.

Margaret and Julian use traditional media, primarily press features in quality news and fashion magazines, such as *Image*, *Irish Tatler* and *The Gloss*. Select sponsorship, such as the launch of the new Irish Times building and the *Irish Tatler* magazine in October 2006, has been fruitful in generating awareness and opportunities for feature articles in the press. Merchandising within the shops, branding and product packaging have been Cloon Keen's strongest forms of promotion. Margaret and Julian are interested in using electronic media, to generate the opportunity for audience involvement. Interactivity can facilitate brand objectives and be a powerful tool for eliciting an immediate response from customers. Cloon Keen aims to build a website, not only to serve as an online retail environment, but also as a platform to initiate a lifestyle blog, which would work as a source for stimulating viral marketing.

So far, Cloon Keen's branding strategy seems to have paid off. Even with fairly limited promotional efforts, Cloon Keen has garnered a loyal customer base, as 80 per cent are repeat customers. Their marketing efforts primarily target working women, aged 25 to 50 years, who have traditionally purchased premium scented candles and skin care products in department stores. They use these high quality products on a daily basis as affordable luxuries. Cloon Keen's loyal customers are well travelled, have reasonably high levels of disposable income, are open to trying new products and are increasingly seeking better pricing without sacrificing high quality and service. Cloon Keen's strategy has also been successful in attracting other consumers beyond its primary target, such as metrosexual males, who are attracted to the good quality toiletries, as well as young teenage girls, who are attracted to Cloon Keen's gourmet range of candles.

One of the main purposes of the branding and product development strategy has been to differentiate Cloon Keen from its competitors. The company operates in two overlapping markets: candles and home fragrances, as well as the personal care market. There are numerous rivals that manufacture functionally similar products, sold through a variety of channels. Many of these rivals have substantially greater resources, better name recognition, and sell through broader distribution channels. Some of these competitors are speciality retailers of personal care products, including international chains such as The Body Shop and L'Occitane, as well as local speciality retailers, such as The Burren Perfumery. The lack of significant barriers to entry in this market may result in new competition, including possible imitators to Cloon Keen.

The challenge for Cloon Keen Atelier is to find the optimum market position that provides a strategic advantage amongst robust competition. How will it maintain the high quality, good value and premium position in the market against new competitors? And how can Cloon Keen effectively promote itself and communicate with customers to the extent that it may be considered a lifestyle brand, rather than just a product brand?

Sources: Cloon Keen Atelier example has been informed by the following reports: Datamonitor Reports, 'Market Watch: Personal Care', March 2006; 'Personal Care: Industry Update', August 2006; 'Hand and Body Care in Ireland Industry Profile', December 2006; Euromonitor International Reports, 'Country Market Insight: Retailing Ireland', September 2006; Skin Care: Ireland', May 2006; 'Cosmetics and Toiletries: World', February 2007; 'Air Care: Ireland', March 2007. Margaret Mangan, co-owner of Cloon Keen Atelier, provided information in relation to the firm. The author thanks Margaret Mangan and Julian Checkley, of Cloon Keen Atelier, for their time and assistance in the writing of this case.

Finally, companies need periodically to audit their brands' strengths and weaknesses.[32] They should ask: Does our brand excel at delivering benefits that consumers truly value? Is the brand properly positioned? Do all of our consumer touch points support the brand's positioning? Do the brand's managers understand what the brand means to consumers? Does the brand receive proper, sustained support? The brand audit may turn up brands that need more support, brands that need to be dropped, or brands that must be rebranded or repositioned because of changing customer preferences or new competitors.

SERVICES MARKETING

Services have grown dramatically in recent years. Services account for the largest proportion of economic activity in the EU, although the percentage of economic activity (measured by the percentage of the workforce employed in the service industries) varies considerably from country to country. For example, in the UK 73 per cent of the workforce is employed in services, and the figure is very similar for Sweden. However, in Germany and Ireland a smaller proportion works in services. In both of these countries about 63 per cent of the workforce is employed in services – Germany has retained more of its manufacturing industries than other rich European countries, while Ireland has retained a fairly large agricultural sector. Nevertheless, even in these countries the service sector is the largest part of the economy. And the service sector is growing in size all across Europe. Services are growing fast in the world economy, making up 20 per cent of the value of all international trade.[33]

Service industries vary greatly. *Governments* offer services through courts, employment services, hospitals, the armed forces, police and fire services, postal service and schools. *Private not-for-profit organisations* offer services through museums, charities, churches, universities and hospitals. A large number of *business organisations* offer services – airlines, banks, hotels, insurance companies, consulting firms, medical and legal practices, entertainment companies, property (estate) agents, retailers and others.

Nature and characteristics of a service

A company must consider four special service characteristics when designing marketing programmes: *intangibility*, *inseparability*, *variability* and *perishability* (see Figure 7.5).

Service intangibility means that services cannot be seen, tasted, felt, heard or smelled before they are bought. For example, people undergoing cosmetic surgery cannot see the result before the purchase. Airline passengers have nothing but a ticket (these days, often an e-ticket) and the promise that they and their luggage will arrive safely at the intended destination, hopefully at the same time. To reduce uncertainty, buyers look for 'signals' of service quality. They draw conclusions about quality from the place, people, price, equipment and communications that they can see.

Therefore, the service provider's task is to make the service tangible in one or more ways and to send the right signals about quality. One analyst calls this *evidence management*, in which the service organisation presents its customers with organised, honest evidence of its capabilities. The famous American not-for-profit medical service provider the Mayo Clinic practices good evidence management:

FIGURE 7.5

Four service characteristics

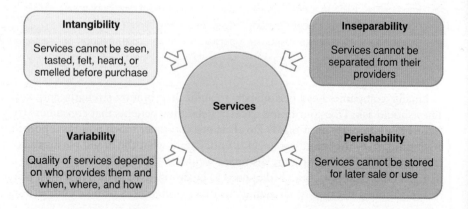

When it comes to hospitals, it's very hard for the average patient to judge the quality of the 'product'. You can't try it on, you can't return it if you don't like it, and you need an advanced degree to understand it. And so, when we're considering a medical facility, most of us unconsciously turn detective, looking for evidence of competence, caring, and integrity. The Mayo Clinic doesn't leave that evidence to chance. By carefully managing a set of visual and experiential clues, Mayo offers patients and their families concrete evidence of its strengths and values. For example, staff people at the clinic are trained to act in a way that clearly signals its patient-first focus. 'My doctor calls me at home to check on how I am doing,' marvels one patient. 'She wants to work with what is best for my schedule.' Mayo's physical facilities also send the right signals. They've been carefully designed to relieve stress, offer a place of refuge, create positive distractions, convey caring and respect, signal competence, accommodate families, and make it easy to find your way around. The result? Exceptionally positive word-of-mouth and abiding customer loyalty, which have allowed Mayo Clinic to build what is arguably the most powerful brand in health care – with very little advertising.[34]

Very similar strategies are pursued by similar private healthcare organisations in Europe, such as the UK-based BUPA, which is now expanding internationally and operates in Spain through its Sanitas subsidiary and in Ireland as Quinn Healthcare.

Physical goods are produced, then stored, later sold and still later consumed. In contrast, services are first sold, then produced and consumed at the same time. **Service inseparability** means that services cannot be separated from their providers, whether the providers are people or machines. If a service employee provides the service, then the employee becomes a part of the service. Because the customer is also present as the service is produced, *provider–customer interaction* is a special feature of services marketing. Both the provider and the customer affect the service outcome.

Service variability means that the quality of services depends on who provides them as well as when, where and how they are provided. For example, some hotels – say, Ibis – have reputations for providing better service than others. Still, within a given Ibis hotel, one registration-desk employee may be cheerful and efficient, whereas another standing just a few feet away may be unpleasant and slow. Even the quality of a single Ibis employee's service varies according to his or her energy and frame of mind at the time of each customer encounter.

Service perishability means that services cannot be stored for later sale or use. Some dentists charge patients for missed appointments because the service value existed only at that point and disappeared when the patient did not show up. The perishability of services is not a problem when demand is steady. However, when demand fluctuates, service firms often have difficult problems. For example, because of rush-hour demand, public transport companies have to own much more equipment than they would if demand were even throughout the day. Thus, service firms often design strategies for producing a better match between demand and supply. Hotels and holiday resorts charge lower prices in the off-season to attract more guests. And restaurants hire part-time employees to serve during peak periods.

Marketing strategies for service firms

Just like manufacturing businesses, good service firms use marketing to position themselves strongly in chosen target markets. Retailer John Lewis promises to be 'never knowingly undersold'. Ritz-Carlton Hotels positions itself as offering a memorable experience that 'enlivens the senses, instils well-being, and fulfills even the unexpressed wishes and needs of our guests'. These and other service firms establish their positions through traditional marketing mix activities.

However, because services differ from tangible products, they often require additional marketing approaches. In a product business, products are fairly standardised and can sit on shelves waiting for customers. But in a service business, the customer and front-line service employee *interact* to create the service. Thus, service providers must interact effectively with customers to create superior value during service encounters. Effective interaction, in turn, depends on the skills of front-line service employees and on the support processes backing these employees.

The service profit chain

Successful service companies focus their attention on *both* their customers and their employees. They understand the **service-profit chain,** which links service firm profits with employee and customer satisfaction. This chain consists of five links:

- Internal service quality: *superior employee selection and training, a quality work environment and strong support for those dealing with customers, which results in . . .*
- Satisfied and productive service employees: *more satisfied, loyal and hardworking employees, which results in . . .*
- Greater service value: *more effective and efficient customer value creation and service delivery, which results in . . .*
- Satisfied and loyal customers: *satisfied customers who remain loyal, repeat purchase, and refer other customers, which results in . . .*
- Healthy service profits and growth: *superior service firm performance.*[35]

Therefore, reaching service profits and growth goals begins with taking care of those who take care of customers. In fact, Starbucks CEO Howard Schultz goes so far as to say that 'customers always come in second – employees matter more'. The idea is that happy employees will unleash their enthusiasm on customers, creating even greater customer satisfaction. 'If the battle cry of the company [is] to exceed the expectations of our customers,' says Schultz, 'then as managers, we [must] first exceed the expectations of our people.'[36]

Thus, service marketing requires more than just traditional external marketing using the Four Ps. Figure 7.6 shows that service marketing also requires *internal marketing* and *interactive marketing*. **Internal marketing** means that the service firm must effectively train and motivate its customer-contact employees and supporting service people to work as a *team* to provide customer satisfaction. Marketers must get everyone in the organisation to be customer-centred. In fact, internal marketing must *precede* external marketing.

Interactive marketing means that service quality depends heavily on the quality of the buyer–seller interaction during the service encounter. In product marketing, product quality often depends little on how the product is obtained. But in services marketing, service quality depends on both the service deliverer and the quality of the delivery. Service marketers, therefore, have to master interactive marketing skills.

FIGURE 7.6

Three types of service marketing

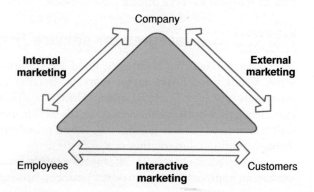

In today's marketplace, companies must know how to deliver interactions that are not only 'high touch' but also 'high tech'. For example, customers can log on to the Deutsche Bank Private Wealth Management site and access account information, investment research, real-time stock prices and personal financial advice. Customers seeking more personal interactions can contact service reps by phone or visit a local Deutsche Bank branch office. Thus, Deutsche Bank has mastered interactive marketing at all three levels – calls, clicks *and* visits.

Today, as competition and costs increase, and as productivity and quality decrease, more service marketing sophistication is needed. Service companies face three major marketing tasks: they want to increase their *service differentiation*, *service quality* and *service productivity*.

Managing service differentiation

In these days of intense price competition, service marketers often complain about the difficulty of differentiating their services from those of competitors. To the extent that customers view the services of different providers as similar, they care less about the provider than the price.

The solution to price competition is to develop a differentiated offer, delivery and image. The *offer* can include innovative features that set one company's offer apart from competitors' offers. Some hotels offer car hire, banking and business centre services in their lobbies and high-speed Internet connections in their rooms. Airlines differentiate their offers though frequent-flyer award programmes and special services. For example, Qantas offers personal entertainment screens at every seat and 'Skybeds' for international business class flyers. Lufthansa provides wireless Internet access and real-time surfing to every seat – it makes 'an airplane feel like a cyber café'. And British Airways offers spa services at its arrivals lounge at Heathrow airport. Says one ad: 'You can step off the plane and straight into a shower, a robe, even a Molton Brown facial – all while your suit is being pressed.'

Service companies can differentiate their service *delivery* by having more able and reliable customer-contact people, by developing a superior physical environment in which the service product is delivered, or by designing a superior delivery process. For example, many grocery chains now offer online shopping and home delivery as a better way to shop than having to drive, park, queue up and carry groceries home.

Finally, service companies also can work on differentiating their *images* through symbols and branding. Telecommunications group BT adopted the 'world' symbol to demonstrate its commitment to offering global services. Other well-known service symbols include the red and white HSBC 'triangles' symbol, McDonald's Golden Arches, and the London Underground red roundel with a blue rectangle familiar to London residents and millions of London tourists!

Managing service quality

One of the major ways a service firm can differentiate itself is by delivering consistently higher quality than its competitors do. Like manufacturers before them, most service industries have now joined the customer-driven quality movement. And like product marketers, service providers need to identify what target customers expect concerning service quality.

Unfortunately, service quality is harder to define and judge than is product quality. For instance, it is harder to agree on the quality of a haircut than on the quality of a hair dryer. Customer retention is perhaps the best measure of quality – a service firm's ability to hang on to its customers depends on how consistently it delivers value to them.[37]

Top service companies set high service quality standards. They watch service performance closely, both their own and that of competitors. They do not settle for merely good service; they aim for 100 per cent defect-free service. A 98 per cent performance standard may sound good, but using this standard, 310,000 UPS packages would be lost each day, 10 words would be misspelled on each printed page, 225,000 prescriptions would be misfilled daily, and drinking water would be unsafe 7 days a year.[38]

Unlike product manufacturers who can adjust their machinery and inputs until everything is perfect, service quality will always vary, depending on the interactions between employees and customers. As hard as they try, even the best companies will have an occasional late delivery, burned steak, or grumpy employee. However, good *service recovery* can turn angry customers into loyal ones. In fact, good recovery can win more customer purchasing and loyalty than if things had gone well in the first place. Therefore, companies should take steps not only to provide good service every time but also to recover from service mistakes when they do occur.

The first step is to *empower* front-line service employees – to give them the authority, responsibility and incentives they need to recognise, care about and tend to customer needs. At Radisson, for example, well-trained employees go through the 'Yes I Can!' training programme to give them the confidence to do whatever it takes, on the spot, to keep guests happy. They are also expected to help management ferret out the cause of guests' problems and to inform managers of ways to improve overall hotel service and guests' comfort.

Managing service productivity

With their costs rising rapidly, service firms are under great pressure to increase service productivity. They can do so in several ways. They can train current employees better or hire new ones who will work harder or more skilfully. Or they can increase the quantity of their service by giving up some quality. The provider can 'industrialise the service' by adding equipment and standardising production, as in McDonald's assembly-line approach to fast-food retailing. Finally, the service provider can harness the power of technology. Although we often think of technology's power to save time and costs in manufacturing companies, it also has great – and often untapped – potential to make service workers more productive.

However, companies must avoid pushing productivity so hard that doing so reduces quality. Attempts to industrialise a service or to cut costs can make a service company more efficient in the short term. But they can also reduce its longer-term ability to innovate, maintain service quality, or respond to consumer needs and desires. In short, they can take the 'service' out of service.

ADDITIONAL PRODUCT CONSIDERATIONS

Here, we discuss two additional product policy considerations: social responsibility in product decisions and issues of international product and service marketing.

Product decisions and social responsibility

Product decisions have attracted much public attention. Marketers should consider carefully public policy issues and regulations involving acquiring or dropping products, patent protection, product quality and safety, and product warranties.

Regarding new products, governments may prevent companies from adding products through acquisitions if the effect threatens to reduce competition. Companies dropping products must be aware that they have legal obligations, written or implied, to their suppliers, dealers and customers who have a stake in the dropped product. Companies must also obey patent laws when developing new products. A company cannot make its product illegally similar to another company's established product.

Manufacturers must comply with specific laws regarding product quality and safety. The European Food Safety Authority is responsible for maintaining food standards within the EU, and individual countries have their own authorities, such as the Food Safety Authority of Ireland, and the Food Standards Agency in the UK. Several EU laws protect consumers from unsafe and adulterated food, drugs and cosmetics. Safety legislation has been passed to regulate fabrics, chemical substances, vehicles, toys, and drugs and poisons. If consumers have been injured by a product that has been designed defectively, they can sue manufacturers or dealers.

This phenomenon has resulted in huge increases in product liability insurance premiums, causing big problems in some industries. Some companies pass these higher rates along to consumers by raising prices. Others are forced to discontinue high-risk product lines. Some companies are now appointing 'product stewards', whose job is to protect consumers from harm and the company from liability by proactively identifying potential product problems.

International product and services marketing

International product and service marketers face special challenges. First, they must figure out what products and services to introduce and in which countries. Then, they must decide how much to standardise or adapt their products and services for world markets.

On the one hand, companies would like to standardise their offerings. Standardisation helps a company to develop a consistent worldwide image. It also lowers the product design, manufacturing and marketing costs of offering a large variety of products. On the other hand, markets and consumers around the world differ widely. Companies must usually respond to these differences by adapting their product offerings. Something as simple as an electrical outlet can create big product problems:

> Those who have travelled across Europe know the frustration of electrical plugs, different voltages, and other annoyances of international travel . . . Philips, the electrical appliance manufacturer, has to produce 12 kinds of irons to serve just its European market. The problem is that Europe does not have a universal [electrical] standard. The ends of irons bristle with different plugs for different countries. Some have three prongs, others two; prongs protrude straight or angled, round or rectangular, fat, thin, and sometimes sheathed. There are circular plug faces, squares, pentagons, and hexagons. Some are perforated and some are notched. One French plug has a niche like a keyhole. Looking for a fix? One online travel service sells an elaborate 10-piece adapter plug set for international travellers for $65.00.[39]

Packaging also presents new challenges for international marketers. Packaging issues can be subtle. For example, names, labels and colours may not translate easily from one country to another. A firm using yellow flowers in its logo might fare well in the United States but meet with disaster in Mexico, where a yellow flower symbolises death or disrespect. Similarly, although Nature's Gift might be an appealing name for gourmet mushrooms in America, it would be deadly in Germany, where *gift* means poison. Packaging may also have to be tailored to meet the physical characteristics of consumers in various parts of the world. For instance, soft drinks are sold in smaller cans in Japan to fit the smaller Japanese hand better. Thus, although product and package standardisation can produce benefits, companies must usually adapt their offerings to the unique needs of specific international markets.

Service marketers also face special challenges when going global. Some service industries have a long history of international operations. For example, the commercial banking industry was one of the first to grow internationally. Banks had to provide global services in order to meet the foreign exchange and credit needs of their home country clients wanting to sell overseas. In recent years, many banks have become truly global. Germany's Deutsche Bank, for example, serves more than 12 million customers in 74 countries. For its clients around the world who wish to grow globally, Deutsche Bank can raise money not only in Frankfurt but also in Zurich, London, Paris and Tokyo.[40]

Professional and business services industries such as accounting, management consulting and advertising have only recently globalised. The international growth of these firms followed the globalisation of the client companies they serve. For example, as their clients began to employ worldwide marketing and advertising strategies, advertising agencies responded by globalising their own operations. McCann-Erickson Worldwide, a global advertising agency, operates in more than 130 countries. It serves international clients such as Coca-Cola, General Motors, ExxonMobile, Microsoft, MasterCard, Johnson & Johnson and Unilever in markets ranging from the United States and Canada to Korea and Kazakhstan. Moreover, McCann-Erikson is one company in the Interpublic Group of companies, an immense, worldwide network of advertising and marketing services companies.[41]

Retailers are among the latest service businesses to go global. As their home markets become saturated, American retailers such as Wal-Mart, Toys 'R' Us, Office Depot and Saks Fifth Avenue are expanding into faster-growing markets abroad. For example, every year since 1995 Wal-Mart has entered a new country. Other retailers are making similar moves. Asian shoppers can now buy American products in French-owned Carrefour stores. Carrefour, the world's second-largest retailer behind Wal-Mart, now operates in more than 11,000 stores in 31 countries. It is the leading retailer in Europe, Brazil and Argentina and the largest foreign retailer in China.[42]

The trend towards growth of global service companies will continue, especially in banking, airlines, telecommunications and professional services. Today service firms are no longer simply following their manufacturing customers. Instead, they are taking the lead in international expansion.

THE JOURNEY YOU'VE TAKEN Reviewing the concepts

A product is more than a simple set of tangible features. In fact, many marketing offers consist of combinations of both tangible goods and services, ranging from *pure tangible goods* at one extreme to *pure services* at the other. Each product or service offered to customers can be viewed on three levels. The *core product* consists of the core problem-solving benefits that consumers seek when they buy a product. The *actual product* exists around the core and includes the quality level, features, design, brand name and packaging. The *augmented product* is the actual product plus the various services and benefits offered with it, such as warranty, free delivery, installation and maintenance.

1 **Define *product* and the major classifications of products and services.**

Broadly defined, a *product* is anything that can be offered to a market for attention, acquisition, use or consumption that might satisfy a want or need. Products include physical objects but also services, events, persons, places, organisations, ideas or mixes of these entities. *Services* are products that consist of activities, benefits or satisfactions offered for sale that are essentially intangible, such as banking, hotel, telephone and home-repair services.

Products and services fall into two broad classes based on the types of consumers that use them. *Consumer products* – those bought by final consumers – are usually classified according to consumer shopping habits (convenience products, shopping products, speciality products and unsought products). *Industrial products* – purchased for further processing or for use in conducting a business – include materials and parts, capital items, and supplies and services. Other marketable entities – such as organisations, persons, places and ideas – can also be thought of as products.

2 Describe the decisions companies make regarding their individual products and services, product lines and product mixes.

Individual product decisions involve product attributes, branding, packaging, labelling and product support services. *Product attribute* decisions involve product quality, features, and style and design. *Branding* decisions include selecting a brand name and developing a brand strategy. *Packaging* provides many key benefits, such as protection, economy, convenience and promotion. Package decisions often include designing *labels*, which identify, describe and possibly promote the product. Companies also develop *product support services* that enhance customer service and satisfaction and safeguard against competitors.

Most companies produce a product line rather than a single product. A *product line* is a group of products that are related in function, customer-purchase needs or distribution channels. *Line stretching* involves extending a line downwards, upwards, or in both directions to occupy a gap that might otherwise by filled by a competitor. In contrast, *line filling* involves adding items within the present range of the line. All product lines and items offered to customers by a particular seller make up the *product mix*. The mix can be described by four dimensions: width, length, depth and consistency. These dimensions are the tools for developing the company's product strategy.

3 Discuss branding strategy – the decisions companies make in building and managing their brands.

Some analysts see brands as *the* major enduring asset of a company. Brands are more than just names and symbols – they embody everything that the product or service *means* to consumers. *Brand equity* is the positive differential effect that knowing the brand name has on customer response to the product or service. A brand with strong brand equity is a very valuable asset.

In building brands, companies need to make decisions about brand positioning, brand name selection, brand sponsorship and brand development. The most powerful *brand positioning* builds around strong consumer beliefs and values. *Brand name selection* involves finding the best brand name based on a careful review of product benefits, the target market and proposed marketing strategies. A manufacturer has four *brand sponsorship* options: it can launch a *manufacturer's brand* (or national brand), sell to resellers who use a *private brand*, market *licensed brands*, or join forces with another company to *co-brand* a product. A company also has four choices when it comes to developing brands. It can introduce *line extensions, brand extensions, multibrands* or *new brands*.

Companies must build and manage their brands carefully. The brand's positioning must be continuously communicated to consumers. Advertising can help. However, brands are not maintained by advertising but by the *brand experience*. Customers come to know a brand through a wide range of contacts and interactions. The company must put as much care into managing these touch points as it does into producing its ads. Thus, managing a company's brand assets can no longer be left only to brand managers. Some companies are now setting up brand asset management teams to manage their major brands. Finally, companies must periodically audit their brands' strengths and weaknesses. In some cases, brands may need to be repositioned because of changing customer preferences or new competitors. Other cases may call for completely *rebranding* a product, service or company.

4 Identify the four characteristics that affect the marketing of a service and the additional marketing considerations that services require.

Services are characterised by four key characteristics: they are *intangible, inseparable, variable* and *perishable*. Each characteristic poses problems and marketing requirements. Marketers work to find ways to make the service more tangible, to increase the productivity of providers who are inseparable from their products, to standardise the quality in the face of variability, and to improve demand movements and supply capacities in the face of service perishability.

Good service companies focus attention on *both* customers and employees. They understand the *service profit chain*, which links service firm profits with employee and customer satisfaction. Services marketing strategy calls not only for external marketing but also for *internal marketing* to motivate employees and *interactive marketing* to create service delivery skills among service providers. To succeed, service marketers must create *competitive differentiation*, offer high *service quality* and find ways to increase *service productivity*.

5 Discuss two additional product issues: socially responsible product decisions and international product and services marketing.

Marketers must consider two additional product issues. The first is *social responsibility*. This includes public policy issues and regulations involving acquiring or dropping products, patent protection, product quality and safety, and product warranties. The second involves the special challenges facing international product and service marketers. International marketers must decide how much to standardise or adapt their offerings for world markets.

NAVIGATING THE KEY TERMS

NOTES AND REFERENCES

1 Based on material from http://www.business2000.ie/cases/cases_8th/case18.htm.

2 See 'The Celebrity 100', *Forbes*, accessed at www.forbes.com, June 2005; Siddhartha Finch 'Tiger Woods Signs Long-term Deal with Apple Computer as Mac OS X "Tiger" Spokesperson,' *Mac Daily News*, 1 April 2005, accessed at www.macdailynews.com; and www.tigerwoods.com, accessed March 2005.

3 For more on marketing places, see Philip Kotler, Donald Haider and Irving J. Rein, *Marketing Places* (New York: Free Press, 2002). Information for examples found in Steve Dougherty, 'In a Cold Country, the Nights Are Hot', *New York Times*, 19 December 2004, sect. 5, p. 1; and at www.TravelTex.com, www.michigan.org, and www.iloveny.state.ny.us, August 2005.

4 Accessed online at www.social-marketing.org/aboutus.html, August 2005.

5 See Alan R. Andreasen, Rob Gould and Karen Gutierrez, 'Social Marketing Has a New Champion', *Marketing News*, 7 February 2000, p. 38. See also Philip Kotler, Ned Roberto and Nancy Lee, *Social Marketing: Improving the Quality of Life*, 2nd edn (Thousand Oaks, CA: Sage Publications, 2002); and www.social-marketing.org, August 2005.

6 Quotes and definitions from Philip Kotler, *Kotler on Marketing* (New York: Free Press, 1999), p. 17; and www.asq.org, July 2005.

7 Abby Ghobadian, Simon Speller and Matthew Jones, 'Service Quality: Concepts and Models', *International Journal of Quality & Reliability Management*, 11(9), 1994, pp. 43–66.

8 See Roland T. Rust, Anthony J. Zahorik and Timothy L. Keiningham, 'Return on Quality (ROQ): Making Service Quality Financially Accountable', *Journal of Marketing*, April 1995, pp. 58–70; Roland T. Rust, Christine Moorman and Peter R. Dickson, 'Getting Return on Quality: Revenue Expansion, Cost Reduction, or Both?', *Journal of Marketing*, October 2002, pp. 7–24; and Roland T. Rust, Katherine N. Lemon and Valerie A. Zeithaml, 'Return on Marketing: Using Customer Equity to Focus Marketing Strategy', *Journal of Marketing*, January 2004, p. 109.

9 http://www.design-council.org.uk/en/Case-Studies/All-Case-Studies/Invotek/ Developing-a-design-led-business-model/. © Design Council, 2006. Reproduced with permission. www.designcouncil.org.uk.

10 See Kate Fitzgerald, 'Packaging Is the Capper', *Advertising Age*, 5 May 2003, p. 22.

11 Based on Thomas J. Ryan, 'Labels Grow Up', *Apparel*, February 2005, pp. 26–9.

12 http://www.dwp.gov.uk/lifeevent/benefits/dcs/customer_survey.asp.

13 Example adapted from Michelle Higgins, 'Pop-Up Sales Clerks: Web Sites Try the Hard Sell', *Wall Street Journal*, 15 April 2004, p. D.1.

14 Information accessed online at www.marriott.com, August 2005.

15 Information about Colgate's product lines accessed at www.colgate.com/app/Colgate/US/Corp/Products.cvsp, August 2005.

16 See 'McAtlas Shrugged', *Foreign Policy*, May–June 2001, pp. 26–37; and Philip Kotler and Kevin Lane Keller, *Marketing Management*, 12th edn (Upper Saddle River, NJ: Prentice Hall, 2006), pp. 290–1.

17 David C. Bello and Morris. B. Holbrook, 'Does an Absence of Brand Equity Generalize Across Product Classes?', *Journal of Business Research*, October 1995, p. 125; and Scott Davis, *Brand Asset Management: Driving Profitable Growth through Your Brands* (San Francisco: Jossey-Bass, 2000). See also Kevin Lane Keller, *Building, Measuring, and Managing Brand Equity*, 2nd edn (Upper Saddle River, NJ: Prentice Hall, 2003), ch. 2; and Kusum Ailawadi, Donald R. Lehman and Scott A. Neslin, 'Revenue Premium as an Outcome Measure of Brand Equity', *Journal of Marketing*, October 2003, pp. 1–17.

18 'Best Global Brands 2007', Interbrand, accessed at http://www.ourfishbowl.com/images/surveys/Interbrand_BGB_2007.pdf, 14th July 2008.

19 See Rust, Lemon and Zeithaml 'Return on Marketing: Using Customer Equity to Focus Marketing Strategy', p. 109.

20 See Scott Davis, *Brand Asset Management*, 2nd edn (San Francisco: Jossey-Bass, 2002). For more on brand positioning, see Kotler and Keller, *Marketing Management*, 12th edn, ch. 10.

21 http://www.aquafresh.co.uk/extremeClean.aspx.

22 http://www.spar.co.uk/customers/spar-brand/.

23 See Laura Petrecca, '"Corporate Brands" Put Licensing in the Spotlight', *Advertising Age*, 14 June 1999, p. 1; and Bob Vavra, 'The Game of the Name', *Supermarket Business*, 15 March 2001, pp. 45–6; Jim Cioletti, 'Making the Brand: Behind the Badge', *Beverage World*, 15 December 2004, pp. 36–7.

24 Judith H. Washburn, Brian D. Till and Randi Priluck, 'Co-branding: brand equity and trial effects', *Journal of Consumer Marketing*, 17(7), 2000, pp. 591–604.

25 Henrik Uggla, 'The corporate brand association base: A conceptual model for the creation of inclusive brand architecture', *European Journal of Marketing*, 40(7/8), 2006, pp. 785–802.

26 Laura Liebeck, 'Two Tastes Can Be Better Than One', *Retail Merchandiser*, February 2005, p. 20.

27 Based on information from Kate McArthur, 'Cannibalization a Risk as Coke Diet Brand Tally Grows to Sever,' *Advertising Age*, 28 March 2005, pp. 3, 123; and 'Coca-Cola Zero Pops Into Stores Today', *Atlanta Business Chronicle*, 13 June 2005, accessed at http://atlanta.bizjournals.com/atlanta/stories/2005/06/13/daily7.html.

28 http://www.brandchannel.com/papers_review.asp?sp_id=634.

29 For more on the use of line and brand extensions and consumer attitudes toward them, see Subramanian Balachander and Sanjoy Ghose, 'Reciprocal Spillover Effects: A Strategic Benefit of Brand Extensions', *Journal of Marketing*, January 2003, pp. 4–13; Eva Martinez and Leslie de Chernatony, 'The Effect of Brand Extension Strategies Upon Brand Image',

Journal of Consumer Marketing, 2004, p. 39; and Devon DeiVecchio and Danile Smith, 'Brand-Extension Price Premiums: The Effect of Perceived Fit and Extension Product Category Risk', *Journal of Academy of Marketing Science*, Spring 2005, pp. 184–92.

30 'Top 200 Megabrands', accessed at www.adage.com, June 2005.

31 Stephen Cole, 'Value of the Brand', *CA Magazine*, May 2005, pp. 39–40.

32 See Kevin Lane Keller, 'The Brand Report Card', *Harvard Business Review*, January 2000, pp. 147–57; Kevin Lane Keller, *Strategic Brand Management*, 2nd edn (Upper Saddle River, NJ: Prentice Hall, 2003), pp. 766–7; and David A. Aaker, 'Even Brands Need Spring Cleaning', *Brandweek*, 8 March 2004, pp. 36–40.

33 See CIA, *The World Factbook*, accessed at http://www.cia.gov/cia/publications/factbook/geos/us.html, July 2005; *International Trade Statistics 2004*, World Trade Organisation, p. 23, accessed at www.wto.org, July 2005; and information from the Bureau of Labor Statistics, www.bls.gov, accessed April 2005.

34 Adapted from information in Leonard Berry and Neeli Bendapudi, 'Clueing in Customers', *Harvard Business Review*, February 2003, pp. 100–6 and information accessed at www.mayoclinic.org, August 2005.

35 See James L. Heskett, W. Earl Sasser Jr. and Leonard A. Schlesinger, *The Service Profit Chain: How Leading Companies Link Profit and Growth to Loyalty, Satisfaction, and Value* (New York: Free Press, 1997); Heskett, Sasser, and Schlesinger, *The Value Profit Chain: Treat Employees Like Customers and Customers Like Employees* (New York: Free Press, 2003); and Garry A. Gelade and Stephen Young, 'Test of the Service Profit Chain Model in the Retail Banking Sector,' *Journal of Occupational and Organisational Psychology*, March 2005, pp. 1–22.

36 Jeremy B. Dann, 'How to Find a Hit as Big as Starbucks', *Business 2.0*, May 2004, pp. 66–8.

37 For discussions of service quality, see Valerie A. Zeithaml, A. Parasuraman and Leonard L. Berry, *Delivering Quality Service: Balancing Customer Perceptions and Expectations* (New York: The Free Press, 1990); Zeithaml, Berry and Parasuraman, 'The Behavioral Consequences of Service Quality', *Journal of Marketing*, April 1996, pp. 31–46; Y. H. Hung, M. L. Huang and K. S. Chen, 'Service Quality Evaluation by Service Quality Performance Matrix', *Total Quality Management & Business Excellence*, January 2003, pp. 79–89; and Bo Edvardsson, 'Service Quality: Beyond Cognitive Assessment', *Managing Service Quality*, 2(2), pp. 127–31.

38 See 'UPS 4th Quarter Shows 10% Revenue Gain', accessed at http://pressroom.ups.com, April 2005.

39 See Philip Cateora, *International Marketing*, 8th edn (Homewood, IL: Irwin, 1993), p. 270; David Fairlamb, 'One Currency – But 15 Economies', *BusinessWeek*, 31 December 2001, p. 59; and www.walkabouttravelgear.com/elect.htm, July 2005.

40 Information accessed online at www.deutsche-bank.com, July 2005.

41 Information accessed online at www.interpublic.com and www.mccann.com, July 2005.

42 See 'Wal-Mart International Operations', accessed at www.walmartstores.com, July 2005; '2005 Global Powers of Retailing', *Stores*, January 2005, accessed at www.stores.org; and information accessed at www.carrefour.com/english/groupecarrefour/profil.jsp, July 2005.

CHAPTER 9

Pricing: Understanding and capturing customer value

AFTER STUDYING THIS CHAPTER, YOU SHOULD BE ABLE TO

- Understand the importance of customer value perceptions and company costs when setting prices
- Identify and define the other important internal and external factors affecting a firm's pricing decisions
- Describe the major strategies for pricing imitative and new products
- Explain how companies find a set of prices that maximises the profits from the total product mix
- Discuss how companies adjust their prices to take into account different types of customers and situations
- Discuss key issues related to initiating and responding to price changes

THE WAY AHEAD Previewing the concepts

We continue your marketing journey with a look at a second major marketing mix tool – pricing. Firms successful at creating customer value with the other marketing mix activities must capture this value in the prices they earn. According to one pricing expert, pricing involves 'harvesting your profit potential'.[1] If effective product development, promotion, and distribution sow the seeds of business success, effective pricing is the harvest. Yet, despite its importance, many firms do not handle pricing well. In this chapter, we begin with the question, 'What is a price?' Next, we look at customer value perceptions, costs and other factors that marketers must consider when setting prices. Finally, we examine pricing strategies for new-product pricing, product mix pricing, price adjustments and dealing with price changes.

Pricing decisions can make or break a company. For openers, consider Primark, whose low-cost, everyday-low-price strategy years has helped it to become a top high street fashion retailer. Everything that Primark does is focused on the goal of delivering clothes that people want at prices that other retailers cannot match.

Primark

Clothing retailer Primark is one of Europe's most spectacular retailing successes. When it opened a flagship store on London's Oxford Street in 2007, eager customers queued through the night and blocked up the whole street just to be among the first visitors. How did it achieve this kind of success? Well, in simple terms, by offering the kind of clothes that young women want to buy at prices that are so low they might be thought to be 'loss-leaders' or 'sale prices'. But Primark doesn't do loss-leaders or sale prices, it just does low prices in all of its stores all of the time: 'everyday low pricing' or EDLP in today's jargon. This has raised suspicions that Primark's prices are too good to be true. How can Primark offer good products at such low prices? Why can't their rivals match them? In June 2008 it looked like the 'trick' had been exposed, as a BBC TV *Panorama* documentary claimed that Primark was sourcing its products from factories in India employing child labour. But Primark hit back, immediately ceasing to do business with those factories and reinforcing its systems for monitoring the ethical standards employed by all Primark suppliers. The company was determined to prove that everything it has achieved is firmly based on the company's ethical code of conduct:

- Employment is freely chosen.
- Freedom of association and the right to collective bargaining are respected.
- Working conditions are safe and hygienic.
- Child labour shall not be used.
- Living wages are paid.
- Working hours are not excessive.

- No discrimination is practised.
- Regular employment is provided.
- No harsh or inhumane treatment is allowed.

In other words, according to the company's management team, Primark clothing is manufactured under exactly the same conditions as the clothing sold by other major high street chains. The low prices that Primark offers its customers are not achieved through a special 'trick' involving the exploitation of the workforce in developing countries; in fact, the labour conditions at Primark suppliers are just the same as the conditions at factories supplying other major high street clothing stores. The question is, then, if there is no 'special trick', just how does it manage to deliver the products that customers want at prices that are so strikingly low?

Primark Stores Ltd is a subsidiary of Associated British Foods, a diversified international food, ingredients and retail group with global sales of £6.8 billion and 85,000 employees in 43 countries. Primark operates a total of 177 stores in Ireland (where it trades under the Penneys brand), Spain and the UK. The company employs in excess of 25,000 people. In Britain, in terms of market share, Primark is ranked as the second largest clothing retailer by volume and the leading retailer in value clothing. Primark has been voted 'Best Value High Street Fashion' by GMTV and ITV viewers, and has won numerous industry awards, including 'Best New Store – Primark Oxford Street' and 'Value

Retailer of the Year' (Drapers Awards 2007); 'The Retail Award' (Juice FM Liverpool Style Awards); 'Fashion Retail Interior of the Year', 'Shop-fitting Excellence Award' and 'Best UK Interior Award' for the Oxford Street store (Retail Interior Awards 2007); and 'Value for Money' and 'Casual Clothes' in the Prima Fashion High Street Awards 2007.

In the financial year 2006/7, 32 new stores were opened and five smaller stores were closed to give 4.8 million sq ft of retail selling space. One of the highlights of that year was the opening of the Oxford Street store in April. This was extremely successful, selling 1 million items in its first ten days of trading, and attracting considerable media coverage. The 85,000 sq ft Liverpool store was opened in September 2007 and was greeted with a similar level of enthusiasm both by customers and media. Recently Primark has been expanding rapidly in Spain. Five additional stores have recently opened in

Source: Getty Images.

Spain: in Bilbao, Jerez, Oviedo and two further stores in Madrid. Primark now has 25 stores trading from over 50,000 sq ft, of which eight trade from over 70,000 sq ft.

Primark explains its success in terms of:

- super-competitive prices (the result of technology, efficient distribution, supply and volume buying), and

- mainstream market product quality (high street locations, superior store interiors, clear focus on the target market).

Primark targets young, fashion-conscious under 35s, offering them high quality, fashion basics at value for money prices. Almost half of sales are in womenswear. A quarter of sales are in menswear and childrenswear, with other items constituting the remaining sales. Buying and merchandising teams in Reading (UK) and Dublin (Ireland) travel internationally to source and buy up-to-the-minute fashion basics that best reflect each season's key fashion trends. Primark's offer to the customer is one of high quality merchandise, at value for money, backed by Primark's service promise. Primark prides itself on its loyal customer base. According to the company:

A strong consumer proposition has been developed for the Primark brand and embodied in the line 'Look Good, Pay Less' which communicates Primark's value-based offering in a precise manner, to its core target audience. The purpose of the advertising in the first instance is to support this strong value proposition and secondly to tailor the media solution to the store. Communication models are created and the imagery of the advertising is young, modern and dynamic to reflect the core target audience. A combination of media is used to create, impact upon and tightly target new customers.

This all leaves the main question unanswered. It is not hard to see that offering customers desirable products in convenient high street locations and at rock-bottom prices is a recipe for success. If there is no simple 'trick' involved, like buying your products from cut-price suppliers who use unethical employment practices, then how can this be done? The answer seems to be that everything about Primark is designed to deliver low costs and low prices. The entire business proposition is built around delivering value to customers. There is a constant emphasis on keeping overhead and operating costs low. Profit margins are lower than the industry average. Primark only invests in advertising that it knows will make a difference, and avoids high-profile, expensive image-building advertising; the management team believes that their customers know what the company stands for and that positive word-of-mouth advertising from satisfied customers is the best kind of promotion. Above all, Primark keeps its product designs simple, concentrates on the most popular sizes, and then buys products in large quantities so benefiting from economies of scale.

Sources: www.primark.co.uk; www.bbc.co.uk.

As the Primark case study shows, companies today face a fierce and fast-changing pricing environment. Increasing customer price consciousness has put many companies in a 'pricing vice'. In the USA they call this the 'Wal-Mart phenomenon', reflecting the aggressive pricing policies adopted by the world's largest retailer.[2] So far Wal-Mart has established only a fairly small presence in Europe, with the acquisition of Asda in the UK. However, Wal-Mart is increasing its global presence and now operates 2,760 stores in 13 markets outside the continental USA: Argentina, Brazil, Canada, China, Costa Rica, El Salvador, Guatemala, Honduras, Japan, Mexico, Nicaragua, Puerto Rico and the UK. The sort of retail power that Wal-Mart exerts in the USA is making its presence felt across the globe. In response, it seems that almost every company is looking for ways to slash prices, and that is hurting their profits.

Yet, cutting prices is often not the best answer. Reducing prices unnecessarily can lead to lost profits and damaging price wars. It can signal to customers that the price is more important than the customer value a brand delivers. Instead, companies should sell value, not price. They should persuade customers that paying a higher price for the company's brand is justified by the greater value they gain. The challenge is to find the price that will let the company make a fair profit by harvesting the customer value it creates. For example, the IKEA business vision is to create a better everyday life for as many people as possible, and they aim to do this 'by offering a wide range of well-designed, functional home furnishing products at prices so low that as many people as possible will be able to afford them'.[3] IKEA aims to make a profit itself by offering customers real value.

WHAT IS A PRICE?

In the narrowest sense, **price** is the amount of money charged for a product or service. More broadly, price is the sum of all the values that customers give up in order to gain the benefits of having or using a product or service. Historically, price has been the major factor affecting buyer choice. In recent decades, non-price factors have gained increasing importance. However, price still remains one of the most important elements affecting a firm's market share and profitability.

Price is the only element in the marketing mix that produces revenue; all other elements represent costs. Price is also one of the most flexible elements of the marketing mix. Unlike product features and channel commitments, prices can be changed quickly. At the same time, pricing is the number-one problem facing many marketing executives, and many companies do not handle pricing well. One frequent problem is that companies are too quick to reduce prices in order to get a sale rather than convincing buyers that their product's greater value is worth a higher price. Other common mistakes include pricing that is too cost-oriented rather than customer value-oriented, and pricing that does not take the rest of the marketing mix into account.

Some managers view pricing as a big headache, preferring instead to focus on the other marketing mix elements. However, smart managers treat pricing as a key strategic tool for creating and capturing customer value. Prices have a direct impact on a firm's bottom line. According to one expert, on average a 5 per cent increase in price increases profits by 22 per cent.[4] More importantly, as a part of a company's overall value proposition, price plays a key role in creating customer value and building customer relationships.

FACTORS TO CONSIDER WHEN SETTING PRICES

The price the company charges will fall somewhere between one that is too high to produce any demand and one that is too low to produce a profit. Figure 9.1 summarises the major considerations in setting price. Customer perceptions of the product's value set the ceiling for prices. If customers perceive that the price is greater than the product's value, they will not buy the product. Product costs set the floor for prices. If the company prices the product below its costs, company profits will suffer. In setting its price between these two extremes, the company must consider a number of factors, including its overall marketing strategy and mix, the nature of the market and demand, competitors' strategies and prices, and a number of other internal and external factors.

FIGURE 9.1

Factors affecting price decisions

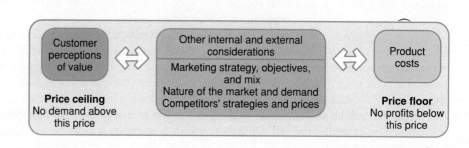

Customer perceptions of value

In the end, the customer will decide whether a product's price is right. Pricing decisions, like other marketing mix decisions, must start with customer value. When customers buy a product, they exchange something of value (the price) in order to get something of value (the benefits of having or using the product). Effective, customer-oriented pricing involves understanding how much value consumers place on the benefits they receive from the product and setting a price that captures this value.

Value-based pricing

Good pricing begins with a complete understanding of the value that a product or service creates for customers. **Value-based pricing** uses buyers' perceptions of value, not the seller's cost, as the key to pricing. Value-based pricing means that the marketer cannot design a product and marketing programme and then set the price. Price is considered along with the other marketing mix variables *before* the marketing programme is set.

Figure 9.2 compares value-based pricing with cost-based pricing. Cost-based pricing is product driven. The company designs what it considers to be a good product, adds up the costs of making the product, and sets a price that covers costs plus a target profit. Marketing must then convince buyers that the product's value at that price justifies its purchase. If the price turns out to be too high, the company must settle for lower mark-ups or lower sales, both resulting in disappointing profits.

Value-based pricing reverses this process. The company sets its target price based on customer perceptions of the product value. The targeted value and price then drive decisions about product design and what costs can be incurred. As a result, pricing begins with analysing consumer needs and value perceptions, and price is set to match consumers' perceived value.

It's important to remember that 'good value' is not always the same as 'low price'. For example, the German luxury goods manufacturer Montblanc, part of the Swiss firm Compagnie Financière Richemont SA, sells exclusive pens for hundreds of euros – a less expensive pen might write just as well, but some consumers place great value on the intangibles they receive from a 'fine writing instrument'. Similarly, many American car buyers consider that the luxurious Bentley Continental GT delivers real value, even at a basic price of $175,000, because of the long tradition of British motor racing excellence and German engineering (Bentley is now part of the Volkswagen Group) associated with the brand:

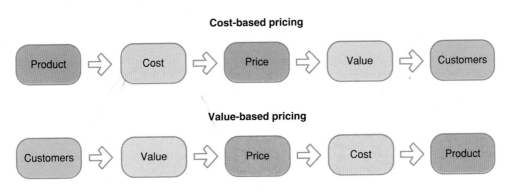

FIGURE 9.2

Value-based pricing versus cost-based pricing

Source: Thomas T. Nagle and Reed K. Holden, *The Strategy and Tactics of Pricing*, 3rd edn (Upper Saddle River, NJ: Prentice Hall, 2002), p. 4. Pearson Education, Inc., Upper Saddle River, New Jersey.

Every Bentley GT is built by hand, an Old World bit of automaking requiring 160 hours per vehicle. Craftsmen spend 18 hours simply stitching the perfectly joined leather of the GT's steering wheel, almost as long as it takes to assemble an entire VW Golf. The results are impressive: Dash and doors are mirrored with walnut veneer, floor pedals are carved from aluminum, window and seat toggles are cut from actual metal rather than plastic, and every air vent is perfectly chromed . . . The sum of all this is a fitted cabin that approximates that of a $300,000 vehicle, matched to an engine the equal of a $200,000 automobile, within a car that has brilliantly incorporated . . . technological sophistication. As I said, the GT is a bargain. [Just ask anyone on the lengthy waiting list.] The waiting time to bring home your very own GT is currently half a year.[5]

A company using value-based pricing must find out what value buyers assign to different competitive offers. However, companies often find it hard to measure the value customers will attach to their products. For example, calculating the cost of ingredients in a meal at a good restaurant is relatively easy. But assigning a value to other satisfactions such as taste, environment, relaxation, conversation and status is very hard. And these values will vary for both different consumers and different situations.

Still, consumers will use these perceived values to evaluate a product's price, so the company must work to measure them. Sometimes, companies ask consumers how much they would pay for a basic product and for each benefit added to the offer. Or a company might conduct experiments to test the perceived value of different product offers. According to an old Russian proverb, there are two fools in every market – one who asks too much and one who asks too little. If the seller charges more than the buyers' perceived value, the company's sales will suffer. If the seller charges much less than buyers' perceived value, its products sell very well, but they produce less revenue than they would if they were priced at the level of perceived value.

We now examine two types of value-based pricing: *good value pricing* and *value-added pricing*.

Good value pricing During the past decade, marketers have noted a fundamental shift in consumer attitudes toward price and quality. Many companies have changed their pricing approaches to bring them into line with changing economic conditions and consumer price perceptions. More and more, marketers have adopted good value pricing strategies – offering just the right combination of quality and good service at a fair price.

In many cases, this has involved introducing less expensive versions of established, brand-name products. For example, Armani offers the less expensive, more casual Armani Exchange fashion line. In other cases, good value pricing has involved redesigning existing brands to offer more quality for a given price or the same quality for less.

An important type of good value pricing at the retail level is *everyday low pricing (EDLP)*. EDLP involves charging a constant, everyday low price with few or no temporary price discounts. In contrast, *high-low pricing* involves charging higher prices on an everyday basis but running frequent promotions to lower prices temporarily on selected items. In recent years, high-low pricing has given way to EDLP in retail settings ranging from Peugeot car dealerships to Carrefour or Tesco supermarkets to upmarket department stores such as John Lewis.

Value-added pricing In many business-to-business marketing situations, the challenge is to build the company's *pricing power* – its power to escape price competition and to justify higher prices and margins without losing market share. To do this, many companies adopt *value-added* strategies. Rather than cutting prices to match competitors, they attach value-added features and services to differentiate their offers and thus support higher prices.

When a company finds its major competitors offering a similar product at a lower price, the natural tendency is to try to match or beat that price. Although the idea of undercutting a competitor's prices and watching customers flock in is tempting, there are dangers. Price cutting can lead to price wars that erode the profit margins of all competitors in an industry. Or worse, discounting a product can cheapen it in the minds of customers. This greatly reduces the seller's power to maintain profitable prices in the long term.

So, how can a company keep its pricing power when a competitor undercuts its price? Often, the best strategy is not to price below the competitor, but rather to price above and convince customers that the product is worth it. The company should ask, 'What is the value of the product to the customer?', then stand up for what the product is worth. In this way, the company shifts the focus from price to value. 'Even in today's economic environment, it's not about price,' says a pricing expert. 'It's about keeping customers loyal by providing service they can't find anywhere else.'[6] Miele is a master at value-added marketing:

> The motto at Miele is 'Immer Besser' which translated means 'Forever Better'. This motto was conceived over 100 years ago by the founders and remains our company motto today, permeating through every aspect of our business. We pride ourselves on having the best products with unsurpassed quality and below are the elements that really set out the Miele difference.

Quality and reliability:

- All products are designed for 20 years use.
- Products are subjected to rigorous endurance testing during development.
- Every product we produce goes through an end line test before passing quality control.
- Many products are then randomly checked against further quality criteria.
- Strict quality control for us means peace of mind for you.

Performance:

- Miele is consistently independently tested in many product categories and consistently comes out on top.
- Whether its washing dishes, clothes or cooking a meal, Miele products deliver optimal results no matter how big or small the task.
- What's more, optimal results are married with gentle performance, which is vital for good fabric care and glassware for example.[7]

So, that's what Miele themselves have to say, but what independent evidence is there that they deliver enhanced value to customers, and that customers are prepared to pay for it? In May 2007 the UK independent consumer testing organisation Which? made four Miele products 'Best Buys' in the dishwasher category, five Miele products 'Best Buys' in the washing machine category, and seven Miele products 'Best Buys' in the vacuum cleaner category. In fact, virtually every Miele product that was tested got the coveted title of a Which? 'Best Buy'. Most of the

The emphasis at Miele is on delivering products with excellent quality and reliability that justify a price premium over other brands. Independent customer test organisations consistently give Miele products the highest ratings.

Source: Miele.

manufacturers tested received no 'Best Buys' at all. It is the quality of the build and the reliability and performance of their products that enables Miele to charge premium prices. For example, you can buy many brands of washing machine, such as Beko, Hoover or Servis, for around £200 in the UK. But if you want a Miele, you will have to pay considerably more; even if you shop around, you are unlikely to find one priced below £500. Miele deliver better value to the customer, and customers are prepared to pay for it.[8]

Company and product costs

Whereas customer value perceptions set the price ceiling, costs set the floor for the price that the company can charge. The company wants to charge a price that both covers all its costs for producing, distributing and selling the product, and delivers a fair rate of return for its effort and risk. A company's costs may be an important element in its pricing strategy. Many companies, such as Ryanair and Aldi, work to become the 'low-cost producers' in their industries. Companies with lower costs can set lower prices that result in greater sales and profits.

Types of costs

A company's costs take two forms, fixed and variable. **Fixed costs** (also known as overheads) are costs that do not vary with production or sales level. For example, a company must pay each month's bills for rent, heating, interest and managerial salaries, whatever the company's output. **Variable costs** vary directly with the level of production. Each personal computer produced by Dell involves a cost of microprocessors, wires, plastic, packaging and other inputs. These costs tend to be the same for each unit of the same model produced. They are called variable because their total varies with the number of units produced – the more computers are produced, the higher are the variable costs. **Total costs** are the sum of the fixed and variable costs for any given level of production. Management wants to charge a price that will at least cover the total production costs at a given level of production.

The company must watch its costs carefully. If it costs the company more than competitors to produce and sell its product, the company will have to charge a higher price or make less profit, putting it at a competitive disadvantage.

Cost-based pricing

The simplest pricing method is **cost-plus pricing** – adding a standard mark-up to the cost of the product. For example, an electrical retailer might pay a manufacturer €20 for a toaster and mark it up to sell at €30, a 50 per cent mark-up on cost. The retailer's gross margin is €10. If the store's operating costs amount to €8 per toaster sold, the retailer's profit margin will be €2.

The manufacturer that made the toaster probably used cost-plus pricing. If the manufacturer's standard cost of producing the toaster was €16, it might have added a 25 per cent mark-up, setting the price to the retailers at €20. Similarly, construction companies submit job bids by estimating the total project cost and adding a standard mark-up for profit. Lawyers, accountants, architects and other professionals typically price by adding a standard mark-up to their costs. Some sellers tell their customers they will charge cost plus a specified mark-up; for example, aerospace companies price this way to the government.

Using standard mark-ups to set prices is generally not a good idea. Any pricing method that ignores customer value and competitor prices is not likely to lead to the best price. Still, mark-up pricing remains popular for many reasons. First, sellers are more certain about costs than about customer value perceptions and demand. By tying the price to cost, sellers simplify pricing – they do not have to make frequent adjustments as demand changes. Second, when all firms in the industry use this pricing method, prices

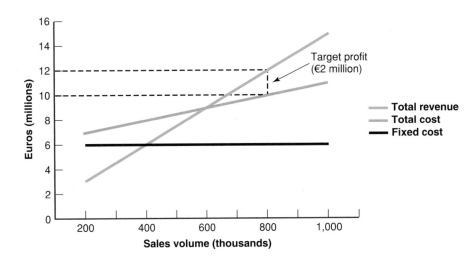

FIGURE 9.3

Break-even chart for
determining price

tend to be similar and price competition is thus minimised. Third, many people feel that cost-plus pricing is fairer to both buyers and sellers. Sellers earn a fair return on their investment but do not take advantage of buyers by raising prices when buyers' demand is very high.

Another cost-oriented pricing approach is **break-even pricing**, or a variation called **target profit pricing**. The firm tries to determine the price at which it will break even or make the target profit it is seeking. Target pricing uses the concept of a *break-even chart*, which shows the total cost and total revenue expected at different sales volume levels. Figure 9.3 shows a break-even chart for the toaster manufacturer discussed here. Fixed costs are €6 million regardless of sales volume, and variable costs are €5 per unit. Variable costs are added to fixed costs to form total costs, which rise with volume. The slope of the total revenue curve reflects the price. Here, the price is €15 (for example, the company's revenue is €12 million on 800,000 units, or €15 per unit).

At the €15 price, the company must sell at least 600,000 units to *break even* (break-even volume = fixed costs ÷ (price − variable costs) = €6,000,000 ÷ (€15 − €5) = 600,000). That is, at this level, total revenues will equal total costs of €9 million. If the company wants a target profit of €2 million, it must sell at least 800,000 units to obtain the €12 million of total revenue needed to cover the costs of €10 million plus the €2 million of target profits. In contrast, if the company charges a higher price, say €20, it will not need to sell as many units to break even or to achieve its target profit. In fact, the higher the price, the lower the company's break-even point will be.

The major problem with this analysis, however, is that it fails to consider customer value and the relationship between price and demand. As the *price* increases, *demand* decreases, and the market may not buy even the lower volume needed to break even at the higher price. For example, suppose the company calculates that, given its current fixed and variable costs, it must charge a price of €30 for the product in order to earn its desired target profit. But marketing research shows that few consumers will pay more than €25. In this case, the company will have to reduce its costs in order to lower the break-even point so that it can charge the lower price consumers expect.

Thus, although break-even analysis and target profit pricing can help the company to determine minimum prices needed to cover expected costs and profits, they do not take the price-demand relationship into account. When using this method, the company must also consider the impact of price on sales volume needed to realise target profits and the likelihood that the needed volume will be achieved at each possible price.

Other internal and external considerations affecting price decisions

Customer perceptions of value set the upper limit for prices, and costs set the lower limit. However, in setting prices within these limits, the company must consider a number of other internal and external factors. Internal factors affecting pricing include the company's overall marketing strategy, objectives and marketing mix, as well as other organisational considerations. External factors include the nature of the market and demand, competitors' strategies and prices, and other environmental factors.

Overall marketing strategy, objectives and mix

Price is only one element of the company's broader marketing strategy. Thus, before setting price, the company must decide on its overall marketing strategy for the product or service. If the company has selected its target market and positioning carefully, then its marketing mix strategy, including price, will be fairly straightforward. For example, when Toyota developed its Lexus brands to compete with German luxury performance cars in the higher-income segment, this required charging a high price. In contrast, when it introduced its Aygo model, a small car with excellent fuel economy and low running costs aimed at budget-conscious car buyers, this positioning required charging a low price. Thus, pricing strategy is heavily influenced by decisions on market positioning.

General pricing objectives might include survival, current profit maximisation, market share leadership, or customer retention and relationship building. At a more specific level, a company can set prices to attract new customers or to profitably retain existing ones. It can set prices low to prevent competition from entering the market or set prices at competitors' levels to stabilise the market. It can price to keep the loyalty and support of resellers or to avoid government intervention. Prices can be reduced temporarily to create excitement for a brand. Or one product may be priced to help the sales of other products in the company's line. Thus, pricing may play an important role in helping to accomplish the company's objectives at many levels.

Price is only one of the marketing mix tools that a company uses to achieve its marketing objectives. Price decisions must be coordinated with product design, distribution and promotion decisions to form a consistent and effective marketing programme. Decisions made for other marketing mix variables may affect pricing decisions. For example, a decision to position the product on high-performance quality will mean that the seller must charge a higher price to cover higher costs. And producers whose resellers are expected to support and promote their products may have to build larger reseller margins into their prices.

Companies often position their products on price and then tailor other marketing mix decisions to the prices they want to charge. Here, price is a crucial product positioning factor that defines the product's market, competition and design. Many firms support such price positioning strategies with a technique called **target costing**, a potent strategic weapon. Target costing reverses the usual process of first designing a new product, determining its cost, and then asking, 'Can we sell it for that?' Instead, it starts with an ideal selling price based on customer value considerations, and then targets costs that will ensure that the price is met.

Other companies de-emphasise price and use other marketing mix tools to create *non-price* positions. Often, the best strategy is not to charge the lowest price, but rather to differentiate the marketing offer to make it worth a higher price. For example, Sony builds more value into its consumer electronics products and charges a higher price than many competitors. Customers recognise Sony's higher quality and are willing to pay more to get it. Some marketers even *feature* high prices as part of their positioning (see Marketing at Work 9.1). For example, Belgian beer brand Stella Artois has long been advertised as 'reassuringly expensive', with the 'expensive' image of the brand designed to convey both quality and European sophistication to the customer.

MARKETING AT WORK 9.1

Steinway: Price is nothing; the Steinway experience is everything

A Steinway piano – any Steinway piano – costs a lot. A Steinway grand piano typically runs anywhere from €40,000 to €165,000. The most popular model sells for around €72,000. But Steinway buyers aren't looking for bargains. In fact, it seems the higher the prices, the better. High prices confirm that a Steinway is the very best that money can buy – the epitome of hand-crafted perfection. As important, the Steinway name is steeped in tradition. It evokes images of classical concert stages, sophisticated dinner parties, and the celebrities and performers who've owned and played Steinway pianos across more than 150 years. When it comes to Steinway, price is nothing, the Steinway experience is everything.

To be sure, Steinway & Sons makes very high quality pianos. With 115 patents to its credit, Steinway & Sons has done more than any other manufacturer to advance the art of piano building. Steinway pioneered the development of a one-piece piano rim produced out of 17 laminations of veneer. It invented a process for bending a single 22-foot long strip of these laminated sheets inside a massive piano-shaped vice. It's this strong frame that produces Steinway's distinctive clear tones. Steinway & Sons has continued perfecting this design, and today a Steinway piano's 243 tempered, hard-steel strings exert 35 tons of pressure – enough force to implode a three-bedroom house if the strings were strung between attic and cellar.

In addition to cutting edge technology, Steinway & Sons uses only the finest materials to construct each piano. Rock maple, spruce, birch, poplar and four other species of wood each play a crucial functional role in the physical and acoustical beauty of a Steinway. The expansive wooden soundboard, which turns the string vibrations into sound, is made from select Alaskan Sitka spruce – one grade higher than aircraft grade. Through delicate hand craftsmanship, Steinway transforms these select materials into pianos of incomparable sound quality. From start to finish, it takes 450 skilled workers more than a year to handcraft and assemble a Steinway piano from its 12,000 component parts. Thus, Steinway is anything but mass market. Each year, Steinway's factories in Astoria, New York, and Hamburg, Germany, craft approximately 5,000 pianos. (By comparison, Yamaha produces 100,000 pianos per year.)

Steinway's precision quality alone would command the best prices, but Steinway buyers get much more than just a well-made piano. They also get the Steinway mystique. Owning or playing a Steinway puts you in some very good company. Fully 98 per cent of piano soloists with the world's major symphony orchestras prefer playing on a Steinway. More than 90 per cent of the world's concert pianists, some 1,300 in all, bear the title of Steinway Artist – an elite club of Steinway-owning professional musicians.

But Steinways aren't just for world-class pianists and the wealthy. Ninety-nine per cent of all Steinway buyers are amateurs who perform only in their own homes. 'We see a lot of corporate executives and physicians buying Steinway grands,' says a Steinway marketer. 'But it is not unusual at all for a middle-income person to come in and buy a grand.'

Performers of all kinds sing Steinway's praises. 'Steinway is the only piano on which the pianist can do everything he wants. And everything he dreams,' declares premier pianist and conductor Vladimir Ashkenazy. At the other end of the performing spectrum, contemporary singer-songwriter Randy Newman puts it this way: 'I have owned and played a Steinway all my life. It's the best Beethoven piano. The best Chopin piano. And the best Ray Charles piano. I like it, too.' Whereas some people want a Porsche in the garage, others prefer a Steinway in the living room – both cost about the same, and both make a statement about their owners.

Even in the worst of times, Steinway & Sons has held true to its

A Steinway piano costs a lot, but buyers are not looking for bargains. When it comes to a Steinway, price is nothing, the Steinway experience is everything.
Source: Courtesy of Steinway & Sons.

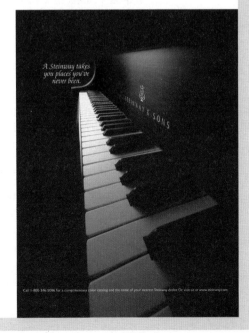

tradition and image – and to its pre-mium prices. Although the company is no longer owned by the Steinway family, its current owners still prize and protect the brand's exclusivity. When they bought the troubled com-pany in 1984, new management was burdened with 900 pianos of excess inventory. But rather than slashing prices to make a quick profit at the risk of tarnishing the brand, man-agers restored the company's health by holding the line on prices and renewing its commitment to quality. Through such actions, Steinway has retained its cult-like following and continues to dominate its market. Despite its very high prices – or more

likely because of them – Steinway enjoys a 95 per cent market share in concert halls.

So, you won't find any promo-tional sales on Steinway pianos. Charging significantly higher prices continues to be a cornerstone of the company's 'much more for much more' value proposition. To cus-tomers, whatever a Steinway costs, it's a small price to pay for the experience of owning one. Classical pianist Krystian Zimerman sums up his Steinway experience this way: 'My friendship with the Steinway piano is one of the most important and beautiful things in my life.' Who can put a price on such feelings?

Sources: Rosemary Barnes, 'The Price of Perfection: Steinway Piano Commands a Premier Price', *Knight Ridder Tribune Business News*, 26 February 2005, p. 1; Andy Serwer, 'Happy Birthday Steinway', *Fortune*, 17 March 2003, p. 94; 'Books and Arts: Making the Sound of Music; Piano Manufacturers', *The Economist*, 7 June 2003, p. 102; Brian T. Majeski, 'The Steinway Story', *Music Trades*, September 2003 p. 18; 'The Most Famous Name in Music', *Music Trades*, September 2003, pp. 118–30; Stephan Wilkinson, 'High-Strung. Powerful. Very Pricey', *Popular Science*, 1 March 2003, p. 32; 'Steinway Musical Instruments, Inc.', *Hoover's Company Capsules*, 15 March 2004, p. 48052; Michael Z. Wise, 'Piano Versus Piano', *New York Times*, 9 May 2004; and quotes and information found at www.steinway.com, August 2005.

Thus, marketers must consider the total marketing strategy and mix when setting prices. If the product is positioned on non-price factors, then decisions about quality, promotion and distribution will strongly affect price. If price is a crucial positioning factor, then price will strongly affect decisions made about the other marketing mix elements. But even when featuring price, marketers need to remember that customers rarely buy on price alone. Instead, they seek products that give them the best value in terms of benefits received for the price paid.

Organisational considerations

Management must decide who within the organisation should set prices. Companies handle pricing in a variety of ways. In small companies, prices are often set by top manage-ment rather than by the marketing or sales departments. In large companies, pricing is typically handled by divisional or product line managers. In industrial markets, sales-people may be allowed to negotiate with customers within certain price ranges. Even so, top management sets the pricing objectives and policies, and it often approves the prices proposed by lower-level management or salespeople.

In industries in which pricing is a key factor (airlines, aerospace, steel, railways, oil companies), companies often have pricing departments to set the best prices or to help others in setting them. These departments report to the marketing department or top management. Others who have an influence on pricing include sales managers, production managers, finance managers and accountants.

The market and demand

As noted earlier, good pricing starts with an understanding of how customers' percep-tions of value affect the prices they are willing to pay. Both consumer and industrial buyers balance the price of a product or service against the benefits of owning it. Thus, before setting prices, the marketer must understand the relationship between price and demand for its product. In this section, we take a deeper look at the price–demand relationship and how it varies for different types of markets. We then discuss methods for analysing the price–demand relationship.

Pricing in different types of markets The seller's pricing freedom varies with different types of markets. Economists recognise four types of markets, each presenting a different pricing challenge.

Under *pure competition* (also known as *perfect competition*), the market consists of many buyers and sellers trading in a uniform commodity such as wheat, copper, or financial securities. No single buyer or seller has much effect on the going market price. A seller cannot charge more than the going price, because buyers can obtain as much as they need at the going price. Nor would sellers charge less than the market price, because they can sell all they want at this price. If price and profits rise, new sellers can easily enter the market. In a purely competitive market, marketing research, product development, pricing, advertising and sales promotion play little or no role. Sellers in these markets do not spend much time on marketing strategy.

Under *monopolistic competition*, the market consists of many buyers and sellers who trade over a range of prices rather than a single market price. A range of prices occurs because sellers can differentiate their offers to buyers. Either the physical product can be varied in quality, features or style, or the accompanying services can be varied. Buyers see differences in sellers' products and will pay different prices for them. Sellers try to develop differentiated offers for different customer segments and, in addition to price, freely use branding, advertising and personal selling to set their offers apart. Thus, Dulux paint is differentiated through strong branding and advertising, reducing the impact of price. Because there are many competitors in such markets, each firm is less affected by competitors' pricing strategies than in oligopolistic markets.

Under *oligopolistic competition*, the market consists of a few sellers who are highly sensitive to each other's pricing and marketing strategies. The product can be uniform (steel, aluminium) or non-uniform (cars, computers). There are few sellers because it is difficult for new sellers to enter the market. Each seller is alert to competitors' strategies. If a steel company slashes its price by 10 per cent, buyers will quickly switch to this supplier. The other steelmakers must respond by lowering their prices or increasing their services.

In a *pure monopoly*, the market consists of one seller. The seller may be a government monopoly, a private regulated monopoly or simply a private company that has a monopoly because it has introduced a unique, new product. In many European countries telecommunications services were, until recently, run by government monopolies, but in recent years it has become normal to allow competition. Utility services, such as water and gas, are often run by private companies (such as the French firm SUEZ – formerly Suez Lyonnaise des Eaux) but regulated by the government. W.L. Gore is a good example of a company that obtained a monopoly through the introduction of a unique product, namely the Gore-Tex waterproof and breathable membrane used extensively in both consumer and industrial products. In a regulated monopoly, the government appoints a regulator whose job it is to see that the monopolist charges reasonable prices, offering good value to the customer and fair returns to shareholders. Non-regulated monopolies are free to price at what the market will bear. However, they do not always charge the full price for a number of reasons: a desire not to attract competition, a desire to penetrate the market faster with a low price, or a fear of government regulation.

Analysing the price–demand relationship Each price the company might charge will lead to a different level of demand. The relationship between the price charged and the resulting demand level is shown in the **demand curve** in Figure 9.4. The demand curve shows the number of units the market will buy in a given time period at different prices that might be charged. In the normal case, demand and price are inversely related; that is, the higher the price, the lower the demand. Thus, the company would sell less if it raised its price from P_1 to P_2. In short, consumers with limited budgets probably will buy less of something if its price is too high.

Demand curve

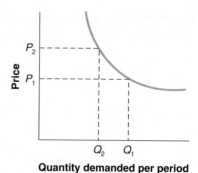

In the case of prestige goods, the demand curve sometimes slopes upwards. This is because consumers believe that higher prices mean higher quality. For example, the Gibson Guitar Corporation recently toyed with the idea of lowering its prices to compete more effectively with Japanese rivals such as Yamaha and Ibanez. To its surprise, Gibson found that its instruments didn't sell as well at lower prices. 'We had an inverse [price–demand relationship],' noted Gibson's chief executive. 'The more we charged, the more product we sold.' At a time when other guitar manufacturers have chosen to build their instruments more quickly, cheaply and in greater numbers, Gibson still promises guitars that 'are made one-at-a-time, by hand. No shortcuts. No substitutions'. It turns out that low prices simply aren't consistent with 'Gibson's century-old tradition of creating investment-quality instruments that represent the highest standards of imaginative design and masterful craftsmanship'.[8] Still, even for a product like this there will be a limit on price beyond which price increases will reduce the level of demand.

Most companies try to measure their demand curves by estimating demand at different prices. The type of market makes a difference. In a monopoly, the demand curve shows the total market demand resulting from different prices. If the company faces competition, its demand at different prices will depend on whether competitors' prices stay constant or change with the company's own prices. For example, in a town with several competing petrol stations, if one petrol retailer raises its price when the others do not, then one would expect demand for its petrol to decline sharply because customers will buy from the lower-priced competitors.

Price elasticity of demand Marketers also need to be aware of **price elasticity** – how responsive demand will be to a change in price. If demand hardly changes with a small change in price, we say demand is *inelastic*. If demand changes greatly, we say the demand is *elastic*.

If demand is elastic rather than inelastic, sellers will consider lowering their prices because a lower price will produce more total revenue. This practice makes sense as long as the extra costs of producing and selling more do not exceed the extra revenue. At the same time, most firms want to avoid pricing that turns their products into commodities. In recent years, forces such as deregulation and the instant price comparisons afforded by the Internet and other technologies have increased consumer price sensitivity, even turning products like mobile phones, laptop computers and MP3 players into commodities in some consumers' eyes.

Marketers need to work harder than ever to differentiate their offerings when many different competitors are selling virtually the same product at a comparable or lower price. More than ever, companies need to understand the price sensitivity of their customers and prospects and the trade-offs people are willing to make between price and product characteristics. In the words of marketing consultant Kevin Clancy, those who target only the price sensitive are 'leaving money on the table'.

Competitors' strategies and prices

In setting its prices, the company must also consider competitors' costs, prices and market offerings. Consumers will base their judgements of a product's value on the prices that competitors charge for similar products. A consumer who is considering the purchase of a Sony digital camera will evaluate Sony's customer value and price against the value and prices of comparable products made by Nikon, Kodak, Canon and others.

In addition, the company's pricing strategy may affect the nature of the competition it faces. If Sony follows a high-price, high-margin strategy, it may attract competition. A low-price, low-margin strategy, however, may stop competitors or drive them out of the market. Sony needs to benchmark its costs and value again competitors' costs and value. It can then use these benchmarks as a starting point for its own pricing.

In assessing competitors' pricing strategies, the company should ask several questions. First, how does the company's market offering compare with competitors' offerings in terms of customer value? If consumers perceive that the company's product or service provides greater value, the company can charge a higher price. If consumers perceive less value relative to competing products, the company must either charge a lower price or change customer perceptions to justify a higher price.

Next, how strong are current competitors and what are their current pricing strategies? If the company faces a host of smaller competitors charging high prices relative to the value they deliver, it might charge lower prices to drive weaker competitors out of the market. If the market is dominated by larger, low-price competitors, the company may decide to target unserved market niches with value-added products at higher prices. For example, your local independent bookshop isn't likely to win a price war against Amazon.com, Blackwell or Waterstone's. It would be wiser to add special customer services and personal touches that justify higher prices and margins.

Finally, the company should ask, How does the competitive landscape influence customer price sensitivity?[10] For example, customers will be more price sensitive if they see few differences between competing products. They will buy whichever product costs the least. The more information customers have about competing products and prices before buying, the more price sensitive they will be. Easy product comparisons help customers to assess the value of different options and to decide what prices they are willing to pay. Finally, customers will be more price sensitive if they can switch easily from one product alternative to another.

What principle should guide decisions about what price to charge relative to those of competitors? The answer is simple in concept but often difficult in practice: no matter what price you charge – high, low, or in between – be certain to give customers superior value for that price.

Other external factors

When setting prices, the company also must consider a number of other factors in its external environment. *Economic conditions* can have a strong impact on the firm's pricing strategies. Economic factors such as boom or recession, inflation and interest rates affect pricing decisions because they affect both consumer perceptions of the product's price and value and the costs of producing a product. The company must also consider what impact its prices will have on other parties in its environment. How will *resellers* react to various prices? The company should set prices that give resellers a fair profit, encourage their support and help them to sell the product effectively. The *government* is another important external influence on pricing decisions. Finally, *social concerns* may have to be taken into account. In setting prices, a company's short-term sales, market share and profit goals may have to be tempered by broader societal considerations. We will examine public policy issues in pricing later in the chapter.

MAKING CONNECTIONS Linking the concepts

The concept of customer value is critical to good pricing and to successful marketing in general. Slow down for a minute and be certain that you appreciate what value really means.

■ In an earlier example, one car critic called the Bentley Continental GT great value at $175,000 – a real bargain even at this price. Does this fit with your idea of value?

■ Pick two competing brands from a familiar product category (watches, perfume, consumer electronics, restaurants) – one low priced and the other high priced. Which, if either, offers the greatest value?

■ Does 'value' mean the same thing as 'low price'? How do these concepts differ?

We've now seen that pricing decisions are subject to an incredibly complex array of customer, company, competitive and environmental forces. To make things even more complex, a company sets not a single price but rather a *pricing structure* that covers different items in its line. This pricing structure changes over time as products move through their life cycles. The company adjusts product prices to reflect changes in costs and demand and to account for variations in buyers and situations. As the competitive environment changes, the company considers when to initiate price changes and when to respond to them.

We now examine the major dynamic pricing strategies available to marketers. In turn, we look at *new-product pricing strategies* for products in the introductory stage of the product life cycle, *product mix pricing strategies* for related products in the product mix, *price adjustment strategies* that account for customer differences and changing situations, and strategies for initiating and responding to *price changes*.

NEW-PRODUCT PRICING STRATEGIES

Pricing strategies usually change as the product passes through its life cycle. The introductory stage is especially challenging. Companies bringing out a new product face the challenge of setting prices for the first time. They can choose between two broad strategies: *market-skimming pricing* and *market-penetration pricing*.

Market-skimming pricing

Many companies that invent new products set high initial prices to 'skim' revenues layer by layer from the market. Sony frequently uses this strategy, called **market-skimming pricing**. When Sony introduced the world's first high-definition television (HDTV) to the Japanese market in 1990, the high-tech sets cost €43,000. These televisions were purchased only by customers who could afford to pay a high price for the new technology. Sony rapidly reduced the price over the next several years to attract new buyers. By 1993 a 28-inch HDTV cost a Japanese buyer just over €6,000. In 2001, a Japanese consumer could buy a 40-inch HDTV for about €2,000, a price that many more customers could afford. An entry level HDTV set now sells for less than €1,000 in Europe, and prices continue to fall. In this way, Sony skimmed the maximum amount of revenue from the various segments of the market.[11]

Market skimming makes sense only under certain conditions. First, the product's quality and image must support its higher price, and enough buyers must want the product at that price. Second, the costs of producing a smaller volume cannot be so high that they cancel the advantage of charging more. Finally, competitors should not be able to enter the market easily and undercut the high price.

Market-penetration pricing

Rather than setting a high initial price to skim off small but profitable market segments, some companies use **market-penetration pricing**. They set a low initial price in order to *penetrate* the market quickly and deeply – to attract a large number of buyers quickly and win a large market share. The high sales volume results in falling costs, allowing the company to cut its price even further. For example, Aldi, Lidl and other discount retailers use penetration pricing. And Dell used penetration pricing to enter the personal computer market, selling high-quality computer products through lower-cost direct channels. Its sales soared when HP, Apple and other competitors selling through retail stores could not match its prices.

Several conditions must be met for this low-price strategy to work. First, the market must be highly price sensitive so that a low price produces more market growth. Second, production and distribution costs must fall as sales volume increases. Finally, the low price must help keep out the competition, and the penetration pricer must maintain its low-price position – otherwise, the price advantage may be only temporary. For example, Dell faced difficult times when other competitors established their own direct distribution channels. However, through its dedication to low production and distribution costs, Dell has retained its price advantage and established itself as the industry's number-one personal computer maker. Nevertheless, the pricing challenges in this market just go on and on – in 2005 the Chinese company Lenovo took over IBM's personal computer business, opening up the prospect of even more cut-throat competition for Dell to deal with.

PRODUCT MIX PRICING STRATEGIES

The strategy for setting a product's price often has to be changed when the product is part of a product mix. In this case, the firm looks for a set of prices that maximises the profits on the total product mix. Pricing is difficult because the various products have related demand and costs and face different degrees of competition. We now take a closer look at the five product mix pricing situations summarised in Table 9.1: *product line pricing*, *optional-product pricing*, *captive-product pricing*, *by-product pricing* and *product bundle pricing*.

Product line pricing

Companies usually develop product lines rather than single products. For example, you can buy a small Samsung LCD television for the bedroom or kitchen and it will cost around €300, but if you want the top-of-the-range 52-inch Samsung model it is

TABLE 9.1 Product mix pricing strategies

Strategy	Description
Product line pricing	Setting price steps between product line items
Optional-product pricing	Pricing optional or accessory products sold with the main product
Captive-product pricing	Pricing products that must be used with the main product
By-product pricing	Pricing low-value by-products to get rid of them
Product bundle pricing	Pricing bundles of products sold together

going to cost you more like €2,500, and there is a whole range of models in between. If you want to buy a Sony digital camera then even for the simpler models (rather than the more expensive and more complicated models with exchangeable lenses) you can pay anything from €100 for a basic model to €550 for a model with top-of-the-range features.

In **product line pricing**, management must decide on the price steps to set between the various products in a line.

The price steps should take into account cost differences between the products in the line, customer evaluations of their different features and competitors' prices. In many industries, sellers use well-established *price points* for the products in their line. Thus, men's clothing stores might carry men's suits at three price levels: €185, €325 and €495. The customer will probably associate low-, average- and high-quality suits with the three price points. Even if the three prices are raised a little, men normally will buy suits at their own preferred price points. The seller's task is to establish perceived quality differences that support the price differences.

Optional-product pricing

Many companies use **optional-product pricing** – offering to sell optional or accessory products along with their main product. For example, a car buyer may choose to order air-conditioning and a CD changer. Some hi-fi systems offer the option of an MP3 interface socket.

Pricing these options is tricky. Car companies have to decide which items to include in the base price and which to offer as options. Until recent years, the major American car companies' normal pricing strategy was to advertise a stripped-down model at a base price to bring people into showrooms and then to devote most of the showroom space to showing option-loaded cars at higher prices. The economy model was stripped of so many comforts and conveniences that most buyers rejected it. European and Japanese car manufacturers had always tended to offer more in the base price model, and eventually GM and other American car makers followed their example and included more desirable features in the base models. Most advertised prices today represent a well-equipped car.

Captive-product pricing

Companies that make products that must be used along with a main product are using **captive-product pricing**. Examples of captive products are razor blades, video games and printer cartridges. Producers of the main products (razors, video games consoles and printers) often price them low and set high mark-ups on the supplies. Thus, Gillette sells low-priced razors but makes money on the replacement cartridges. HP makes very low margins on its printers but very high margins on printer cartridges and other supplies. Sony and other video games makers sell games consoles at low prices and obtain the majority of their profits from the video games. Sales of video games software are worth about four times as much in market value as sales of the games consoles themselves.

In the case of services, this strategy is called *two-part pricing*. The price of the service is broken into a *fixed fee* plus a *variable usage rate*. Theme parks such as EuroDisney charge an admission fee that gives customers access to most of the attractions, but then hope that customers will pay more for the food, drinks, merchandise and other services – like photographs taken of you on the roller-coasters – when they visit the park. Sports events, such as professional football and tennis, charge an admission fee and then offer customers a range of additional products and services to buy – again, merchandise, like football shirts and player photographs, is a big part of this. Mobile phone companies charge a flat rate for a fixed number of call minutes and SMS text messages, then charge for extra minutes and texts over what the plan allows. The service firm must decide how much to charge for the basic service and how much for the variable usage. The fixed amount should be low enough to induce usage of the service; profit can be made on the variable fees.

By-product pricing

In producing processed meats, petroleum products, chemicals and other products, there are often by-products. If the by-products have no value and if getting rid of them is costly, this will affect the pricing of the main product. Using **by-product pricing**, the manufacturer will seek a market for these by-products and should accept any price that covers more than the cost of storing and delivering them.

By-products can even turn out to be profitable. For example, papermaker MeadWestvaco has turned what was once considered chemical waste into profit-making products:

> MeadWestvaco created a separate company, Asphalt Innovations, which creates useful chemicals entirely from the by-products of MeadWestvaco's wood-processing activities. In fact, Asphalt Innovations has grown to become the world's biggest supplier of specialty chemicals for the paving industry. Using the salvaged chemicals, paving companies can pave roads at a lower temperature, create longer-lasting roads, and more easily recycle road materials when roads need to be replaced. What's more, salvaging the by-product chemicals eliminates the costs and environmental hazards once associated with disposing of them.[12]

Sometimes, companies don't realise how valuable their by-products are. For example, most zoos don't realise that one of their by-products – their occupants' manure – can be an excellent source of additional revenue. Chessington Zoo in London sells the manure from its tigers to people who want to deter domestic cats from entering their property – apparently the scent of tiger manure is enough to scare off even the most determined pet cat. More widely than this, of course, animal manure is a natural by-product of many agricultural activities (raising animals) and is a very desirable input to other agricultural activities (growing crops). So chicken farmers can sell the manure that their chickens produce to companies that will process it into chicken manure pellets for use by farmers or by gardeners. General farmyard manure is a highly desirable, natural fertiliser and soil-improver which you can buy from any garden centre or agricultural supplier.

By-products can be a valuable source of revenue. Animal manure can be converted into excellent fertiliser.

Source: Westland Horticultural.

Product bundle pricing

Using **product bundle pricing**, sellers often combine several of their products and offer the bundle at a reduced price. For example, fast-food restaurants bundle a burger, fries and a soft drink at a combo price. Theatres and sports teams sell season tickets at less than the cost of single tickets. Resorts sell specially priced holiday packages that include airfare, accommodations, meals and entertainment. And computer makers include attractive software packages with their personal computers. Price bundling can promote the sales of products consumers might not otherwise buy, but the combined price must be low enough to get them to buy the bundle.[13]

PRICE ADJUSTMENT STRATEGIES

Companies usually adjust their basic prices to account for various customer differences and changing situations. Here we examine the seven price adjustment strategies summarised in Table 9.2: *discount and allowance pricing, segmented pricing, psychological pricing, promotional pricing, geographical pricing, dynamic pricing and international pricing.*

TABLE 9.2 Price adjustment strategies

Strategy	Description
Discount and allowance pricing	Reducing prices to reward customer responses such as paying early or promoting the product
Segmented pricing	Adjusting prices to allow for differences in customers, products or locations
Psychological pricing	Adjusting prices for psychological effect
Promotional pricing	Temporarily reducing prices to increase short-term sales
Geographical pricing	Adjusting prices to account for the geographical location of customers
Dynamic pricing	Adjusting prices continually to meet the characteristics and needs of individual customers and situations
International pricing	Adjusting prices for international markets

Discount and allowance pricing

Most companies adjust their basic price to reward customers for certain responses, such as early payment of bills, volume purchases and off-season buying. These price adjustments – called *discounts* and *allowances* – can take many forms.

The many forms of **discounts** include a *cash discount*, a price reduction to buyers who pay their bills promptly. A typical example is '2/10, net 30,' which means that although payment is due within 30 days, the buyer can deduct 2 per cent if the bill is paid within 10 days. A *quantity discount* is a price reduction to buyers who buy large volumes. Such discounts provide an incentive to the customer to buy more from one given seller, rather than from many different sources.

A *functional discount* (also called a *trade discount*) is offered by the seller to trade-channel members who perform certain functions, such as selling, storing and record keeping. A *seasonal discount* is a price reduction to buyers who buy merchandise or services out of season. For example, lawn and garden equipment manufacturers offer seasonal discounts to retailers during the autumn and winter months to encourage early ordering in anticipation of the heavy spring and summer selling seasons. Seasonal discounts allow the seller to keep production steady during an entire year.

Allowances are another type of reduction from the list price. For example, *trade-in allowances* are price reductions given for turning in an old item when buying a new one. Trade-in allowances are most common in the car industry but are also given for other durable goods. *Promotional allowances* are payments or price reductions to reward dealers for participating in advertising and sales support programmes.

Segmented pricing

Companies will often adjust their basic prices to allow for differences in customers, products and locations. In **segmented pricing**, the company sells a product or service at two or more prices, even though the difference in prices is not based on differences in costs.

Segmented pricing takes several forms. Under *customer-segment* pricing, different customers pay different prices for the same product or service. Museums, for example, may charge a lower admission for students and for retired people. Under *product-form pricing*, different versions of the product are priced differently but not necessarily according to differences in their costs.

Using *location pricing*, a company charges different prices for different locations, even though the cost of offering each location is the same. For instance, concert halls vary their seat prices because of audience preferences for certain locations, and British universities charge higher tuition fees for students from outside the EU. Finally, using *time pricing*, a firm varies its price by the season, the month, the day, and even the hour. Some public utilities vary their prices to commercial users by time of day and weekend versus weekday. Holiday resorts may give weekend and seasonal discounts.

Segmented pricing goes by many names. Robert Cross, a consultant to the airlines, calls it *revenue management*. According to Cross, the practice ensures that 'companies will sell the right product to the right consumer at the right time for the right price'. Airlines, hotels and restaurants call it *yield management* and practise it religiously. The airlines, for example, routinely set prices hour-by-hour – even minute-by-minute – depending on seat availability, demand and competitor price changes.

Continental Airlines launches more than 3,000 flights every day. Each flight has between 10 and 20 prices. Continental starts booking flights 330 days in advance, and every flying day is different from every other flying day. As a result, at any given moment, Continental may have nearly 7 million prices in the market. It's a daunting marketing task – all of those prices need to be managed, all of the time. For Continental, setting prices is a complex process of balancing demand and customer satisfaction against company profitability.

The airlines know full well that we are puzzled by the frantic pricing and repricing that they do – puzzled, that is, when we aren't infuriated. 'I do not set the prices,' says Jim Compton, senior vice president of pricing and revenue management at Continental Airlines. 'The market sets prices.' That's point one. Point two: 'I have a really perishable product. It's gone when the door of the plane closes. An empty seat is lost revenue.' The most valuable airline seat is the one that somebody must have an hour before take-off and is willing to pay almost any price for. An airline seat gets more profitable with time – right up to the moment it goes from being worth $1,000 one-way to being worth $0.

Here's how Compton and his colleagues think about this: You want to sell every seat on the plane, except that you also want to have a handful left at the very end, for your most profitable (not to mention most grateful) customers. The airlines could easily sell out every seat, every flight, every day. They'd price 'em pretty low, book 'em up, and wait for take-off. But that would mean there'd

Segmented pricing: at any given moment, Continental may have nearly 7 million prices in the market. All of those prices need to be managed, all of the time.

Source: PA Photos/David J. Phillip/AP.

never be any seats available two or three weeks before a flight took off. How exasperated would customers be to call and find no seats three days out? When you understand that dilemma, all of a sudden, airline prices don't seem so exploitive. Although all of the seats on that New York–Miami flight are going to the same place, they aren't the same product. You pay less when you commit to a ticket four weeks in advance; Continental assumes a risk for holding a seat until the end – and wants to be paid a lot to balance the times when saving that last seat for you means that the seat flies empty.[14]

For segmented pricing to be an effective strategy, certain conditions must exist. The market must be segmentable, and the segments must show different degrees of demand. The costs of segmenting and watching the market cannot exceed the extra revenue obtained from the price difference. Of course, the segmented pricing must also be legal. Most importantly, segmented prices should reflect real differences in customers' perceived value. Otherwise, in the long run, the practice will lead to customer resentment and ill will.

Psychological pricing

Price says something about the product. For example, many consumers use price to judge quality. A €100 bottle of perfume may contain only €3 worth of scent, but some people are willing to pay the €100 because this price indicates something special.

In using **psychological pricing**, sellers consider the psychology of prices and not simply the economics. For example, consumers usually associate price with quality; they generally assume that a higher-priced product also offers higher quality. When they can judge the quality of a product by examining it or by calling on past experience with it, they use price less to judge quality. But when they cannot judge quality because they lack the information or skill, price becomes an important quality signal:

> Some years ago, Heublein produced Smirnoff, then America's leading vodka brand. Smirnoff was attacked by another brand, Wolfschmidt, which claimed to have the same quality as Smirnoff but was priced at one dollar less per bottle. To hold on to market share, Heublein considered either lowering Smirnoff's price by one dollar or holding Smirnoff's price but increasing advertising and promotion expenditures. Either strategy would lead to lower profits and it seemed that Heublein faced a no-win situation. At this point, however, Heublein's marketers thought of a third strategy. They *raised* the price of Smirnoff by one dollar! Heublein then introduced a new brand, Relska, to compete with Wolfschmidt. Moreover, it introduced yet another brand, Popov, priced even *lower* than Wolfschmidt. This clever strategy positioned Smirnoff as the elite brand and Wolfschmidt as an ordinary brand, producing a large increase in Heublein's overall profits. The irony is that Heublein's three brands were pretty much the same in taste and manufacturing costs. Heublein knew that a product's price signals its quality. Using price as a signal, Heublein sold roughly the same product at three different quality positions.

Another aspect of psychological pricing is **reference prices** – prices that buyers carry in their minds and refer to when looking at a given product. The reference price might be formed by noting current prices, remembering past prices, or assessing the buying situation. Sellers can influence or use these consumers' reference prices when setting price. For example, a company could display its product next to more expensive ones in order to imply that it belongs in the same class. Department stores often sell women's clothing in separate departments differentiated by price: clothing found in the more expensive department is assumed to be of better quality.

For most purchases, consumers don't have all the skill or information they need to figure out whether they are paying a good price. They don't have the time, ability or inclination to research different brands or stores, compare prices and get the best deals. Instead, the may rely on certain cues that signal whether a price is high or low. For example, the fact that a product is sold in a prestigious department store might signal that it's worth a higher price.

Interestingly, such pricing cues are often provided by sellers. A retailer might show a high manufacturer's suggested price next to the marked price, indicating that the product was originally priced much higher. Or the retailer might sell a selection of familiar products for which consumers have accurate price knowledge at very low prices, suggesting that the store's prices on other, less familiar products are low as well. The use of such pricing cues has become a common marketing practice (see Marketing at Work 9.2).

MARKETING AT WORK 9.2

Quick, what's a good price for . . .? We'll give you a cue

It's Saturday morning and you stop by your local supermarket to pick up a few items for tonight's garden barbecue. Cruising the aisles, you're bombarded with price signs, all suggesting that you just can't beat this store's deals. A 4 kilo bag of Heat Beads® barbecue briquets goes for only £3.97. Cans of Heinz Baked Beans are four for £1.86. An aisle display advertises big bags of Walker's potato crisps at an 'everyday low price' of just £1.99. And a sign on top of a huge mass of Coke 10-packs advertises two for £5.50.

These certainly look like good prices, but *are* they? If you're like most shoppers, you don't really know. In a recent *Harvard Business Review* article, two pricing researchers conclude, 'for most of the items they buy, consumers don't have an accurate sense of what the price should be'. In fact, customers often don't even know what prices they're actually paying. In one recent study, researchers asked supermarket shoppers the price of an item just as they were putting it into their shopping carts. Less than half the shoppers gave the right answer.

To know for sure if you're paying the best price, you'd have to compare the marked price to past prices, prices of competing brands and prices in other stores. For most

purchases, consumers just don't bother. Instead, they rely on a most unlikely source. 'Remarkably . . . they rely on the retailer to tell them if they're getting a good price,' say the researchers. 'In subtle and not-so-subtle ways, retailers send signals [or pricing cues] to customers, telling them whether a given price is relatively high or low.' In their article, the researchers outline the following common retailer pricing cues.

■ *Sale signs*. The most straightforward retail pricing cue is a sale sign. It might take any of several familiar forms: 'Sale!', 'Reduced!', 'New low price!', 'Price after discount!' or 'Now 2 for only . . . !' Such signs can be very effective in signalling low prices to consumers and increasing sales for the retailer. The researchers' studies in retail stores and mail-order catalogues reveal that using the word 'sale' beside a price

(even without actually varying the price) can increase demand by more than 50 per cent.

While sales signs can be effective, overuse or misuse can damage both the seller's credibility and its sales. Unfortunately, some retailers don't always use such signs truthfully. Still, consumers trust sale signs. Why? 'Because they are accurate most of the time,' say the researchers. 'And besides, customers are not that easily fooled.' They quickly become suspicious when sale signs are used improperly.

■ *Prices ending in 9*. Just like a sale sign, a 9 at the end of a price often signals a bargain. You see such prices everywhere. For example, browse the websites of discounters such as Aldi or Carrefour and you will see that

Pricing cues such as sales signs and prices ending in 9 can be effective in signalling low prices to consumers and increasing sales for the retailer.
Source: Getty Images/Tim Boyle.

a lot of prices end in 9. 'In fact, this pricing tactic is so common', say the researchers, 'you'd think customers would ignore it. Think again. Response to this pricing cue is remarkable.' Normally, you'd expect that demand for an item will fall as the price goes up. Yet in one study involving women's clothing, raising the price of a dress from €34 to €39 *increased* demand by a third. By comparison, raising the price from €34 to €44 yielded no difference in demand.

But are prices ending in 9 accurate as pricing cues? 'The answer varies,' the researchers report. 'Some retailers do reserve prices that end in 9 for their discounted items. For instance, J. Crew and Ralph Lauren generally use 00-cent endings on regularly priced merchandise and 99-cent endings on discounted items. Comparisons of prices at major department stores reveal that this is common, particularly for apparel. But at some stores, prices that end in 9 are a miscue – they are used on all products regardless of whether the items are discounted.'

■ *Signpost pricing (or loss-leader pricing)*. Unlike sale signs or prices that end in 9, signpost pricing is used on frequently purchased products about which consumers tend to have accurate price knowledge. For example, you probably know a good price on a 10-pack of Coke when you see one. New parents usually know how much they should expect to pay for disposable nappies. Research suggests that customers use the prices of such 'signpost' items to gauge a store's overall prices.

If a store has a good price on Coke or Pampers or Persil, they reason, it probably also has good prices on other items.

Retailers have long known the importance of signpost pricing, often called 'loss-leader pricing'. They offer selected signpost items at or below cost to pull customers into the store, hoping to make money on the shopper's other purchases.

■ *Pricing-matching guarantees*. Another widely used retail pricing cue is price matching, whereby stores promise to meet or beat any competitor's price. Department store John Lewis, for example, uses 'Never Knowingly Undersold' as its catchphrase. If you find a better price within 28 days on something you bought at John Lewis, the retailer will refund the difference. While this is certainly a promise that John Lewis will fulfil if necessary, it is not a promise that it expects to have to meet very often, because the company monitors prices carefully and always aims to give the lowest local price for every product.

Evidence suggests that customers perceive that stores offering price-matching guarantees have overall lower prices than competing stores, especially in markets where they perceive price comparisons to be relatively easy. But are such perceptions accurate? 'The evidence is mixed,' say the researchers. Consumers can usually be confident that they'll pay the lowest price on eligible items. However, some manufacturers make it hard to take advantage of price-matching policies by introducing 'branded variants'

– slightly different versions of products with different model numbers for different retailers. At a broader level, some pricing experts argue that price-matching policies are not really targeted at customers. Rather, they may serve as a warning to competitors: 'If you cut your prices, we will, too.' If this is true, price-matching policies might actually reduce price competition, leading to higher overall prices.

Used properly, pricing cues can help consumers. Careful buyers really can take advantage of signals such as sale signs, 9-endings, loss-leaders and price guarantees to locate good deals. Used improperly, however, these pricing cues can mislead consumers, tarnishing a brand and damaging customer relationships.

The researchers conclude: 'Customers need price information, just as they need products. They look to retailers to provide both. Retailers must manage pricing cues in the same way that they manage quality . . . No retailer . . . interested in [building profitable long-term relationships with customers] would purposely offer a defective product. Similarly, no retailer who [values customers] would deceive them with inaccurate pricing cues. By reliably signalling which prices are low, companies can retain customers' trust – and [build more solid relationships].'

Sources: Quotes and other information reprinted by permission of *Harvard Business Review*, excerpt from 'Mind Your Pricing Cues' by Eric Anderson and Duncan Simester, September 2003. Copyright © 2003 by the Harvard Business School Corporation; all rights reserved. See also Joydeep Srivastava and Nicholas Lurie, 'Price-Matching Guarantees as Signals of Low Store Prices: Survey and Experimental Evidence', *Journal of Retailing*, 2004; and Michael J. Barone, Kenneth C. Manning and Paul W. Minard, 'Consumer Response to Retailers' Use of Partially Comparative Pricing', *Journal of Marketing*, July 2004, pp. 37–47.

Even small differences in price can signal product differences. Consider a stereo priced at €300 compared to one priced at €299.95. The actual price difference is only 5 cents, but the psychological difference can be much greater. For example, some consumers will see the €299.95 as a price in the €200 range rather than the €300 range. The €299.95 will more likely be seen as a bargain price, whereas the €300 price suggests more quality. Some psychologists argue that each digit has symbolic and visual qualities that should be considered in pricing. Thus, 8 is round and even and creates a soothing effect, whereas 7 is angular and creates a jarring effect.

Promotional pricing

With **promotional pricing**, companies will temporarily price their products below list price and sometimes even below cost to create buying excitement and urgency. Promotional pricing takes several forms. Supermarkets and department stores will price a few products as *loss-leaders* to attract customers to the store in the hope that they will buy other items at normal mark-ups. For example, supermarkets often sell disposable nappies at less than cost in order to attract family buyers who make larger average purchases per trip. Sellers will also use *special-event pricing* in certain seasons to draw more customers. That's why a lot of retailers have post-Christmas sales to attract shoppers back into their stores.

Manufacturers sometimes offer *cash rebates* ('cash back') to consumers who buy the product from dealers within a specified time; the manufacturer sends the rebate directly to the customer. Rebates have been popular with car companies and producers of durable goods and small appliances, but they are also used with consumer packaged goods. Some manufacturers offer *low-interest financing*, *longer warranties*, or *free maintenance* to reduce the consumer's 'price'. This practice has become a favourite of the car industry. Or, the seller may simply offer *discounts* from normal prices to increase sales and reduce inventories.

Promotional pricing, however, can have adverse effects. Used too frequently and copied by competitors, price promotions can create 'deal-prone' customers who wait until brands go on sale before buying them. Or constantly reduced prices can erode a brand's value in the eyes of customers. Marketers sometimes use price promotions as a quick fix instead of working through the difficult process of developing effective longer-term strategies for building their brands. In fact, one observer notes that price promotions can be addictive for both the company and the customer: 'Price promotions are the brand equivalent of heroin: easy to get into but hard to get out of. Once the brand and its customers are addicted to the short-term high of a price cut it is hard to wean them away to real brand building . . . But continue and the brand dies by 1,000 cuts.'[15]

The frequent use of promotional pricing can also lead to industry price wars. Such price wars usually play into the hands of only one or a few competitors – those with the most efficient operations. For example, until recently, the computer industry avoided price wars. Computer companies showed strong profits as their new technologies were snapped up by eager consumers. When the market cooled, however, many competitors began to unload PCs at discounted prices. In response, Dell, the industry's undisputed low-cost leader, started a brutal price war that only it could win. The result was nothing short of a rout. IBM has since sold off its PC unit, and HP continues to struggle for profitability, with PC profit margins averaging just 1 per cent compared to Dell's 6 per cent. Dell has emerged top in the worldwide PC industry.[16]

The point is that promotional pricing can be an effective means of generating sales for some companies in certain circumstances. But it can be damaging for other companies or if taken as a steady diet.

MAKING CONNECTIONS Linking the concepts

Here's a good place to take a brief break. Think about some of the companies and industries you deal with that are 'addicted' to promotional pricing.

■ Many industries have created 'deal-prone' consumers through the heavy use of promotional pricing – fast food, cars, airlines, tyres, furniture and others. Pick a company in one of these industries and suggest ways that it might deal with this problem.

■ How does the concept of value relate to promotional pricing? Does promotional pricing add to or detract from customer value?

Geographical pricing

A company must also decide how to price its products for customers located in different parts of the country or world. Should the company risk losing the business of more distant customers by charging them higher prices to cover the higher shipping costs? Or should the company charge all customers the same prices regardless of location? We will look at five **geographical pricing** strategies for the following hypothetical situation:

The Peerless Paper Company is located in Rotterdam, Holland, and sells paper products to customers all over Europe. The cost of transport is high and affects the companies from whom customers buy their paper. Peerless wants to establish a geographical pricing policy. It is trying to determine how to price a €100 order to three specific customers: Customer A (Oslo, Norway), Customer B (Milan, Italy) and Customer C (Lisbon, Portugal).

One option is for Peerless to ask each customer to pay the shipping cost from the Rotterdam factory to the customer's location. All three customers would pay the same factory price of €100, with Customer A paying, say, €10 for shipping; Customer B, €15; and Customer C, €25. Called *FOB-origin pricing*, this practice means that the goods are placed *free on board* (hence, *FOB*) a carrier. At that point the title and responsibility pass to the customer, who pays the freight from the factory to the destination. Because each customer picks up its own cost, supporters of FOB pricing feel that this is the fairest way to assess freight charges. The disadvantage, however, is that Peerless will be a high-cost firm to distant customers.

Uniform-delivered pricing is the opposite of FOB pricing. Here, the company charges the same price plus freight to all customers, regardless of their location. The freight charge is set at the average freight cost. Suppose this is €15. Uniform-delivered pricing therefore results in a higher charge to the Oslo customer (who pays €15 freight instead of €10) and a lower charge to the Lisbon customer (who pays €15 instead of €25). Although the Oslo customer would prefer to buy paper from another local paper company that uses FOB-origin pricing, Peerless has a better chance of winning over the Portuguese customer. Other advantages of uniform-delivered pricing are that it is fairly easy to administer and it lets the firm advertise its price nationally.

Zone pricing falls between FOB-origin pricing and uniform-delivered pricing. The company sets up two or more zones. All customers within a given zone pay a single total price; the more distant the zone, the higher the price. For example, Peerless might set up a Northern Europe zone and charge €10 freight to all customers in this zone, and a Southern Europe zone in which it charges €25. In this way, the customers within a given price zone receive no price advantage from the company. For example, customers in Milan and Lisbon pay the same total price to Peerless. The complaint, however, is that the Milan customer is paying part of the Lisbon customer's freight cost.

Using *basing-point pricing*, the seller selects a given city as a 'basing point' and charges all customers the freight cost from that city to the customer location, regardless of the city from which the goods are actually shipped. For example, Peerless might set Paris as the basing point and charge all customers €100 plus the freight from Paris to their locations. This means that a Rotterdam customer pays the freight cost from Paris to Rotterdam, even though the goods may be shipped from Rotterdam. If all sellers used the same basing-point city, delivered prices would be the same for all customers and price competition would be eliminated. Industries such as sugar, cement, steel and vehicles used basing-point pricing for years, but this method has become less popular today. Some companies set up multiple basing points to create more flexibility: they quote freight charges from the basing-point city nearest to the customer.

Finally, the seller who is anxious to do business with a certain customer or geographical area might use *freight-absorption pricing*. Using this strategy, the seller absorbs all or part of the actual freight charges in order to get the desired business. The seller might reason that if it can get more business, its average costs will fall and more than compensate for its extra freight cost. Freight-absorption pricing is used for market penetration and to hold on to increasingly competitive markets.

Dynamic pricing

Throughout most of history, prices were set by negotiation between buyers and sellers. *Fixed price* policies – setting one price for all buyers – is a relatively modern idea that arose with the development of large-scale retailing at the end of the nineteenth century. Today, most prices are set this way. However, some companies are now reversing the fixed pricing trend. They are using **dynamic pricing** – adjusting prices continually to meet the characteristics and needs of individual customers and situations.

For example, think about how the Internet has affected pricing. From the mostly fixed pricing practices of the past century, the Web seems now to be taking us back – into a new age of fluid pricing. 'Potentially, [the Internet] could push aside sticker prices and usher in an era of dynamic pricing,' says one writer, 'in which a wide range of goods would be priced according to what the market will bear – instantly, constantly.'[17]

Dynamic pricing offers many advantages for marketers. For example, Internet sellers such as Amazon (through its .com and national web addresses in Europe) can mine their databases to gauge a specific shopper's desires, measure his or her means, instantaneously tailor products to fit that shopper's behaviour, and price products accordingly.

Many direct marketers monitor inventories, costs and demand at any given moment and adjust prices instantly. For example, Dell uses dynamic pricing to achieve real-time balancing of supply and demand for computer components. Author Thomas Friedman describes Dell's dynamic pricing system this way:

[Dell's] supply chain symphony – from my order over the phone to production to delivery to my house – is one of the wonders of the flat world . . . Demand shaping goes on constantly . . . It works like this: At 10 am Austin time, Dell discovers that so many customers have ordered notebooks with 40-gigabyte hard drives since the morning that its supply chain will run short in two hours. That signal is automatically relayed to Dell's marketing department and to Dell.com and to all the Dell phone operators taking orders. If you happen to call to place your Dell order at 10.30 am, the Dell representative will say to you, 'Tom, it's your lucky day! For the next hour we are offering 60-gigabyte hard drives with the notebook you want – for only $10 more than the 40-gig drive. And if you act now, Dell with throw in a carrying case along with your purchase, because we so value you as a customer.' In an hour or two, using such promotions, Dell can reshape the demand for any part of any notebook or desktop to correspond with the projected supply in its global supply chain. Today memory might be on sale, tomorrow it might be CD-ROMS.[18]

Buyers also benefit from the Web and dynamic pricing. A wealth of websites – such as PriceRunner, Ciao, ShopGenie and shopzilla – give instant product and price comparisons from thousands of vendors. For example, Ciao (**www.ciao.de** in Germany, **www.ciao.fr** in France, **www.ciao.co.uk** in the United Kingdom, **www.ciao.es** in Spain, and so on) lets shoppers browse by category or search for specific products and brands. It then searches the Web and reports back links to sellers offering the best prices. In addition to simply finding the vendor with the best price, customers armed with price information can often negotiate lower prices.

Buyers can also negotiate prices at online auction sites and exchanges. Suddenly the centuries-old art of haggling is back in vogue. Want to sell that antique pickle jar that's been collecting dust for generations? Post it on eBay, the world's biggest online flea market. Want to name your own price for a hotel room or hire car? Visit Priceline (**www.priceline.de** in Germany, **www.priceline.fr** in France, **www.priceline.co.uk** in the United Kingdom, **www.priceline.es** in Spain, and so on) or another reverse auction site.

International pricing

Companies that market their products internationally must decide what prices to charge in the different countries in which they operate. In some cases, a company can set a uniform worldwide price. For example, Boeing sells its planes at about the same price everywhere, whether in the United States, Europe or a Third World country. However, most companies adjust their prices to reflect local market conditions and cost considerations.

The price that a company should charge in a specific country depends on many factors, including economic conditions, competitive situations, laws and regulations, and development of the wholesaling and retailing system. Consumer perceptions and preferences also may vary from country to country, calling for different prices. Or the company may have different marketing objectives in various world markets, which require changes in pricing strategy. For example, Samsung might introduce a new product into mature markets in highly developed countries with the goal of quickly gaining mass-market share – this would call for a penetration pricing strategy. In contrast, it might enter a less developed market by targeting smaller, less price-sensitive segments; in this case, market-skimming pricing makes sense.

Costs play an important role in setting international prices. Travellers abroad are often surprised to find that goods that are relatively inexpensive at home may carry outrageously higher price tags in other countries. A pair of Levi's jeans might sell for €90 in Paris and only €30 in New York. A McDonald's Big Mac selling for a modest €2.90 in the USA might cost €6.00 in Reykjavik, Iceland, and an Oral-B toothbrush selling for €2.49 in the UK may cost €10 in China. Conversely, a Gucci handbag going for only €140 in Milan, Italy, might fetch €240 in the United States. In some cases, such *price escalation* may result from differences in selling strategies or market conditions. In most instances, however, it is simply a result of the higher costs of selling in another country – the additional costs of product modifications, shipping and insurance, import tariffs and taxes, exchange-rate fluctuations and physical distribution.

For example, Campbell found that distribution in the UK cost 30 per cent more than in the United States. US retailers typically purchase soup in large quantities – 48-can cases of a single soup by the dozens, hundreds or carloads. In contrast, English grocers purchase soup in small quantities – typically in 24-can cases of *assorted* soups. Each case must be hand-packed for shipment. To handle these small orders, Campbell had to add a costly extra wholesale level to its European channel. The smaller orders also mean that English retailers order two or three times as often as their US counterparts, bumping up billing and order costs. These and other factors caused Campbell to charge much higher prices for its soups in the UK.[19]

Thus, international pricing presents some special problems and complexities. We discuss international pricing issues in more detail in Chapter 15.

PRICE CHANGES

After developing their pricing structures and strategies, companies often face situations in which they must initiate price changes or respond to price changes by competitors.

Initiating price changes

In some cases, the company may find it desirable to initiate either a price cut or a price increase. In both cases, it must anticipate possible buyer and competitor reactions.

Initiating price cuts

Several situations may lead a firm to consider cutting its price. One such circumstance is excess capacity. Another is falling market share in the face of strong price competition. In such cases, the firm may aggressively cut prices to boost sales and share. But as the airline, fast-food and other industries have learned in recent years, cutting prices in an industry loaded with excess capacity may lead to price wars as competitors try to hold on to market share.

A company may also cut prices in a drive to dominate the market through lower costs. Either the company starts with lower costs than its competitors, or it cuts prices in the hope of gaining market share that will further cut costs through larger volume. Dell has used this strategy effectively in the personal computer market.

Initiating price increases

A successful price increase can greatly increase profits. For example, if the company's profit margin is 3 per cent of sales, a 1 per cent price increase will increase profits by 33 per cent if sales volume is unaffected. A major factor in price increases is cost inflation. Rising costs squeeze profit margins and lead companies to pass cost increases along to customers. Another factor leading to price increases is over-demand: when a company cannot supply all that its customers need, it may raise its prices, ration products to customers, or both.

When raising prices, the company must avoid being perceived as a price gouger. Customers have long memories, and they will eventually turn away from companies or even whole industries that they perceive as charging excessive prices. There are some techniques for avoiding this problem. One is to maintain a sense of fairness surrounding any price increase. Price increases should be supported by company communications telling customers why prices are being raised. Making low-visibility price moves first is also a good technique: some examples include dropping discounts, increasing minimum order sizes, and curtailing production of low-margin products. The company sales force should help business customers find ways to economise.

Wherever possible, the company should consider ways to meet higher costs or demand without raising prices. For example, it can consider more cost-effective ways to produce or distribute its products. It can shrink the product or substitute less expensive ingredients instead of raising the price, as candy bar manufacturers often do. Or it can 'unbundle' its market offering, removing features, packaging or services and separately pricing elements that were formerly part of the offer. IBM, for example, now offers training and consulting as separately priced services.

Buyer reactions to price changes

Customers do not always interpret price changes in a straightforward way. They may view a price *cut* in several ways. For example, what would customers think if Chanel No. 5 perfume, for which 'la feminité est intemporelle' (femininity is timeless) were to cut its price in half? Or what if Sony suddenly cut its personal computer prices drastically?

A high price adds to the aura of exclusivity associated with prestigious brands such as Chanel.

You might think that the computers are about to be replaced by newer models or that they have some fault and are not selling well. You might think that Sony is abandoning the computer business and may not stay in this business long enough to supply future parts. You might believe that quality has been reduced. Or you might think that the price will come down even further and that it will pay to wait and see.

Similarly, a price *increase*, which would normally lower sales, may have some positive meanings for buyers. What would you think if Sony *raised* the price of its latest personal computer model? On the one hand, you might think that the item is very 'hot' and may be un-obtainable unless you buy it soon. Or you might think that the computer is an unusually good performer. On the other hand, you might think that Sony is greedy and charging what the market will bear.

Competitor reactions to price changes

A firm considering a price change has to worry about the reactions of its competitors as well as those of its customers. Competitors are most likely to react when the number of firms involved is small, when the product is uniform, and when the buyers are well informed about products and prices.

How can the firm anticipate the likely reactions of its competitors? The problem is complex because, like the customer, the competitor can interpret a company price cut in many ways. It might think the company is trying to grab a larger market share, or that it's doing poorly and trying to boost its sales. Or it might think that the company wants the whole industry to cut prices to increase total demand.

The company must guess each competitor's likely reaction. If all competitors behave alike, this amounts to analysing only a typical competitor. In contrast, if the competitors do not behave alike – perhaps because of differences in size, market shares or policies – then separate analyses are necessary. However, if some competitors will match the price change, there is good reason to expect that the rest will also match it.

Responding to price changes

Here we reverse the question and ask how a firm should respond to a price change by a competitor. The firm needs to consider several issues: Why did the competitor change the price? Is the price change temporary or permanent? What will happen to the company's market share and profits if it does not respond? Are other competitors going to respond? Besides these issues, the company must also consider its own situation and strategy and possible customer reactions to price changes.

Figure 9.5 shows the ways a company might assess and respond to a competitor's price cut. Suppose the company learns that a competitor has cut its price and decides that this price cut is likely to harm company sales and profits. It might simply decide to hold its current price and profit margin. The company might believe that it will not lose too much market share, or that it would lose too much profit if it reduced its own price. Or it might decide that it should wait and respond when it has more information on the effects of the competitor's price change. However, waiting too long to act might let the competitor get stronger and more confident as its sales increase.

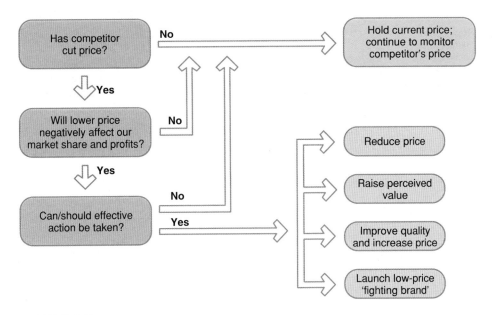

FIGURE 9.5

Assessing and responding to competitor price changes

If the company decides that effective action can and should be taken, it might make any of four responses. First, it could *reduce its price* to match the competitor's price. It may decide that the market is price sensitive and that it would lose too much market share to the lower-priced competitor. Cutting the price will reduce the company's profits in the short term. Some companies might also reduce their product quality, services and marketing communications to retain profit margins, but this will ultimately hurt long-term market share. The company should try to maintain its quality as it cuts prices.

Alternatively, the company might maintain its price but *raise the perceived value* of its offer. It could improve its communications, stressing the relative value of its product over that of the lower-priced competitor. The firm may find it cheaper to maintain price and spend money to improve its perceived value than to cut price and operate at a lower margin. Or, the company might *improve quality and increase price*, moving its brand into a higher price-value position. The higher quality creates greater customer value which justifies the higher price. In turn, the higher price preserves the company's higher margins.

Finally, the company might *launch a low-price 'fighting brand'* – adding a lower-priced item to the line or creating a separate lower-priced brand. This is necessary if the particular market segment being lost is price sensitive and will not respond to arguments of higher quality.

PUBLIC POLICY AND PRICING

Price competition is a core element of a free market economy. In setting prices, companies are not usually free to charge whatever prices they wish. Many European and national laws govern the rules of fair play in pricing. In addition, companies must consider broader societal pricing concerns. Legislation is in place in all of the world's major economies to prohibit anti-competitive pricing practices. For example, in Europe the most important legislation affecting pricing is Article 81 of the EU Treaty.

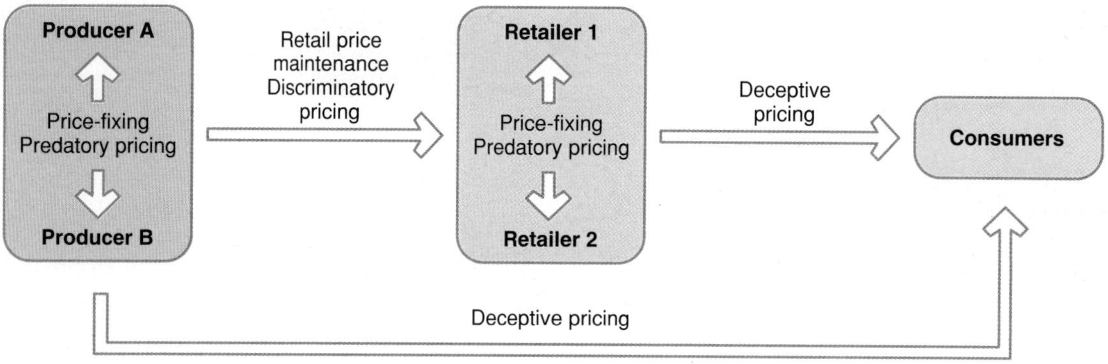

FIGURE 9.6

Public policy issues in pricing

Source: Reprinted with permission from *Journal of Public Policy and Marketing*, published by the American Marketing Association, L.D. Compeau and D. Grewel, 'Pricing and Public Policy: A Research Agenda and Overview of Special Issue', *Journal of Public Policy and Marketing*, Spring 1999, pp. 3–10, Figure 1.

Figure 9.6 shows the major public policy issues in pricing. These include potentially damaging pricing practices within a given level of the channel (price-fixing and predatory pricing) and across levels of the channel (retail price maintenance, discriminatory pricing and deceptive pricing).[20]

In the European Union anti-competitive business practices are prohibited by Article 81 of the EU Treaty:

> The following shall be prohibited as incompatible with the common market: all agreements between undertakings, decisions by associations of undertakings and concerted practices which may affect trade between Member States and which have as their object or effect the prevention, restriction or distortion of competition within the common market, and in particular those which:
>
> (a) directly or indirectly fix purchase or selling prices or any other trading conditions;
>
> (b) limit or control production, markets, technical development, or investment;
>
> (c) share markets or sources of supply;
>
> (d) apply dissimilar conditions to equivalent transactions with other trading parties, thereby placing them at a competitive disadvantage;
>
> (e) make the conclusion of contracts subject to acceptance by the other parties of supplementary obligations which, by their nature or according to commercial usage, have no connection with the subject of contracts.[21]

The aim of Article 81 is to promote free competition and free trade throughout the EU. Many Member States have their own further legislation to prevent anti-competitive practices in general and unfair pricing practices specifically.

THE JOURNEY YOU'VE TAKEN Reviewing the concepts

Before you leave pricing behind, let's review the important concepts. *Price* can be defined as the sum of all the values that customers give up in order to gain the benefits of having or using a product or service. Pricing decisions are subject to an incredibly complex array of company, environmental and competitive forces.

1 Discuss the importance of understanding customer value perceptions and company costs when setting prices.

Good pricing begins with a complete understanding of the value that a product or service creates for customers and setting a price the captures that value. The price the company charges will fall somewhere between one that is too high to produce any demand and one that is too low to produce a profit.

Customer perceptions of the product's value set the ceiling for prices. If customers perceive that the price is greater than the product's value, they will not buy the product. At the other extreme, company and product costs set the floor for prices. If the company prices the product below its costs, its profits will suffer.

Costs are an important consideration in setting prices. However, cost-based pricing is product driven. The company designs what it considers to be a good product and sets a price that covers costs plus a target profit. If the price turns out to be too high, the company must settle for lower mark-ups or lower sales, both resulting in disappointing profits. Value-based pricing reverses this process. The company sets its target price based on customer perceptions of the product value. The targeted value and price then drive decisions about product design and what costs can be incurred. As a result, pricing begins with analysing customer needs and value perceptions, and price is set to match customers' perceived value.

2 Identify and define the other important external and internal factors affecting a firm's pricing decisions.

Other *internal* factors that influence pricing decisions include the company's overall marketing strategy, objectives, mix and organisation for pricing. Price is only one element of the company's broader marketing strategy. If the company has selected its target market and positioning carefully, then its marketing mix strategy, including price, will be fairly straightforward. Some companies position their products on price and then tailor other marketing mix decisions to the prices they want to charge. Other companies de-emphasise price and use other marketing mix tools to create *non-price* positions.

Common pricing objectives might include survival, current profit maximisation, market share leadership, or customer retention and relationship building. Price decisions must be coordinated with product design, distribution and promotion decisions to form a consistent and effective marketing programme. Finally, in order to coordinate pricing goals and decisions, management must decide who within the organisation is responsible for setting price.

Other *external* pricing considerations include the nature of the market and demand, competitors' strategies and prices, and environmental factors such as the economy, reseller needs and government actions. The seller's pricing freedom varies with different types of markets. Ultimately, the customer decides whether the company has set the right price. The customer weighs the price against the perceived values of using the product – if the price exceeds the sum of the values, consumers will not buy. So the company must understand concepts like demand curves (the price–demand relationship) and price elasticity (consumer sensitivity to prices). Consumers also compare a product's price to the prices of competitors' products. A company therefore must learn the customer value and prices of competitors' offers.

3 Describe the major strategies for pricing imitative and new products.

Pricing is a dynamic process. Companies design a *pricing structure* that covers all their products. They change this structure over time and adjust it to account for different customers and situations. Pricing strategies usually change as a product passes through its life cycle. In pricing innovative new products, it can follow a *skimming policy* by initially setting high prices to 'skim' the maximum amount of revenue from various segments of the market. Or it can use *penetration pricing* by setting a low initial price to penetrate the market deeply and win a large market share.

4 **Explain how companies find a set of prices that maximises the profits from the total product mix.**

When the product is part of a product mix, the firm searches for a set of prices that will maximise the profits from the total mix. In *product line pricing*, the company decides on price steps for the entire set of products it offers. In addition, the company must set prices for *optional products* (optional or accessory products included with the main product), *captive products* (products that are required for use of the main product), *by-products* (waste or residual products produced when making the main product), and *product bundles* (combinations of products at a reduced price).

5 **Discuss how companies adjust their prices to take into account different types of customers and situations.**

Companies apply a variety of *price adjustment strategies* to account for differences in consumer segments and situations. One is *discount and allowance pricing*, whereby the company establishes cash, quantity, functional or seasonal discounts or varying types of allowances. A second strategy is *segmented pricing*, whereby the company sells a product at two or more prices to accommodate different customers, product forms, locations or times. Sometimes companies consider more than economics in their pricing decisions, using *psychological pricing* to better

communicate a product's intended position. In *promotional pricing*, a company offers discounts or temporarily sells a product below list price as a special event, sometimes even selling below cost as a loss-leader. Another approach is *geographical pricing*, whereby the company decides how to price to near and distant customers. *Dynamic pricing* involves adjusting prices continually to meet the characteristics and needs of individual customers and situations. Finally, *international pricing* means that the company adjusts its price to meet conditions and expectations in different world markets.

6 **Discuss the key issues related to initiating and responding to price changes.**

When a firm considers initiating a *price change*, it must consider customers' and competitors' reactions. There are different implications to *initiating price cuts* and *initiating price increases*. Buyer reactions to price changes are influenced by the meaning customers see in the price change. Competitors' reactions flow from a set reaction policy or a fresh analysis of each situation.

There are also many factors to consider in responding to a competitor's price changes. The company that faces a price change initiated by a competitor must try to understand the competitor's intent as well as the likely duration and impact of the change. If a swift reaction is desirable, the firm should pre-plan its reactions to different possible price actions by competitors. When facing a competitor's price change, the company might sit tight, reduce its own price, raise perceived value, improve quality and raise price, or launch a fighting brand.

NAVIGATING THE KEY TERMS

NOTES AND REFERENCES

1 Thomas T. Nagle and Reed K. Holden, *The Strategy and Tactics of Pricing*, 4th edn (Upper Saddle River, NJ: Prentice Hall, 2005), ch. 1.

2 George Mannes, 'The Urge to Unbundle', *Fast Company*, 27 February 2005, pp. 23–4.

3 http://franchisor.ikea.com, accessed 7 May 2007.

4 A. Hinterhuber, 'Towards value-based pricing – An integrative framework for decision making', *Industrial Marketing Management*, 33, 2004, pp. 765–78.

5 John Tayman, 'The Six-Figure Steal', *Business 2.0*, June 2005, pp. 148–50.

6 Erin Stout, 'Keep Them Coming Back for More', *Sales & Marketing Management*, February 2002, pp. 51–2. See also Hinterhuber, 'Towards Value-Based Pricing – An Integrative Framework for Decision Making', pp. 765ff; and Helen Atkinson, 'Adding New Value', *Traffic World*, 28 March 2005, pp. 18–22.

7 Extract from www.miele.co.uk, accessed 15 July 2008.

8 Information from www.which.co.uk.

9 Joshua Rosenbaum, 'Guitar Maker Looks for a New Key', *Wall Street Journal*, 11 February 1998, p. B1; and information accessed online at www.gibson.com, July 2005.

10 See Robert J. Dolan, 'Pricing: A Value-Based Approach', *Harvard Business School Publishing*, 9-500-071, 3 November 2003.

11 See Philip Kotler and Kevin Lane Keller, *Marketing Management*, 12th edn (Upper Saddle River, NJ: Prentice Hall, 2006), p. 438; Cliff Edwards, 'HDTV: High-Anxiety Television', *Business Week*, 10 June 2002, pp. 142–6; Eric Taub, 'HDTV's Acceptance Picks Up Pace as Prices Drop and Networks Sign On', *New York Times*, 31 March 2003, p. C1; and Stephen H. Wildstrom, 'Buying the Right HDTV', *BusinessWeek*, 2 February 2004, p. 22.

12 Michael Buettner, 'Charleston, S.C.-Based Asphalt Innovations Turns Waste into Helpful Product', *Knight Ridder Tribune Business News*, 18 October 2004, p. 1.

13 See Nagle and Holden, *The Strategy and Tactics of Pricing*, 4th edn, 2005, pp. 244–7; Stefan Stremersch and Gerard J. Tellis, 'Strategic Bundling of Products and Prices: A New Synthesis for Marketing', *Journal of Marketing Research*, January 2002, pp. 55–72; and Chris Janiszewski and Marcus Cunha, Jr, 'The Influence of Price Discount Framing on the Evaluation of a Product Bundle', *Journal of Marketing Research*, March 2004, pp. 534–46.

14 Example adapted from Charles Fishman, 'Which Price Is Right?', *Fast Company*, March 2003, pp. 92–6. Additional data from 'Continental Airlines Reports March 2005 Operational Performance', Continental Financial and Traffic Releases, http://www.continental.com/company/investor/news.asp, accessed April 2005. See also Robert G. Cross, *Revenue Management: Hard-Core Tactics for Market Domination* (New York: Broadway Books, 1998); Edward Wong, 'Airline Economics: Fasten Your Seat Belt', *New York Times*, 9 December 2003, p. G6; Lynn DeLain and Edward O'Meara, 'Building a Business Case for Revenue Management', *Journal of Revenue Management and Pricing Management*, January 2004, pp. 338–53; and Dimitris Bertsimas and Sanne de Boer, 'Dynamic Pricing and Inventory Control for Multiple Products', *Journal of Pricing Management*, January 2005, pp. 303–19.

15 Tim Ambler, 'Kicking Price Promotion Habit Is Like Getting Off Heroin – Hard', *Marketing*, 27 May 1999, p. 24. See also Robert Gray, 'Driving Sales at Any Price?', *Marketing*, 11 April 2002, p. 24; and Lauren Kellere Johnson, 'Dueling Pricing Strategies', *MIT Sloan Management Review*, Spring 2003, pp. 10–11; and Peter R. Darke and Cindy M.Y. Chung, 'Effects of Pricing and Promotion on Consumer Perceptions: It Depends of How You Frame It', *Journal of Retailing*, 2005, pp. 35–47.

16 See 'Dell, the Conqueror', *BusinessWeek*, 24 September 2001, pp. 92–102; Andy Serwer, 'Dell Does Domination', *Fortune*, 21 January 2002, pp. 70–5; and Pui-Wing Tam, 'H-P Gains Applause as It Cedes PC Market Share to Dell', *Wall Street Journal*, 18 January 2005, p. C1.

17 Robert D. Hof, 'Going, Going, Gone', *BusinessWeek*, 12 April 1999, pp. 30–2. See also Kotler and Keller, *Marketing Management*, 12th edn, 2006, pp. 432–3.

18 Thomas L. Friedman, *The World is Flat: A Brief History of the Twenty-First Century* (New York: Farrar, Straus & Giroux, 2003), pp. 417–8.

19 Philip R. Cateora, *International Marketing*, 7th edn (Homewood, IL: Irwin, 1990), p. 540. See also Barbara Stottinger, 'Strategic Export Pricing: A Long and Winding Road', *Journal of International Marketing*, 2001, pp. 40–63; and Warren J. Keegan, *Global Marketing Management* (Upper Saddle River, NJ: Prentice Hall, 2002), ch. 12.

20 For discussions of these issues, see Dhruv Grewel and Larry D. Compeau, 'Pricing and Public Policy: A Research Agenda and Overview of Special Issue', *Journal of Public Policy and Marketing*, Spring 1999, pp. 3–10; and Michael V. Marn, Eric V. Roegner and Craig C. Zawada, *The Price Advantage* (Hoboken, NJ: John Wiley & Sons, 2004), Appendix 2.

21 http://europa.eu.

CHAPTER 10
Marketing channels and supply chain management

AFTER STUDYING THIS CHAPTER, YOU SHOULD BE ABLE TO

- explain why companies use distribution channels and discuss the functions these channels perform
- discuss how channel members interact and how they organise to perform the work of the channel
- identify the major channel alternatives open to a company
- explain how companies select, motivate and evaluate channel members
- discuss the nature and importance of marketing logistics and integrated supply chain management

THE WAY AHEAD Previewing the concepts

We now arrive at the third marketing mix tool – distribution. Firms rarely work alone in creating value for customers and building profitable customer relationships. Instead, most are only a single link in a larger supply chain and distribution channel. As such, an individual firm's success depends not only on how well *it* performs but also on how well its *entire distribution channel* competes with competitors' channels. To be good at customer relationship management, a company must also be good at partner relationship management. The first part of this chapter explores the nature of distribution channels and the marketer's channel design and management decisions. We then examine physical distribution – or logistics – an area that is growing dramatically in importance and sophistication. In the next chapter, we'll look more closely at two major channel intermediaries – retailers and wholesalers.

To get us started, we'll take a close look at a medium-sized Spanish paint company, Pinturas Fierro, which has had to solve quite a few distribution and logistical issues as it has grown and entered international markets. Good management of the distribution system has been a key component in enabling this family firm to survive and thrive for over 70 years. Read on and see why.

Pinturas Fierro: Slow but safe growth

Jesús Cambra Fierro

Pinturas Fierro is a Spanish family company devoted to the production and distribution of paint for industrial use, such as the car and the decoration industries; the company also produces solvents and other auxiliary products. It demonstrates some characteristic features for a medium-sized business: a fairly small number of employees, management of the business handled by the owners, and relatively few specialists in management positions. The company was created in 1930 by the family that owns and runs it today. Currently the third generation runs the company while the fourth generation is receiving training in the fields of chemistry and business administration in order to take the control and management of the company in the future.

Since its creation the company has been characterised by great dynamism and an eagerness to grow. Initially, the company was a small local shop that sold paint, varnish and accessories. When the founder's son took charge of the business, in 1943, the location changed to the commercial area of Barbastro, their home town in northern Spain, and they established a provincial and regional network for the exclusive distribution of the most highly-respected paint brands in Spain (such as Titan and Valentine). During this period the company became well established in its home region and began to expand into neighbouring France. In the early 1980s the important decision was made to invest in manufacturing facilities for paint, varnish and solvents. The first production activities coincided with the arrival of the third generation into the

company's management in 1986. However, although members of the family had excellent knowledge of chemistry they had little training in business management, and this began to hamper the company's development. After a period of consolidation, during which managerial skills were developed, the business began to look for expansion opportunities nationally and internationally.

Today the company is divided into two fundamental areas: firstly, production and distribution (wholesaling) to industrial customers, and, secondly, distribution (wholesaling) to commercial customers and retailers. The company has 16 employees, and in 2005 sales turnover amounted to €4.5 million. The centre of operations is still in the Spanish market, especially in Aragon, Catalonia, industrial areas of Madrid, Valencia and Andalusia; there is an international presence through non-exclusive distributors in France, northern Italy and, on a smaller scale, in Portugal and Morocco.

Throughout most of the history of Pinturas Fierro the company has

relied less on formal management principles and more on the intuitive business sense of the owners. Because the people that have run the company always knew that they were dealing with the present and future of their family, they were never tempted to take on excessive risks. Besides, they were chemists rather than businessmen. This has led to a fairly cautious approach to business expansion, with a clear focus on producing high quality products even if this meant that prices sometimes had to be higher than rivals'.

Let's now take a look at how the company has managed its expansion, and how it has consistently and carefully augmented the distribution channels that it employs. The first stage of the expansion was characterised by the creation of a simple distribution network, covering 75–100 kilometres from the physical location of the firm. The problem here was that the area is mountainous (near the Pyrenees) and the transport infrastructure was poorly developed. However, the company exploited the absence of

The retail team at Pinturas Fierro.
Source: Photo by Jesús Cambra Fierro.

competitors interested in the area. This territory was neither attractive nor profitable for distant companies, whereas for Pinturas Fierro, it was their home territory and all they needed was a driver with a van, who could make deliveries and handle logistical matters. Using this simple commercial network the company obtained the exclusive dealership within the local area for several of the most prestigious national and international brands, like Valentine and Titan.

However, growing business led to the need to increase the stock of products stored and to have actual space for it. The company acquired two fairly small warehouses in the same town, one for paints and varnishes, the other for accessory products.

The 1980s saw further expansion of the business and the addition of a new product line: accessory machinery. This line included air compressors and power generators. However, this increased the complexity of the management task considerably. New brands like Peugeot and Pintuc were added to the portfolio, and it became clear that the company needed more space in which to exhibit and store the products, and to offer technical support. In particular, in this industry, customers often give equipment maintenance a low priority, and expect the dealer to sort out any problems quickly when equipment breaks down. Customer service is a priority.

During this period more employees were hired: one as warehouse manager, one to handle the accounts and administration, and two as commercial salespeople. Two delivery vehicles were acquired and agreements on physical distribution were signed with specialised companies so that commercial staff no longer had to handle the phys-

ical distribution of the product. As a result the sales team could spend more time on existing customers and prospecting for new customers.

As transport infrastructure improved in the 1980s, so several competing companies became interested in the home territory of Pinturas Fierro. At the same time several new brands emerged with very aggressive price strategies. All these factors reduced profit margins and meant that the company had to handle a wider range of brands. In any case, Pinturas Fierro had been able to build a commercial network perfectly adapted to the physical and social features of the territory. The company had a good reputation for the technical training of its salespeople, its commitment to meet customer deadlines, the size of its product portfolio and its willingness to meet the specific needs of every customer.

As the company developed its production facilities and began to sell its own products, rather than simply to distribute those of other companies, new challenges emerged. Establishing distribution channels, and handling logistics, for its own products became matters of serious concern. Key target markets were in the industrial centres of Catalonia and, inevitably, in Madrid, where the concentration of business was highest. Although Pinturas Fierro wanted to establish exclusive distributorships, they were not well known as a manufacturer and so found this very difficult. Consequently, they decided to sell their products through distributors that also handled other brands. They looked for distributors who specialised in industrial customers with a wide portfolio. Potential distributors were invited to the factory so that they could learn about the production process and how the product could

be customised to meet the needs of particular industrial customers. Pinturas Fierro managers visited Madrid and Barcelona regularly to meet potential customers. This way they both demonstrated their support to the distributor and surveyed the actual needs of the market. This information, together with the feedback generated by the distributor enriched considerably the company's knowledge of the market.

What about international markets? They were considered to be of secondary importance compared to getting established in Spain. But by the 1990s the management felt that the company was mature enough to expand internationally. The route selected to enter foreign markets was exporting, building relationships with distributors in international markets in the same way that they had built relationships with Spanish distributors. Expanding into international markets was expected to enhance the reputation of the company back home in Spain. Pinturas Fierro followed a typical internationalisation strategy for a medium-sized firm, making the nearby countries of France and Italy their first targets. The company has taken part in trade missions and international trade fairs. Gradually the proportion of exports in total sales is increasing.

What are the challenges that Pinturas Fierro faces for the future? The company, true to its origins, still sells to the retail trade and still distributes Valentine and Titan brands. Although the retail trade is fairly small, it has always been there and has always provided funds for the company's new ventures. Besides, the management of the business are emotionally attached to the retail trade and would not want to see it go. In 2008 the company was working on enlarging the central main warehouse and the manufacturing facilities, and was investing in new, improved logistics technology designed to improve physical stock management. The working relationships with suppliers are very satisfactory, and the managers are working hard to maintain and improve them. Similarly, the company understands that its distributors are the principal point of contact with the customers, and so will continue to invest time and effort in developing excellent distributor relationships. The challenge of further internationalisation is always present. The company is hampered because few employees can speak foreign languages, and, in any case, it currently has limited production capacity with which to expand further in international markets. However, as the next generation of the family comes into the business, fully trained in modern management and marketing techniques, perhaps they will take the plunge and launch Pinturas Fierro decisively into the international arena.

Sources: Based on interviews with the owners and managers.

Just like Pinturas Fierro, most firms cannot bring value to customers by themselves. Instead, they must work closely with other firms in a larger value-delivery network.

SUPPLY CHAINS AND THE VALUE-DELIVERY NETWORK

Producing a product or service and making it available to buyers requires building relationships not just with customers, but also with key suppliers and resellers in the company's *supply chain*. This supply chain consists of 'upstream' and 'downstream' partners. Upstream from the company is the set of firms that supply the raw materials, components, parts, information, finances and expertise needed to create a product or service. Marketers, however, have traditionally focused on the 'downstream' side of the supply chain – on the *marketing channels* or *distribution channels* that look forward towards the customer. Downstream marketing channel partners, such as wholesalers and retailers, form a vital connection between the firm and its customers.

Both upstream and downstream partners may also be part of other firms' supply chains. But it is the unique design of each company's supply chain that enables it to deliver superior value to customers. An individual firm's success depends not only on how well *it* performs, but also on how well its entire supply chain and marketing channel competes with competitors' channels.

The term *supply chain* may be too limited – it takes a *make-and-sell* view of the business. It suggests that raw materials, productive inputs and factory capacity should serve as the starting point for market planning. A better term would be *demand chain* because it suggests a *sense-and-respond* view of the market. Under this view, planning starts with the needs of target customers, to which the company responds by organising a chain of resources and activities with the goal of creating customer value.

Even a demand-chain view of a business may be too limited, because it takes a step-by-step, linear view of purchase-production-consumption activities. With the advent of the Internet and other technologies, however, companies are forming more numerous and complex relationships with other firms. For example, Ford manages numerous supply chains. It also sponsors or transacts on many B2B websites and online purchasing exchanges as needs arise. Like Ford, most large companies today are engaged in building and managing a continuously evolving *value delivery network*.

As defined in Chapter 2, a value-delivery network is made up of the company, suppliers, distributors and ultimately customers who 'partner' with each other to improve the performance of the entire system. For example, Nokia, the leading manufacturer of mobile phones, manages a whole community of suppliers and assemblers of semiconductor components, plastic cases, LCD displays and accessories. Its network also includes offline and online resellers. All of these diverse partners must work effectively together to bring superior value to Nokia's customers.

This chapter focuses on marketing channels – on the downstream side of the value-delivery network. However, it is important to remember that this is only part of the full value network. To bring value to customers, companies need upstream supplier partners just as they need downstream channel partners. Increasingly, marketers are participating in and influencing their company's upstream activities as well as its downstream activities. More than marketing channel managers, they are becoming full value network managers.

The chapter examines four major questions concerning marketing channels. What is the nature of marketing channels and why are they important? How do channel firms interact and organise to do the work of the channel? What problems do companies face in designing and managing their channels? What role do physical distribution and supply chain management play in attracting and satisfying customers? In Chapter 11, we will look at marketing channel issues from the viewpoint of retailers and wholesalers.

THE NATURE AND IMPORTANCE OF MARKETING CHANNELS

Few producers sell their goods directly to the final users. Instead, most use intermediaries to bring their products to market. They try to forge a **marketing channel** (or **distribution channel**) – a set of interdependent organisations that help make a product or service available for use or consumption by the consumer or business user.

A company's channel decisions directly affect every other marketing decision. Pricing depends on whether the company works with national discount chains, uses high-quality speciality stores, or sells directly to consumers via the Web. The firm's sales force and communications decisions depend on how much persuasion, training, motivation and support its channel partners need. Whether a company develops or acquires certain new products may depend on how well those products fit the capabilities of its channel members.

Companies often pay too little attention to their distribution channels, sometimes with damaging results. In contrast, many companies have used imaginative distribution systems to *gain* a competitive advantage. FedEx's creative and imposing distribution system made it a leader in express delivery. Dell revolutionised its industry by selling personal computers directly to consumers rather than through retail stores. Online retailer Amazon pioneered the sales of books and a wide range of other goods via the Internet.

Distribution channel decisions often involve long-term commitments to other firms. For example, companies such as PSA Peugeot Citroën, Samsung or Toshiba can easily change their advertising, pricing or promotion programmes. They can scrap old products and introduce new ones as market tastes demand. But when they set up distribution channels through contracts with franchisees, independent dealers, or large retailers, they cannot readily replace these channels with company-owned stores or websites if conditions change. Therefore, management must design its channels carefully, with an eye on tomorrow's likely selling environment as well as today's.

How channel members add value

Why do producers give some of the selling job to channel partners? After all, doing so means giving up some control over how and to whom they sell their products. Producers use intermediaries because they create greater efficiency in making goods available to target markets. Through their contacts, experience, specialisation and scale of operation, intermediaries usually offer the firm more than it can achieve on its own.

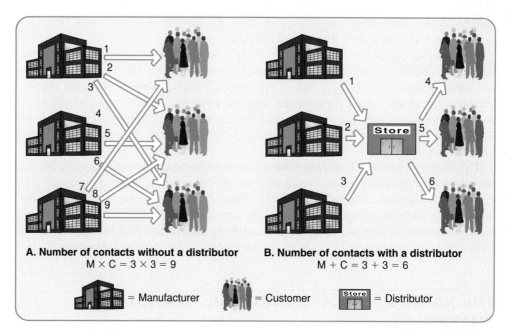

A. Number of contacts without a distributor
$M \times C = 3 \times 3 = 9$

B. Number of contacts with a distributor
$M + C = 3 + 3 = 6$

= Manufacturer   = Customer   = Distributor

FIGURE 10.1

How a distributor reduces the number of channel transactions

Figure 10.1 shows how using intermediaries can provide economies. Figure 10.1A shows three manufacturers, each using direct marketing to reach three customers. This system requires nine different contacts. Figure 10.1B shows the three manufacturers working through one distributor, which contacts the three customers. This system requires only six contacts. In this way, intermediaries reduce the amount of work that must be done by both producers and consumers.

From an economic point of view the role of marketing intermediaries is to transform the assortments of products made by producers into the assortments wanted by consumers. Producers make narrow assortments of products in large quantities, but consumers want broad assortments of products in small quantities. Marketing channel members buy large quantities from many producers and break them down into the smaller quantities and broader assortments wanted by consumers.

For example, Nestlé makes millions of KitKat bars each day, but you want to buy only a few bars at a time. So big food, drug and discount retailers, such as Carrefour, Lidl, Aldi and Tesco, buy KitKat by the truckload and stock it on their stores' shelves. In turn, you can buy a single KitKat, along with a shopping trolley full of small quantities of toothpaste, shampoo and other related products as you need them. Thus, intermediaries play an important role in matching supply and demand.

In making products and services available to consumers, channel members add value by bridging the major time, place and possession gaps that separate goods and services from those who would use them. Members of the marketing channel perform many key functions. Some help to complete transactions:

- *Information*: Gathering and distributing marketing research and intelligence information about actors and forces in the marketing environment needed for planning and aiding exchange.
- *Promotion*: Developing and spreading persuasive communications about an offer.
- *Contact*: Finding and communicating with prospective buyers.
- *Matching*: Shaping and fitting the offer to the buyer's needs, including activities such as manufacturing, grading, assembling and packaging.

■ *Negotiation*: Reaching an agreement on price and other terms of the offer so that ownership or possession can be transferred.

Others help to fulfil the completed transactions:

■ *Physical distribution*: Transporting and storing goods.

■ *Financing*: Acquiring and using funds to cover the costs of the channel work.

■ *Risk taking*: Assuming the risks of carrying out the channel work.

The question is not *whether* these functions need to be performed – they must be – but rather *who* will perform them. To the extent that the manufacturer performs these functions, its costs go up and its prices have to be higher. When some of these functions are shifted to intermediaries, the producer's costs and prices may be lower, but the intermediaries must charge more to cover the costs of their work. In dividing the work of the channel, the various functions should be assigned to the channel members who can add the most value for the cost.

Number of channel levels

Companies can design their distribution channels to make products and services available to customers in different ways. Each layer of marketing intermediaries that performs some work in bringing the product and its ownership closer to the final buyer is a **channel level**. Because the producer and the final consumer both perform some work, they are part of every channel.

The *number of intermediary levels* indicates the *length* of a channel. Figure 10.2A shows several consumer distribution channels of different lengths. Channel 1, called a **direct marketing channel**, has no intermediary levels; the company sells directly to consumers. For example, both Avon and Essentially Yours sell cosmetic products through home and office sales parties, and on the Web; Interflora sells flowers, gifts and greeting cards direct by telephone and on line. The remaining channels in Figure 10.2A are **indirect marketing channels**, containing one or more intermediaries.

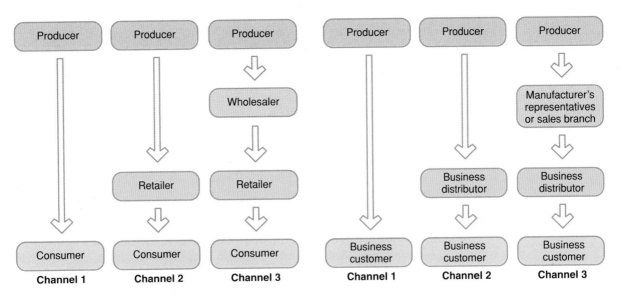

A. Customer marketing channels   **B. Business marketing channels**

FIGURE 10.2

Consumer and business marketing channels

Figure 10.2B shows some common business distribution channels. The business marketer can use its own sales force to sell directly to business customers. Or it can sell to various types of intermediaries, who in turn sell to these customers. Consumer and business marketing channels with even more levels can sometimes be found, but less often. From the producer's point of view, a greater number of levels means less control and greater channel complexity. Moreover, all of the institutions in the channel are connected by several types of *flows*. These include the *physical flow* of products, the *flow of ownership*, the *payment flow*, the *information flow* and the *promotion flow*. These flows can make even channels with only one or a few levels very complex.

CHANNEL BEHAVIOUR AND ORGANISATION

Distribution channels are more than simple collections of firms tied together by various flows. They are complex behavioural systems in which people and companies interact to accomplish individual, company and channel goals. Some channel systems consist only of informal interactions among loosely organised firms. Others consist of formal interactions guided by strong organisational structures. Moreover, channel systems do not stand still – new types of intermediaries emerge and whole new channel systems evolve. Here we look at channel behaviour and at how members organise to do the work of the channel.

Channel behaviour

A marketing channel consists of firms that have partnered for their common good. Each channel member depends on the others. For example, a Peugeot dealer depends on Peugeot to design cars that meet consumer needs. In turn, Peugeot depends on the dealer to attract consumers, persuade them to buy Peugeot cars, and service cars after the sale. Each Peugeot dealer also depends on other dealers to provide good sales and service that will uphold the brand's reputation. In fact, the success of individual Peugeot dealers depends on how well the entire Peugeot marketing channel competes with the channels of other auto manufacturers.

Each channel member plays a specialised role in the channel. For example, Sony's role is to produce consumer electronics products that consumers will like and to create demand through national advertising. The role of electrical retailers like Fnac and Currys digital is to display these Sony products in convenient locations, to answer buyers' questions and to complete sales. The channel will be most effective when each member takes on the tasks it can do best.

Ideally, because the success of individual channel members depends on overall channel success, all channel firms should work together smoothly. They should understand and accept their roles, coordinate their activities and cooperate to attain overall channel goals. However, individual channel members rarely take such a broad view. Cooperating to achieve overall channel goals sometimes means giving up individual company goals. Although channel members depend on one another, they often act alone in their own short-term best interests. They often disagree on who should do what and for what rewards. Such disagreements over goals, roles and rewards generate **channel conflict**.

Horizontal conflict occurs among firms at the same level of the channel. For instance, some Peugeot dealers in Madrid might complain that other dealers in the city steal sales from them by pricing too low or by advertising outside their assigned territories. Or Holiday Inn franchisees might complain about other Holiday Inn operators over-charging guests or giving poor service, hurting the overall Holiday Inn image.

Vertical conflict, conflicts between different levels of the same channel, is even more common. For example, office furniture maker Herman Miller created conflict with its dealers when it opened an online store – **www.hmstore.com** – and began selling its products directly to customers. Although Herman Miller believed that the website was reaching only smaller customers who weren't being served by current channels, dealers complained loudly. As a result, the company closed down its online sales operations.

Similarly, Goodyear created hard feelings and conflict with its premier independent-dealer channel when it began selling through mass-merchant retailers:

> For more than 60 years, Goodyear sold replacement tyres exclusively through its premier network of 5,300 independent Goodyear dealers. In mid-1992, however, Goodyear jolted its dealers by agreeing to sell its tyres through Sears auto centres. Similar pacts soon followed with Wal-Mart and Sam's Club, pitting dealers against the nation's most potent retailers. Goodyear claimed that the change was essential. Value-minded tyre buyers were increasingly buying from cheaper, multibrand discount outlets and department stores. By selling exclusively through its dealer network, Goodyear simply wasn't putting its tyres where many consumers were going to buy them. Unfortunately, as Goodyear expanded into the new channels, it took few steps to protect its prized exclusive-dealer network.
>
> Since the shift, Goodyear's relations with its dealers have steadily deteriorated. Dealers complain not just about competition from mega-retailers but also about shoddy treatment and unfair pricing from Goodyear. For example, to sell more tyres, Goodyear until recently offered bulk discounts to its biggest retailers and wholesalers. 'The result was pricing insanity,' notes one observer. 'Some smaller dealers were paying more for tyres than what Sears charged at retail.' As a result, some of Goodyear's best dealers have defected to competitors, and many others now carry and push competing brands. Says one former dealer, 'After someone punches you in the face a few times, you say, "Enough is enough".' Goodyear's replacement tyre sales – which make up 70 per cent of the company's revenues – have gone flat.

> Patching Goodyear's dealer relations, damaged over many years, will take time. 'We still have a long way to go on this,' admits Goodyear's VP for replacement tyre sales. 'We lost sight of the fact that it's in our interest that our dealers succeed.' Larry Hauck, owner of a tyre distributor in Alton, Illinois, would agree. An exclusive Goodyear dealer for 35 years until the late 1990s, he's the kind of once-loyal dealer that the company says it wants to woo back. Recently, though, Goodyear kicked him out of its dealer network. The reason? He wasn't buying enough tyres. Says Hauck, 'I just don't understand why they would cut the legs out from under people who have been loyal to them all these years.'[1]

Channel conflict: Goodyear's conflicts with its independent dealers have caused hard feelings and flattened the company's replacement tyre sales.

Source: Photo by Joe and Kathy Heiner.

Some conflict in the channel takes the form of healthy competition. Such competition can be good for the channel – without it, the channel could become passive and non-innovative. But severe or prolonged conflict, as in the case of Goodyear, can disrupt channel effectiveness and cause lasting harm to channel relationships. Companies should manage channel conflict to keep it from getting out of hand.

Vertical marketing systems

For the channel as a whole to perform well, each channel member's role must be specified and channel conflict must be managed. The channel will perform better if it includes a firm, agency, or mechanism that provides leadership and has the power to assign roles and manage conflict.

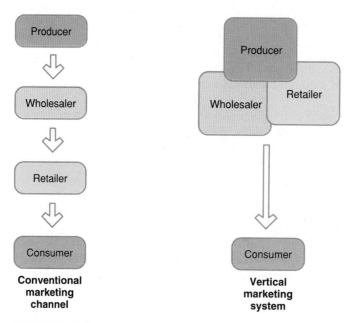

FIGURE 10.3

Comparison of conventional distribution channel with vertical marketing system

Historically, *conventional distribution channels* have lacked such leadership and power, often resulting in damaging conflict and poor performance. One of the biggest channel developments over the years has been the emergence of *vertical marketing systems* that provide channel leadership. Figure 10.3 contrasts the two types of channel arrangements.

A **conventional distribution channel** consists of one or more independent producers, wholesalers and retailers. Each is a separate business seeking to maximise its own profits, perhaps even at the expense of the system as a whole. No channel member has much control over the other members, and no formal means exists for assigning roles and resolving channel conflict.

In contrast, a **vertical marketing system (VMS)** consists of producers, wholesalers and retailers acting as a unified system. One channel member owns the others, has contracts with them, or wields so much power that they must all cooperate. The VMS can be dominated by the producer, wholesaler or retailer.

We look now at three major types of VMSs: *corporate, contractual* and *administered*. Each uses a different means for setting up leadership and power in the channel.

Corporate VMS

A **corporate VMS** integrates successive stages of production and distribution under single ownership. Coordination and conflict management are attained through regular organisational channels. For example, UK confectionery manufacturer Thornton's sells 80 per cent of its products through the company's own stores.[2] The fantasy games company Games Workshop designs, manufactures, distributes and retails its own range of products, so retaining complete control over the entire vertical marketing system.[3] And little-known Italian eyewear maker Luxottica produces many famous eyewear brands – including Ray-Ban, Vogue, Anne Klein, Ferragamo and Bvlgari. It then sells these brands through two of the world's largest optical chains, LensCrafters and Sunglass Hut, which it also owns.[4]

Controlling the entire distribution chain has turned Spanish clothing chain Zara into the world's fastest-growing fashion retailer.

The secret to Zara's success is its control over almost every aspect of the supply chain, from design and production to its own worldwide distribution network. Zara makes 40 per cent of its own fabrics and produces more than half of its own clothes, rather than relying on a hotchpotch of slow-moving suppliers. New styles take shape in Zara's own design centres, supported by real-time sales data. New designs feed into Zara manufacturing centres, which ship finished products directly to 741 Zara stores in 54 countries, saving time, eliminating the need for warehouses, and keeping inventories low. Effective vertical integration makes Zara faster, more flexible, and more efficient than international competitors such as Gap, Benetton, and Sweden's H&M. Its finely-tuned distribution systems makes Zara seem more like Dell or Wal-Mart than Gucci or Louis Vuitton. Zara can make a new line from start to finish in less than 15 days, so a look seen on MTV can be in Zara stores within a month, versus an industry average of nine months. And Zara's low costs let it offer mid-market chic at downmarket prices. The company's stylish but affordable offerings have attracted a cult following, and the company's sales have more than doubled to $4.9 billion in the past six years.[5]

Contractual VMS

A **contractual VMS** consists of independent firms at different levels of production and distribution who join together through contracts to obtain more economies or sales impact than each could achieve alone. Coordination and conflict management are attained through contractual agreements among channel members.

The **franchise organisation** is the most common type of contractual relationship – a channel member called a *franchisor* links several stages in the production-distribution process. Although McDonald's is undoubtedly the best-known franchise in Europe, as it is around the world, Europe boasts many home-grown franchises. Almost every kind of business has been franchised – from hotels and fast-food restaurants to dental centres and dating agencies, from wedding consultants and maid services to fitness centres and undertaker services. The largest European franchise operations include '5 à sec' dry-cleaners from France, Paellador restaurants from Spain, Groscek convenience stores from Poland, and Chemex International commercial cleaning services from the UK.[6]

There are three types of franchises. The first type is the *manufacturer-sponsored retailer franchise system* – for example, Peugeot and its network of independent franchised dealers. The second type is the *manufacturer-sponsored wholesaler franchise system* – Coca-Cola licenses bottlers (wholesalers) in various markets who buy Coca-Cola syrup concentrate and then bottle and sell the finished product to retailers in local markets. The third type is the *service firm-sponsored retailer franchise system* – examples are found in the commercial cleaning business (Chemex International, Swisher), the fast-food service business (McDonald's, Paellador), and the hotel business (Mercure, Ibis, Travelodge).

The fact that most consumers cannot tell the difference between

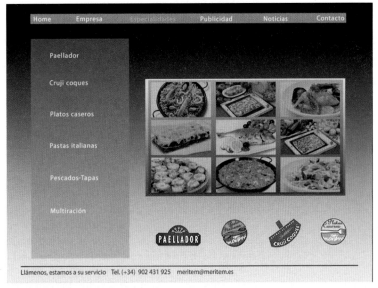

European franchising operations such as Paellador compete with global brands like McDonald's in the fast-food business.

Source: http://www.paellador.es

contractual and corporate VMSs shows how successfully the contractual organisations compete with corporate chains.

Administered VMS

In an **administered VMS**, leadership is assumed not through common ownership or contractual ties but through the size and power of one or a few dominant channel members. Manufacturers of a top brand can obtain strong trade cooperation and support from resellers. For example, Danone, Louis Vuitton and L'Oréal can command unusual cooperation from resellers regarding displays, shelf space, promotions and price policies. Large retailers such as Carrefour and Tesco can exert strong influence on the manufacturers that supply the products they sell.

Horizontal marketing systems

Another channel development is the **horizontal marketing system**, in which two or more companies at one level join together to follow a new marketing opportunity. By working together, companies can combine their financial, production, or marketing resources to accomplish more than any one company could alone.

Companies might join forces with competitors or non-competitors. They might work with each other on a temporary or permanent basis, or they may create a separate company. For example, banks often install automated teller machines (ATMs) on the premises of major retailers, delivering mutual benefits to the customer, the retailer and the bank itself. Similarly, both the coffee bar company Costa and the bookshop chain Waterstone's clearly believe that their businesses benefit from having Costa coffee bars located in Waterstone's stores. Customers can stay in the store longer, rather than leaving to find a separate coffee shop when their book browsing makes them thirsty.

Such channel arrangements also work well globally. For example, because of its excellent coverage of international markets, Nestlé jointly sells General Mills's cereal brands in 80 countries outside North America. Similarly, Coca-Cola and Nestlé formed a joint venture, Beverage Partners Worldwide, to market ready-to-drink coffees, teas and flavoured milks in more than 40 countries worldwide. Coke provides worldwide experience in marketing and distributing beverages, and Nestlé contributes two established brand names – Nescafé and Nestea.[7]

Multichannel distribution systems

In the past, many companies used a single channel to sell to a single market or market segment. Today, with the proliferation of customer segments and channel possibilities, more and more companies have adopted **multichannel distribution systems** – often called *hybrid marketing channels*. Such multichannel marketing occurs when a single firm sets up two or more marketing channels to reach one or more customer segments. The use of multichannel systems has increased greatly in recent years.

Figure 10.4 shows a hybrid channel. In the figure, the producer sells directly to consumer segment 1 using direct-mail catalogues, telemarketing and the Internet, and reaches consumer segment 2 through retailers. It sells indirectly to business segment 1 through distributors and dealers and to business segment 2 through its own sales force.

These days, almost every large company and many small ones distribute through multiple channels. The Spanish banking organisation Grupo Santander is well established in both Europe and Latin America, and reaches customers by telephone, over the Internet, and through its branch offices. The office supplies company Staples originated in the USA but now operates in 22 countries, with stores in the UK, Germany, the Netherlands, Portugal, and catalogue businesses in several other European countries including Italy, Spain, Poland and Hungary. Staples markets through its traditional retail outlets, a direct-response Internet site, virtual malls, and 30,000 links on affiliated sites.

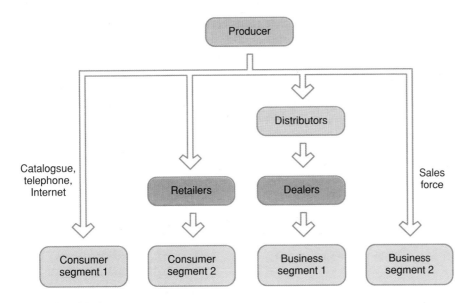

FIGURE 10.4

Hybrid marketing channel

Siemens uses multiple channels to serve dozens of segments and niches, ranging from large corporate and institutional buyers to small businesses to home office buyers. The Siemens sales force sells the company's information technology equipment and services to large and mid-size business customers. Siemens also sells through a network of distributors and value-added resellers, which sell Siemens computers, systems and services to a variety of special business segments. Home office buyers can buy Fujitsu Siemens personal computers and printers from speciality computer stores or any of several large retailers. And both business and home office buyers can buy directly from Siemens by phone or online from the company's websites (the corporate website is **www.siemens.com**, and from there you can navigate to individual country web sites such as **www.siemens.ua**, the Ukrainian site).

Multichannel distribution systems offer many advantages to companies facing large and complex markets. With each new channel, the company expands its sales and market coverage and gains opportunities to tailor its products and services to the specific needs of diverse customer segments. But such multichannel systems are harder to control, and they generate conflict as more channels compete for customers and sales. For example, when Siemens began selling directly to customers through its own website, many of its retail dealers were concerned that they might lose sales.

Changing channel organisation

Changes in technology and the explosive growth of direct and online marketing are having a profound impact on the nature and design of marketing channels. One major trend is toward **disintermediation** – a big term with a clear message and important consequences. Disintermediation occurs when product or service producers cut out intermediaries and go directly to final buyers, or when radically new types of channel intermediaries displace traditional ones.

Thus, in many industries traditional intermediaries are dropping by the wayside. For example, companies such as Dell and easyJet sell directly to final buyers, cutting retailers out of their marketing channels altogether. In other cases, new forms of resellers are displacing traditional intermediaries. For example, e-commerce is growing rapidly, taking business from traditional bricks-and-mortar retailers. Consumers can buy flowers from Interflora (**www.interflora.com**), clothes from H&M (hm.com), and books, videos, toys, jewellery, consumer electronics and almost anything else from amazon.com or their national Amazon website (amazon.co.uk, amazon.fr, amazon.de) – all without ever stepping into a traditional retail store. And online music download services such as iTunes and Napster are threatening the very existence of traditional music-store retailers (see Marketing at Work 10.1).

MARKETING AT WORK 10.1

Disintermediation: The music industry dances to a new iTune

Buying music can be a pretty frustrating experience. Perhaps you can identify with the following scenario:

You whistle a happy tune as you stroll into the Zavvi music store to do a little music shopping. You pick up The Best of 50 Cent *and decide that while it might be somebody's idea of 'best of' it isn't yours and is missing some of your favourite tracks.* Back to Black *by Amy Winehouse looks good, but your friends have found that one or two of the tracks are not quite as good as the rest of the album. Taking a look at Usher's* Here I Stand *you think to yourself that there must be a few great tracks on there but you don't really want to buy all 19 on the album. Why do they keep insisting that you buy an entire CD when you can just go online and get only the tunes you really want from iTunes or the Nokia online Music Store, and pay around one euro, or 80 pence for each track? Fed up, you walk away without buying anything.*

Experiences like these, coupled with revolutionary changes in the way music is being distributed and purchased, have thrown the music industry into turmoil. Today, online music download services offer an attractive alternative to buying standard CDs from the limited assortments of traditional music retailers. Instead, you can go online, choose from hundreds of thousands of individual tracks, digitally download one or a dozen in any of several formats, burn them onto a CD or dump them into your iPod, and listen to them wherever and whenever you please.

It seems like everyone is getting into the music download business these days. Coffee chain Starbucks opened an in-store music service – Hear Music – letting customers burn downloaded tracks onto CDs while sipping their lattes. Today's mobile phone almost always has a built-in MP3 player so that you can download music direct to your phone and carry it with you wherever you go. And fearsome competitors like Microsoft, Yahoo! and Sony have launched their own online music stores.

These new distribution options are great for consumers. But the new channel forms threaten the very existence of traditional music retailers. There's even a fancy word to describe this phenomenon – *disintermediation*. Strictly speaking, disintermediation means the elimination of a layer of intermediaries from a marketing channel – skipping a step between the source of a product or service and its consumers. For example, when Dell began selling personal computers directly to consumers, it eliminated – or disintermediated – retailers from the traditional PC distribution channel.

More broadly, disintermediation includes not only the elimination of channel levels through direct marketing but also the displacement of traditional resellers by radically new types of intermediaries. For example, only a few decades ago, most recorded music was sold through independent music retailers or small chains. Many of these smaller retailers were later disintermediated by large speciality music superstores, such as Tower Records, Virgin Records (now Zavvi) and HMV. The superstores, in turn, have faced growing competition from general discount retailers such as Carrefour and Asda. Believe it or not, American retailer Wal-Mart is currently the world's number one CD seller.

Now, the surge of new online music sellers is threatening to make traditional CD sellers obsolete. Retail CD sales have dropped continuously since 1999 – the year Napster (the original music download site) was launched. Traditional music retailers are finding it difficult to compete and some of them have left the business altogether. Things are not likely to get better for the traditional stores. One retail consultant predicts that half of today's music stores will be out of business within five years and that, eventually, 'CDs, DVDs, and other forms of physical media will become obsolete'.

Disintermediation: online music download services, such as Apple's iTunes, are threatening to make traditional CD sellers obsolete.
Source: PA Photos/Walter Bieri/AP.

per-song rates. Finally, the old retailing model of selling CDs like they were LP vinyl records doesn't work so well any more. That was fine in an era when people had one stereo in the living room and maybe one in the kids' room. But now consumers want music in a variety of formats that they can play anywhere, anytime: on home hi-fi systems, boomboxes, car stereos, computers, MP3 players like the iPod and, of course, on their mobile phones.

Thus, disintermediation is a big word but the meaning is clear. Disintermediation occurs only when a new channel form succeeds in serving customers better than the old channels. Marketers who continually seek new ways to create real value for customers have little to fear. However, those who fall behind in adding value risk being swept aside. Will today's music store retailers survive? It's an open question.

How are the traditional retailers responding to the disintermediation threat? Some are following the 'if you can't beat them, join them' principle by creating their own downloading services. And music stores do still have several advantages over their online counterparts. The stores have a larger base of existing customers, and a physical store provides a shopping experience for customers that's difficult to duplicate online. Retailers can morph their stores into comfortable, sociable gathering spots were people hang out, chat with friends, listen to music, go to album signings, and perhaps attend a live performance.

But the traditional store retailers also face daunting economics. Store rents are rising while CD prices are falling. And running stores generates considerable inventory and store operating costs. New online entrants face none of those traditional distribution costs. Moreover, whereas store retailers can physically stock only a limited number of in-print titles, the music download sites can provide millions of selections and offer out-of-print songs.

What's more, whereas music stores are stuck selling precompiled CDs at album prices, music download sites let customers buy only the songs they want at low

Sources: Opening extract based on Paul Keegan, 'Is the Music Store Over?', *Business 2.0*, March 2004, pp. 114–18. Other quotes and information from Lorin Cipolla, 'Music's on the Menu', *Promo*, 1 May 2004; Sarah E. Lockyer, 'Full Steam Ahead', *Nation's Restaurant News*, 3 May 2004, p. 4; Peter Lewis, 'Drop a Quarter in the Internet', *Fortune*, 22 March 2004, p. 56; Erik Gruenwedel, 'Tower Records Spins Profits, Suitors', *Video Store Magazine*, 5–11 December 2004, p. 8; Mike Hughlett, 'More Companies Enter Musical Phone Field', *Knight Ridder Tribune News*, 16 June 2005, p. 1; and 'How to Get Your Music Mobile', *Music Week*, 25 June 2005, p. S11.

Disintermediation presents problems and opportunities for both producers and intermediaries. To avoid being swept aside, traditional intermediaries must find new ways to add value in the supply chain. To remain competitive, product and service producers must develop new channel opportunities, such as Internet and other direct channels. However, developing these new channels often brings them into direct competition with their established channels, resulting in conflict.

To ease this problem, companies often look for ways to make going direct a plus for the entire channel. For example, Bosch knows that many customers would prefer to buy its power tools and outdoor power equipment online. But selling directly through its website would create conflicts with important and powerful retail partners. So, while

Source: Corbis/Ken Seet.

Rather than selling directly from their own website, Bosch refer buyers to resellers' websites or stores.

Bosch's website provides detailed information about the company's products, you can't buy a Bosch cordless screwdriver, rotary hammer, power saw, or anything else there. Instead, the Bosch site refers you to resellers' websites and stores. Thus, Bosch's direct marketing helps both the company and its channel partners.

CHANNEL DESIGN DECISIONS

We now look at several channel decisions manufacturers face. In designing marketing channels, manufacturers struggle between what is ideal and what is practical. A new firm with limited capital usually starts by selling in a limited market area. Deciding on the best channels might not be a problem. The problem might simply be how to convince one or a few good intermediaries to handle the line.

If successful, the new firm can branch out to new markets through the existing intermediaries. In smaller markets, the firm might sell directly to retailers; in larger markets, it might sell through distributors. In one region, it might grant exclusive franchises; in another, it might sell through all available outlets. Then, it might add a Web store that sells directly to hard-to-reach customers. In this way, channel systems often evolve to meet market opportunities and conditions.

For maximum effectiveness, however, channel analysis and decision-making should be more purposeful. Designing a channel system calls for analysing consumer needs, setting channel objectives, identifying major channel alternatives and evaluating them.

Analysing consumer needs

As noted previously, marketing channels are part of the overall *customer value-delivery network*. Each channel member adds value for the customer. Thus, designing the marketing channel starts with finding out what target consumers want from the channel. Do consumers want to buy from nearby locations or are they willing to travel to more distant centralised locations? Would they rather buy in person, over the phone, through the mail, or via the Internet? Do they value breadth of assortment or do they prefer specialisation? Do consumers want many add-on services (delivery, credit, repairs, installation), or will they obtain these elsewhere? The faster the delivery, the greater the assortment provided, and the more add-on services supplied, the greater the channel's service level.

Providing the fastest delivery, greatest assortment and most services may not be possible or practical. The company and its channel members may not have the resources or skills needed to provide all the desired services. Also, providing higher levels of service results in higher costs for the channel and higher prices for consumers. The company must balance consumer needs not only against the feasibility and costs of meeting these needs but also against customer price preferences. The success of discount retailing shows that consumers will often accept lower service levels in exchange for lower prices.

Setting channel objectives

Companies should state their marketing channel objectives in terms of targeted levels of customer service. Usually, a company can identify several segments wanting different levels of service. The company should decide which segments to serve and the best channels to use in each case. In each segment, the company wants to minimise the total channel cost of meeting customer service requirements.

The company's channel objectives are also influenced by the nature of the company, its products, its marketing intermediaries, its competitors and the environment. For example, the company's size and financial situation determine which marketing functions it can handle itself and which it must give to intermediaries. Companies selling perishable products may require more direct marketing to avoid delays and too much handling.

In some cases, a company may want to compete in or near the same outlets that carry competitors' products. In other cases, producers may avoid the channels used by competitors. Mary Kay Cosmetics, for example, sells direct to consumers through its corps of more than 1 million independent beauty consultants in 34 markets worldwide, among them Finland, Moldova, Norway, Poland, Slovakia and Ukraine, rather than going head-to-head with other cosmetics makers for scarce positions in retail stores. Directline markets insurance directly to consumers via the telephone and the Web rather than through agents.

Finally, environmental factors such as economic conditions and legal constraints may affect channel objectives and design. For example, in a depressed economy, producers want to distribute their goods in the most economical way, using shorter channels and dropping unneeded services that add to the final price of the goods.

Identifying major alternatives

When the company has defined its channel objectives, it should next identify its major channel alternatives in terms of *types* of intermediaries, the *number* of intermediaries and the *responsibilities* of each channel member.

Types of intermediaries

A firm should identify the types of channel members available to carry out its channel work. For example, suppose a manufacturer of test equipment has developed an audio device that detects poor mechanical connections in machines with moving parts. Company executives think this product would have a market in all industries in which electric, combustion or steam engines are made or used. The company's current sales force is small, and the problem is how best to reach these different industries. The following channel alternatives might emerge:

- *Company sales force*: Expand the company's direct sales force. Assign outside salespeople to territories and have them contact all prospects in the area, or develop separate company sales forces for different industries. Or, add an inside telesales operation in which telephone salespeople handle small or mid-size companies.

- *Manufacturer's agency*: Hire manufacturer's agents – independent firms whose sales forces handle related products from many companies – in different regions or industries to sell the new test equipment.

- *Industrial distributors*: Find distributors in the different regions or industries who will buy and carry the new line. Give them exclusive distribution, good margins, product training and promotional support.

Number of marketing intermediaries

Companies must also determine the number of channel members to use at each level. Three strategies are available: intensive distribution exclusive distribution and selective distribution. Producers of convenience products and common raw materials typically seek **intensive distribution** – a strategy in which they stock their products in as many outlets as possible. These products must be available where and when consumers want them. For example, toothpaste, confectionery and other similar items are sold in millions of outlets to provide maximum brand exposure and consumer convenience. Nestlé, Danone, Cadbury-Schweppes and other consumer goods companies distribute their products in this way.

By contrast, some producers purposely limit the number of intermediaries handling their products. The extreme form of this practice is **exclusive distribution**, in which the producer gives only a limited number of dealers the exclusive right to distribute its products in their territories. Exclusive distribution is often found in the distribution of luxury cars and exclusive women's clothing. For example, Bentley dealers are few and far between – even large cities may have only one dealer. By granting exclusive distribution, Bentley gains stronger distributor selling support and more control over dealer prices, promotion, credit and services. Exclusive distribution also enhances the car's image and allows for higher mark-ups.

Between intensive and exclusive distribution lies **selective distribution** – the use of more than one, but fewer than all, of the intermediaries who are willing to carry a company's products. Most television, furniture and home appliance brands are distributed in this manner. For example, Zanussi-Electrolux, Beko and Miele sell their major appliances through dealer networks and selected large retailers. By using selective distribution, they can develop good working relationships with selected channel members and expect a better than average selling effort. Selective distribution gives producers good market coverage with more control and less cost than does intensive distribution.

Responsibilities of channel members

The producer and intermediaries need to agree on the terms and responsibilities of each channel member. They should agree on price policies, conditions of sale, territorial rights and specific services to be performed by each party. The producer should establish a list price and a fair set of discounts for intermediaries. It must define each channel member's territory, and it should be careful about where it places new resellers.

Mutual services and duties need to be spelled out carefully, especially in franchise and exclusive distribution channels. For example, McDonald's provides franchisees with promotional support, a record-keeping system, training at Hamburger University and general management assistance. In turn, franchisees must meet company standards for physical facilities, cooperate with new promotion programmes, provide requested information and buy specified food products.

Evaluating the major alternatives

Suppose a company has identified several channel alternatives and wants to select the one that will best satisfy its long-term objectives. Each alternative should be evaluated against economic, control and adaptive criteria.

Using *economic criteria*, a company compares the likely sales, costs and profitability of different channel alternatives. What will be the investment required by each channel alternative, and what returns will result? The company must also consider *control issues*. Using intermediaries usually means giving them some control over the marketing of the product, and some intermediaries take more control than others. Other things being equal, the company prefers to keep as much control as possible. Finally, the company must apply *adaptive criteria*. Channels often involve long-term commitments, yet the company wants to keep the channel flexible so that it can adapt to environmental changes. A channel that involves long-term commitments must deliver superior economic returns or better control.

Designing international distribution channels

International marketers face many additional complexities in designing their channels. Each country has its own unique distribution system that has evolved over time and changes very slowly. These channel systems can vary widely from country to country. Thus, global marketers usually adapt their channel strategies to the existing structures within each country.

In some markets, the distribution system is complex and hard to penetrate, consisting of many layers and large numbers of intermediaries. Consider Japan:

> The Japanese distribution system stems from the early seventeenth century when cottage industries and a [quickly growing] urban population spawned a merchant class . . . Despite Japan's economic achievements, the distribution system has remained remarkably faithful to its antique pattern . . . [It] encompasses a wide range of wholesalers and other agents, brokers, and retailers . . . There are myriad tiny retail shops. An even greater number of wholesalers supplies goods to them, layered tier upon tier . . . For example, soap may move through three wholesalers plus a sales company after it leaves the manufacturer before it ever reaches the retail outlet . . . The distribution network . . . reflects the traditionally close ties among many Japanese companies . . . [and places] much greater emphasis on personal relationships with users . . . Although [these channels appear] inefficient and cumbersome, they seem to serve the Japanese customer well . . . Lacking much storage space in their small homes, most Japanese homemakers shop several times a week and prefer convenient [and more personal] neighbourhood shops.[8]

Many Western firms have had great difficulty breaking into the closely knit, tradition-bound Japanese distribution network.

At the other extreme, distribution systems in developing countries may be scattered and inefficient, or altogether lacking. For example, China and India are huge markets, each with populations of over 1 billion. However, because of inadequate distribution systems, most companies can profitably access only a small portion of the population located in each country's most affluent cities. 'China is a very decentralized market,' notes a China trade expert. '[It's] made up of two dozen distinct markets sprawling across 2,000 cities. Each has its own culture . . . It's like operating in an asteroid belt.' China's distribution system is so fragmented that logistics costs amount to 15 per cent of the nation's GDP, far higher than in most other countries.[9]

Thus, international marketers face a wide range of channel alternatives. Designing efficient and effective channel systems between and within various country markets poses a difficult challenge. We discuss international distribution decisions further in Chapter 15.

CHANNEL MANAGEMENT DECISIONS

Once the company has reviewed its channel alternatives and decided on the best channel design, it must implement and manage the chosen channel. Channel management calls for selecting, managing and motivating individual channel members and evaluating their performance over time.

Selecting channel members

Producers vary in their ability to attract qualified marketing intermediaries. Some producers have no trouble signing up channel members. For example, with a globally prestigious motorcar brand such as Lexus, there will never be any difficulty in attracting dealers in practically any part of Europe or the rest of the world. But things are different for a less prestigious brand such as Skoda, particularly in the rich economies of Western Europe.

When selecting intermediaries, the company should determine what characteristics distinguish the better ones. It will want to evaluate each channel member's years in business, other lines carried, growth and profit record, cooperativeness and reputation. If the intermediaries are sales agents, the company will want to evaluate the number and character of other lines carried and the size and quality of the sales force. If the intermediary is a retail store that wants exclusive or selective distribution, the company will want to evaluate the store's customers, location and future growth potential.

Managing and motivating channel members

Once selected, channel members must be continuously managed and motivated to do their best. The company must sell not only *through* the intermediaries but *to* and *with* them. Most companies see their intermediaries as first-line customers and partners. They practise strong *partner relationship management (PRM)* to forge long-term partnerships with channel members. This creates a marketing system that meets the needs of both the company *and* its marketing partners.

In managing its channels, a company must convince distributors that they can succeed better by working together as a part of a cohesive value delivery system.[10] Thus, Procter & Gamble and Tesco work together to create superior value for final consumers. They jointly plan merchandising goals and strategies, inventory levels, and advertising and promotion plans.

Many companies are now installing integrated high-tech partner relationship management systems to coordinate their whole-channel marketing efforts. Just as they use customer relationship management (CRM) software systems to help manage relationships with important customers, companies can now use PRM and supply chain management (SCM) software to help recruit, train, organise, manage, motivate and evaluate relationships with channel partners.

Evaluating channel members

The producer must regularly check channel member performance against standards such as sales quotas, average inventory levels, customer delivery time, treatment of damaged and lost goods, cooperation in company promotion and training programmes, and services to the customer. The company should recognise and reward intermediaries who are performing well and adding good value for consumers. Those who are performing poorly should be assisted or, as a last resort, replaced. A company may periodically 'requalify' its intermediaries and prune the weaker ones.

PUBLIC POLICY AND DISTRIBUTION DECISIONS

For the most part, companies are legally free to develop whatever channel arrangements suit them. In fact, the laws affecting channels seek to prevent the exclusionary tactics of some companies that might keep another company from using a desired channel. Most channel law deals with the mutual rights and duties of the channel members once they have formed a relationship.

Many producers and wholesalers like to develop exclusive channels for their products. When the seller allows only certain outlets to carry its products, this strategy is called *exclusive distribution*. When the seller requires that these dealers not handle competitors' products, its strategy is called *exclusive dealing*. Both parties can benefit from exclusive arrangements. The seller obtains more loyal and dependable outlets, and the dealers obtain a steady source of supply and stronger seller support. But exclusive arrangements also exclude other producers from selling to these dealers. This situation brings exclusive dealing contracts under the scope of Article 85(1) of the EU Treaty. One of the principal objectives of establishing the EU was to bring about conditions of free trade, so it is not surprising to find that matters to do with free competition, which can include 'vertical agreements' between channel members, were addressed in the treaty upon which the EU was founded. Article 85(1) prohibits actions which 'have as their object or effect the prevention, restriction or distortion of competition'. In practice, many forms of vertical agreement are allowed under EU competition law, but this is a complex area in which advice from a lawyer with expertise in EU law is likely to be necessary.

Exclusive dealing often includes *exclusive territorial agreements*. The producer may agree not to sell to other dealers in a given area, or the buyer may agree to sell only in its own territory. The first practice is normal under franchise systems as a way to increase dealer enthusiasm and commitment. It is also perfectly legal – a seller has no legal obligation to sell through more outlets than it wishes. The second practice, whereby the producer tries to keep a dealer from selling outside its territory, is a much more contentious issue.

Producers of a strong brand sometimes sell it to dealers only if the dealers will take some or all of the rest of the line. This is called full-line forcing. Such *tying agreements* are not necessarily illegal, but the legal situation will vary depending on the specific anti-competition laws in individual European countries. The practice may prevent consumers from freely choosing among competing suppliers of these other brands.

Finally, producers are free to select their dealers, but their right to terminate dealers is somewhat restricted. In general, sellers can drop dealers 'for cause'. However, they cannot drop dealers if, for example, the dealers refuse to cooperate in a doubtful legal arrangement, such as exclusive dealing or tying agreements.[11]

MARKETING LOGISTICS AND SUPPLY CHAIN MANAGEMENT

In today's global marketplace, selling a product is sometimes easier than getting it to customers. Companies must decide on the best way to store, handle and move their products and services so that they are available to customers in the right assortments, at the right time and in the right place. Physical distribution and logistics effectiveness has a major impact on both customer satisfaction and company costs. Here we consider the nature and importance of logistics management in the supply chain, goals of the logistics system, major logistics functions and the need for integrated supply chain management.

Nature and importance of marketing logistics

To some managers, marketing logistics means only trucks and warehouses. But modern logistics is much more than this. **Marketing logistics** – also called **physical distribution** – involves planning, implementing and controlling the physical flow of goods, services and related information from points of origin to points of consumption to meet customer requirements at a profit. In short, it involves getting the right product to the right customer in the right place at the right time.

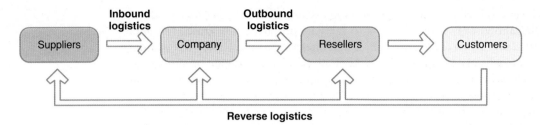

FIGURE 10.5

Supply chain management

In the past, physical distribution typically started with products at the plant and then tried to find low-cost solutions to get them to customers. However, today's marketers prefer customer-centred logistics thinking, which starts with the marketplace and works backward to the factory, or even to sources of supply. Marketing logistics involves not only *outbound distribution* (moving products from the factory to resellers and ultimately to customers) but also *inbound distribution* (moving products and materials from suppliers to the factory) and *reverse distribution* (moving broken, unwanted or excess products returned by consumers or resellers). That is, it involves the entire **supply chain management** – managing upstream and downstream value-added flows of materials, final goods and related information among suppliers, the company, resellers and final consumers, as shown in Figure 10.5.

The logistics manager's task is to coordinate activities of suppliers, purchasing agents, marketers, channel members and customers. These activities include forecasting, information systems, purchasing, production planning, order processing, inventory, warehousing and transportation planning.

Companies today are placing greater emphasis on logistics for several reasons. First, companies can gain a powerful competitive advantage by using improved logistics to give customers better service or lower prices. Second, improved logistics can yield tremendous cost savings to both the company and its customers. As much as 20 per cent of an average product's price is accounted for by shipping and transport alone. This far exceeds the cost of advertising and many other marketing costs. Third, the explosion in product variety has created a need for improved logistics management. For example, 100 years ago a typical grocery store carried only 270 items. The store manager could keep track of this inventory on about 10 pages of notebook paper stuffed in a shirt pocket. Today, the average supermarket carries a bewildering stock of more than 25,000 items. A Carrefour Hypermarché carries more than 100,000 products, 30,000 of which are grocery products. Ordering, shipping, stocking and controlling such a variety of products presents a sizeable logistics challenge.

Finally, improvements in information technology have created opportunities for major gains in distribution efficiency. Today's companies are using sophisticated supply chain management software, Web-based logistics systems, point-of-sale scanners, uniform product codes, satellite tracking, and electronic transfer of order and payment data. Such technology lets them manage the flow of goods, information and finances quickly and efficiently through the supply chain.

Goals of the logistics system

Some companies state their logistics objective as providing maximum customer service at the least cost. Unfortunately, no logistics system can *both* maximise customer service *and* minimise distribution costs. Maximum customer service implies rapid delivery, large inventories, flexible assortments, liberal returns policies and other services – all of which raise distribution costs. In contrast, minimum distribution costs imply slower delivery, smaller inventories and larger shipping lots – which represent a lower level of overall customer service.

The goal of marketing logistics should be to provide a *targeted* level of customer service at the least cost. A company must first research the importance of various distribution services to customers and then set desired service levels for each segment. The objective is to maximise *profits*, not sales. Therefore, the company must weigh the benefits of providing higher levels of service against the costs. Some companies offer less service than their competitors and charge a lower price. Other companies offer more service and charge higher prices to cover higher costs.

Major logistics functions

Given a set of logistics objectives, the company is ready to design a logistics system that will minimise the cost of attaining these objectives. The major logistics functions include *warehousing, inventory management, transportation* and *logistics information management*.

Warehousing

Production and consumption cycles rarely match. Most companies have to store their tangible goods while waiting to sell them. For example, Flymo, Bosch, Honda and other lawnmower manufacturers run their factories all year long and store up products for the heavy spring and summer buying seasons. The storage function overcomes differences in needed quantities and timing, ensuring that products are available when customers are ready to buy them.

A company must decide on *how many* and *what types* of warehouses it needs and *where* they will be located. The company might use either *storage warehouses* or *distribution centres*. Storage warehouses store goods for moderate to long periods. **Distribution centres** are designed to move goods rather than just store them. They are large and highly automated warehouses designed to receive goods from various plants and suppliers, take orders, fill them efficiently, and deliver goods to customers as quickly as possible.

For example, Tesco operates a network of 20 distribution centres in the UK, serving the needs of over 1,250 UK stores. As Tesco expands internationally it opens similar distribution centres in other countries; recently, Tesco has opened new distribution centres in Hungary, Poland and Slovakia. A typical Tesco distribution centre employs around 500 people and handles 100 million cases of products every year.

Like almost everything else these days, warehousing has seen dramatic changes in technology in recent years. Older, multi-storeyed warehouses with outdated materials handling methods are steadily being replaced by newer, single-storeyed *automated warehouses* with advanced, computer-controlled materials handling systems requiring few employees. Computers and scanners read orders and direct lift trucks, electric hoists or robots to gather goods, move them to loading docks and issue invoices.

Inventory management

Inventory management also affects customer satisfaction. Here, managers must maintain the delicate balance between carrying too little inventory and carrying too much. With too little stock, the firm risks not having products when customers want to buy. To remedy this, the firm may need costly emergency shipments or production. Carrying too much inventory results in unnecessarily high inventory carrying costs and stock obsolescence. Thus, in managing inventory, firms must balance the costs of carrying larger inventories against resulting sales and profits.

Many companies have greatly reduced their inventories and related costs through *just-in-time* logistics systems. With such systems, producers and retailers carry only small inventories of parts or merchandise, often only enough for a few days of operations. For example, computer manufacturer Dell is now Ireland's largest exporter. Dell is a master just-in-time producer, and carries just 3–4 days of inventory, whereas competitors might carry 40 days or even 60.[12] New stock arrives exactly when needed, rather than being stored in inventory until being used. Just-in-time systems require accurate forecasting along with fast, frequent and flexible delivery so that new supplies will be available when needed. However, these systems result in substantial savings in inventory carrying and handling costs.

Marketers are always looking for new ways to make inventory management more efficient. It the not too distant future, handling inventory might even become fully automated. For example, in Chapter 3 we discussed RFID or 'smart tag' technology, by which small transmitter chips are embedded in or placed on products and packaging on everything from flowers and razors to tyres. 'Smart' products could make the entire supply chain – which accounts for nearly 75 per cent of a product's cost – intelligent and automated. Companies using RFID would know, at any time, exactly where a product is located physically within the supply chain. 'Smart shelves' would not only tell them when it's time to reorder, but would also place the order automatically with their suppliers. Such exciting new information technology applications will revolutionise distribution as we know it. Many large and resourceful marketing companies, such as Procter & Gamble, IBM and Wal-Mart, are investing heavily to make the full use of RFID technology a reality.[13]

Transportation

The choice of transportation carriers affects the pricing of products, delivery performance and condition of the goods when they arrive – all of which will affect customer satisfaction. In shipping goods to its warehouses, dealers and customers, the company can choose among five main transportation modes: truck, rail, water, pipeline and air, along with an alternative mode for digital products: the Internet.

Trucks have in recent years increased their share of transportation steadily, and offer some advantages that are hard to match. Trucks are highly flexible in their routing and time schedules, and they can usually offer faster service than railways. They are efficient for short hauls of high-value merchandise. Trucking firms have added many services in recent years. For example, Société Norbert Dentressangle SA and most other major carriers now offer everything from satellite tracking and 24-hour shipment information to logistics planning software and 'border ambassadors' who expedite cross-border shipping operations. Norbert Dentressangle is a typical example of a large-scale European trucking operation. Although the company is based in France, 65 per cent of its business serves destinations outside France, and on average the company clocks up 650 crossings of the English Channel every day. However, Norbert Dentressangle and other European transport operators (such as Kühne und Nagel AG of Germany) are all having to face up to the issue of CO_2 emissions; transport in general is a major contributor to Europe's CO_2 emissions, and road transport contributes much the

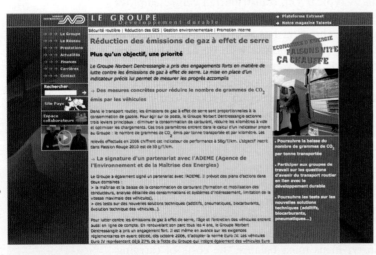

Increasingly, transport operators like Norbert Dentressangle of France have to take account of environmental factors in their strategic planning.

largest share of overall transport emissions. Trucking companies are striving to increase the efficiency of their operations, but with the current European focus on reducing CO_2 emissions in the struggle to avert climate change, they will no doubt come under ever-increasing pressure to reduce the environmental impact of their business.

Railways are one of the most cost-effective modes for shipping large amounts of bulk products – coal, sand, minerals, and farm and forest products – over long distances. In recent years, railways have increased their customer services by designing new equipment to handle special categories of goods, providing flatcars for carrying truck trailers by rail (piggyback), and providing in-transit services such as the diversion of shipped goods to other destinations en route and the processing of goods en route.

Water carriers transport large amounts of goods by ships and barges on European coastal and inland waterways. Although the cost of water transportation is very low for shipping bulky, low-value, non-perishable products such as sand, coal, grain, oil and metallic ores, water transportation is the slowest mode and may be affected by the weather. Both rail transport and water transport produce less CO_2 per kilometre than road transport, so that European policy makers prefer these transport modes to road transport wherever possible.

Pipelines, which account for about 16 per cent of cargo tonne-kilometres, are a specialised means of shipping oil, natural gas and chemicals from sources to markets. Most pipelines are used by their owners to ship their own products.

Although *airfreight* contributes only a small percentage of freight miles, this is still an important freight transportation mode. Airfreight rates are much higher than rail or truck rates, but airfreight is ideal when speed is needed or distant markets have to be reached. Among the most frequently airfreighted products are perishables (fresh fish, cut flowers) and high-value, low-bulk items (technical instruments, jewellery). Companies find that airfreight also reduces inventory levels, packaging costs and the number of warehouses needed. Of course, air transport performs relatively poorly on environmental grounds (for example, in terms of CO_2 emissions). Some consumer activists are encouraging consumers to avoid products that have been transported by air, in order to discourage the use of airfreight other than for essential purposes.

The *Internet* carries digital products from producer to customer via satellite, cable modem or telephone wire. Software firms, the media, music companies and education all make use of the Internet to transport digital products. While these firms primarily use traditional transportation to distribute CDs, newspapers and more, the Internet holds the potential for lower product distribution costs. Whereas planes, trucks and trains move freight and packages, digital technology moves information bits.

Shippers also use **intermodal transportation** – combining two or more modes of transportation. *Piggyback* describes the use of rail and trucks; *fishyback*, water and trucks; *trainship*, water and rail; and *airtruck*, air and trucks. Combining modes provides advantages that no single mode can deliver. Each combination offers advantages to the shipper. For example, not only is piggyback cheaper than trucking alone but it also provides flexibility, convenience and potential environmental benefits.

In choosing a transportation mode for a product, shippers must balance many considerations: speed, dependability, availability, cost and others. Thus, if a shipper needs speed, air and truck are the prime choices. If the goal is low cost, then water or pipeline might be best. Increasingly, shippers will also have to take account of the environmental impact of their operations, because of pressure from European policy makers and consumers.

Logistics information management

Companies manage their supply chains through information. Channel partners often link up to share information and to make better joint logistics decisions. From a logistics perspective, information flows such as customer orders, billing, inventory levels and even customer data are closely linked to channel performance. The company wants to design a simple, accessible, fast and accurate process for capturing, processing and sharing channel information.

Information can be shared and managed in many ways – by mail or telephone, through salespeople, or through traditional or Internet-based *electronic data interchange (EDI)*, the computerised exchange of data between organisations. EDI has existed since well before the emergence of the Internet, and has been advocated as a mechanism by which the less-developed countries of Europe can improve their economic conditions. For example, EDI was developed in Slovenia in the 1990s, with a focus on the automotive, trade, transportation and financial sectors, in order to promote economic growth.[14] Some car manufacturers make the use of EDI compulsory for any supplier that wants to do business with them.[15]

In some cases, suppliers might actually be asked to generate orders and arrange deliveries for their customers. Many large retailers – such as Tesco and Homebase – work closely with major suppliers such as Procter & Gamble or Black & Decker to set up *vendor-managed inventory (VMI)* systems or *continuous inventory replenishment* systems. Using VMI, the customer shares real-time data on sales and current inventory levels with the supplier. The supplier then takes full responsibility for managing inventories and deliveries. Some retailers even go so far as to shift inventory and delivery costs to the supplier. Such systems require close cooperation between the buyer and seller.

Integrated logistics management

Today, more and more companies are adopting the concept of **integrated logistics management**. This concept recognises that providing better customer service and trimming distribution costs require *teamwork*, both inside the company and among all the marketing channel organisations. Inside, the company's various departments must work closely together to maximise the company's own logistics performance. Outside, the company must integrate its logistics system with those of its suppliers and customers to maximise the performance of the entire distribution system.

Cross-functional teamwork inside the company

In most companies, responsibility for various logistics activities is assigned to many different functional units – marketing, sales, finance, operations, purchasing. Too often, each function tries to optimise its own logistics performance without regard for the activities of the other functions. However, transportation, inventory, warehousing and order-processing activities interact, often in unexpected ways. Lower inventory levels reduce inventory carrying costs. But they may also reduce customer service and increase costs from stockouts, back orders, special production runs and costly fast-freight shipments. Because distribution activities involve strong trade-offs, decisions by different functions must be coordinated to achieve better overall logistics performance.

The goal of **integrated supply chain management** is to harmonise all of the company's logistics decisions. Close working relationships among functions can be achieved in several ways. Some companies have created permanent logistics committees, made up of managers responsible for different physical distribution activities. Companies can also create supply chain manager positions that link the logistics activities of functional areas. For example, Procter & Gamble has created supply managers, who manage all of the supply chain activities for each of its product categories. Many companies have a vice president of logistics with cross-functional authority. Finally, companies can employ sophisticated, system-wide supply chain management software, now available from wide range of suppliers.[16] The important thing is that the company must coordinate its logistics and marketing activities to create high market satisfaction at a reasonable cost.

Building logistics partnerships

Companies must do more than improve their own logistics. They must also work with other channel partners to improve whole-channel distribution. The members of a distribution channel are linked closely in creating customer value and building customer relationships. One company's distribution system is another company's supply system. The success of each channel member depends on the performance of the entire supply chain. For example, Carrefour can charge the lowest retail prices only if its entire supply chain – consisting of thousands of merchandise suppliers, transport companies, warehouses and service providers – operates at maximum efficiency.

Smart companies coordinate their logistics strategies and forge strong partnerships with suppliers and customers to improve customer service and reduce channel costs. Many companies have created *cross-functional, cross-company teams*. Other companies partner through *shared projects*. For example, many large retailers are working closely with suppliers on in-store programmes. Clearly, both the supplier and the customer benefit from such partnerships. The point is that all supply chain members must work together in the cause of serving final consumers.

Third-party logistics

Most big companies love to make and sell their products. But many loathe the associated logistics 'grunt work'. They detest the bundling, loading, unloading, sorting, storing, reloading, transporting, customs-clearing and tracking required to supply their factories and to get products out to customers. They hate it so much that a growing number of firms now outsource some or all of their logistics to **third-party logistics (3PL) providers**.

These '3PLs' – companies such as CEVA Logistics, UPS Supply Chain Services, or FedEx Logistics – help clients to tighten up sluggish, overstuffed supply chains, slash inventories and get products to customers more quickly and reliably. CEVA Logistics employs over 50,000 people and operates from over 1,000 locations in over 100 countries. In 2008 CEVA Romania, a subsidiary of CEVA Logistics, announced that it had taken over the planning and supply of Pirelli tyres from Pirelli's warehouse in Slatina to all Romanian customers.[17] For another example, UPS's Supply Chain Services, see Marketing at Work 10.2. According to a recent survey of chief logistics executives at Fortune 500 companies, 81 per cent of these companies use third-party logistics (also called *outsourced logistics* or *contract logistics*) services.[18]

Companies use third-party logistics providers for several reasons. First, because getting the product to market is their main focus, these providers can often do it more efficiently and at lower cost. Outsourcing typically results in 15 per cent to 30 per cent cost savings. Second, outsourcing logistics frees a company to focus more intensely on its core business. Finally, integrated logistics companies understand increasingly complex logistics environments. This can be especially helpful to companies attempting to expand their global market coverage. For example, companies distributing their products across Europe face a bewildering array of environmental restrictions that affect logistics, including packaging standards, truck size and weight limits, and noise and emissions pollution controls. By outsourcing its logistics, a company can gain a complete pan-European distribution system without incurring the costs, delays and risks associated with setting up its own system.

MARKETING AT WORK 10.2

UPS: 'Let us manage the supply chain; you focus on what you do best'

It doesn't matter where you go in Europe, or where you go in the world for that matter, UPS will always be close by and ready to handle your parcels for you. Mention UPS, and most people think of one of those familiar brown trucks with a friendly driver, rumbling around their neighbourhood dropping off parcels. That makes sense. The company's 94,000 delivery vehicles deliver more than 4 billion packages each year. Even the company's brown colour has come to mean something special to customers. 'We've been referred to for years as Big Brown,' says a UPS marketing executive. 'People love our drivers, they love our brown trucks, they love everything we do.' Thus was born UPS's current 'What Can Brown Do for You?' marketing campaign.

However, you might be surprised to learn that most of UPS's revenues come not from the residential customers who receive the packages, but from the business customers who send them. And for these business customers, package delivery is just part of a much more complex logistics process that involves purchase orders, inventory, order status checks, invoices, payments, returned merchandise and fleets of delivery vehicles. UPS knows that all these work-a-day logistical concerns can be a nightmare. Moreover, most companies don't see these activities as strategic competencies that give them competitive advantage.

That's where Big Brown comes in. These are exactly the things that UPS does best. Over the years, UPS has grown to become much more than a neighbourhood small package delivery service. It is now a $50 billion corporate giant providing a broad range of logistics solutions. 'UPS is leveraging decades of experience managing its own global delivery network to serve as the traffic manager for Corporate America's sprawling distribution networks,' observes an industry analyst. If it has to do with logistics, at home or abroad, UPS can probably do it better than anyone can.

UPS has the resources to handle the logistics needs of just about any size business. It employs 425,000 people, some 94,000 vehicles (package cars, vans, tractors and motorcycles), 579 aircraft, and more than 1,000 warehouse facilities in 120 countries. UPS serves 90 per cent of the world population and 99 per cent of businesses in the Fortune 1,000.

Beyond moving their packages efficiently around the world, UPS can provide the advice and technical resources needed to help business customers large and small improve their own logistics operations. UPS Consulting advises companies on redesigning logistics systems to align them better with business strategies. UPS Supply Chain Solutions helps customers to synchronise the flow of goods, funds and information up and down their supply chains. UPS Logistics Technologies supplies software that improves customers' distribution efficiency, including street-level route optimisation, territory planning, mobile delivery execution, real-time wireless dispatch and GPS tracking. For example, UPS applied all of these resources to help Ford overhaul its dated distribution system:

For years, the bane of most Ford dealers was the auto maker's antiquated system for getting cars from factory to showroom. Cars could take as long as a month to arrive – that is, when they weren't lost along the way. And Ford was not always able to tell its dealers exactly what was coming, or even what was in inventory at the nearest rail yards. 'We'd lose track of whole trainloads of cars,' recalls Jerry Reynolds, owner of Prestige Ford in Garland, Texas. 'It was crazy.'

But three years ago, Ford handed its tortuous distribution network to an unlikely source: UPS. In a joint venture with the carmaker, UPS redesigned Ford's entire North American delivery network. Ultimately, UPS deployed a tracking system similar to the one it uses to monitor its own 14.1 million packages daily – right down to slapping bar codes on the windshields of the 4 million cars rolling out of Ford's North American plants each year and onto railcars. The result: UPS has cut the time it takes autos to arrive at dealer lots by 40 per cent, to 10 days on average. In the first year alone, that trimmed Ford's inventory carrying costs by $125 million. And the new system makes it easy for dealers to track down the models most in demand. 'It was the most amazing transformation I had ever seen,' marvels dealer Reynolds. 'My last comment to UPS was: "Can you get us spare parts like this?" '

UPS helped German shoemaker Birkenstock to navigate the complexities of international shipping, saving money while at the same time providing better serve to Birkenstock's retailers and customers:

> Thanks to UPS, Birkenstock has slashed the time and money it takes to get its shoes from factories in Germany to US stores. Here's how. In Germany, Birkenstock packs the shoes in crates bar-coded with their final US destination. Then, UPS takes over. It trucks the crates to Rotterdam, and then ships them across the Atlantic to New Jersey ports (instead of routing them through the Panama Canal to Birkenstock's California warehouses). UPS clears incoming shipments through customs and whisks them away to its nearby distribution hub. Minutes after arriving, the crates are opened, shoes are sorted, and brown trucks speed them to any of 3,000 stores. By handing over its keys to UPS, Birkenstock has cut the time it takes to get shoes to stores from as many as

seven weeks to just three weeks. 'Our spring fashion merchandise shipped 100 per cent on time – and it was the first time in history I've been able to say that,' says Birkenstock's chief operating officer.

In all, UPS will undertake just about any logistics task for customers, anything from fixing busted electronics to answering customer phone calls to issuing corporate credit cards.

> For Jockey International, UPS not only manages a warehouse but also handles Internet order fulfilment. Clothing bought on the Jockey website is boxed for shipping by UPS warehouse staffers and delivered by UPS drivers. And if there's a problem, calls are handled by UPS phone reps. Big Brown also handles laptop repairs for Toshiba America, installs X-ray machines in Europe for Philips Medical Systems, and dresses teddy bears for TeddyCrafters.

Thus, for most residential customers, the answer to the question 'What can Brown do for you?' is pretty simple: 'Deliver my package as quickly as possible.' But for UPS's business customers, Big Brown can do much more than just get a Christmas package there on time. It can be a strategic logistics partner, working hand-in-hand with customers to solve their complex logistics problems. UPS's new logistics pitch can be summed up this way: Let us manage the supply chain; you focus on the things that you do best.

Sources: Examples, quotes, and other information adapted from or found in Dean Foust, 'Big Brown's New Bag', *BusinessWeek*, 19 July 2004, pp. 54–6. Reprinted from 19.6.04 issue of *Business Week* by special permission, copyright © 2004 by The McGraw-Hill Companies, Inc.; www.pressroom.ups.com/mediakits/factsheet/0,2305,866,00.html, August 2005, and http://www.ups.com/content/us/en/about/facts/worldwide.html, August 2008. Birkenstock example used with permission of Birkenstock Orthopädie GmbH & Co. KG. See also Nabil Alghalith, 'Competing with IT: The UPS Case', *Journal of American Academy of Business*, September 2005, pp. 7–16.

THE JOURNEY YOU'VE TAKEN Reviewing the concepts

So, what have you learned about distribution channels and integrated supply chain management? Marketing channel decisions are among the most important decisions that management faces. A company's channel decisions directly affect every other marketing decision. Management must make channel decisions carefully, incorporating today's needs with tomorrow's likely selling environment. Some companies pay too little attention to their distribution channels, but others have used imaginative distribution systems to gain competitive advantage.

1 **Explain why companies use marketing channels and discuss the functions these channels perform.**
Most producers use intermediaries to bring their products to market. They try to forge a *marketing channel* (or *distribution channel*) – a set of interdependent organisations involved in the process of making a product or service available for use or consumption by the consumer or business user. Through their contacts, experience, specialisation and scale of operation, intermediaries usually offer the firm more than it can achieve on its own.

Marketing channels perform many key functions. Some help *complete* transactions by gathering and distributing *information* needed for planning and aiding exchange; by developing and spreading persuasive *communications* about an offer; by performing *contact* work – finding and communicating with prospective buyers; by *matching* – shaping and fitting the offer to the buyer's needs; and by entering into *negotiation* to reach an agreement on price and other terms of the offer so that ownership can be transferred. Other functions help to *fulfil* the completed transactions by offering *physical distribution* – transporting and storing goods; *financing* – acquiring and using funds to cover the costs of the channel work; and *risk taking* – assuming the risks of carrying out the channel work.

2 **Discuss how channel members interact and how they organise to perform the work of the channel.**

The channel will be most effective when each member is assigned the tasks it can do best. Ideally, because the success of individual channel members depends on overall channel success, all channel firms should work together smoothly. They should understand and accept their roles, coordinate their goals and activities and cooperate to attain overall channel goals. By cooperating, they can more effectively sense, serve and satisfy the target market. In a large company, the formal organisation structure assigns roles and provides needed leadership. But in a distribution channel made up of independent firms, leadership and power are not formally set. Traditionally, distribution channels have lacked the leadership needed to assign roles and manage conflict. In recent years, however, new types of channel organisations have appeared that provide stronger leadership and improved performance.

3 **Identify the major channel alternatives open to a company.**

Each firm identifies alternative ways to reach its market. Available means vary from direct selling to using one, two, three or more intermediary *channel levels*. Marketing channels face continuous and sometimes dramatic change. Three of the most important trends are the growth of *vertical*, *horizontal* and *multichannel marketing systems*. These trends affect channel cooperation,

conflict and competition. *Channel design* begins with assessing customer channel service needs and company channel objectives and constraints. The company then identifies the major channel alternatives in terms of the *types* of intermediaries, the *number* of intermediaries and the *channel responsibilities* of each. Each channel alternative must be evaluated according to economic, control and adaptive criteria. Channel management calls for selecting qualified intermediaries and motivating them. Individual channel members must be evaluated regularly.

4 **Explain how companies select, motivate and evaluate channel members.**

Producers vary in their ability to attract qualified marketing intermediaries. Some producers have no trouble signing up channel members. Others have to work hard to line up enough qualified intermediaries. When selecting intermediaries, the company should evaluate each channel member's qualifications and select those who best fit its channel objectives. Once selected, channel members must be continuously motivated to do their best. The company must sell not only *through* the intermediaries but *to* them. It should work to forge long-term partnerships with its channel partners to create a marketing system that meets the needs of both the manufacturer *and* the partners. The company must also regularly check channel member performance against established performance standards, rewarding intermediaries who are performing well and assisting or replacing weaker ones.

5 **Discuss the nature and importance of marketing logistics and integrated supply chain management.**

Just as firms are giving the marketing concept increased recognition, more business firms are paying attention to *marketing logistics* (or *physical distribution*). Logistics is an area of potentially high cost savings and improved customer satisfaction. Marketing logistics addresses not only *outbound distribution* but also *inbound distribution* and *reverse distribution*. That is, it involves entire *supply chain management* – managing value-added flows between suppliers, the company, resellers and final users. No logistics system can both maximise customer service and minimise distribution costs. Instead, the goal of logistics management is to provide a *targeted* level of service at the least cost. The major logistics functions include *order processing, warehousing, inventory management* and *transportation*.

The *integrated supply chain management concept* recognises that improved logistics requires teamwork in the form of close working relationships across functional areas inside the company and across various organisations in the supply chain. Companies can achieve logistics harmony among functions by creating cross-functional logistics teams, integrative supply manager positions, and senior-level logistics executives with cross-functional authority. Channel partnerships can take the form of cross-company teams, shared projects and information-sharing systems. Today, some companies are outsourcing their logistics functions to third-party logistics (3PL) providers to save costs, increase efficiency, and gain faster and more effective access to global markets.

NAVIGATING THE KEY TERMS

Administered VMS 344
Channel conflict 340
Channel level 339
Contractual VMS 343
Conventional distribution channel 342
Corporate VMS 342
Direct marketing channel 339
Disintermediation 345
Distribution centre 355

Distribution channel 337
Exclusive distribution 350
Franchise organisation 343
Horizontal marketing system 344
Indirect marketing channel 339
Integrated logistics management 358
Integrated supply chain management 358
Intensive distribution 350

Intermodal transportation 357
Marketing channel 337
Marketing logistics (or physical distribution) 353
Multichannel distribution system 344
Selective distribution 350
Supply chain management 354
Third-party logistics (3PL) provider 359
Vertical marketing system (VMS) 342

NOTES AND REFERENCES

1 Portions of this example adapted from Kevin Kelleher, 'Giving Dealers a Raw Deal', *Business 2.0*, December 2004, pp. 82–4.

2 David Jennings, 'Thornton's: the vertically integrated retailer, questioning the strategy', *International Journal of Retail and Distribution Management*, **29**(4), 2004 pp. 176–87.

3 http://investor.games-workshop.com/about_us.aspx.

4 Matthew Boyle, 'Brand Killers', *Fortune*, 11 August 2003, pp. 89–100; and information accessed at www.giantfood.com and www.luxottica.com/english/profilo_aziendale/index_keyfacts.html, August 2005.

5 Miguel Helft, 'Fashion Fast Forward', *Business 2.0*, May 2002, p. 60; John Tagliabue, 'A Rival to Gap That Operates Like Dell', *New York Times*, 30 May 2003, p. W-1; Susan Reda, 'Retail's Great Race', *Stores*, March 2004, p. 36; Kasra Ferdows, Michael A. Lewis and Jose A.D. Machuca, 'Rapid-Fire Fulfilment', *Harvard Business Review*, November 2004, pp. 104–10; and www.inditex.com, August 2005.

6 Information accessed at www.franchiseeurope.com.

7 Information accessed at www.mind-advertising.com/ch/nestea_ch.htm, and www.nestle.com/Our_Brands/Breakfast_Cereals/Overview/Breakfast+Cereals.htm, August 2005.

8 See Subhash C. Jain, *International Marketing Management*, 3rd edn (Boston: PWS-Kent Publishing, 1990), pp. 489–91. See also Warren J. Keegan, *Global Marketing Management* (Upper Saddle River, NJ: Prentice Hall, 2002), pp. 403–4.

9 Quotes and information from Normandy Madden, 'Two Chinas', *Advertising Age*, 16 August 2004, pp. 1, 22; Dana James, 'Dark Clouds Should Part for International Marketers', *Marketing News*, 7 January 2002, pp. 9, 13. Russell Flannery, 'Red Tape', *Forbes*, 3 March 2003, pp. 97–100; and Russell Flannery, 'China: The Slow Boat', *Forbes*, 12 April 2004, p. 76.

10 For more on channel relationships, see 'Supply Chain Challenges', *Harvard Business Review*, July 2003, pp. 65–73; James C. Anderson and James A. Narus, *Business Market Management*, 2nd edn. (Upper Saddle River, NJ: Prentice Hall, 2004), ch. 9; Jeffery K. Liker and Thomas Y. Choi, 'Building Deep Supplier Relationships', *Harvard Business Review*, December 2004, pp. 104–13; and David Hannon, 'Supplier Relationships Key to Future Success', *Purchasing*, 2 June 2005, pp. 25–9.

11 For a full discussion of laws affecting marketing channels, see Anne Coughlan, Erin Anderson, Louis Stern and Adel El-Ansary, Marketing Channels (Upper Saddle River, NJ: Prentice Hall, 2006), ch. 12.

12 'Adding a Day to Dell', *Traffic World*, 21 February 2005, p. 1; and William Hoffman, 'Dell Ramps Up RFID', *Traffic World*, 18 April 2005, p. 1.

13 See Ann Bednarz, 'IBM Has Some Tall RFID Plans', *Network World*, 2 May 2005, pp. 17–18; 'RFID: From Potential to Reality', *Frozen Food Age*, April 2005, p. 40; Jack Neff, 'P&G Products to Wear Wire', *Advertising Age*, 15 December 2004, pp. 1, 32; Tom Van Riper, 'Retailers Eye RFID Technology to Make Shopping Easier', *Knight Ridder Tribune Business News*, 23 May 2005, p. 1; John S. McClenahen, 'Wal-Mart's Big Gamble', *Industry Week*, April 2005, pp. 42–6; and information accessed online at www.autoidlabs.org, August 2005.

14 Donald J. McCubbrey and Joze Gricar, 'The EDI project in Slovenia: a case study and model for developing countries', *Information Technology and People*, 8(2), 1995, pp. 6–16.

15 Thomas W. Lauer, 'Side effects of mandatory EDI order processing in the automotive supply chain', *Business Process Management Journal*, 6(5), 2000, pp. 366–75.

16 See Martin Grossman, 'The Role of Trust and Collaboration in the Internet-Enabled Supply Chain', *Journal of American Academy of Business*, September 2004, p. 391; and 'Supply Chain Management Systems', *Logistics Today*, 25 January 2005, pp. 30–2.

17 http://www.cevalogistics.com, accessed April 2008.

18 See 'Add Value to Your Supply Chain – Hire a 3PL,' *Materials Management and Distribution*, January–February 2004, p. A3; and Paul Stastny, 'Outsourcing Global Supply Chain Management', *Canadian Transpotation Logistics*, March 2005, pp. 32–4.

CHAPTER 11
Retailing and wholesaling

AFTER STUDYING THIS CHAPTER, YOU SHOULD BE ABLE TO

- explain the roles of retailers and wholesalers in the distribution channel
- describe the major types of retailers and give examples of each
- identify the major types of wholesalers and give examples of each
- explain the marketing decisions facing retailers and wholesalers

THE WAY AHEAD Previewing the concepts

In the previous chapter, you learned the basics of
distribution channel design and management. Now, we'll
look more deeply into the two major intermediary channel
functions, retailing and wholesaling. You already know
something about retailing – you're served every day by
retailers of all shapes and sizes and there is a good
chance you've had some experience of working in a retail
environment. However, you probably know much less about
the horde of wholesalers that work behind the scenes. In this
chapter, we'll navigate through the characteristics of different
kinds of retailers and wholesalers, the marketing decisions
they make and trends for the future.

To start the tour, we'll look at Aldi. This German
supermarket chain is known as a hard discounter – a retailer
that sells goods without requiring customers to pay for
extras like strong brands or extra packaging.

Aldi: Don't discount them

Sean Ennis, *Department of Marketing, University of Strathclyde, Scotland*

Source: Alamy Images/Vario Images GmbH & Co. KG.

Albrecht **Di**scount (**ALDI**) was established by two brothers in Germany in the 1950s. It emerged in response to the economic difficulties experienced by German society after the Second World War. The two brothers had a major disagreement in 1962 and the company was split into two separate operations: Aldi Nord (concentrating mainly in Denmark, France, the Benelux countries and Poland), and Aldi Sud (focusing its efforts in the United Kingdom, Ireland, Austria and Slovenia). Both entities now cooperate in a friendly manner. As a retailer, its underlying philosophy has evolved from the basic principle of offering low prices, focusing on own branded products, carrying a limited number of items (1,000 as compared to 25,000 in the traditional supermarkets), and operating in a basic, no-frills store, with minimal staffing. This approach contrasts strongly against other retailers in an environment where most European consumers have come to expect a wide choice of brands at varying price points.

In an interview the CEO of Aldi in the United Kingdom – Paul Foley – outlined the Aldi strategy by offering the following observations. 'If you sell more versions of a product, you need a bigger store – the customer will still only buy one product. Aldi stores are a cross between a supermarket, a street market and a warehouse.'[1]

Some retailers try to cater for all segments – Aldi very deliberately does not. Foley went on to say 'the bottom end of the market is not that attractive to us. They don't have much money, they don't travel very far and they are very brand conscious. The very top of the market – where the amount of money spent on food is a very small amount of disposable income – is not attractive either. But everything in the middle is fair game.'

Certainly in the United Kingdom, Aldi would appear to be making inroads into the ABC1 social category, where 50 per cent of their customers fall into this category – up 17 per cent from 2007. As economic times get harder, Aldi is becoming a more attractive proposition to the middle-class shopper hoping to make savings. Indeed, Aldi has promised its customers a saving of £30 on a £100 weekly shop when compared to the 'Big Four' supermarkets (Tesco, Asda, Sainsbury's and Morrisons). How can it deliver on this bold promise?

Because it carries so few items, it can purchase very large quantities from its suppliers and is therefore able to offer lower prices. It applies rigorous cost control procedures over all aspects of its operations. The stores are spartan and facilitate ease of handling and display – another source for cost reduction. Long queues at the checkouts and minimal staffing reinforce this image of low cost, low service operations. It does little or no advertising, apart from periodic newsletters that it circulates locally. It specialises in selling staple products such as food, beverages, sanitary articles and other inexpensive household items. Store managers use PDAs to place their orders in the evening and the store is replenished the next day. This puts Aldi into the category known as the 'hard discounter': an operation that pushes prices even lower than the traditional discounters – for cultural and historical reasons, this retailing category is strongly associated with Germany – Lidl being another prime example.

In terms of international expansion, it finances its new store openings from its cash resources, avoiding potential exposure to high loans. The company shuns publicity and moves quietly into new markets. This quiet expansion has taken it to 3.5 per cent of the total European market. In comparison, the market leader – Carrefour – has captured 6.8 per cent.

It should be noted that shopping culture significantly influences how well or badly Aldi performs in a given market. Until recently, Aldi and Lidl struggled to capture a significant slice of the UK market dominated by the likes of Tesco, Sainsbury's, Asda and Morrison. Almost 70 per cent of food sales fall into the hands of these companies. Traditionally, UK shoppers have been more interested in purchasing well-known branded products. Many have turned up their noses at the thought of buying own brands or little known European brands. By contrast, in its home market of Germany – the third biggest retail market in the world, after the USA and Japan – Aldi is in pole position and discounters hold sway. No social stigma is associated with shopping in such stores there and, as a consequence, the focus on low price works very effectively.

Despite the low, low prices, Aldi has done its best to build up a reputation for selling quality products. Its cabinet displays in its head office attest to this observation – where over 50 awards and citations recognising the quality of various products sit proudly on display. It is also worth noting that surveys consistently show that in the German market Aldi is perceived as the

third most respected brand (after Siemens and BMW).

Aldi continues to refine various aspects of its retail strategy. Up to three years ago, of the 1,000 items carried, only 15 fell into the branded category. These were represented by brands such as Marmite, Tetley Teabags and Budweiser. In late 2005, Aldi started to stock a limited number of premium brands such as the Italian confectioner Ferrero, and Procter & Gamble and Kimberley Clark have also signed deals with Aldi.

As the recession and credit crunch begin to take effect in many European markets, it is likely that Aldi will continue to present an even more attractive option to financially-hit shoppers. Increasingly such shoppers are having to look at smarter and more innovative ways of maximising their value from declining disposable incomes. Aldi provides an attractive alternative. A recent advertising campaign in the UK used the following slogans, capturing the essence of Aldi's appeal to the 'smarter' shopper: 'Don't change your lifestyle, change

your supermarket' and 'Spend a little, live a lot'.

Certainly in the United Kingdom, Aldi has been expanding at an even faster rate than the 'Big Four' competitors. Its target is to open one store a week until 1,200 stores are established. Although only holding 3 per cent of the UK market share, the effective management of its costs means that it is very profitable. It will be interesting to see whether Aldi continues to make inroads into the dominance of the traditional supermarkets such as Tesco and Sainsbury's. A lot will depend on the economic outlook. If European economies pick up, shoppers may quickly revert back to the more expensive, branded items when disposable incomes begin to rise. If not, Aldi may benefit from a change in shopping culture as the type of goods it offers become more acceptable. In any event, Aldi has clearly developed a successful value proposition, making it one of the most profitable and successful retailers in Europe.

Source: See note 1 at the end of this chapter.

The Aldi story sets the stage for examining the fast-changing world of today's resellers. This chapter looks at *retailing* and *wholesaling*. In the first section, we look at the nature and importance of retailing, major types of store and non-store retailers, the decisions retailers make and the future of retailing. In the second section, we discuss these same topics as they relate to wholesalers.

RETAILING

What is retailing? We all know that Tesco, Carrefour and H&M are retailers, but so are Avon representatives, Amazon.com, the local Travelodge and a GP seeing patients. **Retailing** includes all the activities involved in selling products or services directly to final consumers for their personal, non-business use. Many institutions – manufacturers, wholesalers and retailers – do retailing. But most retailing is done by **retailers**: businesses whose sales come *primarily* from retailing.

Although most retailing is done in retail stores, in recent years *non-store retailing* has been grxowing much faster than has store retailing. Non-store retailing includes selling to final consumers through direct mail, catalogues, telephone, the Internet, home-shopping TV, home and office parties, door-to-door contact, vending machines and other direct-selling approaches. We discuss such direct-marketing approaches in detail in Chapter 13. In this chapter, we focus on store retailing.

Types of retailers

Retail stores come in all shapes and sizes and new retail types keep emerging. The most important types of retail stores are described in Exhibit 11.1 and discussed in the

Exhibit 11.1 Major store retailer types

Speciality stores
Carry a narrow product line with a deep assortment, such as clothing stores, sporting-goods stores like JD Sports, furniture stores, florists and bookshops. A clothing store would be a *single-line* store, a men's clothing store would be a *limited-line store*, and a men's custom-shirt store would be a *super-speciality* store. Examples: Zara, Gap, JD Sports.

Department stores
Carry several product lines – typically clothing, home furnishings and household goods – with each line operated as a separate department managed by a specialist buyer or merchandiser. Examples: John Lewis, Macy's, Le Printemps and Gostiny Dvor.

Supermarkets
A relatively large, low-cost, low-margin, high-volume, self-service operation designed to serve the consumer's total needs for grocery and household products. Examples: Carrefour, Aldi, Tesco.

Convenience stores
Relatively small stores located near residential areas, open long hours seven days a week, and carrying a limited line of high-turnover convenience products at slightly higher prices. Examples: 7-Eleven, Londis, Opencor.

Discount stores
Carry standard merchandise sold at lower prices with lower margins and higher volumes. Examples: Wal-Mart, Target.

Off-price retailers
Sell merchandise bought at less than regular wholesale prices and sold at less than retail, often leftover goods, overruns, and irregulars obtained at reduced prices from manufacturers or other retailers. These include *factory outlets* owned and operated by manufacturers (example: the collection at Serravalle); *independent off-price retailers* owned and run by entrepreneurs or by divisions of larger retail corporations (example: TK Maxx [known as TJ Maxx outside the UK, Ireland and Germany); and *warehouse (or wholesale) clubs* selling a limited selection of brand-name groceries, appliances, clothing and other goods at deep discounts to consumers who pay membership fees (e.g. Costco).

Superstores
Very large stores traditionally aimed at meeting consumers' total needs for routinely purchased food and non-food items. Includes *category killers*, which carry a deep assortment in a particular category and have a knowledgeable staff (examples: Tesco, Petsmart, Staples); *supercentres*, combined supermarket and discount stores (example: Wal-Mart Supercenters); and *hypermarkets* with up to 220,000 square feet of space combining supermarket, discount and warehouse retailing (examples: Carrefour, Pyrca).

following sections. They can be classified in terms of several characteristics, including the *amount of service* they offer, the breadth and depth of their *product lines*, the *relative prices* they charge and how they are *organised*.

Amount of service

Different products require different amounts of service and customer service preferences vary. Retailers may offer one of three levels of service – self-service, limited service and full service.

Self-service retailers serve customers who are willing to perform their own 'locate-compare-select' process to save money. Self-service is the basis of all discount operations and is typically used by sellers of convenience goods (such as supermarkets) and nationally branded, fast-moving shopping goods (such as Marks & Spencer).

Limited-service retailers, such as Carphone Warehouse, provide more sales assistance because they carry more shopping goods about which customers need information – expensive electronic items for example. Their increased operating costs result in higher prices. In *full-service retailers*, such as speciality stores and first-class department stores, salespeople assist customers in every phase of the shopping process – think Harrods. Full-service stores usually carry more speciality goods for which customers like to be 'waited on'. They provide more services resulting in much higher operating costs, which are passed along to customers as higher prices.

Product line

Retailers also can be classified by the length and breadth of their product assortments. Some retailers, such as **speciality stores**, carry narrow product lines with deep assortments within those lines. Today, speciality stores are flourishing. The increasing use of market segmentation, market targeting and product specialisation has resulted in a greater need for stores that focus on specific products and segments.

In contrast, **department stores** carry a wide variety of product lines. In recent years, department stores have been squeezed between more focused and flexible speciality stores on the one hand, and more efficient, lower-priced discounters on the other. In response, many have added promotional pricing to meet the discount threat. Others have stepped up the use of store brands and single-brand 'designer shops' to compete with speciality stores – as Marks & Spencer does with Per Uno clothing for women. Still others are trying mail order, telephone and Web selling. Service remains the key differentiating factor. Retailers such as John Lewis, El Corte Ingles in Spain and Portugal, and other high-end department stores are doing well by emphasising high-quality service.

Supermarkets are the most frequently shopped type of retail store. In Europe they are facing slower sales growth because of slower population growth, saturation of the market and increasing restrictions on new shops.

Thus, most supermarkets are making improvements to attract more customers. In the battle for 'share of stomachs', many large supermarket chains are moving upscale, providing improved store environments and higher quality food offerings, such as in-store bakeries, gourmet deli counters and fresh seafood departments – *'It's not just food, it's M&S Food'*. Others are cutting costs, establishing more efficient operations and lowering prices in order to compete more effectively against the discounters like Lidl and Aldi – Asda has taken this route. Many of the major European supermarket chains offer home delivery for groceries bought online – the British Retail Consortium estimates that 4 per cent of all retail transactions are now conducted online.[2] Many speculate on the current and future size of the online portion of retail markets, but Mintel, the market intelligence agency, has suggested it might be about €111 billion across the EU in 2010, representing about 5 per cent of of all retail transactions.[3]

Convenience stores are small stores that carry a limited line of high-turnover convenience goods like newspapers, snacks and drinks. There are chains of these all over

Source: Alamy Images/Swerve.

Convenience stores are becoming ever more sophisticated retailing environments.

Europe – Narvesan in Norway and Pressbyrån in Sweden were both founded in the nineteenth century (the latter specialising in small outlets in railway stations), Londis (London and District Independent Shopkeepers) in the UK, the Spanish Opencor and, of course, Spar over much of the continent (originally Dutch in origin).[4] These specialists are increasingly being joined by small format versions of the leading grocers, such as the Tesco Express and Sainsbury Local chains.

Superstores are much larger than regular supermarkets and offer a large assortment of routinely purchased food products, non-food items and services. Wal-Mart acquired Asda ten years ago, and there seem to be moves to replicate the US format of very large combination food and discount stores in the EU – Wal-Mart has 2,500 of these in the US alone[5] – how and why is discussed in Marketing at Work 11.1 (see p. 381).

Recent years have also seen the explosive growth of superstores that are actually giant speciality stores, the so-called **category killers**. They feature stores the size of aircraft hangars that carry a very deep assortment of a particular line with a knowledgeable staff. Category killers are prevalent in a wide range of categories, including books, baby gear, toys, electronics, home-improvement products, linens and towels, party goods, sporting goods, even pet supplies. Another superstore variation, a *hypermarket*, is a huge superstore, perhaps as large as *six* football pitches. This is a format that emerged in Europe before the USA – Carrefour pioneered hypermarkets in France, and now generates three-quarters of its sales from its four key EU markets in France, Italy, Spain and Belgium. It is also rapidly expanding in China and Eastern Europe.[6]

Finally, for some retailers, the product line is actually a service. Service retailers include hotels, banks, airlines, cinemas, restaurants, garages, hair salons and dry cleaners.

Relative prices

Retailers can also be classified according to the prices they charge (see Exhibit 11.1). Most retailers charge regular prices and offer normal quality goods and customer service. Others offer higher quality goods and service at higher prices. The retailers that feature low prices are discount stores and 'off-price' retailers.

Discount stores A **discount store** sells standard merchandise at lower prices by accepting lower margins and selling higher volume. The early discount stores cut expenses by offering few services and operating in warehouse-like facilities in low-rent, heavily populated areas. Today's discounters have improved their store environments and increased their services, while at the same time keeping prices low through lean, efficient operations. If France brought Europe and the world the hypermarket, then Germany can claim to be the home of the two most significant discounters in Europe – Aldi and Lidl. Other significant players include the Danish Netto and the Spanish Dia. These discounters are increasingly impacting on the retail scene as a whole, as we saw in the opening case about Aldi.

Off-price retailers As the major discount stores traded up, a new wave of **off-price retailers** moved in to fill the ultra-low price, high volume gap. Ordinary discounters buy at regular wholesale prices and accept lower margins to keep prices down. In contrast, off-price retailers buy at less than regular wholesale prices and charge consumers less than retail. Off-price retailers can be found in all areas, from food, clothing, and electronics to no-frills banking and discount brokerages.

The three main types of off-price retailers are *independents, factory outlets* and *warehouse clubs*. **Independent off-price retailers** either are owned and run by entrepreneurs or are divisions of larger retail corporations. Although many off-price operations are run by smaller independents, most large off-price retailer operations are owned by bigger retail chains. Well known off-price retailers in Europe include TK Maxx, Matalan and Makro.

Factory outlets – producer-operated stores sometimes group together in *factory outlet malls* and *value retail centres*, where dozens of outlet stores offer prices as low as 50 per cent below retail on a wide range of items. Factory outlet malls have become one of the hottest growth areas in retailing. While common in the US, these are still relatively scarce in Europe. Serravalle Designer Outlet, near Piedmont in Italy, offers good deals on brands like Cerruti and Dolce and Gabbana. In the UK, Bicester Village is one of a very few example – owned and operated by a company called Value Retail which specialises in this type of retail environment.[7]

Brands such as Polo Ralph Lauren, Giorgio Armani, Gucci, and Versace are increasingly appearing in these outlets, causing department stores to protest to the manufacturers of these brands. Given their higher costs, the department stores have to charge more than the off-price outlets. Manufacturers counter that they send last year's merchandise and seconds to the factory outlet malls, not the new merchandise that they supply to the department stores. Still, the department stores are concerned about the growing number of shoppers willing to make weekend trips to stock up on branded merchandise at substantial savings.

Organisational approach

Although many retail stores are independently owned, others band together under some form of corporate or contractual organisation. The major types of retail organisations – *corporate chains, voluntary chains, retailer cooperatives, franchise organisation*s and *merchandising conglomerate*s – are described in Table 11.1.

Chain stores are two or more outlets that are commonly owned and controlled. They have many advantages over independents. Their size allows them to buy in large quantities at lower prices and gain promotional economies. They can hire specialists to deal with areas such as pricing, promotion, merchandising, inventory control and sales forecasting.

The great success of corporate chains caused many independents to band together in one of two forms of contractual associations. One is the *voluntary chain* – a wholesaler-sponsored group of independent retailers that engages in group buying and common merchandising as discussed in Chapter 10. In Germany, Edeka supermarkets operate like this. The other form of contractual association is the *retailer cooperative* – a group of independent retailers that bands together to set up a jointly owned, central wholesale operation and conducts joint merchandising and promotion efforts. A good example of this would be the Euronics network of independent electrical retailers.[8] These organisations give independents the buying and promotion economies they need to match the prices of larger chains.

Another form of contractual retail organisation is a **franchise**. The main difference between franchise organisations and other contractual systems (voluntary chains and retail cooperatives) is that franchise systems are normally based on some unique product or service, on a method of doing business, or on the trade name, goodwill or patent that

TABLE 11.1 Major types of retail organisation

Type	Description	Examples
Corporate chain stores	Two or more outlets that are commonly owned and controlled, employ central buying and merchandising, and sell similar lines of merchandise. Corporate chains appear in all types of retailing, but they are strongest in department stores, food stores, chemists, shoe stores and women's clothing stores.	Zara, C&A, WHSmith
Voluntary chains	Wholesaler-sponsored groups of independent retailers engaged in bulk buying and common merchandising.	Londis, Edeka
Retailer co-operatives	Groups of independent retailers who set up a central buying organisation and conduct joint promotion efforts.	Euronics
Franchise organisations	Contractual association between a franchiser (a manufacturer, wholesaler or service organisation) and franchisees (independent businesspeople who buy the right to own and operate one or more units in the franchise system). Franchise organisations are normally based on some unique product, service or method of doing business, or on a trade name or patent, or on goodwill that the franchiser had developed.	McDonald's, Subway, Pizza Hut, BodyShop
Merchandising conglomerate	A free-form corporation that combines several diversified conglomerates retailing lines and forms under central ownership, along with some integration of their distribution and management functions.	DSG International

the franchiser has developed. Franchising has been prominent in fast foods, health and fitness centres, hairdressing, car hire and dozens of other product and service areas.

But franchising covers a lot more than just burgers and fitness centres. Franchises have sprung up to meet just about any need. The Swedish company Husse has more than 300 franchisees across Europe, each delivering pet food to owners' homes directly. Benetton is a famous Italian clothing company with franchises all over the globe – but Italy also has smaller businesses like Calzedonia offering franchises in their specialities of swimwear and hosiery, and in Austria and Germany Musikschule Fröhlich offers private music lessons through its franchise partners.[9]

Franchises now command a significant presence on most European high streets. Benetton, McDonald's, Subway, Thorntons, Toni&Guy are present in most UK towns and cities, and across the continent companies like Etam, Bang & Olufson, Depato and Lacoste follow suit.[10]

One of the best-known and most successful franchisers, McDonald's, now has more than 26,000 restaurants in 119 countries serving nearly 40 million customers a day.[11]

Finally, *merchandising conglomerates* are corporations that combine several different retailing forms under central ownership. You might not have heard of DSG International, but you will have heard of their high-street retail outlets like PC World and Currys. Outside the UK they also own Elkjøp and Gigantti in Scandinavia, UniEuro in Italy and Kotsovolus in Greece. Such diversified retailing, similar to a multibranding strategy, provides superior management systems and economies that benefit all the separate retail operations.

MAKING CONNECTIONS Linking the concepts

Slow down and think about all the different kinds of retailers you deal with regularly, many of which overlap in the products they carry.

■ Pick a familiar product: camera, microwave, item of clothing. Shop for this product at two very different store types, say a discount store or category killer on the one hand, and a department store or smaller speciality store on the other. Compare the stores on product assortment, services and prices. If you were going to buy the product, where would you buy it and why?

■ What does your shopping trip suggest about the futures of the competing store formats that you sampled?

Retailer marketing decisions

Retailers are always searching for new marketing strategies to attract and hold customers. In the past, retailers attracted customers with unique product assortments and more or better services. Today, retail assortments and services are looking more and more alike. National brand manufacturers, in their drive for volume, have placed their branded goods everywhere. Such brands are found not only in department stores but also in mass-merchandise discount stores, off-price discount stores and on the Web. Thus, it's now more difficult for any one retailer to offer exclusive merchandise.

Service differentiation among retailers has also eroded. Many department stores have trimmed their services, whereas discounters have increased theirs. Customers have become smarter and more price sensitive. They see no reason to pay more for identical brands, especially when service differences are shrinking. For all these reasons, many retailers today are rethinking their marketing strategies.

As shown in Figure 11.1, retailers face major marketing decisions about their *target market and positioning*, *product assortment and services*, *price*, *promotion* and *place*.

Target market and positioning decision

Retailers first must define their target markets and then decide how they will position themselves in these markets. Should the store focus on upscale, midscale or downscale shoppers? Do target shoppers want variety, depth of assortment, convenience or low prices? Until they define and profile their markets, retailers cannot make consistent decisions about product assortment, services, pricing, advertising, store decor, or any of the other decisions that must support their positions.

Too many retailers fail to define their target markets and positions clearly. They try to have 'something for everyone' and end up satisfying no market well. In contrast, successful retailers define their target markets well and position themselves strongly.

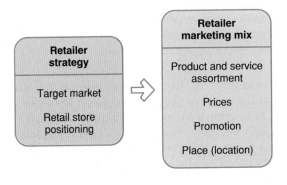

FIGURE 11.1

Retailer marketing decisions

Asda positions itself on being good value for money, Aldi on low-price goods without branding or packaging, Tesco on range and Marks & Spencer on quality.

Product assortment and services decision

Retailers must decide on three major product variables: *product assortment*, *services mix* and *store atmosphere*.

The retailer's *product assortment* should differentiate the retailer while matching target shoppers' expectations. One strategy is to offer merchandise that no other competitor carries, such as private brands or national brands on which it holds exclusives. For example, House of Fraser gets exclusive rights to carry well-known designers' labels. It also offers an exclusive men's fashion line under its own Linea private brand. Another strategy is to feature blockbuster merchandising events – Debenhams is known for running spectacular 24-hour sales at very short notice. Finally, the retailer can differentiate itself by offering a highly targeted product assortment – Long Tall Sally carries clothing for tall and large women, Games Workshop carries a range of table-top games and hobby materials.

The *services mix* can also help set one retailer apart from another. For example, some retailers invite customers to ask questions or consult service representatives in person or via phone or keyboard. B&Q offers a diverse mix of services to do-it-yourselfers, from 'how-to' classes to a proprietary credit card.

The *store's atmosphere* is another element in the reseller's product arsenal. Every store has a physical layout that makes moving around in it either hard or easy. Each store has a 'feel'; one store is cluttered, another cheerful, a third plush, a fourth sombre. The retailer must design an atmosphere that suits the target market and moves customers to buy. In the US, Urban Outfitters sets itself apart by creating a unique store environment, and this atmosphere is deliberately recreated in the European outlets in, amongst other places Glasgow, Dublin, Copenhagen and Antwerp:

The inside of an Urban Outfitters store is a far cry from the stark, cookie-cutter interiors you'll find at Gap or Express. 'Shopping here should be like a treasure hunt,' says Laura O'Connor, Urban's 34-year-old general merchandising manager. O'Connor and her team give every store the feel of a boutique. Urban delivers small batches of new merchandise daily to keep things fresh. New and recycled fashions are sold alongside housewares (think beaded curtains and cocktail shakers), encouraging serious browsing and creating a thrill-of-the-hunt vibe suited to a thrift store. Visual arts teams at each store – typically four artists per location – overhaul each store's look every two weeks. The men's department at one store – this week, at least – is wallpapered with newspaper sports pages dyed pink. That art deco jewellery? O'Connor got the idea while visiting a museum in Prague. The quick-changing assortments and decor get customers stopping in often to see what's new, while the 'organised clutter' design keeps them around by selling unexpected items side by side. Urban even places Xboxes and vintage arcade games in its menswear sections so bored boyfriends won't pressure female shoppers to leave. As a result, Urban's customers stay an average of 45 minutes per visit – more than twice as long as shoppers linger in most clothing stores. That helps the company's stores generate $596 in sales per square foot each year – 80 per cent more than at Limited and Express. That, in turn, makes Urban Outfitters one of the best-performing clothing chains around.[12]

Other retailers practice 'experiential retailing'. At Inglesport, consumers can try out climbing equipment on a huge wall in the store, or they can test Gore-Tex jackets by going under a simulated rain shower. At London's Master Spa, shoppers are invited to wear their bathing suits during a 'tub test'. Similarly, Smeg – Italy's largest producer of kitchen appliances – helps its dealers to install its products in realistic kitchen mock-ups.[13]

Increasingly, retailers are turning their stores into theatres that transport customers into unusual, exciting shopping environments. For example, the largest shopping mall in Europe is Istanbul's Cevahir Mall with an enormous 350 shops on ten floors. Of this huge space, a mere 58,000 square metres is given over to the Atlantis Entertainment Centre, which incorporates an indoor roller-coaster and several IMAX cinema screens, as well as a theatre.[14]

All of this confirms that retail stores are much more than simply assortments of goods. They are environments to be experienced by the people who shop in them. Store atmospheres offer a powerful tool by which retailers can differentiate their stores from those of competitors.

Price decision

A retailer's price policy must fit its target market and positioning, product and service assortment, and competition. All retailers would like to charge high mark-ups and achieve high volume, but the two seldom go together. Most retailers seek *either* high mark-ups on lower volume (most speciality stores) *or* low mark-ups on higher volume (mass merchandisers and discount stores).

Thus, Henry Poole & Co. – a bespoke tailors on Savile Row in London will custom-make a suit or even an outfit appropriate to visit a royal palace that will fit you, and only you, exactly. How much does this cost? If you have to ask, you can't afford it.

At the other extreme, TK Maxx sells brand-name clothing at discount prices, settling for a lower margin on each sale but selling at a much higher volume.

Retailers must also decide on the extent to which they will use sales and other price promotions. Some retailers use no price promotions at all, competing instead on product and service quality rather than on price. For example, it's difficult to imagine Henry Poole holding a two-for-the-price-of-one sale. Other retailers practice '*high-low' pricing* – charging higher prices on an everyday basis, coupled with frequent sales and other price promotions to increase store traffic, clear out unsold merchandise, create a low-price image, or attract customers who will buy other goods at full prices. Still others – such as Asda, Tesco and other mass retailers – practise *everyday low pricing* (EDLP), charging constant, everyday low prices with few sales or discounts. Which strategy is best depends on the retailer's marketing strategy and the pricing approaches of competitors.[15]

A modern shopping mall can be immense. With ten floors, Cevahir in Istanbul is Europe's largest.

Source: Alamy Images/Lilyana Vynogradova.

Henry Poole will make an outfit measured to fit you – and only you.

Source: Alamy Images/Kirsty Mclaren.

Promotion decision

Retailers use any or all of the promotion tools – advertising, personal selling, sales promotion, public relations and direct marketing – to reach consumers. They advertise in newspapers and magazines and on radio, television and the Internet. Advertising may be supported by newspaper inserts and direct mail. Personal selling requires careful training of salespeople in how to greet customers, meet their needs and handle their complaints. Sales promotions may include in store demonstrations, displays, contests and visiting celebrities. Public relations activities, such as press conferences and speeches, store openings, special events, newsletters, magazines and public service activities, are always available to retailers. Most retailers have also set up websites, offering customers information and other features, and often selling merchandise directly.

Place decision

Retailers often point to three critical factors in retailing success: *location, location* and *location*! It's very important that retailers select locations that are accessible to the target market in areas that are consistent with the retailer's positioning. Small retailers may have to settle for whatever locations they can find or afford. Large retailers, however, usually employ specialists who select locations using advanced methods.

Most stores today cluster together to increase their customer pulling power and to give consumers the convenience of one-stop shopping. Historically, European shopping districts have tended to evolve rather than be designed. An excellent example of this is the street in York called The Shambles. Shambles derives from an ancient word – shamel – related to open air meat markets. The combination of smells, noises, chaos and claustrophobia of these medieval streets has led to the modern meaning of the word to describe things being in a mess.[16] Urban planning is a relatively modern concept, meaning these districts don't have an organised layout, have poor infrastructure and facilities and usually aren't big enough for modern purposes. Without very significant reconstruction, there are a limited number of ways to improve these areas – pedestrianisation becoming an increasingly popular option.

A **shopping centre** is a group of retail businesses planned, developed, owned and managed as a unit. A *regional shopping centre*, or *regional shopping mall*, the largest and most dramatic shopping centre, can have several hundred stores and attract customers from a wide area. The Metro Centre in Gateshead, Bluewater in Kent, the Galeria Kazimierz in Cracow and the Olympia in Munich are all good examples and the Cevahir Mall, mentioned before, sits on the historical trade hub between Europe and Asia.

A *community shopping centre* contains between 15 and 40 retail stores. It normally contains a branch of a department store or variety store, a supermarket, speciality stores, professional offices and sometimes a bank. Most shopping centres are there to support the needs of a city district or a complete town. In Europe some of these are quite old. Glasgow has the Argyll Arcade from 1827 and Paris has many that survive from the first half of the nineteenth century, with evocative names like Passage Choiseul, Passage des Panoramas and Grand-Cerf.[17] Many more, generally rather ugly, modern examples exist, like Kringlan in the centre of Reykjavik.

A recent addition to the shopping centre scene is the so-called *retail park*. These huge unenclosed shopping centres consist of a group of retail stores, including large, free-standing anchors such as IKEA, Staples and Next. Each store has its own entrance, with parking directly in front for shoppers who wish to visit only one store. Retail parks have increased rapidly in number during the past few years to challenge traditional indoor malls.

The current trend is towards value-oriented outlet malls and retail parks on the one hand, and smaller 'lifestyle centres' on the other. These lifestyle centres – smaller malls with upscale stores, convenient locations and expensive atmospheres – are usually located near affluent residential districts and cater to the retail needs of consumers in their areas. The future of malls 'will be all about creating places to be rather than just places to buy'.[18]

The future of retailing

Retailers operate in a harsh and fast-changing environment, which offers threats as well as opportunities. For example, the industry suffers from chronic overcapacity, resulting in fierce competition for customers. Consumer demographics, lifestyles and shopping patterns are changing rapidly, as are retailing technologies. To be successful, then, retailers will have to choose target segments carefully and position themselves strongly. They will have to take the following retailing developments into account as they plan and execute their competitive strategies.

New retail forms and shortening retail life cycles

New retail forms continue to emerge to meet new situations and consumer needs, but the life cycle of new retail forms is getting shorter. Department stores took about 100 years to reach the mature stage of the life cycle; more recent forms, such as warehouse stores, reached maturity in about ten years. In such an environment, seemingly solid retail positions can crumble quickly – C&A, the Dutch clothing retailer, had been a presence on the UK high street for 75 years. In 2000, it took the decision to close down all 113 of its UK shops, making nearly 5,000 staff redundant. The reason? A previously strong position selling value for money clothing had been eroded by new retailers like Matalan undercutting prices and established companies like Gap and Next taking away profitable segments.[19]

Many retailing innovations are partially explained by the **wheel-of-retailing concept**.[20] According to this concept, many new types of retailing forms begin as low-margin, low-price, low-status operations. They challenge established retailers that have become 'fat' by letting their costs and margins increase. The new retailers' success leads them to upgrade their facilities and offer more services. In turn, their costs increase, forcing them to increase their prices. Eventually, the new retailers become like the conventional retailers they replaced. The cycle begins again when still newer types of retailers evolve with lower costs and prices. The wheel-of-retailing concept seems to explain the initial success and later troubles of department stores, supermarkets and discount stores, and the recent success of off-price retailers.

Growth of non-store retailing

Most of us still make most of our purchases the old-fashioned way: we go to the shop, find what we want, queue patiently to plunk down our cash or credit card, and bring home our purchases. However, consumers now have an array of alternatives, including mail order, television, phone and online shopping. Shoppers are increasingly avoiding the hassles and crowds by doing more of their shopping by phone or computer. Although such retailing advances may threaten some traditional retailers, they offer exciting opportunities for others. Most store retailers have now developed direct retailing channels. In fact, more online retailing is conducted by 'click-and-brick' retailers than by 'click-only' retailers.[21]

Online retailing is the newest form of non-store retailing. All types of retailers now use the Web as an important marketing tool. The online sales of giant bricks-and-mortar retailers, such as Tesco, John Lewis and Marks & Spencer, are increasing rapidly. Several large click-only retailers – Amazon.com, online auction site eBay, online travel companies such as Travelocity and Expedia, and others – are now making it big on the Web. At the other extreme, hordes of niche marketers are using the Web to gain reach new markets and expand their sales. Today's more sophisticated search engines and comparison shopping sites (Shopping.com, Buy.com, Shopzilla and others) put almost any e-tailer within a mouse click or two's reach of millions of customers.

Still, much of the anticipated growth in online sales will go to multichannel retailers – the click-and-brick marketers who can successfully merge the virtual and physical worlds. Look at Tesco – in nine years its home delivery service for groceries bought online has grown from nothing to a £1.6 billion business as of 2008.[22]

Retail convergence

Today's retailers are increasingly selling the same products at the same prices to the same consumers in competition with a wider variety of other retailers. For example, you can buy books at outlets ranging from independent local bookshop to superstores such as Borders or websites such as Amazon.com. When it comes to brand-name appliances, department stores, discount stores, home improvement stores, off-price retailers, electronics superstores and a slew of websites all compete for the same customers. This merging of consumers, products, prices and retailers is called *retail convergence*:

> Retail convergence is the coming together of shoppers, goods and prices. Customers of all income levels are shopping at the same stores, often for the same goods. Old distinctions such as discount store, speciality store and department store are losing significance: the successful store must match a host of rivals on selection, service and price. Where you go for what you want – that has created the biggest challenge facing retailers. Consider fashion. Once the exclusive of the wealthy, fashion now moves just as quickly from the runways of New York and Paris to retailers at all levels. Ralph Lauren sells in department stores and in the Marshall's at the strip mall. Designer Stephen Sprouse, fresh off a limited edition of Louis Vuitton handbags and luggage, has designed a summer line of clothing and other products for Target.[23]

Such convergence means greater competition for retailers and greater difficulty in differentiating offerings. The competition between chain superstores and smaller, independently owned stores has become particularly heated. In the US, Wal-Mart has been accused of destroying independents in countless small towns around the country. In the UK, this is becoming a significant issue for retailers like Tesco.[24]

Yet the news is not all bad for smaller companies. Many small, independent retailers are thriving. They are finding that sheer size and marketing muscle are often no match for the personal touch small stores can provide or the speciality niches that small stores fill for a devoted customer base.

The rise of mega-retailers

The rise of huge mass merchandisers and speciality superstores, the formation of vertical marketing systems, and a rash of retail mergers and acquisitions have created a core of superpower mega-retailers. Through their superior information systems and buying power, these giant retailers can offer better merchandise selections, good service and strong price savings to consumers. As a result, they grow even larger by squeezing out their smaller, weaker competitors.

The mega-retailers are also shifting the balance of power between retailers and producers. A relative handful of retailers now controls access to enormous numbers of consumers, giving them the upper hand in their dealings with manufacturers. In Europe, this concentration and the problems it can cause are most marked in the supermarket sector.[25]

Growing importance of retail technology

Retail technologies are becoming critically important as competitive tools. Progressive retailers are using advanced information technology and software systems to produce better forecasts, control inventory costs, order electronically from suppliers, send

MARKETING AT WORK 11.1

Wal-Mart: The world's largest company

Wal-Mart's annual sales now exceed $380 billion – making it the world's largest company. This size is reflected in all aspects of its operations. A typical distribution centre serves 70–100 stores out of a global total of more than 7,000, employing 700–1,000 staff in a facility with five miles of conveyor belts. Wal-Mart employs more than 2 million people worldwide. Let's put that into perspective – it is roughly equivalent to the total active manpower of the army of the People's Republic of China. One out of every 235 men, women and children in the United States is a Wal-Mart associate. Wal-Mart has a single day sales record of $1.52 billion.

What are the secrets behind this spectacular success? First and foremost, Wal-Mart is passionately dedicated to its value proposition of 'Always Low Prices, *Always!*' Its mission is to 'lower the world's cost of living'. To deliver on this promise, it

Leading discounters, such as Wal-Mart, now dominate the retail scene. First and foremost, Wal-Mart is passionately dedicated to its value proposition of 'Always Low Prices, Always!'
Source: © Alex Segre/Alamy.

listens to and takes care of its customers, treats employees as partners and keeps a tight rein on costs.

Wal-Mart knows its customers well and takes good care of them. As one analyst puts it, 'The company gospel . . . is relatively simple: Be an agent for customers, find out what they want, and sell it to them for the lowest possible price.' The company stays close to customers – for example, each top Wal-Mart executive spends at least two days a week visiting stores, talking directly with customers and getting a first-hand look at operations. Then, Wal-Mart delivers what customers want: a broad selection of carefully selected goods at unbeatable prices. Concludes Wal-Mart's current president and chief executive, 'We're obsessed with delivering value to customers.'

Beyond listening to and taking care of customers, Wal-Mart also takes good care of employees. It believes that, in the final accounting, the company's people are what really make it better. Wal-Mart was first to call employees 'associates', a practice now widely copied by competitors. The associates work as partners, become deeply involved in operations, and share rewards for good performance.

Everyone at Wal-Mart [is] an associate – from [the CEO] . . . to a cashier named Janet at the Wal-Mart on Highway 50 in Ocoee, Florida. 'We', 'us' and 'our' are the operative words. Wal-Mart department heads, hourly associates who look after one or more of 30-some departments ranging from sporting goods to electronics, see figures that many companies never show general managers: costs, freight

charges, profit margins. The company sets a profit margin for each store, and if the store exceeds it, then the hourly associates share part of the additional profit.

Finally, Wal-Mart delivers real value by keeping a sharp eye on costs. Wal-Mart is a lean, mean, distribution machine – it has the lowest cost structure in the industry. This lets the giant retailer charge lower prices but still reap higher profits. For example, grocery prices drop an average of 10 to 15 per cent in markets Wal-Mart has entered, and Wal-Mart's food prices average 20 per cent less than its grocery store rivals. Wal-Mart's lower prices attract more shoppers, producing more sales, making the company more efficient, and enabling it to lower prices even more.

Wal-Mart's low costs result in part from superior management and more sophisticated technology – its headquarters contains a computer communications system that is second in size only to the US Defense Department, giving managers around the world instant access to sales and operating information. Wal-Mart also spends less than competitors on advertising as a percentage of sales. Because Wal-Mart has what customers want at the prices they'll pay, its reputation has spread rapidly by word-of-mouth. It has not needed more advertising.

Finally, Wal-Mart keeps costs down through good old 'tough buying'. Whereas the company is known for the warm way it treats customers, it is equally well known for the calculated way it wrings low prices from suppliers. The following passage describes a visit to Wal-Mart's buying offices:

▶

Don't expect a greeter and don't expect friendly . . . Once you are ushered into one of the spartan little buyers' rooms, expect a steely eye across the table and be prepared to cut your price. 'They are very, very focused people, and they use their buying power more forcefully than anyone else in America,' says the marketing vice president of a major vendor. 'They talk softly, but they have piranha hearts, and if you aren't totally prepared when you go in there, you'll have your [head] handed to you.'

Some critics argue that Wal-Mart squeezes its suppliers too hard, driving some out of business. Wal-Mart proponents counter, however, that it is simply acting in its customers' interests by forcing suppliers to be more efficient. 'Wal-Mart is tough, but totally honest and straightforward in its dealings with vendors,' says an industry consultant. 'Wal-Mart has forced manufacturers to get their act together.' In fact, in order to sell $380-billion worth of goods each year, Wal-Mart must first develop a network of partners to *supply* those goods. That requires skilful supplier relationship management.

Some observers wonder whether Wal-Mart can be so big and still retain its focus and positioning. They wonder if an ever-larger Wal-Mart can stay close to its customers and employees. The company's managers are betting on it. No matter where it operates, Wal-Mart's announced policy is to take care of customers 'one store at a time'. Says one top executive: 'We'll be fine as long as we never lose our responsiveness to the consumer.'

Sources: Quotes and other information from Bill Saporito, 'Is Wal-Mart Unstoppable?', *Fortune*, 6 May 1991, pp. 50–9; Carol J. Loomis, 'Sam Would Be Proud', *Fortune*, 17 April 2001, pp. 131–44; Cait Murphy, 'Introduction: Wal-Mart Rules', *Fortune*, 15 April 2002, pp. 94–8; Jerry Useem, 'One Nation Under Wal-Mart', *Fortune*, 3 March 2003, pp. 65–78; Bruce Upbin, 'Wall-to-Wall Wal-Mart', *Forbes*, 12 April 2004, p. 76; Sandra O'Loughlin and Barry Janoff, 'Wal-Mart Keeps Smiling, and Rivals Are Not Happy', *Brandweek*, 21 June 2004, p. S62; Don Longo, 'Wal-Mart on Its Way to Becoming the First Trillion Dollar Corporation', *Retail Merchandiser*, March 2005, p. 7; '100 Top Retailers', *Stores*, July 2005, accessed at www.stores.org; and Wal-Mart 2008 Annual Report and Fact Sheets accessed at http://walmartstores.com/FactsNews/FactSheets/ in August 2008.

information between stores, and even sell to customers within stores. They are adopting checkout scanning systems, online transaction processing, electronic data interchange, in-store television and improved merchandise handling systems.

Perhaps the most startling advances in retailing technology concern the ways in which today's retailers are connecting with customers. Many retailers now routinely use technologies such as touch-screen kiosks, customer loyalty cards, electronic shelf labels and signs, handheld shopping assistants, smart cards, self-scanning systems and virtual-reality displays.

Global expansion of major retailers

Retailers with unique formats and strong brand positioning are increasingly moving into other countries. Many are expanding internationally to escape mature and saturated home markets. Over the years, several giant US retailers – McDonald's, Gap, Toys 'R' Us – have become globally prominent as a result of their great marketing prowess. Others, such as the world's largest retailer, Wal-Mart, are rapidly establishing a global presence. Wal-Mart, which now operates more than 7,000 stores in 14 countries abroad, sees exciting global potential, potential which is already being exploited by the three European retailers in the global top five – Carrefour, Tesco and Germany's Metro.[26]

French discount retailer Carrefour, the world's second largest retailer after Wal-Mart, has embarked on an aggressive mission to extend its role as a leading international retailer – with nearly 15,000 stores wordwide selling goods to the value of €82 billion it is rapidly catching up with Wal-Mart, and is pursued in turn by Tesco.

Retail stores as 'communities'

With the rise in the number of people living alone, working at home, or living in isolated and sprawling suburbs, there has been a resurgence of establishments that, regardless of the product or service they offer, also provide a place for people to get together. These places include cafés, tea shops, juice bars, bookshops, superstores, children's play spaces, and urban farmers' markets. Today's bookshops have become part bookshop, part library, part living room and part coffee house. On an early evening at your local Borders, you'll likely find college students doing homework with friends in the coffee bar. Nearby, pensioners sit in cushy chairs thumbing through travel or gardening books while parents read aloud to their children. Borders sells more than just books, it sells comfort, relaxation and community.

Brick-and-mortar retailers are not the only ones creating community. Others have also built virtual communities on the Internet – there is a thriving subculture around eBay and Amazon and many smaller more locally-focused online retailers.

MAKING CONNECTIONS Linking the concepts

Time out! So-called experts have long predicted that non-store retailing eventually will replace store retailing as our primary way to shop. What do you think?

■ Shop for a good book at the Amazon website (**www.amazon.co.uk**), taking time to browse the site and see what it has to offer. Next, shop at a nearby Borders, Waterstone's, or other bookshop. Compare the two shopping experiences. Where would you rather shop? On what occasions? Why?

■ A Borders store creates something of a sense of community. How does Amazon compare in this respect?

WHOLESALING

Wholesaling includes all activities involved in selling goods and services to those buying for resale or business use. We call **wholesalers** those firms engaged *primarily* in wholesaling activities.

Wholesalers buy mostly from producers and sell mostly to retailers, industrial consumers and other wholesalers. As a result, many of the largest and most important wholesalers are largely unknown to final consumers. For example, you may never have heard of a Dutch firm called The Greenery, even though as one of Europe's largest wholesalers of fruit and vegetables you probably eat food supplied by them – see Marketing at Work 11.2 for more detail.

MARKETING AT WORK 11.2

The Greenery: A fresh approach

The Greenery supplies produce to almost all of the major European supermarkets and to similar outlets in North America and the Far East. Around 2,500 people are employed by the company across the globe but mainly in the three Dutch centres at Bleiswijk, Maasland and Barendrecht. These ultra-modern high-tech facilities have every possible aid to make bringing in fragile produce (pre-packed by their suppliers) and directing it on to the right customer as efficient and quick as possible, using 150 specially equipped and fitted lorries.

The shares in the company are all owned by the producers who are members of the horticultural co-operative 'The Greenery UA'. The 1,500 producer-owned member companies market all their products via The Greenery. The main activity of the company is to provide a complete range of vegetables, fruit and mushrooms to supermarket chains in Europe, North America and the Far East throughout the year – generating revenue of about €2 billion annually. Other major target groups are catering companies and industrial processing companies that use the produce in their own operations rather than retailing it.

As an intermediary, The Greenery requires good relationships with buyers and sellers, and the relationships The Greenery has with producers in the Netherlands and abroad give the company direct access to the source of the best produce. Organising the shortest possible chain and optimally matching supply to demand are priorities for The Greenery – the quicker the better the fresher, and old vegetables are donated to charity, not sold. Food safety, sustainability, innovation and logistical efficiency also have a high priority in all The Greenery's activities.

Because of this, programmes to supply the same product all year round are developed in collaboration with customers and suppliers. During one season the products come from Spain, whereas during another season they are grown in the Netherlands. An example of this is a special all-year tomato supply programme for a large chain of supermarkets in the Benelux countries. The Greenery is able to offer this kind of customised concept thanks to its own product quality expertise and its extensive market information network and long-term relationships with professional producers – both in the Netherlands and in the rest of the world.

Food safety and product quality are also continuously subjected to a strict monitoring programme, in which The Greenery supervises and works closely together with all

partners in the chain so that what appears on the supermarket shelf is as fresh and as healthy as possible – and that organic and non-organic produce is never mixed or mislabelled. As part of its commitment to sustainability and ethical trade, The Greenery trains and works with small-scale farmers in Third World countries. Operating in many markets, The Greenery is very aware of national differences. In the German market price is key, but in Benelux and the UK there is rapid growth in organic and convenience products.

At the end of each year, you will find The Greenery working very closely with its UK customers and all its suppliers to prepare for a very short healthy-eating boom immediately after Christmas. This is never a long-term logistical exercise because previous experience suggests the boom lasts no more than three weeks. Kevin Doran, managing director of Greenery UK, said:

The first week after Christmas always sees a huge increase in salad sales. It is not clear if this is because of a wave of New Year resolutions to adopt a healthier diet or just a reaction to the excesses of Christmas week. If it is a result of New Year resolutions, the resolutions appear not to be kept for long – because within three weeks the peak of sales has declined back to the average winter level.

Typically, in the first week of the new year, The Greenery ships 20 per

The Greenery is a leading European wholesaler of fresh produce – it probably supplies your local supermarket. *Source*: Corbis/Gary Holscher.

cent more than its average weekly winter volume of tomatoes and cucumbers – that is several hundred additional tonnes of tomatoes. To ensure that supermarkets can meet the demands of shoppers with a short-term appetite for fresh produce at the start of the year, The Greenery schedules harvesting of salad vegetables over the Christmas period so that they can be delivered to stores immediately after the holidays. This means planning well in advance to ensure that growers have sown crops under glass in time to meet the post-Christmas rush.

Sources: Compiled and edited from The Greenery Annual Report 2007 and Corporate Brochure, available from: www.thegreenery.com, and press releases from Smye Holland Associates, available from: www.smye-holland.com.

But why are wholesalers used at all? For example, why would a producer use whole-salers rather than selling directly to retailers or consumers? Simply put, wholesalers add value by performing one or more of the following channel functions:

- *Selling and promoting*: Wholesalers' sales forces help manufacturers reach many small customers at a low cost. The wholesaler has more contacts and is often more trusted by the buyer than the distant manufacturer.

- *Buying and assortment building*: Wholesalers can select items and build assortments needed by their customers, thereby saving the consumers much work.

- *Bulk-breaking*: Wholesalers save their customers money by breaking large lots into small quantities.

- *Warehousing*: Wholesalers hold inventories, thereby reducing the inventory costs and risks of suppliers and customers.

- *Transportation*: Wholesalers can provide quicker delivery to buyers because they are closer than the producers.

- *Financing*: Wholesalers finance their customers by giving credit, and they finance their suppliers by ordering early and paying bills on time.

- *Risk bearing*: Wholesalers absorb risk by taking title and bearing the cost of theft, damage, spoilage and obsolescence.

- *Market information*: Wholesalers give information to suppliers and customers about competitors, new products and price developments.

- *Management services and advice*: Wholesalers often help retailers train their salespeople, improve store layouts and displays, and set up accounting and inventory control systems.

Types of wholesalers

Wholesalers fall into three major groups (see Table 11.2): *merchant wholesalers, brokers and agents* and *manufacturers' sales branches and offices*. **Merchant wholesalers** are the largest single group of wholesalers, accounting for roughly 50 per cent of all wholesaling. Merchant wholesalers include two broad types: full-service wholesalers and limited-service wholesalers. *Full-service wholesalers* provide a full set of services, whereas the various *limited-service wholesalers* offer fewer services to their suppliers and customers. The several different types of limited-service wholesalers perform varied specialised functions in the distribution channel.

Brokers and *agents* differ from merchant wholesalers in two ways: they do not take title to goods, and they perform only a few functions. Like merchant wholesalers, they generally specialise by product line or customer type. A **broker** brings buyers and sellers together and assists in negotiation. **Agents** represent buyers or sellers on a more per-manent basis. *Manufacturers' agents* (also called manufacturers' representatives) are the most common type of agent wholesaler. The third major type of wholesaling is that done in **manufacturers' sales branches and offices** by sellers or buyers themselves rather than through independent wholesalers.

Wholesaler marketing decisions

Wholesalers now face growing competitive pressures, more demanding customers, new technologies and more direct-buying programmes on the part of large industrial, institu-tional and retail buyers. As a result, they have had to take a fresh look at the marketing strategies. As with retailers, their marketing decisions include choices of target markets, positioning and the marketing mix – product assortments and services, price, promotion and place (see Figure 11.2 on page 387).

TABLE 11.2 Major types of wholesalers

Type	Description
Merchant wholesalers	Independently owned businesses that take title to the merchandise they handle. In different trades they are called *jobbers*, *distributors* or *mill supply houses*. Include full-service wholesalers and limited-service wholesalers:
Full-service wholesalers	Provide a full line of services: carrying stock, maintaining a sales force, offering credit, making deliveries and providing management assistance. There are two types:
Wholesale merchants	Sell primarily to retailers and provide a full range of services, *General merchandise wholesalers* carry several merchandise lines, whereas *general line wholesalers* carry one or two lines in great depth. *Speciality wholesalers* specialise in carrying only part of a line. Examples: health food wholesalers, seafood wholesalers.
Industrial distributors	Sell to manufacturers rather than to retailers. Provide several services, such as carrying stock, offering credit and providing delivery. May carry a broad range of merchandise, a general line or a speciality line.
Limited-service wholesalers	Offer fewer services than full-service wholesalers. Limited-service wholesalers are of several types:
Cash-and-carry wholesalers	Carry a limited line of fast-moving goods and sell to small retailers for cash. Normally do not deliver. Example: a small fish store retailer may drive to a cash-and-carry fish wholesaler, buy fish for cash and bring the merchandise back to the store.
Truck wholesalers (or truck jobbers)	Perform primarily a selling and delivery function. Carry limited lines of semi-perishable merchandise (such as milk, bread, snack foods), which they sell for cash as they make their rounds to supermarkets, small groceries, hospitals, restaurants, factory cafeterias and hotels.
Drop shippers	Do not carry inventory or handle the product. On receiving an order, they select a manufacturer, who ships the merchandise directly to the customer. The drop shipper assumes title and risk from the time the order is accepted to its delivery to the customer. They operate in bulk industries, such as coal, steel and heavy equipment.
Rack jobbers	Serve grocery and health/beauty retailers, mostly in non-food items. They send delivery trucks to stores, where the delivery people set up toys, paperbacks, hardware items, health and beauty aids, or other items. They price the goods, keep them fresh, set up point-of-purchase displays and keep inventory records. Rack jobbers retain title to the goods and invoice the retailers only for the goods sold to consumers.
Producers' co-operatives	Are owned by farmer members and assemble farm produce to sell in local markets. The co-op's profits are distributed to members at the end of the year. They often attempt to improve product quality and promote a co-op brand name, such as Sun Maid raisins or Sunkist oranges.
Mail-order wholesalers	Send catalogues to retail, industrial, and institutional customers featuring jewellery, cosmetics, speciality foods and other small items. Maintain no outside sales force. Main customers are businesses in small outlying areas. Orders are filled and sent by mail, truck or other transportation.
Brokers and agents	Do not take title to goods. Main function is to facilitate buying and selling, for which they earn a commission on the selling price. Generally specialise by product line or customer type.
Brokers	Chief function is bringing buyers and sellers together and assisting in negotiation. They are paid by the party who hired them and do not carry inventory, get involved in financing or assume risk. Examples: food brokers, property brokers, insurance brokers and security brokers.

TABLE 11.2 (*continued*)

Type	Description
Agents	Represent either buyers or sellers on a more permanent basis than brokers do. There are several types:
Manufacturers' agents	Represent two or more manufacturers of complementary lines. A formal written agreement with each manufacturer covers pricing, territories, order handling, delivery service and warranties, and commission rates. Often used in such lines as clothing, furniture and electrical goods. Most manufacturers' agents are small businesses, with only a few skilled salespeople as employees. They are hired by small manufacturers who cannot afford their own field sales forces and by large manufacturers who use agents to open new territories or to cover territories that cannot support full-time salespeople.
Selling agents	Have contractual authority to sell a manufacturer's entire output. The manufacturer either is not interested in the selling function or feels unqualified. The selling agent serves as a sales department and has significant influence over prices, terms and conditions of sale. Found in product areas such as textiles, industrial machinery and equipment, coal and coke, chemicals and metals.
Purchasing agents	Generally have a long-term relationship with buyers and make purchases for them, often receiving, inspecting, warehousing and shipping the merchandise to the buyers. They provide helpful market information to clients and help them obtain the best goods and prices available.
Commission merchants	Take physical possession of products and negotiate sales. Normally, they are not employed on a long-term basis. Used most often in agricultural marketing by farmers who do not want to sell their own output and do not belong to producers' cooperatives. The commission merchant takes a truckload of commodities to a central market, sells it for the best price, deducts a commission and expenses, and remits the balance to the producers.
Manufacturers' and retailers' branches and offices	Wholesaling operations conducted by sellers or buyers themselves rather than through independent wholesalers. Separate branches and offices can be dedicated to either sales or purchasing.
Sales branches and offices	Set up by manufacturers to improve inventory control, selling and promotion. *Sales branches* carry inventory and are found in industries such as lumber and automotive equipment and parts. *Sales offices* do not carry inventory and are most prominent in dry-goods industries.
Purchasing officers	Perform a role similar to that of brokers or agents but are part of the buyer's organisation. Many retailers set up purchasing offices in major market centres such as Paris and Moscow.

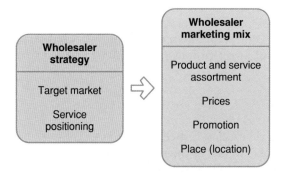

FIGURE 11.2

Wholesaler marketing decisions

Target market and positioning decision

Like retailers, wholesalers must define their target markets and position themselves effectively – they cannot serve everyone. They can choose a target group by size of customer (only large retailers), type of customer (convenience stores only), need for service (customers who need credit), or other factors. Within the target group, they can identify the more profitable customers, design stronger offers and build better relationships with them. They can propose automatic reordering systems, set up management training and advising systems, or even sponsor a voluntary chain. They can discourage less profitable customers by requiring larger orders or adding service charges to smaller ones.

Marketing mix decisions

Like retailers, wholesalers must decide on product assortment and services, prices, promotion and place. The wholesaler's 'product' is the assortment of *products and services* that it offers. Wholesalers are under great pressure to carry a full line and to stock enough for immediate delivery. But this practice can damage profits. Wholesalers today are cutting down on the number of lines they carry, choosing to carry only the more profitable ones. Wholesalers are also rethinking which services count most in building strong customer relationships and which should be dropped or charged for. The key is to find the mix of services most valued by their target customers.

Price is also an important wholesaler decision. Wholesalers usually mark up the cost of goods by a standard percentage – say, 20 per cent. Expenses may run at 17 per cent of the gross margin, leaving a profit margin of 3 per cent. In grocery wholesaling, the average profit margin is often less than 2 per cent. Wholesalers are trying new pricing approaches. They may cut their margin on some lines in order to win important new customers. They may ask suppliers for special price breaks when they can turn them into an increase in the supplier's sales.

Although *promotion* can be critical to wholesaler success, most wholesalers are not promotion-minded. Their use of trade advertising, sales promotion, personal selling and public relations is largely scattered and unplanned. Many are behind the times in personal selling – they still see selling as a single salesperson talking to a single customer instead of as a team effort to sell, build and service major accounts. Wholesalers also need to adopt some of the non-personal promotion techniques used by retailers. They need to develop an overall promotion strategy and to make greater use of supplier promotion materials and programmes.

Finally, *place* is important – wholesalers must choose their locations, facilities and Web locations carefully. Wholesalers typically locate in low-rent, low-tax areas and tend to invest little money in their buildings, equipment and systems. As a result, their materials handling and order processing systems are often outdated. In recent years, however, large and progressive wholesalers are reacting to rising costs by investing in automated warehouses and online ordering systems. The Greenery has invested heavily in these because of the fragile and perishable nature of the produce it works with. Typically, orders are fed from the retailer's system directly into the wholesaler's computer, and the items are picked up by mechanical devices and automatically taken to a shipping platform where they are assembled. Most large wholesalers are using technology to carry out accounting, billing, inventory control and forecasting. Modern wholesalers are adapting their services to the needs of target customers and finding cost-reducing methods of doing business.

Trends in wholesaling

As the wholesaling industry moves into the twenty-first century, it faces considerable challenges. The industry remains vulnerable to one of the most enduring trends of the last decade – fierce resistance to price increases and the winnowing out of suppliers who are not adding value based on cost and quality. Progressive wholesalers constantly watch for better ways to meet the changing needs of their suppliers and target customers. They recognise that, in the long run, their only reason for existence comes from adding value by increasing the efficiency and effectiveness of the entire marketing channel. For example, most people in the UK will be familiar with WHSmith, the leading high street newsagent. Less well known is the fact that until 2006 the company also operated an extremely successful wholesale operation for papers and magazines. This is now an independent company, imaginatively called Smiths, with an annual turnover of £1.2 billion that delivers 60 million items per week to 22,000 retail customers – and then collects the items that weren't sold the next day. In order to assist this process, the company has invested heavily in technology. Its Connect2U website allows each customer to manage their account online, assisting greatly with stock control and order management – critical areas with such a rapid turnaround.[27]

The distinction between large retailers and large wholesalers continues to blur. Many retailers now operate formats such as wholesale clubs and hypermarkets that perform many wholesale functions. In return, many large wholesalers are setting up their own retailing operations. For example, SuperValu is the largest food wholesaler in the USA, and it's also one of the country's largest food retailers. Almost half of the company's $40 billion in sales comes from its Bigg's, Cub Foods, Save-A-Lot, Farm Fresh, Hornbacher's, Laneco, Metro, Scott's Foods, Shop 'n' Save, and Shoppers Food Warehouse stores.[28]

Wholesalers will continue to increase the services they provide to retailers – retail pricing, cooperative advertising, marketing and management information reports, accounting services, online transactions and others. Rising costs on the one hand, and the demand for increased services on the other, will put the squeeze on wholesaler profits. Wholesalers who do not find efficient ways to deliver value to their customers will soon drop by the wayside. However, the increased use of computerised, automated and Web-based systems will help wholesalers to contain the costs of ordering, shipping and inventory holding, boosting their productivity.

Finally, facing slow growth in their domestic markets many large wholesalers are now going global. For example, in 1991, McKesson bought out its Canadian partner, Provigo. The company now receives about 3 per cent of its total revenues from Canada. Its Information Solutions group operates widely throughout North America and Europe.

THE JOURNEY YOU'VE TAKEN Reviewing the concepts

Pull in here and reflect back on this retailing and wholesaling chapter, the last of two chapters on distribution channels. In this chapter, we first looked at the nature and importance of retailing, major types of retailers, the decisions retailers make and the future of retailing. We then examined these same topics for wholesalers. Although most retailing is conducted in retail stores, in recent years, non-store retailing has increased rapidly. In addition, although many retail stores are independently owned, an increasing number are now banding together under some form of corporate or contractual organisation. Wholesalers, too, have experienced recent environmental changes, most notably mounting competitive pressures. They have faced new sources of competition, more demanding customers, new technologies and more direct-buying programmes on the part of large industrial, institutional and retail buyers.

1 **Explain the roles of retailers and wholesalers in the distribution channel.**

Retailing and wholesaling consist of many organisations bringing goods and services from the point of production to the point of use. *Retailing* includes all activities involved in selling goods or services directly to final consumers for their personal, non-business use. *Wholesaling* includes all the activities involved in selling goods or services to those who are buying for the purpose of resale or for business use. Wholesalers perform many functions, including selling and promoting, buying and assortment building, bulk breaking, warehousing, transporting, financing, risk bearing, supplying market information, and providing management services and advice.

2 Describe the major types of retailers and give examples of each.

Retailers can be classified as *store retailers* and *non-store retailers*. Although most goods and services are sold through stores, non-store retailing has been growing much faster than has store retailing. Store retailers can be further classified by the *amount of service* they provide (self-service, limited service or full service), *product line sold* (speciality stores, department stores, supermarkets, convenience stores, superstores and service businesses), and *relative prices* (discount stores and off-price retailers). Today, many retailers are banding together in corporate and contractual *retail organisations* (corporate chains, voluntary chains and retailer cooperatives, franchise organisations and merchandising conglomerates).

3 Identify the major types of wholesalers and give examples of each.

Wholesalers fall into three groups. First, *merchant wholesalers* take possession of the goods. They include *full-service wholesalers* (wholesale merchants, industrial distributors) and *limited-service wholesalers* (cash-and-carry wholesalers, truck wholesalers, drop shippers, rack jobbers, producers' co-operatives and mail-order wholesalers). Second, *brokers and agents* do not take possession of the goods but are paid a commission for aiding buying and selling. Finally, *manufacturers' sales branches and offices* are wholesaling operations conducted by non-wholesalers to bypass the wholesalers.

4 Explain the marketing decisions facing retailers and wholesalers.

Each retailer must make decisions about its target markets and positioning, product assortment and services, price, promotion and place. Retailers need to choose target markets carefully and position themselves strongly. Today, wholesaling is holding its own in the economy. Progressive wholesalers are adapting their services to the needs of target customers and are seeking cost-reducing methods of doing business. Faced with slow growth in their domestic markets and developments such as the North American Free Trade Association and EU enlargement, many large wholesalers are also now going global.

NAVIGATING THE KEY TERMS

NOTES AND REFERENCES

1 'The Retail Boss who says he can save you £30 a week', Interview by Julia Finch, City Editor, *The Guardian*, 11 July 2008, p. 27.

2 http://www.brc.org.uk/latestdata04.asp?iCat=52&sCat=RETAIL+KEY+FACTS.

3   http://www.foodanddrinkeurope.com/news/ng.asp?id=69239-internet-tesco-amazon.

4   SPAR: http://www.spar-international.com/spar-thehistory-1-8-9-en-details.htm;
    Pressbyran: http://www.pressbyran.se/pbweb/pressbyran.nsf/?Open; Opencor:
    http://www.elcorteingles.es/opencor/paginas/home.asp.

5   http://walmartstores.com/AboutUs/7606.aspx.

6   Carrefour Annual Report 2007, available from:
    http://www.carrefour.com/cdc/finance/publications-and-presentations/annual-reports/.

7   Serravalle Deigner Outlet: http://www.mcarthurglen.it/serravalle/home/home.php?lang=en;
    Bicester Village: http://www.bicestervillage.com/bicester/home.asp; Value Retail:
    http://www.valueretail.com/.

8   http://www.euronics.co.uk/about.aspx;
    http://www.edeka.de/EDEKA/Content/DE/Home/index.jsp.

9   http://www.husse.com/; http://www.calzedonia.com/; http://www.musikschule-froehlich.de.

10 http://www.franchiseeurope.com/directory.php?by=Rank.

11 http://www.mcdonalds.co.uk/pages/companyinfo/franchiseinfo.html.

12 Adapted from Susanna Hamner, 'Lessons from a Retail Rebel', *Business 2.0*, June 2005,
    pp. 62–4.

13 See http://www.inglesport.com/wall.php; http://www.masterspas.co.uk/index.asp;
    http://www.smeguk.com/Intro.htm.

14 http://www.istanbulcevahir.com/index_english.html.

15 For a good discussion of retail pricing and promotion strategies, see Kathleen Seiders and
    Glenn B. Voss, 'From Price to Purchase', *Marketing Management*, November–December
    2005, pp. 38–43.

16 http://www.insideyork.co.uk/shambles.

17 http://www.independent.co.uk/travel/europe/welcome-to-the-worlds-first-shopping-malls-
    498317.html; http://www.passagesetgaleries.org/texts/passages/2fiches_passages/fiches/
    choiseul.html.

18 Dean Starkman, 'The Mall, Without the Haul – "Lifestyle Centers" Slip Quietly into
    Upscale Areas, Mixing Cachet and "Curb Appeal"', *Wall Street Journal*, 25 July 2001,
    p. B1; 'To Mall or Not to Mall?', *Buildings*, June 2004, p. 99; Arlyn Tobian Gajilan,
    'Wolves in Shops' Clothing', *Fortune Small Business*, February 2005, pp. 17–18; and
    information accessed on the International Council of Shopping Centers website,
    www.icsc.org, August 2005.

19 http://news.bbc.co.uk/1/hi/business/792028.stm; http://www.c-and-a.com/aboutUs/
    company/history/.

20 See Malcolm P. McNair and Eleanor G. May, 'The Next Revolution of the Retailing
    Wheel', *Harvard Business Review*, September–October 1978, pp. 81–91; Stephen
    Brown, 'The Wheel of Retailing: Past and Future', *Journal of Retailing*, Summer 1990,
    pp. 143–7; Stephen Brown, 'Variations on a Marketing Enigma: The Wheel of Retailing
    Theory', *Journal of Marketing Management*, 7(2), 1991, pp. 131–55; Jennifer Negley,
    'Retrenching, Reinventing and Remaining Relevant', *Discount Store News*, 5 April 1999,
    p. 11; Don E. Schultz, 'Another Turn of the Wheel', *Marketing Management*, March–April
    2002, pp. 8–9; and Carol Krol, 'Staples Preps Easier E-Commerce Site', *B to B*, 14 March
    2005, pp. 3–4.

21 See Sungwook Min and Mary Wolfinbarger, 'Market Share, Profit Margin, and Marketing
    Efficiency of Early Movers, Bricks and Clicks, and Specialists in E-Commerce', *Journal of
    Business Research*, August 2005, pp. 1030ff.

22 From Tesco Preliminary Results 2008, available from:
    http://www.investorcentre.tescoplc.com/plc/ir/pres_results/results/.

23 Excerpt adapted from Alice Z. Cuneo, 'What's in Store?', *Advertising Age*, 25 February 2002, pp. 1, 30–1. See also Robert Berner, 'Dark Days in White Goods for Sears', *BusinessWeek*, 10 March 2003, pp. 78–9.

24 http://news.bbc.co.uk/1/hi/wales/mid/7371372.stm;
http://www.thisismoney.co.uk/news/article.html?in_article_id=417691&in_page_id=2;
http://news.bbc.co.uk/1/hi/england/merseyside/7344045.stm;
http://www.telegraph.co.uk/earth/main.jhtml?xml=/earth/2007/08/27/eatesco127.xml.

25 http://news.bbc.co.uk/1/hi/business/7245944.stm;
http://www.economist.com/world/britain/displaystory.cfm?story_id=10063999;
http://www.economist.com/world/britain/displaystory.cfm?story_id=9725630;
http://search.ft.com/ftArticle?queryText=tesco&y=7&aje=true&x=20&id=080415000266&ct=0&page=2.

26 http://www.nxtbook.com/nxtbooks/nrfe/stores-globalretail08/.

27 http://www.connect2u.co.uk/connect2u/;
http://www.smithnews.co.uk/smithsnews/jsp/SN_SmithsNewsFacts_Page.jsp;
http://www.smithnews.co.uk/smithsnews/jsp/SN_Connect2UInfo_Page.jsp.

28 Facts accessed at www.supervalu.com, Corporate Profile, May 2008.

CHAPTER 12

Communicating customer value: Advertising, sales promotion and public relations

AFTER STUDYING THIS CHAPTER, YOU SHOULD BE ABLE TO

- discuss the process and advantages of integrated marketing communications in communicating customer value
- define the five promotion tools and discuss the factors that must be considered in shaping the overall promotion mix
- describe and discuss the major decisions involved in developing an advertising programme
- explain how sales promotion campaigns are developed and implemented
- explain how companies use public relations to communicate with their publics

THE WAY AHEAD Previewing the concepts

We'll forge ahead now into the last of the marketing mix tools – promotion. Companies must do more than just create customer value. They must also use promotion to communicate that value clearly and persuasively. You'll find that promotion is not a single tool but rather a mix of several tools. Ideally, under the concept of *integrated marketing communications*, the company will carefully coordinate these promotion elements to deliver a clear, consistent and compelling message about the organisation and its products. We'll begin by introducing you to the various promotion mix tools. Next, we'll examine the rapidly changing communications environment and the need for integrated marketing communications. Finally, we'll look more closely at three of the promotion tools – advertising, sales promotion and public relations. In the next chapter, we'll visit the other two promotion mix tools, personal selling and direct marketing.

To start this chapter, let's look behind the scenes at a campaign to improve perception of Renault cars in Germany.

Renault: How a sausage, a sushi roll, a crispbread and a baguette have affected car sales in Europe

Barbara Caemmerer,
*Department of Marketing,
University of Strathclyde, Scotland*

Source: Nordpol + Hamburg Agentur für Kommunikation GmbH.

In Europe, the country-of-origin is a strong factor impacting on consumers' decision-making when buying a car – particularly in the five key markets of Germany, France, Italy, Spain and the UK.[1] Industry data shows that most of the top ten best-selling cars in Germany – the biggest car market in the EU – are produced by Volkswagen, BMW or DaimlerChrysler, while the French and Italians prefer cars that originate in their home markets.[2] This ethnocentric loyalty is the result of clever marketing communications campaigns which have created country-specific, favourable brand images. For example, for German consumers *safety* is one very important criterion when choosing a new car – and they perceive the Mercedes and Volkswagen brands as being the market leaders in this attribute.[3]

Therefore, Joerg-Alexander Ellhof, Director of Marketing Communications at Renault Germany, faced a particular challenge when the French headquarters decided that Renault had to expand its share in the German market. After a phase of thorough market research, he decided that the only way forward was directly to attack the main German competitors as well as other major car import brands on the attribute of *safety*. He believed that a creative, well-integrated marketing communications campaign could have a strong positive impact on

the organisation's fortunes in the German market. However, the task seemed to be immense as – in order to gain market share – he had to convince German car buyers that Renault, a French car manufacturer, was actually building safer cars than the German heavyweights themselves!

Fortunately, Renault had factual evidence for this proposition, as eight of its car models won the Euro NCAP (European New Car Assessment Programme) – Crashtest competition with five stars.[4] This result made Renault officially the manufacturer of the safest cars in Europe – a very good basis on which to build the marketing communications campaign! But various questions remained: How could the campaign be implemented? Which agencies should be involved? What elements of the marketing communications mix should be used? What should the creative execution look like? How should it be evaluated?

After a pitching process during which various agencies were invited to present their campaign suggestions, the Renault Marketing department decided to work with Publicis[5] and Nordpol+ Hamburg,[6] Germany,

on the project. While Publicis is a large and well-established international advertising agency network, Nordpol+ is a relatively new agency with only 25 employees, but has been attracting great industry attention over the last ten years thanks to their extraordinarily creative approaches to campaign planning and design.[7]

The overarching strategic marketing communications objective for the campaign was to increase consumers' awareness of Renault's positive safety attributes and thus enhance desire for the brand amongst German consumers. Therefore, it was decided to use the following message content for the communications campaign: 'Die sichersten Autos kommen aus Frankreich' (*The safest cars come from France*). It was the task of the agencies to identify how this message could be conveyed to the target audience in the most effective and efficient manner. Nordpol+ recommended that the key marketing communications mix elements used in this campaign should consist of cinema advertising, supported by viral marketing initiatives and TV screenings, as well as a new company website that would link into the theme of the campaign.[8] Publicis was responsible for the print advertisements that would also stress the safety message throughout (title: 'Niemand hat mehr ueber Sicherheit zu erzaehlen als Renault'; *No one has more to say about safety than Renault*).[9]

In order to stress the superlative that the *safest* cars come from France, Nordpol+ and Renault decided that the commercial had to demonstrate that Renault cars were safer in comparison to those of other car manufacturers from competing countries-of-origin, mainly Germany, Japan and Sweden. To reinforce the factual basis for this claim, the agency decided to recreate in detail the Euro NCAP – Crashtest scenario for the commercial. However, instead of showing how cars with crashtest dummies slam into the barriers, the agency decided to film the collision of stereo typical national food items with the walls! Firstly, a giant German sausage is driven into the barrier – bursting into thousands of pieces. The same happens to a Japanese Sushi roll and a Swedish crispbread: both pretty much disintegrate on impact. The last contestant is a soft French baguette which is thrust into the barrier, and – surprise – it survives the test with hardly any damage as it can fully absorb the shock (through crumpling and uncrumpling its front). The scenes are shown in slow-motion and the forceful images stand in stark contrast to the accompanying music, the passionate song 'J'attendrai' (*I will wait*) by singer Rina Ketty, which was recorded in 1939.

During the campaign, the market research agency tns sofres[10] was commissioned to track changes in consumers' attitudes to evaluate the effectiveness and efficiency of the marketing communications initiatives used. The data suggests that this commercial – 'Crashtest' – created by Nordpol+ was very successful in changing consumer attitudes towards the brand. There was a strong increase in awareness levels of the safety of Renault cars as well as in intentions to purchase a car from Renault. The two key factors that contributed to this success were the creative execution of the commercial as well as the media strategy that was used to reach the intended audience (in particular potential new car buyers, male, 30–49 years old, with an income of more than €2,000 a month).

Besides the creative execution of the commercial, Nordpol+ and Renault also had to think about what media channels they could use to reach their key target audience. They identified multiplex cinemas, the Internet and TV as appropriate channels and a good media mix – with each channel supporting the other. In the third quarter of 2005 'Crashtest' was shown in multiplex cinemas across 141 German cities. In support of the cinema launch, a viral campaign was started that initiated the diffusion of the commercial on the Internet – by viewers sending the link on to each other by email. Within a few weeks thousands of viewers had seen 'Crashtest' on **www.youtube.com.** From December 2005 to April 2006 the campaign was extended through the broadcasting of the commercial in two-week periods on TV. In support of the TV campaign the commercial was screened again in cinemas in April and May 2006. Finally, from autumn 2006 onwards 'Crashtest' could be seen continuously on TV in commercial breaks during selected programmes. In parallel to the TV campaign, an additional website was developed that was directly linked to the campaign message: **www.sicher.de** (*sicher=safe*). On this website users could identify how safe their car was, according to the latest Euro NCAP – Crashtest results. In addition, the interactive website contained a wide range of additional information on car and road safety.

The unique creative execution as well as the well-integrated integration of messages and media channels used played a crucial role in making this campaign effective and efficient. But it is not only the consumers who have been impressed. The campaign won various prestigious advertising prizes in 2005 and 2006, for example at the ADC (Art Director's Club) Awards and the international advertising festival in Cannes – a result that both client Renault and agency Nordpol+ can be very proud of. For Ellhof the success of the campaign clearly reflects that creativity can be effective and efficient. While the French headquarters of Renault were first sceptical about the rather unconventional approach to the campaign they have recently suggested that the 'Crashtest' commercial should be launched in a further 13 European countries. They believe that Renault Germany has found a very good way of convincing consumers that Renault is building the safest cars in Europe – and as the campaign has been successful in the German market, why should it not have similar effects in other countries, too?

The audience has been screaming for more . . . After the successful implementation of the campaign, client and agency went back to the drawing board to create follow-up commercials for 'Crashtest'. The result? Since 2007 the website **www.sicher.de** has been hosting two new viral commercials called 'Ballett' and 'Kollision', both created by Nordpol+. They have spread quickly through viewers' recommendations across the World Wide Web and have had an impressive number of hits on the YouTube website. Cinema and TV screenings have also been used in support of the viral campaign. Linking into the crashtest theme, 'Ballett' shows the eight Renault NCAP five-star models in a desert in South Africa performing a ballet dance. Built into the performance are quite a few coordinated (but serious!) crashes – however, all cars survive with minor damage and all are able to dance until the end of the piece. The commercial ends with the tagline 'Das sicherste Ensemble der Welt' (*The world's safest ensemble*) and a shot of the eight Renault models. The other follow-up commercial, 'Kollision' is also closely linked to the crashtest theme but, instead of bursting food items, the commercial features scenes of people colliding with each other. Judging from their facial expressions, it is pretty clear that the Sumo wrestlers hurt themselves quite badly during their fight – so do the Swedish and German folk dancers when they bump into each other during a performance. Only the French are exceptionally well coordinated: an elegantly dressed man and woman are about to collide – but instead of hurting themselves they start kissing . . . the tagline of the commercial is 'Der beste Schutz bei einem Zusammenstoss kommt aus Frankreich' (*In case of a collision the best protection comes from France*).

Isn't this exactly the sort of story we expect from the French? The Germans seem to love it – let's see what the rest of the European nations will think.

Sources: With special thanks to Joerg Ellhof and Anne Fritzemeier. For full source details, see notes 1–10 at the end of this chapter.

Building good customer relationships calls for more than just developing a good product, pricing it attractively and making it available to target customers. Companies must also *communicate* that value to customers, and what they communicate should not be left to chance. All of their communications must be planned and blended into a carefully integrated marketing communications programme. Just as good communication is important in building and maintaining any kind of relationship, it is a crucial element in a company's efforts to build profitable customer relationships.

THE PROMOTION MIX

A company's total **promotion mix** – also called its **marketing communications mix** – consists of the specific blend of advertising, sales promotion, public relations, personal selling and direct-marketing tools that the company uses persuasively to communicate customer value and build customer relationships. Definitions of the five major promotion tools follow:[11]

- **Advertising**: Any paid form of non-personal presentation and promotion of ideas, goods or services by an identified sponsor.
- **Sales promotion**: Short-term incentives to encourage the purchase or sale of a product or service.
- **Public relations**: Building good relations with the company's various publics by obtaining favourable publicity, building up a good corporate image, and handling or heading off unfavourable rumours, stories and events.
- **Personal selling**: Personal presentation by the firm's sales force for the purpose of making sales and building customer relationships.
- **Direct marketing**: Direct connections with carefully targeted individual consumers both to obtain an immediate response and to cultivate lasting customer relationships – the use of telephone, mail, fax, email, the Internet and other tools to communicate directly with specific consumers.

Each category involves specific promotional tools used to communicate with consumers. For example, advertising includes broadcast, print, Internet, outdoor and other forms. Sales promotion includes discounts, coupons, displays and demonstrations. Personal selling includes sales presentations, trade shows and incentive programmes. Public relations includes press releases, sponsorships, special events and Web pages. And direct marketing includes catalogues, telephone marketing, kiosks, the Internet and more.

At the same time, marketing communication goes beyond these specific promotion tools. The product's design, its price, the shape and colour of its package, and the stores that sell it – *all* communicate something to buyers. Thus, although the promotion mix is the company's primary communication activity, the entire marketing mix – promotion *and* product, price and place – must be coordinated for greatest communication impact.

INTEGRATED MARKETING COMMUNICATIONS

In past decades, marketers have perfected the art of mass marketing – selling highly standardised products to masses of customers. In the process, they have developed effective mass-media communications techniques to support these mass-marketing strategies. Large companies routinely invested millions or even billions in television, magazine, or other mass-media advertising, reaching tens of millions of customers with a single ad. Today, however, marketing managers face some new marketing communications realities.

The new marketing communications landscape

Two major factors are changing the face of today's marketing communications. First, as mass markets have fragmented, marketers are shifting away from mass marketing. More and more, they are developing focused marketing programmes designed to build closer relationships with customers in more narrowly defined micromarkets. Second, vast improvements in information technology are speeding the movement toward segmented marketing. With today's new information technologies, marketers can amass detailed customer information and keep closer track of customer needs.

Improved information technology has also caused striking changes in the ways in which companies and customers communicate with each other. The digital age has spawned a host of new information and communication tools – from the Internet and mobile phones to satellite and cable television systems and digital video recorders (DVRs). The new technologies give companies exciting new digital tools for interacting with targeted consumers. They also give consumers more control over the nature and timing of messages they choose to send and receive.

The shifting marketing communications model

The shift toward segmented marketing and the explosive developments in information and communications technology have had a dramatic impact on marketing communications. Just as mass marketing once gave rise to a new generation of mass-media communications, the shift towards targeted marketing and the changing communications environment are giving birth to a new marketing communications model. Although television, magazines and other mass media remain very important, their dominance is now declining. Advertisers are now adding a broad selection of more specialised and highly targeted media to reach smaller customer segments with more personalised messages. The new media range from speciality magazines and television channels to product placements in television programmes and video games, to Internet catalogues and email. In all, companies are doing less *broadcasting* and more *narrowcasting*.

Some advertising industry experts even predict a doom-and-gloom 'chaos scenario', in which the old mass-media communications model will collapse entirely. They believe that marketers will increasingly abandon traditional mass media in favour of new digital technologies – from websites and email to mobile phone content and video on demand – technologies that allow conversations with small clusters of consumers who are pro-actively choosing what advertising to consume.[12]

As mass-media costs rise, audiences shrink, and more and more viewers use SkyPlus+ and other DVR systems to skip past disruptive television commercials, the sceptics predict the demise of the old mass-media mainstay – the 30-second television com-mercial. They point out that many large advertisers are now shifting their advertising budgets away from broadcast television in favour of more targeted, cost-effective, interactive and engaging media. Now advertisers have to reach consumers in less conventional ways – on the street, on a mobile phone, online and as we'll see shortly – in-game.

Other industry insiders, however, see a more gradual shift to the new marketing communications model. They note that broadcast television and other mass media still capture a lion's share of the promotion budgets of most major marketing firms, a fact that isn't likely to change quickly. One advertising expert explains: 'TV audiences remain coveted, because – shrinking though they are – they represent the last vestige of mass media and marketing, or as [one executive asserts] "the last surviving conglomeration of human beings in the living room".'[13]

Thus, it seems likely that the new marketing communications model will consist of a gradually shifting mix of both traditional mass media and a wide array of exciting new, more targeted, more personalised media. 'We need to reinvent the way we market to consumers,' says A.G. Lafley, chief executive of Procter & Gamble. 'Mass marketing still has an important role, [but] we need new models to initially coexist with mass marketing, and eventually to succeed it.'[14]

The need for integrated marketing communications

The shift toward a richer mix of media and communication approaches poses a prob-lem for marketers. Consumers today are bombarded by commercial messages from a broad range of sources. But consumers don't distinguish between message sources the way marketers do. In the consumer's mind, messages from different media and promo-tional approaches all become part of a single message about the company. Conflicting messages from these different sources can result in confused company images, brand positions and customer relationships.[15]

All too often, companies fail to integrate their various communications channels. The result is a hotchpotch of communications to consumers. Mass-media advertise-ments say one thing, while a price promotion sends a different signal, and a product label creates still another message. Company sales literature says something altogether different and the company's website seems out of sync with everything else.

The problem is that these communications often come from different parts of the company. Advertising messages are planned and implemented by the advertising depart-ment or an advertising agency. Personal selling communications are developed by sales management. Other company specialists are responsible for public relations, sales pro-motion events, Internet marketing and other forms of marketing communications.

However, whereas these companies have separated their communications tools, customers won't, and it is because of this that more and more companies are adopting the concept of **integrated marketing communications (IMC)**. Under this concept, as illustrated in Figure 12.1, the company carefully integrates its many communications channels to deliver a clear, consistent, and compelling message about the organisation and its brands.[16]

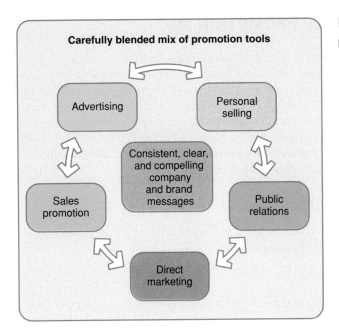

FIGURE 12.1

Integrated marketing communications

IMC calls for recognising all contact points where the customer may encounter the company and its brands. Each *brand contact* will deliver a message, whether good, bad or indifferent. The company wants to deliver a consistent and positive message with each contact. IMC leads to a total marketing communication strategy aimed at building strong customer relationships by showing how the company and its products can help customers solve their problems.

IMC ties together all of the company's messages and images. The company's advertising and personal selling communications have the same message, look and feel as its email promotions. And its public relations materials project the same image as its website.[17] For example, print adverts for Peugeot build consumer preference for the brand. But the ads also point viewers to the company's website, which offers lots of help and very little hype. The site helps serious car buyers build and price a model, find a local showroom online, and learn more about the cars and the company. Later, at the showroom, Peugeot-trained salespeople communicate on a one-to-one basis while customers test-drive the cars.

In the past, no one person or department was responsible for thinking through the communication roles of the various promotion tools and coordinating the promotion mix. To help implement integrated marketing communications, some companies appoint a marketing communications director who has overall responsibility for the company's communications efforts. This helps to produce better communications consistency and greater sales impact. It places the responsibility in someone's hands – where none existed before – to unify the company's image as it is shaped by thousands of company activities.

Integrated marketing communications involve identifying the target audience and shaping a well-coordinated promotional programme to elicit the desired audience response. Too often, marketing communicators focus on creating immediate brand awareness, image or preference in the target market. But this approach to communications is too short-sighted. Today, marketers are viewing communications as helping to *manage the customer relationship over time*. Because customers differ, communications programmes need to be developed for specific segments, niches, and even individuals. And, in these days of new interactive digital communications technologies, companies must ask not only, 'How can we reach our customers?' but also, 'How can we find ways to let our customers reach us?'

SHAPING THE OVERALL PROMOTION MIX

The concept of integrated marketing communications suggests that the company must blend the promotion tools carefully into a coordinated *promotion mix*. But how does the company determine what mix of promotion tools it will use? Companies within the same industry differ greatly in the design of their promotion mixes. For example, Avon spends most of its promotion funds on personal selling and direct marketing, whereas Rimmel spends heavily on consumer advertising. Hewlett-Packard relies on advertising and promotion to retailers, whereas Dell uses more direct marketing. We now look at factors that influence the marketer's choice of promotion tools.

The nature of each promotion tool

Each promotion tool has unique characteristics and costs. Marketers must understand these characteristics in shaping the promotion mix.

Advertising

Advertising can reach masses of geographically dispersed buyers at a low cost per exposure, and it enables the seller to repeat a message many times. For example, television advertising can reach huge audiences who are watching significant sports or entertainment events. About 86 million people watched Barcelona beat Arsenal in the final of the UEFA European Champions League Final in 2006 – a mere fraction of the estimated 600–700 million that watched at least a part of the World Cup Final between France and Italy in Germany on any one of 376 broadcasting channels.[18]

Beyond its reach, large-scale advertising says something positive about the seller's size, popularity and success. Because of advertising's public nature, consumers tend to view advertised products as more legitimate. Advertising is also very expressive – it allows the company to dramatise its products through the artful use of visuals, print, sound and colour. On the one hand, advertising can be used to build up a long-term image for a product (such as Coca-Cola ads). On the other hand, advertising can trigger quick responses (as when Debenhams advertises a 24-hour sale with little advance warning).

Advertising also has some shortcomings. Although it reaches many people quickly, advertising is impersonal and cannot be as directly persuasive as can company salespeople. For the most part, advertising can only carry on a one-way communication with the audience, and the audience does not feel that it has to pay attention or respond. In addition, advertising can be very costly. Although some advertising forms, such as newspaper and radio advertising, can be done on smaller budgets, other forms, such as network TV advertising, require very large budgets.

Personal selling

Personal selling is the most effective tool at certain stages of the buying process, particularly in building up buyers' preferences, convictions and actions. It involves personal interaction between two or more people, so each person can observe the other's needs and characteristics and make quick adjustments. Personal selling also

Rimmel spends heavily on consumer advertising.

allows all kinds of customer relationships to spring up, ranging from matter-of-fact selling relationships to personal friendships. An effective salesperson keeps the customer's interests at heart in order to build a long-term relationship. Finally, with personal selling, the buyer usually feels a greater need to listen and respond, even if the response is a polite 'No thank you'.

These unique qualities come at a cost, however. A sales force requires a longer-term commitment than does advertising – advertising can be turned on and off, but sales force size is harder to change. Personal selling is also the company's most expensive promotion tool, often costing in the hundreds of pounds per call. Many firms spend up to three times as much on personal selling as they do on advertising.

Sales promotion

Sales promotion includes a wide assortment of tools – coupons, contests, money-off deals, premiums and others – all of which have many unique qualities. They attract consumer attention, offer strong incentives to purchase, and can be used to dramatise product offers and to boost sagging sales. Sales promotions invite and reward quick response – whereas advertising says, 'Buy our product', sales promotion says, 'Buy it now'. Sales promotion effects are often short-lived, however, and often are not as effective as advertising or personal selling in building long-term brand preference and customer relationships.

Public relations

Public relations is very believable – news stories, features, sponsorships and events seem more real and believable to readers than ads do. Public relations can also reach many prospects who avoid salespeople and advertisements – the message gets to the buyers as 'news' rather than as a sales-directed communication. And, as with advertising, public relations can dramatise a company or product. Marketers tend to underuse public relations or to use it as an afterthought, yet a well-thought-out public relations campaign used with other promotion mix elements can be very effective and economical.

Direct marketing

Although there are many forms of **direct marketing** – telephone marketing, direct mail, online marketing and others – they all share four distinctive characteristics. Direct marketing is *non-public*: the message is normally directed to a specific person. Direct marketing is *immediate* and *customised*: messages can be prepared very quickly and can be tailored to appeal to specific consumers. Finally, direct marketing is *interactive*: it allows a dialogue between the marketing team and the consumer, and messages can be altered depending on the consumer's response. Thus, direct marketing is well suited to highly targeted marketing efforts and to building one-to-one customer relationships.

Promotion mix strategies

Marketers can choose from two basic promotion mix strategies – *push* promotion or *pull* promotion. Figure 12.2 contrasts the two strategies. The relative emphasis on the specific promotion tools differs for push and pull strategies. A **push strategy** involves 'pushing' the product through marketing channels to final consumers. The producer directs its marketing activities (primarily personal selling and trade promotion) toward channel members to induce them to carry the product and to promote it to final consumers.

Using a **pull strategy**, the producer directs its marketing activities (primarily advertising and consumer promotion) toward final consumers to induce them to buy the product. If the pull strategy is effective, consumers will then demand the product from channel members, who will in turn demand it from producers. Thus, under a pull strategy, consumer demand 'pulls' the product through the channels.

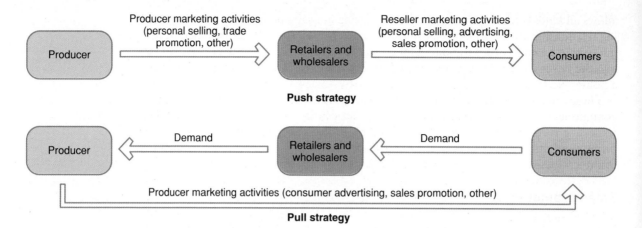

FIGURE 12.2

Push versus pull promotion strategies

Some industrial goods companies use only push strategies; some direct-marketing companies use only pull. However, most large companies use some combination of both. For example, Heinz uses mass-media advertising and consumer promotions to pull its products and a large sales force and trade promotions to push its products through the channels. In recent years, consumer goods companies have been decreasing the pull portions of their mixes in favour of more push. This has caused concern that they may be driving short-term sales at the expense of long-term brand equity.

Companies consider many factors when designing their promotion mix strategies, including *type of product/market* and the *product life-cycle stage*. For example, the importance of different promotion tools varies between consumer and business markets. Business-to-consumer (B2C) companies usually 'pull' more, putting more of their funds into advertising, followed by sales promotion, personal selling and then public relations. In contrast, business-to-business (B2B) marketers tend to 'push' more, putting more of their funds into personal selling, followed by sales promotion, advertising and public relations. In general, personal selling is used more heavily with expensive and risky goods and in markets with fewer and larger sellers.

Now that we've examined the concept of integrated marketing communications and the factors that firms consider when shaping their promotion mixes, let's look more closely at the specific marketing communications tools.

MAKING CONNECTIONS Linking the concepts

Pull over here for a few minutes. Flip back through and link the parts of the chapter you've read so far.

■ How do the *integrated marketing communications (IMC)* and *promotion mix* concepts relate to one another?

■ How has the changing communications environment affected the ways in which companies communicate with you about their products and services? If you were in the market for a new car, where might you hear about various available models? Where would you *search* for information?

ADVERTISING

Advertising can be traced back to the very beginnings of recorded history. The Romans painted walls to announce gladiator fights, and the Phoenicians painted pictures promoting their wares on large rocks along parade routes. Modern advertising, however, is a far cry from these early efforts. Billions upon billions are spent every year on advertising. Exact figures are hard to come by, but one estimate is $654 billion in 2008. Let's take just one country – Austria. One of the more affluent European nations certainly, but far from being the largest in terms of population (less than 9 million). The World Advertising Research Centre estimates that €2.3 billion is spent on advertising annually in Austria, twice what was spent ten years ago, with about 60 per cent being spent on print media in newspapers and magazines. Of the remainder, 20 per cent was on TV advertising and the rest made up of cinema, radio, Internet (the fastest growing media) and outdoor billboards. Indeed, some media agencies expect spending on Internet advertising alone by Europe as a whole to surpass €20 billion by 2010.[19]

Which companies are spending the most on advertising? Globally, the leader is Procter & Gamble, which supports its many familiar brands with heavy investment – $8.5 billion worldwide, with $2.6 billion in Europe. In Europe, the top spenders vary by country – in France it is the entertainment/telecoms conglomerate Vivendi ($390 million), in Italy it is Fiat ($160 million) and in the Republic of Ireland it is the national government ($72 million).[20] Why would the state be the number one advertiser? The answer is of course that advertising is a good way to inform and persuade, whether the purpose is to sell Coca-Cola or new environmentally friendly regulations or to promote new social marketing objectives. (Refer to Table 12.1 for a summary of leading brands around Europe.)

Marketing management must make four important decisions when developing an advertising programme (see Figure 12.3): *setting advertising objectives, setting the advertising budget, developing advertising strategy* (*message decisions* and *media decisions*) and *evaluating advertising campaigns.*

Setting advertising objectives

The first step is to set *advertising objectives*. These objectives should be based on past decisions about the target market, positioning and marketing mix, which define the job that advertising must do in the total marketing programme.

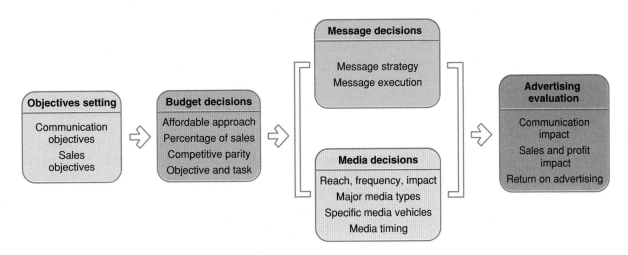

FIGURE 12.3

Major decisions in advertising

TABLE 12.1 Top advertisers in selected European countries

GLOBAL MARKETERS: Top 10 Global Marketers by Country			November 19, 2007	Advertising Age	11

Cyprus
AGB Nielsen Media Research

Advertiser	2006	2005	%CHG
Ortanider	$19.2	NA	NA
Hellenic Bank	17.0	NA	NA
Laiki Bank	15.1	NA	NA
Golden Telemedia	12.8	NA	NA
Bank or Cyprus	12.8	NA	NA
Coca-Cola Co.	12.2	NA	NA
Carrerour	11.0	NA	NA
Procter & Gamble Co.	10.6	NA	NA
Nestle	7.9	NA	NA
Peoplestel	6.4	NA	NA

Figures and U.S. dollars in millions.

Estonia
TNS Emor/TNS Media Inteligence

Advertiser	2006	2005	%CHG
Procter & Gamble Co.	$4.5	$3.5	29.0
EMT	2.4	1.8	34.2
Tele2	2.0	1.1	81.7
Swedtank	1.6	1.5	11.2
Royal Anold	1.4	1.5	-6.5
Coca-Cola Co.	1.3	1.1	22.0
A-Setwer	1.3	1.1	23.3
Elion Ettewotted	1.2	0.8	45.2
L'Oreal	1.2	1.0	21.4
Reckitt Benckiser	1.1	1.0	17.0

Figures are U.S. dollars in millions.

Georgia
TV MR GE (lic. of AGB Nielsen Media Research)

Advertiser	2006	2005	%CHG
Colgate-Falmoliwe Co.	$5.1	NA	NA
Waoti GSM	3.4	NA	NA
Geocell	2.9	NA	NA
Procter & Gamble Co.	2.7	NA	NA
Elite Electronics Trading Network	1.7	NA	NA
Rustaweli Aknmeteli	1.4	NA	NA
Awersi	1.2	NA	NA
Coca-Cola Co.	1.2	NA	NA
Hars Inc.	1.1	NA	NA
PSP	1.1	NA	NA

Figures are U.S. dollars in millions.

Hungary
TNS Media Intelligence

Advertiser	2006	2005	%CHG
Deutscne Telekom	$105.5	$133.4	-20.9
Procter & Gamble Co.	98.4	73.9	33.2
Unilever	87.3	80.3	8.7
Reckitt Benckiser	62.0	57.7	7.4
Telencr	60.5	55.1	9.7
Henkel	53.6	52.1	2.2
Baver	52.3	45.0	16.3
Danone Group	47.1	56.5	-16.6
L'Oreal	45.3	41.5	9.1
Vodarone	41.9	43.2	-3.2

Figures are U.S. dollars in millions.

Czech Republic
TNS Media Intelligence

Advertiser	2006	2005	%CHG
Vodatone	$96.1	$47.4	102.8
Teleronica	95.8	66.3	44.5
Procter & Gamble Co.	70.1	53.8	30.3
Deutsche Telekom	56.8	55.6	2.1
Danone Group	54.5	65.5	-16.8
Henkel	45.9	32.3	42.4
Unilewer	40.7	35.9	13.2
L'Oreal	39.8	28.4	40.3
Volkswagen	36.9	33.8	9.2
Nestle	34.9	27.6	26.3

Figures and U.S. dollars in millions.

Finland
TNS Gallup

Advertiser	2006	2005	%CHG
Elisa	$20.5	$18.9	8.4
TeliaSonera	17.3	19.2	-10.0
Unilewer	17.2	16.1	6.6
Ford Motor Co.	13.7	13.5	2.0
L'Oreal	12.8	9.7	31.3
Procter & Gamble Co.	11.8	9.9	18.6
Volkswagen	11.5	10.0	14.1
Toyota Motor Corp.	10.3	8.3	23.9
Dna Finland	9.9	10.3	-3.0
Valio	9.8	8.4	16.9

Figures are U.S. dollars in millions.

Germany
Nielsen Global Adview

Advertiser	2006	2005	%CHG
Wetro Group	$401.7	$350.4	14.6
Deutsche Telekom	289.6	239.8	20.8
Lidl & Schwarz Stiftung Co.	280.9	268.2	4.8
Procter & Gamble Co.	265.8	237.2	12.1
Volkswagen	257.2	223.1	15.3
L'Oreal	236.6	196.0	20.7
Bertelsmann	227.7	204.5	11.4
A lorecnt, Muelheim	215.9	204.5	5.6
Unilever	204.5	212.8	-3.9
Arel Springer Verlag	193.3	212.9	-9.2

Figures are U.S. dollars in millions.

Ireland
Institute of Advertising Practitioners in Ireland (IAPI)

Advertiser	2006	2005	%CHG
Gowernment – ROI	$71.6	NA	NA
McDonald's Corp.	32.1	6.5	395.3
Unilever	27.4	24.4	12.1
Independent News & Wedia	26.1	NA	NA
Diageo	25.1	27.0	-7.0
Eircom Group	24.2	8.8	173.1
Sherry Fitzgerald	20.7	NA	NA
Frocter & Gamble Co.	20.0	16.8	18.9
DSG International	18.9	20.3	-6.7
Vodarone	16.8	22.8	-26.3

Figures are U.S. dollars in millions.

Denmark
TNS Gallup

Advertiser	2006	2005	%CHG
Dansk Supermarked	$39.4	$35.3	11.6
TDC	37.8	46.5	-18.7
Danske Bank	32.9	38.6	-14.8
Nykedit Realkredit	29.4	23.7	24.1
Carisberg	22.8	22.9	-0.6
Dansk Tipstjeneste	22.4	20.7	8.2
Semler Gruppen	22.2	21.6	2.6
FDB	21.8	20.1	8.4
Telenor	20.9	17.6	18.8
TeliaSonera	20.6	25.3	-18.5

Figures and U.S. dollars in millions.

France
TNS Media Intelligence

Advertiser	2006	2005	%CHG
Viwendi	$389.0	$349.4	11.4
L'Oreal	384.2	347.5	10.6
PSA Peugeot Citroen	336.5	311.3	8.1
France Telecom	295.4	313.4	-5.7
Renault	265.8	242.7	9.5
Association Familiale Wulliez	258.1	277.6	-7.0
Danone Group	224.9	224.3	0.3
Nestle	215.9	226.8	-4.8
Carrelour	201.5	201.1	0.2
Canal + Groupe	186.5	18.06	3.2

Figures are U.S. dollars in millions, discounted by AA.

Greece
Media Services

Advertiser	2006	2005	%CHG
Hellenic Telecom Org. (OTE)	$70.2	$68.9	1.9
Telecom Italia	48.6	35.2	37.9
Procter & Gamble Co.	47.6	33.7	41.0
Vodalone	45.3	41.7	8.6
L'Oreal	43.5	20.3	114.7
OPAP	33.7	30.2	11.5
Nestle	25.1	22.1	13.7
Naspers	24.1	26.3	-8.2
Piraeus Bank	23.2	17.9	29.5
National Bank of Greece	22.3	15.6	43.3

Figures are U.S. dollars in millions.

Italy
Nielsen Global AdView

Advertiser	2006	2005	%CHG
Fiat	$156.5	$131.5	19.0
Frocter & Gamble Co.	125.0	135.8	-8.0
Unilever	122.8	142.0	-13.5
Ferrero	121.7	105.8	15.1
Telecom Italia	111.1	142.3	-21.9
L'Oreal	105.8	93.7	12.9
Vodarone	95.9	94.5	1.5
Barilla Holding	94.1	93.8	0.3
Volkswagen	91.7	87.9	4.3
FSA Peugeot Citroen	84.6	78.6	7.6

Figures are U.S. dollars in millions, discounted by AA.

Source: *Advertising Age*, 'Top 100 Global Marketers', available from http://www.adage.com/datacenter/article?article_id=106350.

An **advertising objective** is a specific communication *task* to be accomplished with a specific *target* audience during a specific period of *time*. Advertising objectives can be classified by primary purpose – whether the aim is to *inform*, *persuade* or *remind*. Table 12.2 lists examples of each of these objectives.

Informative advertising is used heavily when introducing a new product category. In this case, the objective is to build primary demand. Thus, early producers of DVD players first had to inform consumers of the image quality and convenience benefits of the new product. *Persuasive advertising* becomes more important as competition increases. Here, the company's objective is to build selective demand. For example, once DVD players became established, Sony began trying to persuade consumers that *its* brand offered the best quality for their money. As technology moves on, Sony must repeat this with Blu-ray.

Some persuasive advertising has become *comparative advertising*, in which a company directly or indirectly compares its brand with one or more other brands. Comparative advertising has been used for products ranging from soft drinks, beer and pain relievers to computers, batteries, car hire and credit cards. For example, in its classic comparative campaign, the car-hire company Avis positioned itself against market-leading Hertz by claiming, 'We're number two, so we try harder.'

More recently, Three – the mobile telecoms company – wanted to compare its price plans with those of its rivals. Three produced a TV advert in which their lower pricing was highlighted next to air-bubbles containing the numbers for rival price-plans, these bubbles (a theme prominent in the adverts of its arch-competitor O_2) popped each time

TABLE 12.2 Possible advertising objectives

Informative advertising	
Telling the market about a new product	Describing available services
Suggesting new uses for a product	Correcting false impressions
Informing the market of a price change	Reducing consumers' fears
Explaining how the product works	Building a company image

Persuasive advertising	
Building brand preference	Persuading customer to purchase now
Encouraging switching to your brand	Persuading customer to receive a sales call
Changing customer's perception of product attributes	

Reminder advertising	
Building and maintaining the customer relationship	Reminding consumer where to buy the product
Reminding consumer that the product may be needed in the near future	Keeping it in the customer's mind during off-seasons

to emphasise Three's superior value. Apollo, a company manufacturing fire alarms, produced a poster showing their wider range of products when compared against that of a rival, Rafiki. The German advertising agency BBDO created a clever comparison to benefit their client FedEx by creating imagery to imply that UPS relied on FedEx to deliver its packages.[21]

Advertisers use comparative advertising with caution. All too often such ads invite competitor responses, resulting in an advertising war that neither competitor can win – or breaking the European Union's strict rules and regulations in this area. Three was taken to the European Court of Justice by O_2. The court ruled that while the use of the bubbles did infringe on O_2's trademarks, the comparison itself was not unfair.[22]

Reminder advertising is important for mature products – it helps to maintain customer relationships and keep consumers thinking about the product. Expensive Coca-Cola television ads primarily build and maintain the Coca-Cola brand relationship rather than informing or persuading customers to buy in the short term.

Setting the advertising budget

After determining its advertising objectives, the company next sets its *advertising budget* for each product. No matter what method is used, setting the advertising budget is no easy task. Here, we look at four common methods used to set the total budget for advertising: the *affordable method*, the *percentage-of-sales method*, the *competitive-parity method* and the *objective-and-task method*.[23]

Affordable method

Some companies use the **affordable method**: they set the promotion budget at the level they think the company can afford. Small businesses often use this method, reasoning that the company cannot spend more on advertising than it has. They start with total revenues, deduct operating expenses and capital outlays, and then devote some portion of the remaining funds to advertising. Unfortunately, this method of setting budgets completely ignores the effects of promotion on sales. It tends to place advertising last among spending priorities, even in situations in which advertising is critical to the firm's success. It leads to an uncertain annual promotion budget, which makes long-range market planning difficult.

Percentage-of-sales method

Other companies use the **percentage-of-sales method**, setting their promotion budget at a certain percentage of current or forecasted sales. Or they budget a percentage of the unit sales price. The percentage-of-sales method has advantages. It is simple to use and helps management think about the relationships between promotion spending, selling price and profit per unit.

Despite these claimed advantages, however, the percentage-of-sales method has little to justify it. It wrongly views sales as the *cause* of promotion rather than as the *result*. It bases the ad budget on the availability of funds rather than on marketing needs and opportunities. Larger brands tend to receive more advertising, whether they need it or not. Meanwhile, smaller or failing brands receive less spending even though they may need more. Also, under the percentage-of-sales method, because the budget varies with year-to-year sales, long-range planning is difficult. Finally, the method does not provide any basis for choosing a *specific* percentage, except what has been done in the past or what competitors are doing.

Competitive-parity method

Still other companies use the **competitive-parity method**, setting their promotion budgets to match competitors' outlays. They monitor competitors' advertising or get industry promotion spending estimates from publications or trade associations, and then set their budgets based on the industry average.

Two arguments support this method. First, competitors' budgets represent the collective wisdom of the industry. Second, spending what competitors spend helps prevent promotion wars. Unfortunately, neither argument is valid. There are no grounds for believing that the competition has a better idea of what a company should be spending on promotion than does the company itself. Companies differ greatly, and each has its own special promotion needs. Finally, there is no evidence that budgets based on competitive parity prevent promotion wars.

Objective-and-task method

The most logical budget-setting method is the **objective-and-task method**, whereby the company sets its promotion budget based on what it wants to accomplish with promotion. This budgeting method entails the following:

1 defining specific promotion objectives,
2 determining the tasks needed to achieve these objectives,
3 estimating the costs of performing these tasks, and
4 summing these costs to obtain the proposed promotion budget.

The objective-and-task method is the best method for setting advertising budgets. It forces management to spell out its assumptions about the relationship between money spent and promotion results. But it is also the most difficult method to use. Often, it is hard to figure out which specific tasks will achieve specific objectives. For example, suppose Sony wants 60 per cent awareness for its latest Blu-ray model during the six-month introductory period. What specific advertising messages and media schedules should Sony use to attain this objective? How much would these messages and media schedules cost? Sony management would have to consider such questions, even though they are hard to answer.

Developing advertising strategy

Advertising strategy consists of two major elements: creating advertising *messages* and selecting advertising *media*. In the past, companies often viewed media planning as secondary to the message creation process. The creative department first created good advertisements, and then the media department selected the best media for carrying these advertisements to desired target audiences. This often caused friction between creatives and media planners.

Today, however, media fragmentation, soaring media costs, and more focused target marketing strategies have promoted the importance of the media planning function. More and more, advertisers are orchestrating a closer harmony between their messages and the media that deliver them. Among the more noteworthy ad campaigns based on tight media creative partnerships is the pioneering campaign for Absolut vodka, made by V&S Absolut Spirits.

Since the iconic 'bottle' campaign began in 1979, the Absolut team and its ad agency meet once a year with a slew of magazines to set Absolut's media schedule. The agency's creative department then creates media-specific ads. The result is a wonderful assortment of very creative ads for Absolut, tightly targeted to audiences of the media in which they appear. For example, an 'Absolut Bravo' ad in playbills has roses adorning a clear bottle, while business magazines contain an 'Absolut Merger' foldout. In New York-area magazines, 'Absolut Manhattan' ads feature a satellite photo of Manhattan, with Central Park assuming the distinctive outline of an Absolut bottle. In London, ads show the famous entry to the Prime Minister's residence at No. 10 Downing Street with the door in the shape of an Absolut bottle. An 'Absolute Primary' ad run during the political season featured the well-known bottle spattered with mud. In 'Absolut Love', run in February to celebrate Valentine's Day, two Absolut bottles embrace, silhouetted by a shining heart in the background. In some cases, the creatives even develop ads for magazines not yet on the schedule, such as a clever 'Absolut Centerfold' ad for *Playboy* magazine. The ad portrayed a clear, unadorned playmate bottle ('11-inch bust, 11-inch waist, 11-inch hips'). In all, Absolut has developed more than 1,500 ads for the more than two-decades-old campaign. At a time of soaring media costs and cluttered communication channels, a closer cooperation between creative and media people has paid off handsomely for Absolut. Largely as a result of its breakthrough advertising, in the United States, Absolut remains the nation's number one imported vodka and the number three liquor brand overall. The Absolut ads have developed a kind of cult following, and Absolut is one of only three original brands to be inducted into the American Advertising Hall of Fame.[24]

Creating the advertising message

No matter how big the budget, advertising can succeed only if advertisements gain attention and communicate well. Good advertising messages are especially important in today's costly and cluttered advertising environment. The average number of receivable television channels per household has skyrocketed from low single figures in the 1950s to more than 100 today, alongside the thousands of magazines from which to choose.[25] Add the countless radio stations and a continuous barrage of catalogues, direct mail, Internet email and pop-up ads and out-of-home media, and consumers are being bombarded with ads at home, at work and at all points in between. One expert estimates that the average person is exposed to some 1,600 ad messages a day. Another puts the number at an eye-popping 5,000 ads a day.[26]

Breaking through the clutter If all this advertising clutter bothers some consumers, it also causes big problems for advertisers. Take the situation facing television advertisers. As well as the significant costs of creating and filming their commercial – which is usually in the region of £2–300,000 – they must also pay for it to be broadcast. Rates vary considerably, being a function of the length, time of day, time of year, broadcaster and expected share of the total audience the particular channel captures. Here's an example. ITV broadcasts a set of channels across the UK, but the main one is ITV1. A 30-second advert, showing mid-morning, would cost about £8,000 a time. The same advert shown during peak time in the evening would cost £83,000. Having your advert shown only in part of the country costs less. Channel Five quotes prices for the same two time slots of about £2,000 and £17,000 – reflecting generally smaller audiences.[27]

Until recently, television viewers were pretty much a captive audience for advertisers. But today's digital wizardry has given consumers a rich new set of information and entertainment choices. With the growth in cable and satellite TV, the Internet, video on demand (VOD) and DVDs rentals, today's viewers have many more options. Digital technology has also armed consumers with an arsenal of weapons for choosing what they watch or don't watch. Increasingly, consumers are choosing *not* to watch ads. They 'zap' commercials by fast-forwarding though recorded programmes. With the remote control, they mute the sound during a commercial or 'zip' around the channels to see what else is on. Studies have found that nearly half of all television viewers now switch channels when the commercial break starts.

Adding to the problem is the rapid growth of digital video recorder-based and video-on-demand systems like SkyPlus+. Many of these systems allow commercial breaks to be omitted from recordings, missing the adverts altogether. The number of viewers using such systems is expected to increase rapidly over the next few years, meaning that an ever-increasing proportion of the viewing public will be able to watch programming on their own time terms, with or without commercials.

Thus, advertisers can no longer force-feed the same old clichéd ad messages to captive consumers through traditional media. Just to gain and hold attention, today's advertising messages must be better planned, more imaginative, more entertaining and more rewarding to consumers. 'A commercial has to cut through the clutter and seize the viewers in one to three seconds, or they're gone,' says one advertising executive. 'Interruption or disruption as the fundamental premise of marketing' no longer works, says another. 'You have to create content that is interesting, useful, or entertaining enough to invite [consumers].'[28]

In fact, many marketers are now subscribing to a new merging of advertising and entertainment, dubbed 'Madison & Vine'. Madison Avenue is the New York City street that has housed many of the headquarters of the largest advertising agencies in the USA – as shown in the HBO series MadMen. Hollywood & Vine, is the intersection of Hollywood Avenue and Vine Street in Hollywood, California, long the symbolic heart of the US entertainment industry. Now, Madison Avenue and Hollywood & Vine are coming together to form a new intersection – *Madison & Vine* – which represents the merging of advertising and entertainment in an effort to break through the clutter and create new avenues for reaching consumers with more engaging messages (see Marketing at Work 12.1).

Message strategy The first step in creating effective advertising messages is to plan a *message strategy* – to decide what general message will be communicated to consumers. The purpose of advertising is to get consumers to think about or react to the product or company in a certain way. People will react only if they believe that they will benefit from doing so. Thus, developing an effective message strategy begins with identifying customer *benefits* that can be used as advertising appeals. Ideally, advertising message strategy will follow directly from the company's broader positioning and customer value strategies.

Message strategy statements tend to be plain, straightforward outlines of benefits and positioning points that the advertiser wants to stress. The advertiser must next develop a compelling *creative concept* – or '*big idea*' – that will bring the message strategy to life in a distinctive and memorable way. At this stage, simple message ideas

MARKETING AT WORK 12.1

Madison & Vine: The new intersection of advertising and entertainment

Welcome to the ever-busier intersection of Madison & Vine, where the advertising industry meets the entertainment industry. In today's cluttered advertising environment, Madison Avenue knows that it must find new ways to engage ad-weary consumers with more compelling messages. The answer? Entertainment! And who knows more about entertainment than the folks at Hollywood & Vine? The term 'Madison & Vine' has come to represent the merging of advertising and entertainment. It takes one of two primary forms: *advertainment* or *branded entertainment*.

The aim of *advertainment* is to make ads themselves so entertaining, or so useful, that people *want* to watch them. It's advertising by invitation rather than by intrusion. There's no chance that you'd watch ads on purpose, you say? Think again. For example, the Super Bowl has become an annual advertainment showcase. Tens of millions of people tune in to the Super Bowl each year, as much to watch the entertaining ads as to see the game – a tradition since the famous '1984' ad for Apple which was directed by Ridley Scott of *Gladiator* and *Black Hawk Down* fame.

And rather than bemoaning TiVo and other DVR systems, many advertisers are now using them as a new medium for showing useful or entertaining ads that consumers actually volunteer to watch. For example, Best Buy created a TiVo showcase, which offered subscribers a chance to access two exclusive videos, win a CD, and opt in to six entertaining product vignettes. Sixty-three per cent of TiVo subscribers opted in to the showcase, staying an average of 3.36 minutes. Interestingly, a recent study found that DVR users aren't necessarily skipping all the ads. According to the study, 55 per cent of DVR users take their finger off the fast-forward button to watch a commercial that is entertaining or relevant, sometimes even watching it more than once. 'If advertising is really entertaining, you don't zap it,' notes an industry observer. 'You might even go out of your way to see it.'

Branded entertainment (or *brand integrations*) involves making the brand an inseparable part of some other form of entertainment. The most common form of branded entertainment is product placements – imbedding brands as props within other programming. The nature of the placement can very widely, from a brief glimpse of a Tropicana carton sitting on the kitchen table on HBO's *The Sopranos* to having products scripted into the theme of the programme.

For the right price, a brand can even play the starring role in a popular show. For example, by its second season, Donald Trump's *The Apprentice* had evolved into a lush outlet for brand integrations. Blue-chip companies like Procter & Gamble, General Motors, Staples, Unilever and Burger King paid $1–4 million per episode to integrate their brands into the hit reality show. Most of these placements have been hugely successful. In one episode, *Apprentice* teams competed to promote a new variant of P&G's Crest toothpaste. An online contest held in conjunction with the show generated the heaviest single day of traffic ever for a P&G brand website, with more than 3 million hits. A spokesperson for P&G's oral-care group called it 'The best money we've ever spent.'

Welcome to Madison & Vine. As this book cover suggests, in today's cluttered advertising environment, Madison Avenue must find new ways to engage ad-weary consumers with more compelling messages. The answer? Entertainment!

Source: Scott Donaton (2006), *Madison and Vine*, copyright © 2006, The McGraw-Hill Companies, Inc.

Perhaps no company has had more mileage out of such brand integrations than GM's Pontiac division. It all started with an extraordinary giveaway on a popular talk show. When *The Oprah Winfrey Show* opened its 19th season with a 'Wildest Dreams' theme, Oprah electrified the studio audience by giving every one of the 276 people in attendance a new, fully loaded Pontiac G6 sedan worth $28,400. The programme also included footage of Oprah helping on the G6's production line and praising a variety of the car's features. On later shows, Oprah revisited two audience members to explore how their Pontiacs changed their lives. The Oprah giveaway set a new benchmark in the field of branded entertainment. The effort cost Pontiac about $8 million but generated an estimated $20 million in unpaid media coverage and favourable PR. 'It's got talk value, PR spin, there's an emotional connection,' said a branding expert. 'It is something you couldn't have paid for.'

Pontiac followed quickly with another stunningly successful placement, this time on *The Apprentice*. Generally viewed as the most successful *Apprentice* brand integration yet, Pontiac used the show to announce a national early-order programme for its new Solstice two-seat roadster. In a show that included photo shoots of the sleek new car and discussions of Solstice benefits, *Apprentice* teams pulled all-nighters to create Solstice promotion brochures. The result? Pontiac's website traffic skyrocketed 1,400 per cent the night the episode aired, and some 41,000 people filled out online registration forms. When the car went on sale at 2 pm the next day, Pontiac sold 1,000 vehicles within 41 minutes and 7,100 within ten days, selling out all the Solstices it planned to build for the year.

Originally created with TV in mind, branded entertainment has spread quickly into other sectors of the entertainment industry. It's widely used in films – think about Ray Ban sunglasses and *Men in Black*, or Audi's sleek concept car in *I, Robot*. And when DreamWorks built the terminal for its film *The Terminal*, along with United Airlines, more than 35 companies chipped in millions to build real stores – Brookstone, Discovery Store, Borders Books, Paul Mitchell – as well as a working food court with Starbucks, Baskin-Robbins, Burger King and Baja Fresh.

So, Madison & Vine is *the* new meeting place for the advertising and entertainment industries. When done right, advertainment and branded entertainment can pay big dividends. However, experts caution that Madison & Vine can also be a dangerous crossing. They worry that making ads too entertaining might detract from the seller's brand message – consumers will remember the clever ad but forget the brand or advertiser. And they note that the intersection is getting pretty congested. With all these new ad formats and product placements, Madison & Vine threatens to create even more of the very clutter that it's designed to break through.

They also worry about potential customer resentment and backlash. Some TV shows bristle outright with product placements. A heavily branded show like *American Idol* contains, on average, more than 66 product placement shots per hour. In the second quarter of 2005, the ten prime-time TV shows with the most placements included 11,579 'brand shout-outs'. At what point will consumers decide that the intersection of Madison & Vine is just too congested and take yet another different route?

Sources: Pontiac example adapted from portions of Gail Schiller, 'Win, Draw for Burnett Branding', *The Hollywood Reporter*, 1 June 2005, accessed at www.hollywoodreporter.com; and Jean Halliday and Claire Atkinson, 'Pontiac Gets Major Mileage Out of $8 Million "Oprah" Deal', *Advertising Age*, 20 September 2004, p. 12. Other quotes and information from '10 Biggest Madison & Vine Deals', *Advertising Age*, 20 December 2004; Stuart Elliott, 'Seinfeld and Superman Join Forces Again in Spots for American Express, This Time on the Web', *New York Times*, 30 March 2004, p. C.5; Marc Graser, 'Product-Placement Spending Poised to Hit $4.25 Billion in '05', *Advertising Age*, 4 April 2005, p. 16; Jim Edwards, 'Will Product Placement Get Its Own Comeuppance?', *Brandweek*, 25 July–1 August, p. 13; and 'Study Spots Ad-Skipping Trends', *The Hollywood Reporter*, 19 August 2005, accessed at www.hollywoodreporter.com.

become great ad campaigns. Usually, a copywriter and art director will team up to generate many creative concepts, hoping that one of these concepts will turn out to be the big idea. The creative concept may emerge as a visualisation, a phrase or a combination of the two.

The creative concept will guide the choice of specific appeals to be used in an advertising campaign. *Advertising appeals* should have three characteristics. First, they should be *meaningful*, pointing out benefits that make the product more desirable or interesting to consumers. Second, appeals must be *believable* – consumers must believe that the product or service will deliver the promised benefits.

However, the most meaningful and believable benefits may not be the best ones to feature. Appeals should also be *distinctive* – they should tell how the product is better than the competing brands. For example, the most meaningful benefit of owning a wristwatch is that it keeps accurate time, yet few watch ads feature this benefit. Instead, based on the distinctive benefits they offer, watch advertisers might select any of a number of advertising themes. Dolce & Gabbana consistently features style and fashion, whereas Rolex stresses luxury and status.

Message execution The advertiser now has to turn the big idea into an actual ad execution that will capture the target market's attention and interest. The creative team must find the best style, tone, words and format for executing the message. Any message can be presented in different *execution styles*, such as the following:

- ■ *Slice of life*: This style shows one or more 'typical' people using the product in a normal setting. For example, two mothers at a picnic discuss the nutritional benefits of Dairylea cheese spread.

- ■ *Lifestyle*: This style shows how a product fits in with a particular lifestyle. For example, an ad for Mongoose mountain bikes shows a serious biker traversing remote and rugged but beautiful terrain and states, 'There are places that are so awesome and so killer that you'd like to tell the whole world about them. But please, *don't*.'

- ■ *Fantasy*: This style creates a fantasy around the product or its use. For instance, many ads are built around dream themes. Gap even introduced a perfume named Dream. Ads show a woman sleeping blissfully and suggests that the scent is 'the stuff that clouds are made of'.

- ■ *Mood or image*: This style builds a mood or image around the product or service, such as beauty, love or serenity. Few claims are made about the product except through suggestion. For example, ads for Singapore Airlines feature soft lighting and refined flight attendants pampering relaxed but happy customers.

- ■ *Musical*: This style shows people or cartoon characters singing about the product. For example, one of the most famous ads in history was a Coca-Cola ad built around the song 'I'd Like to Teach the World to Sing'.

Humour in advertising: the Got Milk? campaign. 'Smash hit by Hayden. Body by milk. You don't have to be a hero to feel invincible. That's why I drink milk. The protein helps build muscle and some studies suggest teens who choose it tend to be leaner. Cheers to that.'

■ *Personality symbol:* This style creates a character that represents the product. The character might be *animated* (Tony the Tiger for Kellogg's cereals) or *real* (the Marlboro man).

■ *Technical expertise:* This style shows the company's expertise in making the product. Thus, Maxwell House shows one of its buyers carefully selecting coffee beans, and Gallo tells about its many years of wine-making experience.

■ *Scientific evidence*: This style presents survey or scientific evidence that the brand is better or better liked than one or more other brands. For years, Crest toothpaste has used scientific evidence to convince buyers that Crest is better than other brands at fighting cavities.

■ *Testimonial evidence or endorsement*: This style features a highly believable or likeable source endorsing the product. It could be ordinary people saying how much they like a given product or a celebrity presenting the product. For example, Lucozade supported their Isotonic brand with a series of ads featuring professional sports coaches saying how important hydration was for top sportsmen.

The advertiser also must choose a *tone* for the ad. Procter & Gamble always uses a positive tone: its ads say something very positive about its products. P&G usually avoids humour that might take attention away from the message. In contrast, many advertisers now use edgy humour to break through the commercial clutter.

The advertiser must use memorable and attention-getting *words* in the ad. For example, rather than claiming simply that 'a BMW is a well-engineered automobile', BMW uses more creative and higher impact phrasing: 'The ultimate driving machine.' It's not Häagen-Dazs is 'a good-tasting luxury ice cream,' but rather 'Our passport to indulgence: passion in a touch, perfection in a cup, summer in a spoon, one perfect moment.'

Finally, *format* elements make a difference in an ad's impact as well as in its cost. A small change in ad design can make a big difference in its effect. In a print ad, the *illustration* is the first thing the reader notices – it must be strong enough to draw attention. Next, the *headline* must effectively entice the right people to read the copy. Finally, the *copy* – the main block of text in the ad – must be simple but strong and convincing. Moreover, these three elements must effectively work *together* to persuasively present customer value.

Selecting advertising media

The major steps in media selection are:

1 deciding on *reach, frequency* and *impact*;
2 choosing among major *media types*;
3 selecting specific *media vehicles*; and
4 deciding on *media timing*.

Deciding on reach, frequency and impact To select media, the advertiser must decide on the reach and frequency needed to achieve advertising objectives. *Reach* is a measure of the *percentage* of people in the target market who are exposed to the ad campaign during a given period of time. For example, the advertiser might try to reach 70 per cent of the target market during the first three months of the campaign. *Frequency* is a measure of how many *times* the average person in the target market is exposed to the message. For example, the advertiser might want an average exposure frequency of three.

The advertiser also must decide on the desired *media impact* – the *qualitative value* of a message exposure through a given medium. For example, for products that need to be demonstrated, messages on television may have more impact than messages on radio because television uses sight *and* sound. The same message in one newspaper (say, the *Financial Times*) may be more believable than in another (say, the *Daily Mail*). In general, the more reach, frequency and impact the advertiser seeks, the higher the advertising budget will have to be.

TABLE 12.3 Profiles of major media types

Medium	Advantages	Limitations
Newspapers	Flexibility; timeliness; good local market coverage; broad acceptability; high believability	Short life; poor reproduction quality; small pass-along audience
Television	Good mass-marketing coverage; low cost per exposure; combines sight, sound and motion; appealing to the senses	High absolute costs; high clutter; fleeting exposure; less audience selectivity
Direct mail	High audience selectivity; flexibility; no ad competition within the same medium; allows personalisation	Relatively high cost per exposure; 'junk mail' image
Radio	Good local acceptance; high geographic and demographic selectivity; low cost	Audio only, fleeting exposure; low attention ('the half-heard' medium); fragmented audiences
Magazines	High geographic and demographic selectivity; credibility and prestige; high-quality reproduction; long life and good pass-along readership	Long ad purchase lead time; high cost; no guarantee of position
Outdoor	Flexibility; high repeat exposure; low cost; low message competition; good positional selectivity	Little audience selectivity; creative limitations
Internet	High selectivity; low cost; immediacy; interactive capabilities	Small, demographically skewed audience; relatively low impact; audience controls exposure

Choosing among major media types The media planner has to know the reach, frequency and impact of each of the major media types. As summarised in Table 12.3, the major media types are newspapers, television, direct mail, radio, magazines, outdoor and the Internet. Each medium has advantages and limitations. Media planners consider many factors when making their media choices. They want to choose media that will effectively and efficiently present the advertising message to target customers. Thus, they must consider each medium's impact, message effectiveness and cost.

The mix of media must be re-examined regularly. For a long time, television and magazines have dominated in the media mixes of national advertisers, with other media often neglected. However, as discussed at the start of the chapter, the media mix appears to be shifting. As mass-media costs rise, audiences shrink and exciting new digital media emerge, many advertisers are finding new ways to reach consumers. They are supplementing the traditional mass media with more specialised and highly targeted media that cost less and target more effectively.

For example, cable and satellite television systems are booming. Such systems allow narrow programming formats such as all sports, all news, nutrition, arts, home improvement and gardening, cooking, travel, history, finance and others that target select groups. BSkyB and other cable operators are even testing systems that will let them target specific types of ads to specific types of customers. For example, only pet owners would see ads from pet food companies.[29] Advertisers can take advantage of such 'narrowcasting' to target specific market segments. Satellite television and set-top box-based broadcast media seem to make good sense with their multitude of channels, each with a specific set of audience characteristics. But, increasingly, ads are popping up in far less likely places. In their efforts to find less costly and more highly targeted ways to reach consumers, advertisers have discovered a dazzling collection of 'alternative media', including computer games (see Marketing at Work 12.2).

MARKETING AT WORK 12.2

Advertising in computer games

In recent years, advertising professionals have become increasingly concerned that traditional media is being ignored by key consumer segments – especially young men and/or highly educated urban residents. Research suggests that these key groups are spending less and less time watching television or reading magazines and newspapers and are instead using the Internet and playing games, whether it be on a PC, a console or on a handheld device like a mobile phone, an iPhone or a Nintendo DS.

Electronic Arts, one of the world's largest video games companies, is releasing a free online version of its popular Battlefield games, called *Battlefield Heroes*. Why would it do this? EA hopes that the money lost from not selling the game will be more than made up for by reduced costs (mass production and distribution) and by advertising revenue from brand managers keen to place their products where they might be seen by these elusive groups. Adverts will not appear in the game itself, but rather during pauses as a new game is waiting to start, or a new level is loading. EA will periodically release new content – levels, equipment – which will come with updated ads from new sponsors.[30]

The growth and potential of this media has not gone unnoticed by established companies. Activision now works with the market research agency Neilson to collect and interpret audience measurement figures for computer game adverts.[31] Google and Yahoo! have already invested heavily, and Microsoft recently bought out a specialist outfit called Massive.

Analysts say the in-game advertising market is worth about $514 million today. And dynamic in-game advertising, which allows advertisers to change the advertisements at will, is expected to reach $675 million by 2012 in the United States, according to consumer research group Parks Associates.[32]

Microsoft sees its early lead in the in-game advertising market as a strategic opportunity that fits well into the company's overall advertising strategy.

'The idea is to have advertisements appear and fit in naturally to the games just as they would in real life,' said Jay Sampson, vice president of North American and Asia Pacific sales for Massive, Microsoft's in-game advertising marketplace. *'But these advertisements are also dynamic. So the ads can be updated or changed by the advertiser at any time.'*

'Emerging media, like in-game advertising, is a huge component of our overall strategy,' said Matthew Carr, senior director of Microsoft Digital Advertising Solutions. 'We're already in a leadership position here. And we see this as being where the future growth will be.'[33]

TABLE 12.4 Game ads – recall numbers

KEY METRIC	GAMERS NOT EXPOSED TO ADS	GAMERS EXPOSED TO ADS	% INCREASE
Brand Familiarity	20%	40%	+100%
Brand Rating	14%	25%	+79%
Purchase Consideration	28%	47%	+68%
Ad Recall	38%	55%	+45%
Positive Ad Rating	30%	41%	+37%

Source: http://www.massiveincorporated.com/casestudies.html. Massive, Inc.

Adverts are everywhere these days – this neon sign was added to the game world of Splinter Cell.
Source: http://www.trendwatching.com/img/briefing/2006-07/SplinterCell_axe.jpg

Does advertising your products in a game bring any advantages? IGA Worldwide, a company specialising in matching brands with games, believes that in fact there are five clear advantages, and that work done for them by Nielsen supports this:[34]

1   *Realism* – as the real world is filled with advertising, the plausibility and credibility of game worlds can be enhanced by incorporating brand imagery and simulated posters/displays in the game setting. Neilson found that most gamers actually liked the extra realism ads brought to the games – whether the AXE (Lynx) deodorant neon sign in *Splinter Cell* or a Coke vending machine in *Second Life*.

2   *Non-interruptive* – we all hate pop-up ads on websites, and we grow impatient in waiting for an interstitial to close, but would we think our gaming experience had been lessened by a Toyota advert appearing on a hoarding as we screamed round the Nürburgring, or the advertising for Adidas or Nike around the pitch in many football games?

3   *Engaging* – as one 'media futures' advertising executive said, 'The killer benefit of gaming is attention. We live in a multimedia world and you can't guarantee people will take any notice of your TV ad, but gamers have to concentrate on what they're doing, or their character dies. Your message is much more likely to get through.'[35] If the product and brand can be incorporated into the game in a credible way this enhances the engagement immensely – the neon AXE sign

in *Splinter Cell* was designed into the game so that it became an obstacle the gamer has to negotiate. Once this is accomplished, the in-game hero then uses the sign to tether a rope line to as he abseils his way towards the bad guys.

4   *Recall, awareness and purchase intention* – if brands are making the game more realistic and enjoyable, then gamers will be much more likely to recall those products at a later date and also be more likely to consider purchasing them.

5   *Measurable* – the number of people that see a TV advert or drive past a roadside hoarding can only be estimated. Some online multi-player games like *Second Life*® produce extraordinarily accurate and detailed data about the in-game behaviour of players – where they were, what they looked at and for how long. This data is fascinating for social scientists as well as brand managers. See Table 12.4 in Marketing at Work 12.2 for Example data.

So are all brands suitable for in-game advertising? The answer appears to be no – with two reasons. First, if the brand is not one which could credibly appear in the context of the game, it will look inauthentic. Second, some groups are becoming increasingly concerned that in-game adverts may be just too effective with certain vulnerable groups – such as young children, as one newspaper columnist reports:

What is also striking is that advergaming is almost entirely unregulated. The Advertising Standards Agency in the UK

oversees adverts that play before a game starts, but not adverts within the game, which are classed as sponsorship.

'I think the ASA ought to have its brief expanded to cover computer games properly,' says John Beyer, a director of Mediawatch UK, the lobby group formerly known as the National Viewers' and Listeners' Association.

So far, tobacco advertising has been kept out of computer games by the software companies themselves. For example, Sony, which publishes the current Formula One *game, and Electronic Arts, which used to publish it, both refuse tobacco adverts. Also, a game with alcohol advertising would be unlikely to get an age rating below 18 from Pan European Game Information, the trade body that certifies games as suitable for particular age groups. Even so, Electronic Arts and Activision, among other publishers, have worked with fast-food companies despite growing concerns about levels of obesity in the population. More adverts in games are also likely to lead to more calls for regulation.*[36]

Sources: See notes 30–36 at the end of this chapter.

Another important trend affecting media selection is the rapid growth in the number of 'media multitaskers', people who absorb more than one medium at a time:

It looks like people who aren't satisfied with 'just watching TV' are in good company. According to a recent survey, three-fourths of US TV viewers read the newspaper while they watch TV, and two-thirds of them go online during their TV time. According to the study, 70 per cent of media users say they at one time or another try to absorb two or more forms of media at once. What's more, if today's kids are any indication, media multitasking is on the rise. Nearly a third of kids 8 to 18 say when they're doing schoolwork at home, they're often talking on the phone, surfing the Web, instant messaging, watching TV or listening to music at the same time.[37]

Media planners need to take such media interactions into account when selecting the types of media they will use.

Selecting specific media vehicles The media planner now must choose the best *media vehicles* – specific media within each general media type. For example, television vehicles include *Coronation Street* and ITV's *News at Ten*. Magazine vehicles include *Vogue*, the Italian *Corriere della Sera*, and *FHM*.

Media planners must compute the cost per thousand persons reached by a vehicle. A full-page colour advert in the *Daily Telegraph* costs about £60,000 per day – and daily readership averages around 2.1 million, meaning that the cost per thousand is about £29. In the *Guardian*, a similar advert will cost £18,000 but, with a readership of 1.1 million, a cost per thousand of £16.[38] The media planner ranks each magazine by cost per thousand and favours those magazines with the lower cost per thousand for reaching target consumers. The media planner must also consider the costs of producing ads for different media. Whereas newspaper ads may cost very little to produce, flashy television ads may cost millions.

In selecting specific media vehicles, the media planner must balance media costs against several media effectiveness factors. First, the planner should evaluate the media vehicle's *audience quality*. For a Huggies disposable nappy advertisement, for example, *You and Your Baby* magazine would have a high exposure value; *GQ* would have a low exposure value. For the numbers given above for the *Telegraph* and the *Guardian*, the planner must consider the make-up of the readership – the *Guardian* may be cheaper per thousand, but is a higher proportion of the *Telegraph*'s readership more likely to conform to the targeted segments – those interested in luxury cars, for example? Second, the media planner should consider *audience attention*. Readers of *Vogue*, for example, typically pay more attention to ads than do *The Economist* readers. Third, the planner should assess the vehicle's *editorial quality* – the *Financial Times* is more believable and prestigious than the *Daily Mail*, *Speigel* over *Bild*.

Deciding on media timing The advertiser must also decide how to schedule the advertising over the course of a year. Suppose sales of a product peak in December and drop in March. The firm can vary its advertising to follow the seasonal pattern, to oppose the seasonal pattern, or to be the same all year. Most firms do some seasonal advertising – for example, before major annual events or holidays like Christmas, Easter and Valentine's Day. Some marketers do *only* seasonal advertising. For instance, Bell's advertises its whisky only in the period leading up to Christmas.

Finally, the advertiser has to choose the pattern of the ads. *Continuity* means scheduling ads evenly within a given period. *Pulsing* means scheduling ads unevenly over a given time period. Thus, 52 ads could either be scheduled at one per week during the year or pulsed in several bursts. The idea behind pulsing is to advertise heavily for a short period to build awareness that carries over to the next advertising period. Those who favour pulsing feel that it can be used to achieve the same impact as a steady schedule but at a much lower cost. However, some media planners believe that although pulsing achieves minimal awareness, it sacrifices depth of advertising communications.

Evaluating advertising effectiveness and return on advertising investment

Advertising accountability has become a hot issue for most companies. Increasingly, top management is asking: 'What return are we getting on our advertising investment?' and 'How do we know that we're spending the right amount?' According to a recent survey by the US Association of National Advertisers (ANA), measuring advertising's efficiency and effectiveness is the number one issue in the minds of today's advertisers. In the survey, 61.5 per cent of respondents said that it is important that they define, measure and take action in the area of advertising accountability.[39]

Advertisers should regularly evaluate two types of advertising results: communication effects and the sales and profit effects. Measuring the *communication effects* of an ad or ad campaign tells whether the ads and media are communicating the ad message well. Individual ads can be tested before or after they are run. Before an ad is placed, the advertiser can show it to consumers, ask how they like it, and measure message recall or attitude changes resulting from it. After an ad is run, the advertiser can measure how the ad affected consumer recall or product awareness, knowledge and preference. Pre- and post-evaluations of communication effects can be made for entire advertising campaigns as well.

Advertisers have become pretty good at measuring the communication effects of their ads and ad campaigns. However, the *sales and profits* effects of advertising are often much harder to measure. For example, what sales and profits are produced by an ad campaign that increases brand awareness by 20 per cent and brand preference by 10 per cent? Sales and profits are affected by many factors besides advertising – such as product features, price and availability.

One way to measure the sales and profit effects of advertising is to compare past sales and profits with past advertising expenditures. Another way is through experiments. For example, to test the effects of different advertising spending levels, Coca-Cola could vary the amount it spends on advertising in different market areas and measure the differences in the resulting sales and profit levels. More complex experiments could be designed to include other variables, such as differences in the ads or media used.

However, because so many factors affect advertising effectiveness, some controllable and others not, measuring the results of advertising spending remains an inexact science. Despite the growing importance of advertising accountability, only 19 per cent of the ANA study respondents were satisfied with their ability to measure return on advertising investments. When asked if they would be able to 'forecast the impact on sales' of a 10 per cent cut in advertising spending, 63 per cent said no.

Other advertising considerations

In developing advertising strategies and programmes, the company must address two additional questions. First, how will the company organise its advertising function – who will perform which advertising tasks? Second, how will the company adapt its advertising strategies and programmes to the complexities of international markets?

Organising for advertising

Different companies organise in different ways to handle advertising. In small companies, advertising might be handled by someone in the sales department. Large companies set up advertising departments whose job it is to set the advertising budget, work with the ad agency, and handle other advertising not done by the agency. Most large companies use outside advertising agencies because they offer several advantages.

How does an **advertising agency** work? Advertising agencies were started in the mid to late 1800s by salespeople and brokers who worked for the media and received a commission for selling advertising space to companies. As time passed, the salespeople began to help customers prepare their ads. Eventually, they formed agencies and grew closer to the advertisers than to the media.

Today's agencies employ specialists who can often perform advertising tasks better than can the company's own staff. Agencies also bring an outside point of view to solving the company's problems, along with lots of experience from working with different clients and situations. So, today, even companies with strong advertising departments of their own use advertising agencies.

Some ad agencies are huge – the US based Omnicon Group had revenues exceeding $11.4 billion. In Europe, WPP in London was the biggest ($10.8 billion) with the French Publicis Group in second place ($5.9 billion).[40] Most large advertising agencies have the staff and resources to handle all phases of an advertising campaign for their clients, from creating a marketing plan to developing ad campaigns and preparing, placing and evaluating ads.

International advertising decisions

International advertisers face many complexities not encountered by domestic advertisers. The most basic issue concerns the degree to which global advertising should be adapted to the unique characteristics of various country markets. Some large advertisers have attempted to support their global brands with highly standardised worldwide advertising, with campaigns that work as well in Bangkok as they do in Birmingham or Berlin. For example, Range Rover has created a worldwide brand image of ruggedness and reliability; Coca-Cola's Sprite brand uses standardised appeals to target the world's youth. Ads for Gillette's Venus razors are almost identical worldwide, with only minor adjustments to suit the local culture.

Standardisation produces many benefits – lower advertising costs, greater global advertising coordination and a more consistent worldwide image. But it also has drawbacks. Most importantly, it ignores the fact that country markets differ greatly in their cultures, demographics and economic conditions. Thus, most international advertisers 'think globally but act locally'. They develop global advertising *strategies* that make their worldwide advertising efforts more efficient and consistent. Then they adapt their advertising *programmes* to make them more responsive to consumer needs and expectations within local markets.[41] For example, Coca-Cola has a pool of different commercials that can be used in or adapted to several different international markets. Some can be used with only minor changes – such as language – in several different countries. Local and regional managers decide which commercials work best for which markets.[42]

Global advertisers face several special problems. Advertising media costs and availability differ vastly from country to country, for instance. Countries also differ in the extent to which they regulate advertising practices. Many countries have extensive systems of laws restricting how much a company can spend on advertising, the media used, the nature of advertising claims and other aspects of the advertising programme. Such restrictions often require advertisers to adapt their campaigns from country to country. For example, alcoholic products cannot be advertised or sold in Muslim countries. In many countries, Sweden and Norway for example, food ads are banned from kid's TV. To play it safe, McDonald's advertises itself as a family restaurant in Sweden. Comparative ads, while acceptable and even common in the United States and Canada, are less commonly used in the UK, unacceptable in Japan, and illegal in India and Brazil.

China has restrictive censorship rules for TV and radio advertising; for example, the words 'the best' are banned, as are ads that 'violate social customs' or present women in 'improper ways'. McDonald's recently avoided government sanctions there by publicly apologising for an ad that crossed cultural norms by showing a customer begging for a discount. Similarly, Coca-Cola's Indian subsidiary was forced to end a promotion that offered prizes, such as a trip to Hollywood, because it violated India's established trade practices by encouraging customers to buy in order to 'gamble'.[43]

Thus, although advertisers may develop global strategies to guide their overall advertising efforts, specific advertising programmes must usually be adapted to meet local cultures and customs, media characteristics and advertising regulations.

MAKING CONNECTIONS Linking the concepts

Think about what goes on behind the scenes for the ads we all tend to take for granted.

■ Pick a favourite print or television ad. Why do you like it? Do you think that it's effective? Can you think of an ad that people like that may not be effective?

■ Dig a little deeper and learn about the campaign *behind* your ad. What are the campaign's objectives? What is its budget? Assess the campaign's message and media strategies. Looking beyond your own feelings about the ad, is the campaign likely to be effective?

SALES PROMOTION

Advertising often works closely with another promotion tool, sales promotion. *Sales promotion* consists of short-term incentives to encourage purchase or sales of a product or service. Whereas advertising offers reasons to buy a product or service, sales promotion offers reasons to buy *now*.

Examples of sales promotions are found everywhere. A free-standing insert in the Sunday newspaper contains a coupon offering £1 off a classical CD. An email from Ocado.com offers a £5 discount on your next home delivery. The end of the aisle display in the local supermarket tempts impulse buyers with a wall of beer multi-packs. A businessman buys a new Sony laptop and gets a free carrying case, or a family buys a new car and receives a rebate of £500. A DIY chain might receive a 10 per cent discount on selected Black & Decker portable power tools if it agrees to advertise them in local newspapers. Sales promotion includes a wide variety of promotion tools designed to stimulate earlier or stronger market response.

Rapid growth of sales promotion

Sales promotion tools are used by most organisations, including manufacturers, distributors, retailers and not-for-profit institutions. They are targeted toward final buyers (*consumer promotions*), retailers and wholesalers (*trade promotions*), business customers (*business promotions*), and members of the sales force (*sales force promotions*). According to Institute of Sales Promotion estimates, more than £20 billion was spent on Sales Promotion in 2006 in the UK alone – £1 billion more than was spent on broadcast, outdoor and press advertising combined.[44]

Several factors have contributed to the rapid growth of sales promotion, particularly in consumer markets. First, inside the company, product managers face greater pressures to increase their current sales, and promotion is viewed as an effective short-term sales tool. Second, externally, the company faces more competition and competing brands are less differentiated. Increasingly, competitors are using sales promotion to help differentiate their offers. Third, advertising efficiency has declined because of rising costs, media clutter and legal restraints. Finally, consumers have become more deal-oriented, and ever larger retailers are demanding more deals from manufacturers.

The growing use of sales promotion has resulted in *promotion clutter*, similar to advertising clutter. Consumers are increasingly tuning out promotions, weakening their ability to trigger immediate purchase. Manufacturers are now searching for ways to rise above the clutter, such as offering larger coupon values or creating more dramatic point-of-purchase displays.

In developing a sales promotion programme, a company must first set sales promotion objectives and then select the best tools for accomplishing these objectives.

Sales promotion objectives

Sales promotion objectives vary widely. Sellers may use *consumer promotions* to increase short-term sales or to help build long-term market share. Objectives for *trade promotions* include getting retailers to carry new items and more inventory, getting them to advertise the product and give it more shelf space, and getting them to buy ahead. For the *sales force*, objectives include getting more sales force support for current or new products or getting salespeople to sign up new accounts. Sales promotions are usually used together with advertising, personal selling or other promotion mix tools. Consumer promotions must usually be advertised and can add excitement and pulling power to ads. Trade and sales force promotions support the firm's personal selling process.

In general, rather than creating only short-term sales or temporary brand switching, sales promotions should help to reinforce the product's position and build long-term *customer relationships*. If properly designed, every sales promotion tool has the potential to build both short-term excitement and long-term consumer relationships. Increasingly, marketers are avoiding 'quick fix', price-only promotions in favour of promotions designed to build brand equity. Examples include all of the 'frequency marketing programmes' and loyalty clubs that have mushroomed in recent years. Most hotels, supermarkets and airlines now offer frequent-guest/buyer/flyer programmes offering rewards to regular customers. For example, Air France, offers a loyalty programme called Flying Blue, a programme that targets its core market of not so frequent leisure travellers.

Major sales promotion tools

Many tools can be used to accomplish sales promotion objectives. Descriptions of the main consumer, trade and business promotion tools follow.

Consumer promotion tools

The main *consumer promotion tools* include samples, coupons, cash refunds, price packs, premiums, advertising specialities, patronage rewards, point-of-purchase displays and demonstrations, and contests, sweepstakes and games.

Samples are offers of a trial amount of a product. Sampling is the most effective – but most expensive – way to introduce a new product or to create new excitement for an existing one. Some samples are free; for others, the company charges a small amount to offset its cost. The sample might be delivered door to door, sent by mail, handed out in a store, attached to another product or featured in an ad. Sometimes, samples are combined into sample packs, which can then be used to promote other products and services. Sampling can be a powerful promotional tool. Consider this example of cough sweets originating in Fleetwood, UK:

> Fisherman's Friend throat lozenges used sampling as the centrepiece of a very successful brand-building programme. It began by passing out 250,000 samples of its lozenges at more than 25 fairs, sporting events, and other happenings where it was a sponsor. Each

sample contained an invitation to visit the Fisherman's Friend website, where customers could enter a contest to win a Mini Cooper by submitting a slogan to be used in the future 'Tell a Friend' (about Fisherman's Friend) ad campaign. The sampling promotion was a complete success. US sales of Fisherman's Friend lozenges grew 115 per cent for the year, 25 per cent better than expectations. Some 5,000 people submitted a slogan for the company's new ad campaign. The winner suggested the slogan, 'Lose a Cough. Gain a Friend', which is now featured in ads and on the website. The successful sampling campaign continues via the company's website, which invites consumers to sign themselves and a friend up to receive free samples of Fisherman's Friend in the mail.[45]

Coupons are certificates that give buyers a saving when they purchase specified products. UK firms alone issued coupons with a redeemable value of £4 billion in 2007. Coupons can promote early trial of a new brand or stimulate sales of a mature brand. However, as a result of coupon clutter, redemption rates have been declining in recent years.[46] Thus, most major consumer goods companies are issuing fewer coupons and targeting them more carefully. Marketers are also cultivating new outlets for distributing coupons, such as supermarket shelf dispensers, electronic point-of-sale coupon printers, or even text messaging systems. Text message couponing is popular in Europe, India and Japan, and it's slowly gaining popularity in the United States. For instance, if a local nightclub is having a slow night, it can log in and blast out a special offer coupon. Some companies also offer coupons on their websites or through online coupon services.

Cash refunds (or rebates) are like coupons except that the price reduction occurs after the purchase rather than at the retail outlet. The consumer sends a 'proof of purchase' to the manufacturer, who then refunds part of the purchase price by mail. For example, Citroën often offer customers a mix of cash refunds and part-exchange on new cars and Barratt offers relatively substantial rebates to people who buy newly built houses from them.

Price packs (also called money-off deals) offer consumers savings off the regular price of a product. The reduced prices are marked by the producer directly on the label or package. Price packs can be single packages sold at a reduced price (such as two for the price of one), or two related products banded together (such as a toothbrush and toothpaste). Price packs are very effective – even more so than coupons – in stimulating short-term sales.

Premiums are goods offered either free or at low cost as an incentive to buy a product, ranging from toys included with kids' products to phone cards and DVDs. A premium may come inside the package (in-pack), outside the package (on-pack), or through the mail. Kellogg's are past masters at this – their *Galactic Gadgets* promotion offered *Star Wars* prizes via an assortment of channels. Packages of Frosted Flakes contained a free light-up Saberspoon. Other cereals offered an R2-D2 snack bowl that beeps and whistles. And if your specially-marked package of Pop-Tarts played Darth Vader music, you won a Darth Vader Voice Changer.

Advertising specialities, also called *promotional products*, are useful articles imprinted with an advertiser's name, logo, or message that are given as gifts to consumers. Typical items include T-shirts and other apparel, pens, coffee mugs, calendars, key rings, mouse pads, matches, tote bags, coolers, golf balls, and caps. Such items can be very effective. In a recent study, 71 per cent of all consumers surveyed had received at least one promotional product in the last 12 months. Seventy-six per cent of those were able to recall the advertiser's name on the promotional product they received, compared to only 53.5 per cent who could recall the name of an advertiser in a print publication they had read in the past week.[47]

Patronage rewards are cash or other awards offered for the regular use of a certain company's products or services. For example, airlines offer frequent flyer plans, awarding points for miles travelled that can be turned in for free airline trips. And supermarkets issue frequent shopper cards that dole out a wealth of discounts at the checkout. Baskin-Robbins offers frequent purchase awards – for every ten purchases, customers receive a free ice cream.

Point-of-purchase (POP) promotions include displays and demonstrations that take place at the point of purchase or sale. Think of your last visit to the local Tesco, WHSmith or Boots. Chances are good that you were tripping over aisle displays, promotional signs, 'shelf talkers', or demonstrators offering free tastes of featured food products. Unfortunately, many retailers do not like to handle the hundreds of displays, signs and posters they receive from manufacturers each year. Manufacturers have responded by offering better POP materials, tying them in with television or print messages, and offering to set them up.

Contests, sweepstakes and *games* give consumers the chance to win something, such as cash, trips, or goods, by luck or through extra effort. A *contest* calls for consumers to submit an entry – a jingle, guess, suggestion – to be judged by a panel that will select the best entries. A *sweepstakes* calls for consumers to submit their names for a draw. A *game* presents consumers with something – bingo numbers, missing letters – every time they buy, which may or may not help them win a prize. A sales contest urges dealers or the sales force to increase their efforts, with prizes going to the top performers.

Trade promotion tools

Manufacturers direct more sales promotion cash toward retailers and wholesalers (78 per cent) than to consumers (22 per cent).[48] Trade promotion can persuade resellers to carry a brand, give it shelf space, promote it in advertising and push it to consumers. Shelf space is so scarce these days that manufacturers often have to offer price-offs, allowances, buy-back guarantees, or free goods to retailers and wholesalers to get products on the shelf and, once there, to keep them on it.

Manufacturers use several trade promotion tools. Many of the tools used for consumer promotions – contests, premiums, displays – can also be used as trade promotions. Or the manufacturer may offer a straight discount off the list price on each case purchased during a stated period of time (also called a *price-off, off-invoice* or *off-list*). Manufacturers also may offer an allowance (usually so much off per case) in return for the retailer's agreement to feature the manufacturer's products in some way. An *advertising allowance* compensates retailers for advertising the product. A *display allowance* compensates them for using special displays.

Manufacturers may offer *free goods*, which are extra cases of merchandise, to resellers who buy a certain quantity or who feature a certain flavour or size. They may offer *push money* – cash or gifts to dealers or their sales forces to 'push' the manufacturer's goods. Manufacturers may give retailers free *speciality advertising items* that carry the company's name, such as pens, pencils, calendars, paperweights, memo pads and mouse mats.

Business promotion tools

Companies spend billions each year on promotion to industrial customers. *Business promotion tools* are used to generate business leads, stimulate purchases, reward customers and motivate salespeople. Business promotion includes many of the same tools used for consumer or trade promotions. Here, we focus on two additional major business promotion tools – conventions and trade shows, and sales contests.

Many companies and trade associations organise *conventions and trade shows* to promote their products. Firms selling to the industry show their products at the trade show. Vendors receive many benefits, such as opportunities to find new sales leads, contact customers, introduce new products, meet new customers, sell more to present customers, and educate customers with publications and audiovisual materials. Trade shows also help companies reach many prospects not reached through their sales forces.

Some trade shows are huge. For example, at the BAUMA mining and construction equipment trade show in Munich, Germany, some 2,800 exhibitors from 47 countries presented their latest product innovations in half a million square metres of space to more than 50,000 attendees from 191 countries.[49]

A *sales contest* is a contest for salespeople or dealers to motivate them to increase their sales performance over a given period. Sales contests motivate and recognise good company performers, who may receive trips, cash prizes or other gifts. Some companies award points for performance, which the receiver can turn in for any of a variety of prizes. Sales contests work best when they are tied to measurable and achievable sales objectives (such as finding new accounts, reviving old accounts, or increasing account profitability).

Developing the sales promotion programme

Beyond selecting the types of promotions to use, marketers must make several other decisions in designing the full sales promotion programme. First, they must decide on the *size of the incentive*. A certain minimum incentive is necessary if the promotion is to succeed; a larger incentive will produce more sales response. The marketer also must set *conditions for participation*. Incentives might be offered to everyone or only to select groups.

Marketer must also decide how to *promote and distribute the promotion* programme itself. A money-off coupon could be given out in a package, at the store, via the Internet, or in an advertisement. Each distribution method involves a different level of reach and cost. Increasingly, marketers are blending several media into a total campaign concept. The *length of the promotion* is also important. If the sales promotion period is too short, many prospects (who may not be buying during that time) will miss it. If the promotion runs too long, the deal will lose some of its 'act now' force.

Evaluation is also very important. Many companies fail to evaluate their sales promotion programmes, and others evaluate them only superficially. Yet marketers should work to measure the returns on their sales promotion investments, just as they should seek to assess the returns on other marketing activities. The most common evaluation method is to compare sales before, during and after a promotion. Marketers should ask, Did the promotion attract new customers or more purchasing from current customers? Can we hold on to these new customers and purchases? Will the long-term customer relationship and sales gains from the promotion justify its costs?

Clearly, sales promotion plays an important role in the total promotion mix. To use it well, the marketer must define the sales promotion objectives, select the best tools, design the sales promotion programme, implement the programme and evaluate the results. Moreover, sales promotion must be coordinated carefully with other promotion mix elements within the integrated marketing communications programme.

PUBLIC RELATIONS

Another major mass-promotion tool is *public relations* – building good relations with the company's various publics by obtaining favourable publicity, building up a good corporate image, and handling or heading off unfavourable rumours, stories and events. Public relations departments may perform any or all of the following functions:[50]

■ *Press relations or press agency:* Creating and placing newsworthy information in the news media to attract attention to a person, product or service.

■ *Product publicity*: Publicising specific products.

■ *Public affairs*: Building and maintaining national or local community relations.

■ *Lobbying*: Building and maintaining relations with legislators and government officials to influence legislation and regulation.

■ *Investor relations*: Maintaining relationships with shareholders and others in the financial community.

■ *Development*: Public relations with donors or members of non-profit organisations to gain financial or volunteer support.

Public relations is used to promote products, people, places, ideas, activities, organisations, and even nations. Companies use public relations to build good relations with consumers, investors, the media and their communities. Trade associations have used public relations to rebuild interest in declining commodities such as eggs, apples, milk and potatoes. The state of New York turned its image around when its 'I ♥ New York!' publicity and advertising campaign took root, bringing in millions more tourists. Whole nations have used public relations to attract more tourists, foreign investment and international support – as we saw with the case on VisitScotland in Chapter 4.

The role and impact of public relations

Public relations can have a strong impact on public awareness at a much lower cost than advertising can. The company does not pay for the space or time in the media. Rather, it pays for a staff to develop and circulate information and to manage events. If the company develops an interesting story, it could be picked up by several different media, having the same effect as advertising that would cost millions. And it would have more credibility than advertising.[51]

Public relations results can sometimes be spectacular. Think how each new Harry Potter book launch was used to turn a commercial release into a social and cultural event. The launches of the seven Harry Potter novels became increasingly linked in with promotional efforts as the series neared its conclusion. For the release of the final book, J.K. Rowling read out excerpts to 500 competition winners at the Natural History Museum in London, while tens of thousands of children took part in activities around the world involving costumes, parties and freebies – a frenzy whipped up by the publishers. The result? One UK supermarket chain sold 250,000 copies in nine hours of trading.[52]

Despite its potential strengths, public relations is sometimes described as a marketing stepchild because of its often limited and scattered use. The public relations department is usually located at corporate headquarters. Its staff is so busy dealing with various publics – stockholders, employees, legislators, the press – that public relations programmes to support product marketing objectives may be ignored. Marketing managers and public relations practitioners do not always talk the same language. Many public relations practitioners see their job as simply communicating. In contrast, marketing managers tend to be much more interested in how advertising and public relations affect brand building, sales and profits, and customer relationships.

This situation is changing, however. Although public relations still captures only a small portion of the overall

Source: Getty Images.

Public relations results can sometimes be spectacular. The release of the last book in the Harry Potter series saw events globally.

marketing budgets of most firms, PR is playing an increasingly important brand-building role. Public relations can be a powerful brand-building tool. Two well-known marketing consultants even go so far as to conclude that advertising doesn't build brands, PR does. The consultants proclaim that the dominance of advertising is over, and that public relations is quietly becoming the most powerful marketing communications tools.

> The birth of a brand is usually accomplished with [public relations], not advertising. Our general rule is [PR] first, advertising second. [Public relations] is the nail, advertising the hammer. [PR] creates the credentials that provide the credibility for advertising . . . Anita Roddick built the Body Shop into a major brand with no advertising at all. Instead, she travelled the world on a relentless quest for publicity . . . Until recently Starbucks Coffee Co. didn't spend a hill of beans on advertising, either. In ten years, the company spent less than $10 million on advertising, a trivial amount for a brand that delivers annual sales of [in the billions]. Wal-Mart Stores became the world's largest retailer . . . with very little advertising . . . On the Internet, Amazon.com became a powerhouse brand with virtually no advertising.[53]

While most advertisers wouldn't agree about the 'fall of advertising' part of the title, the point is a good one. Advertising and public relations should work hand in hand to build and maintain brands.

Major public relations tools

Public relations uses several tools. One of the major tools is *news*. PR professionals find or create favourable news about the company and its products or people. Sometimes news stories occur naturally, and sometimes the PR person can suggest events or activities that would create news. *Speeches* can also create product and company publicity. Increasingly, company executives must field questions from the media or give talks at trade associations or sales meetings, and these events can either build or hurt the company's image. Another common PR tool is *special events*, ranging from news conferences, press tours, grand openings and fireworks displays to laser shows, hot air balloon releases, multimedia presentations, star-studded spectaculars, or educational programmes designed to reach and interest target publics.

Public relations people also prepare *written materials* to reach and influence their target markets. These materials include annual reports, brochures, articles, and company newsletters and magazines. *Audiovisual materials*, such as films, slide-and-sound programmes, and video and audio CDs, are being used increasingly as communication tools. *Corporate identity materials* can also help create a corporate identity that the public immediately recognises. Logos, stationery, brochures, signs, business forms, business cards, buildings, uniforms, and company cars and trucks – all become marketing tools when they are attractive, distinctive and memorable. Finally, companies can improve public goodwill by contributing money and time to *public service activities*.

As we discussed in Chapter 5, many marketers are now also designing *buzz marketing* campaigns to generate excitement and favourable word-of-mouth for their brands. Buzz marketing creates publicity by getting consumers themselves to spread information about a product or service to others in their communities. Procter & Gamble understands the importance of buzz. It created a separate marketing arm called Tremor, which has enlisted an army of buzzers to create word-of-mouth not just about P&G products, but for those of other client companies as well.

Another recent public relations development is *mobile marketing* – travelling promotional tours that bring the brand to consumers. Mobile marketing has emerged as an effective way to build one-to-one relationships with targeted consumers. These days, it seems that almost every company is putting its show on the road – the German firm mm Promotions provides vehicles and mobile-exhibit design for a large number of firms. Recent 'tours' have included Electrolux, Samsung, Nivea and the trade union IG Metall. These tours take new products, free samples, literature and salespeople out and about – bringing the company to where potential customers are. Charmin's 'Potty Palooza' serves as a rolling showcase for – you guessed it – toilet paper and makes an appearance at music festivals where its facilities are appreciated.[54]

A company's website can be a good public relations vehicle. Consumers and members of other publics can visit the site for information and entertainment. Such sites can be extremely popular and can also be ideal for handling crisis situations. In all, in this age where 'it's easier to disseminate information through email marketing, blogs, and online chat', notes an analyst, 'public relations is becoming a valuable part of doing business in a digital world'.[55]

As with the other promotion tools, in considering when and how to use product public relations, management should set PR objectives, choose the PR messages and vehicles, implement the PR plan and evaluate the results. The firm's public relations should be blended smoothly with other promotion activities within the company's overall integrated marketing communications effort.

THE JOURNEY YOU'VE TAKEN Reviewing the concepts

In this chapter, you've learned how companies use integrated marketing communications (IMC) to communicate customer value. Modern marketing calls for more than just creating customer value by developing a good product, pricing it attractively and making it available to target customers. Companies also must clearly and persuasively *communicate* that value to current and prospective customers. To do this, they must blend five communication-mix tools, guided by a well-designed and implemented integrated marketing communications strategy.

1 Discuss the process and advantages of integrated marketing communications in communicating customer value.

Recent shifts toward targeted or one-to-one marketing, coupled with advances in information and communications technology, have had a dramatic impact on marketing communications. As marketing communicators adopt richer but more fragmented media and promotion mixes to reach their diverse markets, they risk creating a communications hotchpotch for consumers. To prevent this, more companies are adopting the concept of *integrated marketing communications (IMC)*. Guided by an overall IMC strategy, the company works out the roles that the various promotional tools will play and the extent to which each will be used. It carefully coordinates the promotional activities and the timing of when major campaigns take place. Finally, to help implement its integrated marketing strategy, the company appoints a marketing communications director who has overall responsibility for the company's communications efforts.

2 Define the five promotion tools and discuss factors that must be considered in shaping the overall promotion mix.

A company's total *promotion mix* – also called its *marketing communications mix* – consists of the specific blend of *advertising, personal selling, sales promotion, public relations* and *direct-marketing* tools that the company uses to persuasively communicate customer value and build customer relationships. Advertising includes any paid form of non-personal presentation and promotion of ideas, goods or services by an identified sponsor. In contrast, public relations focuses on building good relations with the company's various publics by obtaining favourable unpaid publicity. Personal selling is any form of personal presentation by the firm's sales force for the purpose of making sales and building customer relationships. Firms use sales promotion to provide short-term incentives to encourage the purchase or sale of a product or service. Finally, firms seeking immediate response from targeted individual customers use non-personal direct-marketing tools to communicate with customers.

The company wants to create an integrated *promotion mix*. It can pursue a *push* or a *pull* promotional strategy, or a combination of the two.

The best specific blend of promotion tools depends on the type of product/market and the product life-cycle stage. People at all levels of the organisation must be aware of the many legal and ethical issues surrounding marketing communications.

3 Describe and discuss the major decisions involved in developing an advertising programme.

Advertising – the use of paid media by a seller to inform, persuade and remind about its products or organisation – is a strong promotion tool that takes many forms and has many uses. *Advertising decision-making* involves decisions about the objectives, the budget, the message, the media and, finally, the evaluation of results. Advertisers should set clear *objectives* as to whether the advertising is supposed to inform, persuade or remind buyers. The advertising *budget* can be based on what is affordable, on sales, on competitors' spending, or on the objectives and tasks. The *message decision* calls for planning a message strategy and executing it effectively. The *media decision* involves defining reach, frequency and impact goals; choosing major media types; selecting media vehicles; and deciding on media timing. Message and media decisions must be closely coordinated for maximum campaign effectiveness. Finally, *evaluation* calls for evaluating the communication and sales effects of advertising before, during and after the advertising is placed and measuring advertising return on investment.

4 Explain how sales promotion campaigns are developed and implemented.

Sales promotion covers a wide variety of short-term incentive tools – coupons, premiums, contests, buying allowances – designed to stimulate final and business consumers, the trade and the company's own sales force. Sales promotion spending has been growing faster than advertising spending in recent years. A sales promotion campaign first calls for setting sales promotion objectives (in general, sales promotions should be *consumer relationship building*). It then calls for developing and implementing the sales promotion programme by using consumer promotion tools (*samples, coupons, cash refunds* or *rebates, price packs, premiums, advertising specialities, patronage rewards* and others); trade promotion tools (*discounts, allowances, free goods, push money*); and business promotion tools (*conventions, trade shows, sales contests*). The sales promotion effort should be coordinated carefully with the firm's other promotion efforts.

5 Explain how companies use public relations to communicate with their publics.

Public relations involves building good relations with the company's various publics. Its functions include *press agency, product publicity, public affairs, lobbying, investor relations*, and *development*. Public relations can have a strong impact on public awareness at a much lower cost than advertising can, and public relations results can sometimes be spectacular. Despite its potential strengths, however, public relations sometimes sees only limited and scattered use. Public relations tools include *news, speeches, special events, buzz marketing, mobile marketing, written materials, audiovisual materials, corporate identity materials* and *public service activities*. A company's website can be a good public relations vehicle. In considering when and how to use product public relations, management should set PR objectives, choose the PR messages and vehicles, implement the PR plan and evaluate the results. Public relations should be blended smoothly with other promotion activities within the company's overall integrated marketing communications effort.

NAVIGATING THE KEY TERMS

NOTES AND REFERENCES

1 http://www.netzeitung.de/wirtschaft/unternehmen/382766.html.

2 Michael Loeffler, 'A multinational examination of the "(non-)domestic product" effect', *International Marketing Review*, **19**(4/5), 2002, p. 482.

3 http://www.gwa.de/images/effie_db/2007/270700_032_Renault_OK_1109-2.pdf.

4 http://www.euroncap.com/home.aspx.

5 http://www.publicis.com/.

6 http://www.nordpol.com/nordpol.php.

7 http://www.welt.de/print-welt/article321794/Mit_Nordpol_auf_kreativer_Expedition.html.

8 http://www.gwa.de/images/effie_db/2007/270700_032_Renault_OK_1109-2.pdf.

9 http://www.publicis.de/html/pages/presse_frankfurt_archiv2006_data8399.htm.

10 http://www.tns-sofres.com/.

11 The first four of these definitions are adapted from Peter D. Bennett, *The AMA Dictionary of Marketing Terms*, 2nd edn (New York: McGraw-Hill, 2004). Other definitions can be found at www.marketingpower.com/live/mg-dictionary.php?, August 2005.

12 Bob Garfield, 'The Chaos Scenario', *Advertising Age*, 4 April 2005, pp. 1, 57ff; and 'Readers Respond to "Chaos Scenario"', *Advertising Age*, 18 April 2005, pp. 1ff.

13 Garfield, 'The Chaos Scenario', p. 57.

14 Jack Neff, 'P&G Chief: We Need New Model Now', *Advertising Age*, 15 November 2004, pp. 1, 53.

15 See: O. Holm, 'Integrated marketing communication: from tactics to strategy', *Corporate Communications: An International Journal*, **11**(1), 2006, pp. 23–33.

16 See Chapters 3 and 4. See also Don E. Schultz and Philip J. Kitchen, *Communication Globally: An Integrated Marketing Approach* (New York: McGraw-Hill, 2000); and Don E. Schultz and Heidi Schultz, *IMC: The Next Generation* (New York: McGraw-Hill, 2004).

17 For more on integrated marketing communications, see Don E. Schultz, Stanley I. Tannenbaum and Robert F. Lauterborn, *Integrated Marketing Communications* (Chicago, IL: NTC, 1992); Schultz and Kitchen, *Communication Globally: An Integrated Marketing Approach*; Prasad A. Naik and Kalyan Raman, 'Understanding the Impact of Synergy in Multimedia Communications', *Journal of Marketing Research*, November 2003, pp. 375–88; and Schultz and Schultz, *IMC: The Next Generation*.

18 Fifa – World Cup and Television report: http://www.fifa.com/mm/document/fifafacts/ffprojects/ip-401_06e_tv_2658.pdf; EUFootball Biz: http://www.eufootball.biz/Television/050107-World-Cup-final-most-viewed-sporting-event.html.

19 Estimates for 2008: world advertising spend estimate from Universal McCann: http://www.universalmccann.com/; ad-spend per country – Austria – available from WARC: http://www.warc.com/Trial/Samples/Default.asp#Checklists; online advertising spend: http://www.iabeurope.ws/Home/OnlineAdvertising2007.aspx and http://www.clickz.com/showPage.html?page=3627779.

20 All numbers are for 2007 and from AdAge: http://adage.com/datacenter/article?article_id=106350.

21 FedEx example from: http://adsoftheworld.com/media/ambient/fedex_truck – BBDO at: http://www.bbdo.de/de/home.html.

22 http://www.out-law.com/page-7563.

23 For more on advertising budgets, see George E. Belch and Michael A. Belch, *Advertising and Promotion: An Integrated Marketing Communications Perspective*, 6th edn (New York: McGraw-Hill, 2004), pp. 211–32.

24 Information from Gary Levin, ' "Meddling" in Creative More Welcome', *Advertising Age*, 9 April 1990, pp. S4, S8; 'Absolut Vodka Turns 25 Tomorrow', press release, 19 April 2004, accessed at www.absolut.com; and the Q&A section at www.absolut.com, August 2004; Matthew Miller, 'Absolut Chaos', *Forbes*, 13 December 2004, p. 84; and Stuart Elliott, 'Vodka Goes Beyond Plain Vanilla', *The New York Times*, 16 June 2005, p. C6.

25 '500 Channels with Nothing On? Nah – No Channels at All', 2 July 2004, accessed at www.corante.com/importance/archives/004736.html; and 'Number of Magazines by Category', accessed at www.magazine.org/editorial/editorial_trends_and_magazine_handbook/1145.cfm, August 2005.

26 Charles Pappas, 'Ad Nauseam', *Advertising Age*, 10 July 2000, pp. 16–18; and Mark Ritson, 'Marketers Need to Find a Way to Control the Contagion of Clutter', *Marketing*, 6 March 2003, p. 16.

27 Channel Five figures from: http://www.five.tv/aboutfive/sales/mediapack/container/; ITV estimates from In The Picture at: http://www.itpmag.demon.co.uk/welcome.html.

28 Edward A. Robinson, 'Frogs, Bears, and Orgasms: Think Zany if You Want to Reach Today's Consumers', *Fortune*, 9 June 1997, pp. 153–6. See also Tobi Elkin, 'Courting Craftier Consumers', 1 July 2002, p. 28; Devin Leonard, 'Nightmare on Madison Avenue', *Fortune*, 28 June 2004, pp. 93–108; and Theresa Howard, ' "Viral" Advertising Spreads through Marketing Plans', *USA Today*, 6 June 2005, accessed at www.usatoday.com/money/advertising/2005-06-22-viral-usat_x.htm.

29 See David Kiley, 'Cable's Big Bet on Hyper-Targeting', *BusinessWeek*, 4 July 2005, pp. 58–9.

30 See: http://www.guardian.co.uk/technology/2008/jan/22/games.advertising.

31 See: Game on for advertisers – *Daily Telegraph*: http://www.telegraph.co.uk/money/main.jhtml?xml=/money/2004/04/18/ccgame18.xml.

32 http://www.parksassociates.com/.

33 Edited from: Microsoft demos in-game advertising: http://news.cnet.com/8301-10784_3-9784685-7.html.

34 This section compiled from The Internet Advertising Bureau's report on in games advertising – available from: http://www.iabuk.net/en/1/mmogsandingameadvertising.html, and IGA Worldwide: http://www.igaworldwide.com/aboutus/index.cfm.

35 From IAB Report on in-game advertising, p. 10. Available from: http://www.iabuk.net/en/1/mmogsandingameadvertising.html.

36 From: Game on for advertisers – *Daily Telegraph*: http://www.telegraph.co.uk/money/main.jhtml?xml=/money/2004/04/18/ccgame18.xml.

37 Adapted from information found in 'Multi-Taskers', *Journal of Marketing Management*, May–June 2004, p. 6; and 'Kids Today: Media Multitaskers', 9 March 2005, accessed at www.cbsnews.com/stories/2005/03/09/tech/main678999.shtml.

38 *Telegraph* rates: http://advertising.telegraph.co.uk/ChannelDetail.aspx?channel=1&editorial=18&tab=Rate+Card; *Guardian* rates and readership from: http://www.adinfo-guardian.co.uk/the-guardian/guardian-circulation-and-readership.shtml.

39 Stuart Elliot, 'How Effective Is This Ad, in Real Numbers? Beats Me', *The New York Times*, 20 July 2005, p. C8.

40 Adage – Agency Profiles Yearbook 2007, available from: http://adage.com/datacenter/article?article_id=116341.

41 See: M.R. Nelson and H-J. Hye-Jin Paek, 'A content analysis of advertising in a global magazine across seven countries: Implications for global advertising strategies', *International Marketing Review*, **24**(1), 2007, pp. 64–86; and Kara Chan, Lyann Li, Sandra Diehl and Ralf Terlutter, 'Consumers' response to offensive advertising: a cross cultural study', *International Marketing Review*, **24**(5), pp. 606–28.

42 See: N. Kshetri, N.C. Williamson and A. Schiopu, 'Economics and politics of advertising: evidence from the enlarging European Union', *European Journal of Marketing*, **41**(3/4), 2007, pp. 349–66 and D. Petrovici and M. Marinov, 'Determinants and antecedents of general attitudes towards advertising: A study of two EU accession countries', *European Journal of Marketing*, **41**(3/4), 2007, pp. 307–26.

43 See Alexandra Jardine and Laurel Wentz, 'It's a Fat World After All', *Advertising Age*, 7 March 2005, p. 3; George E. Belch and Michael A. Belch, *Advertising and Promotion*, (New York: McGraw-Hill/Irwin, 2004), pp. 666–8; and Jonathan Cheng, 'China Demands Concrete Proof of Ads', *Wall Street Journal*, 8 July 2005, p. B1.

44 Institute of Sales Promotion research archive: http://www.isp.org.uk/news.php?pid=258.

45 'Casting the Net Wider', *Candy Industry*, February 2005, p. 24; Damian J. Troise, 'Fisherman's Friend Coughs Up Mini Cooper for Slogan Contest Winner', *Knight Ridder Tribune Business News*, 25 February 2005, p. 1; and www.fishermansfriendusa.com, accessed May 2005.

46 ISP: http://www.isp.org.uk/news.php?pid=258.

47 See 'Promotional Products – Impact, Exposure, and Influence' at Promotional Products Association International website, www.ppai.org, May 2005.

48 'Rusty Relations', *Convenience Store News*, 3 August 2005, accessed at www.csnews.com.

49 Numbers from: http://www.bauma.de/en/Home.

50 Adapted from Scott Cutlip, Allen Center and Glen Broom, *Effective Public Relations*, 9th edn (Upper Saddle River, NJ: Prentice Hall, 2006), ch. 1.

51 See: C. Valentini, 'Global versus cultural approaches in public relationship management: The case of the European Union', *Journal of Communication Management*, **11**(2), 2007, pp. 117–33.

52 Information from http://news.bbc.co.uk/1/hi/entertainment/6907855.stm.

53 Al Ries and Laura Ries, 'First Do Some Publicity', *Advertising Age*, 8 February 1999, p. 42. Also see Al Ries and Laura Ries, *The Fall of Advertising and the Rise of PR* (New York: HarperBusiness, 2002). For points and counterpoints, see O. Burtch Drake, ' "Fall" of Advertising? I Differ', *Advertising Age*, 13 January 2003, p. 23; Robert E. Brown, 'Book Review: The Fall of Advertising & the Rise of PR', *Public Relations Review*, March 2003, pp. 91–3; and Mark Cheshire, 'Roundtable Discussion – Making & Moving the Message', *The Daily Record*, 30 January 2004, p. 1.

54 Mm Productions: http://www.truckpromotion.com/index.php?id=3; see Kate Fitzgerald, 'Marketing on the Move', *Advertising Age*, 18 March 2002, p. 59; Jeff St John, 'Microsoft Sends Mobile Marketing Van to Kennewick, Wash., Area', *Knight Ridder Tribune Business News*, 28 April 2004, p. 1; and Lucas Conley, 'On a Roll', *Fast Company*, February 2005, p. 28.

55 Paul Holmes, 'Senior Marketers Are Sharply Divided About the Role of PR in the Overall Mix', *Advertising Age*, 24 January 2005, pp. C1–C2.

PART FOUR

Extending marketing

CHAPTER 14
Marketing in the digital age

AFTER STUDYING THIS CHAPTER, YOU SHOULD BE ABLE TO

- ■ discuss how the digital age is affecting both consumers and the marketers who serve them
- ■ explain how companies have responded to the Internet and other powerful new technologies with e-business strategies, and how these strategies have resulted in benefits to both buyers and sellers
- ■ describe the four major e-marketing domains
- ■ discuss how companies go about conducting e-marketing to deliver more value profitably to customers
- ■ overview the promise and challenges that e-commerce presents for the future

THE WAY AHEAD Previewing the concepts

We've learned that the aim of marketing is to create value *for* customers in order to capture value *from* consumers in return. Good marketing companies win, keep and grow customers by understanding customer needs, designing customer-driven marketing strategies, constructing value delivering marketing programmes, and building customer and marketing partner relationships. In the final three chapters, we'll extend this concept to three special areas – marketing in the digital age, global marketing, and marketing ethics and social responsibility. Although we've visited these topics regularly in each previous chapter, because of their special importance, we will focus exclusively on them in this part.

In this chapter, we look into marketing in the rapidly changing digital environment. Marketing strategy and practice have undergone dramatic changes during the past decade. Major technological advances, including the explosion of the Internet, have had a major impact on buyers and the marketers who serve them. To thrive in this digital age – even to survive – marketers must rethink their strategies and adapt them to today's changing environment and even new virtual worlds.

We'll begin by looking at how companies are coming to terms with the existence of the virtual world and the fact that their brands and products need to be supported here as well as on the high street.

Second Life®: Second market?

Janet Ward, *School of Agriculture, Food and Rural Development, University of Newcastle, UK*

If it surprises you to hear that platinum selling recording artists, major television networks, and global hotel chains are setting up shop in a virtual online space – one that might be mistaken for a video game – that surprise should not last long. As more and more people and companies discover the rich expressive power and social networking capabilities of virtual worlds, the phenomenon will become commonplace.[1]

Second Life® (SL) is one example of an 'open' virtual world with over 65,000 virtual acres and 12,485,596 residents from over 100 countries.[2] SL offers a free basic membership, compared to the monthly subscription charged by World of Warcraft (WoW) which itself has more than 10 million users globally. In SL residents (avatars) can communicate directly with one another, buy land, build properties, set up businesses or just relax and enjoy themselves. The in-world currency is the Linden dollar (L$) which has an exchange rate with the US dollar – usually at about the rate of 1US$ = 250L$. The resident profile shows that 36 per cent of users are in the 25–34 age category, with 60 per cent being male and 40 per cent being female.[3] There is currently a strong northern hemisphere bias to residents with the USA having the largest number of users at 36 per cent, closely followed by Europe; however, both Japan and Brazil feature in the top ten countries. An important point about the way SL is designed means that all residents can communicate with each other and are effectively within the same environment. The only limitations within this are real-world time differences.

What makes SL truly distinctive from others of its type, and makes it interesting to marketers, is that it is the first virtual world to allow residents to keep the intellectual property of anything they create in-world. This has meant that major organisations from IBM to Mercedes Benz, to advertising agencies such as Bartle Bogle Hegarty (BBH) and charities such as The American Cancer Society, as well as over 200 universities, have now established a presence in SL. This is a completely new marketing environment.

Online environments like Second Life have some common characteristics; they simulate a 3D environment, they are persistent, i.e. they continue to exist and develop 24/7, they use avatars, as visual representations of the individual, and the main communication is text-based chat. These characteristics create an immersive environment which means 'virtual online worlds provide an additional level of personality that is missing from the typical chat room environment'.[4] As the individual customises their own avatar this creates a sense of belonging and involvement. As one researcher explains, 'Avatars are endowed with mannerisms, skills, and wardrobes that their users create (employing a variety of software tools), purchase (from in-world stores), receive as gifts (from other avatars), or earn (through in-game achievements). Indeed while avatars' anonymity is

part of their appeal, many people take considerable pride in their creations as public expressions of hidden aspects of their identity.'[5] For marketers this raises the opportunity to understand different aspects of consumer behaviour that might not be perceivable or examinable using traditional forms of research. An analysis of all items for sale using SL Exchange by Kzero Research[6] gives a breakdown of the virtual items for sale, of which the top items are: clothing (35 per cent), home furnishings (17 per cent), avatar accessories (14 per cent) and avatar appearance changes (7 per cent).[6] This emphasises the time, effort and Linden dollars spent in creating an individual appearance and environment.

So what marketing opportunities are there in Second Life? Companies can decide whether to have an open public presence or a closed presence. IBM is an example of a company using both options. Their closed islands are effectively an internal marketing environment allowing collaborative working for staff worldwide without intrusion. 'One of the key advantages of virtual reality over the telephone for example is that it has the potential to provide enhanced support for work and interaction between remote participants by delivering a common world of digital data and virtual objects for co-participants to discuss.'[7] IBM call Innovation Island the 'front door' to their presence in SL. Visitors find an interactive environment where they can take part in activities, attend events in the theatre, or be signposted to specialist areas such as the IBM Business Centre to meet support staff or University Relations Island to see examples of collaborative projects.

Other real world brands have also developed sites including Mercedes Benz, where you can test-drive a virtual car, or Nissan Sentra, where you first have to solve a puzzle before looping the loop in your car. These obviously have some PR value but do not give such a strong corporate message because the sites are much smaller. American Apparel opened a store in SL along with lots of publicity. This was open just over a year and sold virtual T-shirts. It has now closed and has a message explaining, '. . . we feel like our time is up here. So we're closing our doors on Lerappa Island for now. This doesn't mean we're finished with the virtual world. Stay tuned to see what we do next.' So real world businesses are still testing SL out, just like in the early days of the Internet, with companies trying to work out it if they should have a presence in SL and what kind of presence it should be.

Who is currently making money in Second Life? Well, interestingly, it's the people selling the virtual products. Resident Anshe Chung became the first Second Life L$ millionaire by selling virtual real estate, and now has interests in several other virtual worlds. There are increasing numbers of people earning a living or a substantial part of their income through SL – as with eBay for a decade. Second Life provides an opportunity to develop and test new brands and products/services cheaply – it is a way to save money as well as generate income. There are a wide range of shops, malls and clubs to suit all tastes. However, can these brands then be transferred back into the real world? One success story: 'Tringo, a cross between Tetris and Bingo was invented in SL by Nathan Keir (aka Kermitt Quirk). The

game became so popular that it has been licensed for Nintendo's Game Boy advance and for desktop PCs.'[8]

There are now an increasing number of media companies trying to make links between the real world and SL. At the Vodafone site you can phone from SL to the real world, and Sky News has an SL studio for a virtual version of its continuous news channel. Universities and other not-for-profit organisations are also using SL for public engagement. 'Working in conjunction with the UK's National Physical Laboratory (NPL), Imperial College London (ICL) has created a virtual hospital in the 3D virtual world of Second Life and a series of machinima documentary films that describe the future of healthcare.'[9] This potentially provides a strong message; however, from a marketing perspective it is not totally clear who the target audiences are and if they will be sufficiently computer literate to take advantage of this site.

What is the future for these virtual worlds? According to Gartner Research, by 2010, 80 per cent of Fortune 500 global companies will have some form of massive multi-player online or virtual-world presence.[10] As time goes by they will become more experienced and sophisticated at marketing in these virtual environments – just as has happened with other Internet-based media.

Many virtual worlds unlike dot.coms are already profitable.

Sources: See notes 1–10 at the end of this chapter.

As this case makes clear, recent technological advances have created a digital age. Widespread use of the Internet and other powerful new technologies is having a dramatic impact on marketers and buyers. In this chapter, we examine how marketing strategy and practice are having to change constantly to take advantage of today's new technologies.

THE DIGITAL AGE

It is likely that you'll know quite a bit about these technologies already, but some of the terminology is bandied about very loosely so we'll define a few terms first for the sake of clarity. **Intranets** are networks that connect people within a company to each other and to the company network – sets of pages and online resources available only to those in that organisation, even if the geographical spread of these people is global. If you are currently studying, it is likely that your college or university will have an intranet for staff and students – you can access the library, download class materials and perhaps even find out how well you did in your assessments. **Extranets** connect a company with its suppliers, distributors and other outside partners – big retailers and wholesalers use these to manage the movement of goods more effectively. The **Internet**, a vast public web of computer networks, connects users of all types all around the world to each other and to an amazingly large information repository.

The wonderful world of Internet statistics

This chapter – just like all the others – contains many facts and figures. It is in the nature of Internet-related statistics and estimates that any accuracy they may possibly have had will be momentary – the rapidity and fluidity of the medium, and the inherent difficulty in obtaining accurate information, means many such figures are guesstimates at best, wild speculation at worst. During the lifespan of this, and any, book, technologies, capacities and activities can increase or reduce by several orders of magnitude. That warning being given, let's have a peek into the wonderful world of Internet statistics.

With the creation of the World Wide Web and Web browsers in the 1990s, the Internet was transformed from a mere communication tool into a certifiably revolutionary technology. The Internet continues to grow explosively. It is estimated that about 1.4 billion people have regular access to the Internet – approximately one person in five in the world. In detail, we can see that Internet use is not evenly distributed across the globe – nearly three-quarters of North Americans have access but only one in 20 Africans.

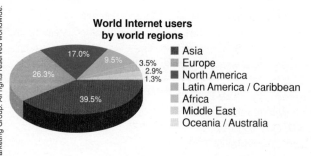

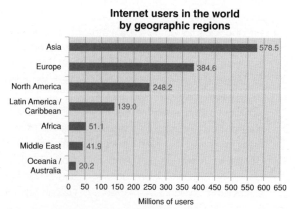

World Internet statistics.

Generally there is a significant correlation between wealth and development levels and Internet usage. Europe has about half of its population as regular users, but this varies very significantly by country. Greece, Hungary and Romania come near the bottom of the league with fewer than a third online, while the Netherlands and Iceland are at the top with more than 80 per cent. The UK and Germany are towards the top end and are 10 per cent higher than France, Italy and the Czech Republic.[11]

You may think of the Internet as being an English-speaking phenomenon, and indeed English is the most common language used on webpages. Unsurprisingly Chinese is in second place and Spanish, French, German, Italian and Portuguese make up most of the rest of the top ten.[12] Quality of access varies just as much as quantity. One recent report found that broadband users in France and Sweden had an average connection speed of 17mbps, nearly three times that of Germany, six times that of the UK and 15 times that of Spain.[13] Even within countries access can vary widely – rural parts of Portugal, Russia and Scotland (the highlands and islands) are not well served, even when a major city in the same country might be. Residents of London get twice the speed of those living in Belfast.[14] This does matter – the changing culture and demographics of web-usage and availability mean that marketers cannot treat all Internet customers the same.[15]

This explosive worldwide growth in Internet usage forms the heart of the digital age. The Internet has been *the* revolutionary technology of the new millennium, empowering consumers and businesses alike. The Internet enables consumers and companies to access and share huge amounts of information with just a few mouse clicks. Recent studies have shown that more and more consumers are accessing information on the Internet before making major life decisions. One in three consumers relies heavily on the Internet to gather information about buying a car, finding a job, dealing with a major illness, or making investment decisions. The average UK Internet user spent some 45 hours in April 2008 online – with about 27 hours of that at home. In Italy the equivalent total for work and home combined was 43 hours and in France 60 hours.[16] As a result, to be competitive in today's new marketplace, companies must adopt Internet technology or risk being left behind.

The Internet and other digital technologies have given marketers a whole new way to reach and serve customers. The amazing success of early *click-only* companies – the so-called dot-coms such as Amazon.com, eBay, Expedia and hundreds of others – caused existing *brick-and-mortar* manufacturers and retailers to re-examine how they served their markets. Now, almost all these traditional companies have set up their own online sales and communications channels, becoming *click-and-mortar* competitors. It's hard to find a company today that doesn't have a substantial Web presence, and/or a presence in virtual environments like Second Life.

MARKETING STRATEGY IN THE DIGITAL AGE

Conducting business in the digital age calls for a new model for marketing strategy and practice. The Internet is revolutionising how companies create value for customers and build customer relationships. The digital age has fundamentally changed customers' notions of convenience, speed, price, product information and service. Thus, today's marketing requires new thinking and action. Companies need to retain most of the skills and practices that have worked in the past. But they will also need to add major new competencies and practices if they hope to grow and prosper in the changing digital environment.

E-business, e-commerce and e-marketing in the digital age

E-business involves the use of electronic platforms – intranets, extranets and the Internet – to conduct a company's business. Almost every company has set up a website to inform about and promote its products and services. Others use websites simply to build stronger customer relationships.

Most companies have also created intranets to help employees communicate with each other and to access information found in the company's systems. For example, some 14,000 employees regularly log on to the P&G intranet, mNet, to receive training and to research marketing news from around the world. Companies also set up extranets with their major suppliers and distributors to enable information exchange, orders, transactions and payments.

E-commerce is more specific than e-business. E-business includes all electronics-based information exchanges within or between companies and customers. In contrast, e-commerce involves buying and selling processes supported by electronic means, primarily the Internet. *E-markets* are 'market*spaces*', rather than physical market*places*. Sellers use e-markets to offer their products and services online. Buyers use them to search for information, identify what they want, and place orders using credit or other means of electronic payment.

E-commerce includes *e-marketing* and *e-purchasing* (*e-procurement*). **E-marketing** is the marketing side of e-commerce. It consists of company efforts to communicate about, promote, and sell products and services over the Internet. Thus, Amazon.com, LLBean.com and Dell.com conduct e-marketing at their websites. The flip side of e-marketing is e-purchasing, the buying side of e-commerce. It consists of companies purchasing goods, services and information from online suppliers. In business-to-business buying, e-marketers and e-purchasers come together in huge e-commerce networks.

E-commerce and the Internet bring many benefits to both buyers and sellers. Let's review some of these major benefits.

Benefits to buyers

Internet buying benefits both final buyers and business buyers in many ways. It can be *convenient*. Customers don't have to battle traffic, find parking spaces, and trek through shops and aisles to find and examine products. They can do comparative shopping by surfing websites. Web marketers never close their doors. Buying is *easy* and *private*. Customers encounter fewer buying hassles and don't have to face salespeople or open themselves up to persuasion and emotional pitches. Business buyers can learn about and buy products and services without waiting for and tying up time with salespeople.

In addition, the Internet often provides buyers with greater *product access and selection*. Unrestrained by physical boundaries, Web sellers can offer an almost unlimited selection to consumers almost anywhere in the world. Just compare the incredible selections offered by many Web merchants to the more meagre assortments of their brick-and-mortar counterparts. For example, log onto Bulbs.com, 'the Web's no. 1 light bulb superstore', and you'll have instant access to every imaginable kind of light bulb or lamp – incandescent bulbs, fluorescent bulbs, projection bulbs, surgical bulbs, automotive bulbs – you name it. No physical store could offer handy access to such a vast selection.

E-commerce channels also give buyers access to a wealth of comparative *information* about companies, products and competitors. Good sites often provide more information in more useful forms than even the most solicitous salesperson can. For example, Amazon.com offers top-ten product lists, extensive product descriptions, expert and user product reviews, and recommendations based on customers' previous purchases.

Finally, online buying is *interactive* and *immediate*. Buyers can often interact with the seller's site to create exactly the configuration of information, products or services they desire, then order or download them on the spot. Moreover, the Internet gives consumers a greater measure of control. Like nothing else before it, the Internet has empowered consumers. These days, people looking to buy a new laptop or mobile phone will research prices, performance and possibilities online. They may not actually purchase online, but when they come to buy, they will be armed with much more knowledge. This is the new reality of consumer control.[17]

Benefits to sellers

E-commerce also yields many benefits to sellers. First, the Internet is a powerful tool for *customer relationship building*. Because of its one-to-one, interactive nature, companies can interact online with customers to learn more about specific needs and wants. In turn, online customers can ask questions and volunteer feedback. Based on this ongoing interaction, companies can increase customer value and satisfaction through product and service refinements.

The Internet and other electronic channels can also *reduce costs* and *increase speed and efficiency*. By using the Internet to link directly to suppliers, factories, distributors and customers, businesses can cut costs and pass savings on to customers. Internet-only marketer Amazon.com avoids the expense of maintaining a store and the related costs of rent, insurance and utilities. Because customers deal directly with sellers, online selling often results in lower costs and improved efficiencies for channel and logistics functions such as order processing, inventory handling, delivery and trade promotion. Finally, communicating electronically often costs less than communicating on paper through the mail. For instance, a company can produce digital catalogues for much less than the cost of printing and mailing paper ones.

E-marketing can also offer greater *flexibility*. It allows marketers to make ongoing adjustments to offers and programmes, or to make immediate and timely announcements and offers. For example, easyJet and other budget airlines can micromanage their pricing structures to take into account demand for seats, and they can notify customers about changes, delays or other problems very promptly. Argos can use their website to update their online catalogue on a continual basis, something simply not possible with the printed version.

Finally, the Internet is a truly *global* medium that allows buyers and sellers to click from one country to another in seconds. A Web surfer from Paris or Istanbul can access an online L.L. Bean catalogue as easily as someone living in Freeport, Maine, the direct retailer's home town. Even small e-marketers find that they have ready access to global markets.[18]

Companies can now provide applications for use with portable devices like Apple's iPhone so that customers can view and buy wherever they are.

Source: Alamy Images/Helene Rogers.

E-MARKETING DOMAINS

The four major e-marketing domains are shown in Figure 14.1 and discussed below. They include B2C (business to consumer), B2B (business to business), C2C (consumer to consumer), and C2B (consumer to business).

B2C (business to consumer)

The popular press has paid the most attention to **B2C (business-to-consumer) e-commerce** – the online selling of goods and services to final consumers. Online consumer buying continues to grow at a healthy rate. Verdict Research reported that in 2008 it increased

FIGURE 14.1

E-marketing domains

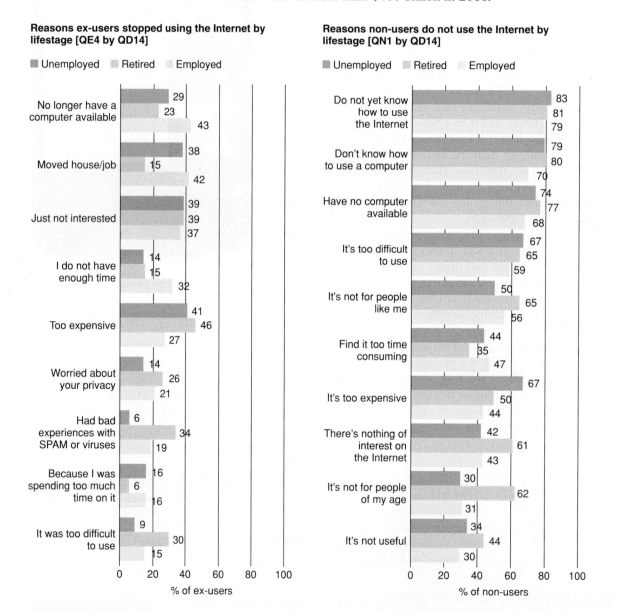

	Targeted to consumers	Targeted to businesses
Initiated by business	B2C (business to consumer)	B2B (business to business)
Initiated by consumer	C2C (consumer to consumer)	C2B (consumer to business)

by more than a third to about £15 billion in the UK alone, while in the three biggest European B2C markets – the UK, France and Germany – it has been estimated that annual growth in the period 2006–11 will be about 25 per cent. Across Europe, B2C commerce will have a value of more than $400 billion in 2011.[19]

Reasons ex-users stopped using the Internet by lifestage [QE4 by QD14]

■ Unemployed ■ Retired ■ Employed

Reason	Unemployed	Retired	Employed
No longer have a computer available	29	23	43
Moved house/job	38	15	42
Just not interested	39	39	37
I do not have enough time	14	15	32
Too expensive	41	46	27
Worried about your privacy	14	26	21
Had bad experiences with SPAM or viruses	6	34	19
Because I was spending too much time on it	16	6	16
It was too difficult to use	9	30	15

% of ex-users

Reasons non-users do not use the Internet by lifestage [QN1 by QD14]

■ Unemployed ■ Retired ■ Employed

Reason	Unemployed	Retired	Employed
Do not yet know how to use the Internet	83	81	79
Don't know how to use a computer	79	80	70
Have no computer available	74	77	68
It's too difficult to use	67	65	59
It's not for people like me	50	65	56
Find it too time consuming	44	35	47
It's too expensive	67	50	44
There's nothing of interest on the Internet	42	61	43
It's not for people of my age	30	62	31
It's not useful	34	44	30

% of non-users

The Oxford Internet Survey.

Source: Dutton, W.H. and Helsper, E.J. (2007) *The Internet in Britain: 2007*, Oxford Internet Institute, University of Oxford (Oxford, UK).

Online consumers

As more people find their way onto the Web, the cyberspace population is becoming more mainstream and diverse. The Web now offers marketers a palette of different kinds of consumers seeking different kinds of online experiences.

Not all types of people use the Internet to the same degree, or in the same proportion. Although the gender gap has narrowed significantly in the last ten years, there is still an imbalance towards men. Age is a significant factor – while ever-increasing numbers of the over 55s are browsing online, a much higher proportion of the young do so. In fact, the Oxford Internet Survey reported that one in three retired people were online, as were more than half of those of working age but almost all – 98 per cent – of those of student age were regular Internet users. They also reported that Internet usage was correlated very strongly with both education and income – 90 per cent of those earning more than £50,000 per year were online, compared to less than a third of those on £12,500 or less.[20]

Internet consumers differ from traditional offline consumers in their approaches to buying and in their responses to marketing. The exchange process via the Internet has become more customer initiated and customer controlled. Traditional marketing targets

Use by income (QH19 by QD19)

'Here is a card showing the range of incomes that people have. Which of the letters on this card best represents the total income of your household before tax?'

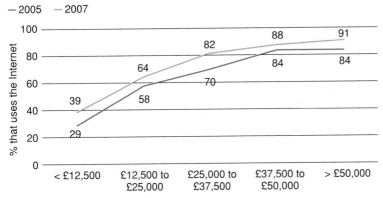

OxIS 2005: N-2,185; OxIS 2007: N-2,350

The percentage of users has increased between 2005 and 2007 across all income groups.

Those in the highest income category are more than twice as likely to use the Internet (91%) than those in the lowest income category (39%).

Use by education (QH19 by QD13)

'What is the last type of educational institution (e.g. school, college or university) that you have attended or which type of educational institution are you attending now?'

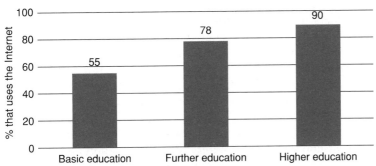

OxIs 2007: N-2,350 Basic: N-1,176; Further: N-640; Higher: N-405I (Note the same data are available excluding current students but percentages are very similar).

Education, like income, is strongly related to Internet use. Only half (55%) of those with basic education (up to secondary school) use the Internet while most (90%) of those with a higher (university) education use the Internet.

Source: Dutton, W.H. and Helsper, E.J. (2007) *The Internet in Britain: 2007*, Oxford Internet Institute, University of Oxford (Oxford, UK).

a somewhat passive audience. In contrast, e-marketing targets people who actively select which websites they will visit and what marketing information they will receive about which products and under what conditions. Thus, the new world of e-commerce requires new marketing approaches.

B2C websites

Consumers can find a website for buying almost anything. The Internet is most useful for products and services when the shopper seeks greater ordering convenience or lower costs. The Internet also provides great value to buyers looking for information about differences in product features and value. However, consumers find the Internet less useful when buying products that must be touched or examined in advance. Still, even here there are exceptions. For example, who would have thought that tens of thousands of people would order cars online each year without seeing and trying them first?

People now go online to order a wide range of goods – clothing from Gap, furniture from IKEA, major appliances from Currys, flowers from Interflora, or even financial services from Egg.

B2B (business to business)

Although the media gives the most attention to business-to-consumer (B2C) websites, consumer goods sales via the Web are dwarfed by **B2B (business-to-business) e-commerce**. The research firm Gartner reported that B2B e-commerce was, by 2005, over $8.5 trillion globally.[21] B2B marketers use trading networks, auction sites, spot exchanges, online product catalogues, barter sites, and other online resources to reach new customers, serve current customers more effectively, and obtain buying efficiencies and better prices.

Within Europe, there is evidence to suggest that there are significant national, industry/sector and functional differences affecting not only the *number* of businesses that trade online, but also, for those that do, the *proportion* of business done online. Industries and sectors with a strong ICT dimension like telecommunications are much more heavily involved with B2B e-commerce than more traditional industries like footwear manufacture or construction. Nationally, some countries stand out. Spain leads in respect of online supply chain management with more than a third of firms doing this – twice as many as in the Netherlands and six times those in Germany. The same countries are not necessarily the most advanced in all areas of B2B e-commerce, however, with Finnish and French organisations much more likely to be able to accept orders online than Spanish firms. As a proportion of all business done B2B e-commerce is 11.7 per cent across the EU, with Italy on 2 per cent, Bulgaria on 0.1 per cent and the UK (17.1 per cent) close behind the leader Denmark on 17.5 per cent.[22]

Most major B2B marketers now offer product information, customer purchasing and customer support services online. For example, corporate buyers can visit Sun Microsystems' website (**www.sun.com**), select detailed descriptions of Sun's products and solutions, request sales and service information, and interact with staff members. Some major companies conduct almost all of their business on the Web. Networking equipment and software maker Cisco Systems takes more than 80 per cent of its orders over the Internet.

Some B2B e-commerce takes place in **open trading exchanges** – huge e-marketspaces in which buyers and sellers find each other online, share information and complete transactions efficiently. For example, PlasticsNet.com, an Internet marketplace for the plastics product industry, connects over 90,000 monthly visitor/buyers with more than 200 suppliers. However, despite the use of such open e-marketspaces, a lion's share of all B2B e-commerce is conducted through private sites. Increasingly, online sellers are setting up their own **private trading exchanges**. Open trading exchanges facilitate transactions between a wide range of online buyers and sellers. In contrast, a private trading exchange links a particular seller with its own trading partners.

C2C (consumer to consumer)

Much **C2C (consumer-to-consumer) e-commerce** and communication occurs on the Web between interested parties over a wide range of products and subjects. In some cases, the Internet provides an excellent means by which consumers can buy or exchange goods or information directly with one another. For example, eBay, Amazon, and other auction sites offer popular marketspaces for displaying and selling almost anything, from art and antiques, coins, stamps and jewellery to computers and consumer electronics. EBay's C2C online trading community consists of more than 240 million users worldwide – 14 million of them in the UK. In the first three months of 2007, some 600 million items were bought and sold globally, with a value of about $15 billion.[23]

In other cases, C2C involves interchanges of information through Internet forums that appeal to specific special-interest groups. Such activities may be organised for commercial or non-commercial purposes. An example is Web logs, or *blogs*, which can be about anything, from politics or football to haiku or cooking.

No one knows how many blogs exist, or what proportion of them are regularly updated, but one report suggests that today's blogosphere consists of about 120 million English-language blogs with another 120,000 being created each day. China adds another 73 million to the global total alone.[24]

Many marketers are now tapping into blogs as a medium for reaching carefully targeted consumers. One way is to advertise on an existing blog or to post content there. For example, Web-savvy Nike created an 'Art of Speed' microsite on blog site Gawker.com. The Art of Speed showcased the work of 15 innovative filmmakers who interpreted the idea of speed. The showcase gave Nike high-quality exposure within a small audience. 'Gawker is a very influential site among a community that appreciates creativity, film, and interesting projects and who are going to dig deeper and find out the back story,' said Nike's communications manager. 'In some circles, Gawker has more authenticity than Nike,' says an online communications analyst. 'That's why blogs really work for advertisers, because of the credibility of the blog.'[25]

Other companies set up their own blogs. For example, Procter & Gamble launched a blog site (sparklebodyspray.com) to promote its Secret Sparkle Body Spray to tweens girls (seven- to twelve-year-olds).

Web logs: Nike created an 'Art of Speed' microsite on blog site Gawker.com, giving it high quality exposure within a small, select audience.

The site features character blogs based on each of four Sparkle Body Spray Girls – Rose, Vanilla, Tropical and Peach. Each character's writing takes on a personality similar to a real pre-teen girl. They blog about things girls are interested in, from fashion to celebrity gossip to sports. Says Secret's brand manager, 'the character blog concept [allows] each visitor to create her own experience'.[26]

As a marketing tool, blogs offer some advantages. They can offer a fresh, original, personal and cheap way to reach today's fragmented audiences. However, the blogosphere is cluttered and difficult to control. 'Blogs may help companies bond with consumers in exciting new ways, but they won't help them control the relationship,' says a blog expert. Such Web journals remain largely a C2C medium. 'If anything, blogs will continue tipping the balance of power toward the consumer,' says the expert. 'That isn't to suggest companies can't influence the relationship or leverage blogs to engage in a meaningful relationship, but the consumer will remain in control.'

In all, C2C means that online buyers don't just consume product information – increasingly, they create it. They join Internet interest groups to share information, with the result that 'word-of-Web' is joining 'word-of-mouth' as an important buying influence. Word about good companies and products travels fast. Word about bad companies and products travels even faster. Many sites, including eComplaints.com, ConsumerReview.com, and Consumerist.com, have cropped up to provide consumers with a forum where they can air complaints and share information about product and service experiences.

Marketers are realising that the issues and trends discussed in the blogosphere often move into the mainstream consciousness of the culture of the society over time – the thoughts and opinions of these bloggers can be used to develop an understanding of the current Zeitgeist, critical in markets where fashions and trends can change quickly. One newspaper recently went to far as to provide a top 50 of the most influential blogs.[27]

C2B (consumer to business)

The final e-commerce domain is **C2B (consumer-to-business) e-commerce**. Thanks to the Internet, today's consumers are finding it easier to communicate with companies. Most companies now invite prospects and customers to send in suggestions and questions via company websites. Beyond this, rather than waiting for an invitation, consumers can search out sellers on the Web, learn about their offers, initiate purchases and give feedback. Using the Web, consumers can even drive transactions with businesses, rather than the other way around. For example, using Priceline.com, would-be buyers bid for airline tickets, hotel rooms, hire cars, and even home mortgages, leaving the sellers to decide whether to accept their offers.

Consumers can also use websites such as PlanetFeedback.com to ask questions, offer suggestions, lodge complaints, ask questions, or deliver compliments to companies. The site provides letter templates for consumers to use based on their moods and reasons for contacting the company. The site then forwards the letters to the customer service manager at each company and helps to obtain a response. 'About 80 per cent of the companies respond to complaints, some within an hour,' said a PlanetFeedback spokesperson.[28]

MARKETING ON THE WEB

Companies of all types are now marketing online. In this section, we first discuss the different types of e-marketers shown in Figure 14.2. Then we examine how companies go about conducting online marketing.

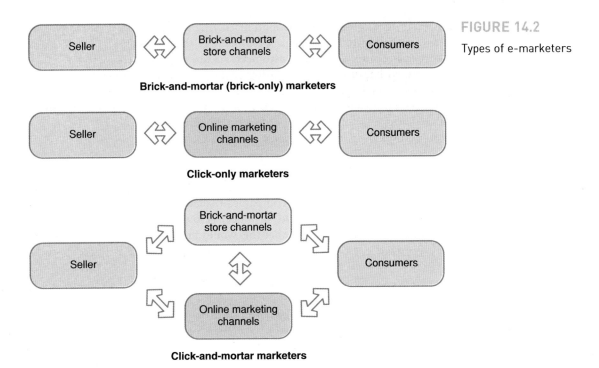

FIGURE 14.2

Types of e-marketers

Click-only versus click-and-mortar e-marketers

The Internet gave birth to a new species of e-marketers – the *click-only* dot-coms – which operate only online without any brick-and-mortar market presence. In addition, most traditional *brick-and-mortar* companies have now added e-marketing operations, transforming themselves into *click-and-mortar* competitors.

Click-only companies

Click-only companies come in many shapes and sizes. They include *e-tailers*, dot-coms that sell products and services directly to final buyers via the Internet. Examples include Amazon.com, Expedia, and iwantoneofthose.com. Lovefilm rent DVDs, just like Blockbuster – but they do their business online and distribute and collect the films by post.

The click-only group also includes *search engines* and *portals*, such as Google, MSN and Yahoo! which began as search engines and later added services such as news, weather, stock reports, entertainment and storefronts hoping to become the first port of entry to the Internet. *Shopping* or *price comparison sites*, such as Froogle.com, Dooyoo.co.uk, Pricerunner.co.uk and Bizrate.com, give instant product and price comparisons from thousands of sellers – often with feedback ratings from customers attached.

Internet service providers (ISPs) such as Deutsche Telecom's T-Online, the Italian Tiscali and of course BT are click-only companies that provide Internet and email connections for a fee. *Transaction sites*, such as auction site eBay, take commissions for transactions conducted on their sites. The hype surrounding such click-only Web businesses reached astronomical levels during the 'dot-com gold rush' of the late 1990s, when avid investors drove dot-com stock prices to dizzying heights. However, the investing frenzy collapsed in the year 2000, and many high-flying, overvalued dot-coms came crashing back to earth. Dot-coms failed for many reasons. Some rushed into the market without proper research or planning. Often their primary goal was simply to launch an initial public offering (IPO) while the market was hot. Many relied too heavily on spin and hype instead of developing sound marketing strategies. They spent lavishly offline on mass marketing to attract new customers to their sites instead of building loyalty and purchasing among current customers. As one industry watcher concluded, many dot-coms failed because they gave a lot of thought to the razzmatazz and very little to the business model. Such companies should start by rethinking how they create value for customers. How can they leverage their Web-only models to compete effectively against traditional brick-and-mortar competitors on the one hand, and against the newer click-and-mortar competitors on the other?

Click-and-mortar companies

As the Internet grew, some established companies rushed to open websites providing information about their companies and products. However, most resisted adding e-commerce to their sites. They worried that this would produce *channel conflict* – that by selling their products or services online they would be competing with their offline retailers and agents. For example, Hewlett Packard feared that its retailers would drop HP's computers if the company sold the same computers directly online. Merrill Lynch hesitated to introduce online stock trading fearing that its own brokers would rebel.

These companies struggled with the question of how to conduct online sales without cannibalising the sales of their own stores, resellers or agents. However, they soon realised that the risks of losing business to online competitors were even greater than the risks of angering channel partners. If they didn't cannibalise these sales, online competitors soon would. Thus, most established brick-and-mortar companies are now prospering as **click-and-mortar companies**.

For example, Office Depot's more than 1,500 office-supply superstores rack up annual sales of $15 billion in more than 42 countries. But you might be surprised to learn that Office Depot's fastest recent growth has come not from its traditional brick-and-mortar channels, but from the Internet – this is despite buying up other stationery supplies companies like the French firm Guilbert, and Papirius of the Czech Republic.[29] In 2007 the company sold $5 billion of goods online – to businesses and individuals. Other retailers are finding the same thing – firms like Tesco and Carrefour recognise online retailing as being increasingly important to the whole of their operations.

Most click-and-mortar marketers have found ways to resolve channel conflicts. For example, Gibson Guitars found that although its dealers were outraged when it tried to sell guitars directly to consumers, the dealers didn't object to direct sales of accessories such as guitar strings and parts. Avon worried that direct online sales might cannibalise the business of its Avon ladies, who had developed close relationships with their customers. Fortunately, Avon's research showed little overlap between existing customers and potential Web customers. Avon shared this finding with the reps and then moved into online marketing. As an added bonus for the reps, Avon also offered to help them set up their own websites.

Despite potential channel conflict issues, many click-and-mortar companies are now having more online success than their click-only competitors. The list of the top ten online retailers is divided evenly between click-only and click-and-mortar.[30]

What gives the click-and-mortar companies an advantage? Established companies such as John Lewis, Dixons, House of Fraser and Debenhams have known and trusted brand names and greater financial resources. They have large customer bases, deeper industry knowledge and experience, and good relationships with key suppliers. By combining online marketing and established brick-and-mortar operations, they can offer customers more options.

For example, consumers can choose the convenience and assortment of 24-hour-a-day online shopping, the more personal and hands-on experience of in-store shopping, or both. Customers can buy merchandise online, and then easily return unwanted goods to a nearby store.

MAKING CONNECTIONS Linking the concepts

Think about the relative advantages and disadvantages of *click-only*, *brick-and-mortar only* and *click-and-mortar* retailers.

■ Visit the Amazon website. Search for a specific book or film – perhaps one that's not too well known – and go through the buying process.

■ Now visit **www.waterstones.com** and shop for the same book or film. Then visit a Waterstone's store and shop for the item there.

■ What advantages does Amazon have over Waterstone's? What disadvantages? How does your local independent bookshop fare against these two competitors?

Setting up an online marketing presence

Clearly, all companies need to consider moving online. Companies can conduct e-marketing in any of the four ways shown in Figure 14.3: creating a website, placing ads and promotions online, setting up or participating in Web communities, or using email.

Creating a website

For most companies, the first step in conducting e-marketing is to create a website. However, beyond simply creating a website, marketers must design an attractive site and find ways to get consumers to visit the site, stay around and come back often.

Types of websites Websites vary greatly in purpose and content. The most basic type is a **corporate website**. These sites are designed to build customer goodwill and to supplement other sales channels, rather than to sell the company's products directly. For example, although you can buy ice cream and other items at the gift shop on benjerry.com, the site's primary purpose is to enhance customer relationships. At the site, you can learn all about Ben & Jerry's

Corporate website: although you can buy some ice cream at the Ben & Jerry's website, the site's primary purpose is to enhance customer relationships.
At the site, you can learn all about the Ben & Jerry's company and do lots of 'fun-related stuff'.

Source: http://www.benjerry.co.uk/

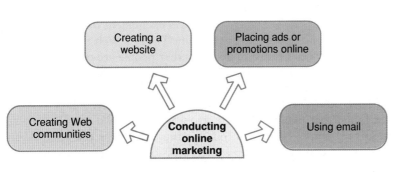

FIGURE 14.3

Setting up for online marketing

company philosophy, products and locations. Or you can visit the Fun Stuff area and send a free e-card to a friend, subscribe to the Chunk Mail newsletter, or while away time playing Scooper Challenge or Virtual Checkers.

Corporate websites typically offer a rich variety of information and other features in an effort to answer customer questions, build closer customer relationships and generate excitement about the company. They generally provide information about the company's history, its mission and philosophy, and the products and services that it offers. They might also tell about current events, company personnel, financial performance and employment opportunities. Most corporate websites also provide entertainment features to attract and hold visitors. Finally, the site might also provide opportunities for customers to ask questions or make comments through email before leaving the site.

Other companies create a **marketing website**. These sites engage consumers in an interaction that will move them closer to a direct purchase or other marketing outcome. Such sites might include a catalogue, shopping tips, and promotional features such as sales events or contests. For example, visitors to SonyStyle.com can search through dozens of categories of Sony products, review detailed features and specifications lists for specific items, read expert product reviews and check out the latest hot deals. They can place an order for the desired Sony products online and pay by credit card, all with a few mouse clicks. Companies aggressively promote their marketing websites in offline print and broadcast advertising and through 'banner-to-site' ads that pop up on other websites.

Mini USA operates a marketing website at **www.miniusa.com**. Once a potential customer clicks in, the car maker wastes no time trying to turn the enquiry into a sale, and then into a long-term relationship. The site offers a garage full of useful information and interactive selling features, including detailed and fun descriptions of current Mini models, tools for designing your very own Mini, information on dealer locations and services, and even tools for tracking your new Mini from factory to delivery.

> Before Angela DiFabio bought her Mini Cooper last September, she spent untold hours on the company's website, playing with dozens of possibilities before coming up with the perfect combination: A chili-pepper-red exterior, white racing stripes on the hood, and a 'custom rally badge bar' on the grill. When DiFabio placed her order with her dealer, the same build-your-own tool – and all the price and product details it provided – left her feeling like she was getting a fair deal. 'He even used the site to order my car,' she says. While she waited for her Mini to arrive, DiFabio logged on to Mini's website every day, this time using its 'Where's My Baby?' tracking tool to follow her car, like an expensive FedEx package, from the factory in Britain to its delivery. 'To be able to check the process made the wait exciting. It definitely gave me a feeling of control in the process,' says DiFabio. It's not that Mini's technology is groundbreaking. Rather, it makes an impact on the customer experience because of how it's integrated with the brand: It's fun, it's individual, it makes users feel like part of the clan. The website does more than just provide information or sell products or services. It keeps customers engaged, and when they're more engaged, they're usually happier, too.[31]

Designing effective websites Creating a website is one thing; getting people to _visit_ the site is another. The key is to create enough value and excitement to get consumers to come to the site, stick around and come back again. Today's Web users are quick to abandon any website that doesn't measure up. 'Whether people are online for work reasons or for personal reasons,' says a Web design expert, 'if a website doesn't meet their expectations, two-thirds say they don't return – now or ever. They'll visit you and leave and you'll never know. We call it the Internet death penalty.'[32] It gets worse – one research team found that many users will give a web page two seconds to give them the information they want – if it fails this test they disappear elsewhere. This means that companies must constantly update their sites to keep them current, fresh and useful – not to mention quick! Doing so involves time and expense, but the expense is necessary if the e-marketer wishes to cut through the increasing online clutter.

In addition, many online marketers spend heavily on good old-fashioned advertising and other offline marketing avenues to attract visitors to their sites. For example, Mitsubishi recently ran a series of ads to draw visitors to its Galant website. The ad featured a cliffhanger of a crash-avoidance test comparing the manoeuvrability of a Gallant GTS versus a Toyota Camry – to find out what happened, viewers had to go to the website. The ads attracted 1.6 million site visits.[33]

For some types of products, attracting visitors is easy. Consumers buying new cars, computers or financial services will be open to information and marketing initiatives from sellers. Marketers of lower involvement products, however, may face a difficult challenge in attracting website visitors. If you're in the market for a computer and you see a banner ad that says, 'The top 10 computers under £500', you'll be likely to click on the banner. But what kind of ad would get you to visit a site like dentalfloss.com?

For low-interest products, the company can create a corporate website to answer customer questions, build goodwill and excitement, supplement selling efforts through other channels and collect customer feedback. Kimberly-Clark does this with a website for its leading toilet paper brand. Making use of the long-standing association with puppies, the website offers simple games for children as well as competitions for their parents.[34]

Applying the 7Cs of effective website design, is this a good site?

Source: Pearson Education Ltd.

A key challenge is designing a website that is attractive on first view and interesting enough to encourage repeat visits. To attract new visitors and to encourage revisits, suggest experts, e-marketers should pay close attention to the seven Cs of effective website design:[35]

- *Context:* the site's layout and design
- *Content:* the text, pictures, sound and video that the website contains
- *Community:* the ways that the site enables user-to-user communication
- *Customisation:* the site's ability to tailor itself to different users or to allow users to personalise the site
- *Communication:* the ways the site enables site-to-user, user-to-site, or two-way communication
- *Connection:* the degree to which the site is linked to other sites
- *Commerce:* the site's capabilities to enable commercial transactions

And to keep customers coming back to the site, companies need to embrace yet another 'C' – constant change.

At the very least, a website should be easy to use and physically attractive. Ultimately, however, websites must also be *useful*. 'The bottom line: People seek substance over style, usefulness over flash,' says one analyst. 'They want to get what they want quickly. Surfers should know almost immediately upon accessing your site why they should stick around, what's in it for them.'[36] Thus, effective websites contain deep and useful information, interactive tools that help buyers find and evaluate products of interest, links to other related sites, changing promotional offers and entertaining features that lend relevant excitement.

From time to time, a company needs to reassess its website's attractiveness and usefulness. One way is to invite the opinion of site-design experts. But a better way is to have users themselves evaluate what they like and dislike about the site. This can be done via a questionnaire or by allowing users to leave comments. Such feedback is useful for all organisations in managing their Web presence, whether they are the European Union or a local council – these organisations can learn who is using their website and how they are using it – or would like to use it.[37]

Placing ads and promotions online

As consumers spend more and more time on the Internet, many companies are shifting more of their marketing budget to **online advertising** to build their brands or to attract visitors to their websites. The amounts spent on online advertising have increased exponentially, and this rate of increase is not expected to slow down in the foreseeable future. The Interactive Advertising Bureau has estimated the amount spent on online advertising in Europe in 2007 as €11.2 billion – up from €7.2 billion in 2006. This compares against US figures of €14.5 billion and €11.1 billion respectively. Two-thirds of the European spend occurred in the three big online markets of the UK, Germany and France – but other, smaller markets grew at incredible speeds – Slovenia by 49 per cent, Spain 55 per cent and Greece an astonishing 91 per cent.

> We are well on the way to achieving the '10 before 10' – that is 10 European countries where online advertising accounts for at least 10 per cent of overall ad spend by the year 2010. At the end of 2007 Denmark, Germany, Netherlands, Norway, Poland, Sweden and the UK had all reached this milestone.[38]

Forms of online advertising Online ads might to appear anywhere on an Internet user's screen. The most common form of online advertising is the *banner ad*, banner-shaped ads found at the top, bottom, left, right, or centre of a Web page. Banners go by many names, including *tickers* (banners that move across the screen), skyscrapers (tall, skinny banner ads at the side of a Web page), and rectangles (block ads appearing in the middle of the screen). Most banner ads contain links to the advertiser's website. For instance, a Web surfer looking up airline schedules or fares might encounter a flashing banner that screams, 'Rent a car from Hertz and get up to 2 days free!' Clicking on the ad takes consumers to the Hertz website, where they can redeem the promotion.

Interstitials are online ads that appear between screen changes on a website, especially while a new screen is loading. For example, visit **www.marketwatch.com** and you'll probably see a ten-second ad for Visa, Verizon or another sponsor before the home page loads. *Pop-ups* are online ads that appear suddenly in a new window in front of the window being viewed. Such ads can multiply out of control, creating a major annoyance. As a result, Internet services and Web browser providers have developed applications that let users block most pop-ups. But not to worry. Many advertisers have now developed *pop-unders*, new windows that evade pop-up blockers by appearing behind the page you're viewing.

Another hot growth area for online advertising is *search-related ads* (or *contextual advertising*), in which text-based ads and links appear alongside search engine results on sites such as Google and Yahoo! What advertisers love about these is that they pay per click – that is, if the advert is ignored, then it doesn't cost the advertiser anything. This compares very favourably with a print ad, for which the rates are fixed dependent on the number of copies of the paper or magazine printed.

Finally, with the increase in broadband Internet access, many companies are developing exciting new *rich media* advertisements, which incorporate animation, video, sound and interactivity. Rich media ads attract and hold consumer attention better than traditional banner ads. They employ techniques such as float, fly and snapback – animations that jump out and sail over the Web page before retreating to their original space. But many media rich ads do more than create a little bit of jumping animation. For example, to attract would-be commodity traders to its website, the Chicago Board of Trade runs a small media-rich banner ad that explodes into a small site when the user's mouse rolls over it. The mouse-over site features free streaming quotes, sample research and a virtual trading account, all of which would never fit into a traditional static ad.[39]

Other forms of online promotion Other forms of online promotion include content sponsorships, microsites, alliances and affiliate programmes, and viral advertising.

Content sponsorships are another form of Internet promotion. Many companies gain name exposure on the Internet by sponsoring special content on various websites, such as news or financial information or special interest topics. For example, Betfair sponsors the Fantasy Football portion of the *Daily Telegraph*'s website, the Edinburgh Fringe Festival website is sponsored by a panel of firms including the Royal Bank of Scotland and Magners Cider. Smaller, more focused websites for niche interests also gain sponsorship of their websites – the UK Games Expo in Birmingham is sponsored by firms like Wizards of the Coast – who market 'Magic: The Gathering' collectable card games. These companies pay for the sponsorship and in return receive exclusive ad and sponsorship recognition alongside the content. Sponsorships are best placed in carefully targeted sites where they can offer relevant information or service to the audience. Similarly, e-marketers can also go online with *microsites*, limited areas on the Web managed and paid for by an external company. For example, an insurance company might create a microsite on a car-buying site, offering insurance advice for car buyers and at the same time offering good insurance deals. Increasingly, firms are adopting this strategy to virtual worlds like Second Life and building a presence as they would on a high street.

Internet companies can also develop *alliances and affiliate programmes*, in which they work with other companies, online and offline, to 'promote each other'. Amazon.com has more than 900,000 affiliates who post Amazon banners on their websites. And Yahoo!, whose ad revenue makes up 84 per cent of its total worldwide revenue, has become a fertile ground for alliances with film studios and TV production companies. In one episode of the US version of *The Apprentice*, teams created and marketed a new flavour of Ciao Bella ice cream. Although Ciao Bella had previous sold its ice cream in only 18 stores in New York and San Francisco, Yahoo! convinced the manufacturer to place the new product in 760 stores around the country. An end-of-episode promotion urged viewers to visit Yahoo!'s local online search engine to look for the store nearest them. The product sold out by 5 pm the next day. And thanks to Yahoo!'s registration database, it was able to provide Ciao Bella with the demographic characteristics of respondents.[40]

Finally, online marketers use **viral marketing**, the Internet version of word-of-mouth marketing. Viral marketing involves creating a website, email message, or other marketing event that is so infectious that customers will want to pass it along to their friends. Because customers pass the message or promotion along to others, viral marketing can be very inexpensive. And when the information comes from a friend, the recipient is much more likely to open and read it. 'The idea is to get your customers to do your marketing for you,' notes a viral marketing expert.[41] When these tactics work, they can create a real buzz around your brand. If done badly, they can fall foul of legislation or create a backlash.

Some firms have gone to extreme lengths – bordering on or even passing legal and moral boundaries. L'Oréal set up a fake blog called *Journal de ma Peau* (Diary of my skin), in order to promote Peel Microabrasion, an anti-wrinkle product. 'Claire' – the purported author of the blog – did not in fact exist, and her endorsement of the product was merely a creation of the company. This tactic spectacularly backfired when the truth became known – many potential consumers were outraged and the negative word-of-mouth and publicity was significant. Recent changes in legislation mean that such actions are now illegal – as well as unethical.[42]

The future of online advertising Although online ad spending is growing rapidly, it still accounts for only a minor portion of the total advertising and marketing expenditures of most companies. This is likely to change in time, and it is playing an increasingly important role in the marketing mixes of many advertisers – one report even suggests it has already achieved parity with TV in terms of spend, and that when campaigns successfully integrate online and offline advertising, the synergy created can be immense – as GroupM found:

> The research found that TV is stronger at telling people about a new brand they haven't heard of before (74 per cent), sparking interest in a brand (74 per cent), providing new information about a brand people are already aware of (72 per cent) and persuading people to try a brand or product (59 per cent). Online advertising can also have these effects but performs relatively better at helping people decide which brands are relevant (50 per cent), causing a re-evaluation of a brand (41 per cent) and giving enough information to make a purchase decision (41 per cent). The findings demonstrated that people have different motivations for watching TV and using the Internet. Although there are overlaps in reasons for use, the Internet is accessed primarily for finding information (75 per cent) and communication (66 per cent), while TV is mainly used for entertainment (80 per cent) and relaxation (73 per cent). Importantly, it also found that consumers are now much more aware of the existence and role of TV and online advertising and what they can do with it for themselves. It was clear from the findings that they appreciate the complete package that TV and online, when used together, offers them. Good news for advertisers concerned with any supposed anti-advertising sentiment.[43]

Although Procter & Gamble spends only a small portion of its ad media budget online, it views the Web as an important medium. According to a P&G marketer, online marketing is 'a permission-based way to offer consumers more information about a product than can be shared in a typical 30-second spot. It opens a two-way exchange where we can better educate consumers about our products.'[44]

The popularity of blogs and other Web forums has resulted in a rash of commercially sponsored websites called **Web communities**, which take advantage of the C2C properties of the Internet. Such sites, like Second Life discussed at the beginning of this chapter, allow members to congregate online and exchange views on issues of common interest. They are the cyberspace equivalent to a Starbucks coffee house, a place where everybody knows your email address.

For example, iVillage.com is a Web community in which women can exchange views and obtain information, support and solutions on families, food, fitness, relationships, relaxation, home and garden, news and issues, or just about any other topic. The site draws more than 16 million unique visitors a month, putting it in a league with magazines such as *Cosmopolitan*, *Glamour* and *Vogue*. Another is Chesspark, a home for those who like to play chess online. It is quite likely that you have your own MySpace, Bebo or Facebook profile – and you may have devoted significant time to personalising it. Alongside the profiles of individuals, it is becoming increasingly common to see profiles for events, bands or brands that think they can use the medium to establish credibility – we certainly saw the logical extension of this in the Second Life case at the beginning of the chapter.

Such communities are often attractive to advertisers because they draw frequent, lengthy visits from consumers with common interests and well-defined demographics.

Using email

Email has exploded onto the scene as an important e-marketing tool. A recent study of email marketing in Europe suggested that we get twice as many commercial messages as work-related and personal emails combined – a result of the estimated €2 billion spent annually by marketers.[45]

To compete effectively in this ever more cluttered email environment – not to mention the increasing sophistication of virus-blockers and other software, marketers are designing 'enriched' email messages – animated, interactive and personalised messages full of streaming audio and video. And they are targeting these attention-grabbers more carefully to those who want them and will act upon them. Consider how Apple uses its weekly email – *New Music Tuesday*. Around the world, millions of iTunes users receive an email that has been customised to them individually. Apple does this by matching up the new releases that week with records of who bought what from the iTunes Store, meaning that you are much more likely to see news and links to music you would be interested in than if you had received the same standardised email as everyone else.

As with other types of online marketing, companies must be careful that they don't cause resentment among Internet users who are already overloaded with 'junk email'. The explosion of **spam** – unsolicited, unwanted commercial email messages that clog up our emailboxes – has produced consumer frustration and anger. According to one research company, spam accounts for as much as 90 per cent of all email.[46] Email marketers walk a fine line between adding value for consumers and being intrusive. Companies must beware of irritating consumers by sending unwanted email to promote their products. Legislation recently enacted across Europe and increasingly around the world is requiring that marketers should ask customers for permission to email marketing pitches. They should also tell recipients how to 'opt in' or 'opt out' of email promotions at any time. This approach, known as *permission-based marketing*, has become a standard model for email marketing.

THE PROMISE AND CHALLENGES OF E-COMMERCE

E-commerce continues to offer both great promise and many challenges for the future. We now look at both the promises of e-commerce and the 'darker side' of the Web.

The continuing promise of e-commerce

Its most ardent apostles still envision a time when the Internet and e-commerce will replace magazines, newspapers, and even stores as sources for information and buying. Most marketers, however, hold a more realistic view. To be sure, online marketing will become a successful business model for some companies, Internet firms such as Amazon.com, eBay, Expedia and Google, and direct-marketing companies such as Dell. Michael Dell's goal is one day 'to have *all* customers conduct *all* transactions on the Internet, globally'. However, for most companies, online marketing will remain just one important approach to the marketplace that works alongside other approaches in a fully integrated marketing mix.

The same applies to not-for-profit organisations like charities. The recent experiences of the International Committee of the Red Cross are a good example of how the internet can impact across many marketing-related issues – see Marketing at Work 14.1 for more on this.

Eventually, as companies become more adept at integrating e-commerce with their everyday strategy and tactics, the 'e' will fall away from e-business or e-marketing. 'The key question is not whether to deploy Internet technology – companies have no

MARKETING AT WORK 14.1

The International Committee of the Red Cross

Ann M. Torres, *Marketing Department, Cairns Graduate School of Business and Economics, National University of Ireland*

The International Committee of the Red Cross (ICRC), established in 1863, is a neutral organisation that works towards ensuring humanitarian protection. The ICRC, headquartered in Geneva, Switzerland, operates in more than 80 countries and employs more than 12,000 staff. It is the world's oldest non-religious organisation dedicated to humanitarian relief and it has a unique place in international law; it is identified by the four 1949 Geneva Conventions as an *impartial humanitarian body* and is mandated by public international law to assist victims of war and violence.

The ICRC's delegations and missions primarily employ nationals of the countries in which it works to carry out a range of activities, such as assisting civilians, individuals deprived of their freedom, dispersed families, the wounded and sick of existing or emerging conflict; preventive action through the cooperation with the national societies; as well as humanitarian coordination and diplomacy. The ICRC and its societies work to uphold seven fundamental principles: humanity, impartiality, neutrality, independence, voluntary service, unity and universality. The principle of humanity forms the central purpose of the ICRC's activities, which is 'to prevent and alleviate human suffering, without discrimination, and to protect human dignity'.

As a consequence of its increased international presence, the ICRC has received more media attention, but as an organisation it is still poorly understood. In July 2001, a review of the Red Cross brand in 15 countries by advertising agency Young & Rubicam found that while the ICRC 'had a high status in all of the 15 countries, people weren't sure what the Red Cross actually did'. Surprisingly, this lack of understanding persists despite the fact the ICRC has won four Nobel Peace Prizes. More importantly, the ICRC began to reassess what it wanted to be known for. As a result, a greater portion of ICRC's marketing communication efforts have been devoted to informing relevant audiences, including the general public, by availing itself of new media to increase its reach – and a major part of this effort has been in revamping the online presence of the organisation.

The ICRC website (**www.icrc.org**) is among its most valuable communication tools – not only as a means to communicate with the general public, but also as a central channel through which it can distribute information and reports to relevant audiences – without having to rely on national governments. It is available in seven languages and consultation of the website continues to rise worldwide; approximately 107 million page views were registered on the ICRC website in 2006. Peak usage of the ICRC website typically occurs around incidents of extraordinary disaster or armed conflict – when the website hosts help and advice for victims and appeals to donors for help. For example, in 2004 peak usage of the ICRC website was in March to May, due to events in Iraq and in December due to the Asian tsunami. In the autumn of 2005, the number of hits peaked with hurricane Katrina and the South Asia earthquake. In response to operational needs and public communication requirements, the

Thousands of Internally Displaced People (IDPs) gather in a field to receive food aid from the Red Cross near a camp for IDPs in the town of Kibati, just north of the provincial capital of Goma, on 5 November 2008. The humanitarian situation remained catastrophic in the North Kivu region, where over 1 million people had been displaced by fighting the week before (*Photo source*: ROBERTO SCHMIDT/AFP/Getty Images).

ICRC continues to add new functions to its website, such as the launch of an RSS feed – a system that makes it possible to deliver newly published press releases and other documents directly to people's desktops. Considerable efforts have also been made to improve the website's editorial content so as to 'strengthen the ICRC's positioning as a global and independent humanitarian organisation'.

Recently the ICRC's Marketing Unit has pursued a number of large-scale research studies so as to develop its communication strategies and to raise 'awareness and influence attitudes on issues of importance' more effectively. The ICRC has focused on two areas of research: examining the communication needs of key audiences, regionally and globally; and measuring perceptions of and attitudes towards humanitarian action, the humanitarian environment, as well as the ICRC logo and emblems. Much of this research has been carried out more quickly at less cost because of the Internet, and the medium is now a key marketing tool in meeting these objectives.

Indeed, the findings from the ICRC's research studies informed its 2006 print, television and Internet campaign strategy, *Abuse Grows Hatred*. The multimedia campaign focused on detention and emphasised the need to abide by the rules of the Geneva Conventions, which prohibit the abuse of detainees. The campaign goes further, stating that abuse and torture perpetuate a cycle of violence. The animated film, created by the agency VCCP City, 'dramatises the point that the ill-treatment of prisoners breeds hatred within the families, communities and countries of the imprisoned' (VCCP 2006: 1). The Internet proved to be by far the most effective and value for money medium through which to distribute this message worldwide.

Learning from this success, in May 2008, the ICRC, as the official charity partner of UEFA for EURO 2008, launched an online fund-raising campaign **www.scorefortheredcross.org**. The campaign prompted Internet users to make donations in support of the Red Cross, where each donation was transformed into virtual goals for the donor's favourite side amongst the 16 qualifiers. The football team with the most goals would win the title of the *Most Humanitarian Team of the EURO 2008*; the campaign's winning team turned out to be Germany, followed by Spain and the Netherlands. The proceeds from the campaign were designated for landmine victims in Afghanistan and to local projects of the 16 European Red Cross societies associated with the campaign. 'This collaboration with the sporting world in a festive competition like EURO 2008 represents an opportunity for the ICRC. It lays the basis for raising the awareness of a large public in a playful way about sensitive topics of humanitarian concern, such as the situation of mine victims in Afghanistan'. The UEFA website also has a link to the ICRC site and frequently provides information about ICRC activities online.

In the future the ICRC will continue to use the Internet to meet its marketing objectives – and so will many other organisations.

Sources: Quotes and information relating to the International Committee of the Red Cross example have been drawn from L.A. Casey and D.B. Rivkin, 'Double-red-crossed', *The National Interest*, 22 March 2005, No. 79, pp. 63–9; Department for International Development, 'Working in Partnership with the International Committee of the Red Cross 2002–2006', 2003; D.P. Forsythe, *The Humanitarians: The International Committee of the Red Cross*, Cambridge University Press, 2005; M. Griffin, 'Emblem crossed out by a crystal', *The Age*, 19 September 2005. International Committee of the Red Cross, 'Discover the ICRC', September 2005; ICRC, 'ICRC 2005 Annual Report'. May 2006; ICRC, 'Emblems of Humanity: The International Red Cross and Red Crescent Movement', July 2007; ICRC, 'ICRC 2006 Annual Report', May 2007; ICRC, 'Study on Operational and Commercial and Other Non-Operational Issues Involving the Use of the Emblems', October 2007; ICRC, 'Score for the Red Cross – Flash Video Spot', May 2008; R. Murphy, 'International Red Cross and Red Crescent Movement: Lecture Notes', 2007, The Centre for Human Rights, National University of Ireland, Galway; Standing Commission of the Red Cross and Red Crescent, 'Strategy for the International Red Cross and Red Crescent', November 2001; VCCP, 'VCCP Creates Detention Ad for ICRC', August 2006. The VCCP campaign's animated film may be viewed at: http://www.icrc.org/web/eng/siteeng0.nsf/html/video-spot-detention-010706. The video spot for the ICRC/UEFA online campaign for Euro 2008 can be seen at: http://www.icrc.org/web/eng/siteeng0.nsf/html/score-for-the-red-cross-ytfilm-050508. The ICRC logo and emblems can be seen at: http://www.icrc.org/web/eng/siteeng0.nsf/htmlall/emblem?OpenDocument.

choice if they want to stay competitive – but how to deploy it,' says business strategist Michael Porter. He continues: 'We need to move away from the rhetoric about "Internet industries", "e-business strategies", and a "new economy", and see the Internet for what it is . . . a powerful set of tools that can be used, wisely or unwisely, in almost any industry and as part of almost any strategy.'[47]

The Web's darker side

Along with its considerable promise, there is a 'darker side' to Internet marketing. Here we examine two major sets of concerns: Internet profitability, and legal and ethical issues.

Internet profitability

One major concern is profitability, especially for B2C dot-coms. While many B2B marketers and B2C click-and-mortar retailers are marketing profitably online, surprisingly few B2C Internet-only companies are profitable. One problem is that, although expanding rapidly, online marketing still reaches only a limited marketspace. The Web audience is becoming more mainstream, but online users still tend to be somewhat more affluent, younger and better educated than the general population. This makes the Internet ideal for marketing financial services, travel services, computer hardware and software, and certain other classes of products. However, it makes online marketing less effective for selling mainstream products. Moreover, in many product categories, users still do more window browsing and product research than actual buying.

Another problem is that the Internet offers millions of websites and a staggering volume of information. Thus, navigating the Internet can be frustrating, confusing and time-consuming for consumers. In this chaotic and cluttered environment, most Web ads and sites go unnoticed or unopened. Even when noticed, online marketers often find it difficult to hold consumer attention. A site must capture Web surfers' attention within only a few seconds or lose them to another site. That leaves very little time for marketers to promote and sell their goods.

Finally, a great number of the click-only online retailers are small, niche marketers. With a growing number of retailers setting up shop online, the niches can become crowded and competitive. Also, consumers are more Web-savvy than ever, and new search technologies and comparison-shopping sites are emerging to help them locate the best deals. This makes the Web an even more competitive marketspace. Finally, dot-com e-tailers are facing stiffer competition from established click-and-mortar retailers entering their markets. Much of the strong recent growth in online sales comes from large companies such as Tesco and Amazon.com, established firms with recognised brands and strong customer bases. Only the most efficient and best-managed dot-coms will be able to survive profitably against such competition.

Legal and ethical issues

From a broader societal viewpoint, Internet marketing practices have raised a number of ethical and legal questions. In previous sections, we've touched on some of the negatives associated with the Internet, such as unwanted email and the annoyance of pop-up ads. Here we examine concerns about consumer online privacy and security, and other legal and ethical issues.

Online privacy and security *Online privacy* is perhaps the number one e-commerce concern. Most online marketers have become skilled at collecting and analysing detailed consumer information. Marketers can easily track website visitors, and many consumers who participate in website activities provide extensive personal information. This may leave consumers open to information abuse if companies make unauthorised use of the information in marketing their products or exchanging databases with other companies. It is because of this that many consumers and policy makers worry that marketers have stepped over the line and are violating consumers' right to privacy. A recent example of this is the furore over a software program called Phorm. This software, trialled on several leading UK ISPs, tracked users' browsing habits and used these to tailor page content with adverts deemed most relevant to that particular user. Privacy groups complained strongly about the difficulties in opting out of the system, further concerns focused on what was being done with highly personal data the user might bring to the screen, such as email read through a browser – like Hotmail or Gmail – or financial or medical information.[48]

Broadband Internet providers BT, TalkTalk and Virgin Media have hit a storm of anger from customers since teaming up with a pioneer in much-hated 'spyware' technology. Last month, the three Internet service providers, with 9 million households between them, signed up to software from an AIM-listed business called Phorm, run by colourful American tycoon Kent Ertugrul. Phorm monitors what content surfers browse on the Net. It will then send to those individuals ads which match the interests they have shown through their browsing. Advertisers pay Phorm a fee, which it shares with the ISP. Phorm says the customer's identity is 'anonymised' so advertisers would not be able to tell who they are. But the IT community is up in arms, dubbing the practice 'data pimping', and is still worried about being spied upon. A website, badphorm.co.uk, has been set up specifically to attack the move. Professor Peter Sommer, author of *The Hacker's Handbook*, claims it is illegal. He argues that it is an interception of a public communication which is in direct contravention of the Regulation of Investigatory Powers Act 2000. Ross Anderson, professor of security engineering at Cambridge University, said: 'The message has to be this: If you care about your privacy, do not use BT, Virgin or TalkTalk as your Internet provider.' Anderson said that, historically, anonymising technology had never worked. Even if it did, he stressed, it still posed huge privacy issues. He gave the example of a woman who had had an abortion without telling their partner. If she had surfed websites like Mothercare or other baby-related retailers and advice centres while making up her mind about the termination, her family's computers might suddenly start receiving baby ads, creating suspicion from the husband or boyfriend. Phorm counters that it will not collect data on sensitive areas like adult or medical data. Ertugrul said: 'I'm not the Prince of Darkness I'm made out to be. The people who have criticised Phorm just haven't seen it. What we are doing will bring greater privacy and fewer rubbish ads people aren't interested in.' He stressed that, unlike Google and other search engines, Phorm would not be storing any details of websites visited or searches made. All it retains is the general category of the sites – for example, fast cars. The Information Commissioner is investigating, having been approached by Phorm. BT, TalkTalk and Virgin Media said they had done due diligence on Phorm and were happy with the privacy situation. Users are also worried about the background of Phorm itself. It, and Ertegrul, were pioneers of software known as spyware, which monitored customer's websurfing and made unwanted pop-up ads appear on screen.[49]

Many consumers also worry about *online security*. They fear that unscrupulous snoopers will eavesdrop on their online transactions or intercept their credit card numbers and make unauthorised purchases. In a recent survey, eight out of ten online shoppers in the UK were concerned about typing in their credit card details.[50] In turn, companies doing business online fear that others will use the Internet to invade their computer systems for the purposes of commercial espionage or even sabotage. There appears to be an ongoing competition between the technology of Internet security systems and the sophistication of those seeking to break them.

In response to such online privacy and security concerns, most national and supra-national governments have attempted to legislate – but the technological and geographical complexity of many issues is a legal minefield. If a shopper in Sweden is browsing the website of a company that is registered in Belgium but is hosted on a server in the Netherlands and pays for her goods using a credit card registered in the UK from a Swiss bank, then which laws do and do not apply if the goods are faulty, if the goods are illegal, if there is a fraud? What taxes are payable? Which governments and agencies have access to personal data generated by that transaction? That is a possible and relatively simplistic illustration of some of the potential issues. Here is a recent example from the world of media:

> Two British newspaper publishers have been fined in French courts because they violated French privacy laws. The publishers were liable because the articles were viewed in France on the Internet. Olivier Martinez, famous in the UK as an ex-boyfriend of Kylie Minogue, sued Mirror Group Newspapers (MGN) and Associated Newspapers for breach of France's strict privacy laws after the newspapers published stories suggesting Martinez and Minogue had recommenced their relationship, which had ended a year previously. The stories also detailed their movements together in Paris earlier this year. MGN was sued because of an article at sundaymirror.co.uk, while Associated was sued over articles at dailymail.co.uk and thisislondon.co.uk. For each title the publishers were ordered to pay €4,500.
>
> The Tribunal de Grande Instance de Paris rejected claims that it did not have the right to hear the case. It had jurisdiction because the online versions of the articles were viewable in France, it found. Though he was only awarded €4,500 per publication, Martinez had claimed €30,000 in total in a series of privacy cases about articles making the same allegations.
>
> His lawyer, Emmanuel Asmar, told out-law.com that French courts usually ordered small payouts. The significance of the case was not financial, he said, but in the setting of a precedent that UK publications could be liable under French privacy legislation. 'The big thing is that for the first time the [court] considered that UK publishers are liable for their contents in France since it is viewable here and the UK is a member of the EU,' he said.
>
> A related case from earlier this year was notable because it held one publisher responsible for material published on its site by another publisher via an RSS syndication feed. That case was also taken by Asmar but on behalf of *La Vie en Rose* director Olivier Dahan. He successfully sued three websites for publishing stories about him and actress Sharon Stone via an RSS feed.
>
> Martinez also won in a case against three websites earlier this year when a court ruled that by publishing a link to offending material the blogs were liable for the privacy invasions of that material.[51]

Of special concern are the privacy and safety of children. Social networking sites like Bebo, Facebook and MySpace are increasingly being used not just by teenagers, but also by younger children. On these sites they are exposed to advertising intended for older children or adults, uncontrolled imagery in other users' profiles and are potentially exposed to abuse from peers and adults. Across Europe, efforts to mitigate these problems and promote safe use of the Internet by children is led by INSAFE.[52] This body, sponsored and endorsed by the EU, is active on four main fronts in respect of online child safety – fighting against illegal content, tackling unwanted and harmful content (whether images or software), promoting a safer online environment and raising awareness amongst parents of online issues. Are such efforts necessary? One group found that three out of four attempts by teenage boys to buy adult DVDs and '18' rated video games were successful, and that an increasing number of teenagers were buying alcohol online.[53]

Many companies have responded to consumer privacy and security concerns with actions of their own. To help foster customer trust, companies such as Expedia have conducted voluntary audits of their privacy and security policies. Since 2000, Expedia has employed PricewaterhouseCoopers to run privacy audits of its online services. Expedia's privacy policy gives customers complete control over the use of the personal information they share with the online travel booker. Expedia also has an independent auditor regularly assess its Web security technology and procedures.[54]

Still others are taking a broadly, industy-wide approach. Founded in 1996, TRUSTe is a non-profit, self-regulatory organisation that works with a number of large corporate sponsors, including Microsoft and AT&T, to audit companies' privacy and security measures and help consumers navigate the Web safely. According to the company's website, 'TRUSTe believes that an environment of mutual trust and openness will help make and keep the Internet a free, comfortable, and richly diverse community for everyone.' To reassure consumers, the company lends it 'trustmark' stamp of approval to websites that meet its privacy and security standards.[55]

Other legal and ethical issues   Beyond issues of online privacy and security, Consumers are also concerned about *Internet fraud*, including identity theft, investment fraud and financial scams.

One common form of Internet fraud is *phishing*, a type of identity theft that uses deceptive emails and fraudulent websites to fool users into divulging their personal data. Some of these messages are obvious attempts at frauds, other are more subtle or more credible – seemingly using plausible email addresses or Web links in order to catch the unwary. Even though Web users are becoming more sophisticated a significant proportion of people can be caught out. The UK banking association APACS listed more than 10,000 phishing incidents in the first quarter of 2008, a more than 200 per cent rise from the same period in 2007. The amount lost from these attacks fell by a third from £33.5 million in 2006 to £22.6 million in 2007.[56]

Phishing also damages the brand identities of legitimate online marketers who have worked to build user confidence in Web and email transactions. Fortunately, companies and governments are taking action. ENISA – the European Network Information Security Agency – is an EU-wide body which coordinates efforts to prevent, address and respond to network and information security problems.[57]

There are also concerns about *segmentation and discrimination* on the Internet. Some social critics and policy makers worry about the so-called *digital divide* – the gap between those who have access to the latest Internet and information technologies and those who don't. They are concerned that in this information age, not having equal access to information can be a social and economic handicap. Socially, lack of Internet access can be an issue for those looking for jobs, somewhere to study, and those considering to whom to give their vote. Economically, at an individual or household level, those who can afford a computer and an Internet connection can browse at Amazon – perhaps saving £5 on a book priced at £20 on the high street. Those without the access pay the high street price – the rich pay less, the poor pay more. Does that strike you as fair? You may recall from the beginning of this chapter how degree and quality of Internet access was so strongly correlated with income and education. This issue scales up across regions and nations – almost all of Europe is an Internet literate and savvy society, used to viewing evaluating and analysing vast quantities of data, but the same cannot be said for much of Africa and Asia. The eighteenth and nineteenth centuries saw the industrial revolution in the West – should we now speak of the digital revolution as the next step?

Despite these challenges and issues, companies large and small are quickly integrating online marketing into their marketing strategies and mixes. As it continues to grow, online marketing will prove to be a powerful tool for building customer relationships, improving sales, communicating company and product information, and delivering products and services more efficiently and effectively.

THE JOURNEY YOU'VE TAKEN Reviewing the concepts

Recent technological advances have created a digital age. To thrive in this digital environment, marketers are adding some Internet thinking to their strategies and tactics. This chapter discusses how marketers are adapting.

1 **Discuss how the digital age is affecting both consumers and the marketers who serve them.**

Much of today's business operates on digital information, which flows through connected networks. Intranets, extranets and the Internet now connect people and companies with each other and with important information. The Internet has grown explosively to become *the* technology of the new millennium, empowering consumers and businesses alike with the blessings of connectivity. Of course, some groups are more blessed than others.[58]

The Internet and other new technologies have changed the ways that companies reach and serve their markets. The Internet enables consumers and companies to access and share huge amounts of information with just a few mouse clicks. In turn, the Internet and other digital technologies have given marketers a whole new way to reach and serve customers. New Internet marketers and channel relationships have arisen to replace some types of traditional marketers. The new technologies are helping marketers to tailor their offers effectively to targeted customers or even to help buyers customise their own marketing offers. It's hard to find a company today that doesn't have a substantial Web presence.

2 **Explain how companies have responded to the Internet and other powerful new technologies with e-business strategies, and how these strategies have resulted in benefits to both buyers and sellers.**

Conducting business in the digital age calls for a new model of marketing strategy and practice. Companies need to retain most of the skills and practices that have worked in the past. However, they must also add major new competencies and practices if they hope to grow and prosper in the digital environment. E-business is the use of electronic platforms to conduct a company's business. E-commerce involves buying and selling processes supported by electronic means, primarily the Internet. It includes e-marketing (the selling side of e-commerce) and e-purchasing (the buying side of e-commerce).

E-commerce benefits both buyers and sellers. For buyers, e-commerce makes buying convenient and private, provides greater product access and selection, and makes available a wealth of product and buying information. It is interactive and immediate and gives the consumer a greater measure of control over the buying process. For sellers, e-commerce is a powerful tool for building customer relationships. It also increases the sellers' speed and efficiency, helping to reduce selling costs. E-commerce also offers great flexibility and better access to global markets.

3 **Describe the four major e-marketing domains.**

Companies can practice e-commerce in any or all of four domains. B2C (business-to-consumer) e-marketing is initiated by businesses and targets final consumers. Despite setbacks following the 'dot-com gold rush' of the late 1990s, B2C e-commerce continues to grow at a healthy rate. Although online consumers are still somewhat higher in income and more technology-oriented than traditional buyers, the cyberspace population is becoming much more mainstream and diverse. This growing diversity opens up new e-commerce targeting opportunities for marketers. Today, consumers can buy almost anything on the Web.

B2B (business-to-business) e-commerce dwarfs B2C e-commerce. Most businesses today operate websites or use B2B trading networks, auction sites, spot exchanges, online product catalogues, barter sites, or other online resources to reach new customers, serve current customers more effectively, and obtain buying efficiencies and better prices. Business buyers and sellers meet in huge marketspaces – or open trading networks – to share information and complete transactions efficiently. Or they set up private trading networks that link them with their own trading partners.

Through C2C (consumer-to-consumer) e-marketing, consumers can buy or exchange goods and information directly from or with one another. Examples include online auction sites, forums and Web logs (blogs). Finally, through C2B (consumer-to-business) e-commerce, consumers are now finding it easier to search out sellers on the Web, learn about their products and services and initiate purchases. Using the Web, customers can even drive transactions with business, rather than the other way around.

4 Discuss how companies can go about conducting e-marketing to profitably deliver more value to customers.

Companies of all types are now engaged in e-commerce. The Internet gave birth to the *click-only* dot-coms, which operate only online. In addition, many traditional brick-and-mortar companies have now added e-marketing operations, transforming themselves into *click-and-mortar* competitors. Many click-and-mortar companies are now having more online success than their click-only competitors.

Companies can conduct e-marketing in any of four ways: creating a website, placing ads and promotions online, setting up or participating in Web communities, or using online email. The first step typically is to set up a website. Beyond simply setting up a site, however, companies must make their sites engaging, easy to use and useful in order to attract visitors, hold them and bring them back again.

E-marketers can use various forms of online advertising to build their Internet brands or to attract visitors to their websites. Beyond online advertising, other forms of online promotion include content sponsorships, microsites, alliances and affiliate programmes, and viral marketing, the Internet version of word-of-mouth marketing. Online marketers can also participate in Web communities, which take advantage of the C2C properties of the Web. Finally, email marketing has become a hot new e-marketing tool for both B2C and B2B marketers.

5 Overview the promise and challenges that e-commerce presents for the future.

E-commerce continues to offer great promise for the future. For most companies, online marketing will become an important part of a fully integrated marketing mix. For others, it will be the major means by which they serve the market. Eventually, the 'e' will fall away from e-business or e-marketing as companies become more adept at integrating e-commerce with their everyday strategy and tactics. However, e-commerce also faces many challenges. One challenge is Web profitability – surprisingly few companies, especially the Web-only dot-coms, are using the Web profitably. The other challenge concerns legal and ethical issues – issues of online privacy and security, Internet fraud and the digital divide. Despite these challenges, companies large and small are quickly integrating online marketing into their marketing strategies and mixes.

NAVIGATING THE KEY TERMS

B2B (business-to-business) e-commerce 482

B2C (business-to-consumer) e-commerce 479

C2B (consumer-to-business) e-commerce 484

C2C (consumer-to-consumer) e-commerce 483

Click-and-mortar companies 486

Click-only companies 485

Corporate website 487

E-business 477

E-commerce 478

E-marketing 478

Extranet 476

Internet 476

Intranet 476

Marketing website 488

Online advertising 490

Open trading exchanges 482

Private trading exchanges 482

Spam 493

Viral marketing 491

Web communities 492

NOTES AND REFERENCES

1 P.J. Ludlow and M. Wallace, *The Second Life Herald:The Virtual Tabloid That Witnessed The Dawn Of The Metauniverse* (Cambridge, MA: MIT Press, 2007).

2 Linden Labs: http://secondlife.com/whatis/economy_stats.php.

3 N. Yee, 'The Demographics, Motivations and Derived Experiences of Users of Massively-Multiuser Online Graphical Environments', *PRESENCE: Teleoperators and Virtual Environments*, **15**, 2006, pp. 309–29.

4 Marcus D. Childress, and Ray Braswell, 'Using Massively Multiplayer Online Role-Playing Games for Online Learning', *Distance Education*, **27** (2), 2006, pp. 187–96.

5 Paul Hemp, 'Avatar-based Marketing', *Harvard Business Review*, June, 2006, pp. 48–57.

6 Kzero Research 2008: http://www.kzero.co.uk/blog/?p=1920, accessed 17 February, 2008.

7 Christian Heath, Jon Hindmarsh and Mike Fraser, '(Im)materiality, virtual reality and interaction: grounding the 'virtual' in studies of technology in action', *The Sociological Review*, **54**(4), 2006, pp. 795–817.

8 SLeducation, 2008: http://sleducation.wikispaces.com/educationaluses, accessed 18 February 2008.

9 Second Health 2008: http://secondhealth.wordpress.com/, accessed 18 February 2008.

10 Mike Macedonia, 'Generation 3D: Living in Virtual Worlds', *Computer*, **40**(10), 2007, pp. 99–101.

11 Data from: http://www.internetworldstats.com/stats4.htm.

12 Top Ten Internet Languages from: http://www.internetworldstats.com/stats7.htm.

13 2008 ITIF Broadband Rankings: http://www.itif.org/index.php?id=143.

14 http://news.bbc.co.uk/1/hi/northern_ireland/7432847.stm.

15 See: I. Burgmann, J. Philip, P.J. Kitchen and R. Williams, 'Does culture matter on the web?', *Marketing Intelligence & Planning*, **24**(1), 2006, pp. 62–76.

16 Data from Nielsen NetRatings: http://www.nielsen-netratings.com/resources.jsp?section=pr_netv&nav=1.

17 Dena Levitz, 'Many Auto Shoppers Consult Internet for Information Before Making Purchase', *Knight Ridder Tribune Business News*, 26 November 2004, p. 1.

18 See: P. Harrigan, E. Ramsey and P. Ibbotson, 'e-CRM in SMEs: An Exploratory study in Northern Ireland', *Marketing Intelligence & Planning*, **26**(4), 2008, pp. 385–404.

19 http://news.bbc.co.uk/1/hi/business/7432643.stm; http://www.verdict.co.uk/; http://www.emarketer.com/Report.aspx?code=emarketer_2000426&src=report_summary_reportsell.

20 Oxford Internet Survey 2007, available from: http://www.oii.ox.ac.uk/microsites/oxis/publications.cfm; http://news.bbc.co.uk/1/hi/business/6913918.stm.

21 http://www.gartner.com/.

22 Data from i2010 – Annual Information Society Report 2007available from: http://ec.europa.eu/information_society/eeurope/i2010/key_documents/index_en.htm#Annual%20Report%202007; e-business survey 2006, available from: http://www.ebusiness-watch.org/statistics/data.htm.

23 Data from: http://news.ebay.com/fastfacts_ebay_marketplace.cfm and http://pages.ebay.co.uk/community/aboutebay/news/pressreleases/fastfacts/04_2005.html.

24 Technorati, State of the Web 2007: http://www.sifry.com/alerts/archives/000493.html; China Internet Information Centre press release: http://www.cnnic.cn/html/Dir/2007/12/27/4954.htm.

25 Chris Oser, 'Nike Assays Blog as Marketing Tool', *Advertising Age*, 14 June 2004, p. 26.

26 'The Secret Is Out: Secret Sparkle Body Spray Launches New Website', 16 May 2005, accessed at www.imc2.com; and Jack Neff, 'Strong Enough for a Man But Made for a Tween', *Advertising Age*, 25 April 2005, p. 26.

27 *The Guardian*, The world's most powerful blogs: http://www.guardian.co.uk/technology/2008/mar/09/blogs.

28 Michelle Slatalla, 'Toll-Free Apology Soothes Savage Beast', *New York Times*, 12 February 2004, p. G4; and information from www.planetfeedback.com/consumer, August 2004.

29 Information from: http://www.officedepot.co.uk/ and Office Depot Investor Presentation, April 2008: http://bnymellon.mobular.net/bnymellon/odp/.

30 http://www.internetretailer.com/top500/list.asp.

31 Adapted from Jena McGregor, 'High-Tech Achiever: MINI USA', *Fast Company*, October 2004, p. 86, with information from www.miniusa.com, August 2005.

32 Sharon Gaudin, 'The Site of No Return', 28 May 2002, accessed at www.graphics-art.com/Site%20of%20no%20return.htm.

33 Marty Bernstein, 'Mitsubishi Super Bowl Ad Lures Viewer to Internet', *Automotive News*, 29 March 2004, p. 56B.

34 http://www.andrex.co.uk/.

35 Jeffrey F. Rayport and Bernard J. Jaworski, *e-Commerce* (New York: McGraw-Hill, 2001), p. 116. Also see Goutam Chakraborty, 'What Do Customers Consider Important in B@B Websites?', *Journal of Advertising*, March 2003, p. 50; and David Sparrow, 'Get 'Em to Bite', *Catalogue Age*, 1 April 2003, pp. 35–6.

36 Reid Goldsborough, 'Creating Web Sites for Web Surfers,' *Black Issues in Higher Education*, 17 June 2004, p. 120.

37 http://europa.eu/survey_en.htm; http://www.rutland.gov.uk/pp/pressrelease/pressdetail.asp?id=6762.

38 Numbers and quote from Interactive Advertising Bureau Europe press release 'Online advertising in Europe surges 40% to €11 billion in 2007', available from: http://www.iabeurope.ws/.

39 Ellis Booker, 'Vivid "Experiences" as the New Frontier', *B to B*, 14 March 2005, p. 14; and Karen J. Bannan, 'Rich Media Demands Attention', *B to B*, 14 March 2005, pp. 24–5.

40 Kris Oser, 'Video in Demand', *Advertising Age*, 4 April 2005, pp. S1–S5.

41 Pete Snyder, 'Wanted: Standards for Viral Marketing', *Brandweek*, 28 June 2004, p. 21.

42 Information from: http://news.bbc.co.uk/1/hi/business/7287413.stm; http://geemodo.blogspot.com/2007/12/sony-flogs-marketing-with-fake-blog.html.

43 Adapted/edited from: Double the Power of Advertising – Marketing Week: http://www.marketingweek.co.uk/cgi-bin/item.cgi?id=60890&u=pg_dtl_art_news&m=pg_hdr_art. (Centaur Media).

44 Jack Neff, 'Taking Package Goods to the Net', *Advertising Age*, 11 July 2005, pp. S1–S3.

45 http://www.forrester.com/Research/Document/Excerpt/0,7211,43165,00.html.

46 http://news.bbc.co.uk/1/hi/technology/7322615.stm.

47 Michael Porter, 'Strategy and the Internet', *Harvard Business Review*, March 2001, pp. 614–78.

48 http://news.bbc.co.uk/1/hi/technology/7283333.stm; http://www.ft.com/cms/s/0/a8704dda-eece-11dc-97ec-0000779fd2ac.html; http://www.badphorm.co.uk/page.php?2; quote from *Evening Standard*, 'Web users angry at ISPs' spyware tie-up: http://www.thisislondon.co.uk/standard-home/article-23449601-details/Web+users+angry+at+ISPs'+spyware+tie-up/article.do.

49 Edited from: http://www.thisislondon.co.uk/standard-home/article-23449601-details/ Web+users+angry+at+ISPs'+spyware+tie-up/article.do.

50 http://www.ft.com/cms/s/0/d90c1178-6520-11dc-bf89-0000779fd2ac.html.

51 Edited from: http://www.out-law.com/page-9155.

52 http://www.saferinternet.org/ww/en/pub/insafe/about.htm;
http://news.bbc.co.uk/1/hi/technology/6332619.stm;
http://ec.europa.eu/information_society/activities/sip/programme/index_en.htm.

53 http://news.bbc.co.uk/1/hi/business/7393449.stm.

54 Information on Expedia at www.expedia.com/daily/press/releases, accessed November 2008.

55 Information on TRUSTe accessed at www.truste.com, September 2005.

56 http://news.bbc.co.uk/1/hi/technology/7348737.stm;
http://news.bbc.co.uk/1/hi/technology/4879468.stm;
http://www.theregister.co.uk/2008/04/17/uk_phishing_trends/.

57 http://www.enisa.europa.eu/index.htm.

58 See: J.A. Schibrowsky, J.W. Peltier and A. Nill, 'The state of internet marketing research: A review of the literature and future research directions', *European Journal of Marketing*, 41(7/8), 2007, pp. 722–33.

CHAPTER 16
Ethics, social responsibility and sustainability

AFTER STUDYING THIS CHAPTER, YOU SHOULD BE ABLE TO

■ identify the major social criticisms of marketing

■ define *consumerism* and *environmentalism* and explain how they affect marketing strategies

■ describe the principles of socially responsible marketing

■ explain the role of ethics in marketing

THE WAY AHEAD Previewing the concepts

You've almost completed your introductory marketing travels. In this final chapter, we'll focus on marketing as a social institution. First, we'll look at some common criticisms of marketing as it affects individual consumers, other businesses and society as a whole. Then, we'll examine consumerism, environmentalism, sustainability and other citizen and public actions to keep marketing in check. Finally, we'll see how companies themselves can benefit from actively pursuing socially responsible, sustainable and ethical practices that bring value not just to individual customers, but to society as a whole. You'll see that social responsibility, sustainable and ethical actions are more than just the right thing to do; many people claim they are also good for business.

Before travelling on, let's take a look at one of the longest running issues in ethics, social responsibility and business, namely the marketing of tobacco products. Today everybody knows that smoking is really bad for your health, but that was not always the case. Did the tobacco companies ever deceive customers about the risks to their health from smoking? Is it morally right to make a profit from selling a product that has well-known health risks? What has the EU been doing to try to persuade people to give up smoking? Read on.

CHAPTER CONTENTS

HELP – For a life without tobacco

Dr Louise Hassan, *Lecturer in Marketing, School of Management, University of St Andrews, Scotland*

Consumers engage in a lot of risky behaviour with potentially damaging consequences for themselves, which also can have a serious impact on the health of others, and on the social and financial well-being of society at large. Most of this risky behaviour (such as binge drinking, speeding and gambling) carries an immediate risk; smoking, on the other hand, is aptly called the secret killer. Smoking is now known to be one of the most hazardous forms of behaviour that a consumer can engage in. Despite this, many young people still take up the habit. Research has shown that taking up smoking is one of the most negative lifestyle choices that an individual can make, with 50 per cent of lifelong smokers dying prematurely because of their habit. Medical data shows that smokers on average live ten years fewer than non-smokers. In fact smoking is thought to be the cause of 30 per cent of all cancer deaths in developed countries. Many illnesses can also be caused by smoking, for instance smoking is known to cause impotence and blindness. Given these stark facts, national governments, the European Commission and health organisations such as the World Health Organization (WHO) continue to work separately and in partnership to reduce the harm caused by tobacco. Indeed the first ever public health treaty, called the Framework Convention on Tobacco Control, is a global effort to tackle the burden of tobacco across the world by providing guidelines on implementable tobacco control policies. So far over 160 countries have signed up to this treaty, with over 130 countries ratifying and implementing its guidelines.

Most countries have targets to reduce smoking, while some countries aim to be entirely smoke-free within the next 50 years. However, there is a lack of consensus on the use of tobacco by consumers and the role of marketing by tobacco companies. Separately, many societies are exploring how marketing, in the form of social marketing, can help to turn the tide and reduce tobacco consumption.

There are various perspectives on the role of tobacco companies in our society. Some people argue that growing tobacco provides jobs and helps a country's economy, others argue that smoking is a personal choice and that in a free society tobacco companies should be allowed to advertise their products and to use other marketing tools, such as price promotions, to increase sales, market share and the size of the overall market. Many countries, such as the USA, Germany and Switzerland, still allow limited tobacco advertising (in newspapers and on hoardings). However, a substantial amount of research into the marketing practices of tobacco companies has demonstrated that legitimate criticisms can be made against them.

First, the tobacco industry did use deceitful practices to encourage young people to take up smoking and worried smokers to switch to so-called 'light' cigarettes through brand imagery and advertising. Other promotional activities took place in bars where marketing representatives of the tobacco companies distributed branded goods, such as branded lighters, matches and bar mats. In a recent court judgment in the USA, Judge Kessler concluded that the tobacco industry had deceived the general public concerning the health risks of smoking over the last 50 years. For these reasons the tobacco companies have been widely criticised, with some consumers now viewing tobacco companies as illegitimate and deceitful. This has been reinforced by public campaigns such

Source: http://en.help-eu.com/pages/index-abzo_pl-ABSURD_ZONE.html. The HELP 'For a life without tobacco' campaign is an initiative of the European Commission's Health and Consumer Directorate (DG SANCO).

as the Truth Campaign in the USA resulting in increased anti-smoking attitudes among young people.

Second, it is known that advertising tobacco products increases tobacco consumption and that only a complete ban on all forms of tobacco promotion is effective. Other elements of the marketing mix have also been found to be effective in reducing tobacco consumptions. Increasing the price of tobacco products decreases the likelihood of young people taking up the habit; tobacco branding can lead to greater intention to smoke. Governments therefore have a key legislative role in the control of tobacco products and tobacco marketing practices in order to protect public health. One aspect of the government's role is to demarket tobacco. Demarketing can be defined as the aspect of marketing that deals with discouraging customers in general or a certain class of customers in particular on either a temporary or permanent basis. In terms of demarketing tobacco many measures can be used, such as smoking bans in public places, a reduction in the number of outlets allowed to sell tobacco, higher taxation on tobacco, free comprehensive smoking cessation support as well as informative and targeted anti-smoking social advertising campaigns.

Within the EU the European Commission (EC) has been taking steps to reduce tobacco consumption. An important EC tobacco control initiative is the 'HELP – for a life without tobacco' campaign which was launched in 2005. This is a four-year, large-scale anti-smoking advertising campaign across the 25 EU Member States (at January 2007: when Bulgaria and Romania joined, the most recent wave of advertisements was also screened in these two new Member States). The HELP campaign's main component is a series of television advertisements using identical visual content with equivalent voice-over messages in the native language of each Member State. The overall aims of the HELP campaign are to highlight the harmful effects of both active and passive smoking, encourage smokers to think more responsibly about their habit (such as the harm it can do to non-smokers) and to consider quitting. Although smokers are a key target group for anti-smoking campaigns (indeed, around 27 per cent of the EU's population are smokers), non-smokers are an increasingly important group given the emphasis across the EU and the world on the harms caused by passive or second-hand smoking. Young people are also a key target group because most experimentation with smoking occurs during adolescence so that anti-smoking advertisements need to promote not only cessation but also prevention. Accordingly the HELP campaign is aimed at adolescents and young adults, typically those aged 15 to 34.

Targeting such a large, varied and multicultural audience with a uniform advertising campaign is a challenge for any marketer, even with a large budget. The budget for the HELP campaign of around €72 million, although one of the largest budgets for a social marketing campaign, is still modest compared with the expenditure on advertising of large multinational corporations. In order to ensure that such a campaign works effectively across countries, extensive pre-testing of advertising concepts is required. The style or persuasive approach of the adverts must also be considered. In the past, different approaches have been used to tackle social problems through advertising. Some authors have found that exposure to an anti-smoking fear appeal can reduce smoking behaviour, others criticise the use of fear as inappropriate. Humour is also used, but humour varies from culture to culture.

Given these observations, the EC and the advertising agency in charge of the development of the HELP campaign used the concept of the 'absurdity of smoking' as a general theme for the campaign. In order to highlight the absurdity of smoking a 'party whistle' was adopted as the substitute for cigarettes in each of the four adverts developed for the campaign. This also reinforces the common creative element of the campaign across each of the advertisements. The adverts used throughout the campaign covered the three themes of prevention, cessation and passive smoking (in social situations and in the home). Over the course of the campaign different lengths of adverts were used. Initially, longer 30-second adverts were produced and aired, with reinforcement spots of 10-second and 20-second adverts. January and February were chosen as the main advertising periods, partly because advertising space is less expensive during these months but additionally because the New Year period is often a time for reflection with many smokers making resolutions to quit. Advertising national quit-line telephone numbers and the HELP campaign website (which contains tips on avoiding smoking, on stopping, and advice about passive smoking) is very important in assisting those wishing to find out more. It is also important to place advertisements on multiple (national and pan-European) channels and at times when the target audience is likely to be watching television, such as during popular soap operas or dramas.

But in today's multichannel era, is television advertising enough to engage a young target audience? Obviously not, since young people spend more time surfing the Internet than watching television. Therefore the HELP campaign has pioneered a multichannel approach to engage its target group, using Internet advertising, an 'absurd zone' on the campaign website with games and an email coaching cessation programme as well as a linked viral marketing campaign (**www.nicomarket.com**). Additionally, interactive and entertaining national events and roadshows took place in many EU capitals. Another key aspect of the HELP campaign is the annual post-exposure evaluation. This allows an independent assessment across each Member State of the level of awareness of the televised campaign, as well as consumers' attitude and liking for the campaign, comprehension of the campaign message and thinking about smoking as a result of the campaign. The results of the evaluation show that awareness of the campaign has increased year on year, with 60 per cent of the target group aware of the campaign. More importantly, message comprehension and liking of the campaign across the Member States is consistently very high. Furthermore, over 55,000 people across the EU took part in the email coaching programme in 2007 alone, while 200,000 have taken part in carbon dioxide testing and over 3 million people have viewed the first viral marketing campaign. Together with the significant press coverage and over 46,000 advertising TV spots as well as 4.2 million hits on the campaign website, these results show that the diverse nature of the campaign generated a huge overall response from the target audience.

Drawing together these findings, the HELP campaign provides a model example of a successful social advertising campaign in terms of engaging with consumers. However, time will tell whether or not smoking uptake or prevalence has been reduced across the EU. Governments require a multifaceted approach to social advertising which allows people to examine their behaviour in a constructive and non-judgemental way. In order to reach a diverse target group multiple approaches such as Internet advertising and viral marketing are required. Today's social marketer cannot simply rely on television advertising as the only way to tackle social problems.[1]

Sources: The author would like to thank the European Commission and all those involved in the development and management of the HELP campaign. For full source details see note 1 at the end of this chapter.

Responsible marketers discover what consumers want and respond with market offerings that create value for buyers in order to capture value in return. The *marketing concept* is a philosophy of customer value and mutual gain. Its practice leads the economy by an invisible hand to satisfy the many and changing needs of millions of consumers.

Not all marketers follow the marketing concept, however. In fact, some companies use questionable marketing practices, and some marketing actions that seem innocent in themselves strongly affect the larger society. Not so long ago the consensus was that tobacco companies should be free to sell cigarettes and smokers should be free to buy them. But, as we saw above, this private transaction involves larger questions of public policy. For example, the smokers are harming their health and may be shortening their own lives. Smoking places a financial burden on the smoker's family and on society at large. Other people around smokers may suffer discomfort and harm from second-hand smoke. Marketing cigarettes to adults might also influence young people to begin smoking. That's why the marketing of tobacco products has sparked substantial debate and negotiation in recent years.[2] In Europe, as the 'HELP – for a life without tobacco' example showed, governments are taking increasingly strong measures to reduce tobacco consumption.

This chapter examines the social effects of private marketing practices. We examine several questions: What are the most frequent social criticisms of marketing? What steps have private citizens taken to curb marketing ills? What steps have legislators and government agencies taken to curb marketing ills? What steps have enlightened companies taken to carry out socially responsible and ethical marketing that creates value for both individual customers and society as a whole?

SOCIAL CRITICISMS OF MARKETING

Marketing receives much criticism. Some of this criticism is justified; much is not. Social critics claim that certain marketing practices hurt individual consumers, society as a whole and other business firms.

Marketing's impact on individual consumers

Consumers have many concerns about how well the Western marketing system serves their interests. Surveys usually show that consumers hold mixed or even slightly un-favourable attitudes toward marketing practices. Consumer advocates, government agencies and other critics have accused marketing of harming consumers through high prices, deceptive practices, high-pressure selling, shoddy or unsafe products, planned obsolescence and poor service to disadvantaged consumers.

High prices

Many critics charge that the Western marketing system causes prices to be higher than they would be under more 'sensible' systems. They point to three factors – *high costs of distribution*, *high advertising and promotion costs* and *excessive mark-ups*.

High costs of distribution A long-standing charge is that greedy intermediaries mark up prices beyond the value of their services. Critics charge that there are too many intermediaries, that intermediaries are inefficient, or that they provide unnecessary or duplicate services. As a result, distribution costs too much and consumers pay for these excessive costs in the form of higher prices.

How do resellers answer these charges? They argue that intermediaries do work that would otherwise have to be done by manufacturers or consumers. Mark-ups reflect services that consumers themselves want – more convenience, larger stores and assort-ments, more service, longer store hours, opportunities to return unwanted goods, and others. In fact, they argue, retail competition is so intense that margins are actually quite low. For example, after taxes, supermarket chains are typically left with barely 1 per cent profit on their sales. If some resellers try to charge too much relative to the value they add, other resellers will step in with lower prices. Low-price stores such as Aldi, Lidl and other discounters pressure their competitors to operate efficiently and keep their prices down.

High advertising and promotion costs Modern marketing is also accused of pushing up prices to finance heavy advertising and sales promotion. For example, a few dozen tablets of a heavily promoted brand of pain reliever sell for the same price as 100 tablets of less promoted brands. Differentiated products – cosmetics, detergents, toiletries – include promotion and packaging costs that can amount to 40 per cent or more of the manufacturer's price to the retailer. Critics charge that much of the packaging and pro-motion adds only psychological value to the product rather than functional value.

Marketers respond that advertising does add to product costs, but it also adds value by informing potential buyers of the availability and merits of a brand. Brand-name products may cost more, but branding gives buyers assurances of consistent quality. Moreover, consumers can usually buy functional versions of products at lower prices. However, they *want* and are willing to pay more for products that also provide psychological benefits – that make them feel wealthy, attractive or special. Also, heavy advertising and promotion may be necessary for a firm to match competitors' efforts – the business would lose 'share of mind' if it did not match competitive spending. At the same time, companies are cost-conscious about promotion and try to spend their money wisely.

Excessive mark-ups Critics also charge that some companies mark up goods excessively. They point to the drug industry, where a pill costing 5 cents to make may cost the consumer €2 to buy. They point to the high rates of interest charged by lending companies on loans made to some of the poorest members of society, and to the high charges for car repair and other services.

Marketers respond that most businesses try to deal fairly with consumers because they want to build customer relationships and repeat business. Most consumer abuses are unintentional. When shady marketers do take advantage of consumers, they should be reported to consumer associations and to government agencies. Marketers also respond that consumers often don't understand the reasons for high mark-ups. For example, the prices of successful new medicines must cover their own development and operating costs *plus* the high research and development costs of formulating and testing many experimental drugs that never make it to market because they turn out to be ineffective or dangerous.

Deceptive practices

Marketers are sometimes accused of deceptive practices that lead consumers to believe they will get more value than they actually do. Deceptive practices fall into three groups: pricing, promotion and packaging. *Deceptive pricing* includes practices such as falsely advertising 'factory' or 'wholesale' prices or a large price reduction from an unrealistically high retail list price. *Deceptive promotion* includes practices such as misrepresenting the product's features or performance or luring the customers to the shop for a bargain that is out of stock. *Deceptive packaging* includes exaggerating the package contents through subtle design, using misleading labelling or describing size in misleading terms.

The toughest problem is defining what is 'deceptive'. For instance, an advertiser's claim that its stimulant drink 'gives you wings', showing cartoon people sprouting wings and flying away, isn't intended to be taken literally. Instead, the advertiser might claim, it is 'puffery' – innocent exaggeration for effect. One noted marketing thinker, Theodore Levitt, once claimed that advertising puffery and alluring imagery are bound to occur – and that they may even be desirable: 'There is hardly a company that would not go down in ruin if it refused to provide fluff, because nobody will buy pure functionality . . . Worse, it denies . . . people's honest needs and values. Without distortion, embellishment, and elaboration, life would be drab, dull, anguished, and at its existential worst.'[3]

However, others claim that puffery and alluring imagery can harm consumers in subtle ways, and that consumers must be protected through education:

> The real danger to the public . . . comes not from outright lies – in most cases facts can ultimately be proven and mistakes corrected. But . . . advertising uses [the power of images and] emotional appeals to shift the viewer's focus away from facts. Viewers who do not take the trouble to distinguish between provable claims and pleasant but meaningless wordplay end up buying 'the sizzle, not the steak' and often paying high. The best defense against misleading ads . . . is not tighter controls on [advertisers], but more education and more critical judgment among . . . consumers. Just as we train children to be wary of strangers offering candy, to count change at a store, and to kick the tires before buying a used car, we must make the effort to step back and judge the value of . . . advertisements, and then master the skills required to separate spin from substance.[4]

Marketers argue that most companies avoid deceptive practices because such practices harm their business in the long run. Profitable customer relationships are built upon a foundation of value and trust. If consumers do not get what they expect, they will switch to more reliable products. In addition, consumers usually protect themselves from deception. Most consumers recognise a marketer's selling intent and are careful when they buy, sometimes to the point of not believing completely true product claims.

High-pressure selling

Salespeople are sometimes accused of high-pressure selling that persuades people to buy goods they had no thought of buying. It is often said that insurance, property and cars are *sold*, not *bought*. Salespeople are trained to deliver smooth, fully prepared talks to entice purchase. They sell hard because sales contests promise big prizes to those who sell the most.

But in most cases, marketers have little to gain from high-pressure selling. Such tactics may work in one-off selling situations for short-term gain. However, increasingly marketers have become convinced that the route to long-term business profitability is through building long-term relationships with customers in order to keep customers coming back (customer retention) because they believe that they receive excellent value. High-pressure or deceptive selling can do serious damage to such relationships. For example, imagine a Procter & Gamble account manager trying to pressure a Carrefour buyer, or an IBM salesperson trying to browbeat a Siemens information technology manager. It simply wouldn't work.

Shoddy, harmful or unsafe products

Another criticism concerns poor product quality or function. One complaint is that, too often, products are not made well and services are not performed well. A second complaint is that many products deliver little benefit, or that they might even be harmful. For example, many critics have pointed out the dangers of today's fat-laden fast food. In fact, McDonald's recently faced a class-action lawsuit charging that its fare has contributed to the nationwide obesity epidemic:

> [Four years ago,] the parody newspaper *The Onion* ran a joke article under the headline 'Hershey's Ordered to Pay Obese Americans $135 Billion'. The hypothesised class-action lawsuit said that Hershey 'knowingly and willfully' marketed to children 'rich, fatty candy bars containing chocolate and other ingredients of negligible nutritional value', while 'spiking' them with 'peanuts, crisped rice, and caramel to increase consumer appeal'. Some joke. [In 2002] New York City attorney Sam Hirsch filed a strikingly similar suit – against McDonald's – on behalf of a class of obese and overweight children. He alleged that the fast-food chain 'negligently, recklessly, carelessly and/or intentionally' markets to children food products that are 'high in fat, salt, sugar, and cholesterol' while failing to warn of those ingredients' links to 'obesity, diabetes, coronary heart disease, high blood pressure, strokes, elevated cholesterol intake, related cancers', and other conditions. Industry defenders decried the suit as frivolous. It is ridiculous, they claimed, to blame the fast-food industry for consumers' 'own nutritional ignorance, lack of willpower, genetic predispositions, failure to exercise, or whatever else may play a role in [their] obesity'. A federal judge agreed and dismissed the suit, explaining that 'it is not the place of the law to protect them from their own excess'.[5]

Who's to blame for the nation's obesity problem? And what should responsible food companies do about it? As with most social responsibility issues, there are no easy answers. McDonald's has worked to improve its products and make its menu and its customers healthier. It cut its 'supersize' option, introduced healthier options such as salads and now offers all-white-meat chicken McNuggets, low-fat 'milk jugs', yogurt, fruit and other healthier choices. However, the McDonald's menu board is still packed with some pretty less-than-healthy selections. And other fast-feeders seem to be going the other way. Hardee's, for example, recently introduced a 1,420 calorie Monster Thickburger, and Burger King launched its Enormous Omelette breakfast sandwich, packing an unapologetic 47 grams of fat. Are these companies being socially irresponsible? Or are they simply serving customers choices they want?[6] (See Marketing at Work 16.1.)

MARKETING AT WORK 16.1

The international obesity debate: Who's to blame?

As you've no doubt heard, many countries in the Western world are facing an obesity epidemic. Everyone seems to agree on the problem. But still unresolved is another weighty issue: who's to blame? Is it the fault of self-indulgent consumers who just can't say no to sticky buns, fat burgers and other tempting treats? Or is it the fault of greedy food marketers who are cashing in on vulnerable consumers, turning us into a nation of overeaters?

Around 10 per cent of British children are classified as 'obese', and 31,000 premature deaths in Britain each year are attributed to poor diet combined with insufficient exercise. The British government has concluded that this is a major social problem and is committed to a public health strategy to minimise the long-term harm. In the United States the 'obesity epidemic' is even more severe, with 31.1 per cent of adults and 15.8 per cent of children aged 6–11 being classified as obese, based on data for the period 1999–2002. Meanwhile, the European Consumers' Organisation, BEUC, claims that in some European countries more than half the adult population is overweight and that one child in five is obese (**www.beuc.eu**).

So, here's that weighty question again. If we know that we're overweight and that it's bad for us, why do we keep putting on the pounds? Who's to blame? The answer, of course, depends on who you ask. However, these days, lots of people are blaming food marketers. In the obesity debate, food marketers have become a favourite target of almost

everyone, from politicians, public policy makers and the press to overweight consumers themselves. And some food marketers are looking pretty much guilty as charged.

Take the American burger chain Hardee's, for example. At a time when other fast-food chains such as McDonald's, Wendy's and Subway were getting 'leaner', Hardee's introduced the decadent Thickburger, featuring one-third of a pound of Angus beef. It followed up with the *Monster* Thickburger: two one-third of a pound Angus beef patties, four strips of bacon and three slices of American cheese, all nestled in a buttered sesame-seed bun slathered with mayonnaise! The Monster Thickburger weighs in at a whopping 1,420 calories and 108 grams of fat, far greater than the government's recommended fat intake for an entire day (they conveniently provide a nutritional calculator at **www.hardees.com/nutrition** so you can work this out for yourself).

Surely, you say, Hardee's made a colossal blunder here. Not so! At least, not from a profit viewpoint. Sales at Hardee's 2,050 outlets have climbed 20 per cent since it introduced the Thickburger line, resulting in fatter profits and a tripling of Hardee's stock price. It seems that some consumers, especially in Hardee's target market of young men aged 18–34, just love fat burgers. A reporter asked a 27-year-old construction worker who was downing a Monster Thickburger if he'd thought about its effect on his health. 'I've never even thought about it,' he replied, 'and to be honest, I don't really care. It just tastes good.'

Hardee's certainly isn't hiding the nutritional facts. Here's how it describes Thickburgers on its website:

There's only one thing that can slay the hunger of a young guy on the move: the Thickburger line at Hardee's. With nine cravable varieties, including the classic Original Thickburger and the monument to decadence, the Monster Thickburger, quick-service goes premium with 100% Angus beef and all the fixings . . . If you want to indulge in a big, delicious, juicy burger, look no further than Hardee's.

So, should Hardee's hang its head in shame? Is it being socially irresponsible by aggressively promoting over-indulgence to ill-informed or unwary consumers? Or is it simply practising good marketing, creating more value for its customers by offering a big juicy burger that clearly satisfies their taste buds, and letting them make their own choices? Critics claim the former; industry defenders claim the latter.

The question of blame gets even murkier when it comes to child obesity. The debate rages over the marketing of everything from fast food and soft drinks in school cafeterias to cereal, biscuits, cakes and other 'not-so-good-for-you' products targeted toward kids and teens, who are seen as especially vulnerable to seductive or misleading marketing pitches. Once again, many public and private advocacy groups point the finger at food marketers. They worry that a 5-year-old watching cute characters and fun ads for a sugary breakfast cereal or chocolate confectionery during a Saturday morning cartoon show probably understands little about good nutrition. These critics have called on food marketers to adopt voluntarily more responsible children's marketing practices. In the UK this issue really hit the headlines when one of the country's leading celebrity chefs, Jamie Oliver, weighed into the argument about the nutritional quality of school meals. After hosting a popular TV show, *Jamie's School Dinners*, the chef was invited to meet influential politicians to promote his argument that the nutritional quality of school meals was dreadful, and that it undermined the ability of children to concentrate in school while putting their long-term health at risk. At first everyone seemed to agree with Jamie that something had to be done to provide schoolchildren with nutritious, freshly cooked lunches made from wholesome ingredients. Government ministers rapidly aligned themselves with Jamie's good food agenda. Then the debate became more acrimonious, with some people even calling the likeable Jamie a 'food fascist'; newspapers and TV stations gave coverage to 'angry mums' who gathered at school gates during the lunch break to provide their offspring with the sugary and fatty products that were now prohibited from the school premises.

So, back to that big question: who's to blame for the obesity

Celebrity chef Jamie Oliver has made a determined effort to improve the nutritional quality of the lunches provided in British schools.
Source: © Peter Dench/Corbis.

epidemic? Is it the marketers who promote unhealthy but irresistible fare to vulnerable consumers? Or is it the fault of consumers themselves for failing to take personal responsibility for their own health and well-being? It's a weighty decision for many food marketers. And, as is the case with most social responsibility issues, finding the answer to that question is

even harder than trying to take off some of those extra pounds.

Sources: Sarah Ellison, 'Kraft Limits on Kid's Ads May Cheese Off Rivals', *Wall Street Journal*, 13 January 2005, p. B3; Steven Gray, 'At Fast-Food Chains, Era of the Giant Burger (Plus Bacon) Is Here', *Wall Street Journal*, 27 January 2005, p. B1; 'Obesity Research Ignites Calls for Food Ad Curbs', *Marketing Week*, 5 May 2005, p. 8; http://www.jamieoliver.com/schooldinners/.

A third complaint concerns product safety. Product safety has been a problem for several reasons, including company indifference, increased product complexity and poor quality control. For years, consumers' associations across Europe, such as BEUC – The European Consumers' Organisation, CAI – The Consumers' Association of Ireland and 'Which?' in the UK, have reported various hazards in tested products: electrical dangers in appliances, carbon monoxide poisoning from room heaters, injury risks from lawn mowers and faults in car design among many others. The organisations' testing and other activities have helped consumers make better buying decisions and encouraged businesses to eliminate product flaws.

However, most manufacturers *want* to produce high quality goods. The way a company deals with product quality and safety problems can damage or help its reputation. Companies selling poor quality or unsafe products risk damaging conflicts with consumer groups and regulators. Moreover, unsafe products can result in product liability suits and large awards for damages. More fundamentally, consumers who are unhappy with a firm's products may avoid future purchases and talk other consumers into doing the same. Thus, quality errors can have severe consequences. Today's marketers know that customer-driven quality results in customer value and satisfaction, which in turn creates profitable customer relationships.

Planned obsolescence

Critics have also argued that some producers follow a programme of planned obsolescence, causing their products to become obsolete before they actually should need replacement. For example, consider printer companies and their toner cartridges:

> Refilled printer cartridges offer the same or improved performance for about half the price of a new one. A number of businesses now offer toner cartridge refill services to businesses. You can refill most cartridges 8–10 times – if you can find the right parts. However, printer companies would prefer to sell their cartridges for €50 or more, rather than allow someone to refill an exhausted one for half the price. So they make it hard for refill operations by continually introducing new models and tweaking inkjet cartridges and laser toner containers. Refill parts manufacturers struggle to keep up, jockeying with the printer companies that are working to thwart refill-enabling rollers, ribbons and other pieces. 'You've got planned obsolescence,' says the owner of a small cartridge refilling company, as he disassembles a cartridge to inspect its drum unit, wiper blade, clips, springs and other mechanisms for signs of wear. 'It's kind of like a 'Mission Impossible': At the end of this tape, the toner cartridge will self-destruct.'[7]

Planned obsolescence: printer companies continually introduce new cartridge models and tweak designs. 'You've got planned obsolescence,' says the owner of Laser Logic, a small cartridge refilling company. 'It's kind of like a *Mission Impossible*: at the end of this tape, the toner cartridge will self-destruct.'

Critics charge that some producers continually change consumer concepts of acceptable styles to encourage more and earlier buying. An obvious example is constantly changing clothing fashions. A particular example is the case of replica football shirts for national teams and famous football clubs; it is alleged that teams issue new shirts too frequently, and that the prices charged for them are too high for many fans to afford. In 2003 the UK Office of Fair Trading fined several businesses, including Manchester United Football Club, for illegally fixing the price of replica shirts.[8] Other producers are accused of holding back attractive functional features, then introducing them later to make older models obsolete. Critics claim that this occurs in the consumer electronics and computer industries. For example, Intel and Microsoft have been accused over the years of holding back their next-generation computer chips and software until demand is exhausted for the current generation.

Marketers respond that consumers *like* style changes; they get tired of the old goods and want a new look in fashion or a new design in cars. No one has to buy the new look, and if too few people like it, it will simply fail. For most technical products, customers *want* the latest innovations, even if older models still work. Companies that withhold new features run the risk that competitors will introduce the new feature first and steal the market. For example, consider personal computers. Some consumers grumble that the consumer electronics industry's constant push to produce 'faster, smaller, cheaper' models means that they must continually buy new machines just to keep up. Others, however, can hardly wait for the latest model to arrive.

> There was a time not so long ago when planned obsolescence was a troubling ghost in the machine. A half a century ago, consumer advocates described engineers at General Electric who intentionally shortened the life of light bulbs and automotive engineers who proposed limiting the lifespans of cars. That was then. In today's topsy-turvy world of personal computers, obsolescence is not only planned, it is extolled by marketers as a virtue. Moreover, there has been hardly a peep from consumers, who dutifully line up to buy each new generation of faster, more powerful machines, eager to embrace the promise of simpler, happier, and more productive lives. Today's computer chips are no longer designed to wear out; in fact, they will last for decades or longer. Even so, hapless consumers now rush back to the store ever more quickly, not to replace broken parts but to purchase new computers that will allow them to work faster, see more vivid colours, or play cooler games.[9]

Thus, most companies do not design their products to break down earlier, because they do not want to lose customers to other brands. Instead, they seek constant improvement to ensure that products will consistently meet or exceed customer expectations. Much of so-called planned obsolescence is the working of the competitive and technological forces in a free society – forces that lead to ever-improving goods and services.

Poor service to disadvantaged consumers

Finally, the Western marketing system has been accused of serving disadvantaged consumers poorly. For example, critics claim that the urban poor often have to shop in smaller stores that carry inferior goods and charge higher prices. The presence of large national chain stores in low-income neighbourhoods would help to keep prices down. However, the critics accuse major chain retailers of 'red-lining', drawing a red line around disadvantaged neighbourhoods and avoiding placing stores there.

Similar red-lining charges have been levelled at the insurance, consumer lending, banking and health-care industries. Home and car insurers have been accused of assigning higher premiums to people with poor credit ratings. The insurers claim that individuals with bad credit tend to make more insurance claims, and that this justifies charging them higher premiums. However, critics and consumer advocates have accused the insurers of a new form of red-lining. Says one writer, 'This is a new excuse for denying coverage to the poor, elderly, and minorities.'[10]

MAKING CONNECTIONS Linking the concepts

Time to take a few moments for reflection. Few marketers *want* to abuse or anger consumers – it's simply not good business. Instead, as you know well by now, most marketers work to build long-term, profitable relationships with customers based on real value and caring. Still, some marketing abuses do occur.

■ Think back over the past three months or so and list the instances in which you've suffered a marketing abuse such as those just discussed. Analyse your list. What kinds of companies were involved? Were the abuses intentional? What did the situations have in common?

■ Pick one of the instances you listed and describe it in detail. How might you go about righting this wrong? Write out an action plan and then do something to remedy the abuse. If we all took such actions when wronged, there would be far fewer wrongs to right!

Marketing's impact on society as a whole

The Western marketing system has been accused of adding to several 'evils' in society at large. Advertising has been a special target.

False wants and too much materialism

Critics have argued that the marketing system encourages too much interest in material possessions. People are judged by what they *own* rather than by who they *are*. This drive for wealth and possessions hit new highs in the 1980s and 1990s, when phrases such as 'greed is good' and 'shop till you drop' seemed to characterise the times.

In the last decade, many social scientists have noted a reaction against the opulence and waste of the previous decades and a return to more basic values and social commitment. However, our infatuation with material things continues. This is causing widespread concern, in particular, about the materialistic attitudes of children. Research undertaken in Britain for the Children's Society in 2007 revealed that 89 per cent of adults believed that today's children were more materialistic than previous generations. The chief executive of the society, Bob Reitemeier, said: 'A crucial question raised by the inquiry is whether childhood should be a space where developing minds are free from concentrated sales techniques', and the Archbishop of Canterbury (head of the Church of England), Dr Rowan Williams, said: 'The selling of lifestyles to children creates a culture of material competitiveness and promotes acquisitive individualism at the expense of the principles of community and cooperation.' Clearly there are influential figures in society who believe that marketing activities are responsible for creating an unhealthy obsession with material things.[11]

The critics do not view this interest in material things as a natural state of mind but rather as a matter of false wants created by marketing. Businesses hire top advertising agencies to stimulate people's desires for goods and advertisers use the mass media to create materialistic models of the good life. People work harder to earn the necessary money. Their purchases increase the output of industry and industry in turn uses advertising to stimulate more desire for the industrial output. Thus, marketing is seen as creating false wants that benefit industry more than they benefit consumers.

Many marketers would say that these criticisms overstate the power of business to create needs. People are quite sceptical of advertising material. Marketers are most effective when they appeal to existing wants rather than when they attempt to create new ones. Furthermore, people seek information when making important purchases and often do not rely on single sources. Even minor purchases that may be affected by advertising messages lead to repeat purchases only if the product delivers the promised customer value. Finally, the high failure rate of new products shows that companies are not able to control demand.

On a deeper level, our wants and values are influenced by many factors including family, peer groups, religion, ethnic background and education. If Europeans are highly materialistic, these values arise out of basic socialisation processes that go much deeper than business and mass media could produce alone.

Too few social goods

Business has been accused of overselling private goods at the expense of public goods. As private goods increase, they often require more public services that may not be available. For example, an increase in car ownership (private good) requires more roads, traffic control, parking spaces and police services (public goods). The overselling of private goods results in 'social costs'. For cars, the social costs include traffic congestion, air pollution, fuel shortages, and deaths and injuries from car accidents.

A way must be found to restore a balance between private and public goods. One option is to make producers bear the full social costs of their operations. The government could require car manufacturers to build cars with even more safety features, more efficient engines and better pollution control systems. The car companies would then raise their prices to cover extra costs. If buyers found the price of some cars too high, however, the producers of these cars would disappear. Demand would then move to those producers that could support the sum of the private and social costs.

A second option is to make consumers pay the social costs. For example, many cities around the world are starting to impose 'congestion charges' in an effort to reduce traffic congestion. To try to unclog its streets, the City of London introduced a congestion charge in 2003. By 2008 the charge was £8.00 per day per car to drive into the congestion charging area, approximately 8 square miles in the very heart of the city. Various plans were under consideration to alter the charging structure and, in particular to increase the charge sharply for the most polluting cars, but with a change of London mayor in May 2008 (with Boris Johnson replacing Ken Livingstone) the future of these changes was put in doubt. Nevertheless, the principle of charging a substantial amount of money to virtually all cars driven into the centre of London was well established. The charge has not only reduced the number of cars entering the zone by 21 per cent, it also raises money to invest in London's public transport system.[12] Other cities in Europe and elsewhere have developed schemes with the same aims as the London congestion charge, although the methods of implementation vary. For example, Stockholm has a very similar congestion charge, while Singapore has a more comprehensive 'electronic road pricing' scheme with charges that vary depending on time and location. Several other major cities are actively considering the introduction of such schemes.

Cultural pollution

Critics charge the marketing system with creating *cultural pollution*. Our senses are being constantly assaulted by marketing and advertising. Advertisements interrupt serious programmes; pages of advertisements obscure magazines; posters obscure beautiful scenery; spam fills our emailboxes. These interruptions continually pollute people's minds with messages of materialism, sex, power or status.

Many people would see these as powerful criticisms, but marketers can try to answer the charges of 'commercial noise' with these arguments: First, they hope that their advertisements reach primarily the target audience. Because of mass-communication channels, some of them are bound to reach people who have no interest in the product and are therefore bored or annoyed. People who buy magazines addressed to their interests rarely complain about the ads because the magazines advertise products of interest; if you buy the motorcycle magazine *Irish Racer* or the magazine for lovers of audio equipment *Hi-Fi World* then you probably look forward to reading the advertisements as well as the articles.

Second, advertisements make much of television and radio free to users and keep down the costs of magazines and newspapers. Many people think this is a small price to pay for these benefits. For example, in many large cities you can pick up one or more free newspapers during the rush hour, paid for completely out of advertising revenue; and judging by the number of people reading such newspapers on the train home, they seem to be popular! Finally, today's consumers have alternatives. For example, they can dodge TV advertisements by using their remote control, or avoid them altogether on many cable or satellite channels. Thus, to hold consumer attention, advertisers are making their work more entertaining and informative.

Too much political power

Another criticism is that business wields too much political power. Large companies in a wide range of industry sectors, including oil, tobacco, pharmaceuticals and alcohol, spend money on public relations material and on specialist PR consultants who lobby (that is, try to influence) people in positions of political power. Advertisers are accused of holding too much power over the mass media, limiting media freedom to report independently and objectively. The critics ask: how can magazines afford to tell the truth about the low nutritional value of packaged foods when these magazines are being subsidised by advertisers who produce high sugar, high fat food products low in nutritional content? How can the major TV companies criticise the practices of the large car companies when such companies invest billions of euros a year in broadcast advertising?

This debate has run for years, and will continue to run for a long time to come. European industries, in fact industries worldwide, do promote and protect their own interests. They have a right to put their views to politicians and to use the mass media. However, their influence can become too great because they wield so much economic power and have so much money to spend on promoting their own point of view. Nevertheless, there are organisations – notably some of the consumer associations that we mentioned earlier in the chapter – that consistently call big business to account and, in their turn, lobby politicians to ensure that there is a counterbalance to the power of big businesses.

Marketing's impact on other businesses

Critics also argue that a company's marketing practices can harm other companies and reduce competition. Three problems are involved: acquisitions of competitors, marketing practices that create barriers to entry and unfair competitive marketing practices.

Critics claim that firms are harmed and competition reduced when companies expand by acquiring competitors rather than by developing their own new products. The large number of acquisitions and rapid pace of industry consolidation over the past several decades have caused concern that vigorous young competitors will be absorbed and that competition will be reduced. In virtually every major industry – retailing, entertainment, financial services, utilities, transportation, vehicles, telecommunications, health care – the number of major competitors is shrinking.

Business acquisition is a complex subject. Acquisitions can sometimes be good for society. The acquiring company may gain economies of scale that lead to lower costs and lower prices. A well-managed company may take over a poorly-managed company and improve its efficiency. An industry that was not very competitive might become more competitive after the acquisition. But acquisitions can also reduce competition and, therefore, are closely regulated by governments.

Critics have also charged that marketing practices prevent new companies from entering an industry. Large marketing companies can use patents and heavy promotional spending, and can tie up suppliers or dealers to keep out or drive out competitors. Those concerned with the regulation of anti-competitive behaviour recognise that some barriers are the natural result of the economic advantages of doing business on a large scale. There are some industries, like aircraft manufacturing, that can only be done efficiently if they are done on a massive scale.

Finally, some firms have actually used unfair competitive marketing practices with the intention of hurting or destroying other firms. They may set their prices below costs, threaten to cut off business with suppliers, or discourage the buying of a competitor's products. Various laws work to prevent such predatory competition. It is difficult, however, to prove that the intent or action was really predatory. Probably the most famous example of anti-competitive allegations in history concerns Microsoft and the Windows operating system:

> Competitors and regulators in both the United States and Europe have accused giant Microsoft of predatory 'bundling' practices. That's the term used to describe Microsoft's practice of continually adding new features to Windows, the operating system installed on more than 90 per cent of desktop computers. Because customers are essentially

locked in to Windows, it's easy for the company to get them to use its other software – even if competitors make better products. That dampens competition, reduces choice and could retard innovation. Since 2000, Microsoft has paid nearly $6 billion to resolve anti-trust suits with other companies for damages caused by its past business practices. For example, it recently paid out more than $775 million to IBM for bullying the company in past years by withholding marketing dollars for selling machines bundled with Netscape instead of Microsoft's browser, Internet Explorer. In another action, the European Commission took dramatic steps to stop what it saw as predatory bundling by Microsoft. It ordered Microsoft to offer a version of Windows with its media-playing software stripped out. The Commission also fined Microsoft more than $600 million for using its 'near monopoly' in the Windows operating system to squeeze out rivals in other types of software.[13]

Although competitors and the government charge that Microsoft's actions are predatory, the question is whether this is unfair competition or the healthy competition of a more efficient company against less efficient ones.

CITIZEN AND PUBLIC ACTIONS TO REGULATE MARKETING

Because some people view business as the cause of many economic and social ills, grass-roots movements have arisen from time to time to keep business in line. The two major movements have been *consumerism* and *environmentalism*.

Consumerism

Businesses have been the target of organised consumer movements on three occasions. The first consumer movement took place in the early 1900s. It was fuelled by rising prices, revelations about conditions in the meat industry and scandals in the drug industry. The second consumer movement, in the mid-1930s, was sparked by an upturn in consumer prices during the Great Depression and another drugs scandal.

The third movement began in the 1960s. Consumers had become better educated, products had become more complex and potentially hazardous, and people were unhappy with American institutions. A prominent champion of consumer rights called Ralph Nader appeared on the scene to force many issues, and other well-known writers, such as the Canadian economist John Kenneth Galbraith, accused big business of wasteful and unethical practices. Since then, many consumer groups have been organised and several consumer protection laws have been passed. The consumer movement has spread internationally and is particularly strong in Europe.

But what is the consumer movement? **Consumerism** is an organised movement of citizens and government agencies to improve the rights and power of buyers in relation to sellers. Traditional *sellers' rights* include:

- The right to introduce any product in any size and style, provided it is not hazardous to personal health or safety; or, if it is, to include proper warnings and controls.

- The right to charge any price for the product provided no discrimination exists among similar kinds of buyers.

- The right to spend any amount to promote the product provided it is not defined as unfair competition.

- The right to use any product message provided it is not misleading or dishonest in content or execution.

- The right to use any buying incentive programmes provided they are not unfair or misleading.

Traditional *buyers' rights* include:

■ The right not to buy a product that is offered for sale.
■ The right to expect the product to be safe.
■ The right to expect the product to perform as claimed.

Comparing these rights, many believe that the balance of power lies on the seller's side. True, the buyer can refuse to buy. But critics feel that the buyer has too little information, education and protection to make wise decisions when facing sophisticated sellers. Consumer advocates call for the following additional consumer rights:

■ The right to be well informed about important aspects of the product.
■ The right to be protected against questionable products and marketing practices.
■ The right to influence products and marketing practices in ways that will improve the 'quality of life'.

Each proposed right has led to more specific proposals by consumerists. The right to be informed includes the right to know the true interest on a loan (truth in lending), the true cost per unit of a brand (unit pricing), the ingredients in a product (ingredient labelling), the nutritional value of foods (nutritional labelling), product freshness (open dating) and the true benefits of a product (truth in advertising). Proposals related to consumer protection include strengthening consumer rights in cases of business fraud, requiring greater product safety and giving more power to government agencies. Proposals relating to quality of life include controlling the ingredients that go into certain products and packaging, reducing the level of advertising 'noise' and putting consumer representatives on company boards to protect consumer interests.

Consumers not only have the *right* but also the *responsibility* to protect themselves instead of leaving this function to someone else. Consumers who believe they got a bad deal have several remedies available, including contacting the company or the media, contacting European, national or local agencies, and going to small-claims courts.

Sustainability

Whereas consumerists consider whether the marketing system is efficiently serving consumer wants, environmentalists are concerned with marketing's effects on the environment and with the costs of serving consumer needs and wants. **Environmentalism** is an organised movement of concerned citizens, businesses and government agencies to protect and improve people's living environment.

Environmentalists are not against marketing and consumption; they simply want people and organisations to operate with more care for the environment. The marketing system's goal, they assert, should not be to maximise consumption, consumer choice or consumer satisfaction, but rather to maximise life quality. And 'life quality' means not only the quantity and quality of consumer goods and services, but also the quality of the environment. Environmentalists want environmental costs included in both producer and consumer decision-making.

The first wave of modern environmentalism was driven by environmental groups and concerned consumers in the 1960s and 1970s. They were concerned with damage to the ecosystem caused by strip-mining, forest depletion, acid rain, loss of the atmosphere's ozone layer, toxic wastes and litter. They also were concerned with the loss of recreational areas and with the increase in health problems caused by bad air, polluted water and chemically-treated food.

The second environmentalism wave was driven by government, which passed laws and regulations during the 1970s and 1980s governing industrial practices affecting the environment. This wave hit some industries hard. Steel companies and utilities had to invest billions in pollution control equipment and costlier fuels. The car industry had to introduce expensive emission controls in cars. The packaging industry had to find ways to reduce litter. These industries and others have often resented and resisted environmental regulations, especially when they have been imposed too rapidly to allow companies to make proper adjustments. Many of these companies claim they have had to absorb large costs that have made them less competitive.

The first two environmentalism waves have now merged into a third and stronger wave in which companies are accepting responsibility for doing no harm to the environment. They are shifting from protest to prevention, and from regulation to responsibility. More and more companies are adopting policies of **environmental sustainability** – developing strategies that both sustain the environment *and* produce profits for the company. According to one strategist, 'The challenge is to develop a *sustainable global economy*: an economy that the planet is capable of supporting indefinitely . . . [It's] an enormous challenge – and an enormous opportunity.'[14] One company that has been striving to be at the forefront of sustainability is the retailer Marks & Spencer. To find out more about how they have been pursuing the sustainability agenda, take a look at Marketing at Work 16.2.

Figure 16.1 shows a grid that companies can use to gauge their progress towards environmental sustainability. At the most basic level, a company can practise *pollution prevention*. This involves more than pollution control – cleaning up waste after it has been created. Pollution prevention means eliminating or minimising waste before it is created. Companies emphasising prevention have responded with 'green marketing' programmes – developing ecologically safer products, recyclable and biodegradable packaging, better pollution controls and more energy-efficient operations.

For example, French transport company Norbert Dentressangle has taken steps to improve fuel efficiency and reduce the emissions from its large fleet of trucks. This includes specific, tough targets for the annual reduction of greenhouse gas emissions, which will be achieved by operating more efficient trucks, reducing the distances that trucks have to cover when empty and optimising vehicle loading to reduce unnecessary miles travelled.

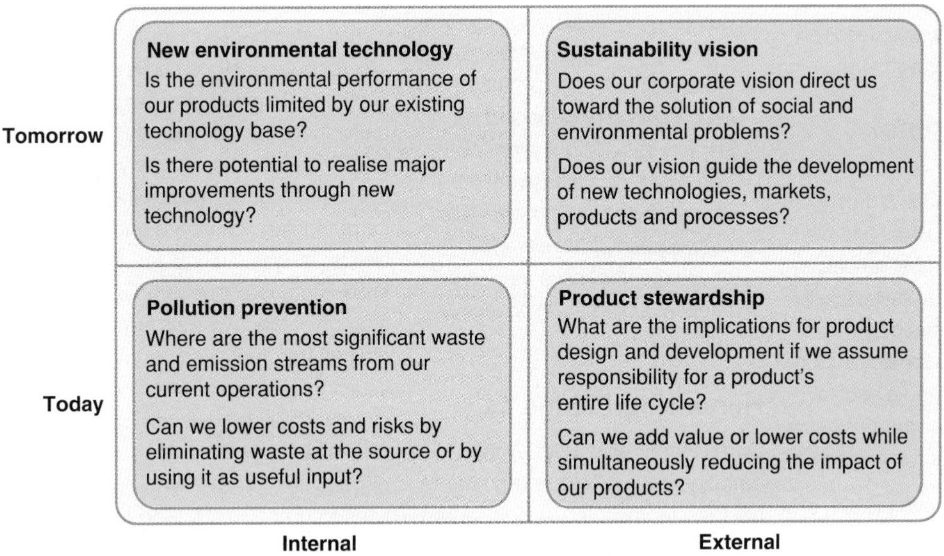

	Internal	**External**
Tomorrow	**New environmental technology** Is the environmental performance of our products limited by our existing technology base? Is there potential to realise major improvements through new technology?	**Sustainability vision** Does our corporate vision direct us toward the solution of social and environmental problems? Does our vision guide the development of new technologies, markets, products and processes?
Today	**Pollution prevention** Where are the most significant waste and emission streams from our current operations? Can we lower costs and risks by eliminating waste at the source or by using it as useful input?	**Product stewardship** What are the implications for product design and development if we assume responsibility for a product's entire life cycle? Can we add value or lower costs while simultaneously reducing the impact of our products?

FIGURE 16.1

The environmental sustainability grid

MARKETING AT WORK 16.2

The Marks & Spencer and Oxfam Clothes Exchange

Professor Ken Peattie,
BRASS Research Centre,
Cardiff Business School, Wales

During the twenty-first century the most significant challenges faced by marketers, and the products, brands and companies they represent, will be linked to aspects of the sustainable development agenda. The relatively unconstrained economic growth of the twentieth century had social and environmental consequences that now threaten the future stability of our society and our economy, and the environmental systems on which we depend. Governments, businesses and many non-governmental organisations (NGOs) are increasingly seeking to address growing concerns about the sustainability of future economic development by taking more account of issues such as climate change, global poverty, resource depletion, waste, biodiversity and population growth.

Marks & Spencer's 'Plan A'

In January 2007 Marks & Spencer launched its £200 million eco-plan 'Plan A', one of the most ambitious strategies to address sustainability concerns to be developed by a leading company. The 100-point plan sought to address the key sustainability challenges that the business faced, grouped under five headings:

- *Climate change*: with the aim of making the business carbon neutral by 2012.
- *Waste*: with the aim of eliminating waste to landfill from its operations by 2012.

- *Sustainable sourcing*: particularly to extend M&S's use of organic and free-range produce.
- *Ethical trading standards*: to use the power of M&S as an own brand retailer to improve the livelihoods of their suppliers and supplier communities worldwide.
- *Helping customers and employees to live a healthier lifestyle.*

In unveiling the plan, M&S Chief Executive, Stuart Rose commented:

Every business and individual needs to do their bit to tackle the enormous challenges of climate change and waste. While M&S will continue to sell great quality, stylish and innovative products, our customers, employees and shareholders now expect us to take bold steps and do business differently and responsibly. We believe a responsible business can be a profitable business. We are calling this 'Plan A' because there is no 'Plan B' . . . This is a deliberately ambitious and, in some areas, difficult plan. We don't have all the answers but we are determined to work with our suppliers, partners and government to make this happen. Doing anything less is not an option.

Honouring Pledge 44

One reason why Plan A was so ambitious was that many of its pledges represented a bold public commitment to change made before the company had fully worked out how that commitment might be met. This was the case for Pledge 44 about helping customers to reduce

their waste clothing by 'making sure that, within five years, you need throw none of our clothing away as waste after you've finished with it. We will start by researching alternatives into clothing disposal, including donation, composting and recycling.' In doing so, M&S would help to address the problem of the estimated 1 million tonnes of clothing annually going into landfill in the UK, much of it suitable for reuse or recycling. The obvious solution for Pledge 44 might have been an in-house clothes reclamation and recycling scheme, but this posed a significant reverse logistics challenge for a retail operation geared towards providing rather than re-acquiring products. Instead, it was the emphasis on partnership that was central to the Plan A project that inspired a solution.

Oxfam is one of the UK's best-known charities with a campaigning and disaster relief remit that seeks to tackle poverty and promote development globally. Many of the issues that Oxfam campaign on, including climate change, fairer trade and the emerging global food crisis, are also central to the strategic agenda for a major food and clothing retailer such as M&S. Since the company sought to maintain good relationships with campaigning charities and other NGOs, it was natural for them to enter into a dialogue with Oxfam on a range of Plan A issues linked to its ethical trading and sustainable sourcing responsibilities and commitments. During this dialogue the realisation grew that there was an opportunity for the two organisations to go beyond talking together, and instead to work together on a mutually beneficial project. With a network of over 750 high-street shops throughout the UK, Oxfam represented the most extensive retail network involved in recycling second-hand goods, particularly clothes. They were also the only UK charity with their own textile sorting operation, Wastesaver, based in Huddersfield. This meant that even the clothes they handled that were unsuitable for resale in the UK could be reused in other countries or recycled in other ways. For M&S they represented the perfect partner for a scheme to recycle customers' used and excess clothing. For Oxfam, the quality of M&S items made them strong sellers within their shops, and an increased flow of M&S items represented a potentially valuable income boost with which to fund their development and disaster relief campaigns. From this opportunity the 'M&S and Oxfam Clothes Exchange' cause-related marketing campaign was born.

The strategic fit between the priorities, needs and capabilities of the two organisations was obvious. There was also a good strategic fit between the strengths of the two brands within their respective worlds, the geographical locations of their stores, and in the nature of their loyal core groups of customers/supporters. Culturally, tactically and operationally, however, there were a number of issues to resolve. For Oxfam a cause-related marketing partnership with a commercial retailer, even one with the strong ethical credentials of M&S, was a new departure. It carried with it an element of reputational risk should M&S find themselves involved in any ethical controversies linked to another aspect of their operations, particularly those close to the heart of Oxfam's agenda such as the treatment of workers in poorer countries. For M&S, it meant an operational link with an organisation that was a social enterprise and not a conventional commercial business, and which depended to a large extent on volunteer workers. So the partnership dialogue to establish the scheme included an operational audit of the Huddersfield Wastesaver facilities to ensure that any operational risks for M&S were addressed, and a review of all elements of the ethical agenda for M&S to ensure that any reputational risks for Oxfam were addressed.

There were some other unusual aspects to the scheme. Although it was a strategically important campaign, it was developed without specific performance targets. Since it was considered central to honouring Pledge 44, and was also a relatively unique campaign for which no obvious precedents or benchmarks existed, it was established on a 'try it and see' basis. The scheme was also developed in considerable secrecy to prevent competitors becoming aware of what was planned. Therefore instead of the normal regional trial to assess the success of such a scheme, a national launch was planned. The nationwide scope and emphasis on secrecy together posed a challenge given that the scheme's success depended on informing and training (and gaining the support of) 23,000 Oxfam staff and volunteers in 790 shops and 65,000 M&S employees across its 375 stores. This was tackled by holding back informing and training people until two weeks before the launch, at which point the Oxfam store managers who had been brought together in London ostensibly for a national 'training day' instead found themselves being briefed and trained on the new joint venture with M&S.

Launching the Clothes Exchange

The scheme was announced, on a six-month trial basis, in January 2008 to mark the first anniversary of Plan A. To add impetus to the campaign launch, the two organisations commissioned market research into the nation's wardrobes from YouGov. This showed that an estimated 2.4 billion items (representing 46 per cent of people's clothes) had sat in a wardrobe without being worn once in the past year. Consumers in the 25–34 age group had the most expensive unworn clothes collection, worth an average of £228. As unworn clothes they were providing no value to the consumer, yet represented a store of value that could be converted into clothes that Oxfam could use to fund their work tackling poverty and which other consumers could purchase and benefit from.

As Oxfam director Barbara Stocking said:

This partnership is an enormous opportunity and Oxfam is very excited to be working with M&S to help make a real difference to global poverty. Recycling and reusing clothes – and anything else we can sell – has always been central to Oxfam's fundraising, as well as being good for the environment. Through our unique textile sorting facility and the resourcefulness and skills of our specialist staff, Oxfam is able to make the most from all the clothes we receive. People's unwanted clothes really will raise much needed money to help people living in poverty.

The offer to M&S customers was that if they made a donation to Oxfam containing at least one piece of M&S labelled clothing or accessory (excluding underwear and swimwear) they would be given a special M&S and Oxfam Clothes Exchange voucher. The voucher was valid for one month, and provided a £5 discount at M&S if customers spent more than £35 on clothing, beauty or products for the home. The deal was structured to reward people through the discount voucher, rather than simply to appeal to their ethical instincts by asking for surplus M&S clothes to be donated to Oxfam. The one-month expiry date on the coupon also acted as a motivator to encourage people to follow through on obtaining the personal benefits from making their clothes donation.

The details of the scheme were communicated to customers through several channels. The launch, backed by a national press advertising campaign, attracted widespread media coverage. Point-of-sale material was developed for use within both M&S stores and Oxfam shops in the UK and Republic of Ireland; it was featured in the M&S customer magazine and through both organisations' websites. The communications campaign generated considerable public interest and follow-up research showed it reached an audience of approximately 45 million people and generated public relations benefits valued at £4.5 million.

The results

The success of the scheme was obvious after only seven weeks when progress was first reviewed. In those seven weeks, Oxfam had issued 140,884 vouchers in exchange for an average of 4.85 items per donation. A total of 683,287 items

were donated, representing a 40 per cent increase on normal donations and equating to an estimated 341 tonnes of clothing which might otherwise have ended up in landfill. By the end of the first six months of the scheme, the forecast additional income for Oxfam would represent around £1.5 million (on an annual basis) to invest in their campaigns. Frontline feedback also suggested that the scheme had attracted thousands of people into an Oxfam shop for the first time, and as the scheme progressed it became clear that its stakeholders approved.

From the M&S perspective, of the vouchers issued during those first seven weeks, over 48 per cent were redeemed (which compares to a typical redemption rate for such vouchers of only 2 per cent). The average value of the basket of goods purchased by customers redeeming vouchers was also just over double the average customer basket, and by the end of the first six months the scheme was generating an average of around £1 million per month in additional sales. The scheme was exemplary in delivering

The M&S and Oxfam Clothes Exchange

The Clothes Exchange, jointly organised with the global charity Oxfam, is one mecanism by which Marks & Spencer are implementing their 'Plan A' commitment to tackle climate change and waste.
Source: © Oxfam and © Marks and Spencer PLC.

the 'triple bottom line' benefits sought by commercial sustainability strategies. It generated valuable funds for Oxfam to spend on social causes in poorer countries. On an annual basis it would benefit the environment by diverting 2 million items of clothing away from landfill. Commercially it benefited M&S through additional sales volume and it benefited consumers by delivering wardrobe space to some and new (to them) clothing to others, and an ethical 'glow' from supporting Oxfam to all of them.

Source: The author would like to thank Mike Barry, Head of Corporate Responsibility, Marks & Spencer, and David McCullough, Trading Director Oxfam, and Fee Gilfeather, Trading Communications & Marketing Manager Oxfam, for their help in developing this case study.

At the next level, companies can practise *product stewardship* – minimising not just pollution from production but all environmental impacts throughout the full product life cycle and all the while reducing costs. Many companies are adopting *design for environment (DFE)* practices, which involve thinking ahead to design products that are easier to recover reuse or recycle. DFE not only helps to sustain the environment, it can be highly profitable for the company. The Commission for Architecture and the Built Environment (CABE) has produced a briefing paper for builders, architects and government organisations offering them advice on how to 'design in' environmental sustainability to construction projects. The aim is to address environmental matters at the very earliest stage in a construction project, for example, at the point where the urban planners start to think about where a new housing development should be built.[15]

At the third level, companies look to the future and plan for *new environmental technologies*. Many organisations that have made good sustainability headway are still limited by existing technologies. To develop fully sustainable strategies, they will need to develop new technologies. For example, in 2005 the Korean car company Hyundai opened its New Environmental Technology R&D Centre in Seoul. The building itself was developed according to environmental standards (including a vacuum toilet system that uses one-tenth as much water as conventional toilets), while the purpose of the R&D facility is to develop the next generation of vehicles and environmental technologies that will cause far less environmental damage than today's cars. This includes projects looking at fuel-cell cars, increasing the recyclability of the materials used in cars, and reducing the use of ferrous (iron-based) materials in car manufacturing.

Finally, companies can develop a *sustainability vision*, which serves as a guide to the future. It shows how the company's products and services, processes and policies must develop and what new technologies must be established to get there. This vision of sustainability provides a framework for pollution control, product stewardship and environmental technology.

Most companies today focus on the lower-left quadrant of the grid in Figure 16.1, investing most heavily in pollution prevention. Some forward-looking companies practise product stewardship and are developing new environmental technologies. Few companies have well-defined sustainability visions. Emphasising only one or a few quadrants in the environmental sustainability grid can be short-sighted. Investing only in the bottom half of the grid puts a company in a good position today but leaves it vulnerable in the future. In contrast, a heavy emphasis on the top half suggests that a company has good environmental vision but lacks the skills needed to implement it. Thus, companies should work at developing all four dimensions of environmental sustainability. The European Commission has created a scheme called the European Business Awards for the Environment to promote just this kind of corporate behaviour. Every two years, a number of European companies are selected as the award winners because of their efforts to promote environmentally-conscious business. In 2006, the winners of these awards came from Spain (two winners, Sotral SpA, a logistics company and DTS-Oabe SL, an insecticide manufacturer), the UK (Windsave Ltd, a wind turbine manufacturer), the Netherlands (iD-L inspired innovations, producer of 'ragbag' fashion products) and Finland (YIT Rakennus Oy, part of the YIT Group which provides a wide range of industrial services).

Environmentalism creates some special challenges for global marketers. As international trade barriers come down and global markets expand, environmental issues are having an ever-greater impact on international trade. Countries in Western Europe, North America and other developed regions are evolving strict environmental standards. The European Union recently passed 'end-of-life' regulations affecting vehicles and consumer electronics products. And the EU's Eco-Management and Audit Scheme provides guidelines for environmental self-regulation.[16]

However, environmental policies still vary widely from country to country. Countries such as Denmark, Germany, Japan, the UK and the United States have fully developed environmental policies and high public expectations. But major countries such as China, India, Brazil and Russia are in only the early stages of developing such policies. Moreover, environmental factors that motivate consumers in one country may have no impact on consumers in another. For example, PVC soft drink bottles cannot be used in Switzerland or Germany. However, they are preferred in France, which has an extensive recycling process for them. Thus, international companies have found it difficult to develop standard environmental practices that work around the world.

FIGURE 16.2

Major marketing decision areas that may be called into question under the law

Source: Photo is © Helene Rogers/Alamy Images.

Instead, they are creating general policies and then translating these policies into tailored programmes that meet local regulations and expectations.

Public actions to regulate marketing

Concerns among the general public about marketing practices will usually lead to government attention and possibly to legislative proposals. Ideas for new laws will be debated – many will be defeated, others will be modified and a few will become workable laws.

Many of the laws that affect marketing were discussed in Chapter 3. The task is to translate these laws into the language that marketing executives understand as they make decisions about competitive relations, products, price, promotion and channels of distribution. Figure 16.2 illustrates the major legal issues facing marketing management.

BUSINESS ACTIONS TOWARDS SOCIALLY RESPONSIBLE MARKETING

At first, many companies opposed consumerism and environmentalism. They thought the criticisms were either unfair or unimportant. But by now most companies have accepted the new consumer rights, at least in principle. They might oppose certain pieces of legislation as inappropriate ways to solve specific consumer problems, but they recognise the consumer's right to information and protection. Many of these companies have responded positively to consumerism and environmentalism as a way to create greater customer value and to strengthen customer relationships.

Enlightened marketing

The philosophy of **enlightened marketing** holds that a company's marketing should support the best long-term performance of the marketing system. Enlightened marketing consists of five principles: *consumer-oriented marketing, innovative marketing, value marketing, sense-of-mission marketing* and *societal marketing.*

Consumer-oriented marketing

Consumer-oriented marketing means that the company should view and organise its marketing activities from the consumer's point of view. It should work hard to sense, serve and satisfy the needs of a defined group of customers. Every good marketing company that we've discussed in this text has had this in common: an all-consuming passion for delivering superior value to carefully chosen customers. Only by seeing the world through its customers' eyes can the company build lasting and profitable customer relationships. By creating value *for* consumers, the company can capture value *from* consumers in return.

Innovative marketing

The principle of **innovative marketing** requires the company always to be seeking real product and marketing improvements. The company that overlooks new and better ways to do things will eventually lose customers to another company that has found a better way. An excellent example of an innovative marketer is Samsung Electronics:

> A decade ago, Samsung was a copycat consumer electronics brand you bought off a shipping pallet at Costco if you couldn't afford a Sony. But today, the brand holds a high-end, cutting-edge aura. In 1996, Samsung Electronics made an inspired decision. It turned its back on cheap knock-offs and set out to overtake rival Sony. The company hired a crop of fresh, young designers, who unleashed a torrent of new products – not humdrum, me-too products, but innovative and stylish products, targeted to high-end users. Samsung called them 'lifestyle works of art' – from brightly colored cell phones and elegantly thin DVD players to flat-panel TV monitors that hung on walls like paintings. Every new product had to pass the 'Wow!' test: If it didn't get a 'Wow!' reaction during market testing, it went straight back to the design studio.[17]

Samsung supported this worldwide goal with substantial advertising expenditure, and reconsidered its distribution strategy so that Samsung products were to be found in upmarket retail outlets where consumers are prepared to pay above-average prices for premium quality products with innovative features. Over the last decade Samsung has successfully repositioned itself as a producer of innovative, high-quality electronics products.

Customer value marketing

According to the principle of **customer value marketing,** the company should put most of its resources into customer value-building marketing investments. Many things marketers do – one-shot sales promotions, minor packaging changes, direct-response advertising – may raise sales in the short term but add less *value* than would fundamental improvements in the product's quality, features or convenience. Enlightened marketing calls for building long-term consumer loyalty and relationships by continually improving the value consumers receive from the firm's market offering.

Sense-of-mission marketing

Sense-of-mission marketing means that the company should define its mission in broad *social* terms rather than narrow *product* terms. When a company defines a social mission, employees feel better about their work and have a clearer sense of direction. For example, Ben & Jerry's ice cream brand is known all over the world (since 2000 Ben & Jerry's has been a business unit of the Anglo-Dutch consumer good giant Unilever), and defined in narrow terms the mission of Ben & Jerry's might be 'to sell ice cream'. However, Ben & Jerry's states its mission more broadly, as one of 'linked prosperity,' including product, economic and social missions (see **www.benjerrys.com/our_company/our_mission/**). Founders Ben Cohen and Jerry Greenfield pioneered the concept of 'values-led business' or 'caring capitalism'. Their mission was to use business to make the world a better place:

> From its beginnings in 1978, Ben & Jerry's bought only hormone-free milk and cream and used only organic fruits and nuts to make its ice cream, which it sold in environmentally-friendly containers. It went to great lengths to buy from minority and disadvantaged suppliers. From its early Rainforest Crunch to its more recent One Sweet Whirled flavours and awareness campaigns, Ben & Jerry's championed a host of social and environmental causes over the years. And from the start, Ben & Jerry's donated a whopping 7.5 per cent of pre-tax profits to support projects that exhibited 'creative problem-solving and hopefulness . . . relating to children and families, disadvantaged groups, and the environment'. By the mid-1990s, Ben & Jerry's had become [America's] number-two super-premium ice cream brand.
>
> However, having a 'double bottom line' of values and profits is no easy proposition. Through the 1990s, as competitors not shackled by their 'principles before profits' missions invaded its markets, Ben & Jerry's growth and profits flattened. Perhaps this was why in 2000, after several years of disappointing financial returns, Ben & Jerry's was acquired by Unilever. Looking back, the company appears to have focused too much on social issues at the expense of sound business management. Cohen once commented, 'There came a time when I had to admit 'I'm a businessman.' And I had a hard time mouthing those words.'[18]

Many entrepreneurial businesses today, like Innocent Drinks, strive to make both profits and a wider contribution to society.

Such experiences taught the socially responsible business movement some hard lessons. The result is a new generation of activist entrepreneurs – not social activists with big hearts who hate capitalism, but well-trained business managers and company builders with a passion for a cause. Innocent Smoothies is a good example of this new kind of caring company with a highly professional approach to business and marketing. They say: 'we want to leave things a little bit better than we find them. We strive to do business in a more enlightened way, where we take responsibility for the impact of our business on society and the environment, and move these impacts from negative to neutral, or better still, positive' – this from a company that started up in 1999 and was approaching an annual turnover of £100 million by 2007, with an estimated 72 per cent of the UK smoothie market.[19]

IMMEDIATE SATISFACTION

FIGURE 16.3
Societal classification of products

	Low	**High**
High	Salutary products	Desirable products
Low	Deficient products	Pleasing products

LONG-TERM CONSUMER BENEFIT

Societal marketing

Following the principle of **societal marketing**, an enlightened company makes marketing decisions by considering consumers' wants and interests, the company's requirements and society's long-term interests. The company is aware that neglecting consumer and societal long-term interests is a disservice to consumers and society. Alert companies view societal problems as opportunities.

A societally-oriented marketer wants to design products that are not only pleasing but also beneficial. The difference is shown in Figure 16.3. Products can be classified according to their degree of immediate consumer satisfaction and long-term consumer benefit. **Deficient products**, such as bad-tasting and ineffective medicine, have neither immediate appeal nor long-term benefits. **Pleasing products** give high immediate satisfaction but may hurt consumers in the long run. Examples include cigarettes and junk food. **Salutary products** have low appeal but may benefit consumers in the long run; for instance, seat belts and air bags. **Desirable products** give both high immediate satisfaction and high long-term benefits, such as a tasty *and* nutritious breakfast food.

Examples of desirable products abound. Low-energy consumption long-life light bulbs are a well-known example, and they are widely available through the biggest retailers (such as Tesco and Carrefour) who stock major brands such as Philips and GE. Toyota's hybrid Prius family car gives both a quiet ride and fuel efficiency. Miele's range of washing machines and dishwashers are recommended by consumer organisations for their excellent performance, and also deliver better energy efficiency and lower water consumption than standard brands.

Companies should try to turn all of their products into desirable products. The challenge posed by pleasing products is that they sell very well but may end up hurting the consumer. The product opportunity, therefore, is to add long-term benefits without reducing the product's pleasing qualities. The challenge posed by salutary products is to add some pleasing qualities so that they will become more desirable in consumers' minds.

MAKING CONNECTIONS Linking the concepts

Pause here, hold your place with your finger, and go back and take another look at the Societal marketing concept section in Chapter 1.

■ How does Figure 1.4 apply to the Enlightened marketing section in this chapter?

■ Use the five principles to assess the actions of a company that you believe exemplifies socially responsible marketing. (If you can't think of one, use Unilever or one of the other companies discussed in this chapter.)

■ Use the principles of enlightened marketing to assess the actions of a company that you believe falls short of socially responsible marketing.

Marketing ethics

Conscientious marketers face many moral dilemmas. The best thing to do is often unclear. Because not all managers have fine moral sensitivity, companies need to develop *corporate marketing ethics policies* – broad guidelines that everyone in the organisation must follow. These policies should cover distributor relations, advertising standards, customer service, pricing, product development and general ethical standards.

The finest guidelines cannot resolve all the difficult ethical situations the marketer faces. Exhibit 16.1 lists some difficult ethical situations marketers could face during their careers. If marketers choose immediate sales-producing actions in all these cases, their marketing behaviour might well be described as immoral or even amoral. If they refuse to go along with *any* of the actions, they might be ineffective as marketing managers and unhappy because of the constant moral tension. Managers need a set of principles that will help them work out the moral importance of each situation and decide how far they can go in good conscience.

Exhibit 16.1 Some morally difficult situations in marketing

1 You work for a cigarette company. Public policy debates over the past few years now leave no doubt in your mind that cigarette smoking and cancer are closely linked. Although your company currently runs an 'if you don't smoke, don't start' promotion campaign, you believe that other company promotions might encourage young (although legal age) non-smokers to pick up the habit. What would you do?

2 Your R&D department has changed one of your products slightly. It is not really 'new and improved', but you know that putting this statement on the package and in advertising will increase sales. What would you do?

3 You have been asked to add a stripped-down model to your line that could be advertised to pull customers into the store. The product won't be very good, but salespeople will be able to switch buyers up to higher-priced units. You are asked to give the green light for the stripped-down version. What would you do?

4 You are thinking of hiring a product manager who has just left a competitor's company. She would be more than happy to tell you all the competitor's plans for the coming year. What would you do?

5 One of your top dealers in an important territory has recently had family troubles and his sales have slipped. It looks like it will take him a while to straighten out his family trouble. Meanwhile you are losing many sales. Legally, you can terminate the dealer's franchise and replace him. What would you do?

6 You have a chance to win a big account that will mean a lot to you and your company. The purchasing agent hints that a 'gift' would influence the decision. Your assistant recommends sending a fine high-definition colour television set to the buyer's home. What would you do?

7 You have heard that a competitor has a new product feature that will make a big difference in sales. The competitor will demonstrate the feature in a private dealer meeting at the annual trade show. You can easily send a spy to this meeting to learn about the new feature. What would you do?

8 You have to choose between three advertising campaigns outlined by your agency. The first (a) is a soft-sell, honest, straight-information campaign. The second (b) uses sex-loaded emotional appeals and exaggerates the product's benefits. The third (c) involves a noisy, somewhat irritating commercial that is sure to gain audience attention. Pre-tests show that the campaigns are effective in the following order: c, b, and a. What would you do?

9 You are interviewing a capable female applicant for a job as salesperson. She is better qualified than the men just interviewed. Nevertheless, you know that some of your important customers prefer dealing with men and you will lose some sales if you hire her. What would you do?

But *what* principle should guide companies and marketing managers on issues of ethics and social responsibility? One philosophy is that such issues are decided by the free market and legal system. Under this principle, companies and their managers are not responsible for making moral judgements. Companies can, according to this principle, in good conscience do whatever the market and legal systems allow.

A second philosophy puts responsibility not on the system but in the hands of individual companies and managers. This more enlightened philosophy suggests that a company should have a 'social conscience'. Companies and managers should apply high standards of ethics and morality when making corporate decisions, regardless of 'what the system allows'. History provides an endless list of examples of company actions that were legal but highly irresponsible. Consider the following amusing, and amazing, example from the USA:

> Prior to the Pure Food and Drug Act, the advertising for a diet pill promised that a person taking this pill could eat virtually anything at any time and still lose weight. Too good to be true? Actually the claim was quite true; the product lived up to its billing with frightening efficiency. It seems that the primary active ingredient in this 'diet supplement' was tapeworm larvae. These larvae would develop in the intestinal tract and, of course, be well fed; the pill taker would in time, quite literally, starve to death.[20]

Each company and marketing manager must work out a philosophy of socially responsible and ethical behaviour. Under the societal marketing concept, each manager must look beyond what is legal and allowed and develop standards based on personal integrity, corporate conscience and long-term consumer welfare.

As with environmentalism, the issue of ethics provides special challenges for international marketers. Business standards and practices vary a great deal from one country to the next. For example, whereas bribes and kickbacks are illegal for EU firms, they are common business practice in many South American countries. One recent study found that companies from some nations were much more likely to use bribes when seeking contracts in emerging-market nations. The most flagrant bribe-paying firms were from Russia and China, with Taiwan and South Korea close behind. Other countries where corruption is common include India, Pakistan and Bangladesh. The least corrupt were companies from Australia, Sweden, Switzerland, Austria and Canada.[21]

The question arises as to whether a company must lower its ethical standards to compete effectively in countries with lower standards. The answer? No. Companies should make a commitment to a common set of shared standards worldwide.

Many industrial and professional associations have suggested codes of ethics and many companies are now adopting their own codes. For example, the European Marketing Confederation, an international umbrella organisation for national marketing associations in European countries, developed the code of ethics shown in Exhibit 16.2. Companies are also developing programmes to teach managers about important ethical issues and help them find the proper responses. They hold ethics workshops and seminars and set up ethics committees. Furthermore, most major EU companies have appointed high-level ethics officers to champion ethical issues and to help resolve ethical problems and concerns facing employees.

Consider Allied Irish Bank (AIB), where they have a CSR Committee which is a subcommittee of the main AIB board – 'CSR', by the way, stands for Corporate Social Responsibility, which is the headline term used for corporate ethical, social and environmental responsibility in many businesses today. At AIB they have an eight-page Code of Business Ethics for all Employees of the AIB Group, which provides detailed guidance to employees about how they are expected to conduct their business ethically. This includes advice on dealing with customer information and protecting customer privacy, dealing with colleagues and ensuring that there is fairness in all employment practices, and advice on general business practice such as forbidding bribery and advising great

Exhibit 16.2 European Marketing Confederation: Code of Conduct
Source: http://www.emc.be/codeconduct.cfm

For a better profession . . .

One of the main objectives of the European Marketing Confederation is to promote and maintain for the benefit of the public high standards of professional skill, ability and integrity among persons engaged in marketing, sales and services.

Members of the EMC are committed to ethical professional conduct. The Confederation requires its Members, as a condition of membership, to adopt and adhere to the following Code of Conduct. The adherence to the Code signifies voluntary assumption of self-discipline.

Confidentiality

Members shall not disclose or use to their own advantage confidential information regarding their employers or business customers without their consent, except where regulations require to do so. The use of data should extend only to those purposes for which consent was received. Lastly privacy is to be respected.

Integrity

Members shall at all time conduct themselves with integrity in such a way as to bring credit to the profession of marketing and to the EMC. Members shall not disseminate any false or misleading information, either on their own behalf, or on behalf of anyone else.

Honesty

Members shall deal honestly with consumers, clients, employees, employers, suppliers and the general public.

Good judgement

Members shall be aware of how their conduct may influence others, such as fellow employees, suppliers or customers. They shall not demand, encourage, coerce or adopt any behaviour which leads to unethical conduct.

Conflict of interest

Members shall seek to avoid conflicts of interest. When a conflict arises a member must withdraw prior to starting the work.

Professionalism

Members shall do their utmost to maintain the highest professional standards and shall endeavour to ensure that those who work with or for them do the same. Members shall regularly extend, develop and maintain their marketing expertise for the benefit of the society. Furthermore members shall assume responsibilities for their activities.

Advertising

Members shall honour the national advertising codes of practice and shall specifically reject and not be involved in false or misleading advertising or misleading sales tactics.

Rights and duties

Members shall have due regard for, and comply with, all the relevant laws of the country in which they are operating.

Expulsion of individuals who are found not to have abided by this Code

In adopting this code and after appropriate investigation of any complaint brought against any individual member, each association which belongs to EMC undertakes to withdraw the membership of an individual found guilty, or to impose an appropriate penalty. All members of EMC recognise and agree that serious and flagrant breaches of this code shall result in the withdrawal of the membership of the individual member concerned.

caution in the acceptance of small gifts or hospitality. Naturally employees are bound to encounter situations that are not directly covered by the code of ethics, and under these circumstances the AIB Code requires employees to ask themselves the following questions:

> Am I being fair and honest?
> Are my intended actions legal?
> Will my action stand the test of time?
> Is anyone's life, health or safety endangered by my action?
> How would my action look in the media and in public?
> Will my actions damage the reputation of the organisation?[22]

Still, written codes and ethics programmes do not ensure ethical behavior. Ethical and social responsibility requires a total corporate commitment. In order to have the best chance of making the corporate ethical code work in practice, companies are advised to keep the code as short as possible, provide employees with concrete examples of correct behaviour, demonstrate that the code receives serious support from top managers, provide training to employees and frequently reinforce the message that ethics is important, and demonstrate that breaches of the code are taken very seriously.[23]

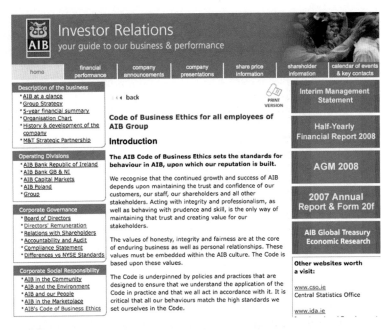

Most large European businesses, like Allied Irish Bank, have codes of ethics that make it clear to employees what is considered ethical, and unethical, behaviour in pursuing profits for the firm.

Source: http://www.aibgroup.com/

THE JOURNEY YOU'VE TAKEN Reviewing the concepts

Well – here you are at the end of your introductory marketing travels. In this chapter, we've closed with many important concepts involving marketing's sweeping impact on individual consumers, other businesses and society as a whole. You learned that responsible marketers discover what consumers want and respond with the right market offerings, priced to give good value to buyers and profit to the producer. A marketing system should deliver customer value and improve the quality of consumers' lives. In working to meet consumer needs, marketers may take some actions that are not to everyone's liking or benefit. Marketing managers should be aware of the main *criticisms of marketing*.

1 Identify the major social criticisms of marketing.

Marketing's *impact on individual consumer welfare* has been criticised for its high prices, deceptive practices, high-pressure selling, shoddy or unsafe products, planned obsolescence and poor service to disadvantaged consumers. Marketing's *impact on society* has been criticised for creating false wants and too much materialism, too few social goods, cultural pollution and too much political power. Critics have also criticised marketing's *impact on other businesses* for harming competitors and reducing competition through acquisitions, practices that create barriers to entry and unfair competitive marketing practices. Some of these concerns are justified; some are not.

2 Define *consumerism* and *environmentalism* and explain how they affect marketing strategies.

Concerns about the marketing system have led to *citizen action movements*. *Consumerism* is an organised social movement intended to strengthen the rights and power of consumers relative to sellers. Alert marketers view it as an opportunity to serve consumers better by providing more consumer information, education and protection. *Environmentalism* is an organised social movement seeking to minimise the harm done to the environment and quality of life by marketing practices. The first wave of modern environmentalism was driven by environmental groups and concerned consumers, whereas the second wave was driven by government, which passed laws and regulations governing industrial practices impacting the environment. Moving into the twenty-first century, the first two environmentalism waves are merging into a third and stronger wave in which companies are accepting responsibility for doing no environmental harm. Companies now are adopting policies of *environmental sustainability* – developing strategies that both sustain the environment and produce profits for the company.

3 Describe the principles of socially responsible marketing.

Many companies originally opposed these social movements and laws, but most of them now recognise a need for positive consumer information, education and protection. Some companies have followed a policy of *enlightened marketing*, which holds that a company's marketing should support the best long-term performance of the marketing system. Enlightened marketing consists of five principles: *consumer-oriented marketing*, *innovative marketing*, *customer-value marketing*, *sense-of-mission marketing* and *societal marketing*.

4 Explain the role of ethics in marketing.

Increasingly, companies are responding to the need to provide company policies and guidelines to help their managers deal with questions of *marketing ethics*. Of course, even the best guidelines cannot resolve all the difficult ethical decisions that individuals and firms must make. But there are some principles that marketers can choose among. One principle states that such issues should be decided by the free market and legal system. A second, and more enlightened principle, puts responsibility not on the system but in the hands of individual companies and managers. Each firm and marketing manager must work out a philosophy of socially responsible and ethical behaviour. Under the societal marketing concept, managers must look beyond what is legal and allowable and develop standards based on personal integrity, corporate conscience, and long-term consumer welfare.

Because business standards and practices vary from country to country, the issue of ethics poses special challenges for international marketers. The growing consensus among today's marketers is that it is important to make a commitment to a common set of shared standards worldwide.

NAVIGATING THE KEY TERMS

Consumerism 555
Consumer-oriented marketing 563
Customer value marketing 563
Deficient products 565
Desirable products 565

Enlightened marketing 563
Environmental sustainability 557
Environmentalism 556
Innovative marketing 563
Pleasing products 565

Salutary products 565
Sense-of-mission marketing 564
Societal marketing 565

NOTES AND REFERENCES

1 Sources: M.J. Thun, C.A. Day-Lally, E.E. Calle, et al., 'Excess mortality among cigarette smokers: changes in a 20-year interval', *American Journal of Public Health*, **85**, 1995, pp. 1223–30; R. Doll, R. Peto, J. Boreham and I. Sutherland, 'Mortality in relation to smoking: 50 years' observations on male British doctors', *British Medical Journal*, **328**, 2004, pp. 1519–27; D.M. Mannino, M. Klevens and W.D. Flanders, 'Cigarette Smoking: an independent risk factor for impotence?', *American Journal of Epidemiology*, **140**, 1994, pp. 1003–8; on blindness, see http://www.rnib.org.uk/xpedio/groups/public/documents/publicwebsite/public_smokingbrusselspr.hcsp; http://www.who.int/gb/fctc/; *Choosing Health: Making Healthy Choices Easier*, Department of Health (2004); http://www.tobaccoleaf.org/about_tobacco/index.asp?op=7&l=en; R.W. Pollay, 'Targeting youth and concerned smokers: evidence from Canadian tobacco industry documents', *Tobacco Control*, **9**, 2000, pp. 136–47; S.K. Katz and A.M. Lavack, 'Tobacco related bar promotions: insights from tobacco industry documents', *Tobacco Control*, **11**(Suppl I), 2002, pp. i92–i101; http://www.usatoday.com/news/washington/2006-08-17-tobacco-lawsuit_x.htm; M.C. Farrelly, C.G. Healton, K.C. Davis, P. Messeri, J.C. Hersey and M.L. Haviland, 'Getting to the truth: evaluating national tobacco countermarketing campaigns', *American Journal of Public Health*, **92**(6), 2002, pp. 901–7; R.L. Andrews and G.R. Franke, 'The determinants of cigarette consumption: a meta-analysis', *Journal of Public Policy and Marketing*, **10**(Spring), 1991, pp. 81–100; H. Saffer and F. Chaloupka, 'The effect of tobacco advertising bans on tobacco consumption', *Journal of Health Economics*, **19**, 2000, pp. 1117–37; F.J. Chaloupka and H. Wechsler, 'Price, tobacco control policies and smoking among young adults', *Journal of Health Economics*, **16**, 1997, pp. 359–73; I.C. Grant, L.M. Hassan, G. Hastings, A-M. MacKintosh and D. Eadie, 'The influence of branding on adolescent smoking behaviour: exploring the mediating role of image and attitudes', *Journal of Nonprofit and Voluntary Sector Marketing*, DOI: 10.1002/nvsm.329, 2007; P. Kotler and S.J. Levy, 'Demarketing, yes, demarketing', *Harvard Business Review*, **49**(6), 1971, pp. 74–80 [p. 75]; US Department of Health and Human Services, *Preventing Tobacco Use Among Young People: A Report of the Surgeon General* (Atlanta, GA: Centers for Disease Control and Prevention, Office on Smoking and Health, 1994); K.H. Smith and M-A. Stutts, 'Effects of short-term cosmetic versus long-term health fear appeals in anti-smoking advertisements on the smoking behaviour of adolescents', *Journal of Consumer Behaviour*, **(3)**, 2003, pp. 157–77; G. Hastings, M. Stead and J. Webb, 'Fear appeals in social marketing: Strategic and ethical reasons for concern', *Psychology and Marketing*, **21**, 2004, pp. 961–86; D.L. Alden, W.D. Hoyer and C. Lee, 'Identifying global and culture-specific dimensions of humor in advertising: a multinational analysis', *Journal of Marketing*, **57**, 1993, pp. 64–75; http://www.eiaa.net/news/eiaa-articles-details.asp?lang=1&id=154; The HELP programme 2005–2007 moving towards a smoke-free Europe. Access at http://ec.europa.eu/health/ph_determinants/life_style/Tobacco/help/docs/2_years.

2 See Winnie Hu, 'The Smoking Ban: Clean Air, Murky Economics', *The New York Times*, 28 December 2003, p. 1.1; 'Smoking Bans Have Their Place, but Outside Isn't One of Them', *The Washington Post*, 5 February 2004, p. T.04; and 'EU Regulations: EU-Wide Ban on Tobacco Ads Imminent', *EIU ViewsWire*, 8 July 2005.

3 Theodore Levitt, 'The Morality (?) of Advertising', *Harvard Business Review*, July–August 1970, pp. 84–92. For counterpoints, see James Heckman, 'Don't Shoot the Messenger: More and More Often, Marketing is the Regulators' Target', *Marketing News*, 24 May 1999, pp. 1, 9.

4 Lane Jennings, 'Hype, Spin, Puffery, and Lies: Should We Be Scared?', *The Futurist*, January–February 2004, p. 16. For recent examples of deceptive advertising, see 'Tropicana Settles Complaint by FTC Over Misleading Ads', *Wall Street Journal*, 3 June 2005, p. B4; and Monty Phan, 'City Sues Wireless Firms', 22 July 2005, accessed at www.newsday.com.

5 Roger Parloff, 'Is Fat the Next Tobacco?', *Fortune*, 3 February 2003, pp. 51–4; '"Big Food" Get the Obesity Message', *New York Times*, 10 July 2003, p. A22; Carl Hulse, 'Vote in House Offers Shield in Obesity Suits', *New York Times*, 11 March 2004, p. A1; and Amy Garber, 'Twice-Tossed McD Obesity Suit Back on Docket', *Nation's Restaurant News*, 7 February 2005, pp. 1ff.

6 'McDonald's to Cut "Super Size" Option', *Advertising Age*, 8 March 2004, p. 13; Dave Carpenter, 'Hold the Fries, Take a Walk', *The News & Observer*, 16 April 2004, p. D1; Michael V. Copeland, 'Ronald Gets Back in Shape,' *Business 2.0*, January/February 2005, pp. 46–7; David P. Callet and Cheryl A. Falvey, 'Is Restaurant Food the New Tobacco?', *Restaurant Hospitality*, May 2005, pp. 94–6; and Kate McArthur, 'BK Offers Fat to the Land', *Advertising Age*, 4 April 2005, pp. 1, 60.

7 Adapted from information found in Mark Fagan, 'Copy Competition Heats Up', *Knight Ridder Tribune Business News*, 4 May 2005, p. 1.

8 www.which.co.uk/reports_and_campaigns/consumer_rights/campaigns/.

9 Adapted from John Markoff, 'Is Planned Obsolescence Obsolete?', *New York Times*, 17 February 2002, p. 4.6. Also see Kevin McKean, 'Planned Obsolescence', *InfoWorld*, 29 September 2003, pp. 38–46.

10 See Brian Grow and Pallavi Gogoi, 'A New Way to Squeeze the Weak?', *BusinessWeek*, 28 January 2002, p. 92; Todd Cooper, 'Redlining Rears Its Ugly Head', *USBanker*, August 2003, p. 64; Marc Lifsher, 'Allstate Settles Over Use of Credit Scores', *Los Angeles Times*, 2 March 2004, p. C.1; and Judith Burns, 'Study Finds Links in Credit Scores, Insurance Claims', *Wall Street Journal*, 28 February 2005, p. D3.

11 'Children "damaged" by materialism', http://news.bbc.co.uk, accessed 14 May 2008; and 'Reflections on Childhood – Lifestyle', report produced by GfK Social Research for The Children's Society, 20 September 2007, available from http://news.bbc.co.uk/1/shared/bsp/hi/pdfs/25_02_08_childhood.pdf.

12 Information obtained from http://www.tfl.gov.uk/roadusers/congestioncharging/, accessed 14 May 2008.

13 Adapted from information found in Steve Hamm, 'Microsoft's Future', *BusinessWeek*, 19 January 1998, pp. 58–68; Dan Carney and Mike France, 'The Microsoft Case: Tying It All Together', *BusinessWeek*, 3 December 2001, pp. 68–9; Paul Meller and Matt Richtel, 'Europeans Rule Against Microsoft: Appeal Is Promised', *New York Times*, 25 March 2004, p. C.1; and Brier Dudley, 'Microsoft Pays IBM to Settle Suit', *Knight Ridder Tribune Business News*, 2 July 2005, p. 1.

14 Stuart L. Hart, 'Beyond Greening: Strategies for a Sustainable World', *Harvard Business Review*, January–February 1997, pp. 66–76. Also see Subhabrata Bobby Banerjee, Easwar S. Iyer and Rajiv K. Kashyap, 'Corporate Environmentalism: Antecedents and Influence of Industry Type', *Harvard Business Review*, April 2003, pp. 106–22; Christopher Laszlo, *The Sustainable Company: How to Create Lasting Value through Social and Environmental Performance* (Washington, DC: Island Press, 2003); Volkert Beekman, 'Sustainable Development and Future Generations', *Journal of Agriculture and Environmental Ethics*, 17(1), 2004, p. 3; and Bill Hopwood, Mary Mellor, and Geoff O'Brien, 'Sustainable Development: Mapping Different Approaches', *Sustainable Development*, February 2005, pp. 38ff.

15 'Sustainable design, climate change and the built environment', briefing paper from the Commission for Architecture and the Built Environment, available at http://www.cabe.org.uk/AssetLibrary/10661.pdf.

16 See 'EMAS: What's New?' accessed at http://europa.eu.int/comm/environment/emas, August 2005; 'Special Report: Free Trade on Trial – Ten Years of NAFTA', *The Economist*, 3 January 2004, p. 13; and Daniel J. Tschopp, 'Corporate Social Responsibility: A Comparison between the United States and Europe', *Corporate Social-Responsibility and Environmental Management*, March 2005, pp. 55–9.

17 Information and quotes from Andy Milligan, 'Samsung Points the Way for Asian Firms in Global Brand Race', *Media*, 8 August 2003, p. 8; Katherine Chen, Michael Jakielski, Nadia Luhr and Joseph Mayer-Salman, 'DigitAll', student paper at the University of North Carolina at Chapel Hill, Spring 2003; Gerry Khermouch, 'The Best Global Brands', *BusinessWeek*, 5 August 2002, p. 92; Leslie P. Norton, 'Value Brand', *Barron's*, 22 September 2003, p. 19; and Samsung Electronics Co. Ltd, *Hoover's Company Capsules*, 15 March 2004; 'Cult Brands', *BusinessWeek Online*, 2 August 2004, accessed at www.businessweek.com; and Samsung Annual Reports and other information accessed at www.samsung.com, September 2005.

18 Information from Mike Hoffman, 'Ben Cohen: Ben & Jerry's Homemade, Established in 1978', *Inc*, 30 April 2001, p. 68; and the Ben & Jerry's website at www.benjerrys.com and www.bodyshop.com, September 2005.

19 http://www.innocentdrinks.co.uk.

20 Dan R. Dalton and Richard A. Cosier, 'The Four Faces of Social Responsibility', *Business Horizons*, May–June 1982, pp. 19–27.

21 See 'Transparency International Bribe Payers Index' and 'Transparency International Corruption Perception Index', accessed at www.transparency.org, August 2005; David Barboza, 'Wave of Corruption Tarnishes China's Extraordinary Growth', *New York Times*, 22 March 2005, p. C1; and Vladimir Kvint, 'The Scary Business of Russia', *Forbes*, 23 May 2005, p. 42.

22 'Code of Business Ethics for all Employees of AIB Group', available at www.aib.com, accessed 14 May 2008.

23 Mark S. Schwartz, 'Effective Corporate Codes of Ethics: Perceptions of Code Users', *Journal of Business Ethics*, 55, 2004, pp. 323–43.

APPENDIX 1

Marketing plan

THE MARKETING PLAN: AN INTRODUCTION

As a marketer, you'll need a good marketing plan to provide direction and focus for your brand, product or company. With a detailed plan, any business will be better prepared to launch a new product or build sales for existing products. Non-profit organisations also use marketing plans to guide their fund-raising and outreach efforts. Even government agencies put together marketing plans for initiatives such as building public awareness of proper nutrition and stimulating tourism.

The purpose and content of a marketing plan

Unlike a business plan, which offers a broad overview of the entire organisation's mission, objectives, strategy and resource allocation, a marketing plan has a more limited scope. It serves to document how the organisation's strategic objectives will be achieved through specific marketing strategies and tactics, with the customer as the starting point. It is also linked to the plans of other departments within the organisation. Suppose a marketing plan calls for selling 200,000 units annually. The production department must gear up to make that many units, the finance department must have funding available to cover the expenses, the human resources department must be ready to hire and train staff, and so on. Without the appropriate level of organisational support and resources, no marketing plan can succeed.

Although the exact length and layout will vary from company to company, a marketing plan usually contains the sections described in Chapter 2. Smaller businesses may create shorter or less formal marketing plans, whereas corporations frequently require highly structured marketing plans. To guide implementation effectively, every part of the plan must be described in considerable detail. Sometimes a company will post its marketing plan on an intranet, which allows managers and employees in different locations to consult specific sections and collaborate on additions or changes.

The role of research

Marketing plans are not created in a vacuum. To develop successful strategies and action programmes, marketers need up-to-date information about the environment, the competition and the market segments to be served. Often, analysis of internal data is the starting point for assessing the current marketing situation, supplemented by marketing intelligence and research investigating the overall market, the competition, key issues, and threats and opportunities issues. As the plan is put into effect, marketers use a variety of research techniques to measure progress toward objectives and identify areas for improvement if results fall short of projections. Finally, marketing research helps marketers learn more about their customers' requirements, expectations, perceptions and satisfaction levels. This deeper understanding provides a foundation for building competitive advantage through well-informed segmenting, targeting and positioning decisions. Thus, the marketing plan should outline what marketing research will be conducted and how the findings will be applied.

The role of relationships

The marketing plan shows how the company will establish and maintain profitable customer relationships. In the process, however, it also shapes a number of internal and external relationships. First, it affects how marketing personnel work with each other and with other departments to deliver value and satisfy customers. Second, it affects how the company works with suppliers, distributors and strategic alliance partners to achieve the objectives listed in the plan. Third, it influences the company's dealings with other stakeholders, including government regulators, the media, and the community at large. All of these relationships are important to the organisation's success, so they should be considered when a marketing plan is being developed.

From marketing plan to marketing action

Companies generally create yearly marketing plans, although some plans cover a longer period. Marketers start planning well in advance of the implementation date to allow time for marketing research, thorough analysis, management review and coordination between departments. Then, after each action programme begins, marketers monitor ongoing results, compare them with projections, analyse any differences and take corrective steps as needed. Some marketers also prepare contingency plans for implementation if certain conditions emerge. Because of inevitable and sometimes unpredictable environmental changes, marketers must be ready to update and adapt marketing plans at any time.

For effective implementation and control, the marketing plan should define how progress towards objectives will be measured. Managers typically use budgets, schedules and performance standards for monitoring and evaluating results. With budgets, they can compare planned expenditures with actual expenditures for a given week, month, or other period. Schedules allow management to see when tasks were supposed to be completed – and when they were actually completed. Performance standards track the outcomes of marketing programmes to see whether the company is moving forward towards its objectives. Some examples of performance standards are: market share, sales volume, product profitability, and customer satisfaction.

SAMPLE MARKETING PLAN FOR SONIC

This section takes you inside the sample marketing plan for Sonic, a hypothetical start-up company. The company's first product is the Sonic 1000, a multimedia personal digital assistant (PDA), also known as a handheld computer. Sonic will be competing with Palm, Hewlett-Packard and other well-established PDA rivals in a crowded, fast-changing marketplace where enhanced mobile phones and many other electronics devices have PDA functionality. The introduction to each section explains more about what that section of the plan should contain and why.

Executive summary
This section summarises the main goals, recommendations and points as an overview for senior managers who must read and approve the marketing plan. Generally a table of contents follows this section, for management convenience.

Executive summary

Sonic is preparing to launch a new multimedia PDA product, the Sonic 1000, in a maturing market. Despite the dominance of PDA leader Palm, we can compete because our product offers a unique combination of features at a value-added price. We are targeting specific segments in the consumer and business markets, taking advantage of opportunities indicated by higher demand for easy-to-use PDAs with expanded communications, entertainment and storage functionality.

The primary marketing objective is to achieve first-year market share in the major European markets of Germany, France, Spain and the UK of 3 per cent with unit sales of 240,000. The primary financial objectives are to achieve first-year sales revenues of €60 million, keep first-year losses to less than €10 million, and break even early in the second year.

Current marketing situation

Sonic, founded 18 months ago by two entrepreneurs with experience in the PC market, is about to enter the now mature PDA market. Multifunction mobile phones and email devices are increasingly popular today, intensifying competition as PDA demand flattens, industry consolidation continues, and downward pricing pressure squeezes profitability. In the peak year for PDA sales, 6.4 million units were sold in the target countries; more recently, yearly PDA sales in these markets totalled about 5 million units. Around the world, fewer than 10 million PDAs were sold last year, compared with 13 million multifunction mobile phones. To gain market share in this dynamic environment, Sonic must carefully target specific segments with features that deliver benefits valued by each customer group.

Market description

Sonic's market consists of consumers and business users who prefer to use a single device for communication, information storage and exchange, and entertainment on the go. Specific segments being targeted during the first year include professionals, corporations, students, entrepreneurs and medical users. Exhibit A1.1 shows how the Sonic 1000 addresses the needs of targeted consumer and business segments.

PDA purchasers can choose between models based on several different operating systems, with particularly popular systems from Palm and Microsoft. Sonic licenses a Linux-based system because it is somewhat less vulnerable to attack by hackers and viruses. Storage capacity is a key issue in this market, and Sonic is equipping its first product with an 8Gb solid state memory for information and entertainment storage. Technology costs are decreasing even as capabilities are increasing, which makes value-priced models more appealing to consumers and to customers with older PDAs who want to trade up to newer, high-end multifunction units.

Product review

Our first product, the Sonic PDA 1000, offers the following standard features:

- Hands-free operation of all functions
- Digital music/video downloading and playback capabilities
- Global positioning system (GPS) for identifying locations, obtaining directions and maps
- Integrated mobile phone with 100-number auto-dial capability
- Wireless Web access, email, instant messaging functionality
- Organisation and communication functions, including calendar, address book, memo pad, Internet browser, email program, word processing and spreadsheet software, text and instant messaging programs
- Large high-resolution colour display
- Virtual keyboard for input without additional accessories
- USB connector for synchronising data with PC
- 8Gb memory with expansion potential
- Wardrobe of PDA cases in different colours, patterns and materials

Current marketing situation
In this section, marketing managers discuss the overall market, identify the market segments they will target, and provide information about the company's current situation.

Market description
By describing the targeted segments in detail, marketers provide context for the marketing strategies and detailed action programmes discussed later in the plan.

Benefits and product features
Exhibit A1.1 clarifies the benefits that product features will deliver to satisfy the needs of customers in each targeted segment.

Product review
The product review should summarise the main features for all of the company's products. The information may be organised by product line, by type of customer, by market, or (as here) by order of product introduction.

EXHIBIT A1.1 Segment needs and features/benefits of Sonic PDA

Targeted segment	Customer need	Corresponding feature/benefit
Professionals (consumer market)	■ Stay in touch conveniently and securely while on the go	■ Built-in mobile phone, wireless email/Web access from anywhere; Linux-based operating system less vulnerable to hackers
	■ Perform many functions hands-free without carrying multiple gadgets	■ Voice-activated phone dialling, Web and IM messaging, music/video playback, file exchange; built-in camera and GPS functions add value
Students (consumer market)	■ Perform many functions hands-free without carrying multiple gadgets	■ Built-in mobile phone, wireless email/Web access from anywhere; hands-free note-taking; built-in camera and GPS functions add value
	■ Express style and individuality	■ Wardrobe of PDA cases in different colours, patterns and materials
Corporate users (business market)	■ Security and adaptability for proprietary tasks	■ Customisable to fit diverse corporate tasks and networks; Linux-based operating system less vulnerable to hackers
	■ Obtain driving directions to business meetings	■ Built-in GPS allows voice-activated access to directions and maps
Entrepreneurs (business market)	■ Organise and access contacts, schedule details, business and financial files	■ No-hands, wireless access to calendar, address book, information files for checking appointments and data, connecting with contacts
	■ Photograph products or business situations to maintain a visual record	■ Built-in camera allows fast and easy photography, stores images for later retrieval
Medical users (business market)	■ Update, access and exchange medical records	■ No-hands, wireless recording and exchange of information to reduce paperwork and increase productivity
	■ Photograph medical situations to maintain a visual record	■ Built-in camera allows fast and easy photography, stores images for later retrieval

First-year sales revenues are projected to be €60 million, based on sales of 240,000 Sonic 1000 units at a wholesale price of €250 each. During the second year, we plan to introduce the Sonic 2000 as a higher-end product with the following standard features:

■ Translation capabilities to translate text between English, French, German and Spanish (other languages to be offered as add-on options)

■ Integrated 8 megapixel camera

Competitive review

The purpose of a competitive review is to identify key competitors, describe their market positions and briefly discuss their strategies.

Competitive review

Competition from mobile phone manufacturers and makers of specialised devices for text and email messaging is an important factor. With non-PDA companies entering the market, current industry participants must continually add features and cut prices or focus on other electronics products. Currently, key competitors include:

- *Palm*. Palm has struggled financially, in part because of the need to reduce prices for competitive reasons. As the best-known maker of PDAs, Palm has achieved good distribution in nearly every channel. The most popular model is the Palm Tungsten which comes in a range of different specifications, but is generally less well equipped than the Sonic 1000.

- *Hewlett-Packard*. HP is targeting business and professional markets with its iPAQ Pocket PC devices. Many have wireless capabilities, large screen displays, longer battery life for extended use and slots for removable memory cards. HP enjoys excellent distribution, and its products are priced from below €300 to more than €600.

- *Acer*. Acer's C530 has a built-in global position system capability as well as a range of business-oriented software applications. Its mapping software and verbal commands eliminate the need for an automotive device. Acer's PDA uses a Windows operating system and has other functions, including a digital voice recorder for brief memos.

- *Dell*. Dell's Axim range of PDA models is characterised by light, slender design and competitive pricing. Most models include Wi-Fi and Bluetooth wireless capabilities. New, more powerful models are expected at regular intervals from this low-cost competitor, which markets directly to customers.

- *Research in Motion*. Known for its highly popular BlackBerry wireless email devices, Research in Motion now offers models that operate as mobile phones and provide email, instant messaging and Web browsing functions. They have built-in keyboards, although the keys are very small. BlackBerry models come in a wide range of prices and specifications. Top-of-the-range BlackBerry models are seen as desirable executive accessories.

Despite this strong competition, Sonic can carve out a definite image and gain recognition among the targeted segments. Our unique communication/entertainment/location combination with hands-free voice command operation is a critical point of differentiation for competitive advantage.

Distribution review

Sonic-branded products will be distributed through a network of retailers in the top 40 cities in Germany, France, the UK and Spain. Among the most important channel partners being contacted are:

- Office supply superstores
- Computer stores
- Electronics speciality stores
- Online retailers

Distribution review
In this section, marketers list the most important channels, provide an overview of each channel arrangement and mention any new developments or trends.

Amazon.co.uk, amazon.fr and amazon.de will carry Sonic PDAs and, for a promotional fee, will give Sonic prominent placement on their home pages during the introduction. Although distribution will initially be restricted to the four specified countries, we plan to expand into other European markets, according to demand. We will emphasise trade sales promotion in the first year.

Strengths, weaknesses, opportunities and threat analysis

Sonic has several powerful strengths on which to build, but our major weakness is lack of brand awareness and image. The major opportunity is demand for multimedia PDAs that deliver a number of valued benefits, eliminating the need for customers to carry more than one device. We also face the threat of ever-higher competition from consumer electronics manufacturers, as well as downward pricing pressure. Exhibit A1.2 summarises Sonic's main strengths, weaknesses, opportunities and threats.

EXHIBIT A1.2 Sonic's strengths, weaknesses, opportunities and threats

Strengths	Weaknesses
■ Innovative combination of functions operated hands-free in one portable device ■ Value pricing ■ Security due to Linux-based operating system	■ Lack of brand awareness and image ■ Heavier than most competing models

Opportunities	Threats
■ Increased demand for multimedia models with diverse functions and benefits ■ Lower technology costs	■ Intense competition ■ Downward pricing pressure ■ Compressed product life

Strengths

Strengths
Strengths are internal capabilities that can help the company reach its objectives.

Sonic can build on three important strengths:

1 *Innovative product*. The Sonic 1000 combines a variety of features that would otherwise require customers to carry multiple devices; these include mobile phone and wireless email functionality, GPS capability, and digital video/music storage and playback – all with hands-free operation.

2 *Security*. Our PDA uses a Linux-based operating system that is less vulnerable to hackers and other security threats that can result in stolen or corrupted data.

3 *Pricing*. Our product is priced lower than competing multifunction models – none of which offer the same bundle of features – which gives us an edge with price-conscious customers.

Weaknesses

Weaknesses
Weaknesses are internal elements that may interfere with the company's ability to achieve its objectives.

By waiting to enter the PDA market until considerable consolidation of competitors has occurred, Sonic has learned from the successes and mistakes of others. Nonetheless, we have two main weaknesses:

1 *Lack of brand awareness*. Sonic has not yet established a brand or image in the marketplace, whereas Palm and others have strong brand recognition. We will address this area with promotion.

2 *Heavier weight*. The Sonic 1000 is slightly heavier than most competing models because it incorporates more features than typical rival products. To counteract this weakness, we will emphasise our unique combination of features and our value-added pricing, two compelling competitive strengths.

Opportunities

Opportunities
Opportunities are external elements that the company may be able to exploit to its advantage.

Sonic can take advantage of two major market opportunities:

1 *Increasing demand for multimedia models with multiple functions*. The market for multimedia, multifunction devices is growing much faster than the market for single-use devices. Customers are now accustomed to seeing users with PDAs in work and educational settings, which is boosting primary demand. Also, customers who bought entry-level models are replacing older models with more advanced models.

2 *Lower technology costs*. Better technology is now available at a lower cost than ever before. Thus, Sonic can incorporate technically advanced features at a value-added price that allows for reasonable profits.

Threats

We face three main threats at the introduction of the Sonic 1000:

1 *Increased competition*. More companies are entering the PDA market with models that offer some but not all of the features and benefits provided by Sonic's PDA. Therefore, Sonic's marketing communications must stress our clear differentiation and value-added pricing.

2 *Downward pressure on pricing*. Increased competition and market-share strategies are pushing PDA prices down. Still, our objective of seeking a 10 per cent profit on second-year sales of the original model is realistic, given the lower margins in the PDA market.

3 *Compressed product life cycle*. PDAs have reached the maturity stage of their life cycle more quickly than earlier technology products. We have contingency plans to keep sales growing by adding new features, targeting additional segments and adjusting prices.

Threats
Threats are current or emerging external elements that may possibly challenge the company's performance.

Objectives and issues

We have set aggressive but achievable objectives for the first and second years of market entry.

First-year objectives

During the Sonic 1000's initial year on the market, we are aiming for a 3 per cent share of the PDA market through unit sales volume of 240,000.

Second-year objectives

Our second-year objectives are to achieve a 6 per cent share based on sales of two models and to achieve break-even early in this period.

Issues

In relation to the product launch, our major issue is the ability to establish a well-regarded brand name linked to a meaningful positioning. We will have to invest heavily in marketing to create a memorable and distinctive brand image projecting innovation, quality and value. We must also measure awareness and response so that we can adjust our marketing efforts as necessary.

Objectives and issues
The company's objectives should be defined in specific terms so management can measure progress and, if needed, take corrective action to stay on track. This section describes any major issues that might affect the company's marketing strategy and implementation.

Marketing strategy

Sonic's marketing strategy is based on a positioning of product differentiation. Our primary consumer target is middle- to upper-income professionals who need one portable device to coordinate their busy schedules, communicate with family and colleagues, get driving directions and be entertained on the go. Our secondary consumer target is high school, university and postgraduate students who want a multimedia device. This segment can be described demographically by age (16–30) and educational status.

Our primary business target is mid- to large-sized corporations that want to help their managers and employees stay in touch and input or access critical data when out of the office. This segment consists of companies with more than €25 million in annual sales and more than 100 employees. A secondary business target is entrepreneurs and small-business owners. We are also targeting medical users who want to reduce paperwork and update or access patients' medical records.

Positioning

Using product differentiation, we are positioning the Sonic PDA as the most versatile, convenient, value-added model for personal and professional use. The marketing strategy

Positioning
A positioning built on meaningful differences, supported by appropriate strategy and implementation, can help the company build competitive advantage.

will focus on the hands-free operation of multiple communication, entertainment and information capabilities differentiating the Sonic 1000.

Product strategy

The Sonic 1000, including all the features described in the earlier Product review section, will be sold with a one-year warranty. We will introduce a more compact, powerful high-end model (the Sonic 2000) during the following year. Building the Sonic brand is an integral part of our product strategy. The brand and logo (Sonic's distinctive yellow thunderbolt) will be displayed on the product and its packaging, and reinforced by its prominence in the introductory marketing campaign.

Pricing strategy

The Sonic 1000 will be introduced at €250 wholesale/€350 estimated retail price per unit. We expect to lower the price of this first model when we expand the product line by launching the Sonic 2000, to be priced at €350 wholesale per unit. These prices reflect a strategy of (1) attracting desirable channel partners and (2) taking share from Palm and other established competitors.

Distribution strategy

Our channel strategy is to use selective distribution, marketing Sonic PDAs through well-known stores and online retailers. During the first year, we will add channel partners until we have coverage in all major geographical markets and the product is included in the major electronics catalogues and websites. We will also investigate distribution through mobile phone outlets maintained by major carriers such as T-Mobile. In support of our channel partners, Sonic will provide demonstration products, detailed specification handouts, and full-colour photos and displays featuring the product. We will also arrange special trade terms for retailers that place volume orders.

Marketing communications strategy

By integrating all messages in all media, we will reinforce the brand name and the main points of product differentiation. Research about media consumption patterns will help our advertising agency choose appropriate media and timing to reach prospects before and during product introduction. Thereafter, advertising will appear on a pulsing basis to maintain brand awareness and communicate various differentiation messages. The agency will also coordinate public relations efforts to build the Sonic brand and support the differentiation message. To attract customer attention and encourage purchasing, we will offer as a limited-time premium a leather carry-case. To attract, retain and motivate channel partners for a push strategy, we will use trade sales promotions and personal selling. Until the Sonic brand has been established, our communications will encourage purchases through channel partners rather than from our website.

Marketing research

Using research, we are identifying the specific features and benefits that our target market segments value. Feedback from market tests, surveys and focus groups will help us develop the Sonic 2000. We are also measuring and analysing customers' attitudes toward competing brands and products. Brand awareness research will help us determine the effectiveness and efficiency of our messages and media. Finally, we will use customer satisfaction studies to gauge market reaction.

Marketing organisation

Sonic's chief marketing officer, Jane Melody, holds overall responsibility for all of the company's marketing activities. Exhibit A1.3 shows the structure of the eight-person marketing organisation. Sonic has hired Worldwide Marketing to handle national sales campaigns, trade and consumer sales promotions and public relations efforts.

EXHIBIT A1.3 Sonic's marketing organisation

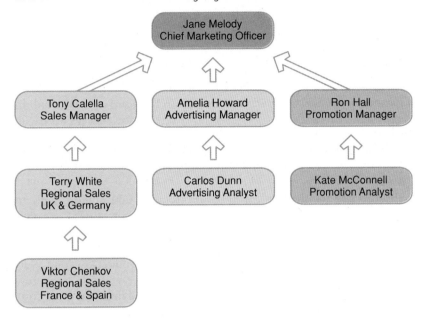

Action programmes

The Sonic 1000 will be introduced in February. Following are summaries of the action programmes we will use during the first six months of next year to achieve our stated objectives.

January

We will initiate a €200,000 trade sales promotion campaign to educate dealers and generate excitement for the product launch in February. We will exhibit at the major consumer electronics trade shows, Webcast the product launch, and provide samples to selected product reviewers, opinion leaders and celebrities as part of our public relations strategy. Our training staff will work with sales personnel at major retail chains to explain the Sonic 1000's features, benefits and competitive advantages.

February

We will start an integrated print/radio/Internet campaign targeting professionals and consumers. The campaign will show how many functions the Sonic PDA can perform and emphasise the convenience of a single, powerful handheld device. This multimedia campaign will be supported by point-of-sale signage as well as online-only specials.

March

As the multimedia advertising campaign continues, we will add consumer sales promotion tactics such giving away leather carry-cases as a premium. We will also distribute new point-of-purchase displays to support our retailers.

April

We will hold a trade sales contest offering prizes for the salesperson and retail organisation that sells the most Sonic PDAs during the 4-week period.

Action programmes
Action programmes should be coordinated with the resources and activities of other departments, including production, finance, purchasing, etc.

May

We plan to roll out a new national advertising campaign this month. The radio ads will feature celebrity voices telling their Sonic PDAs to perform functions such as initiating a phone call, sending an email, playing a song or video, and so on. The print ads will show these celebrities holding their Sonic PDAs.

June

Our radio campaign will add a new voice-over tag line promoting the Sonic 1000 as a graduation gift. We will also exhibit at the annual European electronics trade show and provide channel partners with new competitive comparison handouts as a sales aid. In addition, we will tally and analyse the results of customer satisfaction surveys for use in future promotions and to provide feedback for product and marketing activities.

Budgets

Budgets
Budgets serve two main purposes: to project profitability and to help managers plan for expenditures, scheduling and operations related to each action programme.

Total first-year sales revenue for the Sonic 1000 is projected at €60 million, with an average wholesale price of €250 per unit and variable cost per unit of €150 for unit sales volume of 240,000. We anticipate a first-year loss of up to €10 million on the Sonic 1000 model. Break-even calculations indicate that the Sonic 1000 will become profitable after the sales volume exceeds 267,500, early in the product's second year. Our break-even analysis of Sonic's first PDA product assumes per-unit wholesale revenue of €250 per unit, variable cost of €150 per unit, and estimated first-year fixed costs of €26,750,000.

Controls

Controls
Controls help management assess results after the plan is implemented, identify any problems or performance variations, and initiate corrective action.

We are planning tight control measures to monitor closely quality and customer service satisfaction. This will enable us to react very quickly in correcting any problems that may occur. Other early warning signals that will be monitored for signs of deviation from the plan include monthly sales (by segment and channel) and monthly expenses. Given the PDA market's volatility, we are developing contingency plans to address fast-moving environmental changes such as new technology and new competition.

Sources: Background information and market data adapted from: Sascha Segan, 'A New Driving Force in PDAs', *PC Magazine*, July 2005, p. 40; Sascha Segan, 'Wi-Fi Phone Gets You Connected', *PC Magazine*, 7 June 2005, p. 58; Pui-Wing Tam, 'The Hand-Helds Strike Back', *Wall Street Journal*, 18 May 2005, pp. D1, D6; 'Writing Handhelds', *BusinessWeek*, 6 June 2005, p. 48; 'Our Top PDAs and Phones', *PC Magazine*, 28 June 2005, p. 45; Mike Musgrove, 'Sony Pulling Handheld from US Market', *Washington Post*, 2 June 2004, p. E1; Michael V. Copeland, Om Malik and Rafe Needleman, 'The Next Big Thing', *Business 2.0*, July 2003, pp. 62–9.

OTHER RESOURCES

Professional marketing associations and organisations are another source of information about careers. Marketers belong to many such societies. You may want to contact some of the following in your job search:

- The Chartered Institute of Marketing is the UK professional body – but is growing rapidly in Europe and Asia as well: **www.cim.co.uk**.

- The European Marketing Confederation is a continent-wide professional organisation: **www.emc.be**.

- *Marketing Week* might best be described as the profession's newspaper. Like most other newspapers it has sections on jobs and job hunting: **www.marketingweek.co.uk**.

- *Sales and Marketing Jobs* does what it says on the tin, being a specialist in listing marketing and sales positions: **www.sales-and-marketing-jobs.co.uk/**.

- Many national newspapers have sections specifically for marketing and sales. *The Guardian* is good for non-profit related jobs and also media and creative careers. *The Daily Telegraph* and *The Times* tend to have more brand management and/or market research positions.

GLOSSARY

Adapted marketing mix An international marketing strategy for adjusting the marketing mix elements to each international target market, bearing more costs but hoping for a larger market share and return.

Administered VMS A Vertical Marketing System that coordinates successive stages of production and distribution, not through common ownership or contractual ties, but through the size and power of one of the parties.

Adoption process The mental process through which an individual passes from first hearing about an innovation to final adoption.

Advertising Any paid form of non-personal presentation and promotion of ideas, goods or services by an identified sponsor.

Advertising agency A marketing services firm that assists companies in planning, preparing, implementing and evaluating all or portions of their advertising programmes.

Advertising objective A specific communication task to be accomplished with a specific target audience during a specific period of time.

Affordable method Setting the promotion budget at the level management thinks the company can afford.

Age and life-cycle segmentation Dividing a market into different age and life-cycle groups.

Agent A wholesaler who represents buyers or sellers on a relatively permanent basis, performs only a few functions and does not take title to goods.

Allowance Promotional money paid by manufacturers to retailers in return for an agreement to feature the manufacturer's products in some way.

Approach The step in the selling process in which the salesperson meets the customer for the first time.

B2B (business-to-business) e-commerce Using B2B trading networks, auction sites, spot exchanges, online product catalogues, barter sites and other online resources to reach new business customers, serve current customers more effectively, and obtain buying efficiencies and better prices.

B2C (business-to-consumer) e-commerce The online selling of goods and services to final consumers.

Baby boomers The generation of people born in Europe and North America during the baby boom following the Second World War and lasting until the early 1960s.

Behavioural segmentation Dividing a market into groups based on consumer knowledge, attitude, use or response to a product.

Benefit segmentation Dividing the market into groups according to the different benefits that consumers seek from the product.

Brand A combination of name, term, sign, symbol or design, intended to identify the goods or services of one seller or group of sellers and to differentiate them from those of competitors.

Brand equity The positive differential effect that knowing the brand name has on customer response to the product or service.

Brand extension Using a successful brand name to launch a new or modified product in a new category.

Break-even pricing (target profit pricing) Setting price to break even on the costs of making and marketing a product; or setting price to make a target profit.

Broker A wholesaler that does not take title to goods and whose function is to bring buyers and sellers together and assist in negotiation.

Business analysis A review of the sales, costs and profit projections for a new product to find out whether these factors satisfy the company's objectives.

Business buyer behaviour The buying behaviour of the organisations that buy goods and services for use in the production of other products and services or for the purpose of reselling or renting them to others at a profit.

Business portfolio The collection of businesses and products that make up the company.

Buying centre All the individuals and units that participate in the business buying decision process.

By-product pricing Setting a price for by-products in order to make the main product's price more competitive.

C2B (consumer-to-business) e-commerce Online exchanges in which consumers search out sellers, learn about their offers, and initiate purchases, sometimes even driving transaction terms.

C2C (consumer-to-consumer) e-commerce Online exchanges of goods and information between final consumers.

Captive-product pricing Setting a price for products that must be used along with a main product, such as blades for a razor and film for a camera.

Catalogue marketing Direct marketing through print, video or electronic catalogues that are mailed to selected customers, made available in stores, or presented online.

Category killer Giant speciality store that carries a very deep assortment of a particular line and is staffed by knowledgeable employees.

Causal research Marketing research to test hypotheses about cause-and-effect relationships.

Chain stores Two or more outlets that are owned and controlled in common, have central buying and merchandising, and sell similar lines of merchandise.

Channel conflict Disagreement among marketing channel members on goals and roles – who should do what and for what rewards.

Channel level A layer of intermediaries that performs some work in bringing the product and its ownership closer to the final buyer.

Click-and-mortar companies Traditional brick-and-mortar companies that have added e-marketing to their operations.

Click-only companies The so-called dot-coms, which operate only online without any brick-and-mortar market presence.

Closing The step in the selling process in which the salesperson asks the customer for an order.

Co-branding The practice of using the established brand names of two different companies on the same product.

Cognitive dissonance Buyer psychological discomfort following a purchase arising from anxiety that the buying decision was sub-optimal.

Commercialisation Introducing a new product into the market.

Communication adaptation A global communication strategy of fully adapting advertising messages to local markets.

Competitive advantage An advantage over competitors gained by offering consumers or business buyers greater value, either through lower prices or by providing more benefits that justify higher prices.

Competitive-parity method Setting the promotion budget to match competitors' outlays.

Concentrated (niche) marketing A market coverage strategy in which a firm goes after a large share of one or a few segments or niches.

Concept testing Testing new-product concepts with a group of target consumers to find out if the concepts have strong consumer appeal.

Consumer buyer behaviour The buying behaviour of final consumers – individuals and households who buy goods and services for personal consumption.

Consumer market All the individuals and households who buy or acquire goods and services for personal consumption.

Consumer product Product bought by final consumer for personal consumption, or perhaps as a gift.

Consumerism An organised movement of citizens and government agencies to improve the rights and power of buyers in relation to sellers.

Consumer-oriented marketing The philosophy of enlightened marketing that holds that the company should view and organise its marketing activities from the consumer's point of view.

Contract-manufacturing A joint venture in which a company contracts with manufacturers in a foreign market to produce its product or provide its service.

Contractual VMS A Vertical Marketing System in which independent firms at different levels of production and distribution join together through contracts to obtain more economies or sales impact than they could achieve alone.

Convenience product Consumer product that the customer usually buys frequently, immediately, and with a minimum of comparison and buying effort.

Convenience store A small store located near a residential area that is open long hours seven days a week and carries a limited line of high turnover convenience goods.

Conventional distribution channel A channel consisting of one or more independent producers, wholesalers and retailers, each a separate business seeking to maximise its own profits even at the expense of profits for the system as a whole.

Corporate VMS A Vertical Marketing System that combines successive stages of production and distribution under single ownership – channel leadership is established through common ownership.

Corporate website A website designed to build customer goodwill and to supplement other sales channels, rather than to sell the company's products directly.

Cost-plus pricing Adding a standard mark-up to the cost of the product, e.g. 10 per cent.

Countertrade International trade involving the direct or indirect exchange of goods for other goods instead of cash.

Cultural environment Institutions and other forces that affect society's basic values, perceptions, preferences and behaviours.

Culture The set of basic values, perceptions, wants and behaviours learned by a member of society from family and other important institutions.

Customer database An organised collection of comprehensive data about individual customers or prospects, including geographic, demographic, psychographic and behavioural data.

Customer equity The total combined customer lifetime values of all of the company's customers.

Customer lifetime value The value of the entire stream of purchases that the customer would make over a lifetime of patronage. Often quoted as an amount lost to the company if the customer disappears.

Customer perceived value The customer's evaluation of the difference between all the benefits and all the costs of a marketing offer relative to those of competing offers.

Customer relationship management Nominally to do with the process of creating, developing and maintaining relationships with customers, more typically and accurately referring to the management and use of customer information in databases.

Customer sales force structure A sales force organisation under which salespeople specialise in selling only to certain customers or industries.

Customer satisfaction The extent to which a product's perceived performance matches a buyer's expectations.

Customer value marketing An approach to marketing that emphasises the creation and enhancement of customer value as a route to competitive success.

Decline stage The product life-cycle stage in which a product's sales decline.

Deficient products Products that have neither immediate appeal nor long-term benefits.

Demand curve A curve that shows the number of units the market will buy in a given time period, at different prices that might be charged.

Demands Wants that are backed by buying power.

Demographic segmentation Dividing the market into groups based on demographic variables such as age, sex, family size, family life cycle, income, occupation, education, religion, race and nationality.

Demography The study of human populations in terms of size, density, location, age, gender, ethnicity, occupation and other statistics.

Department store A retail organisation that carries a wide variety of product lines – typically clothing, home furnishings and household goods; each line is operated as a separate department managed by specialist buyers or merchandisers.

Derived demand Business demand that ultimately comes from (derives from) the demand for consumer goods.

Descriptive research Marketing research to better describe marketing problems, situations or markets, such as the market potential for a product or the demographics and attitudes of consumers.

Desirable products Products that give both high immediate satisfaction and high long-term benefits.

Differentiated (segmented) marketing A market coverage strategy in which a firm decides to target several market segments and designs separate offers for each.

Direct investment Entering a foreign market by developing foreign-based assembly or manufacturing facilities.

Direct-mail marketing Direct marketing by sending an offer, announcement, reminder or other item to a person at a particular address.

Direct marketing Direct connections with carefully targeted individual consumers both to obtain an immediate response and to cultivate lasting customer relationships – the use of telephone, mail, fax, email, the Internet and other tools to communicate directly with specific consumers.

Direct marketing channel A marketing channel that has no intermediary levels.

Direct-response television marketing Direct marketing via television, including direct-response television advertising or infomercials and home shopping channels.

Discount A straight reduction in price on purchases during a stated period of time.

Discount store A retail institution that sells standard merchandise at lower prices by accepting lower margins and selling at higher volume.

Disintermediation The cutting out of marketing channel intermediaries by product or service producers, or the displacement of traditional resellers by radical new types of intermediaries.

Distribution centre A large, highly automated warehouse designed to receive goods from various plants and suppliers, take orders, fill them efficiently and deliver goods to customers as quickly as possible.

Distribution channel See Marketing channel.

Diversification A strategy for company growth through starting up or acquiring businesses outside the company's current products and markets.

Downsizing Reducing the business portfolio by eliminating products or business units that are not profitable or that no longer fit the company's overall strategy.

Dynamic pricing Adjusting prices continually to meet the characteristics and needs of individual customers and situations.

E-business The use of electronic platforms – intranets, extranets and the Internet – to conduct a company's business.

E-commerce Buying and selling processes supported by electronic means, primarily the Internet.

Economic community A group of nations organised to work towards common goals in the regulation of international trade.

Economic environment Factors that affect consumer buying power and spending patterns.

E-marketing The marketing side of e-commerce – company efforts to communicate about, promote, and sell products and services over the Internet.

Engel's laws Differences noted over a century ago by Ernst Engel in how people shift their spending across food, housing, transport, health care, and other goods and services categories as family income rises.

Enlightened marketing A marketing philosophy holding that a company's marketing should support the best long-term performance of the marketing system.

Environmental sustainability A management approach that involves developing strategies that both sustain the environment and produce profits for the company.

Environmentalism An organised movement of concerned citizens and government agencies to protect and improve people's living environment.

Exchange The act of obtaining a desired object from someone by offering something in return.

Exclusive distribution Giving a limited number of dealers the exclusive right to distribute the company's products in their territories.

Experimental research The gathering of primary data by selecting matched groups of subjects, giving them different treatments, controlling related factors and checking for differences in group responses.

Exploratory research Marketing research to gather preliminary information that will help define problems and suggest hypotheses.

Exporting Entering a foreign market by selling goods produced in the company's home country, often with little modification.

Extranet A network that connects a company with its suppliers and distributors, often paired with an intranet (see below).

Factory outlet Off-price retailing operation that is owned and operated by a manufacturer and that normally carries the manufacturer's surplus, discontinued or irregular goods.

Fad A fashion that enters quickly, is adopted with great zeal, peaks early and declines very quickly.

Fashion A currently accepted or popular style in a given field.

Fixed costs Costs that do not vary with production or sales level.

Focus group interviewing Personal interviewing that involves inviting typically 6 to 10 people to gather for a few hours with a trained interviewer to talk about a product, service or organisation. The interviewer 'focuses' the group discussion on important issues.

Follow-up The last step in the selling process in which the salesperson follows up after the sale to ensure customer satisfaction and repeat business.

Franchise A contractual association between a manufacturer, wholesaler or service organisation (a franchisor) and independent businesspeople (franchisees) who buy the right to own and operate one or more units in the franchise system.

Franchise organisation A contractual vertical marketing system in which a channel member, called a franchisor, links several stages in the production-distribution process.

Gender segmentation Dividing a market into different groups based on gender.

Generation X The generation of people born between 1965 and 1976 in the 'birth dearth' following the baby boom.

Generation Y The children of the baby boomers, born between 1977 and 1994.

Geographic segmentation Dividing a market into different geographical units such as nations, states, regions, counties, cities or neighbourhoods.

Geographical pricing Setting price based on the buyer's geographical location.

Global firm A firm that operates and/or markets products and services in many nations – potentially in radically different ways. Typically a very large firm with well-known brands.

Group Two or more people who interact to accomplish individual or mutual goals.

Growth-share matrix A portfolio planning method that evaluates a company's strategic business units in terms of their market growth rate and relative market share. SBUs are classified as stars, cash cows, question marks or dogs.

Growth stage The product life-cycle stage in which a product's sales start climbing quickly.

Handling objections The step in the selling process in which the salesperson seeks out, clarifies and overcomes customer objections to buying.

Horizontal marketing system A channel arrangement in which two or more companies at one level join together to follow a new marketing opportunity. (See Vertical marketing system.)

Idea generation The systematic search for new-product ideas.

Idea screening Screening new-product ideas in order to spot good ideas and drop poor ones as soon as possible.

Income segmentation Dividing a market into different income groups.

Independent off-price retailer Off-price retailer that is either owned and run by entrepreneurs or is a division of a larger retail corporation.

Indirect marketing channel Channel containing one or more intermediary levels.

Individual marketing Tailoring products and marketing programmes to the needs and preferences of individual customers – also labelled 'markets-of-one marketing', 'customised marketing' and 'one-to-one marketing'.

Industrial product Product bought by individuals and organisations for further processing or for use in conducting a business.

Innovative marketing A principle of enlightened marketing that requires that a company seeks real product and marketing improvements.

Inside sales force Inside salespeople who conduct business from their offices via telephone, the Internet or visits from prospective buyers.

Integrated direct marketing Direct marketing campaigns that use multiple vehicles and multiple stages to improve response rates and profits.

Integrated logistics management The logistics concept that emphasises teamwork, both inside the company and among all the marketing channel organisations, to maximise the performance of the entire distribution system.

Integrated marketing communications (IMC) The concept under which a company carefully integrates its many communications channels to deliver a clear, consistent and compelling message about the organisation and its products.

Intensive distribution Stocking the product in as many outlets as possible.

Interactive marketing Marketing by a service firm that recognises that perceived service quality depends heavily on the quality of buyer–seller interaction, either face to face or using Internet related tools.

Intermarket segmentation Forming segments of consumers who have similar needs and buying behaviour even though they are located in different countries.

Intermodal transportation Combining two or more modes of transportation.

Internal databases Electronic collections of consumer and market information obtained from data sources within the company network.

Internal marketing Marketing by a service firm to train and effectively motivate its customer-contact employees and all the supporting service people to work as a team to provide customer satisfaction.

Internet A vast public web of computer networks, which connects users of all types all around the world to each other and to an amazingly large 'information repository'.

Intranet A network that connects people within a company to each other and to the company network and excludes those outside this network (see Extranet).

Introduction stage The product life-cycle stage in which the new product is first distributed and made available for purchase.

Joint ownership A joint venture in which a company joins investors in a foreign market to create a local business in which the company shares joint ownership and control.

Joint venturing Entering foreign markets by joining with other companies to produce or market a product or service.

Learning Changes in an individual's behaviour arising from experience.

Licensing A method of entering a foreign market in which the company enters into an agreement with a licensee in the foreign market, offering the right to use a manufacturing process, trade mark, patent, trade secret or other item.of value for a fee or royalty.

Lifestyle A person's pattern of living as expressed in his or her activities, interests and opinions.

Line extension Using a successful brand name to introduce additional items in a given product category under the same brand name, such as new flavours, forms, colours, added ingredients or package sizes.

Local marketing Tailoring brands and promotions to the needs and wants of local customer groups – cities, neighbourhoods and even specific stores.

Macroenvironment The larger societal forces that affect the microenvironment – demographic, economic, legal, technological, political and cultural forces.

Management contracting A joint venture in which the domestic firm supplies the management know-how to a foreign company that supplies the capital; the domestic firm exports management services rather than products.

Manufacturers' sales branches and offices Wholesaling by sellers or buyers themselves rather than through independent wholesalers.

Market The set of all actual and potential buyers of a product or service.

Market development A strategy for company growth by identifying and developing new market segments for current company products.

Market offering Some combination of products, services, information or experiences offered to a market to satisfy a need or want.

Market penetration A strategy for company growth by increasing sales of current products to current market segments without changing the product.

Market-penetration pricing Setting a low price for a new product in order to attract a large number of buyers and a large market share.

Market positioning Arranging for a product to occupy a clear, distinctive and desirable place relative to competing products in the minds of target consumers.

Market segment A group of consumers who respond in a similar way to a given set of marketing efforts.

Market segmentation Dividing a market into distinct groups with distinct needs, characteristics or behaviours who might require separate products or marketing mixes.

Market-skimming pricing Setting a high price for a new product to skim maximum revenues layer by layer from the segments willing to pay the high price; the company makes fewer but more profitable sales.

Marketing The process by which companies create value for customers and build strong customer relationships in order to capture value from customers in return. The AMA defines marketing as 'an organizational function and a set of processes for creating, communicating, and delivering value to customers and for managing customer relationships in ways that benefit the organization and its stakeholders'.

Marketing audit A comprehensive, systematic, independent and periodic examination of a company's environment, objectives, strategies and activities to determine problem areas and opportunities and to recommend a plan of action to improve the company's marketing performance.

Marketing channel (distribution channel) A set of interdependent organisations that help make a product or service available for use or consumption by the consumer or business user.

Marketing concept The marketing management philosophy that holds that achieving organisational goals depends on knowing the needs and wants of target markets and delivering the desired satisfactions better than competitors do.

Marketing control The process of measuring and evaluating the results of marketing strategies and plans, and taking corrective action to ensure that objectives are achieved.

Marketing environment The actors and forces outside marketing that affect marketing management's ability to build and maintain successful relationships with target customers.

Marketing implementation The process that turns marketing strategies and plans into marketing actions in order to accomplish strategic marketing objectives.

Marketing information system (MIS) People, equipment, and procedures to gather, sort, analyse, evaluate and distribute needed, timely and accurate information to marketing decision makers.

Marketing intelligence The systematic collection and analysis of publicly available information about competitors and developments in the marketing environment.

Marketing intermediaries Firms that help the company to promote, sell, and distribute its goods to final buyers; they include resellers, physical distribution firms, marketing service agencies and financial intermediaries.

Marketing logistics (physical distribution) The tasks involved in planning, implementing and controlling the physical flow of materials, final goods and related information from points of origin to points of consumption to meet customer requirements at a profit.

Marketing management The art and science of choosing target markets and building profitable relationships with them.

Marketing mix The set of controllable tactical marketing tools – product, price, place and promotion – that the firm blends to produce the response it wants in the target market.

Marketing myopia The mistake of paying more attention to the specific products a company offers than to the benefits and experiences produced by those products.

Marketing research The systematic design, collection, analysis and reporting of data relevant to a specific marketing situation facing an organisation.

Marketing strategy The marketing logic by which the business unit hopes to achieve its marketing objectives.

Marketing strategy development Designing an initial marketing strategy for a new product based on the product concept.

Marketing supply chain management Managing upstream and downstream value-added flows of materials, final goods and related information among suppliers, the company, resellers and final consumers.

Marketing website A website that engages consumers in interactions that will move them closer to a direct purchase or other marketing outcome.

Maturity stage The stage in the product life cycle in which sales growth slows or levels off.

Merchant wholesaler Independently owned business that takes title to the merchandise it handles.

Microenvironment The actors close to the company that affect its ability to serve its customers – the company, suppliers, marketing intermediaries, customer markets, competitors and publics.

Micromarketing The practice of tailoring products and marketing programmes to the needs and wants of specific individuals and local customer groups – includes local marketing and individual marketing.

Mission statement A statement of the organisation's purpose – what it wants to accomplish in the larger environment.

Modified rebuy A business buying situation in which the buyer wants to modify product specifications, prices, terms or suppliers.

Motive (drive) A need that is sufficiently pressing to direct the person to seek satisfaction of the need.

Multichannel distribution system A distribution system in which a single firm sets up two or more marketing channels to reach one or more customer segments.

Natural environment Natural resources that are needed as inputs by marketers or that are affected by marketing activities.

Needs States of felt deprivation.

New product A good, service or idea that is perceived by some potential customers as new.

New-product development The development of original products, product improvements, product modifications and new brands through the firm's own R&D efforts.

New-task situation A business buying situation in which the buyer purchases a product or service for the first time.

Objective-and-task method Developing the promotion budget by (1) defining specific objectives, (2) determining the tasks that must be performed to achieve these objectives, and (3) estimating the costs of performing these tasks. The sum of these costs is the proposed promotion budget.

Observational research The gathering of primary data by observing relevant people, actions and situations.

Occasion segmentation Dividing the market into groups according to occasions when buyers get the idea to buy, actually make their purchase, or use the purchased item.

Off-price retailer Retailer that buys at less than regular wholesale prices and sells at less than retail. Examples are factory outlets, independents and warehouse clubs.

Online advertising Advertising that appears while consumers are surfing the Web, including banners, interstitials, pop-ups and other forms.

Online databases Computerised collections of information available from online commercial sources or via the Internet.

Online (Internet) marketing research Collecting primary data through Internet surveys and online focus groups.

Open trading exchanges Huge e-marketspaces in which B2B buyers and sellers find each other online, share information and complete transactions efficiently. An 'eBay' for the commercial world.

Opinion leader Person within a reference group who, because of special skills, knowledge, personality or other characteristics, exerts influence on others.

Optional-product pricing The pricing of optional or accessory products along with a main product.

Outside sales force (or field sales force) Outside salespeople who travel to call on customers in the field.

Packaging The activities of designing and producing the container or wrapper for a product.

Partner relationship management Working closely with partners in other company departments and outside the company jointly to bring greater value to customers.

Percentage-of-sales method Setting the promotion budget at a certain percentage of current or forecasted sales or as a percentage of the unit sales price.

Perception The process by which people select, organise and interpret information to form a meaningful picture of the world.

Personal selling Personal presentation by the firm's sales force for the purpose of making sales and building customer relationships.

Personality The unique psychological characteristics that lead to relatively consistent and lasting responses to one's own environment.

Pleasing products Products that give high immediate satisfaction but may hurt consumers in the long run.

Political environment Laws, government agencies and pressure groups that influence and limit various organisations and individuals in a given society.

Portfolio analysis The process by which management evaluates the products and businesses making up the company.

Positioning statement A statement that summarises company or brand positioning – it takes this form: To (target segment and need) our (brand) is (concept) that (point-of-difference).

Pre-approach The step in the selling process in which the salesperson learns as much as possible about a prospective customer before making a sales call.

Presentation The step in the selling process in which the salesperson tells the product 'story' to the buyer, highlighting customer benefits.

Price The amount of money charged for a product or service, or the sum of all the values that customers give up in order to gain the benefits of having or using a product or service.

Price elasticity A measure of the sensitivity of demand to changes in price.

Primary data Information collected for the specific purpose at hand.

Private brand (or store brand) A brand created and owned by a reseller of a product or service.

Private trading exchanges B2B trading networks that link a particular seller with its own trading partners.

Product Anything that can be offered to a market for attention, acquisition, use or consumption that might satisfy a want or need.

Product adaptation Adapting a product to meet local conditions or wants in foreign markets.

Product bundle pricing Combining several products and offering the bundle at a reduced price.

Product concept A detailed version of the new-product idea stated in meaningful consumer terms. Part of the new-product development process.

Product development (1) A strategy for company growth by offering modified or new products to current market segments.

Product development (2) Developing the product concept into a physical product in order to ensure that the product idea can be turned into a workable product.

Product life cycle The course of a product's sales and profits over its lifetime. It involves five distinct stages: product development, introduction, growth, maturity and decline.

Product line A group of products that are closely related because they function in a similar manner, are sold to the same customer groups, are marketed through the same types of outlets or fall within given price ranges.

Product line pricing Setting the price steps between various products in a product line based on cost differences between the products, customer evaluations of different features and competitors' prices.

Product/market expansion grid A portfolio planning tool for identifying company growth opportunities through market penetration, market development, product development or diversification.

Product mix (or product portfolio) The set of all product lines and items that a particular seller offers for sale.

Product position The way the product is defined by consumers on important attributes – the place the product occupies in consumers' minds relative to competing products.

Product quality The ability of a product to perform its functions; it includes the product's overall durability, reliability, precision, ease of operation and repair, and other valued attributes.

Product sales force structure A sales force organisation under which salespeople specialise in selling only a portion of the company's products or lines.

Production concept The idea that consumers will favour products that are available and highly affordable and that the organisation should therefore focus on improving production and distribution efficiency – 'we will sell what we can make'.

Promotion mix (or marketing communications mix) The specific mix of advertising, personal selling, sales promotion, public relations and direct marketing that a company uses to communicate customer value persuasively and build customer relationships.

Promotional pricing Temporarily pricing products below the list price, and sometimes even below cost, to increase short-term sales.

Prospecting The step in the selling process in which the salesperson identifies qualified potential customers.

Psychographic segmentation Dividing a market into different groups based on social class, lifestyle or personality characteristics.

Psychological pricing A pricing approach that considers the psychology of prices and not simply the economics; the price is used to say something about the product.

Public Any group that has an actual or potential interest in, or impact on, an organisation's ability to achieve its objectives.

Public relations (PR) Building good relations with the company's various publics by obtaining favourable publicity, building up a good 'corporate image', and handling or heading off unfavourable rumours, stories and events.

Pull strategy A promotion strategy that calls for spending a lot on advertising and consumer promotion to build up consumer demand that will pull the product through channels.

Push strategy A promotion strategy that calls for using the sales force and trade promotion to push the product through channels.

Reference prices Prices that buyers carry in their minds and refer to when they look at a given product.

Relationship marketing Often defined in opposition to transactional marketing (see below), in that relationship marketing espouses long-term 'management of customers' rather than on a transaction-by-transaction basis. A term often misused to describe loyalty cards.

Retailer Business whose sales come primarily from retailing.

Retailing All activities involved in selling goods or services directly to final consumers for their personal, non-business use.

Return on marketing (or marketing ROI) The net return from a marketing investment divided by the costs of the marketing investment. Often difficult to measure with any degree of accuracy.

Sales force management The analysis, planning, implementation and control of sales force activities. It includes designing sales force strategy and structure and recruiting, selecting, training, supervising, compensating and evaluating the firm's salespeople.

Sales promotion Short-term incentives to encourage the purchase or sale of a product or service.

Sales quota A standard that states the amount a salesperson should sell and how sales should be divided among the company's products.

Salesperson An individual acting for a company by performing one or more of the following activities: prospecting, communicating, servicing and information-gathering.

Salutary products Products that have low appeal but may benefit consumers in the long term.

Sample A segment of the population selected for marketing research to represent the population as a whole.

Secondary data Information that already exists somewhere, having been collected for another purpose.

Segmented pricing Selling a product or service at two or more prices, where the difference in prices is not based on differences in costs.

Selective distribution The use of more than one, but fewer than all, of the intermediaries who are willing to carry the company's products.

Selling concept The idea that consumers will not buy enough of the firm's products unless it undertakes a large-scale selling and promotion effort.

Selling process The steps that the salesperson follows when selling, which include prospecting and qualifying, pre-approach, approach, presentation and demonstration, handling objections, closing and follow-up.

Sense-of-mission marketing A principle of enlightened marketing that holds that a company should define its mission in broad social terms rather than narrow product terms.

Sequential product development A new-product development approach in which one company department works to complete its stage of the process before passing the new product along to the next department and stage.

Service Any activity or benefit that one party can offer to another that is essentially intangible and does not result in the ownership of anything.

Service inseparability A major characteristic of services – they are produced and consumed at the same time and cannot be separated from their providers, whether the providers are people or machines.

Service intangibility A major characteristic of services – they cannot be seen, tasted, felt, heard or smelled before they are bought.

Service perishability A major characteristic of services – they cannot be stored for later sale or use.

Service profit chain The chain that links service firm profits with employee and customer satisfaction.

Service variability A major characteristic of services – their quality may vary greatly, depending on who provides them and when, where and how.

Share of customer The portion of the customer's purchasing that a company gets in its product categories.

Shopping centre A group of retail businesses planned, developed, owned and managed as a unit. Also commonly known as a shopping mall.

Shopping product Consumer good that the customer, in the process of selection and purchase, characteristically compares on such bases as suitability, quality, price and style.

Simultaneous (or team-based) product development An approach to developing new products in which various company departments work closely together, overlapping the steps in the product development process to save time and increase effectiveness.

Single-source data systems Electronic monitoring systems that link consumers' exposure to television advertising and promotion (measured using television meters) with what they buy in stores (measured using store checkout scanners).

Social class Relatively permanent and ordered divisions in a society, the members of which share similar values, interests and behaviours.

Social marketing The design, implementation and control of programmes seeking to increase the acceptability of a social idea, cause or practice among a target group.

Societal marketing concept A principle of enlightened marketing that holds that a company should make good marketing decisions by considering consumers' wants, the company's requirements, consumers' long-term interests and society's long-term interests.

Spam Unsolicited, unwanted commercial email messages.

Speciality product Consumer product with unique characteristics or brand identification for which a significant group of buyers is willing to make a special purchase effort.

Speciality store A retail store that carries a narrow product line with a deep assortment within that line.

Standardised marketing mix An international marketing strategy for using basically the same product, advertising, distribution channels and other elements of the marketing mix in all the company's international markets.

Straight product extension Marketing a product in a foreign market without any change.

Straight rebuy A business buying situation in which the buyer routinely reorders something without any modifications.

Strategic planning The process of developing and maintaining a strategic fit between the organisation's goals and capabilities and its changing marketing opportunities. It involves defining a clear company mission, setting supporting objectives, designing a sound business portfolio and coordinating functional strategies.

Style A basic and distinctive mode of expression.

Subculture A group of people with shared value systems based on common life experiences and situations.

Supermarket Large, low-cost, low-margin, high-volume, self-service store that carries a wide variety of food, laundry and household products.

Superstore A store much larger than a regular supermarket that carries a large assortment of routinely purchased food and non-food items and offers services such as dry cleaning, post office, photo finishing, cheque cashing, bill paying, café, car care and pet care.

Supply chain management See Marketing supply chain management.

Survey research The gathering of primary data by asking people questions about their knowledge, attitudes, preferences and buying behaviour.

SWOT analysis An overall evaluation of the company's strengths (S), weaknesses (W), opportunities (O) and threats (T). A part of the preparation required in drawing up a marketing plan.

Systems selling Buying a packaged solution to a problem from a single seller, thus avoiding all the separate decisions involved in a complex buying situation.

Target costing Pricing that starts with an ideal selling price, then targets costs that will ensure that the price is met.

Target market A set of buyers sharing common needs or characteristics that the company decides to serve.

Target marketing The process of evaluating each market segment's attractiveness and selecting one or more segments to enter.

Team selling Using teams of people from sales, marketing, engineering, finance, technical support, and even upper management, to service large, complex accounts.

Technological environment Forces that create new technologies, creating new product and market opportunities.

Telephone marketing Using the telephone to sell directly to customers.

Territorial sales force structure A sales force organisation that assigns each salesperson to an exclusive geographical territory in which that salesperson sells the company's full line.

Test marketing The stage of new-product development in which the product and marketing programme are tested in more realistic market settings.

Third-party logistics (3PL) provider An independent logistics provider that performs any or all of the functions required to get their client's product to market.

Total costs The sum of the fixed and variable costs for any given level of production.

Transactional marketing A term used pejoratively to describe 'classic' marketing management by numbers – or, rather, the '4Ps'.

Undifferentiated (mass) marketing A market coverage strategy in which a firm decides to ignore market segment differences and go after the whole market with one offer.

Unsought product Consumer product that the consumer either does not know about or knows about but does not normally think of buying.

Value-added pricing Attaching value-added features and services to differentiate a marketing offer and support higher prices, rather than cutting prices to match competitors.

Value analysis An approach to cost reduction in which components are studied carefully to determine if they can be redesigned, standardised or made by less costly methods of production.

Value-based pricing Setting price based on buyers' perceptions of value rather than on the seller's cost.

Value chain The series of departments that carry out value-creating activities to design, produce, market, deliver and support a firm's products.

Value-delivery network The network made up of the company, suppliers, distributors and ultimately customers who 'partner' with each other to improve the performance of the entire system.

Value proposition The full positioning of a brand – the full mix of benefits upon which it is positioned.

Variable costs Costs that vary directly with the level of production.

Vertical marketing system (VMS) A distribution channel structure in which producers, wholesalers and retailers act as a unified system. One channel member owns the others, has contracts with them, or has so much power that they all cooperate. (See Horizontal marketing system.)

Viral marketing The Internet version of word-of-mouth marketing – websites, email messages, or other marketing events that are so infectious that customers will want to pass them along to friends.

Wants The form needs take as shaped by culture and individual personality. (See Needs.)

Web communities Websites upon which members can congregate online and exchange views on issues of common interest.

Wheel-of-retailing concept A concept of retailing that states that new types of retailers usually begin as low-margin, low-price, low-status operations but later evolve into higher-priced, higher-service operations, eventually becoming like the conventional retailers they replaced.

Whole-channel view Designing international channels that take into account all the necessary links in distributing the seller's products to final buyers, including the seller's headquarters organisation, channels among nations and channels within nations.

Wholesaler A firm engaged primarily in wholesaling activity.

Wholesaling All activities involved in selling goods and services to those buying for resale or business use.

INDEX